Impact of Infodemic on Organizational Performance

Muhammad Waseem Bari
Government College University, Faisalabad, Pakistan

Emilia Alaverdov
Georgian Technical University, Georgia

A volume in the Advances in Human Resources Management and Organizational Development (AHRMOD) Book Series

IGI Global
PUBLISHER of TIMELY KNOWLEDGE

Published in the United States of America by
IGI Global
Business Science Reference (an imprint of IGI Global)
701 E. Chocolate Avenue
Hershey PA, USA 17033
Tel: 717-533-8845
Fax: 717-533-8661
E-mail: cust@igi-global.com
Web site: http://www.igi-global.com

Library of Congress Cataloging-in-Publication Data

Names: Bari, Muhammad Waseem, 1980- editor. | Alaverdov, Emilia, 1978- editor.
Title: Impact of infodemic on organizational performance / Muhammad Waseem Bari, and Emilia Alaverdov, editors.
Description: Hershey, PA : Business Science Reference, [2021] | Includes bibliographical references and index. | Summary: "This book offers research on the impact of excessive information circulated due to pandemic (COVID-19) in organizations' performance and how this Infodemic can impact negatively on employees as well as organizations' performance"-- Provided by publisher.
Identifiers: LCCN 2020052953 (print) | LCCN 2020052954 (ebook) | ISBN 9781799871644 (hardcover) | ISBN 9781799871651 (paperback) | ISBN 9781799871668 (ebook)
Subjects: LCSH: Organizational effectiveness--Research. | Organizational behavior--Research. | COVID-19 (Disease)
Classification: LCC HD58.9 .I44 2021 (print) | LCC HD58.9 (ebook) | DDC 302.3/5--dc23
LC record available at https://lccn.loc.gov/2020052953
LC ebook record available at https://lccn.loc.gov/2020052954

This book is published in the IGI Global book series Advances in Human Resources Management and Organizational Development (AHRMOD) (ISSN: 2327-3372; eISSN: 2327-3380)

British Cataloguing in Publication Data
A Cataloguing in Publication record for this book is available from the British Library.

For electronic access to this publication, please contact: eresources@igi-global.com.

Advances in Human Resources Management and Organizational Development (AHRMOD) Book Series

Patricia Ordóñez de Pablos
Universidad de Oviedo, Spain

ISSN:2327-3372
EISSN:2327-3380

Mission

A solid foundation is essential to the development and success of any organization and can be accomplished through the effective and careful management of an organization's human capital. Research in human resources management and organizational development is necessary in providing business leaders with the tools and methodologies which will assist in the development and maintenance of their organizational structure.

The **Advances in Human Resources Management and Organizational Development (AHRMOD) Book Series** aims to publish the latest research on all aspects of human resources as well as the latest methodologies, tools, and theories regarding organizational development and sustainability. The **AHRMOD Book Series** intends to provide business professionals, managers, researchers, and students with the necessary resources to effectively develop and implement organizational strategies.

Coverage

- Employee Benefits
- Corporate Governance
- Organizational Development
- Organizational Behavior
- Change Management
- Employee Relations
- Disputes Resolution
- Upward Feedback
- Employment and Labor Laws
- Skills Management

IGI Global is currently accepting manuscripts for publication within this series. To submit a proposal for a volume in this series, please contact our Acquisition Editors at Acquisitions@igi-global.com or visit: http://www.igi-global.com/publish/.

The Advances in Human Resources Management and Organizational Development (AHRMOD) Book Series (ISSN 2327-3372) is published by IGI Global, 701 E. Chocolate Avenue, Hershey, PA 17033-1240, USA, www.igi-global.com. This series is composed of titles available for purchase individually; each title is edited to be contextually exclusive from any other title within the series. For pricing and ordering information please visit http://www.igi-global.com/book-series/advances-human-resources-management-organizational/73670. Postmaster: Send all address changes to above address.

Titles in this Series

For a list of additional titles in this series, please visit: http://www.igi-global.com/book-series/advances-human-resources-management-organizational/73670

Handbook of Research on Remote Work and Worker Well-Being in the Post-COVID-19 Era
Daniel Wheatley (University of Birmingham, UK) Irene Hardill (Northumbria University, UK) and Sarah Buglass (Nottingham Trent University, UK)
Business Science Reference • © 2021 • 420pp • H/C (ISBN: 9781799867548) • US $265.00

Cases on Critical Practices for Modern and Future Human Resources Management
Devi Akella (Albany State University, USA) Niveen Eid (Birzeit University, Palestine) and Anton Sabella (Birzeit University, Palestine)
Business Science Reference • © 2021 • 322pp • H/C (ISBN: 9781799858201) • US $195.00

Asian Women in Corporate America Emerging Research and Opportunities
Sambhavi Lakshminarayanan (Medgar Evers College, City University of New York, USA)
Business Science Reference • © 2021 • 263pp • H/C (ISBN: 9781799843849) • US $185.00

Critical Issues on Changing Dynamics in Employee Relations and Workforce Diversity
Radha Yadav (Dayananda Sagar University, India) Priyanka Panday (Doon Business School, India) and Naman Sharma (Indian Institute of Foreign Trade, India)
Business Science Reference • © 2021 • 326pp • H/C (ISBN: 9781799835158) • US $215.00

Handbook of Research on Autopoiesis and Self-Sustaining Processes for Organizational Success
Małgorzata Pańkowska (University of Economics in Katowice, Poland)
Business Science Reference • © 2021 • 432pp • H/C (ISBN: 9781799867135) • US $275.00

Designing and Implementing HR Management Systems in Family Businesses
Luca Gnan (University of Rome "Tor Vergata", Italy) and Giulia Flamini (University of Rome "Tor Vergata", Italy)
Business Science Reference • © 2021 • 368pp • H/C (ISBN: 9781799848141) • US $195.00

Transforming Human Resource Functions With Automation
Anchal Pathak (Bule Hora University, Ethiopia) and Shikha Rana (IMS Unison University, India)
Business Science Reference • © 2021 • 192pp • H/C (ISBN: 9781799841807) • US $195.00

Examining the Career Development Practices and Experiences of Immigrants
Jared Keengwe (University of North Dakota, USA) and Kenneth Kungu (Clayton State University, USA)
Business Science Reference • © 2021 • 362pp • H/C (ISBN: 9781799858119) • US $215.00

IGI Global
PUBLISHER of TIMELY KNOWLEDGE

701 East Chocolate Avenue, Hershey, PA 17033, USA
Tel: 717-533-8845 x100 • Fax: 717-533-8661
E-Mail: cust@igi-global.com • www.igi-global.com

Table of Contents

Detailed Table of Contents

that online courses and tests cannot replace traditional teaching techniques, it is not possible to ignore the role of technology and its widespread use in teaching. The study specifically projects the value of technology for academic assistance of online training and evaluation. Moreover, this pandemic has impacted future teaching and learning in many ways. As a result, educators have been facing many challenges during online sessions like no knowledge about online teaching applications. Collaborations between government, technology firms, and higher education institutions in the public, private, and higher education collaboration modes will solve the problem of technological infrastructure.

The 21st century has been fighting against COVID-19, an infection caused by a virus SARS CoV-2. On 30th January 2020, the World Health Organization stated this condition as an international health emergency. Furthermore, on March 11, 2020, it was declared a global pandemic. The pandemic COVID-19 destroyed the health systems at a large scale and the businesses globally. Service, as well as manufacturing industries, faced significant challenges during this pandemic situation of COVID-19. Infodemic is one of the biggest challenges that creates severe problems for the business community. In such circumstances, businesses have to adopt unique business strategies to sustain and gain a competitive edge. The current study evaluates different business strategies like digital servitization, travel insurance, skunkworks structural approach, black swan, etc. adopted by different service sectors, based on a systematic review approach. Mostly, the research paradigm is focused on the aviation industry, and less attention is given to other service sectors like education, banking, etc.

The COVID-19 pandemic is a major challenge for the entire modern world. Since December 2019, the international community has been concerned about the current situation. The World Health Organization declared the disease as a pandemic on March 11, 2020. The countries are doing their best to prevent the spread of disease. Thus, there is an acute health crisis in the world, which leaves its negative results and will continue to affect all areas of society, especially the economy. Existing difficulties are almost universal. The complexity of the situation reflects upon small, developing countries, such as Georgia, where health and economics are the common denominators directly related to environmental protection. Therefore, along with the data about COVID-19, the chapter presents environmental perspectives of Georgia's international cooperation. The current situation in Georgia is reflected in the program documents of the political parties participating in the 2020 parliamentary elections.

The chapter deals with a theoretical generalization and new approaches of solving the scientific problem, which is manifested in the disclosure of the peculiarities of the experience of the threat of COVID-19 by residents of Ukraine, due to Infodemic. To prevent the negative consequences of Infodemic influence, psychological technology has been developed and tested, which is aimed at the formation/development of adaptive potential of the individual, which determines his ability to overcome difficult situations. The peculiarities of the organization and implementation of work in the training group on overcoming negative feelings and frustration caused by individual perception of personal information about the coronavirus and the spread of COVID-19 in the world are described. It is valuable to present the methods of training and the most effective exercises that were used in active social and psychological training. The results of implementation showed high efficiency and expediency of using this psychological technology in the work of a psychologist.

The chapter intends to investigate the influence caused by COVID-infodemic upon the functions carried out by Ukrainian HEIs. As the pandemic and lockdown quickly and unpredictably changed the form of educational activities, HEIs were faced with new challenges and had to demonstrate the updated approaches of their performance not only in educational activities but also as for their social functions. Based on the survey results, the chapter highlights the student's opinion on changes in the performance of the respective universities caused by COVID, infodemic and post-COVID society as well as student understanding of university mission "to contribute to the public good" under the new circumstances. Survey-based research showed that according to the student opinion, modern Ukrainian are to play a more important role in meeting the societal needs of the society, especially under the influence of unpredictable and controversial factors like COVID-infodemic.

This research began with an assumption that what matters to people gets a verbal stamp. Here, the focus is on the social media jokes about online classes, analysed through linguo-cultural approach by Petrova. The analysis revealed that the teachers are facing problems and students are taking advantage of their teachers' technical illiteracy. The highest dense category consists of jokes about students' non-seriousness toward their online lectures. There are serious discipline issues and distractions. Students have devised new excuses to avoid online classes and assigned home-based activities. Some posts even depicted poor prospects for these ill-trained students. Online classes have been depicted as a useless activity. This hierarchical arrangement of the semantic densities revealed the concerns of the current social-media

The different frames used in the COVID-19 coverage in Ecuador by the national and international press were analyzed through their Twitter accounts. This allowed the examination of which aspects of the pandemic were given greater prominence by each newspaper. The study was based on five generic frames, between 17 March and 16 April 2020. The exploration of these frames was carried out by means of an intersubjective content analysis, using four previously trained encoders. The dominant frames for COVID-19 in Ecuador varied according to the media group studied. 1) The concept of heterogeneity was confirmed within framing theory, according to which a single reality, understood as a textual and visual construct, is addressed in multiple ways by the selection of certain aspects that are given greater emphasis or priority; 2) international newspapers and, to a lesser extent, the national press showed their propensity to "internalize" the dynamic of sensationalism; and 3) there are discrepancies in the interests of the readerships with respect to the dominant frames in the media.

This chapter overviews the relationship between international trade and the WTO law, international trade strategy, as well as labour standards, human rights, and the public health in the context of the COVID-19 pandemic crisis. It is stated that the most effective way to overcome the crisis is timely and effective information-sharing since informed community can make better decisions on trade issues. The urgency of effective measures and implementation of new WTO regulations are believed to be vital for providing fair trade in the present circumstances. The right trade policies would not only revive the trade and recover the time lost to the crisis but would also shift toward a more sustainable and inclusive future. The author claims that, in view of the pandemic, the efforts of policymakers and business leaders to find ways to achieve trade balance should imply greater coherency between trade, labour standards, public health, and human rights objectives.

The purpose of this chapter is to understand the business environment for the family businesses in the Gulf Cooperation Council (GCC) based on the theoretical foundation of organisational ecology and open system perspective during the COVID-19 pandemic. More specifically, the reader can understand the business environment of the family firms and how firms can recover from the pandemic by fighting against the infodemic in the GCC region. The authors have used a survey to collect data online from the family firms from Oman during the first and second waves of COVID-19 (i.e., Feb.-Dec. 2020). The results of the study demonstrate that business infodemic negatively moderates the linkage between the business environment-innovation performance nexus and positively moderates between the business environment-commerce association. This research implies the scanning of the Gulf business environment and continuous innovation by family-owned enterprises is vital to avoid a U-shaped recovery in the Arab economies.

The educational institutions face tremendous challenges due to the sudden transition from traditional brick and mortar to online or distance learning in this neo-normal pandemic situation. Meanwhile, the present study examines the influence of faculties' social media literacy and knowledge and awareness of COVID-19 on their resilience via persuasion and coping behavior. Following the essence of the deductive reasoning approach in a positivism paradigm, the study used the partial least square-based structural equation modeling (PLS-SEM) technique to analyze the data. The study collected data using a random sampling method, and results revealed that social media literacy and knowledge and awareness of COVID-19 positively influenced persuasion. Engaging persuasion also positively predicts faculties' resilience. Surprisingly, the study found no significant moderating influence coping behavior. The findings of this study imply beneficial insights for policymakers and educators for ensuring an educational environment. Limitations and directions for future research are also described.

The chapter investigates the degree to which stock market prices were influenced by company financial performance during the period March 2007–September 2020, which included both the beginning of the global financial crisis and the ongoing COVID-19 pandemic crisis. Using quarterly financial data retrieved from the first 34 companies listed on the New York Stock Exchange according to their transaction volumes, empirical results show that, in the period between the two crises, stock market metrics including price to earnings, price to sales, price to book value, and price to free cash flow were shaped by financial performance indicators such as gross margin ratio, operating margin ratio, earnings before interest, taxes, depreciation and amortization margin, pretax margin, and net profit margin.

During the COVID-19 pandemic, the flow of misinformation that appeared in the mass media and especially on social media and was defined as "Infodemic" by the World Health Organization (WHO). In this study, the relationship between the level at which 1.319 social media users in Turkey have been exposed to misinformation during the COVID-19 process, and their views on which sources spread suspicious and misinformation the most and the level of trust in institutions during the pandemic process were investigated. Participants followed developments in the pandemic on social media; 61% were exposed to false information about COVID-19 every day, and most encountered suspicious information on Facebook and Twitter. Social media users who participated in the study found that the institutions they least trusted were the World Health Organization (WHO), pharmaceutical companies, political opposition of Turkey, and traditional media.

The COVID-19 outbreak has prevented students from contributing towards the economic growth of Pakistan. It first disrupted the education system in China and later entered Pakistan to close all levels of educational institutions/sectors since the middle of March 2020. This study aims to highlight the COVID-19 outbreak's effects on educational sector in Pakistan. Pakistan's overall public sector expenditure as a percentage of GDP before the pandemic was already low as compared to regional level, but due to the pandemic, it has dropped down significantly. This study seeks to answer two important questions: (1) What are the impacts of COVID-19 outbreak on Pakistan? (2) Will the closure of educational institutions impact the economic growth of Pakistan? According to empirical and theoretical findings, the results show that the lack of school education for a long period of time will contribute towards unskilled human capital. The COVID-19 outbreak has impacted student learning activities, which may increase the dropout rates, loss of mental health, and consequently, may impact the economic growth of Pakistan later.

Preface

Wuhan Municipal Health Commission, P.R. China on December 31st, 2019 informed several patients of pneumonia in Wuhan, Hubei. Post investigation, it was identified with the name of coronavirus (COVID-19). Almost, throughout the world (195) nations have been affected by COVID-19. The effect of this general wellbeing crisis has influenced nations and networks as far as financial, socio-mental systems, and global relations. United States of America, Brazil, India, France, Russia, United Kingdom, Italy, Turkey, Spain, and Germany are the top 10 affected nations from the COVID-19 respectively. Up to April 5, 2021, 132.186 million people have been affected by COVID-19 across the world, and 2.689 million deaths have been reported. China, United States, Germany, and Belgium are top producers of COVID-19 vaccines respectively.

Along with COVID-19, Infodemic based on pandemic (COVID-19) is another serious issue for the global community. Social media platforms have produced millions of COVID-19 based perspectives of information, however, this information might be based on deception, gossipy tidbits, rumors. Misinformation not only impacts negatively on the human body but also the mental health of the people. The management at WHO's Health Emergencies Program is also worried and understands the negative impacts of infodemic on human health and their professional performance. Likewise, business organizations have and are facing the challenges of pandemic (COVID-19) these days. Due to this infodemic, business organizations are under serious pressure due to financial matters, employees' psychological and physical health, employee performance, and organization s' performance as well. Social media platforms such as Facebook, WhatsApp, etc. are playing a very aggressive role in the growth of this infodemic. Social media has no check and balances on the content and data. The misinformation/wrong information regarding health issucs of the employees, organizations' market share and financial matters, future firing and hiring policies of the organizations, international operations of the companies are the main causes to disturb the business organizations during this pandemic.

A COVID-19 based infodemic has become a global issue for the organization, specifically business organizations. Therefore, this book and its chapters on different phenomena based on COVID-19 are equally important and helpful for all business and social concerns across the world. This book is very helpful for the students of different fields of knowledge. Specifically, this book is very supportive to the students of business administration and business management and its sub-discipline such as human resource management (HRM), Marketing, Finance, Supply Chain Management, and tourism, etc. A brief description of each chapter included in this book as follows.

Chapter 1 highlights the issues related to the mental health of employees during COVID-19. This chapter review the impact of the COVID-19 outbreak on' mental health of employees, and different diseases (such as anxiety, insomnia, and depression) impact employees' behavior and performance. Post-review of the latest articles, blogs, term papers, reports of the World Health Organization (WHO), and newspapers, this study confirms the negative impact of COVID-19 on the physical and mental health of the employees and performance of the organizations. Specifically, this study discussed different psychological problems like anxiety, depression insomnia, social isolation with employees, working in Pakistan. This study also highlights the measures took by the Pakistani government against COVID-19 and their outcomes.

Chapter 2 deals with the most acute situation of the 21st century caused by a new type of infectious disease called COVID-19. This study highlights the situation of such vulnerable groups of society as refugees, asylum seekers, and labor migrants, which even worsens their tough living conditions. In an alarming time of global crises like the COVID-19 pandemic, major international actors are calling for increased protection of the most vulnerable groups, including victims of trafficking, migrants, and refugees, and advocate greater access to health care for all people regardless of their social and migration status.

Chapter 3 discussed the COVID-19 impact on the education sector. The COVID-19 pandemic has propelled a tech-savvy route into the education sector. Online courses and tests cannot replace traditional teaching techniques, it is not possible to ignore the role of technology and its widespread use in teaching. The study specifically projects the value of technology for academic assistance of online training and evaluation. Moreover, this pandemic has impacted a lot on future teaching and learning approaches in many ways. As a result, educators have been facing many challenges during online sessions like no knowledge about online teaching applications. Collaborations among government, technology provider firms, and higher education institutions in the public, private sectors may help to solve the problem during online teaching and learning through effective technological tools.

Chapter 4 explains that pandemic COVID-19 destroyed the health systems at a large scale and the businesses globally. Service, as well as manufacturing industries, faced significant challenges during this pandemic situation of COVID-19. Infodemic is one of the biggest challenges that creates severe problems for the business community. In such circumstances, businesses have to adopt unique business strategies to sustain and gain a competitive edge. The current study evaluates different business strategies like digital servitization, travel insurance, skunkworks structural approach, black swan, etc., adopted by different service sectors, based on a systematic review approach. Mostly research paradigm is focused on the aviation industry, and less attention is given to other service sectors like education, banking, etc.

Chapter 5 discusses that the Covid-19 pandemic is a major challenge for the entire modern world. Since December 2019, the international community has been concerned about the current situation. The World Health Organization declared the disease as a pandemic on March 11, 2020. The countries are doing their best to prevent the spread of disease. Thus, there is an acute health crisis in the world, which leaves its negative results and will continue to affect all areas of society, especially the economy. The complexity of the situation reflects upon small, developing countries, such as Georgia, where health and economics are the common denominators directly related to environmental protection. Therefore, along with the data about the Covid-19, this chapter presents environmental perspectives of Georgia's international cooperation.

Chapter 6 deals with a theoretical generalization and new approaches for solving the scientific problem, which is manifested in the disclosure of the peculiarities of the experience of the threat of COVID-19 by residents of Ukraine, due to Infodemic. To prevent the negative consequences of Infodemic influence, psychological technology has been developed and tested, which is aimed at the formation/development of the adaptive potential of the individual, which determines his ability to overcome difficult situations. The peculiarities of the organization and implementation of work in the training group on overcoming negative feelings and frustration caused by the individual perception of personal information about the coronavirus and the spread of COVID-19 in the world are described. It is valuable to present the methods of training and the most effective exercises that were used in active social and psychological training. The results of implementation showed high efficiency and expediency of using this psychological technology in the work of a psychologist.

Chapter 7 intends to investigate the influence caused by COVID-infodemic upon the functions carried out by Ukrainian higher education institutions (HEIs). As the pandemic and lockdown quickly and unpredictably changed the form of educational activities, HEIs are facing new challenges and had to demonstrate the updated approaches of their performance not only in educational activities but also for their social functions. Based on the survey results, this chapter highlights the student's opinion on changes in the performance of the respective universities caused by COVID-19. Infodemic and post-COVID-19 societies as well as students' understanding of university mission. The results show that modern Ukrainian students' opinions play an important role in meeting societal needs under the influence of unpredictable and controversial factors such as COVID-19 and infodemic.

Chapter 8 begins with an assumption that what matters to people get a verbal stamp. Here, the focus is on the social media jokes about online classes, analyzed through the Linguo-Cultural approach. The analyses revealed that the teachers are facing problems and students are taking advantage of their teachers' technical illiteracy. The highest dense category consists of jokes about students' non-seriousness toward their online lectures. There are serious disciplinary issues and distractions. Students have devised new excuses to avoid online classes and assigned home-based activities. Some posts even depicted poor prospects for these ill-trained students. Online classes have been depicted as a useless activity. This hierarchical arrangement of the semantic densities revealed the concerns of the current social-media users in Pakistan. Policymakers and content creators should come up with sagacious measures to make the best of these virtual classrooms and address the genuine concerns of all the stakeholders.

Chapter 9 examines the problems of Russian youth adaptations in the condition of self-isolation under COVID 19 such as online education supported technologies, psychological and physical health, and the experience of the traditional confession. The authors collected the data from the students of Don State Technical University to prove that the student youth have several problems caused by self-isolation as well as to specify what methods can be applied to overcome COVID-19 based challenges. Sports and spirituality can provide a solid foundation for all health factors and purposefully contribute to the adaptation to post COVID-19 social reality.

In Chapter 10, the authors explain that the modern world is facing the acute captivity of pandemics. Despite the modern world's technological and scientific development, coronavirus has appeared to be stronger, infects people regardless of their social status, place of residence, financial status, origin, intellectual level, and, most importantly, age, seems to be unbelievable. However, the situation is much more complicated especially when the number of deaths increases and it enslaves people almost the world's whole population. Causing certain stress, the pandemic has changed the lifestyles, education system, and economic activities of the world. All these changes have their consequences and influence, which are presented in this chapter. Moreover, it reflects the results of infodemic during the pandemic stress and deals with the psycho-physiological indicators of students and scientific circles.

Chapter 11 addresses how the pandemic has transformed the world at a surprising speed in terms of consumer behaviors and applicable virtual strategies to capture new opportunities. Although, there have been some short-term sharp declines in consumer spending, confident changes have been realized through consumers' evolution into "digitalization" or the use of contactless, functional, and appropriate business models. Accordingly, the pandemic has also brought digitalization forward for companies, making it almost obligatory. This chapter discusses exemplary, inspirational practices of companies that have developed business models, products, and services by managing changes accelerated by the pandemic.

Chapter 12 explains the different frames used in the COVID-19 coverage in Ecuador by the national and international press were analyzed through their Twitter accounts. This allowed the examination of which aspects of the pandemic were given greater prominence by each newspaper. The study was based on five generic frames, between 17 March and 16 April 2020. The exploration of these frames was carried out using inter-subjective content analysis, using four previously trained encoders. The dominant frames for COVID-19 in Ecuador varied according to the media group studies as, the concept of heterogeneity was confirmed within framing theory, according to which a single reality, understood as a textual and visual construct, is addressed in multiple ways by the selection of certain aspects that are given greater emphasis or priority. The international newspapers and, to a lesser extent, the national press showed their propensity to "internalize" the dynamic of sensationalism. There are discrepancies in the interests of the readerships concerning the dominant frames in the media.

Chapter 13 explains the relationship between international trade, WTO law, international trade strategy, labor standards, human rights, and public health in the context of the COVID-19 Pandemic crisis. The most effective way to overcome the crisis is timely and effective information-sharing since an informed community can make better decisions on trade issues. The urgency of effective measures and implementation of new WTO regulations are believed to be vital for providing fair trade in the present circumstances. The right trade policies would not only revive the trade and recover the time lost to the crisis but would also shift toward a more sustainable and inclusive future.

Chapter 14 provides insights to understand the business environment for the family businesses in the Gulf Cooperation Council (GCC) based on the theoretical foundation of organizational ecology and open system perspective during the COVID-19 pandemic. More specifically, the reader can understand the business environment of the family firms and how firms can recover from the pandemic by fighting against the infodemic in the GCC region. We have used a survey to collect data online from the family firms from Oman during the first and second waves of COVID-19 (i.e., Feb-Dec 2020). The results of the study demonstrate that business infodemic negatively moderates the linkage between business environment and innovation performance nexus, while positively moderates between business environment and commerce association. This research implies the scanning of the Gulf business environment and continuous innovation by family-owned enterprises is vital to avoid U-Shape recovery in the Arab economies.

Chapter 15 examines the influence of faculties' social media literacy, knowledge, and awareness of COVID-19 on their resilience via persuasion and coping behavior. Following the essence of the deductive reasoning approach in a positivism paradigm, the study used the partial least square-based structural equation modeling (PLS-SEM) technique to analyze the data. The study collected data using a random sampling method, and results revealed that social media literacy, knowledge, and awareness of COVID-19 positively influenced persuasion. Engaging in persuasion also positively predicts faculties' resilience. Surprisingly, the study found no significant moderating influence on coping behavior. The findings of this study imply beneficial insights for policymakers and educators for ensuring an educational environment.

Chapter 16 investigates the stock market prices influenced by company financial performance during the period March 2007 to September 2020, which included both the beginning of the global financial crisis and the ongoing COVID-19 pandemic crisis. Using quarterly financial data retrieved from the first 34 companies listed on the New York Stock Exchange. According to their transaction volumes, empirical results show that in the period between the two crises, stock market metrics including price to earnings, price to sales, price to book value, and price to free cash flow were shaped by financial performance indicators such as gross margin ratio, operating margin ratio, earnings before interest, taxes, depreciation, and amortization margin, pretax margin and net profit margin.

Chapter 17 sheds light on social media users in Turkey and their misinformation reporting during Covid-19, their views on which sources spread suspicious and misinformation the most, and the level of trust in institutions during the pandemic process. After investigation, it was found that participants followed developments in the pandemic on social media, 61 percent were exposed to false information about Covid-19 every day, and most encountered suspicious information on Facebook and Twitter. Social media users who participated in the study found that the institutions they least trusted were the World Health Organization (WHO), pharmaceutical companies, political opposition of Turkey, and traditional media.

Chapter 18 explains that the COVID-19 outbreak has prevented students to contribute to the economic growth of Pakistan. This study aims to highlight the COVID-19 outbreak's effects on the educational sector in Pakistan. Pakistan's overall public sector expenditure as a percentage of GDP before the pandemic was already low as compared to the regional level, but due to the pandemic, it has dropped down significantly. According to empirical and theoretical findings, the results show that the lack of school education for a long time develop unskilled human resource. The COVID-19 outbreak has impacted students learning activities which may increase the dropout rates, loss of mental health and consequently may impact the economic growth of Pakistan later.

This is one of the first books that focus on the COVID-19 based pandemic, infodemic, and the performance of organizations across the world. The chapters of this book cover the three key areas (HRM, Finance, and Marketing) of business management.

Acknowledgment

This book is developed, edited, and compiled during the period of COVID-19. It was a challenge to approach the authors and collect the chapters within the time limit. Therefore, I acknowledge and appreciate the true efforts of my co-editor *Prof. Dr. Emilia Alaverdov*, all the authors, and the staff of IGI Global for their unconditional support. I am also thankful to my family for giving me time to complete this book while working at home during COVID-19. Especially, I acknowledge the moral support of Muhammad Ibrahim (Billi), Shahnoor, and Mahnoor.

Chapter 1
Mental Health and Employee Performance:
A COVID-19-Based View

Muhammad Waseem Bari
https://orcid.org/0000-0003-2329-3857
Government College University, Faisalabad, Pakistan

Qurrahtulain Khan
University of Kotli, Pakistan

ABSTRACT

The objective of this descriptive study is to highlight the issues related to the mental health of employees during COVID-19. This chapter reviews the impact of the COVID-19 outbreak on mental health of employees, and different diseases (such as anxiety, insomnia, and depression) impact employees' behavior and performance. Post-review of the latest articles, blogs, term papers, reports of the World Health Organization, and newspapers confirms the impact of COVID-19 on the physical and mental health of the employees and performance of the organizations negatively. Specifically, this study has discussed the different psychological problems like anxiety, depression, insomnia, social isolation with employees working in Pakistan. This study also highlights the measures took by the Pakistani government against COVID-19 and their results.

INTRODUCTION

Human history has faced several ups and downs in the shape of different pandemics, epidemics, and world wars. For instance, Prehistoric epidemic: Circa (3000 B.C)., Flu pandemic (1889-1890), Spanish Flu (1918-1920), Asian Flu (1957-1958), AIDS pandemic and epidemic (1981-present day) Swine Flu pandemic (2009-2010), West African Ebola epidemic (2014-2016)(Jarus, 2020), world war I (1914-1918), world war II (1939-1945), and COVID-19 (2019-present). Coronavirus disease of 2019 (COVID-19) began spreading at the end of 2019 and was seen toward the beginning of January 2020. It began spread-

DOI: 10.4018/978-1-7998-7164-4.ch001

ing in China (Wuhan) in mid-to-late January. Upwards of 184 out of 195 nations have been affected by COVID-19. Comprehending the helpful test is the key need through legitimate preventive measures to stop its spread, just as a corrective measure to build up an antibody. The effect of this general wellbeing crisis has influenced nations and networks as far as financial, socio-mental issues, and universal relations. United States of America, Brazil, Italy, and India are the most affected nations by COVID-19 respectively. Millions of people are affected by COVID-19 across the world.

The COVID-19 is not the only global challenge that the world is facing these days. Infodemic based on pandemic (COVID-19) is another serious challenge for the world. Each flare-up is joined with a sort of big wave of data and information, however, this data can be based on deception, gossipy tidbits, rumors, and so on. Misinformation not only impacts negatively on the human body but also the mental health of the people. The management at WHO's Health Emergencies Program is also worried and understands the impact of infodemic on human health and their professional performance.

Business organizations are facing the challenges of pandemic (COVID-19) and may also start to face the glitches of infodemic in 2020. Due to COVID-19 based infodemic, business organizations are facing serious consequences from the perspective of financial matters, employees' psychological and physical health, employee performance, and organization s' performance. Social media such as Facebook, WhatsApp, etc. played a very aggressive role in the growth of this infodemic. Social media has no check and balances on the reliability of the content and data. The misinformation/wrong information regarding health issues of the employees, organizations' market share and financial matters, future firing and hiring policies of the organizations, international operations of the companies are the main causes to disturb the organizations during this pandemic. The COVID-19 based infodemic has also disturbed the psychological contract between the employer and the employees. The impact of pandemic (COVID-19) may be decreased in 2021, however, the impact of relevant infodemic will continue on organizations several years in the future.

From the beginning of the COVID 19 pandemic, misinformation, rumors, and conspiracies have surfaced which has undermined the trust in health care organizations or even the government. Work-life has been profoundly impacted by the pandemic in terms of economic/social life disruption, loss of livelihoods, and impaired wellbeing. Although the World Health Organization (WHO) has developed the guidelines of workplace measures of employees during COVID 19, the wellbeing and mental health of the employees will greatly determine the safety measures implementation and sustainability.

As COVID 19 has been declared to be long lasting by the World Health Organization, the adaptation to the changes in lifestyle will have to be understood from a long-term perspective. From an organizational point of view, this is a period of an opportunity to redesign workplace environments in a manner that they are equally adaptable to the current demands and enhance the wellbeing of its employees. Employees being the greatest assets in current challenging times, their needs must be taken care of to build an effective and sustainable work environment.

There has been a massive growth in the number of COVID 19 cases all across the globe. For most of the employees, work from home or flexible work hours has been the new norm since lockdown. Except for the essential services providers (such as medical doctors, nurses, and emergency staff) who do not have an option to work from home, all of the employers had to undertake sudden precautionary measures in terms of safety and social distancing. According to a survey, 90% of employers believe that work from home and other adaptive measures were necessary during this time and have rather more advantages such as employees becoming more self-reliant and robust. Several governing bodies across the world have issued guidelines for employees in terms of prevention for COVID 19. Some of the safety measures include allowing sick employees to work from home, reducing unnecessary official visits, and avoiding social gatherings. Unfortunately, there have been instances where employees have not been prepared well before the implementation of these guidelines by a few organizations. Some organizations have made it compulsory for their employees to work as usual. Furthermore, a large proportion of employees have reported greater fear, anxiety, and distress due to work pressure. These outcomes can impact an employee's productivity. Hence it is important to assess whether workplace environments are adequately prepared to follow the measures which can eventually reduce the COVID 19 related fear and maintain a productive work profile. So far, accurate data regarding the mental health of employees during COVID 19 is lacking, however past literature has identified a broad range of psychological impacts on essential and non-essential workers.

In Italy, a study that was conducted on 260 healthcare employees showed that, amongst various factors, stigma had a very high impact on the employees' outcomes when they come across COVID-19 patients (Ramaci, Barattucci, Ledda, & Rapisarda, 2020). On the other hand, in Chinese hospitals a study conducted on 1257 healthcare employees, it was found that healthcare employees reported experiencing symptoms of anxiety 44.6%, insomnia 34%, depression 50.4%, and distress 71.5% – especially in female nurses. It shows that nurses suffer a lot and intervention, psychological support is required for them. According to Greenberg and his colleague's mental health challenges which were faced by health care employees in COVID-19 and it was suggested that staff and managers need to help each other through psychological well-being.

According to Greenberg, Docherty, Gnanapragasam, & Wessely (2020), this situation could enhance psychological pressure, and such decisions normally divided into four types: caring for severely unwell patients, allocation of resources and balancing the physical, aligning patient needs with the family and mental health needs of employees. Jiménez-Pavón, Carbonell-Baeza, & Lavie (2020))in their earliest studies have mentioned that COVID-19 is more prevalent among individuals with comorbidities, such as diabetes, hypertension, and heart disease, breathing issues, and especially among old people.

A study which was conducted in Italy showed that the human age itself plays a critical role in increasing the number of COVID-19 affected cases. Onder, Rezza, & Brusaferro (2020) mentioned in their studies that 23% of the population in Italy have been infected with COVID-19. According to Ammar et al. (2020) this situation of the pandemic, there is a need to control the increased psychosocial health, psychosocial stressors, and wellbeing through psychosocial support, many different intervention strategies, and behavioral change.

Studies show that health care professionals are facing problems due to heavy workload, poor infrastructure, and limited resources. According to Sandesh et al. (2020), health care workers are affected by stress, anxiety, depression, and the government should take necessary actions to reduce their burden or workload. Feeling of helplessness, loneliness may result in depression, anxiety, and stress. Poor infrastructure and due to lack of awareness among the community increase the level of stress, depression, and anxiety in Pakistan. Many studies show that even after the pandemic high level of depression, anxiety and stress was found in health care professionals

Human is a social animal. Therefore, interactions and social relations are mandatory for the survival of human beings. Contrary, social distancing is one the key point of the standard operating procedures (SOPs) designed by WHO and the government of Pakistan as well(World Health Organization, 2020). Therefore, social distancing (means isolation)has badly affected the mental health of employees. In this situation, employers need to stay connected with employees and offer job crafting policy. In these unusual circumstances if the employers do not cooperate then employees can be frustrated and demotivated. During this pandemic of COVID-19, the general public was hesitant and fearful to go out of homes. However, several professional workers such as doctors and paramedical staff were bound to go out for the job. Lai et al. (2020) conduct a survey on the healthcare workers serving in Wuhan (China), the suspected origin of COVID-19. Lai et al. (2020) reported that frontline healthcare staff who were directly involved in diagnosis, treatments, and care of COVID-19 patients have clear symptoms of depression, anxiety, insomnia, and distress.

Zvolensky et al. (2020) presented a heuristic model, where they explained the COVID-19 related behavioral outcomes. For instance, COVID-19have psychological and behavioral effects like insomnia, bereavement and insecurity, increased use of tobacco and alcohol, pains, aches, and lack of energy. COVID-19 also increased the rate of depression and anxiety among healthcare workers(Zvolensky et al., 2020). COVID-19 brings global changes in behaviors, societies, and organizational behaviors. Doreen Marshall discusses in his web blog that "Any change can bring with it stress, but we know that stress of longer duration and more intensity without remitting can harm one's mental health"(Marshall, 2020). Given the unique nature of challenges imposed by the lockdown itself, mental health issues need to be addressed as a top priority. From insights obtained from other studies based on past pandemic experiences, some of the pandemic's effect on employees' mental health were reported as, isolation, adverse mental health, insomnia, anxiety, and depression.

Working individuals (like to work from home) have suffered from unique challenges such as managing domestic/financial stress, adapting to the new work parameters, etc. The employees working from home are putting in more hours, managing increased responsibilities, and quite often their way of coping is unhealthy. On the other side, the employees working from their offices also take psychological burden at the workplace where organizations are not sensitized adequately regarding COVID-19.COVID-19 has severely affected employees (of both the public and private sectors) especially in the psychological and financial domains, however, the private sector employees suffered more severely as compared to public sector employees.

ANXIETY, DEPRESSION, AND INSOMNIA SYMPTOMS AMONG EMPLOYEES

COVID-19 has challenged the mental health of millions of workers globally. Almost 65-70% of the total workforce available is females and facing anxiety, depression, and insomnia in the fight against COVID-19(Lai et al., 2020).Unlike housewives and others who have not been exposed directly while staying at home during the lockdown nationwide/globally. Emergency need-based health workers in particular and others in general have faced several effects of COVID-19. They have not only faced the loss of their dear ones' lives but also faced social isolation and financial pressure, resulting in further stress and depression. The strict lockdown affected small business entrepreneurs more severely. Contrary, some businesses such as medical testing labs /pharmacies have benefitted from the COVID-19 period.

In Pakistan, workers affected by COVID-19 have been reported an average of 42% moderate depression, 26% have been affected severely by anxiety (Dain & Pappadopulos, 2020). On the other side, in China, as per the WHO policy brief 50%of workers affected by COVID-19 have been affected by depression, 45% anxiety, and about 34% have been suffering from insomnia(Lai et al., 2020). During the COVID-19 period, the occurrence of mental health issues (anxiety, depression and insomnia, and suicides) in health workers such as nurses, doctors, and supporting staff remained at a higher ratio as compared to the general population. Even, 40% of health workers have been said goodbye to their jobs(Limb, 2016). As per the WHO report, it is estimated that about 18-20 million health workers will be deficient worldwide in the next decade. Therefore, by 2030, stress and pressure on the health care sector will increase(Limb, 2016). There is a need for time to launch an awareness campaign globally to focus on the mental health problems of frontline health workers. It is also required to restructuring the existing health system in the provision of mental health support in emergencies. In this regard, the WHO campaign "stay at home" and COVID-19 vaccine for medical staff steps are appreciable. The countries with more population especially South Asian countries India, Pakistan, and Bangladesh should consider these WHO steps seriously. The world needs to spend more budget on mental health out of the total health budget(Dain & Pappadopulos, 2020).

SOCIAL ISOLATION AND ANXIETY

COVID-19 has changed the lifestyle and working behaviors of the working class. The new normal lifestyle has changed the working approach of the professional, and it is not easy to accept this change for workers. Human beings are social animals and they produce incredible results as a team and believe in teamwork in general. However, the workers in social isolation become the victims of anxiety and depression which decrease the productivity of workers and increase the threats of job security. Hence, it is very important to deal with anxiety head-on to avoid unnecessary stress on workers which seriously affects their mental health and overall performance. Employers can play a vital role in helping to ease their employee job when workers showed psychological safe to work under COVID-19 SOPs.

A stressful environment makes difficult for managers to influence their workers effectively. In the countries where complete lockdown and isolation were applied by the governments, the performance of workers and organizations decreased there. During the period of stay at home to maintain the social distancing, the level of anxiety and tension was increased in workers. Post lockdown, the abilities of workers to perform their jobs are decreased(Kenny, 2020). On the other side, in the countries where smart lockdown/ semi-lockdown was applied, the mental health of those countries' workers was much better. Pakistan was the first country that introduced the notion of smart lockdown and applied it effectively. The results of this smart lockdown were great. Pakistani business organizations and workers did not suffer much financially and socially due to regular business activities under the control of SOPs. Pakistani exports in textiles pharmaceutical industries have increased in 2020 as compared to previous fiscal years. The workers associated with the textile and pharma industries of Pakistan are working 24/7 in multiple shifts to meet the export targets/orders placed by foreign importers(Geo News, 2020).

COVID-19 has introduced new normal social and economic lifestyles. The majority of workers are attempting to manage a wide range of professional and personal responsibilities with the restrictions of COVID-19. With the stress of responsibilities and uncertainty of career due to COVID-19, the workers are facing various psychological issues. Therefore, to maintain the productivity of the organizations and the performance of workers, there is a dire need to address the mental health issues owing to exposures in COVID-19 environments. According to a study, approximately 50% of students across the world who are exposed to COVID-19, are hunting their mental health (Son, Hegde, Smith, Wang, & Sasangohar, 2020). As the pandemic has lingered for a considerable time above one year, the social distancing, remote working, business shutdowns, schools, college closures, and economic uncertainty have led to greater stress thus putting more pressure challenges for a common worker to manage routine affairs. In this stressed environment, workers are working for more time, juggling more responsibilities, and dealing with the additional workload in an unhealthy way. This practice usually leads to reduced employee engagement, satisfaction, and productivity. In nutshell, it also affects the overall performance of the company/organization

EMPLOYEE ENGAGEMENT, SATISFACTION, AND PRODUCTIVITY

Since February 2020, employees with soft skills are working from home because of COVID-19. Two thousand and twenty is a year of stress and tension for the organizations and employees as well. The employers and employees are experiencing the virtual workplace. The employees are facing a lot of problems in the virtual workplace. It is the responsibility of leaders /managers to motivate the workers and increase their engagement in the virtual workplace. The managers should focus on the workers to improve their mental health in the present COVID-19 situation. The workers should be engaged in the planning /execution of various strategies against COVID-19 environments. It is time to design the policies and strategies by keeping in mind COVID-19 impact to motivate, engage, and to enhance their performance. Managers should redesign various teams at the virtual workplace to produce maximum, frustration at all stages should be managed, and the communication gap should be minimized. With such measures not only workers/organization output will increase but also raise their morale and satisfaction level. Job security should be offered to workers to increase productivity.Covid-19has provided human resource managers with opportunities to think more to win the hearts and minds of the workers to gain their loyalties to perform better(Nisha Chanana, 2020).

PAKISTAN AND BATTLE OF COVID-19

Covid-19 has seriously affected the mental health of employees of both the public and private sectors. As employees being head of families are responsible for managing all livelihoods for their respective families. Since the announcement of restrictive measures for pandemic containment, Pakistan implemented various types of lockdown measures (such as full, partial, smart, and macro lockdowns) which appeared to give promising results (NCOC, 2020; Sandesh et al., 2020). As an outcome of these strict and consistent measures adopted by the current Government, Pakistan is one of the few countries with a low death rate, had a high compliance rate and therefore disease spread has been restrictive (NCOC, 2020). One of the reasons for the successful implementation of these programs was adherence to the quarantine instructions. Due to various forms of psychological nudges (such as using mobile for awareness messaging, social media, and electronic/print media), the masses understood that precautionary measures are necessary. Otherwise, the situation in Pakistan can be dangerous because of the huge population in big cities of Pakistan.

Unlike the rest of the world, Pakistan at the national level worked under a single declared platform of NCOC (National Command And Operation Center) where all decisions by the federal government were made in the light of pandemic effects on all segments of society (NCOC, 2020). It leaves a negative impact on the employee's mental health and their families. In China, COVID-19 brought problems like stress, depression, job insecurity, and financial losses to the employers and employees. These problems eventually affected the mental health of the working class which creates obstacles for mental health services (Lai et al., 2020). Psychologically disturbed professionals also decreased their performance and productivity as well. A survey conducted by mental health provider Ginger in which 7 out of 10 employees agreed that the COVID-2019 pandemic is the most stressful time of their entire professional career (Gavidia, 2020). Due to the downsizing policy of multinational organizations, the forthcoming threats of losing Jobs have badly affected workers 'mental health.

The root causes of this impact were financial and social because thousands of small and medium scale business organizations shut down their operations, and several big organizations applied the policy of right-sizing as per the situation developed by COVID-19. The financial crisis and social isolation lead the employees to certain forms of depression. Culturally, Asian people are more socially knitted with each other than western society. Therefore, COVID-19 based social distancing created more impact on the mental health of Asian societies. Moreover, in south Asian societies goodwill gestures of affection and love are related to a handshake or hug which are not allowed as per COVID-19 SOPs. The COVID-19 health crisis has turned into a global economic crisis, putting at risk the health, jobs, and incomes of millions of people around the world. The strict containment measures adopted by all the countries in the first half of 2020 to stop the spread of the disease, put a substantial brake on economic and social activities. Although, Pakistan has not suffered from COVID-19 as India, however, still Pakistan has a projected economic loss of up to 2.5 trillion rupees because of the COVID-19 pandemic in 2020. Moreover, the government of Pakistan figured out that around 3 million jobs are anticipated to be lost in the first round of the COVID-19 outbreak (Bashir, 2020).

REFERENCES

Ammar, A., Trabelsi, K., Brach, M., Chtourou, H., Boukhris, O., Masmoudi, L., ... Ahmed, M. (2020). Effects of home confinement on mental health and lifestyle behaviours during the COVID-19 outbreak: Insight from the" ECLB-COVID19" multi countries survey. *Biology of Sport*, *38*(1), 9–21. doi:10.5114/biolsport.2020.96857 PMID:33795912

Bashir, S. (2020, September 12). The Impact Of Covid-19: How Pakistani Workers Are Living With The New Reality. *Dawn News*. Retrieved from https://www.dawn.com/news/1560876

Dain, K., & Pappadopulos, E. (2020). *Opinion: Depression, anxiety, insomnia — health workers, and the side effects of COVID-19*. Retrieved September 22, 2020, from https://www.devex.com/news/opinion-depression-anxiety-insomnia-health-workers-and-the-side-effects-of-covid-19-97607

Gavidia, M. (2020). *How Has COVID-19 Affected Mental Health, Severity of Stress Among Employees?* Retrieved December 11, 2020, from https://www.ajmc.com/view/how-has-covid19-affected-mental-health-severity-of-stress-among-employees

Geo News. (2020). *Pakistan's exports increase by 7.2% amid the COVID-19 pandemic*. Retrieved December 5, 2020, from https://www.geo.tv/latest/321785-pakistans-exports-increase-by-72-amid-covid-19-pandemic

Greenberg, N., Docherty, M., Gnanapragasam, S., & Wessely, S. (2020). Managing mental health challenges faced by healthcare workers during a covid-19 pandemic. *BMJ (Clinical Research Ed.)*, 368. doi:10.1136/bmj.m1211 PMID:32217624

Jarus, O. (2020). *20 of the worst epidemics and pandemics in history*. Retrieved December 26, 2020, from https://www.livescience.com/worst-epidemics-and-pandemics-in-history.html

Jiménez-Pavón, D., Carbonell-Baeza, A., & Lavie, C. J. (2020). Physical exercise as a therapy to fight against the mental and physical consequences of COVID-19 quarantine: Special focus in older people. *Progress in Cardiovascular Diseases*, *63*(3), 386–388. doi:10.1016/j.pcad.2020.03.009 PMID:32220590

Kenny, R. (2020). *How Can We Combat Post-Lockdown Anxiety?* Retrieved September 12, 2020, from https://www.thehrdirector.com/business-news/employee-engagement/one-simple-tip-from-mental-health-experts-to-boost-staff-wellbeing-and-combat-post-lockdown-workplace-anxiety/

Lai, J., Ma, S., Wang, Y., Cai, Z., Hu, J., Wei, N., Wu, J., Du, H., Chen, T., Li, R., Tan, H., Kang, L., Yao, L., Huang, M., Wang, H., Wang, G., Liu, Z., & Hu, S. (2020). Factors Associated With Mental Health Outcomes Among Health Care Workers Exposed to Coronavirus Disease 2019. *JAMA Network Open*, *3*(3), e203976. doi:10.1001/jamanetworkopen.2020.3976 PMID:32202646

Limb, M. (2016). The world will lack 18 million health workers by 2030 without adequate investment, warns UN. *BMJ (Clinical Research Ed.)*, *1*, 1. https://www.who.int/hrh/com-heeg/bmj.i5169.full.pdf. doi:10.1136/bmj.i5169 PMID:27660102

Marshall, D. (2020). *Taking Care of your Mental Health in the Face of Uncertainty*. American Foundation of Suicide Prevention. Retrieved from https://www.easton.wednet.edu/docs/3-18-20-MentalHealthSupport.pdf

NCOC. (2020). *SOPs*. Retrieved October 13, 2020, from https://ncoc.gov.pk/sop.php

Nisha Chanana, S. (2020). Employee engagement practices during COVID-19 lockdown. *Journal of Public Affairs*, *2*. https://www.ncbi.nlm.nih.gov/pmc/articles/PMC7536939/

Onder, G., Rezza, G., & Brusaferro, S. (2020). Case-fatality rate and characteristics of patients dying in relation to COVID-19 in Italy. *Journal of the American Medical Association*, *323*(18), 1775–1776. doi:10.1001/jama.2020.4683 PMID:32203977

Ramaci, T., Barattucci, M., Ledda, C., & Rapisarda, V. (2020). Social Stigma during COVID-19 and its impact on HCWs outcomes. *Sustainability*, *12*(9), 3834. doi:10.3390u12093834

Sandesh, R., Shahid, W., Dev, K., Mandhan, N., Shankar, P., Shaikh, A., & Rizwan, A. (2020). Impact of COVID-19 on the mental health of healthcare professionals in Pakistan. *Cureus*, *12*(7), 1–5. doi:10.7759/cureus.8974 PMID:32775056

Son, C., Hegde, S., Smith, A., Wang, X., & Sasangohar, F. (2020). Effects of COVID-19 on college students' mental health in the United States: An interview survey study. *Journal of Medical Internet Research*, *22*(9), 1–36. doi:10.2196/21279 PMID:32805704

World Health Organization. (2020). *Population-based age-stratified seroepidemiological investigation protocol for coronavirus 2019 (COVID-19) infection, 26 May 2020*. World Health Organization.

Zvolensky, M. J., Garey, L., Rogers, A. H., Schmidt, N. B., Vujanovic, A. A., Storch, E. A., Buckner, J. D., Paulus, D. J., Alfano, C., Smits, J. A. J., & O'Cleirigh, C. (2020). Psychological, addictive, and health behavior implications of the COVID-19 pandemic. *Behaviour Research and Therapy*, *134*(May), 103715. doi:10.1016/j.brat.2020.103715 PMID:32891956

KEY TERMS AND DEFINITIONS

Anxiety: Anxiety means emotion developed by feelings of tension, apprehensive feelings, and physical changes such as a rise in blood pressure.

Depression: Depression refers to a mood syndrome that origins a tenacious feeling of grief and loss of interest.

Employee Engagement: The extent to which employees feel enthusiastic about their work and remain loyal, committed to their organization.

Infodemic: Infodemic denotes a fast and far-reaching spread of equally correct and erroneous information about some phenomenon, such as a disease (COVID-19).

Pandemic: Pandemic refers to a global epidemic, pandemic spreads several countries at the same time and effects a large number of people.

Productivity: Productivity denotes a ratio between input volume and volume of output.

Chapter 2
The Impact of COVID-19 on the Vulnerable Groups:
Refugees and Labor Migrants-Based View

Emilia Alaverdov
https://orcid.org/0000-0003-3282-172X
Georgian Technical University, Georgia

ABSTRACT

The chapter deals with the most acute situation of the 21st century caused by a new type of infectious disease called COVID-19. It highlights the situation of such vulnerable groups of society as refugees, asylum seekers, and labor migrants, which even worsens their tough living conditions. In an alarming time of global crises like the COVID-19 pandemic, major international actors are calling for increased protection of the most vulnerable groups, including victims of trafficking, migrants, and refugees, and advocate greater access to healthcare for all people regardless of their social and migration status.

INTRODUCTION

Millions of people cross state borders in search of a new place of residence or work, for study or various types of internships, for rest or medical treatment, fleeing political, national, racial, etc. persecution or environmental disasters. Here, it is important to note that migration between countries includes not only irretrievable migrants, migrant workers, and refugees, but also students, businessmen, etc., including tourists, given that short trips usually precede subsequent long-term migrations. These and other types of migration movements are often combined into the concept of international migration of population. There is hardly any country which managed to escape from migration flows and sharp modern contradictions between national and foreign citizens expressed in the growth of social tension in places of concentration of migrants, caused, in particular, by the intensification of competition in national labor markets, increased racial and national hostility, xenophobia, etc.

The relevance of the topic is also explained by the great impact of international migration on the population, and will be one of the important demographic processes for the demographic development

DOI: 10.4018/978-1-7998-7164-4.ch002

of individual countries and regions of the world. At the same time, we are talking not only about the impact on the dynamics of the total population of a particular region of the world, or an individual state but about deeper demographic changes, including for humanity as a whole (Iontsev,1999). Since ancient times, the population has been characterized by the desire to migrate, or relocations from one country to another, from one continent to another, in other words, from one place of residence and employment to another. From the very inception of human history, these migrations were considered one of the most important types of population movement, the essence of which was that a certain part of the people or tribe stood out from a more or less closed union and created a new center of human culture.

Here we have to say that international migration of the population is one of the factors in improving the health of the world's population, which is achieved as a result of the "mixing" of nations and nationalities, thus improving the genetic fund of all mankind. However, these people are in great danger and appear in a very tough and insecure situation during the new and very dangerous challenge which faces the modern world, the unknown for mankind disease called COVID 19.

LITERATURE REVIEW

The tutorial *Methodology and Study Methods Migration Processes* edited by Zh. Zayonchkovskaya, I. Molodikova, V. Mukomel (2007) and published by the Center for Migration Studies focuses on methodological and methodological issues in the study of population migration. Moreover, it shows the Western approaches to the study of migration and describes the sociological approaches to the study of migration, and as well as the highly developed migration theories; highlights the methodological and practical aspects of studying integration migration, with its legal aspects of interdisciplinary study. The book is focused on the migration policy, its management, and the proper ways to represent migration processes.

The book *Migration Processes in the European Union: Contemporary Problems and Challenges MIGRATION* edited by O. Trofimova (2019) examines the existing situation in European countries, as well as the impact of high migration, flows on individual structural components. The book shows national features of the regulation of migration processes in each European country. Moreover, it assessed the effectiveness of the EU supranational policy. It deals with the social, economic, and political challenges associated with the growth of migration from the Middle East and the problems of their adaptation and integration into the host communities. Here the most important is that the authors explain certain theoretical approaches such as classical migration theories, modern and European theories of migration.

Policy Brief: COVID-19 and People on the Move the report issued by United Nations (2020) describes the tough situation of such vulnerable groups of people as migrants, refugees, asylum-seekers, and internally displaced persons (IDPs) which is worsened by the COVID 19. The study is mostly focused on the three aspects of their lives: a poor health care situation and their limited access to health services. The first is due to the following obstacles: legal, because many of them have entered the country illegally, and language, as most of the newcomers do not know the language of the hosting country). Then second is cultural aspects and their severe socio-economic conditions; and the third is unsecure lives.

United Nations Development Program, *Human Rights Due Diligence, and COVID-19: a Rapid Self-Assessment for Business (2020)* gives us a valuable review and assessment of the socio-economic upheavals caused by the global spread of COVID-19, which occurs in times of acute inequality and environmental volatility. The study highlights that the pandemic strongly affects especially vulnerable and marginalized groups with fewer resources, to protect themselves from health risks; it describes the lack of their access to the healthcare system, or purchase essential goods.

Analytical notes *How to protect workers migrants in conditions pandemic COVID-19* issued by the International Labor Organization (2020), gives very strong recommendations for policymakers and constituents. It is obvious that the purpose of this Policy Brief is to provide the necessary information and several substantive recommendations in helping governments and other stakeholders to develop policy responses to the COVID-19 pandemic to protect migrant workers, refugees, and displaced persons working outside of their home countries. Furthermore, the document says that it will be regularly updated according to the development of the situation.

Another valuable document by the Working Group on the Smuggling of Migrants (2020), was developed at the Conference of participants of the *Organization conventions of United Nations against transnational organized crime* held by the Organization of United Nations. The background of the document is prepared by the Secretariat of UN, which deals with the impact of natural disasters, conflicts, and such crises as the COVID-19 pandemic and their impact on the organized crime groups and smuggling routes of migrants. Moreover, it is focused on successful experience in supporting effective cooperation of law enforcement agencies during such crises to identify and investigate relevant crimes and implementation of criminal persecution.

Guidance for Monitoring of places of deprivation freedom during a pandemic COVID-19, published by the OSCE Office for Democratic Institutions and human rights (ODIHR) which has been prepared as part of ODIHR's ongoing efforts to respond to the challenges in the field of human rights emerged in the OSCE area as a result of the COVID-19 pandemic. The purpose of the joint by ODIHR and the Association for the Prevention of Torture publication is to provide strategic supporting national preventive mechanisms and other institutions monitoring places of detention around the world.

The following research *Measures, Policies and Pandemic* (2020) conducted by the International Monetary Fund deal with the measures and responses of governments to the challenges caused by the pandemic and illustrates complex political aspects of world cooperation. It highlights such aspects as a hope to cope with the existing poverty, long-run crisis, and the world after pandemics.

The valuable work by L. Guadagno *Migrants and the COVID-19 pandemic: An initial analysis* (2020) published by the International Organization for Migration studies the migrant's conditions in certain countries during the pandemic. It gives a clear analysis of different vulnerable groups and their socio-economic situation, which has a direct impact on the health conditions. The work highlight the certain challenges that migrants have encountered due to the restricted international mobility connected with pandemic prevention and the rise of xenophobia in the world communities. The work also shows the suffering of migrants from COVID-19 and having fewer chances to recover.

NEW CHALLENGE FOR SOCIAL VULNERABLE GROUPS

According to the official governmental sources, international migrations flows greatly increased by the start of the COVID 19. Thus by the end of 2019 the modern world's had approximately 272 million migrants, asylum-seekers, and refugees (UN, 2019) Here is worth estimating that it is the officially registered number of newcomers, and actually, its number is higher as not every migrant pass the boarders legally and is registered in the host country. According to the United Nations report, we can state that a large number of migrants is distributed among 20 countries most of them are residing in the United

States. Here the number of international migrants is about 51 million, then it is followed by Germany hosting approximately 13 million and the same number is in Saudi Arabia. The third place is given to the Russian Federation with 12 million migrants, here we have to highlight that Russia has mostly labor migrants from Post-Soviet countries. The last among the five major migrant-receiving countries is the United Kingdom with 10 million newcomers (UN, 2020).

Migration greatly affects both the country of origin and the host country, and as well as the living there social circles and communities. If the migration has a properly developed policy, it will have a positive impact on the country of destination and the migrants' welfare: the host country will have a cheap labor force and migrants will improve their social status. It is worthy to say that there is a significant link between migration and development. Thus, the United Nations Member States developed and approved such certain agreements and programs as: the 2030 Agenda for Sustainable Development adopted in 2015; the New York Declaration for Refugees and Migrants from 2016; and the based especially on the following declarations and acts supporting human rights such as the Universal Declaration of Human Rights; the International Covenant on Civil and Political Rights; the International Covenant on Economic, Social and Cultural Rights (UN General Assembly, 2019). Another important is Global Compact for Safe, Orderly and Regular Migration, which was validated by the UN General Assembly on 19 December 2018 and entered in force on 11 January 2019. Here we have to note that in 2019 the number of migrants whose age was 65 years or over was about 32 million, which constitutes 12% of the whole number.

Objective 22: Establish mechanisms for the portability of social security entitlements and earned benefits of the final draft of the adopted document about the Global Compact for Safe, Orderly and Regular Migration states that the hosting countries must assist migrants and ensure their social protection and security and benefit of such provisions as pensions, healthcare, etc. At the same time, when analyzing the work of certain scientists, it is necessary to realize that international migration of the population is only one of the main types of migration movement and, accordingly, is conditioned by certain general laws and patterns inherent by the movement, acting both throughout the history of mankind and in its periods or stages.

The reasons for labor migration are factors of both economic and non-economic character. Non-economic reasons include political, national, religious, racial, family, etc. The reasons for the economic nature are rooted in an economic level of development of individual countries. The labor force moves from countries with low living standards to countries with higher living standards, which is usually related to national differences in wages. Besides, an important economic factor in international labor migration is the presence of a high level of unemployment in some countries, primarily in the underdeveloped ones. An important factor in international labor migration is also the export of capital, the functioning of international corporations, which either carry out the movement of labor to capital or move their capital to the so-called "labor surplus" regions of the world.

International migrants can be divided into several main categories:

- legally arrived immigrants, who are subsequently provided with jobs and take their place in the labor market;
- labor migrants or contract workers, hosted by countries dependent on foreign labor;
- illegal immigrants, including labor migrants, which usually replace jobs at the lowest level of the labor hierarchy;

- asylum seekers for political reasons, as well as the force of the difficult economic situation in their countries (Allakhverdieva, Gabzalilova, 2007).

However, according to the UN report not all the members of UN countries have such policies and provide equal services and access to the essential or emergency health care system, which means any kind of required medical care to preserve a person's life. The report states that only 86% of states, essential services apply to all the migrants despite their status and only a few states provide the essential service to the migrants with legal status (Global Compact for Migration, 2018). In this regard, it is obvious that such vulnerable groups as migrants, refugees, and asylum seekers are in great danger in the term of worldwide pandemic called COVID-19. Here we have to highlight that the situation is even more complicated in COVID-19 conditions, which caused unexpected and insecure circumstances for both the local population and refugees, however, the second is much more vulnerable.

IMPACT OF THE COVID-19 ON ILLEGAL MIGRATION

The smuggling of migrants is an extremely lucrative business and criminal networks thrive on it due to the high demand for smuggling services and the low risk of detection and prosecution. Factors such as political instability and conflict, dire socio-economic conditions, and a lack of prospects, including for children and young people, favor these crimes. A significant proportion of those traveling along these routes come from countries in which conflicts and humanitarian crises are unfolding, political instability reigns for a long time, and there are mass disturbances and/or criminal prosecutions, therefore such persons are potentially entitled to international protection.

During the COVID-19 pandemic, most countries around the world, are to retain the spread of the virus, closed land, sea, and air borders, and took other measures to restrict internal movements, such as both quarantine and forced isolation. The closure of major entry points often leads to increased and improved patrolling at official points of entry to prevent illegal border crossings.

As the world scales up the public health response to the COVID-19 pandemic, countries are urged to take decisive action and provide all people in need with the services they need, including diagnostics. Countries are encouraged to take an integrated approach based on certain circumstances, with the focus on containing the epidemic. As in all cases of rapidly developing epidemics, especially in accidental spread of disease from person to person, it is imperative that the response is in strict accordance with human rights. The program urges that all human rights are inalienable, universal, interdependent, and interrelated. Human rights apply to all people, without exception and discrimination, and are indivisible: one category of rights hardly satisfices another category of rights. The principle of universality is the foundation of international human rights law. Governmental bodies must refrain from acting and directly or indirectly discriminate against individuals or groups, try to prevent negative consequences of public policies, and protect people from any kind of discrimination. It is worthy to say that due to existing inequalities and vulnerabilities, both the epidemic and the response to it, can have a disproportionate impact on certain groups, and this requires appropriate action to reduce inequality. Associating a virus with a specific region, city, nationality or race can lead to an increase in racism, xenophobia, and even stigmatization of regions and cities. This can create a significant stigma against certain groups; contribute to discriminatory behavior, forced additional isolation of people and communities, or violation of their privacy, in all cases affecting both mental health and access to services. In some cases, this can create the real threat of violence and lead to politically motivated responses: motivated not by facts but by fear and stigma.

Here is worth highlighting the existing practice, which shows that while fighting with illegal migration, administrative detention of migrants solely based on immigration status in the absence of real prospects of expulsion or deportation cannot be justified. Under international human rights law, the detention of immigrants can be legal only if there is a real possibility of expulsion or deportation. In the current situation, it is obvious that there are no such prospects. Security interest of public health is not applicable as an excuse to detain migrants without compelling legal basis. The Council of Europe Commissioner for Human Rights called on member states to assess the situation of persons detained in special migration centers and to release the maximum possible number of such persons from prisons. Following the Convention relating to the Status of Refugees and its 1967 Protocol, persons fleeing persecution are entitled to protection in the country where they find themselves and, under established customary law, the Refoulement principle, which means that person should not be returned to the country where they are at risk should be applicable (UNHCR, 1979).

In France, the NPM recommended the temporary closure of detention centers for administratively detained migrants in the light of the conditions existing there and the lack of prospects for deportation. In Spain, the human rights ombudsman, making similar arguments, called on the government to release persons held in migrant detention centers. In the United Kingdom, Detention Action civil society organization, mainly dealing with assisting detained migrants, questioned the legality of the administrative detention of migrants. Although the court eventually stated that the government's actions were legal, the trial itself has contributed to the adoption of positive measures to reduce the number of detained persons and to review all decisions to detain migrants (OSCE & APT, 2020).

Both the virus itself and government responses can create additional discrimination. An epidemic often reveals existing inequalities in society, and mostly, already marginalized and vulnerable people are victims of epidemic. For example, people, who do not have money for medical care, are more likely to refuse testing for the virus; people in prisons will practically not be able to control their access to medical services. It is hardly possible, without investing significant additional resources, to organize self-isolation or simply bathrooms for people in informal settlements or communities, especially if there is no running water or soap. The burden of caring for family members falls primarily on women, so closing schools or quarantining will have a disproportionate impact on women, their ability to work and earn money, and even their ability to self-isolate (UNAIDS, 2020).

THE POLICY OF SETTLEMENT AND SEGREGATION

All over the world, migrants live in a crowded environment with limited access to water and hygiene products. In such conditions, it is difficult to follow the principles of social distance and other basic preventive measures, for example, self-isolation in case of illness. To address these issues, countries should include migrants in temporary housing programs, improve their conditions of stay, and ensure their access to health services at transit points and reception centers.

In this regard, we have to highlight the problem of refugee children, which is especially acute, according to the UN, affects about 14 million people: 12.7 million refugees and 1.1 million asylum seekers. Displaced children have the most limited access to prevention services, diagnosis, treatment, and other necessary support. The COVID-19 crisis will also negatively affect their safety and access to education. EU initiate the resettlement process for 1,600 unaccompanied refugee children. On 15 April, 12 children-seeking asylum were relocated from overcrowded refugee reception centers in Lesvos, Samos, and Chios (Greece) to Luxembourg (UNICEF, 2020).

The problematic field of migration policy is rooted in ambiguity and contradictions of both political and migration spheres. The variety of approaches to the concepts of politics and the migration process generates different points of view on the vision of migration policy. The contradictions are manifested in the difference in definitions of migration policy: most of its existing definitions are too narrow in nature and do not fully disclose its essence. However, the issue of the nature, content, and effectiveness of state migration policy strategies, is still far from resolved. In this regards the attention should be paid to the entire range of proposed interpretations, approaches to understanding, and be focused on the methods of implementation of migration policy.

From the existing definitions of migration policy, it is worthy to highlight the following points and realize that migration policy is a product of political systems. Thus, it is the prerogative of not only the state but also of the various public institutions - parties, churches, etc. Public organizations - may have different points of view on the goals and means of migration policy; migration policy is a process of reconciliation of interests the state in the field of migration regulation at the federal and regional levels with the interests of migrants, local communities, political and economic elites, parties, public institutions. The most important is that migration policy is a process of interaction between states in which the transfer of jurisdiction takes place, since migrants, ceasing to be members of one society, become members of another (Volosenkova, Kabachenko, & Tarasova, 2007).

Thus, we can claim that the migration policy is one of the directions of state policy and is determined by the nature of the state structure, goals, which are persecuted by the state. It represents a state doctrine or concept regulation of migration processes; inextricably linked with the ongoing economic, social, demographic, national, cultural policies.

The specific settlement of Muslims in European cities is the result of a whole complex of processes. One of the main problems in the housing sector remains the relatively high level of segregation, and generally the concentration of minorities in low-income districts. The type of neighborhood in which a person live is influenced by his social and economic integration: lack of connections necessary to find a job, the involvement of young people in criminal activities, negative reputation of poor areas among employers - all these factors contribute to a decrease in economic activity. A significant proportion of the Muslim population lives in low-income districts. However, on the other hand, it should be noted that there are some advantages of living in an area with a large concentration of representatives of one ethnic group: it helps to preserve ethnic and cultural identity, integration is felt at least within its minority, there is an opportunity to rely on close social ties, etc. In addition, the following positive moment is noted: very often, a representative of the "district culture" successfully integrated into the external society is inclined to invest in improving the socio-economic situation in his native district. However, in European countries, the segregation of ethnic and religious minorities is a matter of concern at the municipal and state levels; they believe that the concentration of ethnoreligious minorities in a particular area undermines the natural process of integration. Here it worth mentioning that in most cases, migrants live in special hostels, temporary reception centers for migrants, training centers, detention centers, temporary camps, or communal dwellings. These may include migrants who arrived just before the outbreak of COVID-19, refugees seeking asylum, migrants awaiting a residence or work permit, people seeking family recovery, those who are passing through the area, and others. Housing conditions in such places are often cramped, people use shared washbasins, kitchens, and eating places, in other words, in such housing it is impossible to protect from COVID-19 either those who are there or those who live in the neighborhood. Authorities should take certain measures and ensure in dormitories or communal housing basic utilities such as water supply, sewerage, food, property storage, heating.

There is ample evidence that ethnic and religious discriminations play a vital role in the poor position of ethnic and religious minorities in the labor market. Along with discrimination based on ethnicity, forms of discrimination based on religion are also noted. When looking at the various religious groups within ethnic minorities, it was found that all Muslim groups are the most disadvantaged in terms of employment, and it does not matter which ethnic minority they belong to (Berthoud & Blekesaune, 2007). One of the notable facts is that when considering the questionnaire, the employer draws attention to the name of the applicant. Another fact of discrimination is the demonstration of religious affiliation in an interview that significantly reduces the chances of getting a job.

Supportive Mechanisms for Migrants to Overcome the Pandemic

The socioeconomic upheaval caused by the global spread of COVID-19 occurs at a time of acute inequality and environmental instability. The pandemic is particularly hard-hitting vulnerable and marginalized groups with fewer resources to protect themselves from health risks, access health care, or purchase essential goods. If business units, government departments, and civil society do not develop certain strategies and take timely and proactive actions, the COVID-19 pandemic could spoil much of the progress made towards the 2030 Sustainable Development Agenda (UNDP, 2020).

Business today is threatened with a bankruptcy on an unprecedented scale, leaving millions of people unemployed. In this context, confidence in the resilience of the global economy, and thus the norms and institutions that support it, are being tested like never before. Indeed, business has responded to the challenge posed by COVID-19 by supplying medical supplies, implementing employee support and welfare initiatives, and providing relief to victims. In some cases, factories have shifted to the production of life-saving masks and ventilators, which are in short supply.

However, leading companies also know that they need to go beyond activities that support public welfare and consider any negative consequences that these innovations can have on society and the environment. These companies understand that showing respect for human rights, especially in these difficult economic circumstances, is a reflection of their core values. They understand that preventing, mitigating, and addressing negative human rights impacts will be the key to maintaining the trust of customers, consumers, employees, shareholders, and communities long after the crisis is over. For this, the United Nations developed a certain program aiming to ensure and guarantee health and safety at work for all the nationals or non-nationals of any country. Particularly to develop, test, implement an effective emergency preparedness plan that includes COVID-19 response protocols; ensure access to health-care supplies, such as facemasks, for all employees without any gender, racial, religious, linguistic, ethnic or national discrimination, despite the migration status, sexual orientation, gender identity or membership of social groups facing marginalization/stigma. It means that the program is based on the basic standards of universal human rights and states that every person must have the guarantee either at the workplace or in the country. The program ensures that employees infected with COVID-19 should not be discriminated against at works or during the interviews. Moreover, the program urges to guarantee that migrants and other vulnerable groups are not associated with COVID-19 in advertising, marketing campaigns, or corporate communications to prevent the spread of stereotypes, misinformation, and stigma against marginalized groups (UNDP, 2020).

In many countries, labor migrants are a much more significant part of the labor force, make a significant contribution to the well-being of society and economies is in the forefront among those who perform basic duties in areas such as healthcare, transport, service sector, construction, agriculture, and food industry. At the same time, the majority of labor migrants are concentrated in those sectors of the economy where temporary, informal, unprotected forms of work are widespread, characterized by low wages and lack of social protection. It should be noted that foreign citizens legally working in one or another country, gain access to public social services - public health, education, social security, and unemployment insurance. Here it is worthy to say that financial resources for these purposes are generated from taxes. At the same time, it is clear that the main contribution to the budget is made by local taxpayers, simply because as a rule, they prevail against foreigners working in the country. Migrant workers pay taxes: primarily income tax, as well as a tax on remittances, property tax, etc. Besides, the cost of a migrant's labor, which ultimately determines their wages, includes all taxes paid by the company or enterprise where they work: income tax; social security tax; tax on education; health care tax; contributions to the pension fund; road tax; housing tax, etc. Therefore, considering the fact that the labor migrants are as important for the host country's economy as the local citizens are we can say that the foreign forces should have the same protection mechanism as the locals. However, there is still evidence that labor migrants are one of the most vulnerable categories of workers. Certain information indicates that migrants face increasing discrimination and xenophobia, in some cases - food shortages, layoffs, deterioration of working conditions, including a decrease or non-payment of wages, constrained or unsatisfactory housing conditions, increased restrictions on movement or forced return to their homeland (where they, as suspected carriers of the virus, may face social exclusion). Unfortunately, labor migrants are usually the first candidates for dismissal, but the last in line for testing or treatment, where local citizens are preferred. They are often excluded from the COVID-19 crisis response in their host countries, such as wage subsidies, unemployment benefits, welfare, and social protection measures. Even when they have the opportunity to be tested for COVID19 or receive medical care, they do not always respond to it, fearing being detained or deported, especially illegal migrants. If we talk about domestic workers, house workers, agricultural workers, and other kinds of foreign workforce in the informal economy, we can say that they are marginalized in many countries because local legislation does not treat them as workers.

Lack of income forces people to keep working even during illness, exacerbating the public health risks associated with the further spread of COVID-19. Migrant workers, along with local citizens, should be included in risk-sharing mechanisms - this will ensure universal coverage of social insurance and solidarity financing. Sickness provision can protect both migrants themselves, and their host local communities. In this case, the costs of providing access to affordable health care should be covered collectively through common risk-sharing mechanisms. Moreover, prescribed recurring contributions should be financed. This may be in the form of social security contributions or taxes or be a combination of the two sources. Labor migrants must also have access to quarantine areas, equipped with appropriate medical equipment, sanitary and assisting personnel. All labor migrants, including those who have lost registration or legal status, should have access to remedies against unfair treatment, including those related to reduction or non-payment of wages, denial of other rights, and discrimination in the workplace. They should be provided with access to legal assistance and translation services. To solve the existing labor problems governments, employers' organizations, and workers must contribute to concerted efforts when developing measures countering COVID-19. Among such problems are health and safety workers, insurance of the proper working conditions, support for business and small enterprises, expansion of social protection, and the creation of opportunities for employment of migrants. In this regard, the

International Organization of Employers (IOE) and International Trade Union Confederation (ITUC) issued a joint statement on COVID-19, urging all parties to strengthen coordination, and international financial institutions - to provide support accepted in socio-economic area measures (ILO, 2020).

According to the legal right of international protection and the 1951 UN Convention on the Status of Refugees, a person can be considered as a refuge if he has fled from persecution or from the dangers of war (Convention Relating to the Status of Refugees, 1951). Due to the imposed obligations of accepting countries, have to give asylum to refugees or those who need international protection and guarantee their safety (EUAFR, 2020).

States around the world are taking large-scale measures to support the most vulnerable populations from the threat of coronavirus infection. The main types of assistance include food distribution, payment social benefits and employment support; medical care, and the creation of conditions to reduce the risk of infection. In connection with the recommendations and the need to observe social self-isolation to minimize the risk of the spread of infection, governments are especially concerned about the situation of the homeless, for whom additional support must be provided.

The crisis caused by the outbreak of COVID-19 has affected almost all spheres of society and all segments of the population, but in particular, it has been disastrous for representatives of the most vulnerable social groups, including the elderly people, people with disabilities, and people without housing, orphans, and migrants. The problems of violence in families are becoming more acute, primarily affecting women and children. The number of unemployed people is increasing which will lead to the most acute consequence, such as the loss of home, etc. Poor people are disproportionately burdened by the health and financial impact of the crisis. If not properly addressed, the social crisis caused by the COVID-19 pandemic could also exacerbate inequality, discrimination, and unemployment, globally in both the medium and long term.

The International Organization for Migration notes several challenges for migrants in the context of the spread of COVID-19. The most vital is the lack of access to the health care system. In many countries, migrants, especially in cases of staying in the country on short-term visas or in other non-standard situations, cannot access health services on an equal basis with local citizens. In such conditions, it is important to ensure access to medical services for all groups of the population, including migrants. If governments do not include these populations in certain programs to overcome the consequences of COVID-19, then efforts to combat the outbreak of the virus will be less effective: more people will be infected; the emergency mode will be longer (Account Chamber RF, 2020).

BENEFICIARY GUESTS

Intensification of labor migration among developing countries started its activities in the early 1990s. Its most typical example is the attraction of cheap labor by the oil-producing countries of the Middle East for heavy, low-paid jobs. Workers come mainly from neighboring Arab countries, as well as from India, Pakistan, Bangladesh, Korea, and the Philippines. Migration from developing to economically developed countries represents the main in its scope direction of international labor migration. For economically developed countries, foreign labor from developing countries means providing several industries, infrastructure services with the necessary workers, without which a normal production process is impossible. Migrant workers tend to agree to do work for less pay than local workers do: this makes them attractive to employers.

International labor migration has become an important functioning element in the world economy, within its framework. In this regard, several main directions can be distinguished: migration from developing to economically developed countries; migration within developed countries; migration of highly qualified specialists and scientists (the so-called "brain drain"), etc. Thus within the framework of this theory, international migration is considered as a result of the constant demand for foreign labor, characteristic of economically developed countries, due, in particular, to the cheapness of this labor. A characteristic feature of this theory is the emphasis on significant differences in the levels of development of individual countries and regions of the world, which constantly generates migration flows. At the same time, it is worth saying that if legal migration is considered as a curing source for the state economy illegal migration is a rather profitable criminal type business, which harms it. According to expert estimates, the annual total income of shadow dealers who specialize in transporting Africans and Asians to Western Europe is tens of billions of dollars. At the same time, the costs of finding, temporary detention, and deportation of illegal immigrants often cause significant damage to the economy of the host countries. In this regard, to protect the national labor market from uncontrolled labor force inflow, it is necessary to know the number of illegal migrants arriving and already arrived on the territory of the state. However, the determination of the quantitative parameters of illegal migration is one of the most difficult problems. For several reasons, illegal migrants, in contrast to the legal form, for the most part, avoid any form of control over their stay, movement, and activities (Krainov, Maslenkova & Chelidze, 2007).

Migrants make up the bulk of the workforce in areas that continue to work during the crisis: agriculture, construction, logistics and delivery, waste collection, cleaning services. Inability to provide such services on a remote basis, limited access to personal transport, physical contact with colleagues. The social affect of the COVID-19 pandemic and the inclusiveness of customers, as well as a lack of personal protective equipment and hygiene, make these types of activities dangerous in terms of spread COVID-19.

A large number of migrants are employed in the areas most affected by the crisis. In this regard, it is necessary to include migrants in state support programs as part of the fight against the consequences of the COVID-19 pandemic (unemployment benefits, food stamps, subsidies for rental payments).

CONCLUSION

Representatives of vulnerable groups such as migrants, refugees, asylum seekers, etc. are subject to a greater risk of contracting coronavirus infection and at the same time have fewer opportunities to cope with a difficult life situation.

Broad coverage of inclusiveness in the activities of international organizations and national governments is developed to ensure that the rights and interests of socially vulnerable groups are respected in the process of the global fight against the spread of COVID-19. Despite the significant contribution of the taken measures to ensure the access of these population groups to quality health care, education, and employment, in several cases, forced restrictions are the main factor of negative impact on the living conditions of representatives of these groups. We have to highlight that this necessitates a comprehensive analysis of government policies in the current conditions and coordination of efforts of the state, society and business spheres.

The widespread introduction of a self-isolation regime due to the spread of COVID-19 contributes to an increase in cases of violence committed for the first time against women and children. In this case, in the conditions of limited employment, the need to pay rent, utility and mortgage payments, make the workers with a low income the most vulnerable.

Ignoring the problem of the spread of COVID-19 among migrants can make the efforts of states to overcome the consequences of the pandemic less effective: more people will be infected; the regime the emergency will be longer. Lifestyles, difficulties in obtaining medical care, and non-compliance with sanitary measures make homeless people especially vulnerable to threat. The social consequences of the COVID-19 pandemic and the inclusiveness of the spread of COVID-19 require additional supportive measures from the state and public organizations. Currently, most international, intergovernmental organizations and social movements, addressing issues of inclusion, lead it to not only ensuring the full participation of vulnerable groups in the country's social life and the enjoying of the basic standards of human rights but also to eliminating discrimination of any population groups that may be vulnerable based on gender, age, orientation, ethnicity and nationality, physical capabilities and health status, level of well-being and conditions.

RECOMMENDATIONS

- There should be considered the specific need for inclusion of migrants in COVID-19 response and the effort for their recovery. In most of the countries, such vulnerable groups as migrants, do not have equal health care condition as natives, it means that the expenses for their visits to the health care units are not covered by the state. In most cases, migrants due to the language barriers, illegal statement, etc. their admission to the health care units are practically impossible. Furthermore, irregular migrants are frightened of being reported to the immigration authorities and which will directly lead to their deportation (Guadagno, 2020).
- In this regards the main attention has to be paid to housing, which is an element of the right to a decent standard of living and becomes an instrument of protection against coronavirus.
- It is necessary to establish special control over the provision of health care and sanitation in orphanages, boarding schools for orphans with disabilities to minimize disruptions in children's access to basic and vital health services and prevent outbreaks of COVID-19 in these institutions.
- Particular attention should be paid to the situation of migrants in countries with a high proportion of migrants.
- Particularly, the government must follow the Copenhagen Declaration on Social Development, which the UN report on the creation of an inclusive society refers to, and outlines international obligations to form such a society, which would be stable, secure and fair, and which would be based on the principles of the promotion and protection of all human rights. As well as to be focused on the principles of non-discrimination, tolerance, respect for diversity, equality of opportunity, solidarity, security and participation of the entire population, including the number of disadvantaged groups and individuals and vulnerable groups and individuals (United Nations, 2007).

REFERENCES

Account Chamber of Russian Federation. (2020). *Social Impact of the COVID-19 Pandemic and Inclusiveness*. Government of Russian Federation.

Allakhverdieva, L., & Gabzalilova, V. (2007). Migration and Labor Market. In Z. M. Zayonchkovskaya (Ed.), *Methodology and Study Methods Migration Processes* (pp. 294–315). Center for Migration Studies.

Berthoud, R., & Blekesaune, M. (2007). *Persistent Employment Disadvantage*. The University of Essex.

European Union Agency for Fundamental Rights. (2020). *Fundamental Rights Report.* Luxemburg: Office of European Union.

Global Compact for Migration. (2018). *Global Compact for Safe, Orderly, and Regular Migration.* Global Compact for Migration.

Guadagno, L. (2020). *Migrants and the COVID-19 Pandemic: An Initial Analysis*. International Oganization for Migration.

International Labor Organization. (2020). *How to Protect Workers Migrants in Conditions Pandemic COVID-19*. International Labor Organization.

Iontsev, V. (1999). *International Migration for Population: Theory and History of Studying*. Dialogue.

Krainov, V., Maslenkova, E., & Chelidze, N. (2007). Impact of Migration on the Economy. In Z. M. Zayonchkovskaya (Ed.), *Methodology and Study Methods Migration Processes* (pp. 294–315). Center for Migration Studies.

Organization of Security and Cooperation in Europe and Association for the Prevention of Torture. (2020). *Guidance Monitoring Places of Detention through the COVID-19 Pandemic*. Office for Democratic Institutions and Human Rights.

United Nations. (1951). *Convention Relating to the Status of Refugees*. United Nations Office.

United Nations. (1979). *Handbook on Procedures and Criteria for Determining Refugee Status under the 1951 Convention and the 1067 Protocol relating to the Status of Refugees*. United Nations for Human Rights.

United Nations. (2007). *Practical Strategies to Promote Social Integration*. United Nations Office.

United Nations. (2019). *Population Division International Migration. ST/ESA/SER.A/438*. Department of Economic and Social Affairs.

United Nations. (2019). *Population Division International Migration 2019. ReportSTESA/SER.A/438.* Department of Economic and Social Affairs.

United Nations. (2019). *Report ST/ESA/SER.A/438. Global Compact for Safe, Orderly, and Regular Migration 2019.* United Nations General Assembly.

United Nations. (2020). *Joint United Nations Program on HIV/AIDS. Human Rights in COVID-19. Lessons from the HIV Epidemic: an Effective Community Response*. United Nations Office for Human Rights.

United Nations. (2020). *United Nations Development Program. Comprehensive Analysis of Human Rights and COVID-19. Rapid Self-Assessment of Business Areas*. United Nations Office for Human Rights.

United Nations Assembly. (2019). *Global Compact for Safe, Orderly and Regular Migration*. Report A/RES/73/195. Author.

United Nations International Cildren's Emergency Fund. (2020). *UN agencies welcome the first relocation of unaccompanied children from Greece*. Retrieved October 18, 2020, from www.unicef.org: www.unicef.org/eca/press-releases/un-first-relocation-greece

Volonsenkova, E., Kabachenko, P., & Tarasova, E. (2007). Migration Policy. Migration Management Processes. In Z. M. Zayonchkovskaya (Ed.), *Methodology and Study Methods Migration Processes* (pp. 9–13). Center for Migration Studies.

KEY TERMS AND DEFINITIONS

Conditions: Denoting the relation of an object to the subject or surrounding reality.

COVID-19: The infection disease caused by a new previously unknown coronavirus, which contains a whole family of more than 30 types of viruses.

European Union: A political and economic unification of the initially six countries with the aim of the expansion of the economic cooperation among Belgium, Germany, France, Italy, Luxembourg, and the Netherlands. Which later increased up to 28 countries, however, after the United Kingdom left the European Union on January 31, 2020, the EU has 27 member countries.

Human Migration: Movement or relocation of human beings within the country or from one country to another.

Human Rights: The certain rules that protect the dignity and freedom of each individual. Fundamental rights form and represent the basis of the legal status of each individual.

Politics: Activities of public authorities and their officials; as well as issues and events of public life related to the functioning of the state. The scientific study of politics is conducted within the framework of political science.

Society: A human community, the specifics of which are the relations of people, and represents the form of interaction and association.

Support: The ability to provide help, assistance, moral support, encourage someone, express approval, etc.

Chapter 3
Challenges and Implications During COVID-19 at the Workplace and Future Learning Strategies

Vikas Garg
https://orcid.org/0000-0002-1421-5980
Amity University, Noida, India

Neha Puri
Amity University, Noida, India

ABSTRACT

The COVID-19 pandemic has propelled a tech-savvy route into the education sector. While it is clear that online courses and tests cannot replace traditional teaching techniques, it is not possible to ignore the role of technology and its widespread use in teaching. The study specifically projects the value of technology for academic assistance of online training and evaluation. Moreover, this pandemic has impacted future teaching and learning in many ways. As a result, educators have been facing many challenges during online sessions like no knowledge about online teaching applications. Collaborations between government, technology firms, and higher education institutions in the public, private, and higher education collaboration modes will solve the problem of technological infrastructure.

INTRODUCTION

One of the greatest problems that economies and industries have encountered is COVID-19 pandemic. It would only be possible to resolve this obstacle if we work together to avoid the transmission of this epidemic and provide all home-based telecommunication workers and those returning to their normal workplaces with a secure and stable working atmosphere. A collection of advice articles, awareness-raising content, and more links on the subject are provided in this segment. In workplaces where employees

DOI: 10.4018/978-1-7998-7164-4.ch003

may be exposed to a virus that belongs to the group of biological agents, employers must carry out a risk evaluation in the workplace and take necessary steps. The advice offered on this page is meant to assist employers in these activities. The Biological Agents Directive lays out the basic legal requirements.

Following the 2019 Novel Coronavirus Disease (COVID-2019) pandemic, a range of steps, including those affecting workplaces, have been placed in motion by most Member States of the European Union (EU) to combat the transmission of the disease. During this crisis, the world of work is seriously affected, so all parts of society, including corporations, employers, and social partners, must play a role in supporting staff, their families, and society at large.

If an adequate reduction in COVID-19 transmission rates has been accomplished through physical distancing steps, national administrations are allowed to gradually resume work activities. This is done step by step, with work that is first deemed necessary for health security and approved by the economy and work that can be done easily when working from home last. However, it is extremely conceivable that certain steps will continue regardless of how and to what degree regular job practices can be resumed.

The COVID-19 crisis is placing pressure on employers and staff, whether they have to introduce new policies and methods in a very short period or to cancel their jobs and business operations. Practical assistance for returning to the workplace is offered by occupational safety and health: adequate prevention strategies can help to achieve a stable and secure return to work following physical distance relaxation measures and can lead to the reduction of COVID-19 transmission.

The detection and evaluation of risks in both physical and psychosocial working settings are as in regular working circumstances, the starting point for the administration of occupational safety and health (OSH) under COVID-19 steps. When there is a transition to the job process, employers are obliged to revise their risk assessment and to consider all risks, including those concerning mental health.

MINIMISING EXPOSURE TO COVID-19 AT WORK

Implementing healthy work practices to reduce occupational sensitivity to COVID-19 involves first evaluating the risks, and then implementing the management hierarchy. This involves placing control mechanisms to eliminate the danger first and mitigate employee awareness if this is not feasible. Start with joint measures first and complement them, if necessary, with individual measures, such as personal protection devices (PPE). Some examples of control measures are given below, but not all of them are not all of them will apply to all workplaces or jobs due to their nature.

- For the time being, only critical work should be carried out other work can be delayed until the risk is smaller. Deliver services remotely (telephone or video) if possible, instead of in person. Ensure that only employees are present at the office who are important to the job and minimize the involvement of third parties.
- Reducing physical interaction between workers, to the extent practicable (e.g. during meetings or breaks). Isolate employees who can comfortably perform their duties individually and who do not need specialized machines or facilities that cannot be transferred. For example, plan for them to work alone in a spare office, staff room, canteen, or conference room, if possible.
- Eliminate physical contact with and between clients, and if not possible, restrict it. For eg, contactless distribution or controlled access (while still preventing crowding outside and physical distancing both inside and outside the premises by online or telephone orders.

- Advise drivers on proper cab grooming and supply them with suitable gel and wipes for sanitation. Delivery staff must be licensed to use services such as bathrooms, cafeterias, dressing rooms, and toilets, but with adequate precautions (such as allowing only one user at a time and regular cleaning).
- Place an impermeable barrier between employees particularly if they cannot sustain a distance of two meters from each other. Using things like plastic sheeting, walls, handheld drawers, or storage units, barriers may be purpose-made or improvised. It is important to avoid items that are not sturdy or that have holes, such as pot plants or trolleys, or that cause a new danger, such as tripping or dropping objects.
- Maintain it for less than 15 minutes if direct contact is inevitable. Reduce interaction at the start and end of transitions between various areas of the business. To minimize the number of persons sharing a cafeteria, staff room, or kitchen, coordinate the scheduling of meal breaks. Make sure that there is only one worker in the toilets and dressing rooms at a time.
- Supply soap and water or appropriate hand sanitizer at suitable locations and remind staff regularly to wash their hands. Frequently clean your premises, especially counters, door handles, instruments, and other surfaces that people frequently touch, and if possible, provide good ventilation.
- Avoid excessive workload on cleaning staff by taking appropriate measures, such as assigning additional staff to the tasks and asking workers to leave their workspace tidy. Provide workers with tissues and waste bins lined with a plastic bag so that they can be emptied without contacting the contents.

However, it is important to note that online learning platforms offer socialization as well opportunity. They not only integrate class-based interaction and communication with each other, (including one-to-one contacts and group projects), but they also often provide extracurricular activities, such as online clubs, for example. One benefit of socialization online is that it eliminates, or significantly reduces, social barriers among students (Watson and Gemin 2008). Although some commentators claim that there is no significant distinction between Online learning socialization vs. traditional high school, which is probably not the case for the lower levels of education. The US National Education Association, for example, argues that kids in primary school need the experience of the classroom as they are significantly more chances to interact with their peers or team.

Education online is conducted in two ways. The first is through the use of recorded classes, referred to as the Massive Open Online Course when open to the public (MOOCs). The second is conducted as webinars, or zoom sessions, via live online classes. Besides stable IT infrastructure and faculty members who are comfortable teaching online, universities require high-speed internet and education delivery platforms or learning management systems. To attend these sessions or watch pre-recorded classes, students also need high-speed internet and computers / mobiles.

Higher education is not about exams, lectures, or grades. Instead, it is about an opportunity that trains a pupil, with required skills, talents, and life experiences, to become a functioning part of the workforce. Most educators around institutions believe that there is a need to invest and educate both students and teachers in building structured online education systems and not just using mobile and Google hangouts. Others emphasize the need to dig at the essence of these networks and how students are taught using numerous multimedia resources and processes, while taking into account the issues of inclusion and equality. The need to learn all this through academic disciplines and institutions is also important.

Student mobility opportunities and realistic experience by exchange projects, internships, conference attendance, and more will possibly be off the table for some time. The push for learning, study and teaching needs creative new ways of collaboration and alternate paradigms.

COPING WITH A HIGH RATE OF ABSENCE

Many of the employees could be unavailable because of COVID-19, based on the infection rates in your local region and the procedures in place. They will be able to resume their job remotely (see below) if a worker is in quarantine at home as a precaution, even if this is not the case, the worker may not be able to work for a while.

Employees who are known to have COVID-19 may be absent and unable to function for much longer and once cured of the infection, those who become severely ill may need a further recovery period. Moreover, certain employees may be absent because they need to take care of a relative.

- The lack of a significant number of staff, even if only temporary, can put a burden on continuing operations. Although the staff available should be versatile, they mustn't find themselves in a position that will jeopardize their safety or health. Keep as minimal as possible any extra workload to ensure it does not last for long. In controlling the situation and ensuring that individual employees are not overburdened, line managers play a significant role
- When modifying work to deal with a diminished workforce, such as by introducing new strategies and systems and adjusting positions and duties, determine whether employees need extra preparation and assistance and ensuring that all employees can fulfill the job they are expected to perform.

MANAGING TO WORK FROM HOME

As part of the physical distance steps taken in most of the organizations, if the essence of their job requires it, workers are allowed or obligated to work from home. It's their first day as 'teleworkers' for most of these staff and their professional atmosphere is expected to be lacking in certain ways relative to their workplace. Depending on the worker's condition and the time and energy required for adaptation, the degree to which the home atmosphere may be changed can vary.

Below are some suggestions to minimize the risks to workers who have not been able to prepare their homework properly.

- Conduct a risk appraisal concerning telecommuting staff and their members.
- Enable staff to temporarily take away appliances they use at home at work (if they cannot fetch it themselves, consider arranging its delivery). Items such as a screen, display, keyboard, mouse, printer, chair, footrest, or lamp may be used. To prevent misunderstanding as regular work returns, maintain a list of who takes what things.
- Provide recommendations to teleworkers on setting up a workstation at home that applies good ergonomics, such as good posture and frequent movement, as far as possible.
- Encourage staff to take daily breaks to get up, walk, and stretch (around every 30 minutes).

- Offer assistance to teleworkers by using IT equipment and tools. Teleconferencing and video conferencing technologies may become important for work, but for workers not accustomed to them, they may be problematic.
- Ensure that there is effective contact that affects those employed at home at all stages.
- Do not underestimate the danger of becoming alone and under strain by staff, which can lead to mental health concerns in the absence of care.
- It is necessary to have good communication and support from the manager and peers and to be able to establish casual interaction with colleagues. When a slow return to work has been begun, consider hosting daily staff or team meetings online or rotating what workers will be available at the office.
- Assist workers in setting healthy boundaries between work and free time by communicating clearly when they are expected to be working and available.

INVOLVING EMPLOYEES

The role of staff and their members in the administration of OSH is a prerequisite to progress and a legitimate responsibility. This also refers to steps taken at the workplace concerning COVID-19; a phase of accelerated progression of activities, with a high degree of confusion and distress among workers and the general public.

It is important that you meet soon on with your staff and/or their representatives and the representatives of health and safety about proposed improvements and how temporary procedures can operate in operation. Engaging with the team in risk management and solution growth is an integral aspect of good practice in the area of health and safety. Health and safety members and health and safety boards are in a special role to aid in the implementation of prevention initiatives and to ensure that they are enforced effectively.

POTENTIAL IMPACTS OF COVID-19 TO CO-WORKING

The COVID-19 pandemic has altered every person worldwide's way of working, behaviors, and lifestyle and will have medium-long-term consequences. To reduce the chances of transmission of the virus, though, at different degrees, all sectors of the economy had to respect "social distance" In particular, as in the case of the imaginative and creative class, most service employees had to shift from conventional jobs in the workplace to work at home by smart or remote work.

The present chapter attempts to analyze the impact of the COVID-19 pandemic on co-working spaces within this context by presenting the findings of an international survey addressed to co-working managers worldwide. It is debated whether and how the "nature" of these workspaces has been compromised and what actions have been taken by administrators of co-working spaces to counter the pandemic. Also, potential developments for the business model of co-working as well as its position dynamics are presented together with policy implications.

The company shakeup of the coronavirus is wide and constant. From the complete closing of co-working spaces to comparatively undisturbed cubicle farms, different workplaces have experienced differing degrees of destruction. The COVID-19 influence has not been as cut-and-dry on versatile office space, and many firms face concerns and considerations about their flexible spaces.

During the coronavirus pandemic, are scalable workspaces safe? Can they even be employed in the same capacity as employees? What improvements do administrators of facilities make?

Is it Dead with the Dynamic Office?

Not at least at all! The notion of accessible office space has simply shifted, like other facets of work since the COVID-19 crisis. Flexible workspaces are also targeted at supplying workers with the right atmosphere, but there is more flexibility about how and when they use the area.

For starters, consider co-working. Pessimism about flex space's potential undoubtedly comes from the fact that during the pandemic several co-working spaces locked their doors. But that's not to claim flex room

Conversely, in the office, look at hot tables or hotels. Employers can control how and where they use these rooms. The effect is improved flex room utilization, as well as the potential for protections such as touch tracing. It's the same premise as with greater implementation, a co-working room.

Flexible space is more important than ever at a time of broad adaptation in the workplace. It provides firms with the means to pivot and regroup during a new floor plan or an unpredictable operating climate.

How can Flexible Workplaces Pivot?

In certain situations, as they move to modern floor plans and socially distant workplace strategies, corporations may lean on flex space. Hot desks, when teams split into different workstations, will take the place of desk neighbourhoods. The new meeting rooms can become open-air breakout spaces. In the coronavirus climate, flex room becomes a solution to desk structures made unsuitable.

Flex spaces are not a solution to the end-all, be-all. Many industries that are now leaning on flex space need to make improvements to ensure that these locations can continue to work safely. To comply with wider business expectations around COVID-19 initiatives, adaptive workspaces need to pivot. Examples are:

- Transform hot desks via a reservation system into hotel desks
- Shift occupancy of breakout spaces and other flex areas of the company
- Put up partitions and several flex spaces in open-air settings
- Reconfigure flex space layouts for distance implementation

Projections for the Flexible Space Market

The flexible space market was booming before the pandemic. Estimates place the market share of modular space in office space at as much as 25% before coronavirus, and industry analysts expect it to return to these values not long ago.

For the open space industry, what does the future hold? According to leading business market research company JLL, more of the same. A recent company study says, "while we expect operational models to shift to investor-driven flexible space solution models,"

A second JLL[1] the analysis predicts that as much as 30% of all office space in the U.S. will come under the moniker of flex space by 2030, with usage rates as high as 80%. While all of this is related to co-working, as a group, open space predicts tremendous growth as enterprises merge their advantages with those of a growing decentralized workforce. When remote work becomes a pillar, space can flex as well.

CURRENT SCENARIO OF TEACHING AND LEARNING DURING PANDEMIC

- COVID-19 has resulted in schools being closed all over the country. About 1.2 billion children are out of the classroom worldwide.
- Education has drastically improved as a result, with the distinctive emergence of e-learning, whereby instruction is carried out online and on multimedia platforms.
- Research shows that online learning has been shown to improve data retention and take less time, suggesting the improvements caused by coronavirus could be here to remain.

Though nations are at varying stages of COVID-19 contamination, there are currently more than 1.2 billion children worldwide in 186 countries afflicted by school disruptions due to the pandemic. Children up to the age of 11 are returning to nurseries and schools in Denmark after initially closing on 12 March, but students in South Korea are responding to online roll calls from their teachers.

With this abrupt change away from the classroom in many parts of the world, others are questioning if post-pandemic acceptance of online learning would continue to exist, and how such a shift will affect the education sector worldwide.

Also before COVID-19, there was still strong growth and penetration of education technology, with global edu tech investments exceeding US$18.66 billion in 2019 and the potential demand for online education expected to reach $350 Billion by 2025. There has been a big growth in use since COVID-19, whether it be language applications, immersive tutoring, video conferencing tools, or online learning software.

How is COVID-19 Addressed by the Education Sector?

Many online learning companies provide free access to their services in response to major demand, including platforms such as BYJU'S, a Bangalore-based educational technology and online tutoring firm established in 2011, which is now the most highly regarded edutech business in the world. BYJU has seen a 200 percent rise in the number of new students using its product since announcing free live classes on its Think and Learn app, according to Mrinal Mohit, Chief Operating Officer of the firm.

The COVID-19 pandemic has had a significant impact on the education sector. As colleges reopened their premises to further education, in reaction to the lockdown, countries closed their borders and Measurements. While institutions of higher education were quickly founded, to substitute online instruction for face-to-face lessons, these training and exams were influenced by closures as well as the international students' protection and legal standing in their respective fields of the research host nation.

Figure 1.

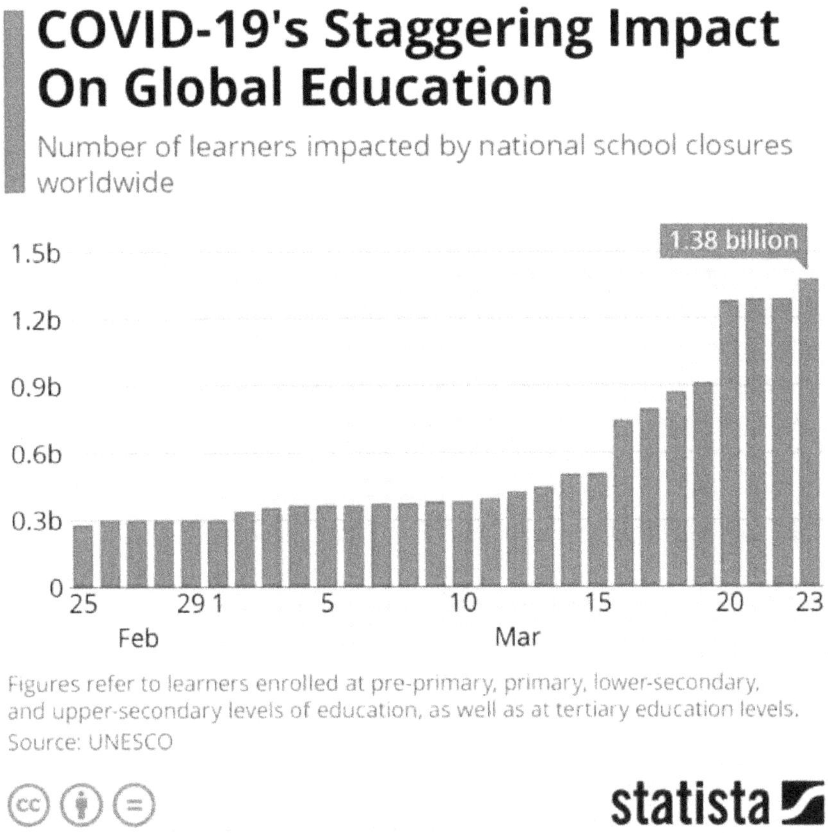

Future Learning

Although some agree that the unplanned and accelerated transition to online learning would result in a weak user interface that is unfavorable to sustainable development without instruction, inadequate space, and little planning, others believe that a new hybrid paradigm of education will emerge with substantial benefits. The incorporation of IT into education will be more increased and that online education will ultimately become an integral part of education in schools.

The Challenges of Online Learning

There are, however, obstacles to resolve. Some students fail to engage in digital learning without reliable internet connections and/or technology; this difference is seen across countries and income brackets within countries. For instance, although 95 percent of students in Switzerland, Norway, and Austria have a computer to use for their schoolwork, according to OECD data, only 34 percent in Indonesia do.

There is a substantial difference between people from affluent and deprived backgrounds in the United States: while almost all 15-year-olds from a privileged background said they had a device to run on almost 25% of those from disadvantaged backgrounds did not. Although some schools and states, such as in New South Wales, Australia, have been supplying wireless equipment to students in need, many are also worrying that the digital gap would broaden the pandemic.

Is Learning Online as Effective?

There is evidence that learning online can be more useful in a variety of areas for those who already have access to the right technologies. Some study indicates that students maintain 25-60% more content on average while studying online, compared to only 8-10% in a classroom. This is mainly due to the willingness of students to study online faster; e-learning takes 40-60 percent less time to learn than in a typical classroom environment so students can learn, go back and re-read at their speed.

Nevertheless, within age groups, the efficacy of online learning varies. The general opinion among children, especially younger ones, is that since children are more easily distracted, and the organized atmosphere is needed. To get the full value of online learning, a deliberate effort must be made to include this framework and go beyond replicating a physical class/reading through video technologies.

IMPLICATIONS OF VIRTUAL TEACHING AND LEARNING

The present scenario is daunting, but it has also created resources for online learning, a virtual class where teachers can interact with their pupils. In contrast to the school teaching dynamic, online learning dynamics are unique. The implementation of a modern approach, though, would have difficulties and encouraging encounters. Technology has been an indispensable part of the life of any person in today's world, making difficult activities simpler and smooth.

Teaching is beyond just a profession; it allows a teacher to strive to grow and widen the horizons for tomorrow's future to be served and shaped. Remote learning has created an incentive for teachers to use evaluation tools for innovation and imagination. It also allows the relationship between teacher and student to be evaluated and improvements worked on. There could be students unable to deal with remote learning and there could be some challenges without having to face peers at school.

As the situation is challenging for the students, it is similarly difficult to handle the schedule to communicate with fellow teachers. Also, colleagues have been helped to work in more productive ways by the simulated training situation. Discussing on Zoom or other video chat applications remotely at face time or community sessions has helped to recreate unique forms to help students train for their academics. Teachers have also been supported by remote learning to consider the mental state of learners. It has made them more caring and resilient, allowing students to preserve their mental well-being. Teachers are going past their conventional teaching concepts and constructing with their students a dialogue bridge. Students need to realize that they are not working in a bubble because the instructors communicate with each pupil personally.

Teachers have since begun to incorporate new technologies to communicate with pupils. Teachers are researching multiple innovations or methods for their students to illustrate different topics from the syllabus. Online learning is not only about a Skype classroom, but rather about connecting students with the topics concerned. Teachers, for example, explore YouTube and other sites to present images of everyday life or to illustrate scientific processes, experiments, etc. Teachers are going beyond traditional textbooks to teach about a particular subject.

Innovation and improvement as a reaction to the challenges of culture are an important part of the teaching career that takes into account the present situation. Teachers are learning to make available online notes, videos, and research resources for students who have access to different technology and knowledge to make the transfer seamless. There are complex concepts such as math, science, etc. for which teachers develop a game approach, an experimental or realistic approach to help students learn and understand.

With remote instruction, it has also become clearer to evaluate the weekly assessments or tasks. The imaginative and interactive activities helped teachers measure each student's success while designing new approaches to better direct them. More than ever, learning modules such as game-based or tech-based are seeing active student engagement. Teachers are helping students interact with diverse research groups across the globe to best train them for their academics. This led to a great team effort.

These days, teachers have followed the digital social media mode to conduct discussions on assignments, topics, competition, etc as students are largely linked to social media. To help students with their academics, teachers can implement any means of communication and technology. The current condition is a challenge for teachers to make their learners succeed in any aspect and to ensure that teachers themselves experience comprehensive learning modules.

Due to the present situation, the dynamic of teaching is shifting, but imparting knowledge is a process that persists. Teachers around the world will need to upskill themselves to make their students have a brighter future.

Around 264 million children and teenagers are not in school (UNESCO, 2017), and this pandemic has made it even worse. As the COVID-19 pandemic spreads, there has been a rising change towards online teaching due to the indefinite shutdown of schools, colleges, and universities as the only alternative left (Martinez, 2020).

Therefore, in the intensely pressing need for an extraordinary existing situation, now is the time to gravely reconsider, revamp, and upgrade our education system. It is also significantly influenced by informal and non-formal schooling. However, owing to teacher-taught direct contact, it is a well-established fact that no pedagogical method will replace the peak position of informal education.

Since the COVID-19 crisis, however, online education became a pedagogical change from the conventional system to the new teaching-learning approach from the classroom to the Zoom, from personal to interactive, and from seminars to webinars. Previously, e-learning, distance education, and correspondence courses were generally viewed as part of non-formal education, but as of now, if the factors remain indefinitely over time, it seems that it will eventually replace the formal education system.

Start.me, Neo, Classtime, Classwize, Ted-Ed, Coursera, Google Classroom, Bakpax, Pronto, Skillshare, ClassDojo, Edmodo, Blackboard Learn, Parlay, Docebo, Feedback Fruits, Udemy, WeVideo, WizIQ, Flipgrid, Codeacadem, are some of the most common online networking channels that will shift the destination and trajectory of the entire education system worldwide in post-COVID-19 circumstances.

GOVERNMENT OF INDIA INITIATIVES AND STRATEGIES ON ONLINE TEACHING-LEARNING IN HEIS

With a focus on ICT[2] and the use of online education as part of the compulsory teaching-learning process at the tertiary level, the Government of India began thinking seriously on this issue. Also, the planning of a draft national education policy for 2019, which at the time of this pandemic was considered a constructive and highly techno-efficient phase, is mirrored. SWAYAM (Study Webs of Active-Learning for Young Aspiring Minds) is a software launched by the Massive Open Online Courses (MOOC) network.

SWAYAM PRABHA is a network of 32 DTH channels committed during the week to telecasting high-quality education programs. The Annual Refresher Course in Teaching (ARPIT) is an online skill learning initiative introduced on the SWAYAM website by the MHRD on 13 November 2018. E-PG Pathshala, run by the University Grants Commission (UGC), was another MHRD project that offered high-quality curriculum-based and engaging e-content across all disciplines in 70 subjects.

E-Pathshala is a portal launched on November 7, 2015, jointly run by the MHRD and the National Council of Educational Research and Training (NCERT), which has provided educational opportunities through an online learning network for teacher educators, academics, research scholars, students, and parents. It can also be seen that we were not ignorant of online education's difficulties and opportunities.

The Indian Top Higher Education Regulatory Body, UGC, has taken the current educational situation very seriously and has proactively made some attempts to overcome the impasse on completion of courses and exams in the current semesters, as well as released a circular on the academic calendar following the recommendations of one of the committees appointed by UGC itself. The completion of the 25 percent syllabus via online teaching mode and 75 percent of faculty has now become mandatory for all universities in India.

It would not be possible to tackle teaching-learning scenarios without rigorously using online teaching tools in the educational scenario of the post-COVID-19 epidemic. Since seeing the fearful coronavirus beast, it can be expected that students will face many obstacles of educational difficulties in the coming time, including quality instruction, hands-on experience, laboratory study, visit the library, peer tutoring, remedial training, analysis, and creativity.

Implementation of Online Teaching-Learning in HEIs

Several challenges have emerged since the COVID-19 crisis in introducing the mechanism of reform in the education system; these difficulties are due to the novel experiences of online education and its technical complexity. Online education is known as the education offered by open universities in India before this pandemic.

But online teaching-learning became a big obstacle to contend with in COVID-19 triggered time, and stakeholders are not likely fit to respond to the rapid educational transition as they are not technologically capable to acknowledge the new situation. Therefore, the consequences of transition need to be discussed to effectively incorporate instructional change (in this case, it relates to the move from conventional teaching-learning methods to online teaching-learning methods).

The introduction of online education across the nation, taking into account the need for an hour, was overwhelmingly decided by central and state governments. The vision of online teaching-learning modes with the blend of opinion bags was half-heartedly and hesitantly endorsed by numerous national state and university level teacher and student groups as a result of enthusiasm to try emerging technologies and the new style of the teaching-learning process in the education system; it is due to the lack of preparedness, orientation and incentives of stakeholders in using online mode of teaching.

Challenges Faced by Teaching Professionals

COVID-19, a contagious virus, has spread across the world and has negatively impacted all areas of the economy. This economic earthquake has entered an astonishing number of several industries, to a great degree mutilating them. The effect of COVID-19 on the Indian economy is expected to cross approximately 8.8tn Indian rupees in 2020 (Keelery, 2020).

The pandemic caused a major economic decline and had a staggering effect on global education. 63 million teachers have been displaced in 165 countries, according to UNESCO. A total of 1.3 billion students worldwide have not been able to attend school or university, and about 32,07,13,810 students are affected in India alone (UNESCO, 2020).

In India, as a rational response to impose social distancing within societies, the government declared the lockdown and closing of education institutions. In their press release (March 21, 2020), the Ministry of Human Resource Development shared numerous free digital e-learning tools such as digital e-learning platforms to support their decision like "the National Programme on Technology Enhanced Learning, Study Web for Active Young Expiring Minds (SWAYAM), e-Pathshala, DIKSHA portal, SWAYAM Prabha, National Repository of Open Educational", etc. for students so that they may capitalize and continue their learning during lockdown (MHRD, 2020a). The ministry also released an advisory to HEIs to continue online education and urged teachers to teach from home. The conventional teaching model was modified to the educational technology (EdTech) model by COVID-19, where teachers and students were introduced to new innovative methodologies for education.

It is worth noting, however, that many HEIs in India are not well equipped with institutionally funded technology such as Moodle, Blackboard (teaching app), Microsoft Teams, and Zoom; however, teachers have been required to use open-source online teaching tools such as WhatsApp, YouTube, Skype and Google hangout for online sessions. Online instruction is stirring at an untested and unparalleled stage and online examinations of students are still carried out with many uncertainties.

It is important that without the presence of teachers, online teaching will not be effective, as they are the frontline employees of any educational institution. In numerous developed countries such as Germany, Luxembourg (Stoffregen), Japan (Sutherland), FL (Shea), few studies have tackled the barriers to online teaching, but very limited studies have been carried out in developing countries. (Stoffregen *et al.*, 2016; Sutherland, 2014; Shea, 2007). In developed countries like India, online education is a comparatively recent idea. The COVID-19 crisis has made it compulsory for teachers in developed countries to use teaching and appraisal tools online to boost the education sector. Teachers need to adapt the program for the effective application of online training and reviews.

In the homeworld, online training and appraisal have distinct problems from online teaching and evaluation in the university environment. The university community has a favorable climate where all the services are readily accessible. This study aims to recognize certain obstacles faced by teachers in the Indian context during online teaching and appraisal in the home environment.

Teachers have faced several difficulties when teaching in the home setting. A whiteboard, marker, and printer are required for the basic facilities for successful teaching and evaluation. Teaching and appraisal entail discipline and dedication, but there were many indigenous factors in home conditions, such as noise, guests, music, family interference, and household jobs, which adversely influenced the consistency of teaching and evaluations (Press Trust of India (2020). Therefore, in-home atmosphere environments, online training, and review have an undesirable detrimental impact. It can be explicitly mentioned that teachers both face stress in teaching and evaluations using either open-source or institutional support technologies. A suitable setup that should be free of external distraction and family disruption is required, and basic facilities should be accessible in the home environment for successful teaching and evaluation.

It was specifically noted that teachers were able to properly instruct and evaluate using institutional-supported technology. It may also be said that institutional assistance can make the activities of teachers simple and stress-free. The value of classroom schooling is undeniable and this pandemic shows that both HEIs and teachers are not yet qualified to manage online instruction (Mahesh, 2020; Azevedo *et al.*, 2020).

It can also be shown that teachers in both grades have encountered technological difficulties (open-sources or institutional-supported technologies). For successful teaching and evaluation, adequate technical resources and technical assistance must be provided. In the research conducted by Shenoy et al. (2020), similar results were recorded that teachers had a great deal of disruption in the minds to implement online teaching technologies.

Teachers have faced personal teaching and appraisal challenges. Many of them did not have experience of online teaching and tests, but they were compelled to do so because of the demand from their organization resulting in their pessimistic attitude. Teachers who had a strong knowledge of institutional-supported technology were not encouraged to hold online sessions because it was a tiring and time-consuming task.

They encountered difficulties such as online teaching unique courses (numerical and practical), answering the doubts of students, and developing online reviews. Any courses containing numerical, experimental, and personal contact were not comfortable for teachers. Language considerations are mitigated during face-to-face instruction when teachers use bilingual conversation to satisfy the questions and inquiries of learners (Mahajan, 2020).

FUTURE PERSPECTIVES FOR TEACHING AND LEARNING

It is important to have an exclusive department committed to improving the institution's technical infrastructure to integrate technology-driven teaching into actual or virtual teaching. It would place the institute, teachers, and students in a different league to educate teachers in LMSs and make it obligatory for all educational purposes.

India's education sector should be aware of the value of technology and should take strict steps to introduce technology-driven teaching and evaluation sessions. By designing new policies and technical mechanisms, HEI has to revise its current policy frameworks to help its educators effectively adopt EdTech to cope with any potential crisis. This study advocates that HEIs should use all facets of technology, starting with "engagement, distribution, assignment, examinations, devices, software, internet connectivity, and power back-up, evaluations and results".

RECOMMENDATIONS

This chapter illuminated the perspectives of teachers in home environments during a lockout in India during COVID-19. First, it was difficult to locate the related literature in the Indian sense due to the uniqueness of the subject and problem discussed. However, during the pandemic case, we wanted to use the literature that influenced the education system for online training and evaluation in other nations. The qualitative analysis technique, IPA[3], was used in this study. These approaches have some drawbacks, such as the likelihood that participants would not have revealed their true intentions and reacted during the interview in a more socially appropriate and attractive manner. Nevertheless, we made sure that all the interventions proposed by Smith and Osborn (2008) were meticulously observed. Despite retaining objectivity in every phase of the current analysis, there is a risk that the opinions of other researchers may vary and they may distinguish. The research can be extended by the triangulation approach using different techniques and methods to get more valid and reliable results.

REFERENCES

Agarwal, K., Fortune, L., Heintzman, J. C., & Kelly, L. L. (2020). Spiritual experiences of long-term meditation practitioners diagnosed with breast cancer: An interpretative phenomenological analysis pilot study. *Journal of Religion and Health*, *59*(5), 1–17. doi:10.100710943-020-00995-9 PMID:32062734

Al-Senaidi, S., Lin, L., & Poirot, J. (2009). Barriers to adopting technology for teaching and learning in Oman. *Computers & Education*, *53*(3), 575–590. doi:10.1016/j.compedu.2009.03.015

Alase, A. (2017). The interpretative phenomenological analysis (IPA): A guide to a good qualitative research approach. *International Journal of Education and Literacy Studies*, *5*(2), 9–19. doi:10.7575/aiac.ijels.v.5n.2p.9

Arora, A. K., & Srinivasan, R. (2020). Impact of pandemic COVID-19 on the teaching-learning process: A study of higher education teachers. *Prabandhan: Indian Journal of Management*, *13*(4), 43–56. doi:10.17010/pijom/2020/v13i4/151825

Azevedo, J.P., Hasan, A., Goldemberg, D., Iqbal, S.A., & Geven, K. (2020). *Simulating the potential impacts of covid-19 school closures on schooling and learning outcomes: a set of global estimates.* Academic Press.

Berge, Z. L., & Mrozowski, S. E. (1999). *Barriers to Online Teaching in Elementary, Secondary, and Teacher Education.* UMBC Faculty Collection. doi:10.21432/T2P59B

Buabeng-Andoh, C. (2012). Factors influencing teachers adoption and integration of information and communication technology into teaching: a review of the literature. *International Journal of Education and Development Using ICT, 8*(1).

Cassidy, E., Reynolds, F., Naylor, S., & De Souza, L. (2011). Using interpretative phenomenological analysis to inform physiotherapy practice: An introduction with reference to the lived experience of cerebellar ataxia. *Physiotherapy Theory and Practice*, *27*(4), 263–277. doi:10.3109/09593985.2010.488278 PMID:20795878

Chaudhary, N. S., Phoolka, S., Sengar, R., & Pande, S. (2019). Whistleblowing in Indian higher education sector: A qualitative study. *International Journal of Learning and Change*, *11*(2), 145–168. doi:10.1504/IJLC.2019.101662

Chen, R. J. (2010). Investigating models for preservice teachers' use of technology to support student-centered learning. *Computers & Education*, *55*(1), 32–42. doi:10.1016/j.compedu.2009.11.015

Dipboye, R. L., & Foster, J. B. (2002). Multi-level theorizing about perceptions of organizational politics. *Research in Multi-Level Issues*, *1*(1), 255–270. doi:10.1016/S1475-9144(02)01035-4

Farmer, L. B., & Byrd, R. (2015). Genderism in the LGBTQQIA community: An interpretative phenomenological analysis. *Journal of LGBT Issues in Counseling*, *9*(4), 288–310. doi:10.1080/15538605.2015.1103679

Gill, M. J. (2015). A phenomenology of feeling: Examining the experience of emotion in organizations. *New Ways of Studying Emotions in Organizations*, *11*, 29–50. doi:10.1108/S1746-979120150000011003

Gratz, E., & Looney, L. (2020). Faculty resistance to change: an examination of motivators and barriers to teaching online in higher education. *International Journal of Online Pedagogy and Course Design, 10*(1), 1-14.

Gupta, K. P., & Chaudhary, N. S. (2017). Prioritizing the factors influencing whistle blowing intentions of teachers in higher education institutes in India. *Procedia Computer Science*, *122*, 25–32. doi:10.1016/j.procs.2017.11.337

Haber, J., & Mills, M. (2008). Perceptions of barriers concerning effective online teaching and policies: Florida community college faculty. *Community College Journal of Research and Practice*, *32*(4-6), 266–283. doi:10.1080/10668920701884505

Kaup, S., Jain, R., Shivalli, S., Pandey, S., & Kaup, S. (2020). Sustaining academics during COVID-19 pandemic: The role of remote teaching-learning. *Indian Journal of Ophthalmology*, *68*(6), 1220. doi:10.4103/ijo.IJO_1241_20 PMID:32461490

Keelery, S. (2020). *India – estimated economic impact of COVID-19 by sector 2020.* Statista. Available at: www.statista.com/statistics/1107798/india-estimated-economic-impact-of-coronavirus-by-sector/

Keengwe, J., Onchwari, G., & Wachira, P. (2008). The use of computer tools to support meaningful learning. *AACE Journal*, *16*(1), 77–92.

Lloyd, S. A., Byrne, M. M., & McCoy, T. S. (2012). Faculty-perceived barriers of online education. *Journal of Online Learning and Teaching*, *8*(1).

Mahajan, S. (2020). *Technological, social, pedagogical issues must be resolved for online teaching* [Web log post]. Available at: https://indianexpress.com/article/opinion/columns/india-coronavirus-lockdown-online-education-learning-6383692/

Mahesh, S. (2020). *A need now but no replacement: teachers share concerns about online classes during COVID-19* [Web log post]. Available at: www.newindianexpress.com/education/2020/may/06/a-need-now-but-no-replacement-teachers-share-concerns-about-online-classes-during-covid-19-2139605.html

MHRD. (2020a). *Students to continue their learning by making full use of the available digital e-Learning platforms – Shri Ramesh Pokhriyal 'Nishank'*. Available at: https://pib.gov.in/PressReleasePage.aspx?PRID=1607521

MHRD. (2020b). *UGC guidelines on examinations and academic calendar for the universities in view of COVID-19 and subsequent lockdown.* **Error! Hyperlink reference not valid.**Available at: https://pib.gov.in/PressReleasePage.aspx?PRID=1619368

MHRD. (2020c). *National education policy 2020*. Available at: https://static.pib.gov.in/WriteReadData/userfiles/NEP_Final_English_0.pdf

Mishra, S. V. (2020). *COVID-19, online teaching, and deepening digital divide in India*. SocArXiv.

Moustakas, C. (1994). *Phenomenological Research Methods*. Sage Publications. doi:10.4135/9781412995658

Peart, A., Lewis, V., Barton, C., & Russell, G. (2020). Healthcare professionals providing care coordination to people living with multimorbidity: An interpretative phenomenological analysis. *Journal of Clinical Nursing*, *29*(13/14). PMID:32221995

Peralta, H., & Costata, F. A. (2007). *Teachers's competence and confidence regarding the use of ICT*. Sísifo-Educational Sciences Journal.

Phutela, N., & Dwivedi, S. (2020). A qualitative study of students' perspective on e-learning adoption in India. *Journal of Applied Research in Higher Education*, *12*(4), 545–559. doi:10.1108/JARHE-02-2019-0041

Press Trust of India. (2020). *From technological queries to distress calls, teachers struggle with challenges posed by lockdown*. Available at: www.ndtv.com/education/from-technological-queries-to-distress-calls-teachers-struggle-with-challenges-posed-by-lockdown-2208957

Pringle, J., Drummond, J., McLafferty, E., & Hendry, C. (2011). Interpretative phenomenological analysis: A discussion and critique. *Nurse Researcher*, *18*(3), 20–24. doi:10.7748/nr2011.04.18.3.20.c8459 PMID:21560922

Prottas, D. J., Cleaver, C. M., & Cooperstein, D. (2016). Assessing faculty attitudes towards online instruction: A motivational approach. *Online Journal of Distance Learning Administration*, *19*(4).

Punit, I.S. (2020). *For many of India's teachers, online classes amid lockdown have been an awful experience*. Available at: https://scroll.in/article/961738/for-many-of-indias-teachers-online-classes-amid-lockdown-have-been-an-awful-experience

QS-ERA. (2020). *COVID-19: a wake-up call for Indian internet service providers*. Available at: www.igauge.in/news/2020/4/covid-19-a-wake-up-call-for-indian-internet-service-providers

Ryan, G.W., & Bernard, H.R. (2000). *Data management and analysis methods*. Academic Press.

Saini, D., & Chaudhary, N. S. (2019). What drives research in higher education? An Indian context. *Journal of Applied Research in Higher Education*.

Sharma, A. K. (2020). COVID-19: creating a paradigm shift in India's education system. *Economic Times Blog*. Available at: https://economictimes.indiatimes.com/blogs/et-commentary/covid-19-creating-a-paradigm-shift-in-indias-education-system/

Shea, P. (2007). Bridges and barriers to teaching online college courses: A study of experienced online faculty in thirty six colleges. *Journal of Asynchronous Learning Networks*, *11*(2), 73–128.

Shenoy, V., Mahendra, S., & Vijay, N. (2020). COVID 19 lockdown technology adaption, teaching, learning, students engagement and faculty experience. *Mukt Shabd Journal*, *9*(4), 698–702.

Smith, J. A. (1996). Beyond the divide between cognition and discourse: Using interpretative phenomenological analysis in health psychology. *Psychology & Health*, *11*(2), 261–271. doi:10.1080/08870449608400256

Smith, J. A. (2011). Evaluating the contribution of interpretative phenomenological analysis. *Health Psychology Review*, *5*(1), 9–27. doi:10.1080/17437199.2010.510659

Smith, J. A., & Eatough, V. (2007). *Interpretative phenomenological analysis. Analysing Qualitative Data in Psychology.*

Smith, J. A., & Osborn, M. (2003). Interpretative phenomenological analysis. Qualitative Psychology: A Practical Guide to Research Methods, 53-80.

Smith, P. K., Smith, C., Osborn, R., & Samara, M. (2008). A content analysis of school anti-bullying policies: Progress and limitations. *Educational Psychology in Practice*, *24*(1), 1–12. doi:10.1080/02667360701661165

Stoffregen, J. D., Pawlowski, J. M., Ras, E., Tobias, E., Šćepanović, S., Fitzpatrick, D., Mehigan, T., Steffens, P., Przygoda, C., Schilling, P., Friedrich, H., & Moebs, S. (2016). Barriers to open e-learning in public administrations: A comparative case study of the European countries Luxembourg, Germany, Montenegro. *Technological Forecasting and Social Change*, *111*, 198–208. doi:10.1016/j.techfore.2016.06.030

Sutherland, S. (2014). Team teaching: Four barriers to native English speaking assistant teachers' ability to model native English in Japanese classrooms. *Asian EFL Journal: Quarterly Journal*, *16*(2), 156–180.

Taylor, C. R. (2002). E-learning: The second wave. *T and D*, *56*(10), 24–31.

UNESCO. (2020). *COVID-19 Educational Disruption and Response*. UNESCO. Available at: https://en.unesco.org/covid19/educationresponse

Verma, G., Campbell, T., Melville, W., & Park, B.Y. (2020). *Science teacher education in the times of the COVID-19 pandemic*. Academic Press.

Watson, J., & Gemin, B. (2008). *Socialization in online programs. Promising practices in online learning*. North American council for online learning. (ERIC Document Reproduction Service ED509631)

Yuen, A. H., & Ma, W. W. (2008). Exploring teacher acceptance of e-learning technology. *Asia-Pacific Journal of Teacher Education*, *36*(3), 229–243. doi:10.1080/13598660802232779

Chapter 4
Emergence of Services Business Strategies During COVID-19

Muhammad Abrar
https://orcid.org/0000-0002-1128-5350
Government College University, Faisalabad, Pakistan

Rizwan Shabbir
https://orcid.org/0000-0003-0859-7465
Government College University, Faisalabad, Pakistan

Iqbal Hussain
Government College University, Faisalabad, Pakistan

ABSTRACT

The 21st century has been fighting against COVID-19, an infection caused by a virus SARS CoV-2. On 30th January 2020, the World Health Organization stated this condition as an international health emergency. Furthermore, on March 11, 2020, it was declared a global pandemic. The pandemic COVID-19 destroyed the health systems at a large scale and the businesses globally. Service, as well as manufacturing industries, faced significant challenges during this pandemic situation of COVID-19. Infodemic is one of the biggest challenges that creates severe problems for the business community. In such circumstances, businesses have to adopt unique business strategies to sustain and gain a competitive edge. The current study evaluates different business strategies like digital servitization, travel insurance, skunkworks structural approach, black swan, etc. adopted by different service sectors, based on a systematic review approach. Mostly, the research paradigm is focused on the aviation industry, and less attention is given to other service sectors like education, banking, etc.

INTRODUCTION

From many centuries, human race is transforming its growth from agricultural sector to information/communication sector and this economic development has not only develop different sectors like manu-

DOI: 10.4018/978-1-7998-7164-4.ch004

facturing and service but also change lifestyles. During 20th century, developed countries have shifted their economic plans based on service industry and same pattern is followed by developing world (Cheng, 2013). Globally, the expansion in service sector is driven by digital technologies that focused on cost-advantage strategies in developed world due to accessibility of information. Coronaviruses mostly trigger pandemics and epidemics with a high infection rate, and it mutates very quickly. So, these pathogens can cause unexpected outbreaks at any time. In the past, it has been noticed that coronaviruses spread mostly from animals to human beings. Then, those infected human-beings pass on the infection to other people through their droplets or smear. In 2002, the world was attacked by severe acute respiratory syndrome (SARS) virus spread from birds to human beings. Tse and Leo Sin (2006) concluded that SARS epidemic as one of the natural environmental situations that demand hotel/restaurants to design recovery strategies by following crisis management.

Similarly, Middle East Respiratory Syndrome (MERS) was identified in 2012 and transmitted from camels (Al-tawfiq & Zumla, 2014). It is admitted that SARS in 2003 triggered by a coronavirus was the first time declared as an epidemic in the age of the internet and globalization. It was identified in South Asia, and more or less 8000 people were infected from November 2002 to June 2003. The most affected countries were P.R.China and Hong Kong (Mackey & Liang, 2012), followed by Taiwan, Singapore, and Canada. Although the SARS infection rate was meager among people, it affected the global economy (Uğur & Akbıyık, 2020).

The twenty-first century has been fighting against COVID-19, an infection caused by a virus SARS CoV-2. This virus was identified in Wuhan (Hubei province), the People's Republic of China, in December 2019 and spread globally within no time. Initially, COVID-19 appeared in the market of live animals from where it was transmitted to human beings. It was found as the causative agent in several patients who suffered from pneumonia. From China, this infection spread out all over the world and struck the global economy. On 30th January 2020 - World Health Organization (WHO) declared this situation an international health emergency. Further, on March 11th, 2020 – it was announced as a global pandemic situation (Lai, Shih, Ko, Tang, & Hsueh, 2020). According to WHO's weekly briefing, dated 29th November 2020 - there have been over 61.8 million cases and over 1.4 million deaths globally ("Weekly epidemiological update - 1 December 2020," n.d.).

According to Strong & Wellburn (2020), general practices recommended by WHO regarding social distancing and staying at home taught people with ways to recalibrate their daily routines. This change in customers' lifestyle have direct effect on business operations and procedures, especially when considering business related to service providers such as educational organizations, entertainment organizations and transportation organizations. Based on the information provided by health agencies, government officials of every country have adopted an inhibition strategy to control the outbreak, through wider social distance, wearing a mask in public places, and by using soup and sanitizers repeatedly. Various measures have been taken by nations to reverse the pandemic growth and to survive their healthcare systems against such pandemic pressure. Such actions provoked worse effects in the form of border restrictions that caused complete/partial lockdowns of cities, temporarily closing public and private institutions, including schools, colleges, universities, restaurants, hotels, convention centers, and markets.

Such epidemics and pandemics on a large scale affect human health and ruin every country's economic condition, especially developing countries, which face substantial financial losses. According to medical experts, the course and duration of the COVID-19 outbreak is still unpredictable, so to estimate its impact on the global economy is not possible for economists and business communities. However, it damages the global economy much more than the SARS outbreak and other global epidemics and pandemics in its current states. In the short-run, this lockdown situation might temporarily reduce job offers in the service sector due to the higher risk of employee-customer interaction. If high mortality has been observed, this situation might prolong that transformed marketing strategies based on Infodemic. These measures showed a negative impact on consumer spending in the short-run and a slowdown in economic growth on business investment in the long-run (Kumar & Managi, 2020).

In the early stage of COVID-19 breakout, the business community did not significantly estimate the impact of pandemic due to limited information about the scenarios and its effect on business world. Time to response to a crisis play a pivotal role in organization decision making process and its effects may not be evaluated easily. Prior studies in management sciences concluded that time has proved a key resource to gain a first or late mover advantage for an organization (Grzymala-Busse, 2011). Among various factors related to time management, few important variables are information availability, resources and cost that play an important role in determining whether an organization or policy-maker act proactively or reactively during a crisis (Grzymala-Busse, 2011). Therefore, time management has short-term as well as long-term dimensions for effective and sustainable firm's response in the time of a crisis (Aguinis & Bakker, 2020).

Globally, the current situation of COVID-19 is articulated in electronic media as well as on print media. Therefore, the global business environment confronts myriad and unseen challenges that force business communities, regular authorities, and governments to respond. Previous literature highlighted many research efforts to investigate such pandemic types, mostly focused on mortality rates, government policies, and disease transmission modes (Lipsitch, Phil, Swerdlow, & Finelli, 2020; Choi, 2020). The existing literature showed a significant shortcoming regarding business response under such pandemic circumstances (Amankwah-amoah, 2020). The recent outbreak of COVID-19 forced practitioners and scholars to investigate the businesses' responses in detail (Wenzel, 2020).

World has been fighting not only with diseases but also struggling for a new emerging phenomenon of infodemcs (Zarocostas, 2020). Service, as well as manufacturing industries, are facing significant challenges during this pandemic situation of COVID-19. It has highlighted issues regarding healthcare systems and their public implications on a large scale. Regarding the service industry, business and consumer markets have faced recession due to many reasons. Infodemic is one of the biggest challenges that create severe problems for the business community as described by World Health Organization (WHO) "Director General: Tedros Adhanom Ghebreyesus" at the Munich Security Conference on February 15th, 2020 "*we are not just fighting an epidemic; we are fighting an Infodemic*." Infodemic is explained as a blend of "information" and "Epidemic," which indicate a rapid and far-reaching diffusion of authentic and non-authentic information regarding anything, like disease, pandemic, or social issue.

The study of Cifuentes-Faura (2020) suggested that COVID-19 pandemic brought bundle of information that includes: how to control its spread, how to prevent from the disease and its consequences are disseminating through information and communication Technologies (ICTs) such as electronic, print and social media. The advancement in ICTs have created innovative tools for users to communicate on different social media networks and provide unique marketing strategies for users to interact. Nowadays, users of social media networks are part of information contributors that not only suggest new transformation strategies but also develop new networks on behalf of organization. In digital age, any news about global crisis spread out within no time through social media networks and reach millions of people without any official journalist intervention and authenticity (Cifuentes-Faura, 2020). So, information/news without any credibility and authenticity may become a part of infodemics. Such types of data create a situation of mistrust among the business community and customers. Many businesses have collapsed worldwide under the influence of such Infodemic.

During crises like COVID-19 ICTs played an important role by promoting effective strategies to handle infodemics. They could create a sense of unity at large scale and also highlighted misinformation and discrimination (Cifuentes-Faura, 2020). Infodemics might cause panic among people and they share misinformation with some fear that is not necessarily true by spreading hoaxes. So, as a part of global nation; we should have a spirit to detect such fake news on ICTs and play our role in stopping their dissemination. Journalism should play its role to elaborate such misinformation and to denounce any kind of hoax. At the time of crises communication could be made effective by avoiding the confusion and to minimize the creation of fake news. In the perspective of COVID-19, Cifuentes-Faura, (2020) suggested some recommendations for media users to avoid infodemics which are consisted on easy and understandable content, must avoid speculating about worst-case scenarios as much possible, guides the readers according to experts recommendations, consult officially before breaking the news, avoid to spread of hoaxes, sensational language should be avoided to prevent panic situation, and give the current scenario about COVID-19 as much as possible. In such circumstances, companies have to adopt some unique business strategies to sustain and to gain a competitive edge in the marketplace like e-marketing, online selling, multi-channel, cross channel, and omnichannel business strategies or maybe a blend of all these.

To deal with infodemic situations, business managers have to explore suitable ways to operate under geographic restrictions along with managing their supply chains. Service organizations also manage business strategies for maintaining their image in pandemic situations. Therefore, the hour's question is; which business strategies would be fruitful for businesses in a situation like Infodemic. Many academic scholars and practitioners tried their best to suggest and recommend different business strategies for the service industry to answer this question. Management and executive have to develop strategies to cope with this COVID-19 and for future when the immediate crises will over and restrictions will gradually lift up. Following these lines, this chapter comprises different strategies adopted worldwide during this pandemic by applying a systematic literature review approach.

UNDERSTANDING SERVICE SECTOR AND INFODEMIC

Service sector is not only the major contributor for develop countries, but it has been seen that Asian economics which are considered as manufacturing export-oriented hubs also showed significant contribution in Asian economic growth (Park & Shin, 2012). Similar suggestion have been highlighted by Lee and McKibbin (2014) which provide indications that productivity growth in Asian service sector have showed a sustainable developments. According to IMF (2020), Global lockdown situation with no production pointed out that recovery from this pandemic might be prolonged and those industries that involve social interaction should impose permanent measures for their survival. The study of Das and Raut (2014) suggested that sustainable development in service sector is based on building human capital that design adaptive strategies.

The work by Talwar (2020) concluded that in current pandemic situation of COVID-19, organizations should be design strategies by considering their actions according to three intervals: Firstly, during six months – organization have to deal with strategies related to employees protection plan, supply chain strategies, cash management and operations. Secondly, in next 12 months – organizations have to revisit their strategic plans along with business model and lastly, in next three years – organizations have a shape new business models by finding new product/service offerings that mutate its supply chain as per environmental requirements. When organizations provide services with digital tools, they usually less relied on human interaction. Nevertheless, the shifts behind expansion and realization of digital strategic offering that focus on long-run processes such as (Tronvoll, Sklyar, Sörhammar, & Kowalkowski, 2020) and have thoughtful effect on organizational operations (Paiola & Gebauer, 2020). These strategies are fundamentally diversified from business processes as they recover organizations from pandemic.

Pandemic also induce economic chaos at a result of heavy monetary and economic cost related to its control (Goodell, 2020). The suggestion from prior pandemic provide experience to plan future policies for risk management and finding suitable supply chain alternatives. The study of Cepoi (2020) explored the impact of pandemic related information on stock markets and revealed that COVID-19 relevant information brought uneven outcomes, therefore people need to identify reliable sources for communication channel in order to get balance trade.

To cater Infodemic consequences, service organization perform task that require innovative thinking for designing value networks (king & Baatartogtokh, 2015). The modern service business models demand for disruptive innovations (Adner, 2002) because that could encourage them to improve their performance and maintain an environmental transformation. In time of crisis with environmental complexity and turmoil, Organization change their structure and strategic plans to smoothen their incremental and radical transformation of services (Uotila, 2018). As stated by Christopher (2000), agility is the basic component which organizations needed in time of crisis such as pandemic. Agility strategies are considered as organizational ability to promptly adopt/response to external environmental factors (Swafford, Ghosh, & Murthy, 2006). Such strategies are specify considerable when unpredictable market situation prevail.

In COVID-19, the world production have fallen by 23% when complete lockdown was applied by every country (Mandel & Veetil, 2020). However, initial impact of COVID-19 on Chinese economy have decreased global production by 7% which means that businesses all around the world are somehow connected with each other in terms of buyer-supplier ties or customer-to-customer ties. In current pandemic situation, it is estimated that for survival of small businesses 410 Billion USD is required only in United States for covering necessary operating expenses (Bartik et al., 2020). The balanced relocation of monetary activities in various sectors during COVID-19 is an alleviation factor, even when government officials are not intervening (Krueger et al., 2020). The outcome suggested by "Swedish Model Solution" that business managers should adopt such actions that assure economic and behavioral cost related to COVID-19 which significantly moderated.

According to Visnjic & Van Looy (2013) those organizations that provide service offering with customer acceptability not only enhance satisfaction but engage them in new services that provide sustainable solution for both (customers and organization), especially in time of crisis (Kindström, Kowalkowski, & Sandberg, 2013). During pandemic situation, service organizations think about diversification strategies that are not only critical for multinational organizations but also for national economy. If service organizations properly follow strategies to apply diversification during pandemic situation, they could minimize the operational loss.

METHODOLOGY

This chapter applied a systematic literature-based approach to research articles to elaborate on different business strategies adopted by the services industry during the pandemic COVID-19. At the first stage of the literature review, the authors sorted out the Social Science Citation Index (SSCI) journals based on their authenticity. They found articles from these publishers: Science Direct (Elsevier), Emerald Insight, Springer, and Wiley. Due to convenience, authors only target "Elsevier" Publisher for exploring key terms. The authors searched the phrases "*New business strategies during COVID-19*" and "*Innovative business strategies during COVID-19*" in the second step.

Moreover, the critical terms of innovative business strategies, COVID-19, service industry, developing business strategies, and new business strategies are used in different combinations. The time span of extracting articles was from January 2020 to November 2020, which provides a list of 22 articles. The third step focused on reviewing the extracted articles based on relevance with the topic, which lead to 10 scholarly articles as given in (Table-1). The articles that were eliminated were review paper, conference paper, or irrelevant with scope. A summarized table is given below that highlights the strategies applied by authors along with industry.

INNOVATIVE BUSINESS STRATEGIES

The selected studies identified the following business strategies most suitable during COVID-19 and such pandemic in the future to gain a competitive edge in the marketplace:

1. Digital Servitization

Rapaccini, Saccani, Kowalkowski, Paiola, & Adrodegari, (2020) conducted research on Italian manufacturing and service firms and found that digital servitization business strategy could be fruitful for organizations during pandemic COVID-19 and also after that to sustain a better position in the market place. Based on their findings, they developed a four-stage business model, i.e., calamity, quick & dirty, restart, and adapt. To shift from a product-centric business to a service-centric business model is called servitization (Kowalkowski, Gebauer, Kamp, & Parry, 2017) that is helpful for manufacturing firms in the time of market turbulent. In the current situation of COVID-19, firms can adopt digital servitization, that is, "*a service strategy that exploits extensively digital breakthroughs such as smart connected products, industrial internet platforms, predictive analytics, digital offerings, and advanced services*" (Rapaccini et al., 2020). Digital servitization will make organization less dependent on man interaction and travel, however the transformation on digital servitization is a long process and have a deliberate effect on business model (Tronvoll, Sklyar, Sörhammar, & Kowalkowski, 2020; Paiola & Gebauer, 2020). From their research, Rapaccini et al., (2020) proposed that digital servitization is a proactive weapon for acceleration and implementation to respond to the crisis.

2. Use of Advanced Industry 4.0 (I4.0) Technology

Belhadi et al., (2020) conducted a study to observe the impact of COVID-19 on supply chain resilience in manufacturing and service operations in automobiles and airlines industries. Based on SCRes theory, this study was conducted in three phases using quantitative and quantitative methods. The results of this study identified the best strategies for the automobile industry were to develop localized supply sources and use advanced industry 4.0 (I4.0) technologies. The study also found that the airline industry perceived that it should define its operations at airports and within the flights to get ready for business continuity challenges posed by COVID-19. Moreover, the study also suggested that both industries use their big data analytics to play a significant role in overcoming the challenges posed by COVID-19 by providing real-time information.

Table 1. Summary of articles published

Sr. No	Topic	Publisher	Journal	Industry	Strategy
1	Navigating disruptive crises through service-led growth: The impact of COVID-19 on Italian manufacturing firms	Elsevier	Industrial Marketing Management	Manufacturing firms	Digital servitization, four-stage model—calamity, quick & dirty, restart, and adapt
2	Impact of COVID-19 on the travel and tourism industry	Elsevier	Technological Forecasting & Social Change	Travel and tourism industry	Four-time economic strategy
3	Note: Mayday, Mayday, Mayday! Responding to environmental shocks: Insights on global airlines' responses to COVID-19	Elsevier	Transportation Research Part E	Airline	Multiple strategies
4	Impacts of COVID-19 on global tourism industry: A cross-regional comparison	Elsevier	Tourism Management Perspectives	Global tourism industry	Travel insurance
5	Structuring for innovative responses to human resource challenges: A skunkworks approach	Elsevier	Human Resource Management Review	Manufacturing firms and service	*Skunkworks* structural approach
6	Airport user experience unpacked: Conceptualizing its potential in the face of COVID-19	Elsevier	Journal of Air Transport Management	Airline	*User Experience*
7	Ultra Long-Haul: An emerging business model accelerated by COVID-19	Elsevier	Journal of Air Transport Management	Airline	Ultra Long Haul (ULH)
8	The future of airports post COVID-19	Elsevier	Journal of Air Transport Management	Airline	Multiple strategies
9	Independent restaurant operator perspectives in the wake of the COVID-19 pandemic	Elsevier	International Journal of Hospitality Management	Restaurant	Multiple strategies
10	COVID-19 social distancing and the US service sector: What do we learn?	Elsevier	Research in International Business and Finance	Service sector	Black Swans

3. Four-Part Economic Strategy

A study was conducted on the tourism industry by Škare, Soriano, & Porada-Rochoń, (2020) to evaluate the potential effects of the COVID-19 pandemic. The study compared the results of the previous pandemic with the current pandemic of COVID-19 and found that the impact of the current pandemic on the industry are worse as compare to the previous one. On the quantitative data analysis base, the study proposed a four-part economic strategy for the tourism industry. The strategy comprises accepting fiscal losses, providing information about people suffering from unexpected income losses by expanding public security support programs, providing healthcare policies, looking after productive capacities, and utilizing financial capabilities until this pandemic weakened. Furthermore, they suggested that businesses should support an innovative crisis-readiness mechanism for survival and preparation of unforeseen pandemics in the coming future. They also found that COVID-19 affected the whole industry in parallel, so after the crisis the industry would require a mutual cooperation rather than a competition for its revival and to minimize the costs of COVID-19.

4. Multi-Facet Strategy

Amankwah-Amoah (2020) conducted a study to investigate the impact of COVID-19 on the airline industry globally. He developed a unified conceptual framework to capture internally and externally strategic and tactical responses over short and long terms. The study found the responses and reactions taken by different airlines against the actions taken by governments like travel restrictions, quarantines, and social-distancing schemes. Under the pressure of social distancing factor, airlines introducing innovative airline business model with long-term implication like in-flight arrangements, high-density seating, and in-flight services. Moreover, airlines are sighting to minimize the erosion of long-developed market capabilities, rout networks, and the prior relationship of trust with customers.

According to the International Air Transport Association (IATA), the current impact of COVID-19 on the aviation industry forced the industry to adapt to the situation as soon as possible. A significant decrease in demand of travelers forced the sector to ground a large number of aircraft; thus, the airlines are trying to identify alternate, quick, and effective measures to survive the industry in the current global crisis of COVID-19 (International Air Transport Association., 2020). In its press release International Air Transport Association. (2020) highlighted that over 2.7 million jobs in the airline industry are at risk, so governments should play their role in surviving the aviation industry of the world. The association directed to governments that they should support the through direct financial support, loans as well as through tax relief also. Under the influence of this press release and the current uncertain situation of the aviation industry impacted by COVID-19, Serrano & Kazda, (2020) found that the rebounding curve of the aviation industry is V-shape and U-shape, which means the sector is rebounding at a very slow pace. They also identified that almost 70 to 80 percent of airline capacity has down as compared to April 2019 that is forcing to multiple airlines to cease their operations temporarily. In early April 2020, almost 60 percent globally was grounded (Curley, Dichter, Krishnan, Riedel, & Saxon, 2020). Serrano & Kazda (2020) suggested that strategies regarding new sources of revenue generation, cost control, and integration of innovations are the future of the aviation industry during and post COVID-19.

Brizek, Frash, McLeod, & Patience, (2020) conducted a research study to assess the attitudes and perceptions of full-service independent restaurant operators under the impact of the pandemic COVID-19 in the South Carolina region. They used a mixed-method approach that comprised a short survey with local administration and government bodies. This survey was open to respondents and was conducted when restaurants were permitted for indoor dining operations following the COVID-19 SOP, i.e., ensuring social distancing when restaurants' seating planning was planned. The second stage of their study consisted of a qualitative approach comprising semi-structured post-survey interviews with selected restaurant operators. The study highlighted the worse impact of the COVID-19 pandemic on independent restaurants, as 25 percent of the restaurants were not able to survive after the lockdown of nearly two months. The results of the study identified that less than a quarter of respondents failed to bring back their employees to pre-pandemic level due to financial crisis occur during a pandemic, and 65 percent of the respondents claimed that they would not be able to keep their restaurants in working position if they have to face pandemic restrictions up to 2021. On the future viability of the tourism and hospitality industry, thethe respondents showed a vibrant response that was surprisingly ambivalent. Based on the findings of their study, Serrano & Kazda, (2020) suggested multiple strategic tools for the industry's survival. They included independent restaurants in tourist regions want hotel guests with some additional component of tourism visits like tours, golf courses, meetings and events, and different ways of attraction. The study also suggested that independent restaurant operators should have to work with local community leaders, convention and visitors' bureaus, and local associations of restaurants to improve the general appeal of the region. In this way, they may create favorable packages with the collaboration of other hospitality and tourism businesses.

5. Travel Insurance

Before the pandemic COVID-19 in the 21st century, the tourism industry was considered one of the greatest markets in the world (Uğur & Akbıyık, 2020). To investigate the travelers' reactions during this pandemic of COVID-19 Uğur & Akbıyık, (2020) conducted a study based on text mining techniques. The data was collected from December 30, 2019, to March 15, 2020. The study indicated that the tourism sector was affected seriously by COVID-19, and travelers mostly decided to cancel or delay their trips. Furthermore, the study highlighted that travelers highly demanded a refund of their canceled trips. Based on these results, Uğur & Akbıyık, (2020) proposed that the tourism industry adopt a travel insurance business strategy during and after the pandemic to revive the business.

6. Skunkworks Structural Approach

COVID-19 is also creating issues for organizations regarding human resource (HR) management like substantial shift to remote working environment, transformation in industrial outlook, shifting learning and growth, and observing government restrictions. Under such unexpected situations, Biron et al., (2020) proposed on the basis of their study conducted on three organizations during this pandemic COVID-19 that skunkworks strategy will be best to deal with HR-related challenges in such type of turbulent environment.

7. User Experience

Tuchen, Arora, & Blessing, (2020) conducted a literature review on the aviation industry and found that most research has been conducted on consumer involvement and service quality as compared to customer experience. They also found that the concept of user experience is quite different for passengers and others like employees, airport workers, visitors, and other stakeholders. The authors proposed that user experience can play an important role in strategic planning involved in managing not only daily operation effectively during this pandemic COVID-19, but also after the pandemic to recover the major events. Furthermore, the user experience strategy would help future planning deal with such types of pandemics.

8. Ultra Long-Haul

"Ultra Long-Haul refers to flights of 14.5h or more… with a minimum greater-circle distance of 12,842 Km" (Bauer, Bloch, & Merkert, 2020). The study conducted by Benjamin et al., (2020) proved that Ultra Long-Haul business strategy not only maintains an essential features for producing a competitive environment in the aviation industry but also it could be applied in other business models too. They also found that it has proved a successful business strategy in the aviation industry during the COVID-19 era.

9. Black Swans

Gunay & Kurtulmuş, (2020) conducted a research study on the service sector in the USA to investigate the impact of pandemic COVID-19. They considered service industries from four areas, including hotels, amusements, air-transportation, and restaurants, which led them to summarize that a conditional association exists between index pairs that showed a sizeable increase during pandemic COVID-19. Moreover, by applying a dynamic conditional correlation based on "Cumulative sums of squares," it was found that an unstable relation exists between the airline industry and the entertainment industry. While they found a stable connection between hotels and restaurant industries as both showed co-movement during pandemic COVID-19. The results of the regression analysis showed that the airline and entertainment industry affected more as compared to the hotel industry, which showed a gradually slow deterioration during the COVID-19 pandemic. While they found no indication regarding an adverse impact on the restaurant industry in the current pandemic situation, and this result regarding the restaurant industry supports the Maslow's hierarchy of needs. Based on the evidences of their study, they recommended that affected industries should utilize a productive working capital along with advanced tools for managing the supply chain to survive in such pandemic situations. They also suggested Black Swans and appropriate utilization of risk measuring methods for all other industries to integrate an additional accurate likelihood of unforeseen actions like COVID-19.

CONCLUSION

The world is attacked by a severe pandemic in the 21st century, called COVID-19. The pandemic affected the whole economy globally, forcing businesses to change their strategies to cope with this pandemic. All industries, either manufacturing or services, are struggling to save their life threatened by COVID-19. Along with other factors, infodemic appeared an essential element that had a significant influence on the business community all over the world during this pandemic situation as coronavirus was appeared surprisingly with little information about its nature, structure, and remedies. Hence, at the initial stage, people were unable to handle the situation created by a coronavirus. Under such circumstances, people shared their thoughts and experiences on print media and electronic media; thus, all these elements combined to develop infodemic globally. Such unrealistic and nonscientific information regarding pandemic COVID-19 hit the business community badly, and many businesses are taking their last breath. Many are forced to change their strategy to sustain alive.

It is too tough to detect a false information, as it often looks like a real one and people give less attention on evaluation before sharing such fake information. So managers should focus on detecting fake news before taking strategic decisions. They can detect such misinformation by font of the text, content and shape of the message and language used for the text. Management should evaluate the information prior to make decisions, in this way it may save its business in this time of COVID-19 crises. World health organization along with some other world-wide organizations like UNICEF, google etc. has established information counter to provide necessary authentic and reliable information regarding COVID-19 related to all over the world. So management should confirm any update to avoid infodemic prior to any decision relevant to business strategy.

This chapter tried to elaborate on sustainable business strategies adopted by different businesses that belong to the service industry worldwide. Through a brief literature review, the authors found that the airline industry is most affected by this current pandemic of COVID-19. The basic reason behind this disaster is the restrictions imposed by different countries to limit the locomotion of the people within the countries and between the countries. Since the coronavirus pandemic was spreading rapidly in the world and the only confirmed precaution suggested by WHO against this pandemic was to limit the people's movement, so every country imposed stick restrictions to control the movements of the people within the countries as well as out of the nations. The aviation industry suffered a lot under such circumstances, and it has to adopt different new strategies or modify existing ones to survive the industry. For instance, Bauer et al., (2020) suggested Ultra Long Haul services as a innovative business strategy for the aviation industry to gain political, economic, social, technological, legal, and environmental benefits during this pandemic of COVID-19. This strategy promised a long-distance flight and will provide bases to save the industry against this pandemic.

Similarly, Tuchen et al. (2020) proposed that users' experience in a new perspective can be used as a new business strategy in the aviation industry to gain a competitive edge during this pandemic. They claimed that user experience in terms of employees, visitors, stakeholders, and other persons working for airports could be fruitful for the aviation industry in such pandemics because the experience of these people can be helpful to understand the real picture of the industry and the pandemic as well.

The chapter also highlighted some other strategies like the skunk work structural approach for the service industry. This business strategy allowed people to work at their places by limiting their movement with modern technology. Another strategy for the service industry that is elaborated in this chapter is a black swan. This strategy requires the service industry to update its risk management approach and risk calculation and demand more space for unexpected events like COVID-19. These measures will prove helpful for survival in worse condition. As the current chapter also highlighted strategies like digital servitization, travel insurance, and many multifaceted service industries, authors still have the point of view that a lot of struggle has been required from the practitioners and academics to save the business community from such type of pandemic. This chapter will prove a milestone in the current literature of service industries, as it has elaborated many new and modified business strategies in the service sector of the world that will help the practitioners and managers in their fighting against COVID-19. With all its blessings, this study has some limitations as usual. The authors of this study only focused on the research published in Science Direct journals that have a limited share in the world research publication. So it is suggested that in the future, other scholars should consider the journals of other publishers like Emerald Insight, Springer, Wiley, etc., to clear the full scene of the industry. Secondly, the authors only touched on the service industry in their literature review and ignored the manufacturing industry damaged in this pandemic. The manufacturing industry also adopted different strategies during this pandemic to survive and sustain a competitive advantage during this pandemic, but this chapter did not elaborate on them. The authors suggest that readers and scholars also comprise the manufacturing industry to save the business community during such a pandemic.

REFERENCES

Adner, R. (2002). When are technologies disruptive? A demand-based view of the emergence of competition. *Strategic Management Journal*, *23*(8), 667–688. doi:10.1002mj.246

Aguinis, H., & Bakker, R. M. (2020). Time is of the essence: Improving the conceptualization and measurement of time. *Human Resource Management Review*, *100763*(March), •••. doi:10.1016/j.hrmr.2020.100763

Al-tawfiq, J. A., Zumla, A., & Memish, Z. A. (2014). ScienceDirect Travel implications of emerging coronaviruses : SARS and MERS-CoV. *Travel Medicine and Infectious Disease*, *12*(5), 422–428. doi:10.1016/j.tmaid.2014.06.007 PMID:25047726

Amankwah-amoah, J. (2020). Note : Mayday, Mayday, Mayday! Responding to environmental shocks : Insights on global airlines' responses to COVID-19. *Transportation Research Part E, Logistics and Transportation Review*, *143*(September), 1–9. doi:10.1016/j.tre.2020.102098 PMID:33013185

Bartik, A. W., Bertrand, M., Cullen, Z., Glaeser, E. L., Luca, M., & Stanton, C. (2020). The impact of COVID-19 on small business outcomes and expectations. *Proceedings of the National Academy of Sciences of the United States of America*, *117*(30), 17656–17666. doi:10.1073/pnas.2006991117 PMID:32651281

Bauer, L. B., Bloch, D., & Merkert, R. (2020). Ultra Long-Haul: An emerging business model accelerated by COVID-19. *Journal of Air Transport Management*, *89*(August), 101901. doi:10.1016/j.jairtraman.2020.101901 PMID:32839647

Belhadi, A., Kamble, S., Jabbour, C. J. C., Gunasekaran, A., Ndubisi, N. O., & Venkatesh, M. (2020). Manufacturing and service supply chain resilience to the COVID-19 outbreak: Lessons learned from the automobile and airline industries. *Technological Forecasting and Social Change*, *120447*(November). doi:10.1016/j.techfore.2020.120447 PMID:33518818

Biron, M., De Cieri, H., Fulmer, I., & Lin, C. H. (2019, May). (Veronica), Mayrhofer, W., Nyfoudi, M., … Sun, J. M. (James). (2020). Structuring for innovative responses to human resource challenges: A skunk works approach. *Human Resource Management Review*, *100768*. Advance online publication. doi:10.1016/j.hrmr.2020.100768

Brizek, M. G., Frash, R. E., McLeod, B. M., & Patience, M. O. (2020). Independent restaurant operator perspectives in the wake of the COVID-19 pandemic. *International Journal of Hospitality Management*, *93*, 102766. doi:10.1016/j.ijhm.2020.102766 PMID:33230361

Cepoi, C. O. (2020). Asymmetric dependence between stock market returns and news during COVID19 financial turmoil. *Finance Research Letters*, *36*, 101658. doi:10.1016/j.frl.2020.101658 PMID:32837370

Cheng, D. (2013). The development of the service industry in the modern economy: Mechanisms and implications for China. *China Finance and Economic Review*, *1*(1), 3. doi:10.1186/2196-5633-1-3

Choi, T. M. (2020). Innovative "Bring-Service-Near-Your-Home" operations under Corona-Virus (COVID-19/SARS-CoV-2) outbreak: Can logistics become the Messiah? *Transportation Research Part E, Logistics and Transportation Review*, *140*(March), 101961. doi:10.1016/j.tre.2020.101961 PMID:32346356

Christopher, M. (2000). The agile supply chain: Competing in volatile markets. *Industrial Marketing Management*, *29*(1), 37–44. doi:10.1016/S0019-8501(99)00110-8

Cifuentes-Faura, J. (2020). Infodemics during COVID-19: Resources and recommendations to combat it. *Online Information Review*. Advance online publication. doi:10.1108/OIR-08-2020-0352

Curley, A., Dichter, A., Krishnan, V., Riedel, R., & Saxon, S. (2020). *Coronavirus: Airlines brace for severe turbulence*. McKinsey. Retrieved from https://www.mckinsey.com/industries/travel-logistics-and-transport-infrastructure/our-insights/coronavirus-airlines-brace-for-severe-turbulence

Das, L., & Raut, R. (2014). Impact of changes in Service Sector in India in shaping the future of Business & Society. *Procedia Economics and Finance*, *11*, 795–803. doi:10.1016/S2212-5671(14)00243-3

Goodell, J. W. (2020). COVID-19 and finance: Agendas for future research. *Finance Research Letters*, *101512*. Advance online publication. doi:10.1016/j.frl.2020.101512 PMID:32562472

Grzymala-Busse, A. (2011). Time will tell? temporality and the analysis of causal mechanisms and processes. *Comparative Political Studies*, *44*(9), 1267–1297. doi:10.1177/0010414010390653

Gunay, S., & Kurtulmuş, B. E. (2020). Covid-19 Social Distancing and the Us Service Sector: What Do We Learn? *Research in International Business and Finance*, *101361*. Advance online publication. doi:10.1016/j.ribaf.2020.101361

IMF. (2020) https://www.imf.org/en/Publications/WEO/Issues/2020/04/14/weo-april-2020

International Air Transport Association. (2020). *Airport Development Reference Manual*. Retrieved from https://www.iata.org/en/publications/store/airport-development-reference-manual/

Kindström, D., Kowalkowski, C., & Sandberg, E. (2013). Enabling service innovation: A dynamic capabilities approach. *Journal of Business Research*, *66*(8), 1063–1073. doi:10.1016/j.jbusres.2012.03.003

King, A. A., & Baatartogtokh, B. (2015). How useful is the theory of disruptive innovation? *MIT Sloan Management Review*, *57*(1), 77.

Kowalkowski, C., Gebauer, H., Kamp, B., & Parry, G. (2017). Servitization and deservitization: Overview, concepts, and definitions. *Industrial Marketing Management*, *60*, 4–10. doi:10.1016/j.indmarman.2016.12.007

Krueger, D., Uhlig, H., & Xie, T. (2020). *Macroeconomic dynamics and reallocation in an epidemic* (No. w27047). National Bureau of Economic Research. https://www.nber.org/papers/w27047.pdf

Kumar, S., & Managi, S. (2020). Does Stringency of Lockdown Affect Air Quality? Evidence from Indian Cities. *Economics of Disasters and Climate Change*, *4*(3), 481–502. doi:10.100741885-020-00072-1 PMID:32838121

Lai, C. C., Shih, T. P., Ko, W. C., Tang, H. J., & Hsueh, P. R. (2020). Severe acute respiratory syndrome coronavirus 2 (SARS-CoV-2) and coronavirus disease-2019 (COVID-19): The epidemic and the challenges. *International Journal of Antimicrobial Agents*, *55*(3), 105924. doi:10.1016/j.ijantimicag.2020.105924 PMID:32081636

Lipsitch, M., Phil, D., Swerdlow, D. L., & Finelli, L. (2020). Defining the Epidemiology of Covid-19—Studies Needed. *The New England Journal of Medicine*, *382*(13), 1194–1196. doi:10.1056/NEJMp2002125 PMID:32074416

Mackey, T. K., & Liang, B. A. (2012). Lessons from SARS and H1N1/A: Employing a WHO-WTO forum to promote optimal economic-public health pandemic response. *Journal of Public Health Policy*, *33*(1), 119–130. doi:10.1057/jphp.2011.51 PMID:22048060

Mandel, A., & Veetil, V. P. (2020). The economic cost of covid lockdowns: An out-of-equilibrium analysis. *Economics of Disasters and Climate Change*, *4*(3), 431–451. Advance online publication. doi:10.100741885-020-00066-z PMID:32838118

Paiola, M., & Gebauer, H. (2020). Internet of things technologies, digital servitization and business model innovation in BtoB manufacturing firms. *Industrial Marketing Management*, *89*(March), 245–264. doi:10.1016/j.indmarman.2020.03.009

Park, D., & Shin, K. (2012). *The service sector in Asia: is it an engine of growth?* Asian Development Bank Economics Working Paper Series, 322.

Rapaccini, M., Saccani, N., Kowalkowski, C., Paiola, M., & Adrodegari, F. (2020). Navigating disruptive crises through service-led growth: The impact of COVID-19 on Italian manufacturing firms. *Industrial Marketing Management*, *88*(May), 225–237. doi:10.1016/j.indmarman.2020.05.017

Serrano, F., & Kazda, A. (2020). The future of airport post COVID-19. *Journal of Air Transport Management*, *89*(May), 101900. doi:10.1016/j.jairtraman.2020.101900 PMID:32834696

Škare, M., Soriano, D. R., & Porada-Rochoń, M. (2020). Impact of COVID-19 on the travel and tourism industry. *Technological Forecasting and Social Change*, (November). Advance online publication. doi:10.1016/j.techfore.2020.120469

Strong, A., & Welburn, J. W. (2020). *An Estimation of the Economic Costs of Social-Distancing Policies*. RAND Corporation.

Swafford, P. M., Ghosh, S., & Murthy, N. (2006). The antecedents of supply chain agility of a firm: Scale development and model testing. *Journal of Operations Management*, *24*(2), 170–188. doi:10.1016/j.jom.2005.05.002

Talwar, R. (2020). *Help Navigating Covid-19 Impacts on Your Business*. Available at: https://troymedia.com/business/help-navigating-covid-19-impacts-on-yourbusiness/

Tronvoll, B., Sklyar, A., Sörhammar, D., & Kowalkowski, C. (2020). Transformational shifts through digital servitization. *Industrial Marketing Management*, *89*(February), 293–305. doi:10.1016/j.indmarman.2020.02.005

Tse, A. C. B., & Leo Sin, S. S. (2006). Crisis management and recovery: How restaurants in Hong Kong responded to SARS. *International Journal of Hospitality Management*, *25*(1), 3–11. doi:10.1016/j.ijhm.2004.12.001 PMID:32287848

Tuchen, S., Arora, M., & Blessing, L. (2020). Airport user experience unpacked: Conceptualizing its potential in the face of COVID-19. *Journal of Air Transport Management*, *89*(June), 101919. doi:10.1016/j.jairtraman.2020.101919 PMID:32874022

Uğur, N. G., & Akbıyık, A. (2020). Impacts of COVID-19 on global tourism industry: A cross-regional comparison. *Tourism Management Perspectives*, *36*(September), 100744. doi:10.1016/j.tmp.2020.100744 PMID:32923356

Uotila, J. (2018). Punctuated equilibrium or ambidexterity: Dynamics of incremental and radical organizational change over time. *Industrial and Corporate Change*, *27*(1), 131–148. doi:10.1093/icc/dtx018

Visnjic, I. K., & Van Looy, B. (2013). Servitization: Disentangling the impact of service business model innovation on manufacturing firm performance. *Journal of Operations Management*, *31*(4), 169–180. doi:10.1016/j.jom.2013.02.001

Weekly epidemiological update. (n.d.). Retrieved December 6, 2020, from https://www.who.int/publications/m/item/weekly-epidemiological-update---1-december-2020

Wenzel, M. (2020). Strategic responses to crisis. *Strategic Management Journal*, *42*(March), 7–18. doi:10.1002mj.3161

Zarocostas, J. (2020). How to fight an infodemic. *Lancet*, *395*(10225), 676. doi:10.1016/S0140-6736(20)30461-X PMID:32113495

KEY TERMS AND DEFINITIONS

Black Swans: "A business strategy that requires to update risk measurement and risk management models and force to allocate more space for unexpected events in the tails of probability distributions" as defined by Gunay and Kurtulmuş (2020).

Digital Servitization: Kowalkowski et al. (2017) and Baines and Lightfoot (2014) described servitization which "refers to a firm's transition from a product-centric business logic, focusing on selling products, to a more service-oriented business logic that focuses on facilitating customer value creation through the provision of advanced services and solutions that better fulfill customers' specific needs."

Ultra-Long Haul (ULH): "The term Ultra Long-Haul refers to flights of 14.5/h or more with a minimum greater-circle distance of 12,842 km" as mention by Bauer (2019).

Chapter 5
COVID-19 Data and Environmental Perspectives:
A Case From Georgia

Manana Darchashvili
Georgian Technical University, Georgia

ABSTRACT

The COVID-19 pandemic is a major challenge for the entire modern world. Since December 2019, the international community has been concerned about the current situation. The World Health Organization declared the disease as a pandemic on March 11, 2020. The countries are doing their best to prevent the spread of disease. Thus, there is an acute health crisis in the world, which leaves its negative results and will continue to affect all areas of society, especially the economy. Existing difficulties are almost universal. The complexity of the situation reflects upon small, developing countries, such as Georgia, where health and economics are the common denominators directly related to environmental protection. Therefore, along with the data about COVID-19, the chapter presents environmental perspectives of Georgia's international cooperation. The current situation in Georgia is reflected in the program documents of the political parties participating in the 2020 parliamentary elections.

INTRODUCTION

The modern world has been facing a common threat since December 2019. As a result of the rapid spread of the deadly infection Covid-19, thousands of people die, there are a number of restrictions in the countries, isolation, quarantine, every state is in the tough and acute situation, which leads to a severe social background.

To stop the disease, the world's famous scientists worked hard all year to create a vaccine against the virus and to achieve the desired results.

Even the world's leading, economically strong countries are facing problems, such difficulties are almost universal. The whole world is facing great challenges and we have to admit that in small countries like Georgia the situation is even more. Here, the authorities, start to work over the situation on January

DOI: 10.4018/978-1-7998-7164-4.ch005

28, 2020, a month before the confirmation of the first fact (February 26): the government started the fight against Covid-19, and on March 21 already declared a state of emergency.

Like the rest of the world, the coronavirus crisis (COVID-19) has posed new challenges to Georgia, with the pandemic affecting all areas of public life. The main goal of the government is to overcome the crisis created by the pandemic, the rapid recovery, and development of the economy, to create a stable and secure environment for every citizen.

Everywhere, including in Georgia, it is a matter for all governments to care for their population health and to adjust the situation of a number of sectors to the appropriate level.

The existing reality has shown that the whole of humanity faces a common problem. The problem does not differ poor from reach people, strong from a weak political actor, developing from a developed country; it affects everyone.

The world is battling with the public health and economic crisis caused by COVID-19, and this situation has made even more clear the power of infectious diseases and their connection to environmental problems.

An important challenge is faced primarily by health systems, as well as, especially for small, developing countries in various areas of the social sphere, we consider it a matter of universal importance because it never loses its relevance at the international level. At the same time, the issue of environmental protection is directly related to the economy. Accordingly, along with the data of Covid-19 in the paper, the environmental issue in Georgia is presented.

Naturally, the situation in the Georgian reality, during the election campaign in a very noisy situation against the background of the pandemic, was reflected in the program documents of the political entities participating in the 2020 parliamentary elections. It is noteworthy to highlight the issue addressing the health and environmental issues in the context of the Covis-19 situation which has its negative impact on the political spectrum as well. Thus, by studying their approaches, we can develop ways of future frameworks based on the findings and recommendations of the goal of overcoming the existing problems.

The paper aims: to study and present the existing reality in Georgia concerning Covid-19 conditions; to observe the effective steps of the government for the stability of the situation and the attitude of political parties to the problems of health and environmental issues and the search for solutions.

Research method: the chapter is based on the qualitative method, extensive analysis is made based on materials, official documents, decisions, resolutions, resolutions, a number of empirical materials, search-processing, and observation of primary sources from various media.

The task of the paper is: based on the available documentary material to present the following:

- how the world's largest, most common problem is perceived in a small country;
- how a small country tries to cope with the challenge;
- what is directly related to this problem;
- what should be addressed in the country to avoid impending threats;
- how the major political entities in the country view the issue, creating the political climate in the country.

The research hypothesis is: the Georgian government, political parties, and the private sector are actively involved in resolving the current situation, and their plans include efforts to address common issues such as healthcare and the importance of the environment. The conclusion/recommendations developed by the analysis of the empirical material based on the study documents taken from the relevant agencies in the paper have educational-practical significance for the interested persons.

LITERATURE REVIEW

The discussion on COVID - 19 first, should be started with StopCoV.ge, which is the first official website on this issue in the Georgian reality. Which has all the existing latest information of government data, from the governmental sites, and governmental and healthcare hotline (Government of Georgia, 2020).

Every citizen of the country has the opportunity to get all the necessary and interesting information through this website. Particularly, the current anti-crisis economic plan adopted by the government, which includes the decisions taken by the government regarding the global pandemic, all the details are written in time indicating the deadline for implementation, various benefits for citizens, targeted social assistance, and negative impact of the pandemic on the country's economy. Moreover, it includes the description of an anti-crisis plan for tourism, an anti-crisis plan for education, an anti-crisis plan of the Ministry of Health for targeted social assistance to citizens, etc.

Besides a large number of official websites, in this regard, analytical articles published in existing media are also very vital and important.

In addition to the pre-election programs published on the official websites of political parties, the chapter deals with the materials published by each party on the official website - partiebi.ge, funded by the Embassy of the Kingdom of the Netherlands. Here it is worth saying that together with various materials the website is significant support for researchers to compare and observe the existing reality.

GEORGIAN REALITY RELATING TO THE COVID - 19

The World Health Organization declared COVID 19 as a global threat on January 30, 2020, and as a pandemic on March 11. Originally detected in the Chinese city of Wuhan in late 2019, the virus, was known to occur initially in bats, and later transmitted to humans through intermediate animals and lead to the transmission from human to human after its mutation.

In this regard, on January 28, 2020, the Interagency Coordination Council was established in Georgia. As a result of the joint effective work of the Ministry of Health, relevant agencies, and the Interagency Coordinating Council, on February 26, the first COVID-19 fact was detected at the border, so that this case, had no contact with the citizens of Georgia. The situation gradually worsened, which led to the declaration of a state of emergency on March 21, 2020.

From the very first day, the following important steps were taken: were restricted direct flights, first from the People's Republic of China, Iran, and then from/to different directions, and was suspended ground traffic. The borders with neighboring Armenia, Azerbaijan, and Russia were closed. Additional quarantine measures were introduced, including a curfew from 9:00 pm to 6:00 am; Meetings of more than 10 people were banned, public and other mass events, schools and universities were switched to online and distance learning methods. The government decided to provide all medical care related to COVID-19 for free, regardless of whether the citizens had medical insurance. The Ministry of Health of Georgia and the Government fully cooperated with the World Health Organization.

The Prime Minister of the country G. Gakharia constantly appeals to the population that the state alone will not be able to defeat the virus, that it is a global crisis, and is necessary to learn how to manage the situation and the virus itself. He keeps urging people to learn to co-exist with the virus and realize that everyone has his/her responsibility in this battle with the invisible enemy.

Periodically, to manage the situation in the country, cerian restrictions are imposed for almost a year.

At present, on November 28, due to the current epidemiological situation, the Interagency Coordination Council adopted and introduces certain restrictions, which means to tighten and expand already existing particular restrictions, such as closing shops, restaurants, fitness centers, and swimming pools, public transport and intercity transport stopped working (these restrictions last for almost two months).

Restaurants and food outlets have completely switched to takeaway and drive service, all kinds of events are held only in an online format. Educational institutions (except medical education programs) are fully switched to remote mode.

According to the official data available in Georgia, due to the newly mutated type of coronavirus in the UK, the Interagency Coordination Council has decided that all persons, including Georgian citizens with a history of travel to the UK during the last 14 days, will be subject to a 12-day quarantine. At the same time, the Interagency Coordinating Council is actively working with experts, specialists, epidemiologists, as well as business representatives on the expediency of easing the restrictions imposed from December 24 (the decision was taken on 28 November), as well as on strict safety regulations in case of such a decision.

According to official statistics, the total number of confirmed cases since the outbreak of the Covid-19 pandemic in the country is 209,462. The number of recovered - up to 184 668. Unfortunately, the total number of death is high for such a small country as Georgia, 2,140 people have died from the virus since the spread of the pandemic (Government of Georgia, 2020).

It should also be noted the coordinated activities of the Government of Georgia, the Prime Minister, the current government in the fight against the Covid-19 pandemic with the WHO Regional Center for Europe, which has had its positive impact in combating the situation.

Negotiations with international partners, vaccine manufacturers, are in an active phase with the involvement of the Ministry of Foreign Affairs and Georgian diplomatic missions abroad, so the country will receive the first doses of the vaccine as soon as possible.

It is important to note the government's concern for Georgian citizens living abroad, in connection with the announcement of the coronavirus (COVID-19) pandemic in the world, hotline numbers were opened in Georgian diplomatic missions abroad. The addresses of the social media channels of the embassies were also published, where the schedule of international flights was regularly published, as well as information on what international flights were performed in Georgia. For the mentioned Georgian citizens who want to travel abroad to Georgia, it is possible to plan appropriate routes in the direction of Georgia.

The COVID-19 pandemic has posed a major challenge to the world in many ways. In connection with the situation in Georgia, the leaders of the country's leading directions are actively working to overcome the situation, because these challenges have severely tested them. One of these is the educational field. In the current situation, the main goal was/is to maintain the continuous process of gaining an education. With the joint efforts of teachers, lecturers, the Ministry, the state, and international organizations, the challenges facing the education system during the pandemic are almost overcome.

The process of distance learning, despite the enthusiasm and creative approach of teachers, is noteworthy. It is worth to highlight the support of international organizations, with which the Ministry was in constant communication during this period and received useful recommendations and advice, is also important. It is also noteworthy that since all universities faced one common challenge, the process was successful through mutual assistance and sharing of experience between universities. Besides, universities were recommended to be guided by the e-learning and quality assurance guidelines developed by the Association of European Higher Education Quality Assurance Agencies (ENQA). In order to ensure universal access to education, a project was also set up in cooperation with the Public Broadcaster at the TV-School, where all classes and subjects are taught by experienced teachers, which received a very positive response from the public (Chkhenkeli, 2020).

According to the current situation in the country, it is very tough, but still, the government does its best to overcome the difficulties and obstacles in almost all directions.

Environmental and Social Impact Management Framework (ESMF) has been developed to address the need for a COVID19 Rapid Response Action Plan, funded by the International Bank for Reconstruction and Development (IBRD) and the Asian Infrastructure and Investment Bank (AIIB). The project is being implemented by the Ministry of Internally Displaced Persons from the Occupied Territories, Labor, Health, and Social Affairs (MoILHSA). ESMF is the guide for the project. As required (Government of Georgia, 2020).

COVID - 19 AND THE ISSUE OF PUBLIC HEALTHCARE IN THE ELECTORAL PROGRAM OF POLITICAL PARTIES IN GEORGIA (2020)

As soon as Georgian regained its independence, the political parties started to become more active in the political process and contributed to improving the electoral process. The parties are constantly involved in the discourse on many topical issues, which is reflected in their program documents, applications. At the current stage and generally, in recent years, the activities of the parties are the subject of active debates, and many questions arise regarding their action plans, their attitude to issues relevant to the country. Consequently, in the current period, when the interest of the whole Georgian political spectrum, as well as the public sphere, were directed towards the October 31, 2020, parliamentary elections, the parties were actively involved in informing the public about fascinating promises, trying to make their program documents as comprehensive as possible.

According to the urgency of the research issue, it is interesting to see to what extent the country's politicians consider the importance of the environmental issue before occupying the places in the Georgian parliament and whether this is reflected in their pre-election documents.

The table deals with the subjects which overcame the electoral threshold (50 subjects participated in the 2020 parliamentary elections, out of which there were two blocs and political seven subjects totally 9) (see table # 1).

Table 1. Votes received in percentages

Election Number	Name of the Electoral Political Entity	Number of Votes in Percentage
2	"Bakradze, Ugulava, Bokeria - European Georgia - Movement for Freedom"	3.79%
5	Bloc "United National Movement - United Opposition" Power in Unity "	27.18%
8	"David Tarkhan-Mouravi, Irma Inashvili - Alliance for Georgian Patriots"	3.14%
10	"Shalva Natelashvili - Georgian Labor Party"	1.00%
24	"Aleko Elisashvili - Citizens"	1.33%
27	Block "Giorgi Vashadze - Strategy Builder"	3.15%
36	„Girchi"	2.89%
41	Georgian Dream - Democratic Georgia	48.22%
56	Lelo-Mamuka Khazaradze	3.15%

Along with several topical issues, all the political parties that gained enough votes to enter the parliament support and state their position on environmental issues, because they are well aware of its urgency.

In this regard, we have to highlight that the materials published by them within the framework of the project funded by the Embassy of the Kingdom of the Netherlands partiebi.ge along with various materials are important contributions to informing the public, comparing and observing scholars' researches (EECMD, 2020).

The ruling party, **"Georgian Dream-Democratic Georgia"** intends to implement large-scale healthcare reforms: fundamental refinement of the primary health care system, ensuring early detection of the disease, which will improve the health of the population; one of the main priorities of the state will be the diagnosis and treatment of oncological diseases; within the framework of state programs to achieve universal access to health care, all beneficiaries will receive the highest quality services, without delay in a place convenient for them; continue to provide the necessary medications for effective management of chronic diseases; the pension for elderly people will gradually increase.

"The United National Movement - United Opposition" "Power in Unity" bloc believes that the goal of the healthcare reform is to create a national healthcare system focused on disease prevention and a healthy and long life-oriented population. The leaders of the party criticized the government's approaches to healthcare. They think it is necessary to: increase state investment in citizens' health; to reduce the medical service price; to introduce thorough preventive health-check at least once a year; to improve universal health care services and provide within the country; to fully fund emergency and planned operations; to make free childbirth, as well as to finance dental services; to double the salaries of healthcare workers; to introduce the private medical practice to strengthen the quality and accessibility of the primary health care system; to increase the of state oncology programs and open a regional oncology center - equipped with modern technologies and staffed with high-class specialists; to be focused on medical tourism (the describe a possible outcome in details). Regarding the current situation, they say that they are ready for it according to the rules set by the World Health Organization so as not to harm any kind of business and, as a result, not to reduce working places. At the same time, they claim that they will exclude selectivity and restrictions on political grounds - the imposed regulation should be applied most evenly.

The block **"Giorgi Vashadze - Strategy Builder"** offers the population a new Georgian model of healthcare, which aims to create a highly cost-effective Georgian model of healthcare based on innovation and high technology, which will offer high-quality medical services to patients. The quality and financial availability of services provided to citizens will be a key feature of the new model. The political team has detailed the main initiatives of the new model of healthcare, the initiatives include the initiative "Individual health plan for all citizens of Georgia"; comprehensive oncology management and full financial coverage at all stages: full digitization of the healthcare system - full integration of electronic healthcare systems at all levels of healthcare, which will make the system more personalized, cost-effective and facilitate the creation of reliable statistics; "Georgia - Regional Health Center", by arranging medical resorts, attracting investment, introducing high standards of safety and services, they ensure that Georgia will appear worldwide attractive place for medical tourism; reducing the price of medicines by at least 30% in price transparency, the so-called introduction of European standards of reference and pricing. Based on the current COVID-19 situation, they have decided to take action to tighten/change the measures in public places due to the specific epidemic situation.

The political union "**European Georgia - Movement for Freedom"** criticizes the government's course and said that despite the increase in public spending on health care, citizens still pay from their pockets to their medical services, leaving many Georgians vulnerable to poverty: improving access to medicines and to overcome poverty is a necessary (though insufficient) condition; the universal health care program should include co-financing components for up to 400 types of medicines (in different proportions for different income groups); efficient spending of state (and non-state) funding on health care is also a prerequisite for improving quality.

In the reality of Covid-19, **"European Georgia - Movement for Freedom"** considers it necessary that the restrictions imposed on public health objectives should be based on mutual trust and cooperation between the government and the public; the government will offer reasonable recommendations to the public, which the citizens will accept and follow accordingly. This is exactly what "coexisting with the virus" means, and it is this approach that will prevent the weakening of the economic sector and a psychological or financial depletion of society that we can endure the marathon of fighting the virus for as long as possible. The leaders of the party also criticize the government's policy in the fight against the virus.

The model of the health care system of the political entity **"Lelo"** envisaged the transition to the principles of insurance medicine - the state would ensure all citizens through private insurance companies. In addition, they offer a number of reforms, with detailed descriptions, in such areas as quality and affordable medicine; health system management (administration) reform; primary health care; Electronic Medicine (E-Health); medical education.

New Political Center - **"Girchi"** believes that in order to improve access to health care and its quality, the state must allow free development in this area; Girchi members have criticized the government for believing that healthcare is the most regulated area where everything is controlled; In fact, it is a merged state that manages this field through businessmen who are kind to it and their business and does not allow private initiatives.

As for the current pandemic situation, they say that they will lift any restrictions imposed by the Georgian government on the people of the country in the framework of the fight against the coronavirus and call on everyone to observe the norms of hygiene.

"Aleko Elisashvili - Citizens" believes that access to a quality health care system can be achieved by proper management. If people's money is to be spent on anything, it is, above all, the health of the people themselves, and healthcare must be available anywhere in the country. Health care reform should be the result of universal consensus and aimed at the long-term perspective, to ensure quality, doctors, clinic founders should be held accountable. Given the current situation, it is believed that the country should follow the recommendations of the World Health Organization, which provides for the rules of careful behavior in society, protection of distance and hygiene, wearing personal clothes. However, it is unacceptable for people to have unreasonable, unsubstantiated, and illogical regulations, which imply strange rules of movement of the curfew, car, and transport, a lack of logic in cities.

The **"Georgian Labor Party"** considers it necessary to provide full health care to those citizens who do not have the resources for medical services. It includes outpatient, inpatient, rehabilitation, and medical treatment; the existence of a multi-profile hospital in all regions of Georgia; de-monopolization of the healthcare and pharmaceutical sectors, resulting in drastic reductions in the cost of medicines and treatment; fund state health programs aimed at reducing drug treatment, alcoholism, and tobacco use (Georgian Labor Party, 2020).

The political union - **"David Tarkhan-Mouravi, Irma Inashvili - Alliance for Patriots of Georgia"** believes that in parallel with the development of paid medical services, free health care should be developed; socially vulnerable citizens and retirees should have free services and also the necessary medicines should be free; the state should take care of regulating the prices of medicines (Alliance for Patriots of Georgia, 2020).

From the pre-election promises of the political parties, it seems that they were maximally motivated to take care of the population as much as possible in their program documents, to improve the existing health issues. Moreover, they are often focused on free medical care, which in some cases is impossible.

APPROACH TO ENVIRONMENTAL ISSUES IN GEORGIA

Protecting the natural environment is a priority for all progressive countries. This is a certain indicator of the level of their development, for example in 1969, when the United States adopted one of the first environmental laws, the National Environmental Policy Act (NEPA), it showed a broad national environmental concern(United States Environmental Protection Agency, 1969).

Georgian Law on Environment, adopted in 1996, regulates the field of environmental protection and natural resource management. Georgian policy has been trying for years to bring the country as close as possible to the environmental conditions and regulations of the developed countries. Article 6/2 of the Constitution of Georgia states that the international treaty or agreement of Georgia if it does not contradict the Constitution of Georgia, has the supreme legal force over domestic state normative acts (The Parliament on Georgia, 1995).

In Georgia, international development-oriented approaches are crucial for the country. Consequently, while the importance of environmental issues and economic development is gradually increasing over the international political agenda, it is more likely that the latter can be achieved only if the balance between the country's development and the utilization of natural resources is maintained. Moreover, it states that public welfare can be ensured when environmental and social aspects are as important as economic growth. Georgia is trying to introduce internationally recognized environmental approaches and regulations to the country, to bring the existing conditions closer to the developed international community. Due to this, in the early 20th century, in 2000, with the support of the World Bank, along with international and national legislation, which further strengthened the cooperation of Georgia with international donor organizations the Georgian government, established the first National Environmental Action Program in the country.

It should be noted that when Georgia joined the European Neighborhood Policy Area (together with 16 countries) in 2004 and the Action Plan was approved in 2006, its implementation was immediately considered as an important step for Georgia in terms of integration into European economic and social structures. In the strategic goals of cooperation between Georgia and the European Union, together with the multilateral cooperation, the issue of protection of the natural environment was considered as well (Pataraia, 2010). Then, in 2014, when the Association Agreement was signed, the European Neighborhood Policy Action Plan was replaced by the Association Agreement Implementation Action Plan, which represents one of the key issues in the field of environment. The agreement envisages certain measures in the field of environment protection, the implementation of which will help to provide appropriate environmental conditions for humans and ecosystems, as well as improve environmental governance and effective decision-making procedures. On this basis was launched the Second National Environmental Program, which was implemented with more intensified international cooperation 2012-2016. Then based on the experience gained from the implementation process of the above-mentioned program and considering the opinion of European and local experts there was developed the third program, which represents the main strategic document of the country in the field of environment and natural resources protection. It presents a specific five-year action plan for 2017-2021, which envisages three main policy trends: 1. "Georgia-EU Association Agreement"; 2. "UN Sustainable Development Goals" and the international environmental agreements with the participation of Georgia and 3. National and sectoral strategic documents related to environmental protection and natural resource management. The strategic objectives of the Third National Environmental Program must be -1. Improving the state of the environment, ensuring the protection / sustainable utilization of natural resources, and avoiding/minimizing the risks that endanger human health and the well-being of the population. 2. Ensuring Georgia's fulfillment of the taken obligations under regional and global environmental agreements and further aligning with EU environmental policy, framework legislation, and the requirements of specific directives. 3. Strengthen administrative structures to ensure effective environmental management and enforcement of environmental legislation. 4. Promoting sustainable development through the integration of environmental aspects in social and economic policy (Davitashvili, Tandilashvili, 2018). These goals are defined considering the country's financial and economic situation, the process of rapprochement with the European Union, international environmental treaties, conventions, and implementation of legislation. At the same time, it worth saying that the implementation of environmental requirements should be achieved only by the active involvement of both the governmental level and civic sector. A sustainable development approach will be established through program activities and ensure the integration of environmental areas in the activities of various fields (Ministry of Environment and Natural Resources of Georgia, 2017).

The Ministry of Environment and Agriculture of Georgia and the Green Climate Fund (GCF) with the assistance of the United Nations Framework Convention on Climate Change (UNFCCC) in 2010 established a joint program intending to assist developing countries with funding resources. At the current stage (2019-2026) the country implements the project: "Expanding the Multilateral Early Warning System and the Use of Climate-Related Information in Georgia", which aims to assist the Government of Georgia at the national level to take several actions to address the climate-related threats to the population.

Georgia is trying to meet its national commitments to some extent. The UN Framework Convention on Paris's Framework Convention on Climate Change entered into force in 2017 (Paris Agreement: essential elements, 2015), according to which to achieve its goals Georgia should (at least) update its climate strategy and action plan every 5 years. Therefore, Georgia has developed a 2030 Climate Change Strategy at the national level. Besides, the Action Plan for 2021-2023 has been developed by experts from various sectors of the economy sector and civil society, which is considered as a mechanism for pursuing and achieving the national goals (analysis of seven sectors and relevant measures). As well as it includes the other tasks and international commitments and is in the framework of Georgia and the EU legal acts (Sikharulidze, Abulashvili, Kunchulia, 2020).

According to the EU-Georgia Association Agenda 2017-2020, it is necessary to provide public access to environmental information and to improve the mechanism for sharing them. It seems to be insufficient, however, it is implemented in several projects, including the Ministry of Environment and Agriculture and LEPL Environment and the joint projects of the Education Center.

PRE-ELECTION DOCUMENTS OF POLITICAL PARTIES ON ENVIRONMENTAL PROTECTION

Georgian politics reflects the complex nature of environmental problems - in the areas of health, economic development and other social welfare. Since 1991, the Ministry of Environment has been responsible for a number of decisions on various issues. According to Article 9 of the Constitution of Georgia, which represents the supreme law of the country: everyone has the right to live in a safe environment, to enjoy the natural environment and public space. Moreover, to receive the complete information about the state of the environment and take care for the environment, as well to participate in environmental decision-making processes. Also, considering the interests of current and future generations, to protec the environment and call for the rational use of natural resources, that are provided by law (The Parliament of Georgia, 1995).

According to the urgency of the research issue, it is interesting to see to what extent the country's politicians consider the importance of the environmental issue before occupying the places in the Georgian parliament and whether this is reflected in their pre-election documents (Senaklen, Arifen, 2014).

It should also be noted that the only political party having an environmental name - Gachechiladze - Green Party (# 9) also participated in the elections however, the party failed to occupy the place in the Georgian Parliament, since it got only 0.07%.

Along with several topical issues, all the political parties that gained enough votes to enter the parliament support and state their position on environmental issues, because they are well aware of its urgency (Government of Georgia, 2020).

The ruling party, **"Georgian Dream-Democratic Georgia"** intends to implement large-scale environmental reforms in its next four years term to ensure a healthy living environment based on the principles of sustainable development and a green economy. These include protected areas, efficient utilization of forest, promotion of ecotourism, the introduction of European environmental standards to minimize environmental pollution, proper urban development, landscaping, and high air quality, including proper transport policies. At the same time, according to their promises, the Georgian legislation in the field of environmental protection will be qualitatively closer to the EU legislation, including the involvement of its citizen. The nine-point environmental plan of the ruling party includes almost every detail and can be considered as a progressive and well-thought scheme (Davitashvili, Tandilashvili, 2018).

"The United National Movement", which is the largest oppositional party and gained the second place among the other oppositional parties, summarizes its commitment regarding the issue and aims to: reduce the air pollution, especially in urban areas; encourage waste recycling; increase the share of renewable energy in total consumption; to construct the hydro electricities only in cases of extreme necessity and based on an internationally qualified conclusion; expand recreational zones in urban centers; regulate the construction with transparent criteria, and to achieve compliance with environmental principles, and to encourage a green economy.

The bloc **"Giorgi Vashadze – Strategy the Builder"** starts by criticizing the existing situation and states that Georgian people have suffered from numerous cases of environmental pollution in recent years. The leader of the bloc refers to the utilization of asbestos-containing products in Bolnisi and Dmanisi municipalities, which threaten human health. They consider it necessary to refine the relevant legislation and introduce effective enforcement mechanisms against companies that pollute the environment. The same approach is used to consider building standards when construction dust pollutes the environment and increases the risk of developing carcinogenic diseases. According to the EU Association Agreement, they plan to create a transparent system in the field of energy and switch to the production of renewable energy (solar, wind, water, geothermal), which will be entirely focused on consumers and safe use of green energy. Another priority for them is the development of green cover strategies for green cover development in cities, including vertical and roof planting.

„European Georgia - Movement for Freedom“ believes that responding to environmental challenges is an integral part of caring for the quality of life and health of future generations, which includes: the protection of Georgia's biodiversity and sustainability of ecosystems; protection and maintenance of a safe environment for human health; facilitate the implementation of international, first and foremost, environmental requirements and standards provided for in the Association Agreement between the EU and Georgia; expansion of Georgia's protected areas; continue to work on creating a full-fledged sewerage system in large cities, attracting international donors and foreign partners; creating a modern information base on the nature of Georgia.

Another political party **„Lelo for Georgia“** starts discussing environmental issues by criticizing the existing data and says that the sphere of the environment leaves much to be desired, that it requires a great afford to first maintain the area, then to save and last to restore it. He considers that the following steps are necessary for the stability of ecological and physical systems; pursuing an environmental policy based on the principles of sustainable development by harmonizing national legislation with EU legislation; to construct the large hydropower plants, which could be subject to the European standard of environmental impact, and shall be discussed widely before its adoption, especially with international environmental organizations. All these must be implemented in the framework of the regulatory impact analysis, and the mandatory environmental impact analysis of each new project. As for its promotion it needs: the extensive utilization of renewable energy; reduction of air pollution; improvement of water and waste management; settlement of green plant quotas in cities; restoration of green cover and cultivating new ones; strengthening the system of protected areas; creating motivational systems for the private sector. Along with the health care system, there are to be ensured the safety of the living environment; to create an effective system of predicting, preventing, and dealing with them, informing the population and education, with minimal loss of the departmental labyrinths. At the same time, animal welfare policy is on the agenda as well. Due to the lack of the policy, the number of stray animals in Georgia is increasing, their condition is deteriorating, the population is threatened and public perceptions of animals are distorted.

New political center - **"Girchi"** believes that more freedom in the field of environmental protection should be given to the private sector. There is also a requirement to repeal meaningless, pointless regulations and prohibitions that ostensibly protect the environment, but in fact, it has the opposite effect, for instance, the entire forest park of the country is supposed to be state-owned and ownerless, which is thoughtlessly cut down and destroyed with the permission of officials and by those who are currently in power.

"Aleko Elisashvili - Citizens" considers it important to create a more ecologically healthy and safe living environment: to support renewable energy sources, maximum utilization and use of renewable energy resources (solar and wind), and to encourage the process to reduce taxes and promote production; promote the production of biologically pure agricultural products; consider the importance to retrain agricultural workers and train new staff in relevant educational programs. Other vital steps to be curried are the promotion of the mentioned production: by imposing tax benefits; reducing the high rate of air pollution in erosion and urban areas; diversifying the green cover, providing more greenery in urban spaces, planting trees and shrubs, and to reduce erosion processes by planting appropriate trees in the designated areas.

„Georgian Labor Party" considers it necessary to define areas in Tbilisi and other large cities where a temporary moratorium will be imposed on the construction of four-story residential buildings. To achieve compliance with EU standards, the air pollution rate will be monitored for fuel quality, and appropriate vehicle inspection standards will be established. Besides, the party promises to develop a certain budget support program for the population; to develop certain norms for limiting dust generation during construction works, and that the introduction of their implementation will be strictly controlled. In the case of being elected, the party leader promises to develop a program for enterprises to clean the air, water, and soil pollution according to the European standards and activities during its term. The leaders of the party promise the determination of the boundaries of urban green areas. They said that trees will be subject to inventory, and cutting the healthy trees will be completely banned; construction companies, upon obtaining a permit, will be required to plant trees and bushes in the surrounding area following the European standards. In addition, necessary works will be conducted to increase the green area, which will be financed by at least 50% of the central budget. Also, he promises to develop a national program to support and separate waste collection-disposal and promote the recycling process. He says that for the first time in Georgia, there will be established a special landfill for the hazardous waste of local origin; the construction of large hydropower factories and nuclear power plants will be prohibited at the legislative level. The action plan says that if necessary, small hydropower factories will be built only to meet the requirements and consent of the local population. That they will conduct the plebiscite and the mandatory consideration of its results following the European standards. It also says that there will be introduced large-scale programs promoting the introduction of energy-efficient technologies and the development of alternative energy such as water, oil, etc. Among them, the purchase and installation of individual systems and materials will be supported by using budget funds through the issuance of long-term interest-free loans to the citizen.

The political union - **"Davit Tarkhan-Mouravi, Irma Inashvili - Alliance of Georgian Patriots"** did not post any information about its future activities on the portal, their program documents, despite the extensive list, say almost nothing specifically about environmental protection (Alliance of Georgian Patriots, 2020).

At the same time, for all political entities, the implementation of large-scale environmental development projects in various directions is very important.

CONCLUSION

The COVID-19 pandemic has posed a great challenge to the world in all directions, naturally, this is a great challenge for the Georgian reality as well.

In the current situation, the government of the country is responsible for stabilizing the situation. In order to overcome the crisis, a number of vital directions are actively working. Both politicians and health workers are in tough time and experience difficulties in finding the solutions, as challenges have put them under the test.

Thus according to the research materials, we can claim that the paper presents the complexity of the current situation and the government's attempt to regulate a number of issues. It discusses the views on the health problem presented in the policy documents of political entities participating in the parliamentary elections in Georgia in 2020.

An environmental issue that is directly related to the health problem is also discussed. Because the COVID-19 pandemic has once again confirmed the ubiquity of the issues. Such is healthcare and the environment directly related to it.

The presented material shows that the political parties represented in the 2020 parliamentary elections have a proper understanding of the role of international agreements, one of the parties of which is Georgia, and are aware of the importance of formulating the national environmental policy process. Consequently, despite the different assessments of some issues, their common aim is to regulate the existing reality, to harmonize the legislative framework with European standards, and accurately implement them. They pay great importance to raise the citizens' awareness and education about the issue and involve them in the solving process.

RECOMMENDATIONS

Thus, there is no doubt that the issue of infections and health is related to environmental problems, therefore it is important that the state, for the prevention of epidemics and the welfare of citizens, in the implementation of a number of ongoing projects (dams, natural resources), actively involve the local population. In addition, to do their best to raise their knowledge and experience about the potential dangers.

The public must have any information on environmental issues (especially the obligation of the state under a number of conventions). At the same time, increase the rate of public participation in the decision-making process.

REFERENCES

Alliance for Patriont of Georgia. (2020). *Our Program.* Retrieved November 11, 2020, from http://patriots.ge/ka/program

Chkhenkeli, M. (2020). *We Overcome Challenges.* Retrieved November, 05, 2020, from http://mes.gov.ge/content.php?lang=geo&id=10320

Davitashvili, L., & Tandiashvili, N. (2018). *Action Program. Third National Environmental Action Program of Georgia 2017-2021.* United Nations Development Program.

Georgian Labor Party. (2020). *Election Program*. Retrieved November 18, 2020, from Labour. ge: http://www.labor.ge/ka/chvens-shesakheb/programa

Government of Georgia. (2020). *Decision About the Mandatory Quaranteen*. Retrieved November, 11, 2020, from http://gov.ge/indexphp?lang_id=GEO&sec_id=541&info_id=78080

Government of Georgia. (2020). *Georgia-COVID-19 Rapid Response Project. Natural and Social Impact Management Framework*. Retrieved November, 11, 2020, from https://www/moh.gov.ge/uploads/files/2021/06.01.21.pdf

Government of Georgia. (2020). *Prevention of Coronavirus Spread in Georgia*. Retrieved November, 15, 2020, from https://stopcov.ge

Ministry of Environment and Natural Resources of Georgia. (2020). Third International Enviromental Action Program of Georgia (2017-2012). Tbilisi: Author.

National Statistics of Georgia. (2020). *Population and Demography*. Retrieved November, 05, 2020, from https://www.geostat.ge/ka/modules/categories/316/mosakhleoba-da-demografia

Partiebi. ge. (2020). *Compare the Results- Environment Protection*. Retrieved December, 11, 2020, from https://partiebi.ge/2020/geocompeare?party1=10&party2=9&party3=&theme=83

Partiebi.ge. (2020). *Compare the Results - Healthcare*. Retrieved December, 11, 2020, from pttps://partiebi.ge/2020/geo/compeare?party1=10&party2=9&party3=&theme=76.

Senaklen, P., & Arifen, I. (2014). *International Politics, Modern Theories, and Tasks*. Ilia State University.

Sikharulidze, A., Abulashvili, G., & Kunchulia, I. (2020). *Georgia's 2030 Climate Change Strategy and 2021-2023 Action Plan*. Ministry of Environmental Protection and Agriculture of Georgia.

The Parliament of Georgia. (1995). *The Constitution of Georgia*. Author.

United States Environmental Protection Agency. (1969). *Summary of the National Enviromental Policy Act*. Retrieved November 17, 2020 from https://www.epa.gov/law-regulations/summary-national-enviromental-policy-act

KEY TERMS AND DEFINITIONS

COVID-19: An infectious, contagious disease that can be transmitted from an infected person to a healthy person.

Economy: Is a unified economic situation of the country, which brings together various sectors: industry, agriculture, construction, transport, etc.

Electoral Subject: A party, election bloc, or voter initiative group registered by an election commission running for office as a member of a representative body of public authority or as a public official.

Environmental Protection: Is all state and public measures aimed at the harmonious relationship between society and nature and aims to preserve the vital foundations of man and nature as a whole and to eliminate existing environmental damage, protect and restore natural resources.

Georgia: An independent, sovereign state of the Black Sea basin in the South Caucasus, bordered by Armenia, Azerbaijan, the Russian Federation, and Turkey. The population of the country is 3. 716.000 (National Statistics Office of Georgia, 2020).

Health: Human physical, spiritual, and social well-being.

Natural Resources: Water, soil, air, minerals, forest, animals, etc.

Pandemic: A large-scale epidemic when a contagious disease spreads to a wide region, several countries of the world.

Party: A group of people with the same interest, who express the interests of a certain part of the population and aim to realize these interests by acquiring or participating in state governance.

Chapter 6
The Negative Consequences of the Infodemic and Technological Support to Deal With Psychological Issues

Nataliia Svitlychna
https://orcid.org/0000-0001-7891-6295
National University of Civil Defence of Ukraine, Ukraine

Natalia Afanasieva
https://orcid.org/0000-0002-1050-8495
National University of Civil Defense of Ukraine, Ukraine

Iryna Ostopolets
State Higher Educational Institution "Donbass State Pedagogical University", Ukraine

ABSTRACT

The chapter deals with a theoretical generalization and new approaches of solving the scientific problem, which is manifested in the disclosure of the peculiarities of the experience of the threat of COVID-19 by residents of Ukraine, due to Infodemic. To prevent the negative consequences of Infodemic influence, psychological technology has been developed and tested, which is aimed at the formation/development of adaptive potential of the individual, which determines his ability to overcome difficult situations. The peculiarities of the organization and implementation of work in the training group on overcoming negative feelings and frustration caused by individual perception of personal information about the coronavirus and the spread of COVID-19 in the world are described. It is valuable to present the methods of training and the most effective exercises that were used in active social and psychological training. The results of implementation showed high efficiency and expediency of using this psychological technology in the work of a psychologist.

DOI: 10.4018/978-1-7998-7164-4.ch006

INTRODUCTION

The ability of a person to resist the actions of adverse factors is one of the most important conditions for the actualization and realization of his personal potential, subjective sense of well-being and vitality. This is especially important now, at the present stage of human development, when the world has faced serious challenges due to the pandemic and the rapid spread of COVID-19.

Nowadays, the research on the influence of the pandemic and quarantine on human life and how it will affect it psychologically in future is going on. However, a number of interesting data from around the world on how humanity responds to COVID-19 and information on the spread of infection have already been partially presented. Each cultural environment (nationality) has its own characteristics of crisis response, which depends on the level of social and economic development, traditions, maturity of the individual and so on. (Okoro et al., 2020; Nguyen et al., 2020; Durodie, 2020)This is partly due to different quality of life, level of education, individual psychological characteristics of perception of information about Infodemic and response to it.

Literary Review

With the beginning of the pandemic, we witnessed another terrible disease that became dangerous to the human psyche and intellectual abilities. This is an infodemia. Infodemia is the dissemination of an excessive amount of information about a certain problem, which makes its solution even more difficult. The term itself appeared in early 2020, when the General Director of the World Health Organization, Tedros Adhan Gebreesus, legitimized the new term and called to confront the misinformation, exaggeration and intimidation that is sweeping the world today, seriously complicating the real problem of stopping and overcoming the pandemic. COVID-19 (Zarocostas, 2020). Every second the Internet, social media, and instant messaging spread information to a huge audience that was partially dangerously useless, incorrect, or even harmful to physical and mental health.

The concept of infodemia includes all manifestations of destabilization of the information ecosystem, which have significantly intensified in the XXI century: fake news, misinformation, enemy speech, propaganda. Along with the exponential growth of information produced and consumed, it becomes extremely threatening to the main species such as Homo sapiens it is the mind. Excessive emotional content of informational messages and the incredible pressure of their number on the human psyche significantly reduce the ability to perceive reality rationally and make well considered judgments and adequate decisions in everyday life. As a result, the panic and anxiety that accompanies men and women around the world are increasing significantly during important local or global crises, such as wars, economic recessions, and epidemics.

In addition, the modern world has become very dense in terms of information: if earlier, in order to get acquainted with certain events, you had to read a newspaper, listen to the radio, now more and more often the average person has a feeling that he dissolves into the planetary information web with its rapid emotions, fears, anxieties, and environmental threats. This determines the persistence of negative perceptive prejudices and the collective social tendency to panic behavior. (Hua, Yangb, Lib et al., 2020)

Psychologists note that the people with different education, age and social status feel the influence of news releases. TV viewers can be affected, because visual stimuli, together with all the others, give the greatest emotional load on the human psyche and cause the greatest emotional response. For example, people who watch news with special reports on emergencies and catastrophes have symptoms the same as the victims who are at the epicenter of events. The information about emergencies in this case is "tried on" for a person himself and his loved ones. Psychologists highlight these viewers to the group of "secondary victims" of an emergency. At the same time, the lack of information about the circumstances is giving a fertile ground for fantasies and speculation. With a lack of available information, negative emotions appear which reach a maximum in the complete absence of information. Positive emotions arise when the available information exceeds the information needed to meet that need. Thus, in some cases, knowledge, awareness of the individual change of the emotional mood and mental state of the individual, open access to internal human resources.

However, we note that the media transmits not only objective but also subjective information, because its content is the result of a thought process. Subjective information to a greater extent reflects not so much the subject of information as the specifics of its perception. Communication through the media allows a lack of feedback between the communicator (TV presenter, program author) and the mass audience (various groups of the population receiving video information, speech, text or audiovisual messages about events). This is due to the one-sided transmission of information and the loss of part of its content in the process, which is facilitated by various factors, including psychological features of perception, the unpreparedness of the object to perceive information, technical obstacles etc.

The current state of the information space of Ukraine is such that the psychological trauma of the population with the active assistance of the media covers both those directly affected by COVID-19 and huge groups of the population who are in the role of virtual participants in this process. In addition, on Ukrainian TV there are the channels which have a special place. They transmit extreme events, such as natural and man-made disasters, robberies, violence, murders, military conflicts, and so on. Ukrainian media are also characterized by too detailed and tragic coverage of information related to the spread of COVID-19 in the country and the world, mortality and descriptions of complications after the disease, medical problems. COVID-19 reports that contain audiovisual information series with footage of human suffering, helplessness of patients and physicians who work hard to provide care, as well as news repetitions, message duration, emotionally expressive vocabulary, emotional and, in part, unsustainable tone of message use means of fascination, increase the level of emotional perception of the population of information and can lead to various negative psychological and behavioral consequences and effects at both the individual and mass levels. The media have an informational and psychological impact on the public consciousness and the mass psyche, reinforce the existing inadequately high individuality and social responsibility, as well as people's anxiety, which reduces the adaptive potential and leads to regressive social and psychological adaptation. The growth of critical sentiments and even aggression towards the media in all social classes of Ukrainian society shows that, on the one hand, the traumatization of the population is intensifying, and on the other the desire for self-defense is intensifying which is manifested in decreasing in media trust and also in attempts to determine the criteria of «ecological safety" of the information environment.

The study of the psychological impact of information on the spread of COVID-19 in Turkey (in a sample of 1130 people from 28 cities) showed that 52.7% of respondents assessed the overall psychological impact as moderate and severe, 18.6% showed moderate or severe depressive symptoms; 26.5% showed moderate and severe anxiety symptoms; 7.9% showed moderate and severe stress levels (Mustafa, 2020). Most respondents spent from 20 to 24 hours a day at home (88.2%); 78.6% of people under research indicated that they were overwhelmed by the amount of information about the coronavirus. The data which have been obtained from Sri Lanka confirms that women, quarantined people and patients with a psychiatric history are at higher risk of psychological symptoms development due to a pandemic and, in particular, through infodemia (ELLepoLa, Rajapakse, 2020).

Ukraine also suffers from "infodemia". Currently, the results of the study of Ukrainian scientists (Anishchenko, 2020; Ostopolets, Kurilchenko, Ulyanova, 2020; etc.) have also shown an increase of negative consequences, including asthenic emotions and moods among the population, an increase of psychosomatic and post-traumatic stress disorders, depressive states, etc. The consequences of panic mood and panic behavior in society, according to Ignatovych O.M. can be expressed in increasing of mortality rate and lower birth rates, increasing the number of psychosomatic disorders and psychiatric diseases. (Ignatovych, 2020) Hence, there is a need to identify the ways and means to prevent this. The development of psychological technology of overcoming the negative effects of Infodemic is relevant.

Methodological Principles and the Organization of the Research

The experimental work was carried out from March to December in 2020 and included several inter-related stages:

- at the first stage of research the scientific tasks are made, hypotheses are formulated, the purpose and tasks of empirical research are formulated, the analysis of scientific sources concerning a problem is made, the selection and approbation of research methods are carried out, the selection of groups of respondents is carried out;
- at the second stage, it was carried out the empirical study of the peculiarities of experiencing the threat of COVID-19 by the people of Ukraine, due to traumatic experience, gender and age; the psychological features of the citizens of Ukraine with different levels of intensity of experiencing the threat of COVID-19 were studied;
- at the third stage the systematization and generalization of the data obtained in the process of theoretical and empirical analysis are carried out. During this stage, the socio-psychological overcoming of the negative consequences of Infodemic for adult residents of Ukraine was developed and tested.

The purpose of the study is to determine the peculiarities of the experiencing of the threat of COVID-19 by residents of Ukraine and to develop a psychological prophylactic program to minimize the negative effects of Infodemic and the pandemic in general.

The tasks are:

1. to determine the level of intensity of experiencing the threat of COVID-19 in residents of Ukraine with different traumatic experiences.
2. to investigate the features of the psychological characteristics of the residents of Ukraine with different intensity of experience of the threat of COVID-19.
3. to develop and test psychological technology to minimize the negative effects of Infodemic and the pandemic in general on the people of Ukraine.

Research methods. In the process of work both general and special research methods were used:

- theoretical nature: analysis, classification, review and analytical method. The use of these methods allowed to study the developments in this field, to review and analyze the data obtained by other scientists in order to systematize them further;
- empirical nature: a) a method of questionnaires to determine the intensity of the experiencing of the threat of COVID-19 by different categories of residents of Ukraine. The questionnaire is based on the formulated theoretical substantiation for the description of the construct "experiencing of an emergency situation".

The experience of the threat of an emergency can be analyzed in terms of its three components, which differ in their psychological content: cognitive, emotional and behavioral, which were taken into account during the development of the questionnaire.

The questionnaire of experiencing the threat of an emergency.

1. The desire not to leave the house because I feel that I am in danger of getting COVID-19 has appeared.
2. Loud unexpected sounds (for example, the sounds of sirens, flying planes, car exhausts, pyrotechnic effects, etc.) make me think of COVID-19.
3. I have various physiological reactions (rapid heartbeat, muscle tension, trembling in the hands, sweating, headache, etc.) when I think of COVID-19.
4. I was afraid that I might become a victim of COVID-19.
5. At night I wake up from the fact that I have terrible dreams about the possibility of getting COVID-19.
6. Sometimes I want to call the psychological help service because of my experience of the threat of getting COVID-19.
7. I have a desire to insure my property because of the threat of losing it as a result of the COVID-19 pandemic.
8. I lose my temper when I hear about the threat of COVID-19.
9. The threat of getting COVID-19 lowers my self-confidence.
10. The threat of getting COVID-19 affects my emotional state.
11. I have thoughts that pandemics will happen again in the future.
12. Due to the COVID-19 pandemic, it is better not to make plans for the future.
13. I try to follow the news about the COVID-19 pandemic in our country, in the world.
14. From time to time I feel unreasonable fear or sudden anxiety.

The processing of the results: always - 3 points, often - 2 points, sometimes - 1 point, never - 0 points.

b) psychological diagnostic method, which is represented in the study by a number of such psychological diagnostic methods: to clarify the information obtained through the author's questionnaire, it was used "Methodology for assessing experiences in a psychotraumatic situation" by M.B. Dorokhov; to diagnose the structural components of experiencing the threat of an emergency: "Scale of basic beliefs" (Padun, Tarabrina, 2004), "Scale of self-assessment of anxiety" by C. D. Spielberger, "Scale of attitudes to time" by J. Nuttin; method of »Individual measure of reflexivity" by A.V. Karpov; A.G. Maklakov and S.V. Chermyanin's multilevel personal questionnaire "Adaptability" (BOO-AM) was used to study the adaptive potential of a person with different levels of intensity of experiencing the threat of an emergency; to assess the severity of psychopathological symptoms in participants it was used "Symptomatic questionnaire SCL-90-R"; the severity of post-traumatic stress reactions was determined using the civil version of the Mississippi scale;

- methods of mathematical statistics: Cronbach's alpha method for measuring the retest reliability of the author's questionnaire; Student's t-test was used to identify the level of significance in the differences of comparative indicators.

The study involved 1305 residents of Ukraine from different regions, different ages, genders, who had different experiences and levels of awareness about the COVID-19 pandemic, different intensity of experience of the COVID-19 threat.

PECULIARITIES OF EXPERIENCING THE COVID-19 THREAT BY RESIDENTS OF UKRAINE

The number of patients with COVID-19 in the world is constantly growing, so the study of the effects of the pandemic on the human psyche has become one of the most pressing and complex social problems. The residents of Ukraine are also aware that they can get sick at any time or have already fallen ill, which causes (or increases) the level of negative affect in a certain part of the population.

The threat of COVID-19 is a high-intensity stressor that can cause various forms of mental maladaptation in both direct and indirect victims. By direct victims we mean those who:

- directly came down with COVID-19 in severe form and has complications;
- those whose relatives or friends died from COVID-19;
- lost his job during a lockdown or quarantine;
- participated in the care of patients with COVID-19.

By indirect victims we mean the people that receive information about COVID-19 through the media, rumors, stories of patients, etc. and in whom the psychopathological symptoms are determined, there are signs of post-traumatic stress of varying severity, in some cases reaches clinical levels of post-traumatic stress disorder (PTSD).

The consequences of Infodemic for indirect victims can be conditionally grouped into the following groups: clinical and psychological, social and psychological, actually psychological. Clinical and psychological consequences include: psychopathological symptoms in indirect victims, which were caused by the indirect influence of information about COVID-19 from the media and other sources of communication. Clinical and psychological consequences also include sleep and concentration disorders, irritability, nightmares, sad repetitive thoughts and memories of the event. The most pronounced forms of mental disorders that occur are PTSD and maladaptation. Direct participation in a traumatic event and the influence of the media is a combined factor in the formation of post-stress states.

The sense of security is also reduced, that is:

- decreased sense of control of the situation: the inability to control the development of events and the use of one's skills to avoid negative consequences;
- feelings of helplessness, which impairs the effectiveness of social functioning.

The level of reduction in the sense of security and development of PTSD cannot be predicted only by objective measurements of the degree of material damage from a pandemic. Personal and emotional involvement in a traumatic situation plays the leading role in the occurrence of mental trauma. Among the personality traits that contribute to the development of feelings of imminent threat are: infantilism, immaturity of emotions, weak resistance to negatively colored external stimuli, external orientation, rigidity, the predominance of hysterical displacement. The most common mental disorders that develop after the COVID-19 pandemic are depression, anxiety disorders, and post-traumatic stress disorder.

The social and psychological consequences of a pandemic include: victimization, antisocial behavior, rent behavior, alcoholism, family conflicts, stigmatization and discrimination, schoolchildren and students' educational failure, loss of sense of security, and so on. The social and psychological consequences of the pandemic are also manifested in the disbelief of people in the ability of the state (government) to protect people, to provide timely and adequate assistance. At the behavioral level, inactive forms of behavior may appear: intensive search for information to reduce the uncertainty of the situation, the development of a state of constant readiness with its subsequent involuntary reduction. These behaviors are associated with experiencing a state of hyper-alertness, wariness in response to information about the threat of COVID-19. The study of the psychological consequences of a pandemic has shown the prevalence of fear of becoming its victim, as well as the loss of life prospects.

People develop negative expectations of the consequences of COVID-19, which they cannot prevent. This personal assessment is manifested either in increased anxiety or in complete indifference to the threat. In this regard, it is necessary to talk about such a psychological construct as experiencing the threat of COVID-19, which means a subjective assessment of the risk of becoming a victim. Experiencing the threat of COVID-19 is a multifaceted construct that includes cognitive, emotional and behavioral levels, that is the subjective assessment of the risk of becoming a victim of COVID-19 is manifested in thoughts, emotions and changes in habitual behaviors. COVID-19 poses a direct threat to the lives of immediate victims. The aim of the empirical study was to identify the relationship between age, gender and personal characteristics of the experience of the threat of COVID-19 by residents of Ukraine. The study tested the hypothesis that not only in direct but also indirect victims of COVID-19, a vulnerable part of the population (anxious, emotionally unstable, people who are easily affected) under the influence of live TV and audio broadcasts that cover during a pandemic, there may be a specific emotional-cognitive complex-experience of the threat of COVID-19, which is associated with signs of post-traumatic stress disorder (PTSD).

To determine the intensity of the COVID-19 threat, it was used a specially designed author's questionnaire by different categories of Ukrainians. At first we investigated the intensity of experiencing of COVID-19 threat in people with different engagement experiences. Based on the assessment of the degree of involvement of all participants, they were divided into four groups: the first group included victims of COVID-19, the second included those whose relatives were affected, the third included the direct witnesses of the disease, the fourth included those who did not suffer from COVID -19 and have no relatives who were ill.

We identified that the highest intensity of experiencing the threat of COVID-19 was defined in the people under research of the 1st group (34.6 points), the lowest in the people under of the 4th group (11.7 points). The differences are significant at p £ 0.05 levels according to the Student's t-test. It should be emphasized that the psychogenic impact of the COVID-19 pandemic consists not only on a direct, immediate threat to human life, but also on an indirect, expectation of the disease.

People, who have no experience with COVID-19, do not have sick (or sick) relatives; receive information about its course mainly through the media and from doctors, acquaintances and other sources. This is probably why these people's experiences of being at risk are at a lower level. It should be noted that the experience of the threat of COVID-19 is intense in the people under research of 2nd and 3rd groups, those whose relatives and friends were affected and those who witnessed the course of the disease. In our opinion, this is due to the fact that the threat to life relates to the future of a person and it is formed, as a rule, after the person became a victim or witness of COVID-19 and its consequences.

We measured the retest reliability of the questionnaire using the Cronbach's alpha method. As a result of repeated measurements, which were carried out 14 days after the first test, a reliability coefficient was calculated, which amounted to 0.92 points, which indicates the high reliability of the questionnaire. The correlation coefficient between the test scores for the two tests gives another estimate of the reliability coefficient such as stability factor.

The intensity of the experience of the threat of COVID-19 in men and women was further investigated. Significant differences were obtained in the indicators of the intensity of the threat in men and women (p £ 0.01 according to Student's test). We explain this fact by the fact that women and men differ in the type of perception of the outside world and reaction to it. Women are usually more extroverted than men, so they are characterized by a higher intensity of experience, impulsiveness in behavior, decision-making and judgment

We also investigated the level of intensity of COVID-19 threat experience in different age groups: the 1st group includes people from16 to 25 years, the 2d group includes people from 26 to 45 years, and the 3d group includes people from 46 to 65 years. It was found that the most prone to the threat of COVID-19 are residents of Ukraine in the middle age groups, the maximum intensity of the experience is observed in people aged 46 to 65 years. This is the period when a person has an established personal, intimate relationship; professional achievements. Family, friendship, relationships are the basic values for people of this age group. COVID-19 can destroy this fundamental value of the individual. That is why the greatest intensity of experiencing his threat is observed in this age group. A person of this age has something to lose, someone to fear.

It was used "Methods for assessing experiences in a psychotraumatic situation" by M.B. Dorokhov to clarify the information obtained and to solve further problems of the study. Significant differences between the indicators of the participants of the 1st and 2nd groups and the 1st and the 4th groups on the scales were revealed: experiencing the state of frustration, experiencing the significance of the situation, experiencing the duration of the situation. This indicates that Ukrainians living with COVID-19 have the most intense negative experiences associated with this experience. In particular, they feel unable to cope with trauma and its consequences on their own, lack of psychological support from other people; traumatic situation is of great importance to them for a long time.

Further, the peculiarities of feelings about COVID-19 in the population of Ukraine: men and women, as well as representatives of different age groups were studied. Significant differences between the indicators of men and women on the scales were revealed: experience of uncertainty of stressor influence (p £ 0.01), experience of significance of the situation (p £ 0.01), experience of lack of support (p £ 0.01). Indicators on these scales are much higher in women. This indicates that women are experiencing a psychotraumatic pandemic situation much deeper, stronger and longer.

This is due to the fact that when analyzing the development of events, they are less likely than men to have anticipation that means the prediction of the possible occurrence of new events, the possible results of certain actions. Psychotrauma is a vital event that leads to deep psychological experiences, which can result in maladaptation and stress-related disorders. In addition, women need more support from other people than men. It should be noted that communication and social support are a psychological resource for a woman's vitality. Thus, we can state that the impact of the events related to the COVID-19 pandemic on the psyche of women is more destructive and prolonged than on the psyche of men. Although this statement is generalized and does not take into account a large number of individual, personal, typological and social factors.

At the same time, no significant differences in the experience of the pandemic situation were found among the residents of Ukraine of different age groups. We believe that the specificity of these experiences is more influenced by other social and psychological factors than age.

PSYCHOLOGICAL PECULIARITIES OF THE RESIDENTS OF UKRAINE WITH DIFFERENT LEVELS OF INTENSITY OF EXPERIENCE OF THE THREAT COVID-19

During the next stage all participants of the research were divided into two groups according to the criterion of intensity of experience of the threat of COVID-19. The 1st group included residents of Ukraine with a high level of intensity of the threat of COVID-19 (102 people), the 2nd group included people with low level (110 people). Respondents with a medium level of intensity of threat experience did not participate in the study. It should be noted that both the 1st and 2nd groups included residents of Ukraine with different experiences regarding COVID-19.

To assess the severity of PTSD, the Mississippi Scale (civil variant, the version of the methodology adapted by a research team led by N.V. Tarabrina) was used, which reflects the condition of people who have experienced a traumatic situation, who witnessed or were informed about it. Based on the standards proposed in this version of the questionnaire, it can be stated that in the participants of the 1st group there is an increased level of severity of PTSD symptoms; in the participants of the 2nd group this level is reduced. That is, the residents of Ukraine with a high intensity of experience of the threat of COVID-19 have a tendency to a sharp emotional reaction to anything that somehow reminds of it. They tend to return to unpleasant memories and relive the events of the past. In certain situations, there may be loss of endurance and self-control, anxiety, internal tension, decreased efficiency, sleep disturbances. There may be difficulties if you need to enter into emotionally close relationships with other people. That is, we can state that the intensity of the COVID-19 threat is correlated with post-traumatic symptoms: the higher the intensity of the threat, the higher the risk of developing PTSD.

Then the level of reactive and personal anxiety was measured using the "Scale of self-assessment of the level of anxiety" by Ch.D. Spielberger (adapted by Yu. L. Khanin). The obtained results indicate that in the respondents of both groups were not found significant differences between the levels of personal anxiety. This is because most researchers attribute the cause of personal anxiety to the peculiarities of the structure and functioning of the CNS. Significant differences in the indicators of situational or reactive anxiety of the respondents were revealed.

Higher levels of situational anxiety were found in respondents of the 1st group (56.3 points), lower - in respondents of the 2nd group (42.6 points), the differences are significant at the level of p £ 0.05 according to Student's criterion. Situational anxiety is defined as a condition that manifests itself in a person when he expects adverse development of events. This condition includes such components as subjective feelings of tension, anxiety, worry, apprehension, as well as signs of activation of the autonomic nervous system. This type of anxiety is closely related to stress. In this case, reactive anxiety characterizes the level of stress at this time. It should be noted that a person does not react to the events, but to what he thinks about them. A person's reaction to any event depends on his thoughts. Thus, we found that residents of Ukraine with different levels of intensity of experience of the threat of COVID-19 have indicators of a slight difference in personal anxiety, but significantly different indicators of situational anxiety. This allows us to state that the level of expectation of the threat is related to the indicator of situational anxiety. Next, the severity of psychopathological symptoms in the subjects was studied using the "Questionnaire for assessing the severity of psychopathological symptoms" (SCL-90-R, Symptom Check List-90-Revised). Significant differences were found between the indicators of the studied groups on the following scales: obsessive-compulsive disorders are more characteristic for people under research of the 1st group (p £ 0.05 according to Student's test). Obsessive-compulsive disorder is a disorder characterized by intrusive obsessions and compulsions that interfere with normal life. Similarly, the respondents of the 1st group have significantly higher indicators on the scale of depression (p £ 0.01). Most often, depression develops against the background of stress or a situation that traumatizes for the long run. Significant differences were also found on the scales of anxiety and phobic anxiety at p £ 0.05 levels of probability. In the respondents of the 1st group, these figures are much higher. Phobic anxiety is defined as a persistent reaction of fear to certain people, places, objects or situations, is characterized as irrational and inadequate to the stimulus and shapes the behavior of avoidance. Thus, we found some association between the intensity of the COVID-19 threat experience and psychopathological symptoms such as obsessive-compulsive disorder, depression, anxiety, and phobic anxiety; it means that the higher the intensity of the experience, the more pronounced these symptoms are.

At the next stage, the features of social and psychological adaptation were studied using the method of "Adaptability" developed by A.G. Maklakov and S.V. Chermyanin. The obtained results showed that in the respondents of the 1st group in comparison with the respondents of the 2nd group the adaptive possibilities were significantly reduced. Significant differences in indicators on all scales of the questionnaire were obtained. According to the scale "Neuropsychological stability" indicators are much higher in the respondents of the 2nd group (p £ 0.05 according to the Student's t-test). This indicates that residents of Ukraine with a low level of intensity of experience of the COVID-19 threat have a high level of neuropsychological stability and behavioral regulation, adequate self-esteem and a realistic perception of reality. Residents of Ukraine with a high level of intensity of experience have a reduced level of behavioral regulation, a tendency to neuropsychiatric disorders, inadequate self-esteem and perception of reality.

According to the "Communicative abilities" scale, the indicators of the respondents of the 2nd group are much higher than the indicators of the respondents of the 1st group (p £ 0.05). This means that residents of Ukraine with a low level of intensity of experience of the COVID-19 threat have a high level of development of communication skills, easy to establish contacts with others, non-conflict. The respondents with a high level of intensity of experience have difficulty in building relationships with others, may show aggression and increased conflict.

According to the "Moral normativity" scale, the respondents of the 2nd group also have higher indicators than the respondents of the 1st group (p £ 0.05). This indicates that the respondents with a low level of intensity of the threat of COVID-19 really assess their role in the social environment, focus on compliance with generally accepted, group-wide norms of behavior. And in respondents with a high level of intensity of experience there is a decrease in the ability to group effective activities. Often they cannot adequately assess their place and role in a social group; they find it difficult to adhere to generally accepted norms of behavior.

The indicator of personal adaptive potential, respectively, is significantly higher in the participants of the 2nd group compared to the participants of the 1st group (p £ 0.05). The participants with a low level of intensity of experience of the COVID-19 threats are included in the group of high and normal adaptation. The participants with a high level of intensity of experience are included in the group of satisfactory adaptation. Most people in this group have signs of various accentuations, which in normal conditions are partially compensated and can be manifested when changing activities. Thus, the study of the adaptive capacity of residents of Ukraine with different levels of intensity of the threat of COVID-19 showed that with increasing intensity of the threat of COVID-19 there is a marked decrease in adaptive capacity, manifested in various behavioral disorders, emotional instability, and impaired interaction with colleagues and people around.

To clarify the obtained data, an assessment of the time settings of the respondents was performed. The obtained results show a subjective feeling of reduced control over the events of present and future life in respondents with a high level of intensity of experience of the threat of COVID-19, which is fully consistent with the previously obtained results. The reason of the stress of uncontrolled events is that a person is unable to influence them. Awareness of the controllability of events reduces the strength of their impact, even if the possibility of control is not used. The ability to predict the occurrence of a stressful event, even if it cannot be controlled, usually reduces the strength of its stressful effect. People who have relapsed with COVID-19 have a significantly reduced critical attitude to their abilities.

The indicators of basic beliefs of the population of Ukraine with different levels of intensity of experience of the COVID-19 threat were studied according to the "Scale of Basic Beliefs" by M.A. Padun, N.V. Tarabrina. Significant differences were found between the indicators of the respondents on the subscales: "fairness" (p £ 0.05 according to Student's criterion) and "belief in control" (p £ 0.05). The rates are much higher in the responents of the 2nd group. These subscales constitute the basic belief in the justice of the world around and characterize the individual's idea of the principles of distribution of luck and misfortune. That is, COVID-19 respondents with a high level of intensity are convinced that there is no justice in the world, the amount of happiness and unhappiness in a person's life does not depend on his personal characteristics, nor the efforts he makes to achieve goals, or on caution and foresight. Such beliefs contribute to anxiety, the formation of expectations of negative events, fatalism and, ultimately, asthenic emotions and reactions.

During the next stage, we investigated the ability to reflexivity using the method of "Individual measure of reflexivity" by A.V. Karpov. The obtained data indicate that the level of reflexivity in the respondents of the 1st group is significantly higher (7.3 walls) than in the respondents of the 2nd group (4.5 walls) (p £ 0.05 according to the Student's test).That is, people with a high level of experience with the threat of COVID-19 have a developed ability to reflect. Reflexivity is manifested in the analysis of their own actions and deeds, the ability to critically realize their characteristics, to see opportunities in self-regulation of activities and behavior. Reflexivity contains the elucidation of the essence and causes of the phenomena and processes that led to a particular result, the appeal to the assessment of their own mode of action. Reflection that occurs as a result of the impact of emotional situations that lead to fear of failure, guilt, shame, resentment, etc., which leads to a reduction of suffering from negative emotions, is defined as sanogenic. Its main function is to regulate a person's emotional states. We believe that this type of reflection is more common in people with a high level of intensity of the COVID-19 threat.

The obtained results of the empirical research were the basis for the development of social and psychological training aimed at overcoming the negative consequences of Infodemic for adults in Ukraine. Social and psychological training is a psychological technology for the development of personal skills for effective living in emergencies, in particular, the COVID-19 pandemic. In fact, this means the formation / development of some adaptive potential of the individual, which determines its resource capabilities in overcoming difficult situations.

In the training program development, we relied on the understanding of the COVID-19 pandemic as an emergency, unusual conditions for a person that are objectively prevalent, threaten his life, health, core values and have no analogues in his past experience.

The main idea of the proposed program is the idea that the COVID-19 pandemic is essentially a challenge offered to us by life, a complex task that can be solved successfully, efficiently and optimistically. The conditions prevailing in such a situation can promote both the growth and development of the individual and his regression, the formation of new protective mechanisms. One way or another can be chosen, to form resistance to stressful situations, guidelines for their effective living with the help of certain psychological technologies.

We believe, and this is confirmed by many studies, that it is possible to develop resilience to emergencies. This means not only the ability to tolerate these situations without harm, but also with a gain for themselves, which is to gain experience, acquire certain qualities, the formation of resistance to stressful situations. All this promotes the individual to a new stage of development.

The conceptual foundations of the program of social and psychological training are:

1. Personality and situational approach in psychology, which involves taking into account the interaction and interdependence of personal and situational parameters. They determine a person's behavior in an emergency and the various consequences that these situations bring to his mental life and personal experience. It is important to take into account one of the provisions of psychology, which states that the impact of any situation depends on the personal and subjective importance given to it by the person. To predict successfully a person's behavior, we must be able to take into account how he himself interprets this situation.
2. Existential psychological theory is a paradigm that draws us to the issue of "Life-Death", offers the concept of "Challenge-Response", self-development of the individual by giving meaning to events and by choosing to improve and develop, rather than protect or stagnate.

The main goal of the program is to overcome the negative consequences of Infodemic and the COVID-19 pandemic in general for adults in Ukraine, the development of individual opportunities in the use of emergencies as "catalysts" of personal growth.

Tasks of the Program

- Introduction to the concepts of "Emergency", "Sustainability", "Existential content of the emergency", "Personal resources" and "Personal development".
- Forming ideas about the COVID-19 pandemic as an "existential challenge to life."
- Learning constructive ways of self-regulation of emotional states.
- Development of resource components of "I-Concept".
- Development of the ability to self-knowledge, self-observation in conditions of emotional tension.
- Forming ideas about you as a person who successfully solves difficult life problems.
- Gaining experience of overcoming in situations that are artificially modeled.

The Methods Used in Training

- discussions;
- mini-lectures;
- individual and group reflection;
- methods of self-regulation;
- role games;
- meditation, work with imagination;
- psychotechnical exercises.

The Expected Results are

- reduction of adverse effects of Infodemic and the COVID-19 pandemic in general;
- forming a goal to overcome emergencies in response to life's challenge;
- development of ideas about oneself as a strong, successful person who develops and solves difficult life situations;
- development of skills of value comprehension received in emergency situations and gaining experience of overcoming;
- formation of skills of self-regulation of emotional states.

The working duration of the program is 64 hours, 8 days and 8 hours.

The Orientation in the Program:

- group formation;
- initial acquaintance of participants with the conceptual basis of the program;
- testing of participants (before the training);
- self-determination of group members and group definition of the purpose of the work in the program;
- rethinking ideas about emergencies and their consequences;
- the formation of ideas about themselves as a subject that can solve such situations;
- expanding the scope of awareness in the process of living emergencies;
- design and construction by each participant of effective means of overcoming the adverse consequences and effects of the COVID-19 pandemic;
- testing their new qualities in conditions that simulate emergencies;
- correction and refinement of skills and guidelines;
- reflection of the program;
- post-training testing.

This training was conducted with a group of residents of Ukraine who have a high level of intensity of experiencing the threat of contracting COVID-19. From the entire sample, we selected 14 people, men and women aged 25 to 45, with higher education and who has a job. The main thing that was paid attention to when forming the training group was the presence of motivation to learn and volunteerism.

At the first lesson, an introductory conversation was held, during which the trainer explained the peculiarities of functioning of the training group, the basic rules of the group were adopted, the purpose and results to which the participants should strive were discussed. Immediately, a conversation was held with future participants on the topics: "What do I expect from the training?", "What problems do I plan to solve?" etc.

The trainer acquainted the participants with the basic principles of the group, namely: communication in the system of "subject-subject" relationships; adherence to the principle of "here and now"; statements of training participants should be spontaneous, sincere; to accept oneself and others as they are, to avoid judgments within and outside the group, and so on.

During the training, 3 stages of work were identified.

The initial stage lasts about 2-3 days with continuous intensive work. At this stage of the training, there is still a fairly high level of tension of the participants, who are worried about "will the group accept me", "should I speak openly about myself?" etc.). All this is expressed in the relative passivity of the training participants.

At the first stage of the group's work the main task of the trainer is to ensure the spontaneity of the process of active social and psychological learning, so that the specific content of the classes determines the behavior of group members and contributes to the formation of a unique training scenario.

The focus of the trainer-psychologist at this stage is the diagnosis of personal issues of training participants, for whom appropriate exercises are used. Each day of training ends with reflection. This contributes to a deep awareness of all processes of group activity and self-knowledge and cognition of others. In their self-reports, the participants note the improvement of understanding of themselves and others, a positive attitude towards people, the ability to penetrate into the inner world of another person, the growth of self-esteem, positive well-being and etc.

The second stage of the group's development is its working stage. In our training, it lasted for 5 sessions and was characterized by a significant emotional load. It was here that global, multilevel, positive disintegration took place, which arose under the influence of self-analysis and self-awareness. At this stage, sensitivity has increased, values have been revised and rethought, and attitudes have been reoriented. At this stage of the training there was not only the final formulation of hypotheses that allowed to determine the causes of psychological problems of training participants, but also to clarify the system of psychological protection, which is inherent in each member of the group. At this stage, use appropriate exercises, elements of psychodrama, and so on.

The work in a training group allows the protagonists to make personal psychological correction on a deeply psychological level. The most relevant to this goal is the method of analysis of a set of thematic drawings. It involves not only the execution of drawings by the subject in accordance with a particular topic, but also the subsequent dialogue with their author in the process of analyzing drawings. The dialogue is focused on identifying the content of reflection, clarifying the causes that give rise to destructive phenomena of the psyche. It is in the drawings that the unconscious is projected. Moreover, there are no coincidences in the manifestations of the unconscious; they are excluded by the principles of "energy saving" and the subjective significance of the content that has left a "trace". The dialogue with the author is focused on identifying the lines of interaction between the unconscious sphere and consciousness, which allows you to update the reserves of the psyche of the author of the drawings. This promotes deeper reflection, expansion of self-awareness, harmonization of personality through the resolution of internal contradictions, which can be the main cause of frustration. These are the contradictions that arise between the tendency to strength and weakness, to life and death, to communicate with people and psychological inability.

The final stage of the group's development is summarizing, re-examining each of the training participants' capabilities and identifying difficulties that they may encounter in the future. In the seventh and eighth sessions, the participants simulate stressful situations in the context of the COVID-19 pandemic, which can cause frustration, and their reproduction and, especially, analysis, proved to be extremely productive activities.

After the training, a re-diagnosis of the intensity of the experience of the threat of COVID-19 and experiences in a traumatic situation in this group was conducted, which proved the effectiveness of the developed training.

CONCLUSION

The impact of adverse events and situations on human life is determined by internal determinants that identify the assessment of situations. For social situations, the conditionality of the subject's behavior is shown by his or her ideas about this situation. Therefore, the study of a person in emergency conditions implies the need to characterize his or her subjective significance. In this process, the crucial thing is how this person selects events and stimuli, perceives, constructs and evaluates them through their cognitive processes.

We consider the idea of an emergency situation as a set of images that perform the function of reflection, as well as they have a regulatory, motivating, evaluative, prognostic function, and provide effective (or ineffective) living.

A study of the relationship between age, gender and personal characteristics of the experience of the COVID-19 threat by residents of Ukraine proved the following:

- indicators of the intensity of experiencing the threat of COVID-19, experiencing the uncertainty of the impact of stressors, the significance of the situation, the lack of support are much higher in women;
- residents of Ukraine of the middle age group are most exposed to the threat of COVID-19. The maximum intensity of experience is observed in people aged 46 to 65 years;
- the most intense negative experiences associated with the COVID-19 pandemic have residents of Ukraine affected by the disease.

The study of the residents of Ukraine with different levels of intensity of the threat of COVID-19 revealed the following psychological features.

The residents of Ukraine with a low level of intensity of the COVID-19 threat are self-confident, consistent in achieving the goal, balanced and independent, positive; strive to fully express their position through a full life in society. They have high or normal indicators of personal adaptive potential, quickly enter new social communities, adequately navigate the situation, non-conflict, and have high emotional stability.

The participants with a high level of intensity of experience of the threat COVID-19 are characterized by a high level of situational anxiety, sanogenic reflection; subjective feeling of reduced control over the events of the present and future; tend to attribute control over events to external circumstances and other people; to a lesser extent appreciate the possibility of creative realization of one's own personality in activity. They belong to the group of satisfactory adaptation, have low emotional stability, signs of various accentuations, which in normal conditions are partially compensated and can be manifested when changing activities.

Table 1. The examples of some exercises used in the training

Exercise "Aspects of awareness"	
Goal	The formation of skills of self-control and attitude to conscious behavior in difficult situations.
Instruction	Participants imagine themselves in one of the difficult situations of personal experience. They need to answer the questions:
Questions	What is good and what is bad for me in this situation? What way of action in this situation will lead to the purpose I need? What are my little conscious desires now? What are the real possibilities of this situation? What are the consequences of each of the possible solutions? Is awareness enough to solve the situation? It is necessary to formulate a motto in figurative form. A message from oneself to oneself, found as a result of such awareness.
It is necessary to formulate a motto in figurative form. A message from oneself to oneself, found as a result of such awareness.	
Exercise "Look from outside"	
Instruction	Participants who have been divided in three-groups are given the following task: a person sitting on a chair should watch himself as if from the side. He or she chooses a place to watch and is attacked by two other participants. The "observer" says aloud what he is observing. Two other participants are given the task to "annoy" the observer, to provoke him to distraction in all possible ways, of course, without causing pain. During the discussion, only the well-being of everyone as an observer and the success of the task are commented on.
Exercise "Meaning extraction"	
Goal	The development of skills of awareness of meaning and "lessons" of life situations.
Instruction	Participants in a circle recall the last of the problematic, difficult situations that happened to them. The group and the psychologist help everyone to show the personal meaning of the situation, to clarify what, in fact, what was the challenge and lesson of life? The psychologist summarizes the discussion.
Exercise "Traits of a personality resilience"	
Goal	To acquaintance with the main personality traits that contribute to the successful overcoming of emergencies; give the opportunity to assess one's level of "resilience".
Instruction	Each participant receives a form with 15 characteristics of a person resistant to emergencies. First, in column A, "+" is placed opposite those features that are most pronounced; 0 - opposite the least pronounced; in column B is placed "+" opposite the traits that are the most characteristic of a personality resilience. After 5 minutes, the psychologist fills out a general information form on the board. To do this, he asks to raise the hands those participants who indicated in the column B the first quality, enter the number of those who answered, and so on. The three qualities that score the most points are the core of a person resistance to extreme situations from the point of view of the group.
Exercise "Changing attitudes to the situation"	
Goal	The formation of a set of technical means to overcome difficult situations.
Instruction	Participants are given the characteristics of situations written on the cards, which suddenly occurred, everyone should read and imagine themselves in a similar situation, and to capture their first direct impressions and emotions, thoughts - something that immediately came to mind; then the person consciously changes his attitude to the situation using one of the proposed coping strategies. The discussion focuses on the most successful strategies.
Exercise "Commitment, control, challenge"	
Goal	The development of resources for resilience to emergencies.
Instruction	Participants change the descriptions of situations; think through each of their new situations: what the challenge of the situation is, how he will be able to control the development of events, which he undertakes in accordance with himself, society, life in this situation. Everyone is interested in the discussion.
Exercise "Kozub"	
Goal	Gaining experience in forming coping strategies from "improvised means".
Instruction	Casual small objects in quantity which exceed number of participants of group (including cards with inscriptions of qualities or the phenomena, for example "Laziness" or "Strong wind") are put in a kozub. The participant who pulls out the object must tell how with its help he will be able to build his strategy of resilience to the emergency situation.
Exercise "A fairy-tale hero"	
Goal	The consolidation of strategies of sustainable behavior, establishing an emotionally positive connection with such behavior.
Instruction	Each participant chooses an image of a fairy-tale or virtual hero, phenomenon, object-symbol, etc., and on his behalf tells the group how he now, having new resources to withstand difficult situations, will be able to cope with them. The group asks him questions that try to identify the negative qualities of the chosen symbol, and the participant must even find in them resourceful, positive aspects that strengthen resilience. If time and mood of participants allow, with the named subjects it is possible to play a fairy-tale action, having divided, for example, group into two or three subgroups, and having devoted a fairy tale plot to questions of embodiment of stability in emergency situations.

The respondents of this group are convinced that there is no justice in the world, the amount of happiness and unhappiness in a person's life does not depend on his personal characteristics, or on the efforts this person makes to achieve the goal, or on his or her caution and foresight. Such beliefs contribute to anxiety, the formation of expectations of negative events, fatalism and, ultimately, asthenic emotions and reactions in an emergency. The respondents of this group require an individual approach, constant monitoring, and corrective measures.

The obtained psychological peculiarities of the participants with a high level of intensity of experience of the threat COVID-19 was the basis of the program of social and psychological training aimed at overcoming the negative consequences of Infodemic and the pandemic in general.

REFERENCES

Anischenko, L. (2020). Vivchennya okremikh aspects in the injection of EPIDEMIS COVID-19 on the psychosomatic manifestation of the inhabitants of the pivnich regions of Ukraine. *Preview of the covid-19 pandemic: distant psychological awareness.*

Durodiй, B. (2020). *Handling Uncertainty and Ambiguity in the COVID-19 Pandemic.* https://psycnet.apa.org/fulltext/2020-37336-001.html

Ellepola, A., & Rajapakse, R. P. (2020). *Foreseeable psychological impact of COVID 19 in Sri Lanka.* https://www.researchgate.net/publication/340522703

Hua, Z., Yangb, Z., & Lib, Q. (2020). *Infodemiological study on COVID-19 epidemic and COVID-19 infodemic.* doi:10.20944/preprints202002.0380.v3

Ignatovich, O. (2020). Psychological prophylaxis of panika and zasobi podolannya. In V. Ribalka (Ed.), *Psychological Prevention and Hygiene in the Anti-COVID-19 Pandemic.* Institute of Pedagogical Education and Education for Young People Ivan Zyazyun of the National Academy of Sciences of Ukraine.

Nguyen, H., Nguyen, M., Do, B., Tran, C., Nguyen, T., Pham, K., Pham, L., Tran, K., Duong, T., Tran, T., Duong, T., Nguyen, T., Nguyen, Q., Hoang, T., Nguyen, K., Pham, T., Yang, S.-H., Chao, J., & Duong, T. (2020). *People with Suspected COVID-19 Symptoms Were More Likely Depressed and Had Lower Health-Related Quality of Life: The Potential Benefit of Health Literacy.* https://pubmed.ncbi.nlm.nih.gov/32244415/

Okoro, J., Ekeroku, A., Nweze, B., Odionye, T., Nkire, J., Onuoha, M., Ezeonwuka, C., & Owoh, J. (2020). *Attitude and preventive practices towards COVID-19 disease and the impact of awareness training on knowledge of the disease among correctional officers.* https://emeraldopenresearch.com/articles/2-51/v1

Ostopolets, I., Kurilchenko, I., & Ulyanova, T. (2020). Psychic deprivation in the minds of quarantine and self-isolation in connection with COVID-19. Contemporary Issues of Digital Economy and Society. Wyższa Szkoła Techniczna w Katowicach.

Ribalka, V. (Ed.). (2020). *Psychological prophylaxis and hygiene of specialties in the anti-pandemic COVID-19.* Institute of Pedagogical Education and Education for Young People Ivan Zyazyun of the National Academy of Sciences of Ukraine.

Slyusarevsky, M., Nayd'onovoi, L., & Voznesenskoy, O. (Eds.). (2020). Materials of the online seminars "Awareness of quarantine: distance psychological assistance and education". Academic Press.

Zarocostas, J. (2020). How to fight an infodemic. *Lancet, 395*(10225), 676. doi:10.1016/S0140-6736(20)30461-X PMID:32113495

KEY TERMS AND DEFINITIONS

Active Social Training: Is a psychological form of development and improvement of various skills and abilities of communication and behavior of the person, carried out in the conditions of group educational and training activity.

Experience of COVID-19 Threat: Is a stressor of high intensity that is capable to cause various forms of mental distress.

Frustration: Is a negative mental state of a person that arises when he encounters insurmountable obstacles / existing or imaginary / in the way of achieving a meaningful goal.

Infodemic: Is a disseminating of an excessive amount of information about a certain problem, which makes its solution even more difficult. The concept of infodemia includes all manifestations of destabilization of the information ecosystem: fake news, misinformation, enemy speech, propaganda, and so on.

Panic: Is a psychological state caused by the threatening influence of a real / imagined threatening situation, false rumors, versions, scary or unpleasant information for an individual or a group; reaction to a threat (real or imagined), associated with the experience of excessive stress, fear, confusion, insecurity, etc.

Psychological Health: Is a dynamic set of mental properties, a state of mental personal well-being (comfort) that provides harmony between different aspects of a person's personality, as well as between a person and society, the possibility of full human functioning in life.

Psychological Technology: Is an algorithm of influence on the human psyche, methods of creating of certain experiences (feelings, emotions, memories) that motivate the individual to the desired action.

Psychological Training: Is a set of group methods of formation of skills and abilities of self-knowledge, communication and interaction of people in the group.

Chapter 7
COVID-19 Infodemic and Social Responsibility of Ukrainian Higher Education Institutions

Kateryna Tryma
https://orcid.org/0000-0001-5567-1387
Institute of Higher Education, NAESU, Ukraine

ABSTRACT

The chapter intends to investigate the influence caused by COVID-infodemic upon the functions carried out by Ukrainian HEIs. As the pandemic and lockdown quickly and unpredictably changed the form of educational activities, HEIs were faced with new challenges and had to demonstrate the updated approaches of their performance not only in educational activities but also as for their social functions. Based on the survey results, the chapter highlights the student's opinion on changes in the performance of the respective universities caused by COVID, infodemic and post-COVID society as well as student understanding of university mission "to contribute to the public good" under the new circumstances. Survey-based research showed that according to the student opinion, modern Ukrainian are to play a more important role in meeting the societal needs of the society, especially under the influence of unpredictable and controversial factors like COVID-infodemic.

INTRODUCTION

At the end of January 2020, based on the Resolution of the Cabinet of Ministers of Ukraine of March 11, 2020, N° 211 "On prevention of the spread of the coronavirus COVID-19 on the territory of Ukraine" (The Resolution of the Cabinet of Ministers of Ukraine N° 211 "On prevention of the spread of the coronavirus COVID-19 on the territory of Ukraine", March 11, 2020), the Ministry of Education and Science of Ukraine issued several recommendations on strengthening sanitary and epidemiological and preventive measures, including in terms of foreign students and international mobility. Those measures included:

DOI: 10.4018/978-1-7998-7164-4.ch007

- to refuse to hold and participate in mass events on the premises and the territory of educational institutions, particularly trial external independent evaluation, Olympiads, competitions, contests, exhibitions, etc.;
- not to send students and employees of institutions to countries with a high risk of infection;
- to inform students and staff on how to prevent the spread of the disease and action in case of illness;
- to develop measures for conducting classes with the help of remote technologies and for practising classes following the curricula after the normalization of the epidemic situation;
- develop measures for partial transfer of employees to remote work;
- provide preventive measures to prevent the widespread of acute respiratory disease caused by a coronavirus and acute respiratory infections;
- to allocate in the dormitories of vocational schools, professional higher, higher, postgraduate education places for isolation of students with signs of acute respiratory diseases;
- implement the decisions of temporary regional anti-epidemic commissions;
- to limit the holding of planned meetings, inspections, examinations to the normalization of the epidemic situation (Letter of the Ministry of Education and Science /1 / 9-154, March 11, 2020.).

The main task of the Ministry of Education and Science of Ukraine in March 2020 was to prevent the spread of coronavirus infection in Ukraine and to contribute to the development of digital learning and the electronic educational environment.

During 2 months, February-March 2020, the HEIs of Ukraine were implementing or/and developing the system of digital learning. By the end of March, 80% of higher education institutions had started the off-line regime of activities. At the same time, some sectoral subsystems (for example, universities that train professional personnel for the spheres of culture or agriculture) were moving to the new format of the educational process more slowly than others, which was partly due to the peculiarities of the organization of the educational process in them as well as connected with the specificity of the profession (medical universities, etc.).

From the very beginning, the Ministry of Education and Science abandoned the detailed regulation of the work of universities during a pandemic, emphasizing the importance of proactive action by the collectives of universities, depending on specific conditions. The Ministry of Education and Science relied on the independence and competence of university management teams, ensuring the development of a regulatory framework and intensive communication both vertically and horizontally: they concerned not only the organization of distance education but also the work of hostels, the employment of students, the organization of volunteer activities of students, psychological support for students and teachers.

Thus, under the conditions of COVID-2019 the activities carried out by the universities in the sphere of education and science had dramatically changed. The standard view of HEIs as institutions for the creation and dispersion of knowledge and preparation for future careers was supplemented by a wide range of social functions. Apart from educational function, the modern HEIs are to perform their indirect functions – they are social actors whose activities, among other things, are aimed at ensuring the development of society. To achieve this aim, higher education institutions contribute to the dissemination of academic knowledge and practical development of universities, forming a 'knowledge society' and satisfying the needs of the society (Tryma, 2019). Being traditionally a very important part of the public sector, under the conditions of infodemia caused by COVID-2019, the HEIS faced with several principally new social and cultural missions. This, COVID-19 forces higher education institutions to adapt quickly to new forms of organizational performance under the pandemic effect.

While the post-COVID social reality now has just started to function, the author of the chapter has assumed that the HEIs has changed not only their organizational performance, they also are determinants who contribute to the change of the social reality and can promote stability and social welfare during the pandemic period and after it.

The economic and social disruption caused by the pandemic is devastating: tens of millions of people are at risk of falling into extreme poverty, while the number of undernourished people, currently estimated at nearly 690 million, could increase by up to 132 million by the end of the year (Impact of COVID-19 on people's livelihoods, their health and our food systems, 2020). As a consequence, universities were forced to consider not only effective distance learning but also to rethink the social role of the universities and their contribution to society.

Therefore, it is logical that under the post-COVID social the HEIs have two main tasks: traditional, which is connected with the educational services and academic research; and second function – contribution into the social stability of the states in which the HEIs perform. The research task is to investigate how the activities of the Ukrainian universities were carried out during 2019-2020 infodemia and how their activity influenced the COVID-infodemic within the Ukrainian students.

BACKGROUND

The problem of 2019-2020 infodemia and its influence upon society and social behaviour has become a pertinent issue for the modern academic discourse. Up to the present moment, there the most difficult and controversial questions are those connected with the new terminology as well as the practical measurement of the new social reality and the social role of the HEIs in it, especially in individual countries, is not a big number of researches in which the influence of epidemic and the consequences of the global epidemic are investigated.

The present research is based on the classic view on the modern universities, which are characterized by a certain degree of academic freedom in the sense that academics can decide about the subject they pursue in their research, and the topics they teach in their institutes as well as the tendency to enjoy at least some autonomy such that they have some discretion over deciding, for example, about appointments, their curriculum, and various other issues' (Huber, 2016). The third common characteristic is the tendency to internalization of the university performance as well as to the competition among HEIs for students, academics, and funding.

The social function and social responsibility of the universities are closely connected with the theory of the welfare state, in which education is generally state-supported by the state and is to be combined with strong market incentives, as in all other parts of the public sector (Kwiek, 2003). But what is the social mission of the HEIs?

In 2010, the international standard ISO 26000 on social responsibility, which was developed with the participation of 500 international experts, defined the main principles of social responsibility, which are characteristic of both profitable enterprises, public organizations and other social players. These include accountability, transparency, ethical behaviour, respect for the interests of stakeholders, recognition of the rule of law, respect for international standards of conduct, respect for human rights. The standard outlines 7 key thematic blocks that form the social responsibility of the organization: 1) human rights;

2) labour relations; 3) the environment; 4) Fair operating practices; 5) consumer rights; 6) community participation and social development (ISO 26000:2010 social responsibility, 2010).

According to Ukrainian researcher Olena Orzhel, many definitions of university social responsibility can be divided into two groups: those that give a narrow interpretation of university social responsibility: the responsibility to a specific community where the university is located (a specific community), and those that interpret university social responsibility as broadly as possible: responsibility for everything that happens at the university (Orzhel, 2017).

In the present research university, social responsibility is to be considered as social functions of the university which are taken within 2019-2020- Infodemic and post-COVID society.

Infodemic, according to Merriam-Webster Dictionary, is a "portmanteau of information" and "epidemic" that typically refers to a rapid and far-reaching spread of both accurate and inaccurate information about something, such as a disease. As facts, rumours, and fears mix and disperse, it becomes difficult to learn essential information about an issue" (Infodemic:, 2019).

First, this term was used in 2003 by journalist and political scientist David Rothkopf in a Washington Post column, when the world's attention was on the current crisis's less terrifying relation: What exactly do I mean by the "infodemic"? A few facts, mixed with fear, speculation and rumour, amplified and relayed swiftly worldwide by modern information technologies, have affected national and international economies, politics and even security in ways that are utterly disproportionate with the root realities. It is a phenomenon we have seen with greater frequency in recent years - not only in our reaction to SARS, for example, but also in our response to terrorism and even to relatively minor occurrences such as shark sightings (Rothkopf, 2003).

Considering modern 2019-2020 Infodemic, the scientist concluded that "the relevant type of Infodemic is "partly characterized by a high information supply of information of variable quality, and a demand for timely and trustworthy information about 2019-epidemic" ((Zhiwen Hu, Zhongliang Yang, Qi Li, An Zhang, Yongfeng Huang, 2020).

Based on the opinions of the interviewees and the author's position, in the research 'infodemic' is regarded as 'a constant chaotic flow of controversial information, facts, remarks, positions and public opinions in a wide range of spheres based on untrusted and unchecked data'. Infodemic can be characterized by the high level of emotional involvement, aimlessness and tendency to be used by various actors who have informational and technological capabilities to effect infodemic.

Post-COVID society is seen as a new type of social activities which are carried out by social actor under the influence of limitations caused by the pandemic, e.g. medical passports, lockdowns, digital communication and social activity, etc.

Based on a critical review of the academic works, official materials of the Ukrainian universities and the results of the survey, this study aims to consider the role of the universities in post-COVID social reality, to answer the following research questions:

- Did the change of organizational performance of the Ukrainian HEIS reflect their social functions? What were the results of digital learning and their influence on the social functions of the HEIs?
- How was the university social responsibility transformed during the 2019-2020-infodemic and post-COVID society?
- What is the potential contribution of the Ukrainian HEIs into the fight against the COVID-19 infodemic through the means of university social responsibility?

Materials and Methods

The analysis of the academic works as well as the documents and reports of the Universities showed that the COVID-2019 highly influenced the organizational performance of Ukrainian higher education institutions and changed their approaches to the learning process and their social functions. One of the aspects of this change was the impact made by higher education upon infodemic. The research of social responsibility of the Ukrainian HEIS and their influence upon the society within infodemic is based on a big variety of research methods and principles. The first principle of the research is the usage of new terminology to describe the peculiarities of the modern educational process as well as university social responsibility. Using social frames to understand the new type of post-COVID reality. The second principle is based on the application of the standard scientific methods like synthesizing and analyse, comparison and categorization, content analysis. These methods were used to analyse the results of the survey conducted by the author of the chapter.

The survey "Social functions and social responsibility of the universities before and after COVID-2019". The attitude of student youth to a new format of education and social functions of the HEIS were discussed with the students in the form of 30 minutes' interview. using online technologies, namely Zoom. The total number of students who were surveyed consists of 20 students: 10 – from Mariupol State University (Mariupol State University, 2019) and 10 from National University of Life and Environmental Sciences of Ukraine (The National University of Life and Environmental Sciences of Ukraine, 2020), speciality "International relations, social communication and regional studios". The survey was conducted in June 2020. The respondents were aged 17-21.

Questionary includes the following questions:

- Gender
- Age
- Speciality
- Course
- University
- How did the educational activities carried out at the university changed after the lockdown?
- Did you like/dislike changes? Why?
- Do you think distance learning is a modern and effective way of getting professional knowledge in general/in your professional sphere?
- In your opinion what social function does the modern university have? In your opinion what social function must the modern university perform?
- Do you take part in the social initiatives of your university?
- Has CORONOVIRUS-infodemic influence the university?
- Has the social role of the university changed after the lockdown?

The choice of the students of this speciality was connected with their social and international activities. These students have the experience of civic work via NGOs and university activities. All respondents had taken part in international programs and projects so they received an understanding of the activities carried out by foreign universities.

The research hypothesis is that infodemic has become the factor that influences not only the educational responsibilities of the HEIs but also contributes to the development of social responsibility of the HEIs.

THE EDUCATIONAL ACTIVITIES OF THE UKRAINIAN HEIS DURING THE LOCKDOWN IN UKRAINE

Before the beginning of the coronavirus pandemic, distance learning was used by teachers on a rather limited scale, while more than half of the teaching staff of universities did not have relevant practice. At the same time, both technological and methodological deficits became key, because teachers did not have the competencies and skills necessary for the high-quality organization of distance learning.

Nevertheless, the faculties of most universities have managed in rather limited terms the start of on-learning. The applied forms of this training largely depended on the available technical capabilities, not only at the university but also at the students' places. The most popular software applications used were: Moodle, ZOOM, MSTeams (free during a pandemic), Webinar, Skype, etc. These applications are not specifically adapted for lecturing, seminars and other types of group work. But the simplicity of their use made it possible to quickly organize the remote interaction of teachers and students. The process of coordinating classes and developing a convenient schedule of classes, taking into account the interests of both teachers and students, as well as control measures when conducting written work and other forms of checks, turned out to be more difficult.

The State Education Quality Service of Ukraine during 23.04.2020 - 05.05.2020 conducted an anonymous survey of research and teaching staff and applicants for higher education institutions of all types and forms of ownership, based on the need to clarify the situation related to using distance learning technologies in the conditions of the national quarantine introduced by the resolution of the Cabinet of Ministers of Ukraine of March 11, 2020, N° 211 "On prevention of the spread of the coronavirus COVID-19" on the territory of Ukraine (The Resolution of the Cabinet of Ministers of Ukraine N° 211 "On prevention of the spread of the coronavirus COVID-19 on the territory of Ukraine", March 11, 2020). The survey showed that the teaching staff of universities as a whole was able to switch to a distance teaching format by quickly developing the materials necessary for teaching and using the available information resources of the Internet, educational platforms and online courses. At the same time, most of the interviewed teachers (68.1%) did not accept distance education, considering this format only as temporary: they were not ready for the constant use of distance technologies in their practice. At the same time, 40% of respondents admitted that the use of distance learning technologies as accompanying full-time education can be quite effective.

A total of 28,391 respondents took part in the survey - 22,367 applicants for higher education and 6,024 research and teaching staff (Information and analytical report on the results of the survey on the state of use of distance learning technologies in higher education institutions of Ukraine, 2020).

Given the results, we can say that the level of skills and ability to use distance learning technologies among research and teaching staff is quite mediocre, as less than half (44.5%) of respondents used such tools on a regular/regular basis.

The results obtained in the study indicate that the majority of respondents, both from among students and from among research and teaching staff, are satisfied with the introduction of distance learning technologies in higher education institutions. In particular, 70% of students and 91% of research and teaching staff, respectively, expressed their full and partial satisfaction with such forms of education.

Only a small proportion of students (19.2%) and research and teaching staff (8%) expressed their views discontent (Information and analytical report on the results of the survey on the state of use of distance learning technologies in higher education institutions of Ukraine, 2020).

This means that such technologies help to increase the level of cognitive activity of students and achieve certain results in theoretical, practical skills and the forms of final control - this is the right step that helps in training future professionals.

At the same time, the situation concerning directing institutions to the development of distance learning technologies is rather disappointing: almost 83% of Ukrainian free educational institutions, according to respondents, do not consider the development of distance technologies in the organization of the educational process as a separate strategy. Educational technologies are a separate development strategy aimed at expanding access to quality education for EU citizens of different ages and social groups, thus creating opportunities for equal access to education for all. As another threat, teachers consider the departure of older teachers from universities, since it will be difficult for them to master the distance teaching format. For the higher education system, this will be, in their opinion, an irreparable loss.

The results of the respondents' assessment of the level of organization by institutions distance learning technologies have shown that to implement curricula and programs, most higher education institutions have left unchanged the quarantine sequence of disciplines, namely the continuation of work on the existing schedule. In this case, two one third of respondents from both students (64.4%) and teachers (71.7%) confirmed that in the conditions of distance work it was possible to ensure compliance with the previously drawn up schedule of classes (Information and analytical report on the results of the survey on the state of use of distance learning technologies in higher education institutions of Ukraine, 2020).

However, the rest of the respondents stated the opposite: almost every fourth respondent denies full compliance with the schedule in the institution, and some respondents (7% of higher education and 3% of research and teaching staff) are categorical in their opinion - the schedule is not followed (Information and analytical report on the results of the survey on the state of use of distance learning technologies in higher education institutions of Ukraine, 2020).

Analysis of the share of respondents' use of technologies distance learning to provide feedback (transmission/receipt of information) showed that the main tools of distance learning are asynchronous learning tools - messengers (noted more than 2/3 of both applicants and teachers), e-mail (every second respondent in both categories) and electronic classrooms on the websites of institutions (every fifth respondent both from among students and from among scientific and pedagogical workers).

Students quite easily started to use distance learning, since modern students are fluent in information and communication technologies. However, this does not mean that students were satisfied with the distance learning format and would like to continue to study online.

Surveys of students' responds conducted by the author showed a little less than half of the respondents (46%) believe that their education has become less effective after the transition to distance learning. According to the survey conducted by the author, the respondents indicated as the main problem was formed during the period of lockdown and online learning – the absence of self-organization. Though, most students (84%) admit that they cannot act responsibly when there is no social or normative framework for them. They do not know how to act in conditions of uncertainty.

A quarter of the respondents indicated that in the distance format it became easier for them to ask questions to the teacher, 64% of respondents had more time to sleep, 49% - more free time, 55% began to get tired of studying less.

60% of respondents (students of both universities) "experienced great stress on their psychological state" while studying in the new conditions. The distance education format in conditions of self-isolation has exacerbated the importance of face-to-face communication between participants in the educational process. Often, the process of socialization, establishing connections that are necessary for the future, personal qualities are realized and formed in the conditions of direct face-to-face communications between students and teachers in educational organizations. Quarantine has significantly reduced the possibility of this interaction.

Despite these difficulties, students, in general, assess the experience of distance learning more positively than teachers. By the end of the academic year (June), the proportion of students who did not consider the distance learning format less effective than the full-time format was 34%.

The analysis of respondents' answers showed that the most frequently surveyed applicants for higher education face the problem of lack of uninterrupted access to the Internet (48%), one in four notes that they do not have the necessary equipment at home, 15% do not have the necessary skills to work with equipment. lack of self-organization is indicated by every third higher education applicant surveyed. These reasons can complicate the timeliness of joining distance learning during the quarantine.

Besides, the respondents who took part in the survey are serious about other factors that complicate distance learning: one in three respondents admits the possibility of biased assessment, which results in irregular communication with the teacher, which confirmed 25% of surveyed students. Teachers assessed the factors that prevent them from providing quality educational services to students in the distance learning mode. The most significant factor, two-thirds of respondents, determine the lack of live contact between teachers and students. And according to the State Education Quality Service of Ukraine, every third teacher is concerned that at the time of large-scale use of distance technologies there were no developed advanced online courses and their development in an emergency in a short time significantly increases the risk of underdeveloped courses (Information and analytical report on the results of the survey on the state of use of distance learning technologies in higher education institutions of Ukraine, 2020).

The universities which the author investigates in the present chapter were able to organize adequate distance learning according to the students' opinion by implementing the following measures:

- building up the necessary technical and information infrastructure;
- improvement of IT-services, a massive installation of applications that allow organizing distance learning;
- issuing to students and teachers for home use of stationary computers, laptops, scanners;
- granting grants to teachers to upgrade their personal computers (laptops, tablets) and update software for use in distance learning;
- development of IT volunteering on the part of students and IT specialists who help teachers with setting up and using software, as well as solving emerging IT problems;
- issuance of methodological recommendations (manuals) and assistance of IT departments to teachers in conducting classes in remote mode (sites, schedule, thematic plan, timing, preparation of training materials), using applications for working in remote mode (ZOOM, MSTeams, etc.).

The pandemic has become a challenge for higher education systems around the world that can simultaneously turn into a new source of development. In just a few weeks, 95% of students around the planet were forced to switch to distance or blended learning.

The "stress test" in the form of an almost instantaneous transition to various forms of distance learning in March 2020, on the one hand, tested these systems for strength, and on the other hand, it allowed testing new technologies, the introduction of which in previous years was complicated by the lack of funding the level of technical equipment, technical skills and the proper level of motivation.

Most Ukrainian universities responded to the pandemic by abandoning full-time education and starting distance learning, closing campuses, taking measures to help students and teachers master new communication formats, including the provision of the necessary hardware and software. The Universities investigated in the present chapter have started their online courses during the pandemic and lockdown without specific problems because before the pandemic the teaching staff started to use online platforms to deliver their courses. So, the biggest challenges for the respondent in addition to improving the mechanisms for providing materials, assistance and monitoring student performance, there was the issue of bringing to students detailed criteria for assessing the current and final assessment of knowledge. The most difficult for the surveyed students was the information about their success in studying the course (discipline) and further actions to improve the quality of knowledge.

ANALYSIS OF STUDENTS' VIEWS ABOUT THE SOCIAL FUNCTIONS OF THE HEIS BEFORE AND AFTER CORONOVIRUS-INFODEMIC (BASED ON THE SURVEY RESULTS)

Focus-groups interviews (online) with the representatives of the speciality "International relations, public communication and regional studies" helped to specify not only the features of the rapid start of distance learning but also showed the specific learning environment in which students have studied since March 2019. Also, the interviewed students shared their vision of the university social role in the circumstances of the pandemic and lockdown.

87% of respondents believe that the university should perform social functions but mainly in the sphere of guarantying professional knowledge and skills which are in demand on the labour market. 13% of young people specified the social role of the HEI wider: expect of the education they included the research projects for local territories as well as the establishment of the first employment of the students.

Among the students who were interviewed 72% were sure that university must perform social duties, but for them was difficult to specify them. 9% of the interviewees noted that the university should help the graduated with employment, establish a special scholarship and pay more attention to better accommodation. 5% of the respondent add to the abovementioned social functions and responsibilities of the modern HEIs the necessity to be engaged in the local community and provide the researches which would be interesting and useful for the specific village, the town of the city. Moreover, 2% of students specified that now the Ukrainian universities consider the studying process to be their main social responsibility without any contribution to the development of the community where the universities are located. 2% of the respondent, who run their local non-governmental organization shared their opinion that the modern Ukrainian universities are too involved in theoretical research and are not ready to work with the practical cases due to the lack of time, wish and professional expertise. The distribution of respondents by their understanding of the social functions of the universities is presented in Figure 1.

Figure 1. Distribution of respondents by their understanding of the social role of the university

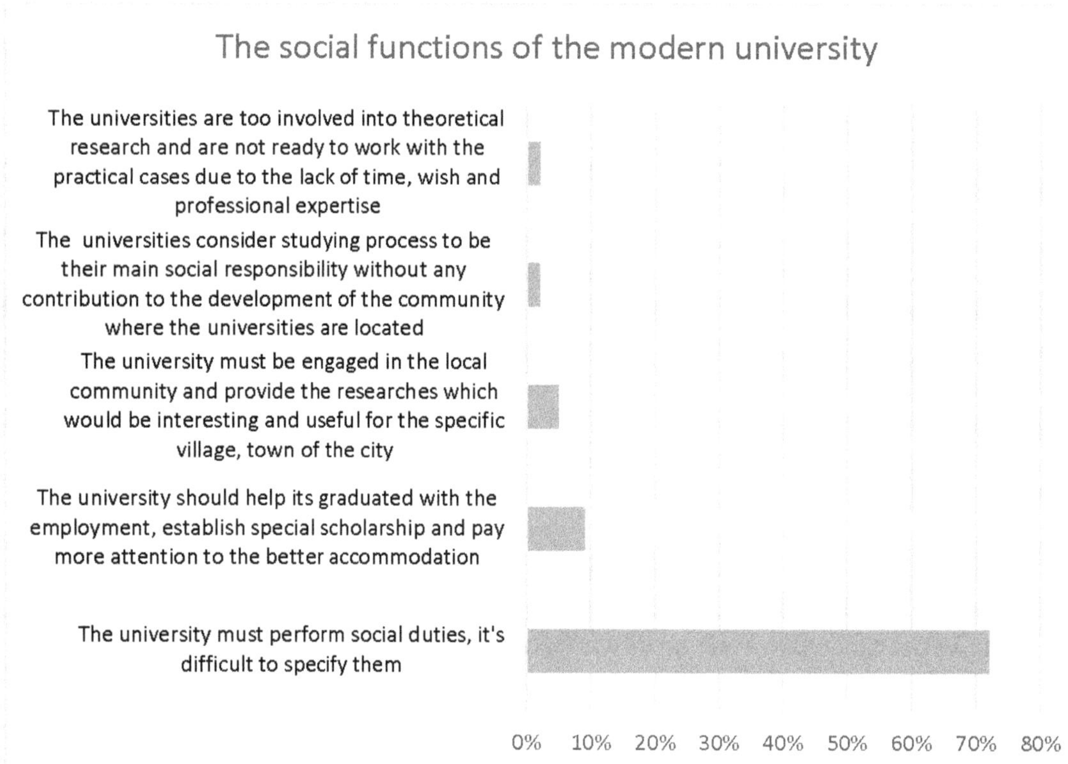

During data collection and analysis, the following inadequacy was faced: the more critical were students from Mariupol state university, as well they presented a wider description of what they think is the social responsibility of the modern HEI. Thus, among 18% of respondents who could describe the social responsibility of the modern university in detail – 15% were from Mariupol.

In our opinion such disproportion could be explained through the following: Mariupol is the city with close and permanent ties among the university, civil society and local authorities; Mariupol state university's staff and students have demonstrated a high level of civic activism after the military attack on the city and contributed to many local civic initiatives, from participation in various activities (exhibitions, public lectures, festivals, etc.) to the establishment of knowledge hubs.

The respondents answered that mainly they don't take part in the social initiatives (as they understand them) of their university (73%). 13% of young people were able to answer this question, and only 14% specified that they take part in such social initiatives as collecting money for charity, participation in charity performances, public concerts and holidays on the territory of their campuses. (Fig.2).

Figure 2. Distribution of respondents by their participation in social initiatives of their university

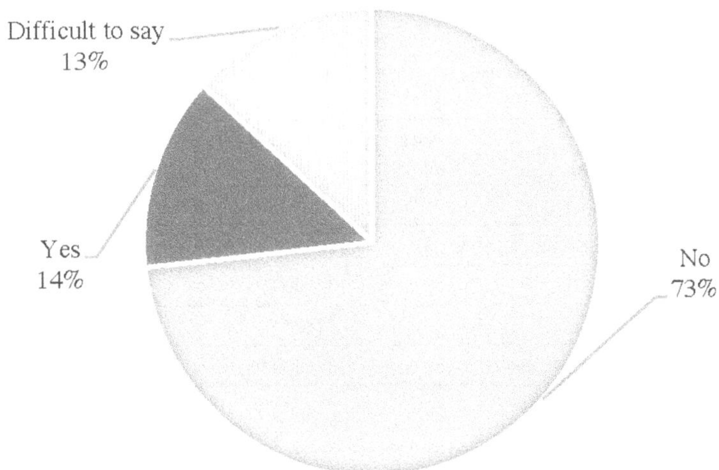

The interviews also showed that the students are not sure about what they consider to be the social responsibility of the university. In most cases, they include to this list all activities connected with the charity, entertainment as well as learning process and study environment. But after the beginning of the pandemic and changes in social life, the students started to reconsider the social role of their universities.

The youth received information, orders and instructions from pedagogical and scientific workers of the proper universities. The teachers were primarily one of the main sources of information for the students if we talk about direct communication and the possibility to ask questions. The knowledge, expertise and common sense of their teachers as well as the position of the management of the faculties and universities was the important factor not only for students but also for their families to understand how to react to the lockdown, what was necessary to do during the pandemic, how to protect themselves and their families. Most respondents (68%) admitted that they had a higher degree of trust in their teachers and a lower degree of trust in the flow of quick and chaotic flow of information in the media and social media and networks like Facebook, Instagram, Telegram which were and are the sources of information for the modern students. The respondents admitted that their relatives, e.g. grandparents and old relatives, used to ask about the pandemic and lockdown, about the information in the media, about the rules they had to follow during the lockdown. 46% of students said that their relatives used to ask about the information and recommendations given in their universities. Thus, the students started to consider the social role and level of trust in the higher educational establishments in the society. The higher number of the students that admitted this correlation was a student from the National University of Life and Environmental Sciences of Ukraine (7 students) and 5 respondents from Mariupol state university. On a personal level, the families of 12 families were surer about the information given at the universities. Therefore, the students were asked again about the social role of modern universities and how the infodemic had changed it. The results of the respondents' ideas and thought about the role of the universities before and after the pandemic are presented in Table. 1. The respondents from both universities proposed variants that were close to one idea which is presented in the table and which is the evidence that such social function is considered equally in different communities. Last variants (*,**) were proposed by the students.

Table 1. Social functions of the modern HEIs after the pandemic and the lockdown

Nº	Social functions of university	National University of Life and Environmental Sciences of Ukraine	Mariupol State University
		Number of interviewed students, %	
1	Create new knowledge and train thinking	10 (100%)	10 (100%)
2	Train skilled personnel	10 (100%)	10 (100%)
3	Manage innovative research	8 (80%)	7 (70%)
4	Provide a community for talent in art and sport	10 (100%)	10 (100%)
5	Perform the role of "agents of social mobility" (equal opportunities for all students to study)	6 (60%)	5 (50%)
6	Contribute to social and cultural development of the local city (public lectures, festivals, etc.)	7 (70%)	6 (60%)
7	Develop the proper infrastructure	10 (100%)	10 (100%)
8	Provide more relevant information from experts on urgent social questions*	9 (90%)	8 (80%)
9	Play the role of social arbitrators on difficult social questions (sexual orientation, gender type, etc.)**	3 (90%)	4 (80%)

Such functions are dominant as to establish new knowledge and to share them with the students; to carry on research and innovation activities and to engage students into the sphere; to develop and train all types of skills which will be interesting for a potential employer; to contribute to the development of personal hobbies in art, sport and culture. In the course of our interviews, the students confirmed the hypothesis of Erik Porfeli and Bora Lee according to which there are many indicators important for the professional socialization of young people and which include, the territorial location of educational institutions, accommodation of the students, the availability of the sports grounds, swimming pool, library and cafes on the territory of the campus. Ukrainian students also consider these conveniences to be part of the social responsibility of the modern university (Lee, 2015). But all new circumstances such as the pandemic and the lockdown undoubtedly affect the activities of the universities - which was described in the first part of the chapter.

Answering the question if COVID-infodemic has influenced the university's performance, most students asked what the term 'infodemic' meant. After some explanations, most of the respondents agreed that after COVID-infodemic not only the system of educational activities carried out by the universities has changed but also the social function of the HEIs. 43%respondents noted that the social responsibility of the university has dramatically changed, 40% agreed that the HEI started to perform new functions. 17% of respondents said that they could not agree with the new functions of the HEIs because everything stayed the same.

After discussing the issue of infodemic the students started to think about the social functions of the modern universities to overcome low knowledge and prejudice, incompetence and to train critical thinking and media literacy not only within the students but also within the local communities (Higher

Education in the World. Towards a Socially Responsible University: Balancing the Global with the Local., 2017). The ideas of the students were close to the concept of "civic university": the universities have to be integrated into the local context, understand the local interests and needs and cooperate with the local authorities (Goddard, 2012).

The understanding of the social role of the universities as a producer of new knowledge and trainer of critical thinking is the most significant social functions the university has to perform according to 70% of the respondents. Considering the new functions of the university caused by CORONOVIRUS-infodemic the thoughts of the students on the wider list of the elements of social responsibility of the university, the respondents pointed a list of social function which to be carried out by the university under the new social conditions:

- the university investigates the world beyond the campus walls and shares the results of research not only with the academic community;
- the modern university provides service that directly benefits the public, in our case, for example, prevention of a disease etc.;
- the university creates local enterprises in which students can practice their skills as well as get their first job;
- the HEIs can form their unique forms of identity, their brands like respected institutions;
- the universities can provide social innovations through their research programs (for example, to create software for local needs, to work out new ways to utilize the garbage, to create new sources of energy beneficial to use in separate communities etc.);
- the universities must be transparent and accountable to various stakeholders like local NGOs (the students who are members of the NGOs admitted the difficulties to organize cooperation with the HEIs);
- the HEIs have to give their expert view in local media and local communities through public lectures, museum exhibitions, cooperation with knowledge hubs and other activities of the sort.

The students described in detail their understanding of the university as an integral part of the society which is close to the triple-helix model of universities, business and government with semi-autonomous centres (Etzkowitz, 2000). It means that Ukrainian students are closer to the European understanding of the social role of the HEIs within society and the model of "truly civic" universities (Goddard, The civic university and the leadership of place., 2012).

The empirical data of the research conducted by a sociological survey among the students have confirmed that not all respondents understand what is the social responsibility of modern universities. The students were more confident when they were discussing the issue of distance learning rather than the social functions of the HEIs.

While discussing with the respondents that inequality we specified that the students are strongly convinced that the primary aim of the university is teaching and instructing rather than performing any social functions. The issue is considered to be rooted in understanding the role of the university within the Ukrainian society: students don't consider their university as serious knowledge hubs (10% of respondents) or they think that universities operate with researches only within the academic community and other universities and they cannot see how the university can cooperate with the local community and business (50%). Moreover, 5% of respondents think that the university produces low-quality knowledge therefore it is impossible to share it with the public. 60% of respondents don't see how the Ukrainian

HEIS can work in the business sphere as Ukrainian legislation limits the universities in this type of activity, but they were not able to specify the legislative acts which do not allow universities to cooperate within the local projects with the enterprises.

The obtained results of students' opinions on social functions of the HEIs make it possible to draw the following conclusions: students don't consider the universities as serious producers of social functions and they do not think the universities, in general, must do it. But after the deeper familiarization with the materials dedicated to the infodemic, the respondents agreed that the universities in Ukraine would be very useful in overcoming the process of misunderstanding and ignorance of information connected with the infodemic and lockdown.

CONCLUSION

Understanding that the pandemic has a continuous effect in modern society, it is necessary to understand the role of usual social intuitions which can contribute to the decision of the problem caused by the pandemic as the consequences of the pandemic will be 'imprinted on the personality of our nation very long,' predicted Anthony Fauci, the Director of the National Institute of Allergy and Infectious Diseases ((Anthony Fauci's security is stepped up as doctor and face of U.S. coronavirus response receives threats, 2020).

The results of the study confirmed the research hypothesis: the infodemic has become the factor that influences the educational responsibilities of the HEIs but partly contributes to the development of social responsibility of the HEIs.

The students noted that after the begging of the pandemic their educational activities have dramatically changed. But moreover, these changes led to the understanding that in the modern world the universities play not only the role of establishers of new knowledge but also as the social actors. Of course, the respondents expressed their idea that Ukrainian HEIs prefer to be distant from community life and societal challenges, focusing on teaching, learning and research. But after the global changes in these activities caused by the pandemic and lockdown students consider that the HEIs can build a wider society together with the local communities. Community life, societal challenges provide impulses for new ideas, stimulating HEIs to generate more knowledge for solving real-life problems such as solving problems in social, political, cultural, technological and other spheres. Thus, the educational activities will be not only of theoretical character but also of practical usage. One of the problems despite all taken measure according to the opinion of the educators and students remains relevant. It' is the need to be patronized. Therefore, students consider themselves to require external guidance and assistance caused by the non-efficient planning of their work and their inability to plan work. Especially this problem was actualized during distance learning assistance when the students did not have an opportunity to be managed by their teacher.

As for the infodemic, the Ukrainian HEIs played an important role for the students and their families because the information received by the university teachers and managers was important for them to operate in their everyday activities as well as to understand how to manage the contradictory and heterogeneous information in the different media. The modern Ukrainian universities have successfully adapted to the pandemic and the lockdown regime: they used to perform their educational activities offline. The students specified that the gravity of social functions is recognized by Ukrainian HEIs, their contribution to social change enhanced, cooperation between academia and community, resulting in a stronger society, nation and state.

REFERENCES

Anthony Fauci's security is stepped up as doctor and face of U.S. coronavirus response receives threats. (2020). *The Washington Post*. Retrieved from https://www.washingtonpost.com/politics/anthony-faucis-security-is-stepped-up-as-doctor-and-face-of-us-coronavirus-response-receives-threats/2020/04/01/ff861a16-744d-11ea-85cb-8670579b863d_story.html

Etzkowitz, H., & Leydesdorff, L. (2000). The dynamics of innovation: From National Systems and "Mode 2" to a Triple Helix of university–industry–government relations. *Research Policy*, *29*(2), 109–123. doi:10.1016/S0048-7333(99)00055-4

Goddard, J., & Vallance, P. (2012). The civic university and the leadership of place. B A. O. In R. Capello (Ed.), *Universities, Cities and Regions: Loci for Knowledge and Innovation Creation (cmp* (pp. 43–63). Routledge.

Higher Education in the World. Towards a Socially Responsible University: Balancing the Global with the Local. (2017). https://unesdoc.unesco.org/ark:/48223/pf0000248150

Hu, Z., Yang, Z., & Li, Q. (2020). *Infodemiological study on COVID-19 epidemic and COVID-19 infodemic*. Research Square.

Huber, B. (2016). The Role of Universities in Society. B C. Y. In N. C. Liu (Ed.), *Matching Visibility and Performance. Global Perspectives on Higher Education* (pp. 92–138). Sense Publishers. doi:10.1007/978-94-6300-773-3_5

Impact of COVID-19 on people's livelihoods, their health and our food systems. (2020.). Joint statement by ILO, FAO, IFAD, and WHO.

Infodemic. (2019). In *Meriam Webster dictionary*. Academic Press.

Information and analytical report on the results of the survey on the state of use of distance learning technologies in higher education institutions of Ukraine. (2020). State Service for the Quality of Education of Ukraine.

ISO 26000:2010 social responsibility. (2010). https://www.iso.org/standard/42546.html

Kwiek, M. (2003). The Social functions of the university in the context of the changing State. *Market Relations*, 2-31.

Lee, D., & Profeli, E. (2015). Youths' socialization to work and school within the family. *International Journal for Educational and Vocational Guidance*, *15*(2), 145–162. doi:10.100710775-015-9302-x PMID:26101556

Letter of the Ministry of Education and Science /1/9-154. (2020).

Mariupol State University. (2019). http://en.mdu.in.ua/

Orzhel, O. (2017). Social responsibility of universities as a factor in shaping the culture of quality of higher education. In Worldview priorities of humanization of higher education: monograph (pp. 140-155). Kyiv: Institute of higher education.

Rothkopf, D. (2003). Article. *The Washington Post.*

The National University of Life and Environmental Sciences of Ukraine. (2020). https://nubip.edu.ua/en

The Resolution of the Cabinet of Ministers of Ukraine N° 211 "On prevention of the spread of the coronavirus COVID-19 on the territory of Ukraine". (2020).

Tryma, K. (2019). Cooperation between Higher Education Institutions and Non-governmental Organizations in Higher Education: International Discourse. *International Scientific Journal of Universities and Leadership*, *2*(8), 102–107. doi:10.31874/2520-6702-2019-8-2-102-107

KEY TERMS AND DEFINITIONS

COVID-19: A contagious disease caused by coronavirus 2 (SARS-CoV-2) which started the 2019-2020 pandemic, lockdown and self-isolation in the world.

Distance Learning, Online Learning: A type of educational activities which take place without a physical presence in the auditoria ethrough the digital technologies and special software in real-time.

Higher Educational Institution: An educational organization that provides students with academic degrees in various academic disciplines.

Infodemic: A constant chaotic flow of controversial information, facts, remarks, positions and public opinions in a wide range of spheres based on untrusted and unchecked data.

Pandemic: A global epidemic that spread across the whole planet, covering the majority of the world population.

Post-COVID Society: A new type of social activities which are carried out by social actor under the influence of limitations caused by the pandemic, e.g. medical passports, lockdowns, digital communication and social activity, etc.

Social Responsibility of the University Within Post-COVID Society: Social functions of the university which are taken after 2019-2020- Infodemic and post-COVID society.

Chapter 8
Knowledge Management in Times of Pandemic:
Insights From Humor on Social Media

Lubna Akhlaq Khan
National University of Modern Languages, Islamabad, Pakistan

ABSTRACT

This research began with an assumption that what matters to people gets a verbal stamp. Here, the focus is on the social media jokes about online classes, analysed through linguo-cultural approach by Petrova. The analysis revealed that the teachers are facing problems and students are taking advantage of their teachers' technical illiteracy. The highest dense category consists of jokes about students' non-seriousness toward their online lectures. There are serious discipline issues and distractions. Students have devised new excuses to avoid online classes and assigned home-based activities. Some posts even depicted poor prospects for these ill-trained students. Online classes have been depicted as a useless activity. This hierarchical arrangement of the semantic densities revealed the concerns of the current social-media users in Pakistan. Policymakers and content creators should come up with sagacious measures to make the best of these virtual classrooms and address the genuine concerns of all the stakeholders.

INTRODUCTION

The episode of COVID-19 worldwide has been obliterating a large number of people's lives while undermining the world's conventional arrangement of living. The brief lockdown has been picked as the best choice to stifle the world's currently dread Covid virus' clutch. The nationwide lockdown approaches lead to schools/colleges/universities' closures, which disturbed the class-based instructional framework and lingered the enrollment of the students of all levels. During the COVID-19 pandemic, teachers and students were not as intense in online classes as they used to be in face-to-face meetings, previously. The training process, which is usually administered in classrooms interactively between teachers and students, is experiencing obstacles within the middle of this pandemic. Before the pandemic, usual greeting activities and sitting together to share experiences were part of the lifestyle of teachers and

DOI: 10.4018/978-1-7998-7164-4.ch008

students. The teacher used to embrace and reinforce with physical intimacy (pat, hugs, claps). Students used to play happily and share their food with their friends. Such an atmosphere is no longer available during this pandemic. Students begin to feel lonely playing alone at home, not getting direct guidance from the teacher to study at home (Supena et al., 2020). Other psychological effects experienced by teachers and students are diverse and complex. Some teachers feel less productive in developing their teacher professionalism by working from home, and vice versa, students are not motivated to study at home. There are sometimes creating misunderstandings related to teacher instructions to students, either through online, semi-online, or offline assignment communication. This affects the level of understanding of students and even parents who accompany them at home. So it becomes a challenge for teachers to transfer meaningful information that is productive for students. In this capricious emergency, new media and new methodologies of schooling are needed to enable the system to go undisrupted. Thus, numerous schools/colleges of the world are offering their services online (Ramij and Sultana, 2020).

The Covid has unfurled numerous difficulties to the world's exceptionally old frameworks, including individuals' ways of life, wellbeing, instructive framework, exchange and organizations, and mechanical framework. The effect of COVID-19 on worldwide schooling can be portrayed as ruinous since numerous students are being denied education for more than six or seven months. UNESCO report showed this interruption in the schooling affected students' lives and, therefore, the general public and the educational network. Along these lines, almost all the nations are managing the topic of how students can learn amid this delayed lockdown situation (Ramij and Sultana, 2020). After the huge number of schools were shut in March 2020, teachers faced critical difficulties in adjusting to the internet-based education, coping up with the least communication with their students, and supporting them learn and progress. In any case, the degree to which instructors have effectively tackled these difficulties and which elements are most pertinent stay obscure (König, Jäger-Biela, and Glutsch, 2020).

In September 2020, the lockdown was practically finished and had influenced almost 90% of the overall students, very nearly 200 nations, and over 1.5 billion students. The mass school closure was essentially a handy solution received in not exactly ideal conditions. The squeezing scramble with which numerous instructive establishments moved to online training may have kept them from tackling its qualities and confronting its restrictions (Giovannella, Passarelli, and Persico, 2020). This research will try to answer the following questions: 1) How is online teaching being perceived by teachers and students as depicted in Corona related social media memes? 2) What are the most frequent concerns related to online teaching during Corona related memes?

SIGNIFICANCE OF THE STUDY

This study will assist in understanding the students' and teachers' perceptions of online teaching during the COVID-19 Pandemic. Based on humorous memes about online teaching, teachers, and students' responses, it tends to open a window in educational setups trying to improve the students' information and abilities through online mode. Other researchers have done their work on serious discourses during this pandemic, which has created a gap to find out different problems during online classes through humorous posts on social media. The systematic analysis of social media jokes would help us see how people sort out their environmental factors and use methods for dealing with stress, for example, by narrating/sharing jokes during times of emergency. Humor improves mindfulness, strengthens agreeability, decreases counterarguments, and does not block the understanding of the message (Xiao, Cauberghe, and

Hudders, 2018). An attempt has been made to feature how humor has been utilized to spread mindfulness and feature public perspectives about COVID-19 regarding online teaching.

LITERATURE REVIEW

All dimensions of societies, and more specifically, education have been negatively influenced by the pandemic. Against the backdrop, various strategies are being presented by governments and tertiary foundations over the world to keep instructing exercises to hold the infection. As no exceptions, universities are also affected negatively due to closure for uncertain time durations. Within no time, the traditional face to face and classroom-based teaching methodology has been replaced by a computer and internet-dependent online education to ensure educational continuity. However, there are obscurity and differences about how to teach, what to teach, the overwork for teachers and students, the teaching environment, and the implications for education equity (Zhang et al.2020). Huge-scale national efforts to utilize technology in support of online teaching, distance education, and remote learning during the COVID-19 pandemic are evolving and advancing rapidly. Literature highlights certain shortcomings of internet-based education, including deficiencies such as weakness of online teaching infrastructure, inexperienced teachers, information gap, and disturbing environment at home. However, despite all difficulties, it was decided that the education of students should not be affected at any cost. For instance, China started a Suspending Classes Without Stopping Learning strategy to see that learning was not traded off during COVID-19 pandemic lockdown (Zhang et al., 2020). To handle the issues, Huang et al. (2020) suggested that governments and education providers need to consider equipping teachers and students with standardized home-based teaching, conduct online teacher training, and support academic research into online education and help students with web-based learning difficulties.

Rouadi and Anouti (2020) saw whether web-based learning was a disappointment or an accomplishment in Lebanon during the Coronavirus crisis (COVID-19) in the tertiary and secondary schools. The investigation targeted at deciding the main reasons that prompted considering the experiment of online learning as fruitful by a few and those that prompted thinking of it as a disappointment by others. They gathered information through the arbitrary sampling strategy. The variety of the clarification strategies, for example, utilization of instructive recordings, the great correspondence between the educator and his students, instructor's capacity to train on the web, and learners' obligation to partake were the principal reasons that drove some to consider the web-based learning a triumph, while the slow internet speed, the power blackouts, not having more than one cell phone or PC at home, and students' absence of support were the fundamental reasons that drove others to think about it as a disappointment. The investigators have recommended the educators accept training on the web and begin adjusting to instructing differently a good ways off when they end up with a need to do so. By following the preventive measures, they were likewise prescribed to isolate their students into gatherings and evaluate them inside the school. Students were prescribed to completely take an interest to make web-based learning productive in Lebanon. Guardians were prescribed and endorsed to guarantee and accept a fundamental part in guaranteeing that their children continue to learn through their cell phones, online media, workstations, or some other particular instrument. The results of the study revealed that the online learning experiment was considered a failure by most of the school principals, teachers, and students. At the time these results cannot be generalized, some people considered online learning successful while others opposed that.

A recent study held in Portugal by Flores, Machado, & Alves (2020) revealed that, on average, teachers were unable to interact with two pupils per class, because of insufficient resources. Teachers also recognized other challenges such as lack of adequate equipment for pupils, insufficient time, absence of satisfactory preparation of internet-based teaching, and absence of help from parents. Moreover, teachers have to rely on their gadgets to instruct. The time spent during online classes is significantly increased as compared to the traditional classrooms while the students' rate of participation in oral assessment is alarmingly decreased. The presence of online platforms for learning is not a new thing in multiple contexts. Some people see it as an opportunity to quickly shift from traditional teaching to online remote teaching. On the other hand, others are worried and doubtful about its implications in terms of social justice and equity. Issues of disparity and prohibition turned out to be considerably more noticeable and basic amid and even after the COVID period (Bozkurt and Sharma, 2020).

Chung, Subramaniam, & Dass (2020) considered internet learning readiness among University Students in Malaysia amid COVID-19 and decide to analyze web-based learning status among college students who have been tossed in at the deep end. It means to explore if demographic factors have any effect on their availability to learn, internet learning experiences, and intention to keep utilizing web-based learning. It additionally analyzed their favored techniques for internet learning and the difficulties they faced. They revealed that the greater part of the respondents demonstrated that whenever given a decision, they would prefer not to proceed with web-based learning later on. Most respondents favored web-based learning through pre-recorded talks transferred to Google Classroom and YouTube. While the greatest test for undergraduates is the quality of the network, for diploma scholars, it is the trouble in understanding the substance of the subject. It is additionally suggested that the public authority, telecom organizations, and colleges ought to put resources into creating a web framework the nation over as web-based learning will be the new standard within an unforeseeable time-frame. The college additionally needs to give further training to upgrade scholastics' internet-based instructing abilities to guarantee lessons are conveyed all the more successfully.

Iivari, Sharma, & Ventä-Olkkonen (2020) have analyzed the digital transformation of everyday life and found out how the pandemic changed the fundamental education of the young generation and pointed out that the students of today have been encircled by advanced innovation since their preliminary introduction to the world. COVID-19 pandemic has unexpectedly and suddenly constrained schools and training centers to participate in such a change. In this investigation, they looked at the computerized change started by the COVID-19 pandemic in the essential schooling of young students. Huang et al. (2020) suggested that governments and educational institutions can come forth to ensure essential online educational information, replenish standardized instructions to teachers and learners regarding distance learning and yield online training and research for the teachers.

Lathifah, Helmanto, & Maryani (2020) examined that the Corona infection related lockdown relocated the learning measure in Indonesia in distance learning. Isolated by time and distance do not intend to overlook classroom management. This investigation expects to discover what degree the act of online classroom management succeeds in the pandemic. It is discovered that the online learning experience costs more time. There are a few things to be considered for better instructing in the online learning system. Improve the accessible recordings instead of making another one. Put the recordings on open access. Guarantee the recorded video outline the instructor's face, with the goal that the students see better as the ordinary classroom goes. Recorded recordings can assist the learning if the web connectivity has got some problem. A brief video is sufficient to cover the material. Consider having meaningful content on little screens. Teach with the goal that the students watch as well as attempt to adhere to the guidance given. Showing true and valued aspects of an instructor helps the enthusiastic learning of the students and will urge them to help the learning cycle together. Educators should locate a reasonable method to advance the learning cycle scholastically and socio-emotionally. The educator should be able to manage an online classroom just like a traditional one.

Online and remote learning has become a necessity to carry on distance learning and ICT based education (Ali, 2020). The transformation of online teaching concerning the traditional educational system has been a technically feasible, safe, asynchronous, and convenient approach to solve the educational system's crisis during this lockdown. The study suggested that the construction of study materials online is similar to those of traditional classrooms and the materials may contain textbooks, supplementary readings like articles, news parts, PDFs, short-span slides, videos, exercises, and case analysis. Structuring materials have also been discussed in the study in light of the SCATE model, i.e. Scope, Content, Activities, Thinking, and Extra by emphasizing the creation of subdivisions of chapters or units based on the learning period i.e. weekly, fortnightly, and/or monthly (Edwards, 2012).

Supena, Umboh, Tarusu, & Kalengkongan (2020) looked at learning methodologies in grade elementary schools during COVID-19 pandemic in North Sulawesi, investigated the experience of primary teachers, and examined the degree of cooperation and supporting components and limitations experienced by instructors in executing learning techniques for primary school students. The findings of the investigation revealed that the learning technique of visiting students straightforwardly at home is done by educators in peripheral regions due to the more limited distance and relatively short travel time to visit students' homes. While the procedure completed by educators in metropolitan regions was more prevalent by using virtual offices through connections utilizing cell phones and learning with web-based applications, the nature of the instructor and student relations in learning interactions does not continue of course. Different learning strategies are employed by the instructors to stay beneficial and proficient in completing their obligations as an instructor and teacher. The learning procedure attempted by the educator is affected by the family spirit that is the sign of the Indonesian country's way of life.

Due to the breakthrough of the education system caused by COVID-19, many countries are struggling hard to continue teaching and learning through alternative online channels. This mode seems to have pros and cons affecting the range of its efficacy. The major factors include availability and adaptability of technology, availability of internet connection and cost of internet, students' perception and acceptability of online learning, teachers' perception and methods for online teaching, etc. Availability of devices for online learning such as computers or mobile phones and internet connection are the basic requirements that are causing hurdles in the effective delivery of online education (Emmungil & Akleylek, 2008; Pathak, 2020).

Bao (2020) explained that the sudden transformation of the traditional teaching system to an online-based system has caused several challenges to the faculty members having a lack of online teaching experience, lack of early preparation, and technology support. Students lack an attitude towards online education, due to a lack of study materials or an appropriate study environment. The adaptability of the students with this new phase of learning is another factor that is required to be examined for the planning and implementation of online classes in developing countries. Adaptability to online courses is also affected by the attributes of the students as age, gender, the origin of the students, prior academic performance, and the subject areas or courses (Xu & Jaggars, 2013).

Cheating through various methods is most likely the greatest weakness in the internet-based assessment. The instructor cannot similarly assign their students they used to do in class. Recognizing cheating is troublesome even with a camcorder that the educator needs to check each student at a time during the test. Shockingly, this reality may provoke powerless examination and a misleading test outcome (Tamm, Fakhri, Martisiute, and Lee, 2019). Alongside the previously mentioned burdens, not being reasonable for all materials stay the greatest obstruction remaining notwithstanding the web-based learning approach. Many believe this sort of learning to be more reasonable for humanities and sociologies instead of logical materials, for example, clinical sciences and technical subjects just because they require a bigger number of practices than hypotheses. Keeping in mind that things may change later on, we are still at a point where web-based learning cannot step up to the advantages of an examination for clinical students or genuine industrial training for students of engineering (Tamm, Fakhri, Martisiute, and Lee, 2019).

Online education seems to have several positive and negative impacts. Kumar (2010) pointed out the pros of online education, describing it as convenient, less expensive, technology-driven, and beneficial. Many other studies also noted the positive aspects of online learning, i.e. convenience, ease of participation, availability of blended courses (Fedynich, 2013). Kumar (2010) identified some cons of distance learning: less social interaction, unequal technology cost, questionable for the effectiveness of assessments, and troublesome for the instructors. Lack of internet access and problems with mobile networks, lack of computer literacy, and internet access (Fedynich, 2013) are also negatively affecting issues regarding the feasibility of online education. Giovannella, Passarelli, & Persico (2020) studied the effect of the pandemic on the Italian learning ecosystem and highlighted how operational conditions and settings can modify the teachers' and learners' expectations and mental setting about online learning and technologies. Furthermore, Agung researched the impact of social psychology due to this pandemic (2020). Likewise, the influence of the COVID-19 pandemic on the implementation of online learning in elementary schools and universities has been investigated by Dewi (2020). The attention given by the teacher is very instrumental in the emotional development of students. These are shown by students expressing feelings of pleasure, both in words and the attitude shown by students (Obergriesser & Stoeger, 2020; Riley, 2011).

The present study aims to find out the reaction of students, teachers, and parents of a developing country like Pakistan for online education amid the COVID-19 situation. This study uncovers the facts regarding online teaching and learning in Pakistan that aggregate some recognizable issues and challenges to embrace web-based learning systems in the country through humorous posts.

THEORETICAL FRAMEWORK AND METHODOLOGY

The Linguo-Cultural Approach by Petrova (2019) is used to analyze the cultural texts of social media jokes about online teaching in Pakistan. This approach prescribes to translate the cultural text in one main substance that it comments, presents, or evaluates as positive or negative. This main substance is named as 'cultureme' and the approach relies on the 'semantic density' (frequency of occurrence) of different positive or negative 'culturemes.' The hierarchical arrangement yielded a tabular representation of the matters of concern regarding online classes. The jokes are collected from the timelines of the authors' social media friends, WhatsApp statuses, and teaching-related forums. A total number of 76 jokes are collected from 15th May 2020 to 15th September 2020. Furthermore, these jokes are thematically grouped and the (Urdu) texts are translated into English, and the representative screenshots/original posts are attached in the Data analysis section. Since humor reflects social perceptions, it is assumed that popular comic texts might provide us with more direct and concise access to valuable data about prevailing attitudes toward the new phenomenon and people's reactions to it.

Table 1. Semantic density of culturemes

	Culturemes	Semantic Density	%
1	Students' Non-serious Response	18	20%
2	Jokes about Difficulties	15	16.66%
3	Insolence during Online Classes	11	12.22%
4	Students' Inappropriate Behavior	7	7.77%
5	Lazy and Unfresh Students	5	5.55%
6	Bunking in 2020	5	5.55%
7	Do not Want Physical Exams	5	5.55%
8	Closure of Educational Institutions is Celebrated	4	4.44%
9	Corona and Research Students	3	3.33%
10	Standards of Performance	3	3.33%
11	Self-defeating jokes	3	3.33%
12	The Reality of Online Classes	3	3.33%
13	After Effects of Online Teaching	3	3.33%
14	Teachers Enjoying during Pandemic	3	3.33%
15	An Excuse to Use Mobile Phones	2	2.22%
	Total	90	100%

Explanation of Semantic Densities

The hierarchical arrangement of 'semantic density' of different culturemes has created a tabular depiction of the concerns regarding humorous posts about online classes. The most frequent cultureme is about the non-serious attitude of students about online classes (18, 20%) and teachers' difficulties (15, 16.66%) and the elements of insolence on the part of students for teachers due to distant mode of work (11, 12.22%). Students' inappropriate response is also covered by a significant number of jokes (7, 7.77%). Students showing up in casual get up, making fun during online classes, and employing technical means to bunk has been mocked in a similar number of posts (5, 5.55%). Students are not ready for on-campus exams due to online learning is another set of memes (5, 5.55%). People are taking the closure of educational institutions as a piece of good news is also conveyed by a significant number of posts (4, 4.44%) Corona/lockdown is being used as a reason to procrastinate by research students working on their MPhil/PhD dissertations (3, 3.33%). Furthermore, the poor future performance of students taught online is also being questioned (3, 3.33%). Teachers are also presented as distressed beings whose pensive work is not acknowledged by the parents or society at large. These jokes have also directed the arrow toward the poor management of online classes in Pakistan as compared to foreign contexts (3, 3.33%). Online classes have been termed as useless and students are expected to come to school with a blank state of mind (3, 3.33%). Teachers are accused of enjoyment during online teaching is conveyed by (3, 3.33%) jokes. Students use mobile phone timelessly during this period without any hesitation (2, 2.22%).

QUALITATIVE DATA ANALYSIS

Students' Non-Serious Response (18-)

Figure 1.

Figure 2.

These posts show how students are behaving during online classes. These memes (Figure 1 and Figure 2) have reiterated that students lack enough motivation to be attentive during online classes. They are facing difficulty in maintaining their concentration and the unattractive online environment is making them sleepy. Most of the memes are depicting different cartoonish characters and animals to delineate the disinterest of the students in the online classes.

Teachers' Difficulty (15-)

Figure 3.

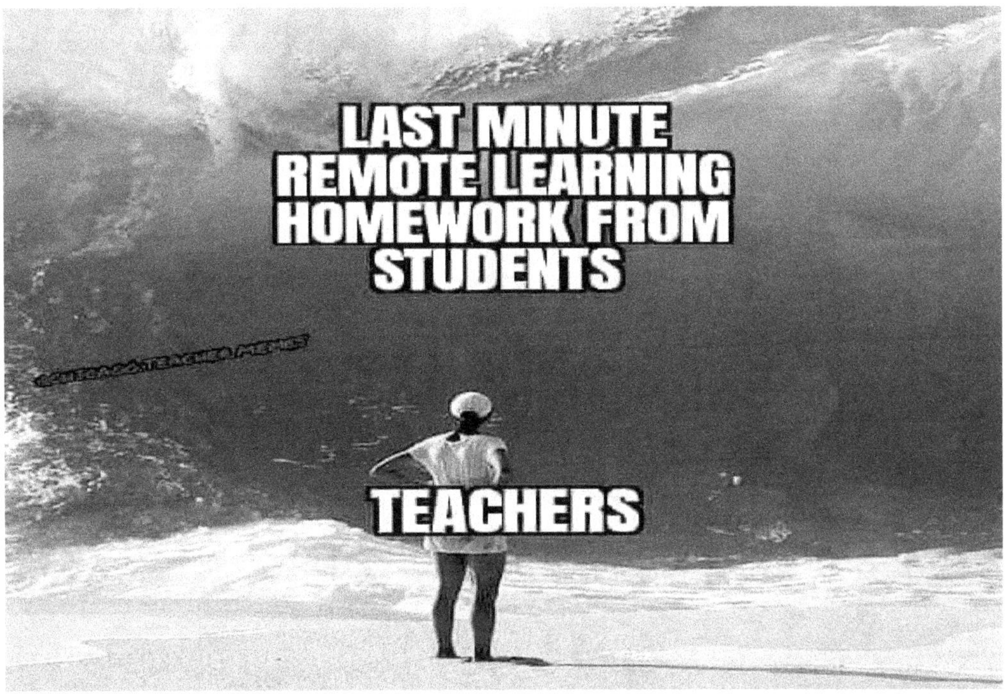

This cultureme is about the difficulty the teachers are having during online teaching. The post depicts a teacher who is looking at a high wave which is captioned as 'last-minute remote learning homework sent by students.' They are supposed to submit their homework in the soft form and it is becoming an uphill task for the teachers to manage and respond properly in a short period.

Insolence during Online Classes (11-)

Students in these memes are depicted as misbehaving with their teachers in different ways. They are not following the instructions issued during online lectures rather they are challenging the teachers. In Figures 4 and 5 students are making illogical excuses and trying to cheat. The teachers are facing severe issues in maintaining the discipline as they do not have any power to punish the trouble creators. Indiscipline created during online classes is creating hurdles to smoothly deliver the lectures and make students learn effectively. Students are relying on technical excuses to evade the burden of responsibility in an online class.

Figure 4.

ONLINE CLASS
PLEASE TURN OFF YOUR PHONE
You have no power here!

Figure 5.

Students' Inappropriate Behavior (7-)

These jokes present the element of faulty learning and informal/inappropriate behavior of students. They are confused and relaxed at the same time. It creates an impact that students are not ready to take these online classes, but they are compelled by their parents and school administration. It is also delineated that students taught through this virtual classroom lack clear understanding and are unable to practically apply the concepts taught. Being at home, students have become too relaxed and they are not absorbing the concepts taught online and when they are required to perform some task based on their online learning they are unable to perform satisfactorily.

Lazy and Unfresh Students (5-)

Students are attending classes from home and they are not fresh as they used to be in their traditional classrooms. The pictorial representation in these memes is also reinforcing the lack of interest and motivation on the part of students. To enhance the comic effect the picture of a negro girl being shot just after she woke up has been compared to her well done get up. A sleepy dog's picture is also reinforcing the same idea.

Figure 6.

Bunking in 2020 (5-)

These posts show a kind of difference in class bunking between 2020 and the previous months/years. The posts highlight that students are feeling easy by muting the App through which they are taking the class. Posts present an easy way to get rid of the drudgery of learning. The sentiments of work shirkers remain the same. Now they have adapted their methodologies to escape the drudgery of online classrooms.

Students Do Not Want Physical Exams (5-)

These posts show the hollow understanding of students during online learning. Students are not ready for physical exams. Figure 13 shows the protest of students against physical exams. Figure 12 also highlights students' rejection of on-campus exams. Figure 12 is designed on the nature of posters having slogans like 'Say No to Corruption' or 'Say No to Injustice'. On the other hand, a student is participating in a protest to conduct exams online just like the classes so the students may have ample chances of cheating.

Figure 7.

Closure of Educational Institutions is Celebrated (4-)

These posts are about students' and teachers' happiness regarding the extended vacations. People are taking this kind of news as well. Figure 14 communicates that at the closure of educational institutions, students and teachers are extremely happy. Figure 15 has stated a caption about the education minister that he is the only person who gives good news in the whole year of 2020 (the closure of schools and colleges).

Corona and Research Students (3-)

The first post (Figure 16) is a statement by a research scholar that 'he/she could not complete the thesis because of Corona this year, previously it was due to my laziness.' The second post (Figure 17) is a statement that 'mask is beneficial for thesis scholars as they were unable to face the public.' These posts mock MPhil and PhD Scholars who have found Covid-19 as an excuse for their incapability to complete their research and thesis in time. It is observed that research scholars mostly suffer from procrastination and imposter syndrome no matter which area and subject they belong to. This lockdown has given such scholars a chance to consider some environmental factors responsible for the delay in their research and thesis writing.

Figure 8.

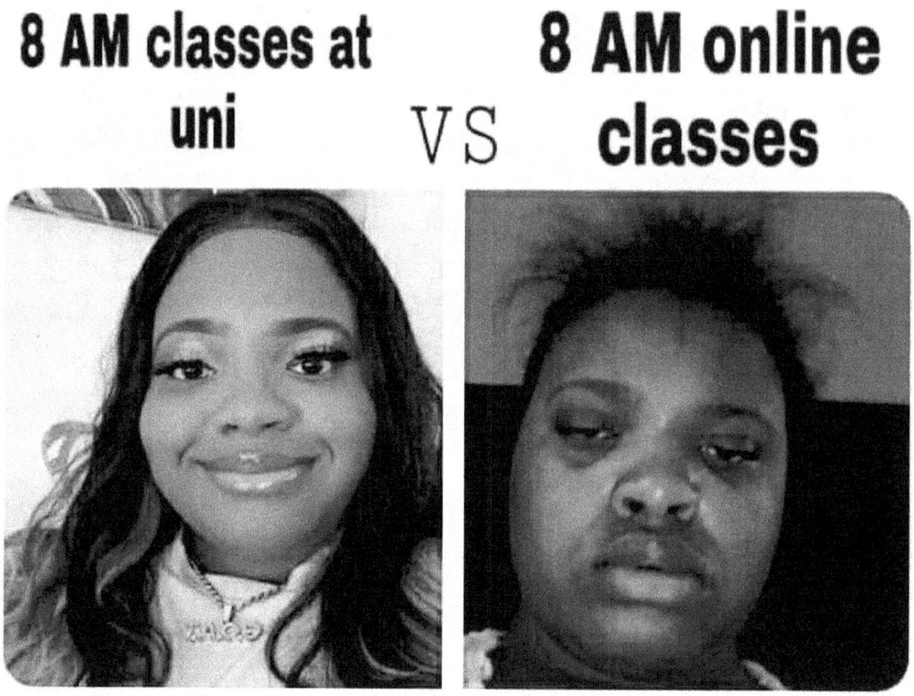

Poor Performance of Online Taught (3-)

These posts are about the quality of online education. The posts show the lack of conceptual clarity and high grades given by the teachers without thinking about the quality of learning by the students. Ramij and Sultana (2020) presented the quality of poor education in a seriousvein and concluded that though the course instructors are highly skilled in terms of academic knowledge, the course materials that are being taught are not compatible enough for online learning. It is due to insufficient time instructors have been allowed to prepare lectures and lack of proper training and infrastructures.

Self Defeating Jokes (3-)

In Figure 20, Pakistani online education has been targeted where teachers are using WhatsApp recordings to teach their students because they lack the required knowledge and technical skills to teach online. Another point to be noted in these memes is the use of images of foreign nationals to enhance the comic effects. Figure 21 shows the selfishness on the part of Pakistani school, they are more concerned about the dues of students instead of the precious lives of the people. On the other hand, people in Italy, the USA, and Britain are more concerned about the impending death.

Figure 9.

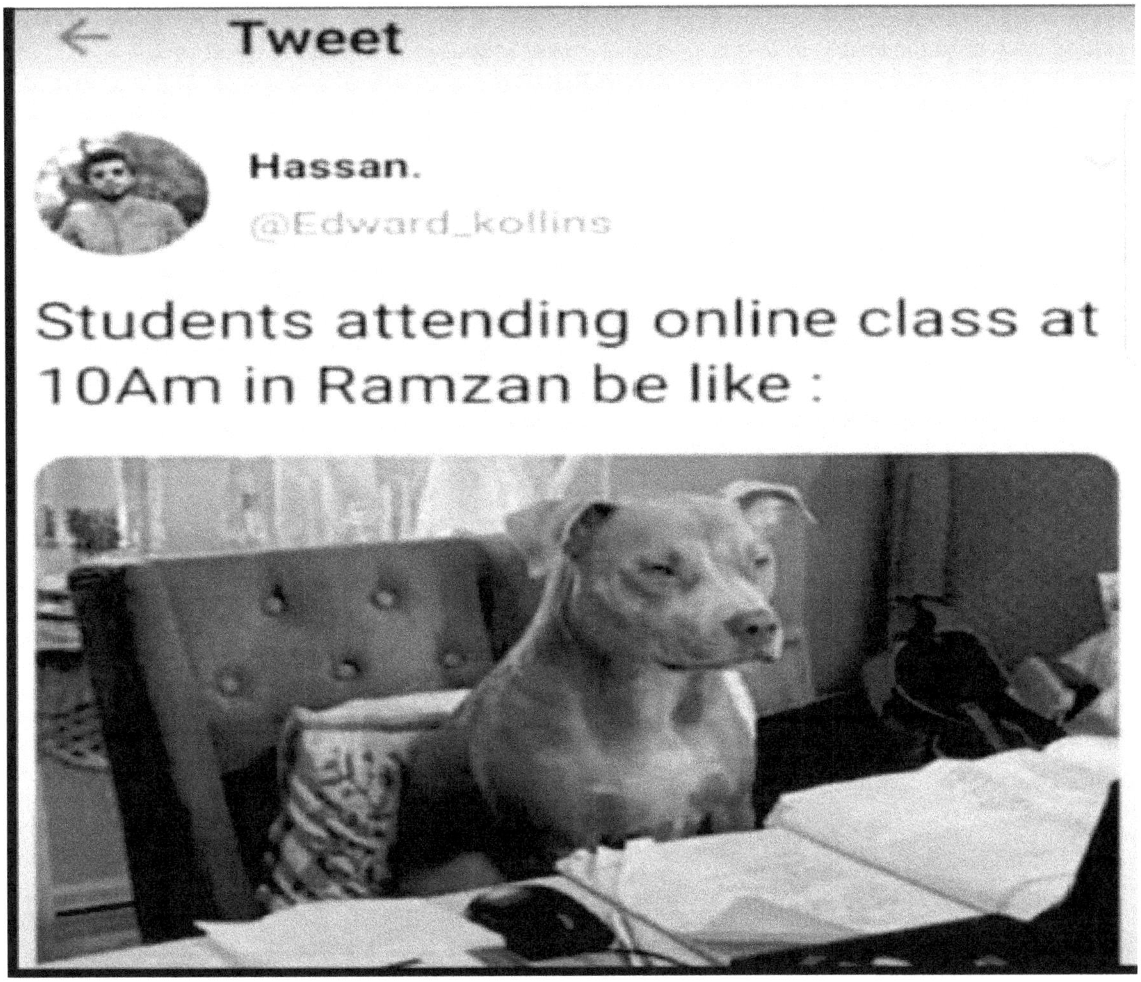

The Reality of Online Classes (3-)

These memes present another dark side of online classes. The students are depicted as not learning during online classes so these are useless. The first post (Figure 22) depicts that parents instead of students are taking the lectures and instructions. In the second post (Figure 23), online classes have been termed as 'useless' as the actress' *dupatta* (a piece of cloth used to cover the head and upper body of a female in Eastern cultures) which is not covering her body at all. In the same manner, online classes are not meeting the objective to impart quality education.

After Effects of Lockdown on Teaching (3-)

These posts show a big challenge for the teachers, after the vacations of COVID-19. Figure 24 depicts a person who is trying to remember in which department, he was studying before lockdown. Students are blank and they have forgotten everything due to not studying during the lockdown (Figure 25). They have wasted their time playing online games. Students are unable to make a reconnection with their on-campus departments, teachers and courses. Playing mobile games has become a part of their reflexes and they answer in the terms of games, even if they are asked some academic questions.

Figure 10.

Teachers Seem to be Enjoying Online Classes (3-)

These posts show that teachers are enjoying online teaching. Figure 26 shows there is no fixed time for these online classes and teachers are not following any fixed timetable. Figure 27 also points out teacher's pleasure during online teaching. A study on a serious discourse during online teaching and time management skill shows that the online learning approach is not suitable for everyone. Time management skills and strong self-motivation are required for a successful E-learning experience. In class, students receive feedback from their teachers and peers, interact with them according to a predetermined schedule, work as a team, grow their communication skills, and be pushed whenever they are needed to be (Tamm, Fakhri, Martisiute, & Lee, 2019).

Figure 11.

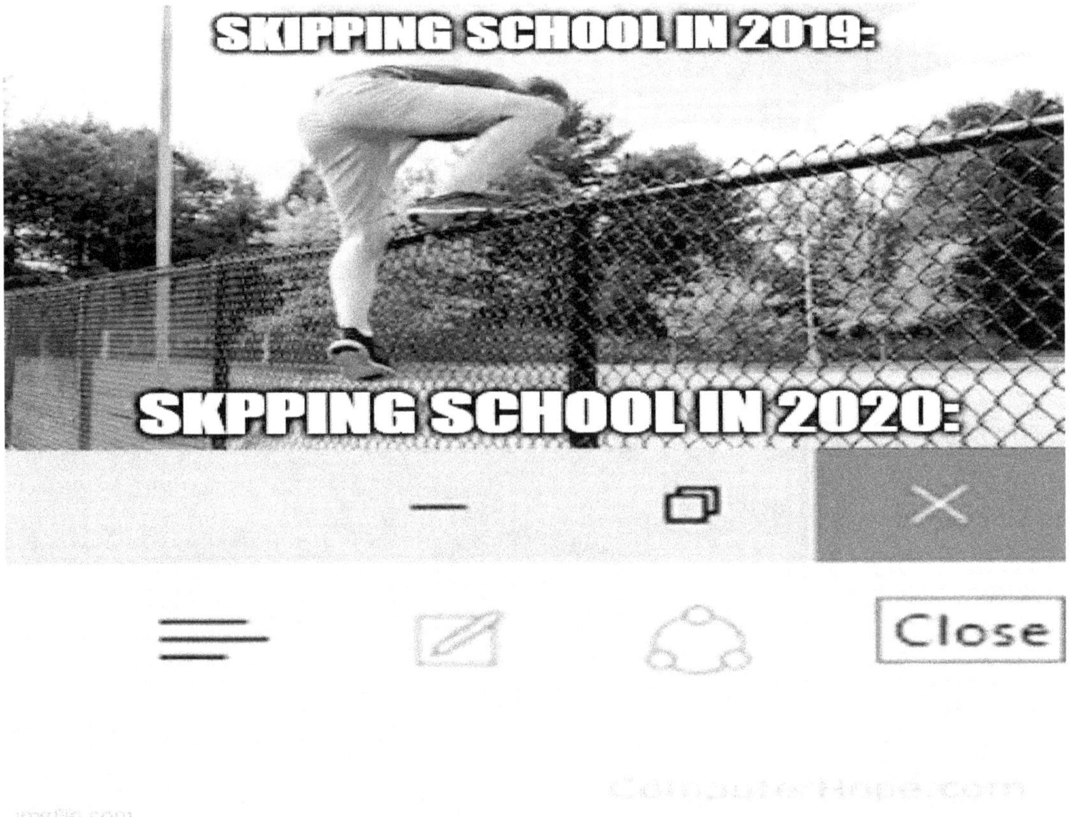

An Excuse to Use Mobile Phone (2-)

These posts show the use of mobile phones for online learning during COVID-19. Figure 28 shows that mobiles are having control over schools now, and Figure 29 explains mobile phones as a lame excuse for online learning. Students can have parents' phones for a long period without any kind of difficulty. Both the posts are self-evident, being written in English.

Not Ready to Learn (2-)

This cultureme is students' tiredness of studies. Figure 30 shows the students' behavior for learning during the period of COVID19. Students are not ready to learn at any cost, they are not concerned about their studies.

Figure 12.

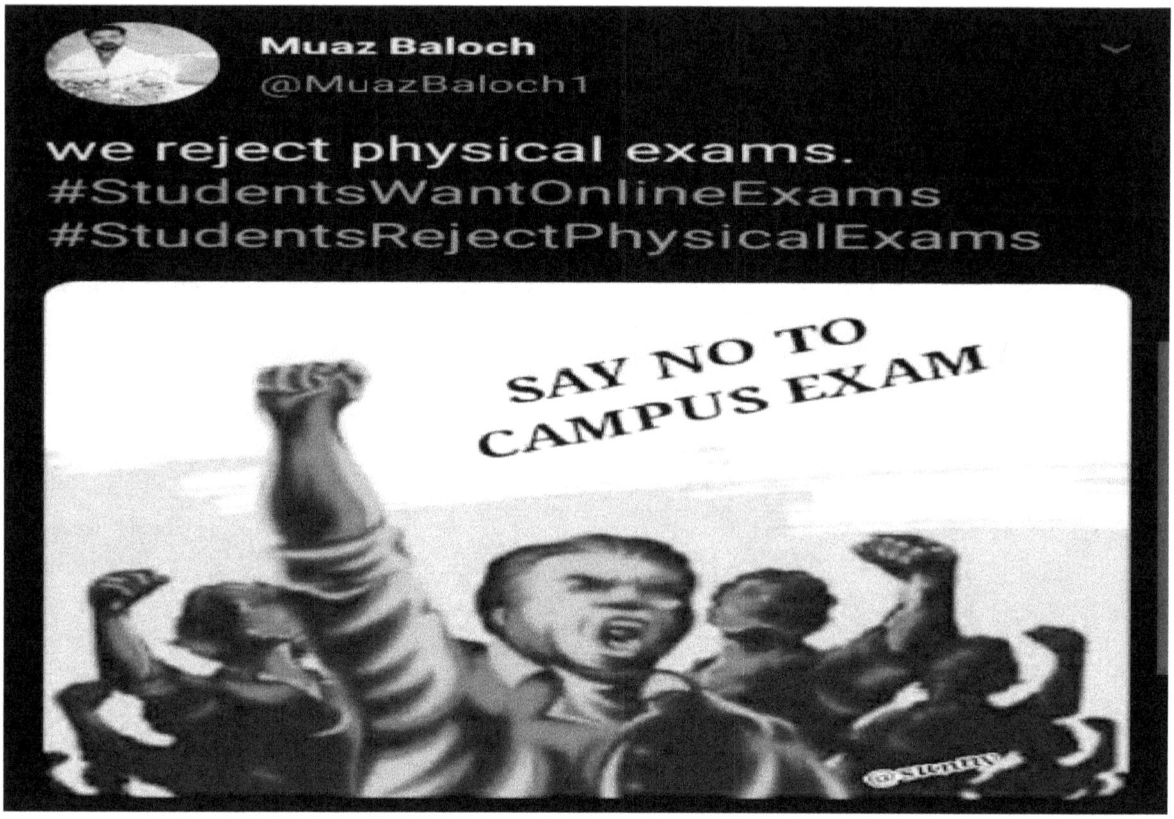

DISCUSSION

Taking insights from the Linguo-Cultural approach, this study has analyzed popular social media jokes/memes concerning COVID-19. Culturemes are a bit of the accumulative memory of a given speech community. Like previous Linguo-cultural scholars (Petrova, 2019), the researcher has used "**semantic density**" to denote the frequency of occurrence of a particular cultureme. The Semantic Density of an idea implies deciphering quantity regarding quality, or in other words, it serves as an indication of cultural centrality and relative significance. The higher the semantic density, the more culturally prominent and significant, would be the cultureme in the respective linguo-culture. The dominant culturemes represent the 'cultural constants' of the linguo-culture in question, while the peripheral ones are an essential addition to its main characteristics.

The culturematic analysis revealed that the majority of COVID19 and online teaching based jokes dealt with non-serious behavior on the part of students. The themes retrieved from the analysis of the comics show that teachers are represented in a derogatory way, where they are represented as helpless and are insulted by the students. These themes are seen as a recurrent subject in the selected comics that are analyzed in terms of linguistic choices and the visual language used in them. The linguistic and visual elements also depict the ways of interaction and communication of teachers and students in the online academic context, which shows the behavior of students with teachers and vice versa. This provides answers to the questions of the study. A power-based relationship between teachers and students is shown in the comics, where teachers are represented as people having no power over students in terms of their behavior and academic discipline. They are not respected by the students, which is not according to the norms of the academic contexts. The posts included in this theme present the idea that students are not ready to learn.

Figure 13.

The second most dense cultureme is highlighting the difficulty of teachers about their lack of expertise in technical education. A poll was conducted among the students that gathered essential information on a few viewpoints that are legitimately related with online education, for example, related knowledge of the online class, specialized ability, kind of gadget and internet service utilized, web speed, span of class, mental anxiety, the appeal of the course substance, financial state of the family and so on. Given this information, a closing comment is drawn that possibly it is a correct chance to embrace web-based learning amid the Covid episode without thinking about the necessary framework(Ramij and Sultana, 2020).

Another set of culturemes shows that students are not ready for on-campus and physical exams. They are protesting against physical exams and are asking for online exams. This shows their lack of understanding during online learning and also their carelessness. The next theme presents students' and teachers' happiness regarding vacations. They are taking this kind of vacation as well and for enjoyment. The next most dense cultureme is highlighting the nuances of online classes from students' perspectives. These teaching and learning related memes reiterated that students want to escape studies, and they want to enjoy these times doing nothing. Students have also delineated certain delaying and bunking tactics, even in online classes. Some of these posts taunt at MPhil and PhD scholars who have found Covid-19 as an excuse for their incapability to complete their research in time. The most emphasized points are the difficulty students, and teachers face to cope with the upsurge of a new medium without any previous homework or expertise.

Figure 14.

Another theme is the quality of online education and its effects on the future of students when they embark on the job market. It is delineated that students taught through this medium would lack clear understanding as well as the practical application of the concepts taught. Power relations between teachers and students are seen to be more on the side of students, as teachers are shown as helpless and not being able to control the misbehaving and disobeying class. The teachers shout at the class, but they are not listened to and made a fool by the students instead. In some comics they are shown as dumb, not knowing anything about the class.

Figure 15.

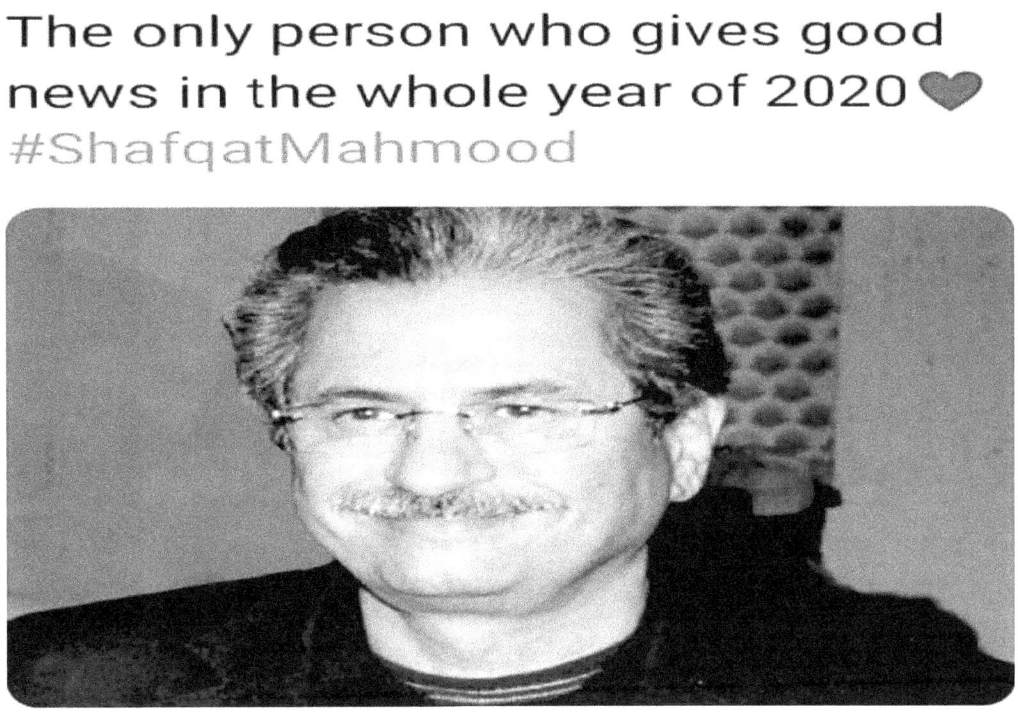

Figure 16.

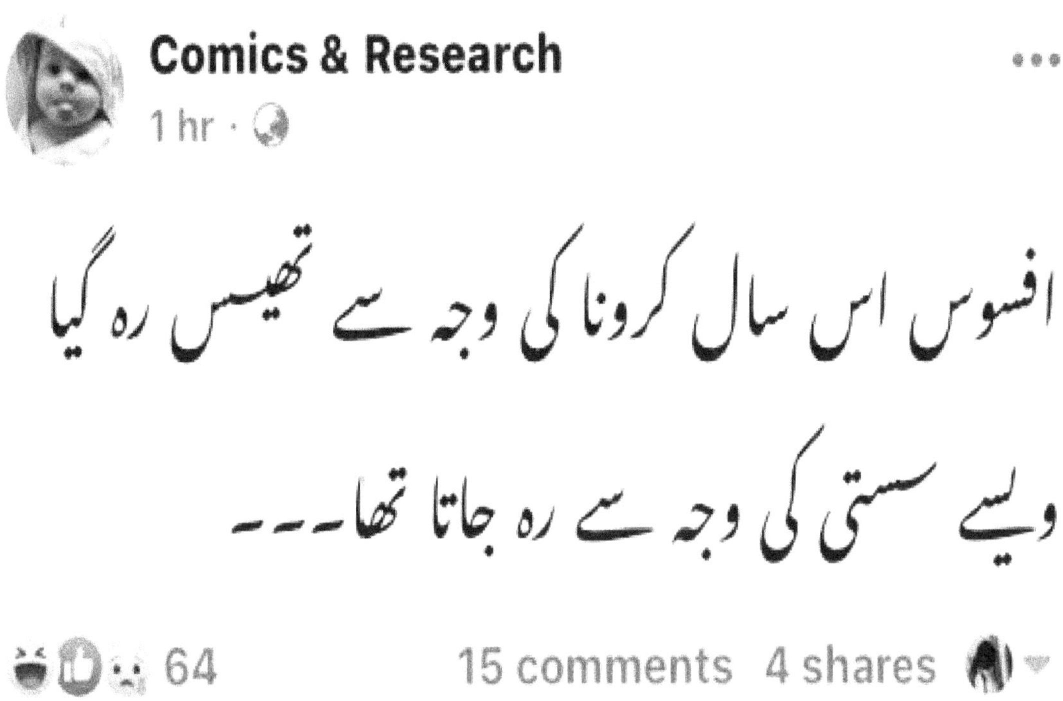

Figure 17.

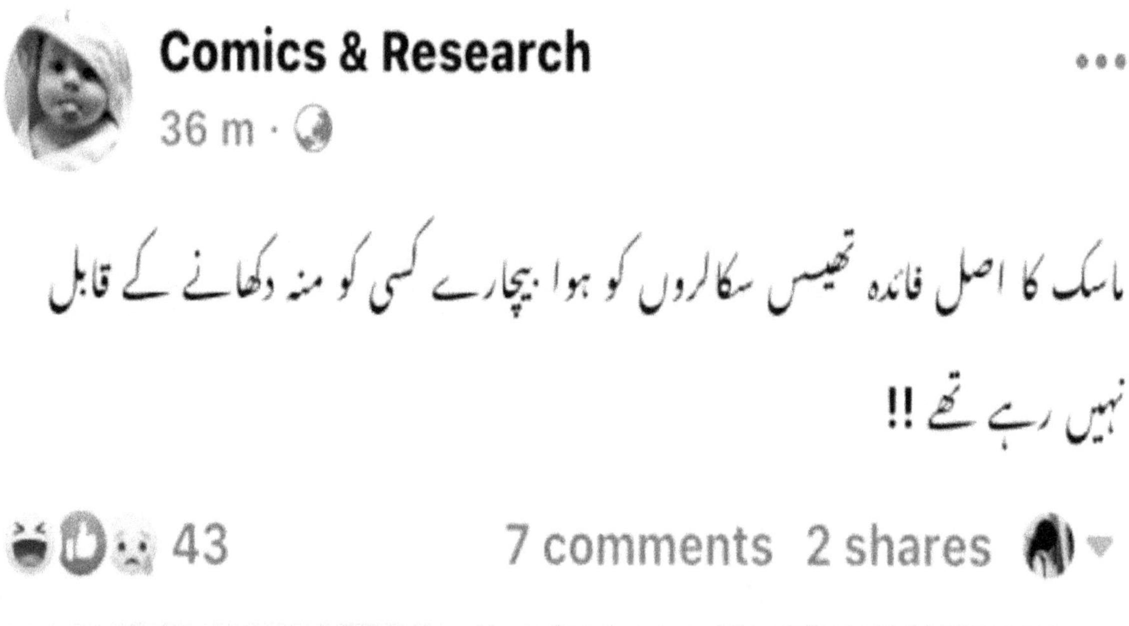

The next most dense cultureme is about unhappy students, which indicates an important issue regarding the mental health of the students. Students have never experienced such a type of pandemic before. They have to maintain social distancing for several months. They are deprived of their healthy lives, of going outside to hang out and play outdoor games using their institutions' physical space. There are many different kinds of Coronaviruses. COVID-19, the newly identified type of Coronaviruses, is considered a pandemic because it causes respiratory illness and can very easily spread among humans. Coughing, having a sore throat, a headache, nausea, losing smell or taste, feeling fever, chills, or pains in the body muscles, dealing with shortness or difficulties in breathing, vomiting, and staying fatigued are the most common symptoms for COVID-19 (Sauer, 2020). So staying at home has made them mentally stressed. In the media, they hear the negative news of new cases of COVID-19 and the increasing death toll. Students who feel mentally stressed are also declining to join online classes or are against the decision to take online classes. There is almost a 43% probability that students are mentally stressed and are unwilling to join an online class(Ramij and Sultana, 2020). The next cultureme in the hierarchy is making fun of the dull and unfresh faces during online classes. It shows that students do not have enough motivation to take online classes. The most emphasized points are the difficulty students and teachers are facing to cope with the upsurge of a new medium without any previous homework or expertise.

Another set of culturemes is that students are making fun during online teaching and they are least bothered about the loss of their studies. Considering the above mentioned aspects related to the online class environment; students should be asked whether it is a right and timely decision to take online classes amid COVID-19 pandemic. Another set represents that teachers are relaxed during vacations, they have no proper schedule to follow. Students are taking mobile phones as an excuse for online classes. Now, they can take phones for a timeless period without any difficulty. As the findings of the present study reveal a non-serious behavior, even when they have a proper place to live. The next cultureme consists of memes making self-defeating humor as compared to other nationalities. The last cultureme reiterated that students want to escape studies, and they want to enjoy these times doing nothing.

Figure 18.

CONCLUSION

Reinforcing Petrova's (2019) assertion, "whatever appears important for our wishing and willing, our hope and anxiety, for acting and doing: that and only that receives the stamp of verbal meaning" (p. 37), the hierarchical arrangement based on culturematic semantic density in a descending order has provided an insight into Pakistani society's matters of concern regarding COVID-19 and online teaching. These humorous texts of the Pakistani nation are in a real sense an ethnography of the people. Teachers' and students' mental stress is presented in a humorous way that they cannot cope up with the online teaching properly. Previously, teachers, as well as students, were used to traditional, face to face interaction and on-campus teaching. The humor produced during normal days was altogether different, which can be covered in a comparative study of the historical evolution of humor to reach the current scenario. The study concludes that the majority of teachers lack technical literacy. The subjects recovered from the investigation of the memes show that teachers are spoken to unfavorably, as defenseless and offended by their students. They are neither taken seriously by their students nor are they respected. The overall image constructed through humorous posts on social media regarding the topic under investigation is that the online classes are a mere waste of time, energy, and resources as students lack motivation and teachers lack enough skills to switch to this new mode efficiently and effectively. The researchers need to conduct quick researches and suggest practical measures to cope up with this anxious situation.

Figure 19.

Figure 20.

Ye Online Classes
kia hoti hain?
PYA
Memes
Pakistan mein
parhty ho?
Han
Whatsapp Recordings ko
kehte hain.

Figure 21.

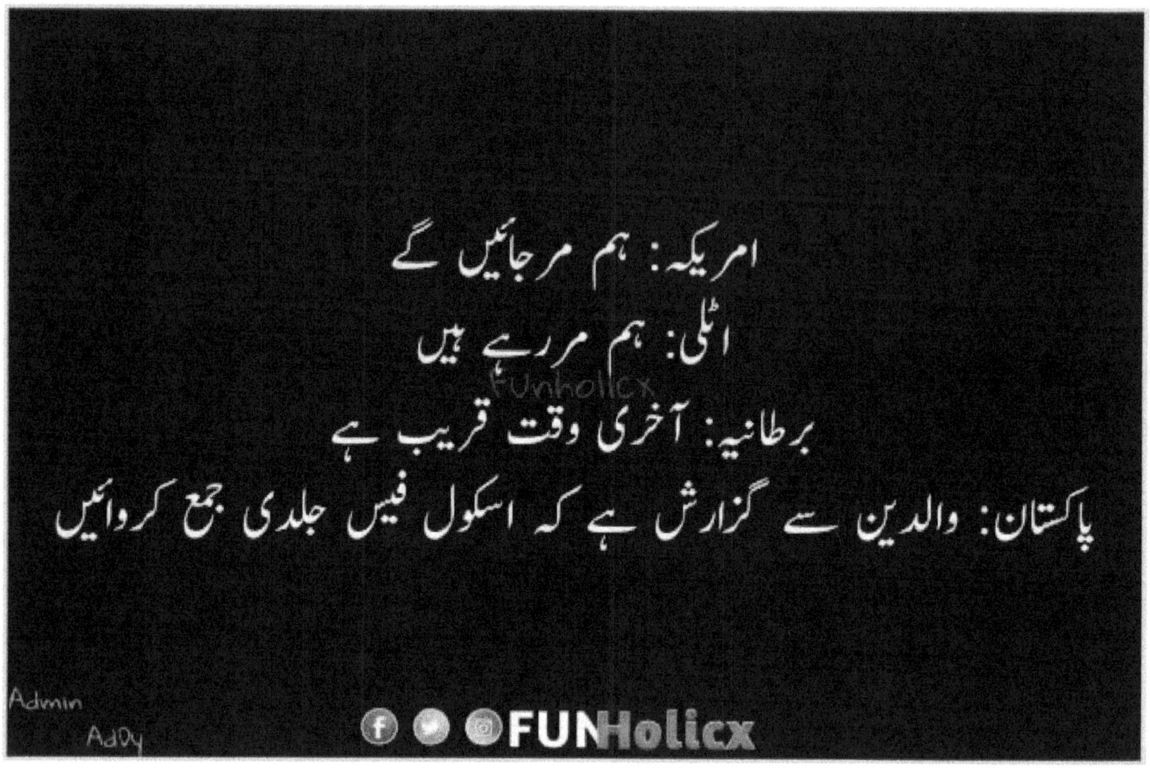
امریکہ: ہم مرجائیں گے
اٹلی: ہم مر رہے ہیں
برطانیہ: آخری وقت قریب ہے
پاکستان: والدین سے گزارش ہے کہ اسکول فیس جلدی جمع کروائیں
Admin
AdDy
FUNHolicx

Figure 22.

Figure 23.

wot iz lyf
@laibanwer
Online classes are as useless as Madhuri's Dupatta in this picture.

Figure 24.

Figure 25.

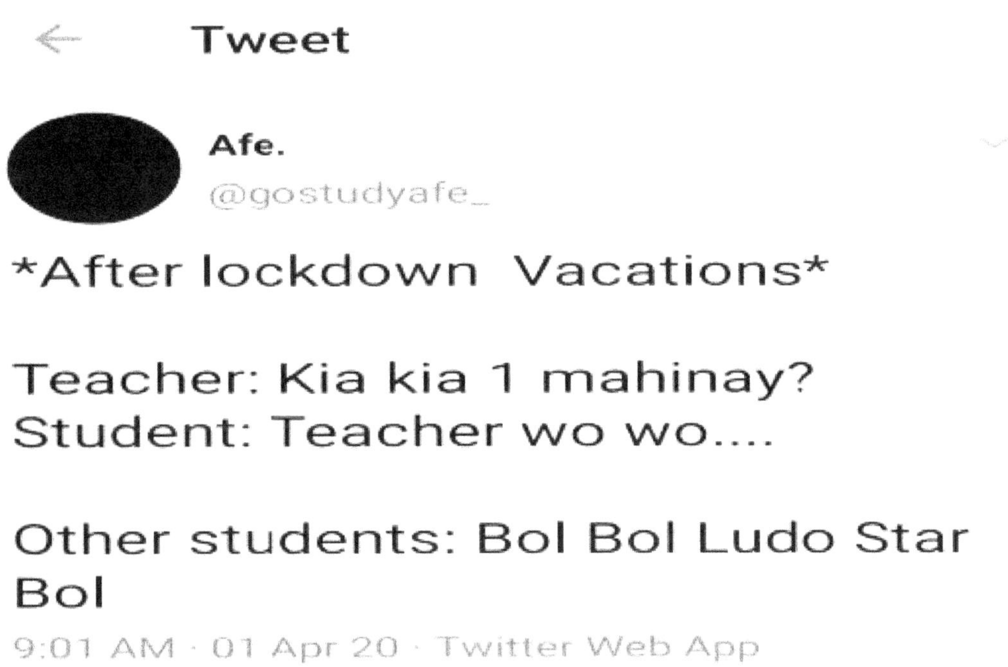

Figure 26.

Me: so when is the class going to be tommorow?
The teacher:
I don't know!
Online classes be like

Figure 27.

Figure 28.

Figure 29.

Figure 30.

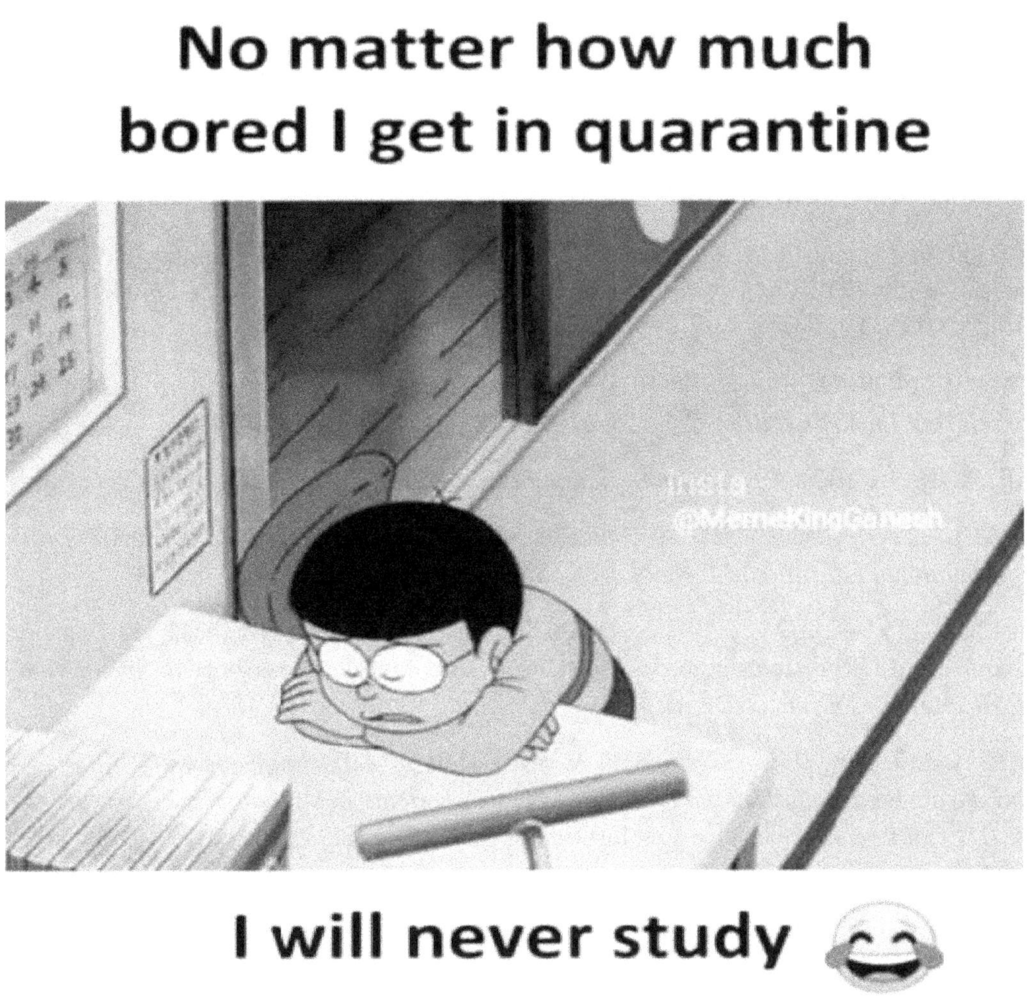

REFERENCES

Agung, I. M. (2020). *Memahami Pandemi Covid-19 Dalam Perspektif Psikologi Sosial.* Psikobuletin: Buletin Ilmiah Psikologi.

Ali, W. (2020). Online and remote learning in higher education institutes: A necessity in light of COVID-19 pandemic. *Higher Education*, *10*(3), 16–25.

Asimov, I. (1971). *Isaac Asimov's Treasury of Humor*. Houghton Mifflin Company.

Assunção Flores, M., & Gago, M. (2020). Teacher education in times of COVID-19 pandemic in Portugal: National, institutional, and pedagogical responses. *Journal of Education for Teaching*, *46*(4), 1–10. doi:10.1080/02607476.2020.1799709

Bao, W. (2020). COVID-19 and online teaching in higher education: A case study of Peking University. *Human Behavior and Emerging Technologies*, *2*(2), 113–115. doi:10.1002/hbe2.191 PMID:32510042

Bozkurt, A., & Sharma, R. C. (2020). Emergency remote teaching in a time of global crisis due to CoronaVirus pandemic. *Asian Journal of Distance Education*, *15*(1), i–vi.

Brom, C., Lukavský, J., Greger, D., Hannemann, T., Straková, J., & Švaříček, R. (2020, July). Mandatory home education during the covid-19 lockdown in the czech republic: A rapid survey of 1st-9th graders' parents. *Frontiers in Education*, *5*, 103. doi:10.3389/feduc.2020.00103

Chung, E., Subramaniam, G., & Dass, L. C. (2020). Online learning readiness among university students in Malaysia amidst COVID-19. *Asian Journal of University Education*, *16*(2), 46–58. doi:10.24191/ajue.v16i2.10294

Dewi, W. A. F. (2020). Dampak Covid-19 terhadap implementasi pembelajaran daring di Sekolah Dasar. *Edukatif: Jurnal Ilmu Pendidikan*, *2*(1), 55–61. doi:10.31004/edukatif.v2i1.89

Edwards, A. (Ed.). (2012). *New Technology and Education*. Continuum Publishing Corporation.

Emmungil, L., & Akleylek, S. (2008). Technical requirements for online education support. *Proceedings of 8th International Educational Technology Conference*, 607-609.

Giovannella, C., Passarelli, M., & Persico, D. (2020). Measuring the effect of the Covid-19 pandemic on the Italian learning Ecosystems at the steady-state: A school teachers' perspective. *Interaction Design and Architecture (s) Journal (IxD&A)*, (45).

Huang, R. H., Liu, D. J., Tlili, A., Yang, J. F., & Wang, H. H. (2020). *Handbook on Facilitating Flexible Learning during Educational Disruption: The Chinese Experience in Maintaining Undisrupted Learning in COVID-19 Outbreak*. Smart Learning Institute of Beijing Normal University.

Huang, R. H., Liu, D. J., Tlili, A., Yang, J. F., & Wang, H. H. (2020). *Handbook on facilitating flexible learning during educational disruption: The Chinese experience in maintaining undisrupted learning in COVID-19 outbreak*. Smart Learning Institute of Beijing Normal University.

Iivari, N., Sharma, S., & Ventä-Olkkonen, L. (2020). Digital transformation of everyday life–How COVID-19 pandemic transformed the basic education of the young generation and why information management research should care? *International Journal of Information Management*, *55*, 102–183. doi:10.1016/j.ijinfomgt.2020.102183 PMID:32836640

König, J., Jäger-Biela, D. J., & Glutsch, N. (2020). Adapting to online teaching during COVID-19 school closure: Teacher education and teacher competence effects among early career teachers in Germany. *European Journal of Teacher Education*, 1–15.

Kumar, D. (2010). *Pros and cons of online education*. North Carolina State University.

Lathifah, Z. K., Helmanto, F., & Maryani, N. (2020). The practice of effective classroom management in COVID-19 time. *International Journal of Advanced Science and Technology*, *29*(7), 3263–3271.

Murgatroyd, S. (2020). COVID-19 and online learning: A SWOT analysis of users' perspectives on learning management system of University of Education, Winneba, Ghana. *International Journal of Learning. Teaching and Educational Research*, *19*(9), 382–401.

Obergriesser, S., & Stoeger, H. (2020). Students' emotions of enjoyment and boredom and their use of cognitive learning strategies–How do they affect one another? *Learning and Instruction*, *66*, 101285. doi:10.1016/j.learninstruc.2019.101285

Pathak, N. V. (2020). Experiencing Online Education. *Purakala*, *31*(40), 211–215.

Radha, R., Mahalakshmi, K., Kumar, V. S., & Saravanakumar, A. R. (2020). E-Learning during a lockdown of a covid-19 pandemic: a global perspective. *International Journal of Control and Automation, 13*(4), 1088-1099.

RamijM.SultanaA. (2020). Preparedness of Online Classes in Developing Countries amid COVID-19 Outbreak: A Perspective from Bangladesh. doi:10.2139srn.3638718

Riley, P. (2011). Attachment theory and the teacher-student relationship: A practical guide for teachers, teacher educators and school leaders. New York: Routledge.

Rouadi, N. E., & Anouti, M. F. (2020). The online learning experiment in the intermediate and secondary schools in Lebanon during the coronavirus (COVID-19) crisis. *Online Learning, 7*(7), 14466-14485.

Samra, C. (1986). *Aspects of internalization*. International Universities Press.

Sauer, L. (2020). *What Is Coronavirus?* Retrieved from Hopkins Medicine: https://www.hopkinsmedicine.org/health/conditions-anddiseases/coronavirus

Supena, A., Umboh, D., Tarusu, D. T., & Kalengkongan, J. (2020, August). Learning Strategies in Elementary Schools During COVID-19 Pandemic in North Sulawesi. In *Proceeding of International Conference on Teaching and Science Education* (Vol. 1, No. 1, pp. 12-19). 10.31098/ictase.v1i1.14

Tamm, S., Fakhri, S., Martisiute, L., & Lee, M. (2019). *Disadvantages of E-Learning*. Retrieved from e-student.org: https://estudent.org/disadvantages-of-e-learning/

Xu, D., & Jaggars, S. S. (2013). Adaptability to online learning: Differences across types of students and academic subject areas. *The Journal of Higher Education*, *85*(5). Advance online publication. doi:10.1353/jhe.2014.0028

Zhang, W., Wang, Y., Yang, L., & Wang, C. (2020). Suspending classes without stopping learning: China"s education emergency management policy in the Covid-19 outbreak. *Journal of Risk and Financial Management*, *13*(55), 1–6. doi:10.3390/jrfm13030055

Ziv, A. (1984). *Personality and Sense of Humor*. Springer.

KEY TERMS AND DEFINITIONS

COVID-19: 2019 novel coronavirus.

Cultureme: The one main substance which is commented, presented, or evaluated as positive or negative

Humor: The quality of being amusing or comic, especially as expressed in literature or speech.

Joke: A thing that someone says to cause amusement or laughter, especially a story with a funny punchline.

Linguo-Culture: Of or pertaining to both language and culture.

Meme: An image, video, piece of text, etc., typically humorous in nature, that is copied and spread rapidly by internet users, often with slight variations.

Online Class: An online class is a course conducted over the internet.

Semantic Density: The frequency of occurrence of a cultureme in a given linguo-culture.

Social Media: Social media are interactive digitally-mediated technologies that facilitate the creation or sharing/exchange of data.

Chapter 9
Adaptation of Young People in Conditions of Self-Isolation in COVID-19 in the Perspectives of Educational Technologies and Sport Spirituality

Tamara Stanislavovna Olenich
https://orcid.org/0000-0002-1212-9181
Don State Tehnical University, Russia

Igor Leonidovich Biryukov
Armavir State Pedagogical University, Russia

ABSTRACT

The chapter examines the problems of Russian youth adaptation in the conditions of self-isolation under COVID-19: educational technologies, psychological and physical health, the experience of the traditional confession. The authors surveyed Don State Technical University to prove that the student youth have a number of problems caused by self-isolation as well as to specify what methods can be applied to overcome COVID-caused challenges. Sports spirituality can provide a solid foundation for all health factors and purposefully contribute to the adaptation to post-COVID social reality. The practical case of the health group in Armavir shows how sports spirituality worked out within the Orthodox Church can be put into practice. Practices of sports spirituality were implemented by the health group in Armavir. They include walking technique and forms of physical activity as health-improving functions, strengthening the body capabilities, breathing exercises, support and interpersonal communication in a thematic conversation in WhatsApp.

DOI: 10.4018/978-1-7998-7164-4.ch009

INTRODUCTION

The epidemiological situation associated with exposure to the COVID- virus 19 appears to be a global challenge to all of humanity. According to the site of the Center for Systems Science and Engineering (CSSE), Johns Hopkins University (JHU), today the world officially recorded 5816706 cases of coronavirus Covid-19 in 188 countries17. Total deaths from coronavirus are 360,437 people (COVID-19 Dashboard by the Center for Systems Science and Engineering, 2020). Confirmed cases of the patients that have recovered after the coronavirus COVID-19 in the world - 2,420,538 (COVID-19 Coronavirus Pandemic, 2020). On the state level, they introduced a lot of specific measures to prevent the threat of the virus spreading in the world.

The spread of coronavirus infection by the nature of the threat and the psychological consequences that it causes can be defined as a psycho-traumatic situation characterized by several distinctive features. One of these features seems to be its multifactoriality (Bykhovets, K., Kogan-Lerner, L., 2020). In the authors' opinion, the sources of stressful experiences are: firstly, the very fact of the existence of a potential danger of infection with coronavirus; secondly, media coverage of these events; third, the economic consequences of the epidemic affecting the entire population (reduction of wages, job loss, etc.); fourthly, changes in the habitual way of life (staying for a long time in a confined space, reducing social activity, switching to home study/work, etc.) in connection with health-preserving measures.

The closures of schools, colleges and universities, compounded by the health and economic crises associated with these crises, pose serious problems for students and their teachers. For the Russian public education system, as for many other education systems of the world, it was a big challenge to cope with this situation. When the lockdown started because of its sudden and extremely quick beginning there were not enough resources to support effective teaching and learning and to provide social and pedagogical support which student youth usually receive in educational institutions offline (Society and Pandemic: Experience and Lessons from COVID-19 Fighting in Russia., 2020). This, COVID-19 forces higher education institutions to fast adapt to new ways of teaching and delivering educational services.

While the exact consequences of COVID-2019 cannot be predicted, the authors of the chapter can make an assumption with high confidence that student performance deteriorates during a pandemic along with their progress in other developmental skills.

It is also worth noting that the different ways in which the crisis has widened existing socioeconomic imbalances, and these imbalances affect learning and educational outcomes, educational inequalities in a negative way (Society and Pandemic: Experience and Lessons from COVID-19 Fighting in Russia., 2020). As a consequence, many of the students who struggle to learn and excel effectively at university under normal circumstances now find that it is difficult, and in some cases even impossible, to receive effective instruction and find it difficult to master the material that is given to them. on distance learning (Titov, 2020).

Under the abovementioned conditions, it is necessary to conduct a holistic study of the problems of youth adaptation in the conditions of self-isolation under COVID 19 and to identify technologies that helped Russian student youth to adapt to the consequences caused by COVID-19.

BACKGROUND

The problem of the epidemic and its influence upon society and social behaviour has become one of the most relevant in the academic discourse. But up to the present moment, there is not a big number of researches in which the influence of epidemic and the consequences of the global epidemic are investigated. The present research is based on the ideas of framing theory which allows us to explain the feeling of social disorientation and social distance which have become one of the most negative results of COVID-2019 (Semetko, H., & Valkenburg, P., 2000).

The second theoretical position is based on the number of works in which specialist in education and psychology research the lockdown and what happens within the student youth within self-isolation but under the necessity to study and to communicate online.

Informational frames allow us "to structure with meaning the social world" therefore framing theory introduces the component of meaning to the facts themselves, as well as other associated interaction processes (De Vreese, 2005). People, especially young people who are only in the process of formation of their critical thinking and social adaptation – in various cases – to the social reality, tend to select certain aspects of reality—even that one which can be fabricated— but at the same time, such frames are given greater emphasis or priority, including parameters such as value judgments, importance, solutions or simply the behaviour (Entman, 2004). Then the frame is transcended from the prime cause highlighted in various sources of information to the audience, who must then decode it through endogenous processes of interpretation and understanding (Chong, D., & Druckman, J.N., 2007). During this process of the information transition complicated with the social isolation, a new social reality has been formed, including individuals' ways of life, wellbeing, instructive framework, exchange and organizations, and mechanical framework. The mainframes of this new post-COVID social reality are normality of digital communication and education as well as physical isolation from the society under discrete lockdown (Cultural-historical activity psychology in extreme situation: the pandemic challenge, 2020).

Communication is a very important factor for the development of the individuals because by introducing individuals to the standards, values, and ways of thinking of their culture (Zalewska, 2019) was limited by lockdown situation. And one of the most important problems is to understand how the youth acquire new habits and behaviours under lockdown and what frames do they construct to overcome the consequences of COVID-2019.

Russian scientists are sure that the process of education within lockdown when the student youth is isolated can be a big challenge to the youth communicational skills as well a big obstacle for the normal socialization of the youth (Bykhovets, K., Kogan-Lerner, L., 2020). Byhovets K. and Kogan-Lerner L. insist on the position that the lockdown and self-isolation, caused by the COVID-19 pandemic, is a multifactor psychotraumal situation which effect can be seen only in a long-term perspective but at the present stage such negative consequences include: neuroticism, introversion, anxiety, and a number of psychopathological signs (Bykhovets, K., Kogan-Lerner, L., 2020). The survey conducted within the students did not show such difficult consequences but students pointed out that they got tired and had more homework which made them feel exhausted.

The expert of the think-tank Russian international affairs council Karpinskaia E. claims that 'the quick start of distance learning has given rise to a number of interrelated problems: some educational institutions have been unable to start online education for various reasons, including lack of logistics and lack of widespread Internet coverage' (Karpinskaya, 2020). According to the expert, 'a significant decrease in the quality of education was recorded during the transition to distance learning in the absence of existing learning management systems in many countries - software for administering training courses within distance learning' (Karpinskaya, 2020). There have also been some technical problems with the usage of online applications which universities apply to conduct distance lectures or seminars. Some universities have announced that they abandoned the Zoom platform and started to apply Google Meet or other applications because of technical easiness and accessibility (Karpinskaya, 2020).

Insufficient accessibility of distance education has proved to be the most important challenge. At the beginning of the period of self-isolation, more than 10% of full-time students did not have equipment that met all the functional requirements for distance learning, while among students from low-income groups of the population, this share reached 30% (Society and Pandemic: Experience and Lessons from COVID-19 Fighting in Russia., 2020).

All abovementioned premises make it interesting research task – to investigate the ways how the youth is adapting to this new social reality, how the student reacts on self-isolation and distance learning. The more ambitious goal is to work out some useful practices and method, psychological or spiritual, which can be used by the youth to adapt to new post-COVID social reality without psychotrauma.

Materials and Methods

The analysis of the literature shows that social framing for such social group as the youth is a necessary element for their adaptation to the new social reality. The research of adaptation of the young people in conditions of self-isolation in COVID 19 to the new social reality intercultural communication is based on a big variety of social science research methods. The first principle of the research is using of social frames to understand the new type of post-COVID reality. The basic method used to investigate the adaptation of the youth is a questionnaire and its content analysis.

The survey "Attitude of student youth to a new format of education using online technologies during the period of self-isolation" was conducted by the Department of Orthodox Culture and Theology, DSTU, located in Rostov-on-Don region of the Russian Federation, and includes analyses of the questionnaire filled in by the student youth aged from 17 to 26. The total number of students who were surveyed consists of 157 people. The survey was conducted in April-June 2020.

The research hypothesis is that influenced by COVID-2019 and self-isolation the Russian student youth have successfully adapted to this new social reality through the set of specific activities and techniques, among which new educational methods, namely, sport spirituality. The authors are strongly convinced that they will provide evidence that development sport spirituality through sports activities can be an effective method to overcome the consequences of COVID-2019 and negative effect of new social frames caused by self-isolation.

New Educational Technologies and Their Influence upon the Youth Performance

The pandemic has become a challenge for higher education systems around the world that can simultaneously turn into a new source of development. In just a few weeks, 95% of students around the planet were forced to switch to distance or blended learning (Society and Pandemic: Experience and Lessons from COVID-19 Fighting in Russia., 2020).

The "stress test" in the form of an almost instantaneous transition to various forms of distance learning in March 2020, on the one hand, tested these systems for strength, and on the other hand, it allowed testing new technologies, the introduction of which in previous years was complicated by the lack of funding the level of technical equipment, technical skills and the proper level of motivation (Gafurov, I., Ibragimov, G., Kalimullin, A. & Alishev, T., 2020).

Most universities responded to the pandemic by abandoning full-time education and switching to distance learning, closing campuses, measures to help students and teachers master new communication formats, including the provision of the necessary hardware and software. At the same time, when starting distance learning, at the first stage of the lockdowns the management of universities did not go to reduce tuition fees, although such a requirement was put forward by student organizations (The storm of the first weeks: how higher education stepped into the reality of a pandemic., 2020). During the pandemic, many governments provided financial assistance to universities: first of all, funds were allocated to higher education institutions with a high proportion of students from low-income strata of the population.

On March 14, 2020 the Ministry of Education and Science of the Russian Federation created an operational headquarters to prevent the spread of new coronavirus infection in the country and recommended that universities, when implementing educational programs, provide for the organization of the work of students and teachers only in the electronic information and educational environment (Society and Pandemic: Experience and Lessons from COVID-19 Fighting in Russia., 2020).

The implementation of distance learning and self-isolation of the youth resulted in many issues. Student academic performance deteriorates during a pandemic along with their progress in other developmental skills (Butz, D., Slautina, I., 2020). It is also worth noting that given the different ways in which the crisis has widened existing socioeconomic imbalances, and how these imbalances affect learning and educational outcomes, educational inequalities are growing. As a result, many of the students who try to learn and excel effectively at university under normal circumstances, now find that it is difficult, and in some cases even impossible, to receive effective instruction, and they have difficulty in mastering the material that is given to them through distance learning (Butz, D., Slautina, I., 2020).

Due to this, the level of satisfaction with education among students falls. To a lesser extent, this affects students studying computer and social sciences, the humanities, economists and managers (Butz, D., Slautina, I., 2020). The worst respondents to distance learning were, as the study polls say, students of creative fields, future engineers and doctors. Many students say that they lack face-to-face communication with the teacher, their assistance, which the teachers because of the lockdown cannot provide to the students (Gafurov, I., Ibragimov, G., Kalimullin, A. & Alishev, T., 2020). Also, students noted that few are capable of self-discipline and self-education. As a result, dissatisfaction and tension was growing. Chronic stress alters the chemical and physical structure of the brain, impairing cognitive skills such as attention, concentration, memory, and creativity (Bykhovets, K., Kogan-Lerner, L., 2020).

It is worth noting that educational institutions are not only a place for acquiring academic and practical knowledge but also a place for socialization. The pandemic has changed the way people interact.

Now the level of live communication is much lower. Naturally, one should not argue that everyone suffers from this. Many people, on the other hand, feel much better isolated from other people. And there are more such people due to the pandemic. The value of the university as a source of communication with peers has lost its strength (Gafurov, I., Ibragimov, G., Kalimullin, A. & Alishev, T., 2020).

However, not only negative consequences have been brought about by COVID-19 and distance learning. Many students noted that they had more time for hobbies and sports. Students of the university under consideration in the present chapter noted that they began to communicate more with friends and family. The contributors to the chapter also noted that distance learning provided more free time, increased resources for preparing for classes and - what is extremely important - for sleep.

When the educators started to apply information and communication technologies in training people under the conditions of lockdown, a number of problems in the transition of knowledge emerged. As the response, new approaches and techniques were worked out and used by the teachers. Nevertheless, there is still a number of tasks in this sphere, primarily, creation of optimal conditions for maintaining continuity and start the process of developing new practices the use of information technology in education (Titov, 2020). Based on the conducted survey and content-analysis of the academic papers the priority tasks still are:

1. Availability of resources and technologies to master the educational program in full without reference to the location of the student.
2. Creation of electronic libraries, provision of access to databases and electronic archives.
3. Conducting training using video lectures, chats, online conferences, the use of which is convenient in practice. Security two-way communication.
4. Development of specialized software, providing the ability to work with information for all participants of the educational process.
5. Close cooperation of specialists in the field of pedagogy, psychology and information technology.
6. Diversity of products created (databases, simulation programs for virtual laboratories, etc.)
7. Identification of the identity of the student passing the exam, credit, thesis or term paper.
8. Clear and uniform criteria for assessing knowledge for all teachers and studied disciplines. Final tests should be accompanied by ongoing testing of knowledge using special systems open to working at any time.
9. Ensuring the smooth operation of the Internet, withdrawing technical problems with the transfer of information. This is especially true (and even critical) when conducting exams.

Experienced Western experts in the field of higher education development Philip Altbach and Hans de Wit, in their recent article “Post pandemic outlook for HE is bleakest for the poorest”, express doubts that the pandemic will entail a technological revolution in higher education (Altbach, P., de Wit, H., 2020). Nevertheless, it is clear that the use of distance learning methods will be expanded.

Distance learning has become a good quick tool to meet the short-term needs of the educational system but during the period of self-isolation and total lockdown, a number of issues have been formed. To identify these issues and to try to provide some guideline for their compensation the authors have conducted the survey.

MAIN FOCUS OF THE CHAPTER: THE EMPIRICAL EVIDENCE OF THE CONSEQUENCES OF COVID-2019 UPON THE YOUTH

The survey “Attitude of student youth to a new format of education using online technologies during the period of self-isolation” was conducted by the Department of Orthodox Culture and Theology, DSTU, located in Rostov-on-Don, the Russian Federation, and includes analyses of the questionnaire filled in by the student youth aged from 17 to 26. The total number of students who were surveyed consists of 157 young people (113 females and 33 males).

The respondents said that they were not happy to study within lockdown: 42% of the students do not like the transition to a distance-learning format. But also, a significant part of the students – 36%, were delighted with the transition to the new format. Almost a quarter of the students found it difficult to answer.

Students formed the frame that it is easy to adjust to all stakeholders of the distance learning to the COVID-circumstances. 78% of students immediately continued their education in a distance format, and only 20% did not immediately start learning in a distance format. 95% of interviewees attended all or almost all distance learning classes and only a few per cent of students (5%) miss classes regularly.

Almost half of the respondents did not like distance learning (43%). A quarter of the respondents (25%) liked the training and 30% of students found it difficult to answer.

The next block of questions is connected with the physical health of the interviewees during lockdown – 42% of the students feel tired after the 2nd online lesson, 17% of students get tired after the 3d lesson and 15% of student didn't get tired after all lessons.

Another picture is about the sleeping patterns of the interviewees. A significant part of the respondents had disrupted sleep patterns and decreased sleep time (65%). A quarter of the respondents did not have any changes, and only 11% marked an improvement in their regime.

The new challenge for the student youth was the volume of homework. A significant part of the respondents (59%) increased their homework during their free time from schooling. For a much smaller part of the respondents (11%), the number of homework has not changed or has decreased.

As a result of self-isolation, the student youth has started to learn less knowledge (50%), only 8% got better results and more knowledge. For 40% of students, their academic performance stayed the same.

Interesting data are about the question: "Has the quality of the presentation of information from teachers improved or has the delivery deteriorated?" – 54% of students think that the teacher kept on giving information on the same level, 34% of teachers gave not high-quality materials and only 10% of teachers improved their academic performance.

70% of students want to return to the university classroom, 15% of interviewees are completely satisfied with the distance learning format. Most students don't like the frame on distance learning: only 17% of students want to study online on an ongoing basis.

Summing up, it's necessary to note that the authors' hypothesis is confirmed. Student youth are looking for new social patterns in a lockdown. For most of the students, distance learning was more negatively than positively affected. The students are unhappy with the current situation and want to return the training to the previous format. Distance learning serves the physical and emotional burnout of students, if this situation continues in the new academic year, this will have some consequences.

For only a small proportion of students, distance learning has become an acceptable social frame and they would not mind continuing their studies in this format.

Some comments from respondents (the respondents gave their agreement to publish these comments; their style and ideas are without changes).

1. "It's terrible. My back hurts (and so is scoliosis of the 2nd degree), so I sit like a shrimp for 8 hours a day, then I move away from this stress for half a day. At the university, we somehow moved around and walked around the buildings. My eyes also hurt, sometimes there is not even time to just bathe, or help mom around the house. Because they started asking a lot, not like before".
2. "Distance learning is not a substitute for full-time education within the walls of the university, information is absorbed better at the university itself, the risk of developing back and vision problems is also unlikely since you need to spend a lot of time sitting at the computer screen or, even worse,

behind the phone screen. But I am satisfied with the work of the teachers at this period, they try to provide us with all the conditions for receiving the relying amount of information for the duration of distance learning".

3. "Studying at the university itself, living in a hostel, in another city, communicating with teachers and classmates ... All this motivates and pushes for development, completing assignments, visiting an educational institution with pleasure. Distance learning, in my opinion, is a vacation where you study, where a lot of things distract you from higher education".
4. "For me, the plus of distance education is that you can wake up later, you don't have to waste time on getting ready to university. I can also do my own thing on a couple while listening to what is happening on an online couple. The downside for me is that the contact with the teachers is going a little worse, but, fortunately, not always significantly. Also, my physical activity has significantly decreased, sometimes an apathetic state appears".
5. "Due to the piling up of homework, couples along with household chores, my health deteriorated greatly. The lost regime, hormonal background, and this entailed bad consequences. I understand that this is a compulsory measure, and in no case do I want to say anything bad to the university, on the contrary, the couples pass on schedule and most of the teachers meet halfway, help and support. But the very fact that distance learning is a compulsory measure and cannot be interrupted is bad for morale in learning".

SOLUTIONS AND RECOMMENDATIONS

Based on the results of the survey and the content-analyses of the questionnaires filled in by the students, the present study highlights the practices which were suggested to the interviewed student to overcome negative effects of self-isolation and to form more positive frames under Post-COVID social reality on the next stage of the research.

The practices the authors suggest for the respondents are worked out by Igor Biryukov, a lecturer of Armavir State Pedagogical University, expert in physical education and a priest of the Russian Orthodox Church in Armavir.

Igor Biryukov calls these practices as 'sport spirituality' – 'as an educational innovation manifested itself as a set of specific communicative techniques associated with mental processes of individuals (cognitive and emotional-volitional), such as thinking, memory, attention, feelings, which in the process of sports activities were aimed at developing interest in a healthy lifestyle and adherence to social rules in the process of sports' (Olenich, T., Terarakelyants, V., Shestopalova, O., & Biryukov, I., 2020). The researcher present practices of sport spirituality within the health group "Yuzhnoe Dolgoleie"/"Southern Longevity" in Armavir within 200 local inhabitants during March 2020 (The priest of the Holy Trinity Cathedral created a health group in Armavir., 2020). On 30th March 2020, the members of the community who joined the thematic group in WhatsApp were asked about their opinion about sport spirituality and the practices Igor Biryukov had done with the. The e-survey in the group showed that 180 members of the community were highly satisfied with the initiative and thought that it was highly sufficient. Moreover, 190 participants expressed their willingness to continue to do the activities worked out by Igor Biryukov. Thus, the community keeps on doing their activities of sport spirituality up to the present moment.

All practices of sports spirituality were implemented in compliance with individual safety measures. Primarily, the sport spirituality was carried out on the base of Nordic walking but Igor Biryukov added some other practices which are described below.

Practical Dimension to the Physical Culture

According to Igor Biryukov, physical exercises are a valuable resource for promoting health, coping with stress and improving quality of life, especially under the lockdown and self-isolation but there are a few basic rules to remember (Biryukov, Spirituality. Tradition. Education. Sacred meanings of bodily practices., 2020):

Physical exercises are essential for health. As a founder of the special system of sport spirituality Igor Biryukov follows the provisions expressed by the other specialist in the sphere of physical education (How physical activity improves mood and health., 2020). Walking as a physical exercise is what the neurologists most often give preference to in their recommendations. There are such benefits of walking regularly: brain health: walking counteracts early dementia, reduces the risk of Alzheimer's and improves overall psychological health; improved vision: walking promotes eye wellness and even helps fight glaucoma; strong heart: cardiologists claim that walking is as beneficial as running in terms of combating heart disease or stroke, and reduces the risk of hypertension and strong lungs: walking as an aerobic exercise increases oxygen flow and helps cleanse the lungs. The next benefit is for the pancreas: walking appears to be even more effective in fighting diabetes than running; improved digestion: 30 minutes of walking every day can reduce the risk of colon disease in the future; elastic muscles: muscle tone and weight loss can also be achieved by walking; strong bones and joints: walking for half an hour daily can increase joint mobility, avoid bone loss and even reduce the risk of fractures. Among the benefits of walking is the relief of back pain: walking promotes more efficient blood flow inside the spine and increases its resilience and flexibility. And the most important thing, under the influence of post-COVID social reality, depression resistance: walking helps to adapt to feelings of depression or emotional exhaustion. What's more, the person can go out with a friend or family or alone if it is necessary because of medical reasons.

The Aspects of Sport Spirituality

The developed and implemented spiritual and sports system is built based on the anthropology of traditionalism in the awareness of the hierarchy of one's being, based on the hesychic practices of the Orthodox Church: bodily, bodily-mental, mental-spiritual and spiritual spheres. With the help of simple walks, the individual can become healthier: stop the development of many diseases of the cardiovascular system, get rid of the problems of low blood pressure and decrease in vitality, as well as improve the psycho-emotional sphere, cheer up, help in getting rid of depression, panic attacks, neuroses.

The sport spirituality according to the ideas of Igor Biryukov consists of 4 spheres.

1. Flesh. Regular physical activity of moderate intensity, such as walking or other sports, has significant health benefits. By being more active throughout the day through relatively simple methods, people can reach the recommended levels of activity quite easily. Physical health directly affects individual spiritual health, promotes spiritual vitality and well-being, or, conversely, an oppressed and dull state of mind.

2. Heart. Sensual nature. Gaining psychological stress resistance, interaction with the environment in the process of social adaptation, through group support and interpersonal communication in thematic conversations of various messengers. Consciousness guides the sensual nature in a direction that is socially acceptable and contributes to the improvement of the sensory nature of the flesh.
3. Mind. The presence of inner strength in a person is also characterized by the presence of a strong will. Therefore, a strong-willed person is, as a rule, a strong-willed person. Willpower is the ability of a person to take action, work to achieve his goals. A person always needs to work hard to achieve the desired results, to have the ability to act purposefully, decisively, persistently; overcoming difficulties, achieve their goals, solve the tasks set for themselves (Biryukov, 2019).
4. Spiritual sphere. At different times Christian men of faith tried to establish in themselves a constant and strong memory of God, so that it merged with consciousness, which they called walking before God. Having reached such a state of spiritual life, a person already completes his or her life path with the thought that God is always before him/her and looks at what and how he/she does.

At different times Christian men of faith tried to establish in themselves a constant and strong memory of God, so that it merged with consciousness, which they called walking with God. Having reached such a state of spiritual life, a person already completes his or her life path with the thought that God is always before him/her and looks at what and how he/she does.

Within the system worked out by Igor Biryukov included social support and interpersonal communication in a thematic conversation in WhatsApp which helped the members of the community to be in connection with their spiritual supporter.

The interviewed students expressed positive attitudes after applying the following spiritual and physical methods to overcome the negative aspect of self-isolation. All students were informed about the system of Igor Biryukov in late April. In the course of May, they tried to follow his recommendations. 67% of students also followed the spiritual practices provided by the Russian Orthodox Church but, of course, this part of the system was not obligatory for the youth. The system created of Igor Biryukov was effective for 137 students (87%), 112 students (65%) said that the spiritual component was also beneficial for their physical and emotional health.

Igor Biryukov considers 'sports spirituality' to become a single integral area of humanitarian knowledge, studying the patterns of formation and development of spiritual processes, forms and methods of functioning of the elements of spirituality in sports (Olenich, T., Terarakelyants, V., Shestopalova, O., & Biryukov, I., 2020). Thus, the component of religious belief not only does not interfere with the process of personal formation, but, on the contrary, significantly enriches it, revealing new opportunities and directions of development. The mechanism of socio-cultural practices of sports reality reveals special forms of work, endowed with a religious context. There the humanity gets a fundamental picture of the manifestations of the phenomenon of sports spirituality in the socio-cultural space of various types of individual activities, not only in the historical aspect, but also in the essential aspect (Biryukov, Spirituality. Tradition. Education. Sacred meanings of bodily practices., 2020). As a consequence, the number of these species affecting the entire society, since if people use the indicated parallel between the life cycle of an individual (ontogeny) and the cycle of existence of all mankind (phylogeny), then the contributors can conclude that ideas about the leading modules of physical activity find their expression, existence and interaction not only with the world of an individual, but are also conditioned by the leading meanings of physical activity of all mankind, being the spiritual experience of the distant ancestors (Biryukov, Sports spirituality concept., 2020).

FUTURE RESEARCH DIRECTIONS

Based on the results of the survey, the practical case in Armavir and the application of the sport spirituality activities by the students of DSTU, the present study makes several noteworthy contributions to the methodology for monitoring spiritual and physical health during self-isolation in COVID 19:

- to monitor the delayed results of the delayed results of spiritual and physical development of the student youth, it is advisable to build, on the one hand, special tracking of the procedural side of the life of university communities (activities, communication) and educational activities of teachers, and on the other, special tracking of the individual success of the students;
- when developing and implementing a monitoring program under the conditions of lockdown and self-isolation, it is necessary to combine the general goals and objectives of spiritual and moral development, education and socialization of students, and specific ones, determined by the social environment of the university, traditions, way of the educational organization and other circumstances;
- a set of monitoring measures must not include strict control of the activities carried out by the university teachers and students because the system created by Igor Biryukov is aimed to ensure the processes of spiritual and moral development rather than to provide reporting process with centralized management;
- monitoring should offer simple, online procedures which can be quick and transparent without bureaucratic formalized procedures;
- the proposed monitoring should not significantly increase the volume of work, introduce additional accountability of the university teachers who contribute to the implementation of the tasks of spiritual and moral development for students;
- it is not recommended to assign responsibility for the spiritual and moral development only to the teaching staff of the university because the system is not obligatory for the students. The experiment has shown that to involve the priests to such practices of extracurricular activities can be expedient;
- in the course of monitoring can show various results of spiritual and moral development in a different university, student communities and concerning different students;
- the work provides for a gradual improvement of the monitoring methodology (it is assumed that this tool is gradually introduced into the practice of educational organizations).

These findings enhance the authors' understanding that the toolkit for monitoring the spiritual and moral development has to include the following element: periodic monitoring of the implementation of sport spiritual activities created within Igor Biryukov's system which it is possible to use easily during lockdown and self-isolation; professional and public examination of reports on the provision of spiritual and moral development for the analysis and reflection of the changes that have occurred due to the activities of the sports teachers or consultants in the life of the university, university communities and individual students.

CONCLUSION

The consequences of the Coronavirus pandemic will be 'imprinted on the personality of our nation very long,' predicted Anthony Fauci, the Director of the National Institute of Allergy and Infectious Diseases (Anthony Fauci's security is stepped up as doctor and face of U.S. coronavirus response receives threats, 2020). The authors of the chapter share Dr. Fauci's conclusion that COVID-19 will have a lasting impact on the basic ways people interact between people and the world. Living at a high risk of infection is likely to shape how people perceive themselves concerning their community, their feelings and behaviour, and their overall riskiness. The longer the threat of coronavirus persists, the more these changes may reflect not only changes in momentary behaviour, but also changes in more sustainable aspects of people's personalities.

The presence of COVID-19 and other viruses will directly and forever change future of the education and the principal thing of this changes is understanding the fact that society must be able to adapt quickly to work and study online for any reason and situation. The pandemic has forced colleges and universities across the country - and around the world - to start online learning.

In conditions of such unpredictable crisis, the idea of sports spirituality becomes especially relevant. There is a shift in emphasis from the competitive plane to the plane of personal development and transcendence. Physical culture activity receives an existential beginning both in the bodily aspect, health and strengthening of the body and in the spiritual - psychological stability and spiritual self-discipline (Olenich, T., Terarakelyants, V., Shestopalova, O., & Biryukov, I., 2020).

With this consideration of sports activities that affect national relations, social status, fashion, ethical values, as well as the way of life of individuals, it becomes clear that sport includes all the achievements accumulated in the process of social and historical practice. Sports spirituality is interesting as a social phenomenon, namely, its special place in sports activities, in various forms of human life, including sports practices within religious systems and religious practices within sports communities (Jirásek, 2018); spiritual culture in social life based on physical culture and sports activities; activities of religious and sports unions, organizations; the sociological dynamics of the development of various processes, international relations (Trothen, 2019) etc.

Physical activity is beneficial not only to the physiological processes of the body but also significantly affects the inner content of a person, his or her spiritual work. Initially considering the pilgrimage practices of movement, the authors can consider the inner aspect and spiritual meaning of walking before God as a special prayer accomplishment on the path of communion with God, filling physical activity with a rethinking of the patristic heritage and its fruitful application in modern conditions (Biryukov, Sports spirituality concept., 2020). All social reality and especially the spiritual sphere stems from the qualitative organization of metaphysical space. The driving force behind this will be the desire to acquire the greatest spiritual volume. All this functional complex of sports spirituality provides a universal preventive form of bodily-spiritual work to resist Coronavirus infection.

Based on the analysis of theoretical approaches to the social changes for the student youth as well as practical usage of sport spirituality as a proposed method of adaptation for students influenced by COVID-2019 and self-isolation, the authors can state that the hypotheses put forward in the research process was confirmed: the development of sport spirituality and the practical experience of Armavir health group as well as the experience of the students of DSTU can be a useful tool to overcome the consequences of COVID-2019.

An essential practical result is also the fact that sport spirituality (in the version of Igor Biryukov's system) can be put into the practical usage of universities within the condition of permanent lockdowns and periodical self-isolation periods and it potentially contributes to:

- - increasing interest in physical education and sports among students who do not pay attention to physical activity;
- attracting a large number of people who are still in search of a good method to cope with traumatic consequences of post-COVID society, thanks to the spread of these ideas among family members, relatives and friend;
- an increase in the number of those students who give up smoking, drinking alcohol and having drugs thanks to an integrated approach to personality;
- creation of optimal conditions for versatile psychophysical training and passing the standards of the Russian Sport;
- sport spirituality can familiarize those people who are not Orthodox but who like sport with Orthodox culture and traditions;
- sport spirituality based on Igor Biryukov's system can be a universal tool for the establishment of social contacts, as well as joint leisure and active recreation not only for student youth but for all social groups;
- sport spirituality can be used as a social glue that keeps society together based on the formation of an Orthodox worldview and a healthy lifestyle.

Thus, the study of post-COVID adaptation methods used by Russian student youth in the process of self-isolation has proved the initial hypothesis stated in the paper. It was verified in the course of research that lockdown and self-isolation affected the youth badly and caused some traumatic psychological and physical consequences. It is increasingly recognized that lockdown and self-isolation have become permanent social phenomena and there is a high risk of their repetition. During lockdown sport, spirituality can be an effective method to adapt to the situation not only for student youth but also for adults. Sport spirituality in the form worked out by Igor Biryukov is aimed at realizing the importance of a healthy lifestyle in life of an individual during the transformational period in social reality. Sport spirituality has the potential to widen an individual's worldview, openness and physical fit. There is an effective and it has an increasing impact on the personality of a young person, as well as educational measures about the national, cultural characteristics of Russian society.

REFERENCES

Altbach, P., & de Wit, H. (2020, April 4). Post pandemic outlook for HE is bleakest for the poorest. *University World News*. Retrieved from https://www.universityworldnews.com/post.php?story=20200402152914362

Anthony Fauci's security is stepped up as doctor and face of U.S. coronavirus response receives threats. (2020, April 2). *The Washington Post*. Retrieved from https://www.washingtonpost.com/politics/anthony-faucis-security-is-stepped-up-as-doctor-and-face-of-us-coronavirus-response-receives-threats/2020/04/01/ff861a16-744d-11ea-85cb-8670579b863d_story.html

Biryukov, I. (2019). Sports spirituality as a subject of theological and philosophical consideration. *Servis+, 4.* Retrieved from: https://cyberleninka.ru/article/n/sportivnaya-duhovnost-kak-predmet-teologo-filosofskogo-rassmotreniya

Biryukov, I. (2020). *Spirituality. Tradition. Education. Sacred meanings of bodily practices*. EPD AGPU.

Biryukov, I. (2020). *Sports spirituality concept*. EPD ASPU.

Butz, D., & Slautina, I. (2020). Formation of a student's personality during a pandemic. Pedagogical sciences: Questions of theory and practice, 170-172.

Bykhovets, K., Kogan-Lerner, L. (2020). The COVID-19 pandemic as a multifactorial traumatic situation. *Social and Economic Psychology, 2*(18), 291-308.

Chong, D., & Druckman, J.N. (2007). Framing theory. *Annual Review of Political Science, 10*, 103-126. . doi:10.1146/annurev.polisci.10.072805.103054

COVID-19 Coronavirus Pandemic. (2020).https://www.worldometers.info/coronavirus/?

COVID-19 Dashboard by the Center for Systems Science and Engineering. (2020). https://coronavirus.jhu.edu/map.html

Cultural-historical activity psychology in extreme situation: the pandemic challenge. (2020). *Chelovek, 4,* 7-40.

De Vreese, C. (2005). News framing: Theory and typology. *News Framing: Theory and Typology*, 13(1), 51-62.

Entman, R. (2004). *Proyection of Power. Framing News, public opinión and U.S. Foreign Policy*. University of Chicago Press.

Gafurov, I., Ibragimov, G., Kalimullin, A. & Alishev, T. (2020). Transforming Higher Education During a Pandemic: Pain Points. *Higher Education in Russia, 10,* 101-112.

How physical activity improves mood and health. (2020). *Armavirskij sobesednik*.

Jirásek, I. (2018). Religion and Spirituality in Sport. In *Oxford Research Encyclopedia of Psychology*. Retrieved from https://oxfordre.com/psychology/view/10.1093/acrefore/9780190236557.001.0001/acrefore-9780190236557-e-149

Karpinskaya, E. (2020). COVID-19: Effects for Higher Education. *Russian International Affairs Council: analytics and commentary.* Retrieved from https://russiancouncil.ru/analytics-and-comments/analytics/covid-19-effekty-dlya-vysshego-obrazovaniya/#short

Olenich, T., Terarakelyants, V., Shestopalova, O., & Biryukov, I. (2020). Sport spirituality as an educational innovation (evidenced-based study). *E3S Web Conference: Innovative Technologies in Science and Education.*

Semetko, H., & Valkenburg, P. (2000). Framing European Politics: A Content Analysis of Press and Television News. *Journal of Communication, 50*, 93–109.

Society and Pandemic: Experience and Lessons from COVID-19 Fighting in Russia. (2020). IPK Pareto-Print LLC.

The priest of the Holy Trinity Cathedral created a health group in Armavir. (2020). *Armavirskij sobesednik*.

The storm of the first weeks: how higher education stepped into the reality of a pandemic. (2020). National Research University Higher School of Economics.

Titov, A. (2020). Distance learning in self-isolation. *Actual Scientific Research in the Modern World, 5*(61),128-130.

Trothen, T. (2019). Sport, Spirituality, and Religion: New Intersections and Global Challenges. *Religions, 10*, 1–8.

Zalewska, J. (2019). Practice Theory Revisited: How Flexible Meta-habit Complements Habitus. *Polish Sociological Review, 205*, 65–84.

KEY TERMS AND DEFINITIONS

Adaptation: Restructuring of the individual's psyche under the influence of objective environmental factors, as well as the person's ability to adapt to various environmental requirements without feeling internal discomfort and without conflict with the environment.

COVID-2019: A contagious disease caused by severe acute respiratory syndrome coronavirus 2 (SARS-CoV-2) which caused a global pandemic, lockdown and self-isolation in most countries in the world.

Education Technology: It is a system of interaction between a teacher and students, the basis of which is a specific concept defined by the goal, objectives, principles, content, methods and means of teaching.

Healthcare: A public sector that organizes and ensures the protection of public health and is a combination of political, economic, social, legal, scientific, medical, sanitary and hygienic, anti-epidemic and cultural measures aimed at preserving and strengthening the physical and mental health of each person, maintaining a healthy life and the provision of medical care for deteriorating health.

Lockdown: A restrictive policy which stipulates limitation of social life for people, local community or the whole nation due to specific risks to themselves or others to fall ill with COVID-2019 if they can move and interact freely.

Pandemic: An unusually strong epidemic that spread across countries and continents, covering the vast majority of the world.

Self-Isolation: It is abstaining from contact with others to reduce the risk of infection.

Sport Spirituality: An educational innovation manifested itself as a set of specific communicative techniques associated with mental processes of individual (cognitive and emotional-volitional), such as thinking, memory, attention, feelings, which in the process of sports activities were aimed at developing interest in a healthy lifestyle and adherence to social rules in the process of physical education and sports. Sport spirituality is aimed at realizing the importance of a healthy lifestyle in life and a person's worldview, openness and desire for cooperation with many sports organizations and associations, and, consequently, the attention of the clergy to this area and the training of specialized personnel.

Chapter 10
Pandemic Stress Caused by the Infodemic Among Youngsters and the Elderly Population

Natavan Karamova
Western Caspian University, Azerbaijan

ABSTRACT

The modern world is facing the acute captivity of pandemics. Despite the modern world's technological and scientific development, the fact that the coronavirus has appeared to be stronger, infects people regardless of their social status, place of residence, financial status, origin, intellectual level, and most importantly, age, seems to be unbelievable. However, the situation is much more complicated especially when the number of deaths increases, and it enslaves almost the world's whole population. Causing certain stress, the pandemic has changed the lifestyles, and education and scientific works are not exceptions. All these changes have their consequences and influence, which are presented in the chapter. Moreover, it reflects the results of Infodemia during the pandemic stress and deals with the psychophysiological indicators of students and scientific circles.

INTRODUCTION

The "coronavirus pandemic" can easily be called the 'tragedy of the century'. In fact, the change in lifestyle that people have been accustomed to for centuries, long homestays, work from home, the transition to online education system, the impossibility of living with national traditions (parties, weddings, mourning ceremonies, etc.), closed cinemas, theaters, bans on sports competitions, etc., naturally, requires adaptation to the new environment, and before this takes place, there is a state of stress emerges, which leads to abnormal psychophysiological indicators, deterioration of health indicators, etc. and causes other pathologies.

A new coronavirus - Coronavirus 2019 (COVID-19), declared a pandemic by the World Health Organization (WHO) on March 11, 2020, has infected more than 4 million people and killed 300,000 people in 188 countries (World Health Organization, 2020). Global efforts continue to create effective

DOI: 10.4018/978-1-7998-7164-4.ch010

therapy for this disease and develop vaccine. Coronavirus 2 (SARS-CoV-2) with increasingly severe acute respiratory syndrome was also detected before. This virus has different and similar features with the viruses we know (Fehr & Perlman, 2015). In fact, these new types of coronaviruses (+) have the largest genomes among viruses with single-stranded RNA genome. The adaptation of viruses in the host organism depends largely on the length of the viral genome. Viruses with small genomes are usually protected by a strong cover. Viruses with large genomes, on the other hand, are more pathogenic and contagious, and have the ability to infect more than one host organism. RNA viruses themselves are divided into 2 groups (+) and (-). (+) RNA chain viruses encode own proteins directly, and the (-) RNA chain must be converted to (+) chain RNA in order to encode the protein because it is a negative copy. This is an additional stage for the reproduction of viruses (Fehr, Perlman, 2015; Leung et. al., 2020; Stadnytskyi, Bax, Bax, Anfinrud, 2020; Richard, Fouchier, 2020).

Coronaviruses include the Nidovirales order, the Coronaviridae family, and the Coronavirinae subfamily. The subfamily includes four genera: Alphacoronavirus, Betacoronavirus, Gammacoronavirus, and Deltacoronavirus. Based on molecular clock analysis on the genomic region of RNA-dependent RNA polymerase (RdRp), scientists believe that the common ancestor of the four coronavirus genes (tMRCA) appeared in 8100 BC. The MRCA of alphacoronavirus, betacoronavirus, gammacoronavirus, and deltacoronavirus was estimated to have appeared around 2400, 3300, 2800, and 3000 BC, respectively. Furthermore, there are assumptions that the history of the natural evolution of coronaviruses has not been properly assessed, and that the history of the coronavirus is older than previous estimations. Coronaviruses like many DNA and RNA viruses, such as herpesviruses, lentiviruses, bornaviruses, filoviruses, and foamy viruses have ancient viral lineage. (Kutter, Spronken, Fraaij, Fouchier, Herfst, 2018; Leung et al., 2020; Richard, Fouchier, 2016).

Different coronaviruses exhibit different host spectra and tissue tropism. Alphacoronavirus and betacoronavirus are commonly transmitted to mammals. In contrast, gammacoronoviruses and deltacoronaviruses can infect birds and fish, and some mammals. By 2019, six coronaviruses were known to infect humans and cause acute respiratory disease. HCoV-229E, HCoV-OC43, HCoV-NL63, and HKU1 cause mild infections of upper respiratory tract, and in rare cases, some of them can cause severe infections in infants, young children, and the elderly. A type of coronavirus identified in 2003, SARS (Severe acute respiratory syndrome), causes atypical pneumonia transmitted by bats. The SARS virus was first reported in Asia and then spread to other continents. The World Health Organization (WHO) has determined that the virus is a new type of coronavirus and named it SARS-CoV. It is estimated that ~ 8,000 people were infected with the virus, and 10% died. Another type of coronaviruses, MERS virus, was identified in the Middle East in September 2012, and Novel Coronavirus 2012 was officially named as Middle East respiratory syndrome coronavirus (MERS-CoV) (Tellier, 2009; Richard, Fouchier, 2020).

The virus, originally named 2019-nCoV by WHO and SARS-CoV-2 (severe acute respiratory syndrome coronavirus-2) by the International Committee on Virus Taxonomy, being a new strain of coronaviruses is also known as Uhan coronavirus, Uhan seafood market pneumonia virus and Uhan pneumonia. The genetic sequence of the new coronavirus genome, a single-stranded RNA virus, has been read. The virus is at least 70% genetically similar to the SARS-CoV virus (also known as atypical pneumonia), which causes severe acute respiratory syndrome. The incubation period of the new coronavirus lasts from 2 days to 10-15 days, and the disease becomes contagious before the onset of symptoms (Richard & Fouchier, 2020).

There are several ways thought which the viruses can spread from person to person. Particles carrying the virus can be a source of danger for people to get infected through coughing, sneezing, hand

and face contact with the source of infection, and the normal breathing of an infected person adound (Kutter, Spronken, Fraaij, Fouchier, Herfst, 2018; Stadnytskyi, Bax, Bax, Anfinrud, 2020). These viral spread mechanisms typically produce large droplets and small aerosols of 5 microns in size to characterize excellent diffusion efficiency and duration of exposure to air, as well as sedimentation patterns along the human respiratory tract. (Fehr, Perlman, 2015; Zhang et al., 2015). The virus is transmitted directly (to humans) or indirectly (infection of surrounding objects); transmitted by live contact and air (droplets and aerosols) (Zhang, Zhang,Wang, Molina. 2020). Large droplets spread easily through the air, infecting people or surrounding objects; on the contrary, aerosols spread very quickly in the air and create conditions for new infections. While direct or indirect transmission occurs over short distances, aerosol transmission can occur over long distances and over time. Of course, when people breathe in viral air, they can be considered potentially infected.

I do not want to talk in detail about the ways of spreading the coronavirus and the symptoms of the disease. The main purpose of this article is to present the results of a study of the negative effects of pandemic stress on humans. The COVID-19 pandemic has had serious socio-economic consequences since the Great Depression, which affected about 265 million people, and the largest global recession since the Great Famine. It has led to the postponement or cancellation of many sporting, religious, political and cultural events and increased extensive supply shopping. Schools, universities and colleges, in general or locally, were closed in 172 countries, which cover about 98.5% of the world's school-age population. Misinformation about the virus has spread on social networks and the media. There are cases of xenophobia and discrimination against the Chinese people and those perceived as Chinese or the highly infected areas (Kutter & Spronken, 2018).

However, the coronavirus pandemic continues to enslave the population, especially those aged 0-18 and over 60 years. In fact, the most sensitive to this disease are people of the mentioned ages. According to the WHO Rules of Procedure, due to the pandemic, people with acute respiratory infections should stay at home, minimize contact with family members and unknown persons, and isolate themselves as soon as they feel any signs of the disease. The spread of coronavirus disease (COVID-19) in the world is already known to cause fear, anxiety, stress and depression in humans. The stress depends on the level of reaction to the event, past life experiences, character, temperament and the society in which we live.

Several factors can specifically cause stress during the spread of an infectious disease:

- Fear and anxiety about own health and the health of relatives;
- Changes in sleep pattern or in diet (insomnia and loss of appetite);
- Difficulty concentrating on work and other issues;
- Severity of other diseases;
- Increased use of alcohol, tobacco, energy drinks or other addictive substances;
- Predominance of sedentary life for days and hypokinesia, etc.

Broken daily habits of people lead to a number of changes. The biggest change is the disruption of circadian clock. At this case, psychological problems such as insomnia, fatigue, stress arise. Furthermore, staying at home for long time, not being able to meet friends, and losing one's freedom can lead to emotional distress and depression. Thinking persistently about the possibility of catching coronavirus causes fear and anxiety. According to studies, it is known that the maximum level of fear and anxiety in the quarantine regime is likely to fall to the minimum level 4-6 months after the quarantine regime.

However, some psychological problems such as depression, post-traumatic stress, and sleep disorders can occur during both quarantine and post-quarantine periods.

Demographic factors (age, gender, marital status, intellectual level, etc.) play a role in the emergence of psychological problems. Studies show that compared to men women are twice as likely to be depressed, that children are more likely to be affected by traumatic events than adults, that people with low intellectual levels are more likely to believe inadequate information, and that the influence of demographic factors is not insignificant (Levy, 2007; Salat, 2001).

As we have note that, people over the age of 60 suffer the most during a pandemic, both due to their susceptibility to the disease and due to their social isolation. Given that, this group of people have higher incidence of cardiovascular disease, diabetes, joint disease and other somatic diseases, weak immunity and difficulty in adapting to the environment are among the most pressing problems. In addition to causing stress, the pandemic itself contributes to the development of stress symptoms. In fact, in conditions of social isolation, older people are mostly sitting motionless, watching TV, lying down or eating. On normal days, the elderly and long-lived, who leave home at least 2-3 times a day, for walk in the park, green areas, social facilities, socialize with their peers, take care for their grandchildren and participate in solution of household problems. However, currently they are locked at houses, which cause certain problem for their nervous and digestive systems, particularly they suffer from loneliness and abnormal metabolism, lack of sunbathing and oxygen intake, which are important for the cardiovascular, skin and nervous system, ensures joint mobility with regular and repetitive walks, avoids depression and neuropsychiatric stress, etc.

Studies have shown that the long-lived leading active life in rural areas have better health indicators than the long-lived residing in urban areas. In the current situation, there is still no serious threat to the health of old people living in villages and districts (Levy, 2007). The fact that they are still engaged in their ordinary and daily life activities, have backyards, are engaged in agriculture, and less likely to be infected in rural areas, live in the same environment with their children and grandchildren, have natural diet, stable sleep regime allows them to safely get out of the pandemic stress situation (Alperovich, 2002; Anisimov, 2003).

The elderlies living in cities, however, face the loss of health indicators against the background of increasing special quarantine regime. Factors such as living in small-size and high-rise buildings, limited mobility, abundance of information, uninterrupted close contact with sources of electromagnetic radiation, low nutritional value (lack of vitamins, minerals, etc.) (Berdyshev, 2003) and weight gain from high calorie, eating or sleeping disorders, social isolation, etc. can lead to the development and aggression of cardiovascular disease, neuropsychiatric stress, the development of endocrine diseases, aggravation of bone and joint diseases, hypoxia and depression, anemia, hypovitaminosis and increased cerebrovascular disease in the elderly (Anisimov, 2003). We conducted a series of personal experiments to investigate the mentioned situation. No compare the level of stress we took two groups of difference generations: elderlies and youngsters. The first group of studies was conducted among the elderlies and the long-lived, and the second group of studies was conducted among the students (Anisimov, 2003; Litvinova et al., 2011; Doremalen et al., 2020; Plotnikova, 2011).

The city of Sumgayit has recently celebrated its 70th anniversary. First of all, I want to tell about the history of the city. Sumgayit was granted the status of city on November 22, 1949. The first settlement in the present territory of the city dates back to the IX century AD. There are historical monuments of that period protected by the state in the territory. Sumgayit is located in thc north of the Absheron Peninsula, 25 km north of the capital Baku. Its area is 108.6 square kilometers.

It is the second industrial city in our republic due to its potential. It has a significant share in the countryəs economy. Sumgayit has large industrial enterprises, construction companies, service and engineering communications, and complex infrastructure.

It was once called the city of youth. Because those who laid the foundation of the city and its first inhabitants were young people. Later, Sumgayit gained new names: industrial city, city of chemists, city of construction workers, ecologically polluted city, city with the only children cemetery in the country, and so on. Now new projects are underway to turn Sumgayit into a free economic zone.

Sumgayit has the most catastrophic environment among Azerbaijan cities. On average, 96,500 tons of harmful substances are released into the air every year. The Aluminum Plant is located 2 km from the city, and most of the toxic substances fall to this Plant. In addition, the "Chemical Industry" Production Unit has played a big role in ecological destruction in Sumgayit. Sumgayit is the only city where 3 enterprises produce chlorine. According to the Resolution of the Council of Ministers No. 567 of July 18, 1991, no chemical plant was to be built in Sumgayit. Nevertheless, since then, 'EP-300' at the Synthesis Rubber Association, 'Polymer-120' at the "Uzvisintez" PU and other enterprises have been built and put into operation. Furthermore, asphalt production plant was built and put into operation at the entrance to the city. Unfortunately, these or other enterprises were constructed without the permission of the relevant authorities (sanitary epidemiological station, nature protection committee, etc.). In addition, the construction of these enterprises had been suffering from grave defects in the projects. Harmful substances emitted into the atmosphere cover the whole city by the wind. From this point of view, of such companies as "Inshaatchilar" and "Kimyatikinti" settlements are in worse situation.

In fact, Sumgayit city has become one of the most tense ecological regions in the world. Numerous shortcomings in the organization of planning and control in placement, construction and operation of enterprises, in some cases, the fact that the city has become a testing ground for harmful technologies, which has no analogues in the world, has been among the main causes of environmental tensions. Conditionally, the history of Sumgayit's ecological life can be divided into several stages. The period from the years of Second World War to the 1970s can be considered as the first stage. During this period, the city's industrial infrastructure was almost fully formed, and most of today's large enterprises had already put into operation. However, even the design of any enterprise did not provide for environmental protection measures, all the wastes of enterprises operating only on the principle of increasing production were released into the environment without any changes. The next stage covers the 1970s and 1990s. During this period, ecology and nature protection came up to agenda. With the serious efforts of the Republic's leadership and the demands before the union authorities, centralized financing of environmental measures was launched. Up to 180 gas dust cleaners in the enterprises, 23 local water treatment plants with a total capacity of 360 thousand m^3/day, a city water treatment plant with a total capacity of 182 thousand m^3/day, which allowed to save 2 thousand m^3 of water per day and which was the most powerful water cycle system, was constructed and put into operation. Recycling technologies for 60 types of toxic industrial wastes with an amount of up to 170,000 tons out more than 300,000 tons annual toxic wastes were mastered. However, in parallel to such activities, the intensive and extensive construction and commissioning of environmentally harmful industrial facilities in Sumgayit by the Soviet Union's decisions sometimes reduced the effectiveness of environmental measures and sometimes negated this effect. For this reason, environmental tensions continued in a number of areas. Therefore, environmental tensions continued in a number of areas. In fact, since no enterprise has the conditions for storage of solid industrial waste, about 5 thousand tons of industrial wastes were dumped in the area, the volume of extremely high levels of wastewater reached 600 thousand m^3 per year, the average annual background concentration of all pollutants in the atmosphere of the city and even residential areas exceeded sanitary norms by 5-10 times, the health of the population set the Union records for premature mortality and morbidity. With the occupation of the lands of our Republic by Armenians and the arrival of 10,000 refugees in the city, the socio-ecological problems deepened, and the financing of environmental measures was challenged. The modern period is characterized by a lot of work done during the independence of our Republic, especially in recent years to resolve the environmental problems of Sumgayit. Along with the operation of important industrial plants in modern Sumgayit, modern environmental equipment is installed. Although incomplete, the environmental measures are giving results for the air in Sumgayit to be relatively clean. Currently, the main environmental problems of Sumgayit are environmental pollution, unauthorized mass destruction of green areas in some cases, unauthorized use of sea sand by construction companies, etc. Furthermore, the use of 1970s facilities at some plants in Sumgayit and their non-compliance with modern standards, as well as the direct discharge of waste into the sea, create environmental tensions in the city. Harmful wastes accumulated by the chemical industry in Sumgayit since the Soviet era still have negative impact on the health of the population and the environment. Environmental problems in Sumgayit are related to the reduction of waste, wastewater, shrinking of greeneries per land and per capita. Most of the waste released into the environment in Sumgayit is carbon dioxide. These include hazardous sulfur oxides, fluorine hydride, hydrogen fluoride and other toxic wastes emitted into the atmosphere by the Aluminum Plant. In Sumgayit, a large amount of hazardous waste is discharged into the Caspian Sea without treatment. The vast majority of environmental problems in Sumgayit are inherited from the Soviet era. Even in one of the recent monitoring, a tense environmental situation was observed in Sumgayit and surrounding areas. The population of the city cannot breathe at night due to the effects of toxic gases (Karamova, Gasimov & Teymurova, 2018; Ahmadov & Veziroglu, 2003).

In 2012, travel.ninemsn.com.au identified seven of the world's most polluted cities. Unfortunately, Sumgayit, one of the largest industrial cities in Azerbaijan, was ranked first in this list. Although Sumgayit, the third largest city in Azerbaijan, was considered as a resort city when it was built, the former Soviet Union leadership turned the city into a center for the production of chemicals for unknown reasons. Even before the collapse of the USSR, the city was not considered as a city with the clean environment and was in one of the 'top' places for infant mortality in the former USSR. Despite the reduction of chemical waste in recent years and the closure of factories that emit toxic waste into the skies of Sumgayit has decreased early deaths, especially infant mortality, the only children's cemetery in the country was built in Sumgayit in 1980. Although the number of child deaths is currently declining, the city ranked first in the region in the number of child deaths from 1984 to 1996. The reason is that the environmental situation was critical: the number of stillbirths, as well as the number of deaths of disabled and weak children had increased. Due to this, the establishment of the children's cemetery turned urgent. Thousands of children have been buried here, and this figure is one of the facts that proves how environmentally stressful the life is in Sumgait.

The study of longevity in such kind of stressful environment is commendable itself. The study of pandemic stress in the long-lived is a topical issue of the modern time (Karamova, Gasimov & Teymurova, 2018).

Despite certain efforts to eliminate the above-described conditions the environmental tensions continue. It worth saying that in spite of the fact that some certain improvements have been observed, however the health status of the population and the longevity index of the population in Sumgayit are very low. The results of our personal studies have proved this.

THE COURSE OF THE FIRST GROUP OF STUDIES AND THE OBTAINED RESULTS

Long-lived people living in Sumgait have been the object of the study since 2012. The age of the long-lived participants in the study ranged from 90 to 105. In fact, we divided the long-lived into two groups according to their period of residence in Sumgait:

1. Those who have lived in Sumgait for at least 50-55 years.
2. Refugees from the Republic of Armenia and IDPs from the formerly occupied territories of Nagorno-Karabakh during 1988-1994 and settled in Sumgait temporarily.

In fact, there are 49 long-lived in the first group and 32 in the second group (90-105 years old). At the same time, 41 old (75-89 years old) and 75 elderly people (65-74 years old) were involved in the study.

Study Method

Comprehensive study methods were used during the studies:

1. Measurement of systolic and diastolic blood pressure by the Korotkov method;
2. Determination of heart rate per minute by palpation;
3. Measurement of lung capacity with "Asta Medica" Peak Flow Meter;
4. Among psychological anxiety indicators, determination of the situational and individual anxiety by the Spielberger-Khanin test, the general anxiety by the Taylor test, and the depression level by the depression scale (Nemov, 2001);
5. Among cognitive indicators, determination of the short-term memory by the "Number Memory Test", the visual memory by the "Image Memory Test", the auditory memory by the Luria's "10 words" test, the attention level by the "Insufficient detail" test;
6. Calculation of vegetative index of Kerdo;
7. Assessment of mental status by MMSE test;
8. Determination of the attention level, logical comprehension and non-verbal intelligence by the Roven's test of increasing difficulty.

The studies was conducted before the pandemic, in 2012-2019 and during the pandemic in May-October 2020.

The Results of the First Group of Studies

In the studies conducted before the pandemic, psychophysiological indicators of long-lived were closer to normal than in the elderlies. In fact, initially, we tested the situational and individual excitement of the long-lived with the Spielberger-Khanin test. It was found that in the first group of the long-lived, situational anxiety was 35.32 ± 3.54 points, individual anxiety was 35.29 ± 2.78 points, and general anxiety was 24.73 ± 4.32 points. In the second group of long-lived, situational anxiety was 44.83 ± 2.87 points, individual anxiety was 46.71 ± 3.18 points, and general anxiety was 39.42 ± 3.74 points (Figure 1). The analysis of the results showed that, while the first group had moderate levels of anxiety, the second group of the long-lived had high levels of anxiety. The level of depression in the first group was 48.54 ± 3.67 points, and in the second group it was 56.64 ± 4.23 points (the norm is 50 points), which indicates the presence of neurotic depression in the second group.

Figure 1. Psychological and emotional indicators of the long-lived people living in Sumgayit. SA - situational anxiety, IA - individual anxiety, GA - general anxiety, D - depression indicator

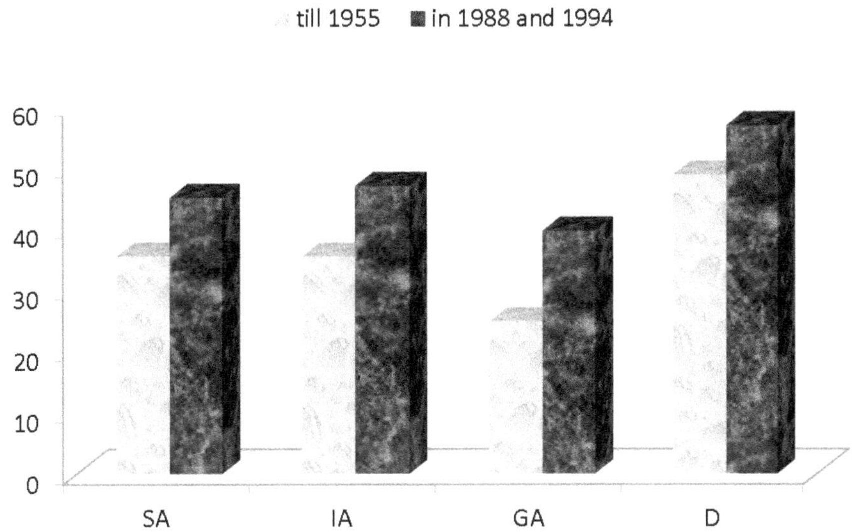

One of the main goals of the research was the study of cognitive processes. In the first group, visual memory was 7.4 ± 2.33 points, auditory memory was 6.1 ± 3.2 points, short-term memory was 6.3 ± 3.34 points, attention was 6.8 ± 2.88 points. In the second group, visual memory was 9.5 ± 2.53 points, auditory memory was 6.58 ± 2.67 points, short-term memory was 5.1 ± 2.4 points, and attention was 5.3 ± 1.81 points. During the analysis of the results, taking into account that the normative limit of visual memory is 6 points, it was found that the second group of long-lived people showed much higher results than the norm. While the hearing and short-term memory test scores were 7, both groups performed below normal. In the attention test, the norm was 6 points, and while the first group showed a result close to the norm, the second group showed a sharply lower level of attention (Figure 2).

The most interesting results were obtained during the determination of non-verbal intelligence by the Roven test. In fact, the first group of long-lived people scored 116.75 ± 4.2 points during testing, and the second group scored 87.93 ± 3.78 points (Figure 3). Intellectual levels are determined based on points scored between 1-9. According to the norm, 115-128 points characterize the 7th intellectual level, and 87-100 points characterize the 5th intellectual level, the first group showed the result belonging to the 7th level, and the second group showed the result of the 5th level.

Figure 2. Cognitive indicators of long-lived living in Sumgayit. VM - visual memory, AM -auditory memory, STM - short-term memory, AI - attention indicator.

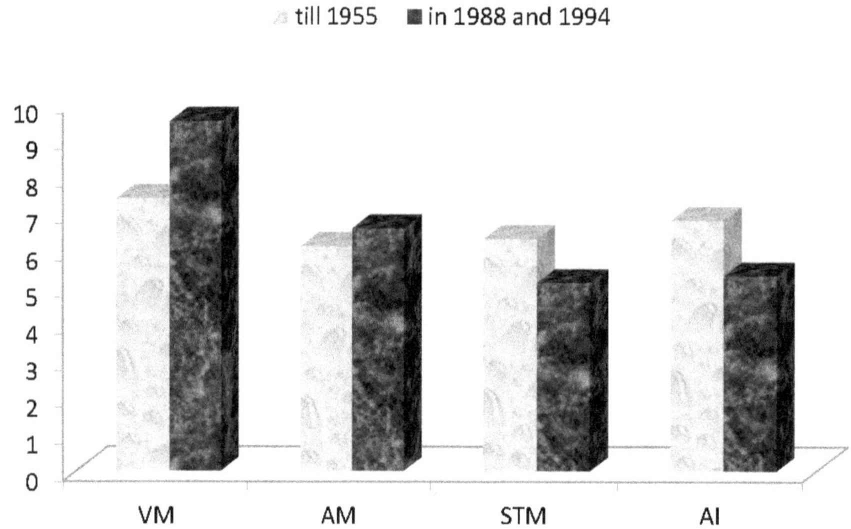

Figure 3. Intellectual level of long-lived people in Sumgait (according to the Roven test).

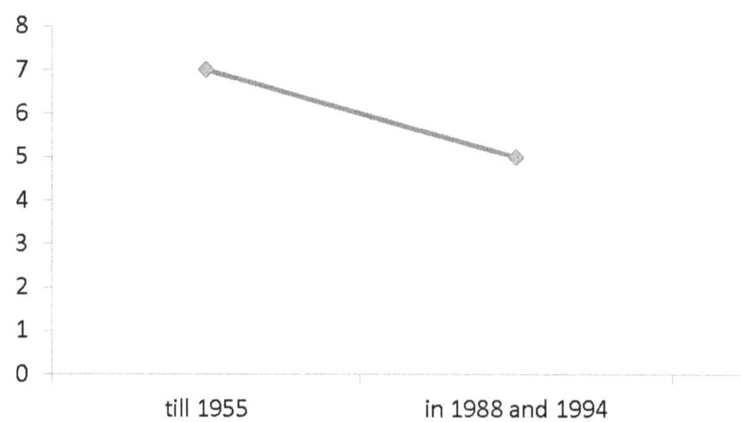

In addition to the above-described facts, blood pressure levels and heart rate were studied, and VCI was determined based on them. The results showed that systolic blood pressure in the first group was 152.06±4.67 mmHg, diastolic blood pressure was 88.15 ± 5.1 mmHg, and heart rate was 75.39±3.89 beats per minute. In the second group, systolic blood pressure was 145.85±3.88 mmHg, diastolic blood pressure was 87.29±4.76 mmHg, and heart rate was 74±2.79 beats per minute (Figure 4).

The advantage of the parasympathetic nervous system in both groups of long-lived was determined during the calculation of VIK (Figure 5).

The air capacity of the lungs in the long-lived was also measured. It was found that in long-lived lung air capacity is 365.69 L/min (Figure 6).

Figure 4. Blood pressure and heart rate of long-lived people in Sumgayit. SBP - systolic blood pressure (mm.Hg), DBP - diastolic blood pressure (mm.Hg), HR-Heart rate (per minute)

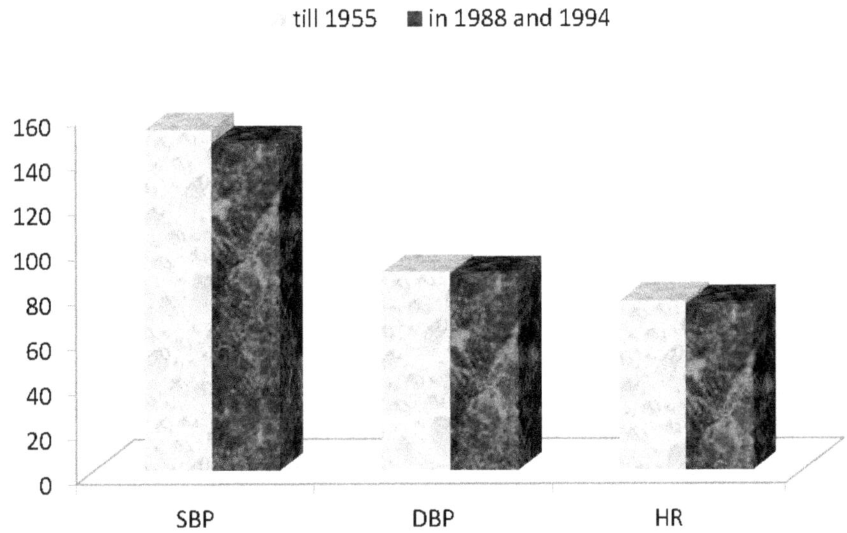

Figure 5. Results of the vegetative Kerdo index.

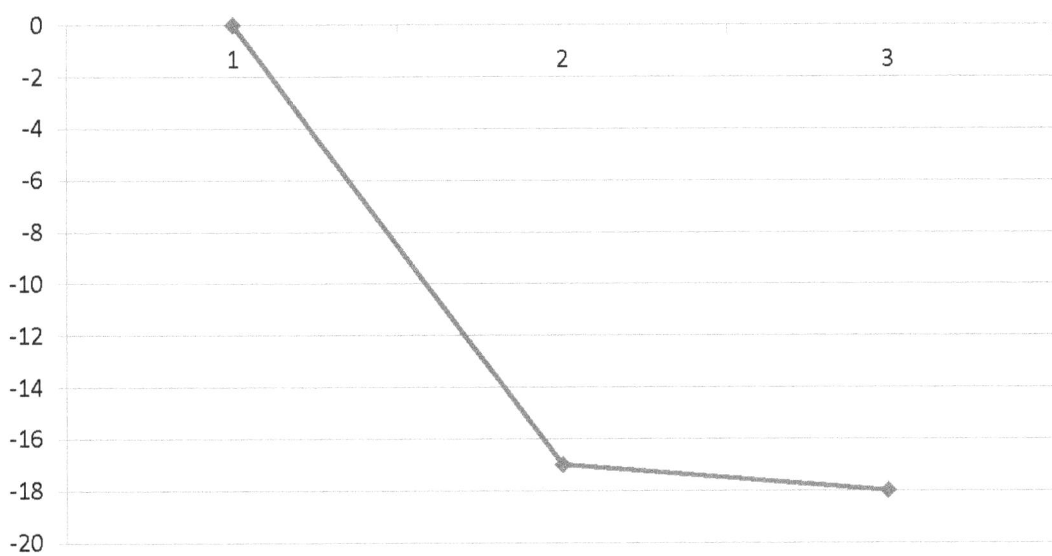

Summarizing the results of the studies, it can be concluded that the harsh environmental conditions in Sumgait or in any others country have seriously affected long-lived and led to decline of health indicators below the norm. This manifests itself the weakening of cognitive and psychophysiological processes. In fact, it should be taken into account that the majority of long-lived people studied have lived in the western part of Azerbaijan for most of their lives, and many of them have inherited the longevity.

Figure 6. Graphic description of lung capacity in long-lived (L/min).

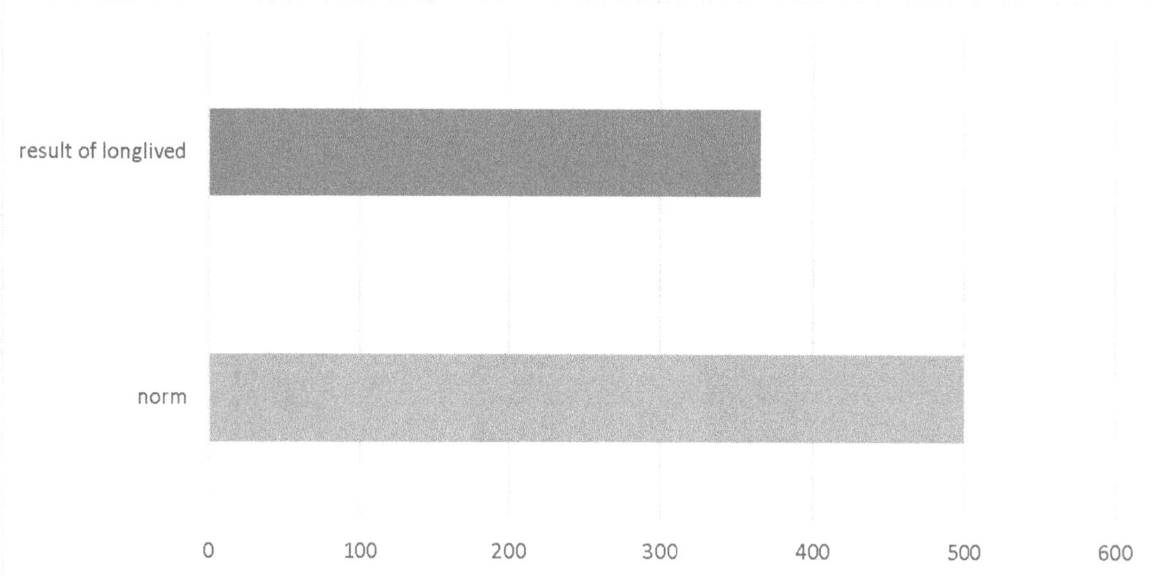

One of the main reasons for dividing the long-lived people in Sumgait into two groups is their length of stay in Sumgait, and the second reason is the difference in the results. In fact, the high level of anxiety in long-lived who moved to Sumgait in 1988 and 1994 is related to numerous factors such as their stressful conditions, the results of the war. Here we can say that the forced separation from their homeland and living environment, moving from the countryside to the environmentally polluted city of Sumgait, suffering severe losses of their relatives, nutritional conditions and change of diet have their negative impacts over their health. As I have already mentioned, most of them are known to be inherited the longevity. However, when the family history was researched, it revealed the information that their children were not as lucky as their ancestors were: they were already seriously ill and died young. According to this fact, we can claim that unfortunately, the number of long-lived will decline sharply in the nearest future (Levy, 2007).

During the analysis of cognitive indicators in the first group of long-lived indicators were observed to comply with the norm compared to the second group. The main reason for this can be attributed to the predominance of intellectuals among the first group of long-lived people, even at this age, some of them read regularly. In the second group of long-lived, on the contrary, the fact that physical and vegetative indicators are close to the norm may be related to their engagement in physical labor and the fresh air and energetic natural foods they enjoyed for many years (Anisimov, 2003; Plotnikova, 2011; Salat, 2001).

The results of research conducted in Sumgait again prove that favorable climatic conditions, fresh air and especially rural conditions, nutrition, and most importantly, living without changing the environment, have serious impact on longevity (Karamova, Gasimov, Teymurova, 2018; Bayramova, & Gasimov, 2012).

During the pandemic, we obtained interesting facts. First, I would like to mention that we were able to involve 22 people in our previous studies in online tests, and we used only psychological-anxiety tests. In fact, situational and individual anxiety, general anxiety, depression scale, "Geriatric depression scale" were tested and MMSE test of mental status was conducted. In addition to psychological testing, anamnesis of long-lived was collected and their health indicators were assessed

The analysis of the results showed that staying home during the pandemic caused serious damage to their health. Elevated blood pressure in those who had never had hypertension before (16 people), tachyarrhythmia (4 people), ischemic heart disease (11 people), and musculoskeletal problems have been reported in almost all 22 people. In addition, digestive disorders, diabetes and various diseases of the nervous system have developed. The results of psychological testing also differed sharply from the results of testing conducted before the pandemic. In fact, high levels of situational and individual anxiety, very high levels of general anxiety, and actual depression (in 4 people) were found.

We used the MMSE test to assess mental status. The results of the tests are obtained by summarizing the answers to each item. It is possible to score a maximum of 30 points, which indicates that the person has high cognitive abilities. Poor cognitive function is indicated by low-test results. Based on the results of various researchers, the test results may show the following results:

- 28 - 30 points - no cognitive dysfunctions
- 24 - 27 points - the pre-dementia phase of cognitive dysfunctions
- 20 - 23 points - mild dementia
- 11 - 19 points - moderate dementia
- 0 - 10 points - severe dementia

In the studies before the pandemic, the long-lived scored 28.13±1.29, indicating that no cognitive function was impaired in them. However, the results of studies conducted during the pandemic were not encouraging. Long-lived the long-lived scored 25.88±2.07 points. This is a sign of the beginning of the pre-dementia phase of cognitive impairment.

In fact, we have witnessed a decrease in cognitive functions against the background of pandemic stress, which seriously harms the health of long-lived, poses a threat to life, and exceeds the norm of psychological and emotional indicators. In order to prevent pandemic stress, it is necessary to take preventive measures, allow the elderly to walk at least 2-3 hours a day in the green areas, follow the doctor's advice, and try to carry out medical treatment if necessary. Doctors working in the gerontology rooms of polyclinics must consult with the elderly and try to prevent the development of any disease.

Figure 7.

THE COURSE AND RESULTS OF THE SECOND GROUP OF STUDIES

The second group of researched was conducted among the first-year students aged 17-19 at Western Caspian University. The research was conducted before the pandemic (2018-2019) and during the pandemic (May-November 2020).

During the research, students' psychological-anxiety indicators (situational and individual anxiety, general anxiety, level of depression) and cognitive indicators (short-term memory, visual and auditory memory, attention and logic) were studied.

There was a reason to conduct research in this direction. In fact, human time is characterized by rapidly evolving and changing socio-economic conditions: sometimes the cases such as the increase in neuropsychological stress due to excessive information intake and the prevalence of similar situations in all areas of human activity. Moreover, the increase in the number of occupations that require a high level of mental resilience and adaptability and the increasing complexity of the education level can cause serious damage to human health. Incomplete physiological maturity especially in adolescence, and incomplete adaptation processes can prevent from getting out of situation caused by emotional stress. Reactions in adolescents during psycho-emotional stress depend on the individual development and the development of typological features of the nervous system, the dynamic characteristics of behavior (stubbornness, dynamism, activity, emotional reactivity, etc.) (Nemov, 2011).

There is a great demand for personal development in human's time. There are several main criteria for assessing personality: social productivity, tolerance to emotional stress, creativity, having special position in society, and so on. All criteria are involved in the full formation of personality and are important for assessing the level of development According to the literature, long-term and frequent emotional reactions lead to persistent irritability in the brain, which is the basis of psycho-emotional stress. Consequently, overexertion of adaptation mechanisms occurs, and leads to serious changes in the endocrine system, metabolism, cardiovascular system, etc. It contributes to the intensification of cognitive processes in the human body and more frequent exposure to stress. One of the most important points is the increasing number of successes and diagnoses in the educational process. It is a topical issue, especially among young people, and the fact that students are exposed to such situation, for sure, has serious impact on the success of the educational process and the mastery of educational material.

The studies before the pandemic aimed to conduct psychophysiological studies on first-year students to determine the effects of emotional stress on memory and to identify these relationships. The colloquium period during the semester is taken as an emotional tension model. The studies were conducted in three stages: on regular school day (20-25 days before the colloquium), 15 minutes before the colloquium and after the colloquium. The object of the studies was 28 first-year students of psychology.

Results Obtained and their Discussion

During the studies conducted on regular school day, it revealed that students had a responsible approach even to ordinary testing process. In fact, short-term memory was determined to be 5.78±1.76 points, and visual memory was 8.1±2.48 points. During the re-testing before the colloquium, the level of short-term memory increased from cognitive indicators to 6.58±1.84 points, and visual memory to 10.5±1.56 points. The results of testing after the colloquium are of particular interest: short-term memory was 7.4±1.04 points (Figure 9) and visual memory was 9.8±1.74 points (Figure 8).

Figure 8.
Photos taken during personal experiments.

Comparative analysis of the results obtained in the study of cognitive indicators showed that the short-term memory of students on regular school day was lower than the norm. This necessitates a responsible approach to the testing process and think that testing is also a source of emotional tension. The results obtained during emotional stress are familiar with the testing process, and at the same time prove that cognitive processes are activated under the influence of emotional stress. For sure, in this case, the activation of general perceptual processes also affects the success indicator and results in success. After the colloquium, short-term memory was higher than normal and showed a perception of the disappearance of the emotional tension process.

The results obtained during the study of visual memory revealed an interesting fact. Thus, the results obtained in all three cases showed a high level of visual memory of students. However, due to the impact of emotional stress, it was found that the performance increased significantly before the colloquium, and that it was still at a higher level than the usual school day, despite a slight decrease after the exam. This proves the positive effect of stress on visual memory and its activity.

Figure 9. The effect of emotional stress on short-term memory

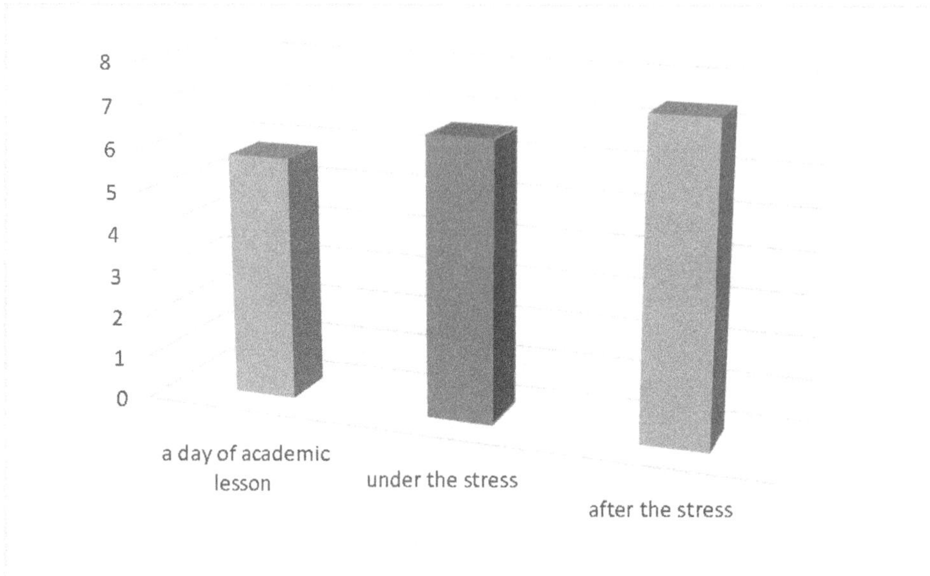

In fact, emotionally stressful situations affect vision and short-term memory, leading to weakening of it, as well as increase in sense of responsibility and, ultimately, increase in success by activating cognitive processes.

During the pandemic, students were involved in the online testing process and the tests used in the studies before the pandemic were applied. However, this time those students were already in the second year, and we got interesting results by testing the same students and comparing the results.

Figure 10. The effect of emotional stress on visual memory

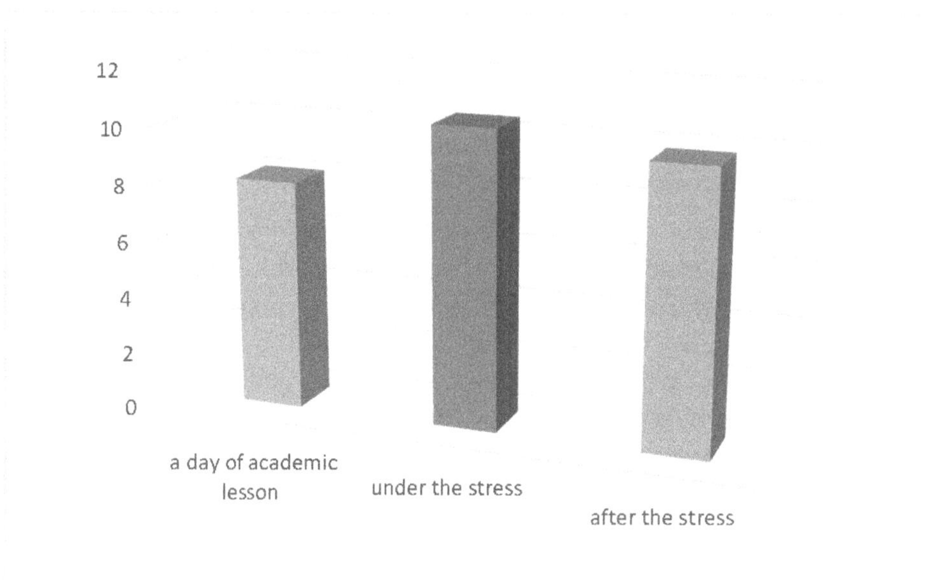

During the testing before the pandemic, students showed moderate situational and individual anxiety, moderate general anxiety, and no depression. The tests conducted during the pandemic, however, revealed high levels of individual and general anxiety in students, actual depression in 3 people, and depression of neurotic origin in 5 people. We investigated the causes of depression: the end of the pandemic, the restoration of normal life, and the transition of students to offline lessons and increase their knowledge. At the same time, students expressed their complains about the online education and lockdown and said that they are not satisfied with this method of education. Moreover, they add that if it continues they will experience and face the following factors:

- luck of sharing emotions;
- boredom (hypokinesia);
- prolonged contact with electromagnetic radiation sources and fatigue;
- attention problems;
- luck of live communication with friends;
- depend only on e-libraries.

During the pandemic, an online colloquium was held and testing was carried out in three stages. The results are presented in the table:

Table 1. Results of cognitive testing conducted before and during the pandemic.

Time of testing	**Before the pandemic**	**During the pandemic**
	Short-term memory	
A day academic lesson	5,78±1,76	5,04±1,97
Before the colloquium	6,58±1,84	5,00±1,23
After the colloquium	7,4±1,04	5,26±1,45
	Visual memory	
A day academic lesson	8,1±2,48	5,63±1,55
Before the colloquium	10,5±1,56	8,91±1,91
After the colloquium	9,8±1,74	8,05±1,28
	Aural memory	
A day academic lesson	7,25±2,0	5,16±1,89
Before the colloquium	8,44±1,99	5,71±1,78
After the colloquium	8,76±1,71	5,43±1,39
	Concentration	
A day academic lesson	8,27±1,35	7,33±1,68
Before the colloquium	11,08±1,99	7,59±1,47
After the colloquium	7,28±1,44	5,25±1,95
	Logic	
A day academic lesson	6,43±1,68	6,74±1,39
Before the colloquium	7,16±1,71	6,09±1,47
After the colloquium	6,91±1,55	5,75±1,81

The analysis of the results showed that if emotional tension before the pandemic caused the activation of cognitive processes, in the online colloquium during the pandemic, against the background of increased excitement, cognitive processes did not activate, and control was below normal. Moreover, there we observed rapid fatigue and delayed adaptation during emotional stress, impaired concentration, and abnormal hearing and short-term memory. All these were reveled during all three experiments; in addition, it is obvious that electromagnetic radiation sources also play a role in impairing cognitive processes. If the same students were not involved in the studies, we probably would not be able to confirm this idea.

In fact, studies among students and long-lived people have once again shown that due to the stress caused by the pandemic, the processes of anxiety increase, cognitive processes weaken, and health indicators fall below normal.

Lack of information on the spread of the coronavirus, the characteristics and mutations of the virus hinders the development of pandemic prevention policies, and as a result, the prevalence of the COVID-19 pandemic is increasing day by day. Outbreaks appear to be exacerbated by airborne infections, especially in densely populated areas, with more serious complications in people over the age of 60, with increased mortality, and delayed vaccination (World Health Organization, 2020).

The role of information and education systems in the prevention of coronavirus infection in Azerbaijan is undeniable. This information fight can be divided into several stages. First of all, the establishment of the Operational Headquarters under the Cabinet of Ministers of the Republic of Azerbaijan and the meetings organized by them resulted in adoption of a number of urgent, pressing and binding decisions. It was decided to postpone the mass events and some social isolation measures were applied in the country from March 14, and the relevant agencies were instructed to ensure the safety of citizens in accordance with the recommendations of the World Health Organization. On the eve of the national quarantine was declared, people had minimal knowledge about the virus. Even very few people in the country were aware of the ways of infection spread, methods of protection against infection, the first symptoms and course of the disease, complications, risk groups, etc. Since the quarantine was announced in March, television, social networks and national Internet resources, newspapers and magazines have started to provide extensive information about the coronavirus, in several languages that the whole population can understand, sometimes very simple, clear, illustrated way, which has enabled to educate children in this way. First, the ways of spreading coronavirus infection are widely explained, and information about prevention methods and the first symptoms began to be disseminated to the population through posters on the streets, at metro stations and bus stops and in buses. Later, the closure of schools, kindergartens, universities and colleges was another step to protect the health of the population aged 0-23. A strict ban on people over the age of 65 to leave home has reduced the incidence of the disease among the elderly population. Most importantly, there were imposed such measures as holding weddings and funerals with limited number of people, the closing of theaters, cinemas, museums, operation of restaurants and cafes. Moreover, all kind of sport competitions were postponed, many kind of jobs and educational processes were transferred to online system. A strict control was imposed over the personal hygiene rules, such as wearing medical mask, hand washing, expansion of the use of soap and other products, to help maintain hygiene, etc. The preference was given to foods rich with vitamins and minerals, explanation of the importance of applying for medical care as soon as they feel the first symptoms of the disease (fever, nausea, weakness, taste) loss of consciousness, etc.). In cases of contacts with infected person, there was a mandatory 14-day special quarantine. Non-compliance with these rules can in some cases result fines and even arrest. This step itself serves to prevent the spread of coronavirus infection. Recently, a number of informational short films have been made in this area, significant scientific articles have been published in periodicals, the scientific conferences, scientific workshops dedicated to coronavirus, and ways of protection, symptoms of the disease, etc. held in higher education and scientific institutions, increased interest in scientific research have been more observed. The closure of access to a number of large cities and villages played an important role to prevent the wide spread of the virus.

Undoubtedly, coronavirus infection also had negative impact on the material well-being of the population.

During the pandemic, the population in the Republic of Azerbaijan enjoy special attention and care. Particularly, the number of unemployed has increased during this period (some enterprises not funded from the state budget became bankrupt which is one of the main causes of unemployment) and most of the population stay home. Here it is worth saying that the "stay home" principle is implemented to prevent the pandemic, with the exception of agricultural facilities, private enterprises do not work, and in which case the situation of the population is unfavorable. Considering the existing situation and certain reasons, the government has implemented certain subsidies, particularly, those who receive salary from the state budget are paid 100%, and the unemployed receive a monthly financial assistance. At the same time, non-governmental organizations (for example, the Red Crescent Society, etc.) supply with material, food, etc. to the people on lower incomes to help them to survive in the hardships caused by pandemic. While concerning about the humans' survival it is worth highlighting that, the treatment of coronavirus patients is at the expense of the government, moreover, it provides the medical care to outpatients. Thus, we can say that the country is actively involved in the process of combating the disease. The closure of schools, universities, colleges and kindergartens, the transition to online education system, the organization of TV lessons both protect the younger generation from this disaster and allow them to continue their education successfully. I believe that by complying with the necessary conditions caused by the pandemic such as staying at home, keeping social distance, following the rules of hygiene, etc., humanity can overcome the existing situation and combat the pandemic.

REFERENCES

Ahmadov, G., & Veziroglu, V. (2003). *Sumgayit and the People in Sumgayit.*

Alperovich, V. (2002). *Social Gerontology*. Rostov State University Journal.

Anisimov, V. (2003). *Molecular and Physiological Mechanisms of Aging*. Journal Nauka.

Bayramova, Y., & Gasimov, Ch. (2012). Features of bioelectrical activity of brain in long-lived in Astana district. Azerbaijan Academy of Ascience, Collection of Scientific Papers of Institute of Physiology named after Garayev, A. and Society of Physiologists.

Berdyashev, G. (2003). *Ecological and Genetic Factors of Aging and Longevity*. Journal Nauka.

Doremalen, V. (2020). Aerosol and Surface Atability of SARS-CoV-2 as Compared with SARS-CoV-1. *English Journal of Medicine.*

Fehr, A., & Perlman, S. (2015). Coronaviruses: An Overview of their Replication and Pathogenesis. *Methods in Molecular Biology (Clifton, N.J.), 1282*, 1–23. doi:10.1007/978-1-4939-2438-7_1 PMID:25720466

Karamova, N., Gasimov, Ch., Teymurova, N. (2018). Features of memory and excitement process in long-living persons. *European Journal of Technical and Natural Sciences.*

Kutter, J., Sporonken, P., Fraaij, R., Founchier, A., & Herfst, S. (2018). Transmission Route of Respiratory Visruses Among Humans. *Current Opinion in Virology, 28*, 142–151. doi:10.1016/j.coviro.2018.01.001 PMID:29452994

Leung, N., Chu, D. K. W., Shiu, E. Y. C., Chan, K.-H., McDevitt, J. J., Hau, B. J. P., Yen, H.-L., Li, Y., Ip, D. K. M., Peiris, J. S. M., Seto, W.-H., Leung, G. M., Milton, D. K., & Cowling, B. J. (2020). Respiratory Virus Shedding in Exhaled Breath and Efficacy of Face Masks. *Nature Medicine, 26*(5), 676–680. doi:10.103841591-020-0843-2 PMID:32371934

Levy, G. (2007). The relationship of Parkinson disease with aging *(pp. 12-42). Archives of Neurology, 64*(9). doi:10.1001/archneur.64.9.1242 PMID:17846263

Litvinova, S. (2011). *Age-related changes in the parameters of saccadic eye movements in healty condition and in Parkinson's disease*. Human Physiology.

Nemov, R. (2001). Psychology. Book 3. Moscow: Academic Press.

Plotnikova, Y. (2011). *Human longevity as a socio-demographic phenomenon.* Dissertation for the degree of Candidate of Social Sciences.

Richard, M. (2016). Influenza "A" Virus via Respiratoty aeroslos or Droplets as it Relates to Pnademic Potential. *FEMS Microbiology Reviews, 40*, 68–85. doi:10.1093/femsre/fuv039 PMID:26385895

Richard, M. (2016). Influenza "A" Virus via Respiratoty aeroslos or Droplets as it Relates to Pnademic Potential. *FEMS Microbiology Reviews, 40*, 68–85. doi:10.1093/femsre/fuv039 PMID:26385895

Salat, D. (2001). Selective presentation and degeneration within the prefrontal cortex in aging and Alzheimer disease. *Archives of Neurology, 658*(1). PMID:11559311

Stadnytskyi, V., Bax, E., Bax, A., & Anfinrud, P. (2020). The Airborne Lifetime of Small Speech Droplets and Their Potential Importance in SARS-CoV-2 Transmission. Proceedings of National Academy of Science of the United States of America, 117.

Tellier, R. (2009). Aerosol Transmission of Influenza "A" Virus: A Review of New Studies. *Journal of Social Interface., 6*(suppl_6), 783–790. doi:10.1098/rsif.2009.0302.focus PMID:19773292

World Health Organization. (2020). *Coronavirus Disease (COVID-2019) situation reports.* Retrieved from https://www.who.int/emergencies/diseases/novel-coronavirus-2019/situation-reports/

Zhang, R., Zhang, A., Wung, Y., & Molina, M. (2020). Conference on Social Science. In *Identifying airborne transmission as the DOminant route for the spread of COVID-19.* National Academy of Science of the United States of America.

KEY TERMS AND DEFINITIONS

Cognitive Processes: Kind of mental processes the performance of the function of the rational cognition, which presents a complex of competence and knowledge, skills, and abilities.

COVID-19: The current pandemic is the result of a coronavirus infection caused by the coronavirus SARS-CoV-2.

Longevity: People aged 90 and over.

Pandemic Stress: Although the pandemic manifests itself at different levels in the world, one of the most serious consequences is the nervous system changes. This area of research is new, and as there are many unanswered questions, the research works conducted in this area are relevant.

Psychophysiological Indicators: Important factors for the assessment of human health, regardless of age, and it is commendable that they can be tested without harm to humans, and that research can be conducted with online testing in modern times.

Stay Home: A demand of the government not to go out and live the dwelling space during the pandemic. Which is one of the acknowledge processes that can help people to survive.

Students: A particular group of people enrolled in a school or other educational institution, undergoing certain trainings for particular purposes of acquiring knowledge, developing a profession and finding employment in a particular filed.

Chapter 11
Changes in Consumer Behaviors During the Pandemic and Virtual Strategies for Acquiring and Keeping Customers

Mustafa Şehirli
https://orcid.org/0000-0002-4800-0283
The University of Health Sciences, Turkey

ABSTRACT

This chapter addresses how the pandemic has transformed the world at a surprising speed in terms of consumer behaviors and applicable virtual strategies to capture new opportunities. Although there have been some short-term sharp declines in consumer spending, confident changes have been realized through consumers' evolution into "digitalization" or the use of contactless, functional, and appropriate business models. Accordingly, the pandemic has also brought digitalization forward for companies, making it almost obligatory. This chapter will also discuss exemplary, inspirational practices of companies that have developed business models, products, and services by managing changes accelerated by the pandemic.

INTRODUCTION

Prior to 2020, the world's most crucial agenda topic was digitalization. In 2020, the pandemic became an important topic at a historic pace, particularly in the business world. This tested our estrangement and accelerated the process between our physical and digital worlds. Inaccurate and worrying data spread across the globe faster than the virus. Remote instruments, such as working from home, distance learning, and digital meetings, changed the business world. Some label this era as the digital pandemic or e-pandemic.

A crucial variable affected by the e-pandemic is customer behavior. In an epidemic with infodemic, consumer (customer) behaviors changed. This study explores these changes, their impacts, strategies to manage these changes, and new opportunities.

DOI: 10.4018/978-1-7998-7164-4.ch011

This section will address consumer/customer behavior (these two terms will be used interchangeably in the research). Customer behavior is influenced by factors like consumer personality traits, attitudes, and necessities, which determine the products and services that will be bought and sold in the markets, as well as when they will be sold, how much will be sold, and at what price. Vital behaviors like consumer brand loyalty and brand recommendation are also effective for companies. In addition to consumers' satisfaction levels, other influential factors emerge, including a company's liquid or fixed assets and company output like profitability.

Accordingly, if today's companies fail to develop strategies aligned with both fundamental trends (digitalization) and current conditions (pandemic) to improve consumer behavior in their favor, they will face the danger of extinction. These strategies can be handled in three ways: (1) strategies directly related to customers (i.e., enriching digital channels, increasing interaction, etc.); (2) employee-related strategies (i.e., remote work, remote training, etc.); and (3) environmental strategies (i.e., digital platform social responsibility projects, etc.). These strategies aim at influencing customer behavior because the "real" bosses of companies and brands are customers. In fact, customers are the only income source for the company (Peppers & Rogers, 2004).

Consequently, this chapter will focus on customer behavior strategies. While evaluating these strategies, however, digital applications will also be considered as they can be implemented during the pandemic in accordance with the department's primary purpose. In a pandemic, it is irresponsible to ignore digitalization strategies for businesses when physical distance between people has increased. It should also be stated that COVID-19 accelerated the already developing digital revolution (Gouveia, Perun, & Daradkeh, 2020).

There are inner (psychological and characteristic features, circumstantial effects) and outer (socio-cultural, cyclical, appealing marketing activities, etc.) factors that play a role in the root of customer behaviors that are affected by the digital strategies. There have been many theories made regarding what types of effects these are. The CAB model which states that the information we gather trigger our emotion and they cause behavior is one of them. Another theory is the Theory of Planned Behaviour (TPB) which states that humans act according to their intentions. It is inevitable for the pandemic to not affect people's behavior within the framework of these theories. The human whose most basic goal is to survive will surely act differently after gaining awareness of the pandemic's dangers (consciousness) which contrasts with their need to survive and society's social impact.

The main indicators that are used worldwide to survey and keep track the consumer behaviors are the Personal Consumption Expenditures (PCE) and Consumer Confidence Index which are created by Gros National Product. The changes that occur within both show how consumer behavior has changed in the current time, thus they make foresight about the future. Also, predictions from certain institutions like IMF, World Bank, etc. regarding the future of the global economy will give a good idea.

There have been important changes within the indicators that state consumer behavior during the pandemic. This change in consumer behavior is not only different in quantity but also in content. While there had been a leaning especially towards security and vital products in the beginning, the products that decreased in demand also have kept up later on. There has not been a decrease in consumption of luxury products but rather diversification. The consuming tools also have been changed meaning contactless or online channels and payment methods have increased in use. On the other hand, an increase in consumers' liquid assets has been observed. Another expected result is the decrease in accommodation and restaurant expenses which requires the use of a social environment. These changes are handled in a more detailed way down below.

Digital strategies fall under four titles: (1) connection technologies (i.e., the internet of objects, etc.); (2) technologies that imitate human behavior (augmented reality [AR], artificial intelligence [AI], etc.); (3) technologies related to socialization (i.e., data mining, etc.); and (4) technologies that develop business models (i.e., learning machines, etc.). The chapter will also discuss prior studies regarding these strategies, characteristics of these strategies, possible effects, and differences. Overall, the chapter will attempt to offer enlightening ideas for both managers and researchers.

At the end of the section, there are practical suggestions given under 3 topics: Pre-Sale, During Sale and After Sale Stages. Every suggestion is based on understanding the customers better, building trust and a long-term personal relationship with them while digitalizing according to the competition of today and the immediate effects of the pandemic.

FACTORS THAT IMPACT CUSTOMER BEHAVIOR IN THE PANDEMIC

This section will explore influential factors regarding customer behaviors in the pandemic. According to the Diderot effect, as defined by McCracken (1988), changes in the consumption habits of consumers requires balance and consistency. In the original incident, Diderot received a new dressing gown, which required all the items in his room to be altered to fit that robe. In other words, habits shield us from new or different consumption. A singular change in our habits can impact all other consumption behaviors. As in the case of Diderot, these changes are not always welcome. In fact, they can come as an unpleasant gift like a pandemic.

In the marketing literature, these effects are generally considered factors that change consumer behaviors. They are typically categorized under the following five titles (Erdoğan, 2009):

1. **Internal-Psychological Factors:** These include perception, learning, and personality traits. For instance, some consumers are open to innovation, learning, and a desire to try new products. Others do not want to change their reliable products or suppliers.
2. **External-Sociocultural Factors:** These include society, family, culture, and religion. For instance, Muslims and Jews do not consume pork.
3. **Demographic Factors:** For example, women are more investigative shoppers. However, men display predatory behaviors.
4. **Marketing Activities:** These include promotional activities, discounts, and distribution conditions. Consumers can always substitute their regular brand with a discounted generic product or brand.
5. **Situational Factors:** These include time, the reason for purchase, and emotional state. For example, umbrella sales increase in sudden rain.

By looking at the above classifications and examples, we can claim that motivated, dynamic, diverse, and problematic consumer behaviors are influenced by environmental factors and differ according to individual characteristics (Wilkie, 1986). Regarding the subject in this chapter, consumer consumption behaviors are, of course, affected by environmental change (Lantos, 2015). Consequently, a pandemic that transforms global conditions can be counted among primarily external (environmental) factors in the above classification. It is evident that the COVID-19 pandemic impacted individuals' internal attitudes, particularly with the contribution of the infodemic. This is because the flow of information about changes in the environment affects human behaviors on a massive scale (Wang, 2015). In other words, the pandemic affects all factors based on the attitude theory and Diderot effect.

Consumer Behavior Literature

It would be helpful to look at basic consumer behavior literature and patterns to gain a deeper understanding of the pandemic's effects on consumers.

Consumer behavior, which is one of the most studied subjects in marketing, is the process and activities people engage in when searching for, selecting, purchasing, using, evaluating and disposing of products and services so as to satisfy their needs and desires (Belch, 1978). So many models have been developed on this subject. One of the oldest of these is Kurt Lewin's theory which claims that behaviors are a function of personal and social impact therefore it is defined as a "black box" (Odabaşı & Barış, 2002). Kotler (1965) has stated that the customers aren't actually a black box and summed up the models of consumer behavior presented so far as:

Marshallian man is concerned chiefly with eco- nomic cues—prices and irieomwand makes a freeh utility calculation before each purchase. Pavlovian man behaves in a largely habitual rather than thoughtful way; certain configurations of cues will set off the same behavior because of rewarded learning in the past. Freudian man'a choiees are influenced strongly by motives and fantasies which take place deep within his private world. Veblenian man acte in a way which is shaped largely by past and present social groups. And finally, Hobbeeian man seeks to reconcile individual gain with organisational gain (p. 45).

Modern consumer behavior models which have come after these models and include models like Assael model, Howard Sheth –HS model ve Nicosia model, see the purchase decision process as a problem-solving process, suppose that it is affected by internal and external factors, and try to explain how the preferences are made rather than what they are influenced by (İslamoğlu & Altunışık, 2010). As one can see, consumer behaviors occurring during the pandemic are also a problem-solving process. It affects consumer behavior as an external impact through attitudes that trigger emotions within the person.

The attitudinal clinical assessment of behavior (CAB) model, developed to understand the process of consumer behavior changes, is critical (Gursoy et al. 2019). The CAB model states that there are three stages of human behavior: (1) cognitive (we know); (2) affective (we feel); and (3) behavioral (we act). In other words, attitudes are developed through specific information and emotions, which allow us to predict our expenses more effectively than our purchasing plans (Adams, 1964).

At this point, the theory of reasoned action (TRA) is one of the most scientifically used models to explain consumer behavior, especially for voluntary reasons (Olson & Zanna, 1993). However, TRA is insufficient in cases where people do not have full willpower. Therefore, Azjen (1991) developed TRA with an additional variable, creating the theory of planned behavior (TPB) (Turan, 2011). According to this theory, a consumer's behavior depends on their intentions. Intentions depend on attitude, their level of control in the behavior, and subjective norms (influence of their environment).

When we use a holistic behavior to study the above theories and factors, the pandemic inevitably affects consumer behavior both internally and externally. Following the CAB model, true or false information (cognitive stage) emerging with the pandemic or infodemic causes emotions (i.e., fear, death, the responsibility to be contagious, insecurity) for individuals, followed by pertinent behavioral intentions. For example, a shortage of goods in the market may cause consumers who learn this information to anxiously stock the goods for future use and a survival drive (Voinea & Filip, 2011). In the formation of these behavioral intentions, both internal attitudinal reactions and factors outside of an individual's control that emerge as a result of the pandemic (i.e., curfew, wearing a mask, maintaining social distance), are effective. In accordance with TPB, the individual's environment, that is relatives' behaviors under the pandemic's influence, is also essential. For instance, a young person's consumption behaviors (eating out) may decrease because their friends did not come along.

We understand how the pandemic changes consumers' behaviors through theories. The following section explores the types of changes.

IMPACTS OF CHANGED CUSTOMER BEHAVIOR

Before studying how the pandemic changed consumer behaviors, this section will discuss changes in consumers' general preferences and intentions via statistical data. A first indicator is per capita domestic product, which can be considered the source of consumer expenditures. If we consider the gross domestic product (GDP) as the average citizen's income, his/her expense is personal consumption expenditures (PCE). Both indicators have undergone severe changes during the pandemic. For instance, in the United States, one of the countries most affected by the pandemic per the Bureau of Economic Analysis (BEA) Second Quarter Report in 2020, the GDP of the country decreased by 31.4% due to COVID-19. PCE decreased by 10.8%. Other decreases included durable goods like automobiles (1.7%), nondurable goods like groceries (15%), and service spending (41.8%). The tourism sector is expected to lose 42.1% of revenue in 2020 (Lock, 2020a). Regarding expenditures in general, there was a severe decrease in the first month (March), especially decreases in the high-income group. However, the situation of expenditures has recovered since the beginning of April (Cox et al., 2020).

Consumer Confidence Index (CCI) is another significant indicator of trends. According to Ipsos's "Global Consumer Confidence Index October 2020" data, there was a severe decline in consumer confidence in 2020 as the pandemic spread across the globe. Moreover, consumers' trust decreased by five points compared to the averages of the last 10 years. It can be argued that there is a decrease in customers' confidence in economic activities during the pandemic, which impacts consumers' spending intention. Still, it is not easy to make such a definite judgment when examining the data. Current research revealed no decrease in consumption expenditures (Gathergood & Guttman-Kenney, 2020). While retail sales decreased by 3.6% in the U.S. compared to the same quarter of the previous year during the pandemic process, shopping shifted from brick-and-mortar to online stores.

On the other hand, the development potential and wealth of experience brought about by digitalization during the pandemic complicate consumption behaviors. In other words, both content and methods of consumer behavior vary. As stated, although offline shopping has decreased due to prohibitions, there has been a severe growth in online shopping. Changing customer preferences may cause USD 2+ trillion of annual value to migrate from public spaces to home-focused industries (Accenture, 2020). In Figure 1, there are some results of a research conducted by McKinsey in many countries. In that research, the online shopping rates of consumers before the pandemic and their predictions about what this rate will be after the pandemic were asked and the difference between them was evaluated on product basis.

Figure 1. The percent growth conversion from physical environment to online shopping before and after the pandemic

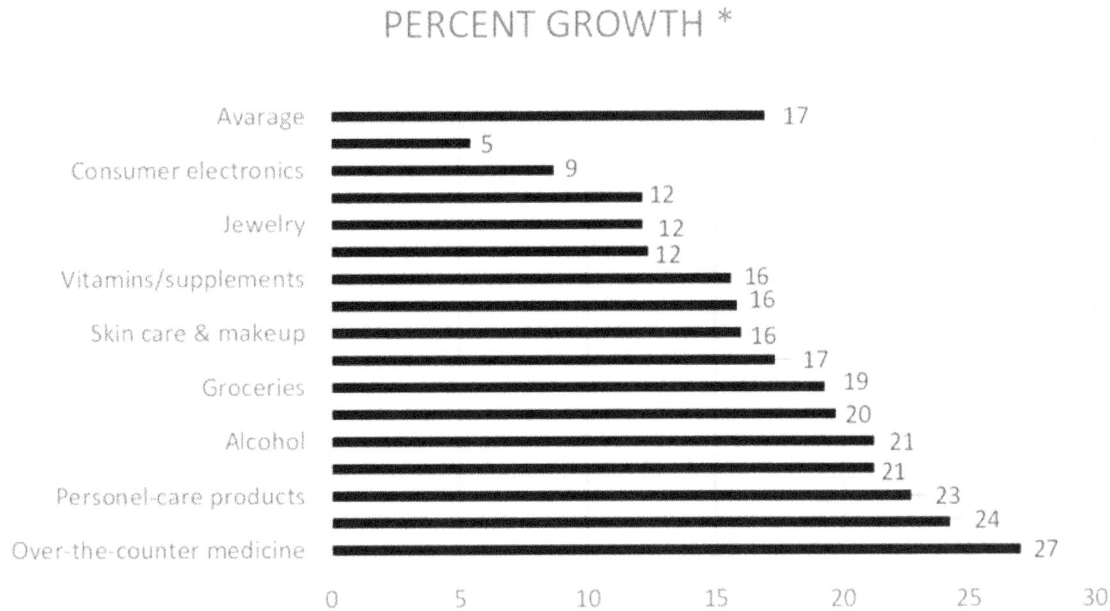

**The average of 8 countries (US,UK, France, Germany, Spain, Italy, India, Japan,China)*

Predictions help develop strategies for consumers. According to the International Monetary Fund (IMF), in 2020, when the pandemic emerged, the world economy was predicted to shrink by 4.9% and grow by 5% in 2021. Although PMI (Purchasing Managers' Index) values, which are among the most critical indicators for investments and growth globally, decreased significantly at the beginning of the pandemic, they peaked after a few months (July 2020), reaching 52.4%. This increase continued in the following months. Based on these data, it is possible to assume that the world's economic situation will start to recover before expected. Accordingly, there are reasons to be optimistic for the year following the pandemic and we should, therefore, establish growth strategies. Moreover, there is great potential for a competitive advantage for companies that can make fast and accurate digital transformations. Fourteen percent of companies have emerged from the previous four significant recessions with both increased turnover and profitability (Jacobides & Reeves, 2020).

Changes in Consuming Preferences

As stated, it would be more accurate to discuss a differentiation rather than a decrease in consumption expenditures in the pandemic. Maslow's hierarchy of needs comes to mind if we recognize that people act with psychological and sociological realities. Under new conditions, those who tried to adapt generally focused on security and survival, placing these factors at the bottom of their pyramid. During the first periods of the pandemic, food, and cleaning products for stockpiling purposes increased. Consequently, expenditures like travel, tourism, entertainment, and education for social and prestige needs have decreased, placing these factors at the upper portion of their pyramid.

Although it does not impact monetary terms in line with this motive, there has been a significant increase in products like hygiene goods, especially face masks and antibacterial gels, across the globe (Conway, 2020). On top of that consumption habits regarding healthy life for survival needs have increased. To exemplify, supplements used in immune system strengthening have increased in consumption and also there has been a 170% growth in the sales of equipment that help to exercise at home (Mukherjee, 2020). Various reports show that sales in consumer goods and products (i.e., food products, beverages, catering, cosmetics, cleaning materials, etc.) increased significantly from early 2020 to mid-year (despite the decrease in March) (Hashem, 2020).

Table 1 illustrates a research report published in Turkey regarding product sales within 10 days after the first case was seen in the country and their rate of increase was determined.

Table 1. Changes in consumption preferences

Product	Increase Rate (%)
Cologne	256
Vinegar	161
Pasta	132
Legumes	111
Flour	98
Yeast	80
Wet wipes	77
Package soup	71
Salt	69
Tomato paste	63

Source: (Ipsos, 2020)

Some people deliberately stocked certain products for an average of two weeks. Simultaneously, all generations of consumers (X, Y, and Z) made more purchases to maintain comfort levels at home as they reduced their frequency of visiting stores (Conmay, 2020). This stocking behavior in the early days of the pandemic later has turned into normal.

A major change in consumer behavior is based on social and physical interaction requirements. The sector most affected by this is the HORECA (hotel and foodservice) sector. Although some restaurants try to survive with takeaway ordering opportunities, hotels in the tourism sector have struggled to manage the pandemic's effects. Two weeks after the pandemic's March 2020 onset, as COVID-19 began to make worldwide impacts, restaurant spending decreased by more than 100% across the globe. The industry started to recoup in May 2020. However, it was only able to recover up to -30% after eight months (Lock, 2020b). Accordingly, even if the increase in the consumption of essential products by those who eat out maintains, the decrease in the amount of spending in other sectors, which has come to a halt, will take significant time to cover the economic damage.

In extraordinary situations, consumers move toward consumer rather than luxury goods because they do not want to fall into a nationwide shortage or fail to meet their basic needs (Campbell & Frei, 2010). On the other hand, a study conducted during the pandemic process revealed that consumers' consumption of luxury goods did not decrease. In the same survey, 49% of consumers in China stated that they consumed more luxury goods during this period. In other words, although there was no severe decrease in the consumption of luxury goods during the pandemic process, some changes occurred in line with cultural and economic differences. For instance, luxury consumption in the U.S. shifted from jewelry (social satisfaction) to feel-good items like alcohol. While this situation in the U.S. can be defined as "new hedonism," the change is considered "optimism" in China and "escapism" in Europe (Hernaez, 2020).

It is possible to interpret these consumer behaviors as changes in habits. Jacobides and Reeves (2020) used the BCG Henderson Institute to show that the most critical change in consumers' habits involves spending more time at home, which impacts three categories: (1) working from home; (2) eating and drinking at home; and (3) entertainment. Consequences in the "work from home" category include painting and renovations, purchasing printers, using digital collaboration applications, and switching network and connection widths. In the "eating and drinking" category, habits include increased home ordering and e-payments and decreased dining in restaurants. Regarding the "entertainment" category, increases are evident in digital channels and games, as well as exercising, reading, and puzzles. Behaviors have decreased in going to the movies and attending sports competitions.

The people who tend to spend more time at home, have started to spend their time spent shopping also online, searching. That way they have started to make more product and price comparisons and have been drawn away from brand loyalty to purchase the best for the cheapest price (Mukherjee, 2020). The important reason for this could again, be interpreted as the need to stay safe and secure as well as liven up life.

The above data revealed that a factor with strong individual and social effects, such as the pandemic, causes reactions appropriate to Maslow's hierarchy of needs. These reactions can have different consequences on consumer segments, as well as social and cultural diversity. The changes manifested themselves in the type of products and/or services consumed and in consumption patterns and/or habits. But it is apparent that these changes are actually a catalyst of the digital revolution happening in the world and it strengthens the need to trust which has been created because of the digital revolution.

Changes in Purchasing Channel

Instruments, such as payment methods, can change behaviors because customers tend to adopt a new behavior based on finances (Czarniewski, 2014). When obligations and fears, such as the pandemic, are determinants, consumers' behaviors are expected to change in terms of payment methods. The World Health Organization (WHO) emphasizes that surfaces and paper money transmit the virus. Therefore, people shifted their payments to e-commerce or e-payment methods to avoid the risk of virus transmission (Hashem, 2020). Digital financial services involve some risks; however, they offer contactless, remote, and practical transactions. It eliminates distance, provides speed, and enables governments to contact citizens more fairly and quickly (International Monetary Found, 2020)

The pandemic had an initial negative impact on mobile banking. However, these adverse effects were partially reversed after a series of positive regulatory measures. The number of payments and financial transactions between banks decreased significantly (Tut, 2020).

People moved from expensive payment methods to cheaper, more manageable methods during this period. Still, the pandemic has accelerated the world's digitalization process. One of them seems to be the field of financial systems. The shift of payments toward contactless digital devices may continue to accelerate, switching paper money to cryptocurrencies in the future.

Changes in Liquid Assets

During the pandemic period, particularly the first months, middle- and low-waged individuals saw a decrease in their expenses. Simultaneously, the government offered financial support forth, which increased the liquid assets (Cox et al., 2020). This situation may serve as a behavior toward security requirements. Moreover, this action reduced income inequality in many countries around the world. It should be recognized that a liquid accumulation that does not return to expenditure would generate a problem in consumption-based economic systems.

UNDERSTANDING AND STRATEGIES AFFECTING CONSUMER BEHAVIOR

The most prominent hardship faced by companies during the pandemic was managing the changing demand (increase vs. decrease) and fluctuation in financial statements. An inadequate response to these changes could result in a company's failure. On the other hand, the response could bring opportunities.

Companies may have a bright future post-pandemic if they were able to supply high-demand products and/or services and create a strong bond with customers during the crisis. First, companies must recognize customers and adapt to their requirements and desires. Second, companies must build trust in consumers. These two points should be considered in the development of a company's strategic plan.

To understand consumers, companies must monitor their behaviors, maintain data, and analyze their needs. Company's must also comply with consumer behavior trends around the world. Attention should be given to the nature of these trends. For instance, the pandemic changed consumer behavior worldwide. However, most of these changes are existing trends. In this sense, the trends can be divided into four classes and two axes, depending on whether they existed before the pandemic and whether they will be long-term needs (Jacobides & Reeves, 2020). These points should be considered in the development of product and service features.

Personalization was an important trend during the pandemic period. As explained, consumer behaviors developed based on security. As a result, there is a transition toward more functional, useful, and low-cost products and services. This situation will continue after restrictions on social contact are lifted. For instance, an instructor may have to continue offering digital training at a more reasonable cost.

The element of trust is more important than ever, especially in the pandemic period. Prior studies show that consumer trust has positive effects on loyalty, fidelity, sales effectiveness, and cooperation (Isaeva, Kira, & Saunders, 2020). Likewise, it is necessary to establish trust to increase customer loyalty and repurchase intentions in the digital environment (Wang, Ngamsiriudom, & Hsieh, 2015).

The following section will explore ways to meet consumers' needs and expectations. It will also discuss how to build relevant, trusting relationships using virtual strategies.

VIRTUAL STRATEGIES AND CONSUMERS' BEHAVIORS

Innovations provided by digitalization emerge in product features, distribution, communication, pricing, or product positioning. These strategies provide economic, functional, and/or psychological benefits to customers. Digital technologies are driven by the needs of customers (Gellweiler & Krishnamurthi, 2020). This section discusses virtual strategies that give managers and academicians ideas to build beneficial consumer behaviors. The strategies are addressed under three stages according to consumer experience processes: (1) pre-sales; (2) sales/experience; and (3) post-sales. Global digitalization occurs under four fields within the three stages (Gellweiler & Krishnamurthi, 2020).

1. **Connection Technologies:** Receivers and transmitters, global connection, the Internet of things (IoT)
2. **Technologies that Imitate Humans:** Application of sensors, AI, AG (for example, remote patient monitoring and surgeries)
3. **Innovations for Changes in Social Trends:** Sharing of confidential information through social media, collecting personal data, sharing assets (i.e., car, office) via devices, smartphones
4. **Creating or Changing Business Models:** New models focused on creating value for the customer
    a. Provide superior products or services
    b. Offer cost advantage
    c. Generate relational value

Note that companies that invest in a transition to new business models via digitalization, especially in crises, will advance by seizing opportunities (Jacobides & Reeves, 2020).

Pre-Sales Stage

Employees

A business must develop "employee first" strategies to increase employee satisfaction and loyalty, as well as protect employee health. Customers' expectations cannot be met without employee satisfaction. During the pandemic period, indispensable employee satisfaction practices included paying employees by forcing financial conditions to the fullest, using government incentives on their behalf, and implementing digital short-time and remote working opportunities.

Trust is the most critical need of both employees and customers. The best way to guarantee trust is to establish open communication and provide accurate information. Sharing the company's financial situation, difficulties, and risks, such as layoffs, with employees will positively affect loyalty. Distance education should be offered to employees to support professional and personal development. An example is LCW, Turkey's largest textile brand, with 47,700 employees and over 1,000 stores in 47 countries. LCW earned employee trust and loyalty by immediately paying three-months' of employee salaries when their stores were closed and unable to do business.

Business Models, Products, and Services

The SARS pandemic in 2003 increased global e-commerce trends. COVID-19 also accelerates the digitalization process. For instance, Microsoft's chief executive officer stated that the company's two-year growth projection in digital transformation was achieved in the first two months of the pandemic (Jacobides & Reeves, 2020). The Internet and virtual business channels have democratized markets to interact with customers in diverse ways, achieve product-market harmony, and stimulate new pursuits. These are consolations for small businesses because small business owners can establish customer connections through new business models during the pandemic. This allows small businesses to strengthen relationships with customers and turn a crisis into an opportunity (Liguori & Pittz, 2020).

The first stage in customer interaction focuses on developing suitable products and services based on customer needs and requests. During times of significant change, such as the pandemic, it is crucial to monitor customer demands and realize business opportunities outside of the existing business models (Liguori & Pittz, 2020). Business leaders can follow social media accounts to identify trends and opportunities. Search trends can be studied using Google Analytics or other data collection tools (Liguori & Pittz, 2020). Mobile applications can also observe how customers behave. For instance, the sports shoe manufacturer ASICS uses Runkeeper data, a fitness-tracking app, to develop products and services (Ikeda & Marshall, 2019).

The digital cloud and big data technologies allow businesses to store, analyze, and use various types of customer information. Companies utilize data-based marketing tools to capture customers' consumption time, frequency, quantity, and profiles. In turn, companies can segment customers, target consumers, and better position their brand (Zhu, 2019). However, handling data presents ethical challenges because it may violate information security (Fernazdez-Rovira et al., 2021). Consequently, attention should be paid to the protection of personal data, security, and competition rules.

The production phase takes place once a company determines which products and services to develop. At this stage using production facilities without a human workforce must be considered. Industry 4.0 adaptations are now compulsory. Thanks to digital innovations, including procurement processes, it is possible to reduce costs, reduce margins of error, and increase delivery times during the production phase. For example, Komatsu, a Japanese construction equipment manufacturer, promoted its "smart construction" concept, which used semi-automated construction equipment with a global positioning system (GPS) to increase performance and positive user experiences. Another example of digitalized production is the Lin Qingxuan cosmetics company in China. The company began to employ beauty professionals in their stores as online influencers after their brick-and-mortar business decreased due to the pandemic process. This decision transitioned the company into a new service experience with its customers (Jacobides & Reeves, 2020). In support of this, according to Kim, Lee, and Jung (2020), virtual reality (VR) videos impacts consumers' intentions to visit those businesses.

The interaction of businesses with suppliers, competitors, professional/sector organizations, and other systems within the government also creates cooperation and synergy to minimize the pandemic's damages. In this sense, digital events (i.e., regular or irregular meetings, gatherings, conferences, or fairs on virtual platforms) may result in new ideas and collaborations. More suitable product and service offerings for customers become available. Therefore, companies should examine virtual platform models and technologies related to their work.

Large companies should consider a digital platform for their ecology and customers, potential customers, dealers, and suppliers. These platforms perform a unique task for win-win interactions between the supplier and the customer. Successful examples (i.e., Cemex, Maersk) exist across the world. For example, 72% of companies with an income of over $10 billion have such a goal (Ikeda & Marshall, 2019). The Shazam app can be cited as a groundbreaking exercise. Apple bought Shazam, which uses a small portion of a musical selection to locate the piece's complete name, in 2017 for $400 million. A Shazam user can use the name of the song to purchase the song from iTunes. The user can also locate the song's lyrics on Google. As a result, the user meets his/her needs through various platforms (Ikeda & Marshall, 2019).

An important point for the firms in product and service development during the pandemic can be analyzed from the change that occurs in the consumption of consumer goods and the increase in at-home activities: People want to connect to life. Then it is important to design products and services according to people's interests and passions, for these to be products and services that make people feel good or give a similar experience. For example, a firm selling dried nuts can gift sunflower seeds to their customers so they can grow them on a balcony. In this time, so many firms have tried to touch their customers through similar activities and presented suggestions to stay at home.

As a final strategy proposal, companies are looking at rural locations to develop innovative products and services.

Sales/Experience Stage

Sales and experience is the process of bringing products and services to customers. During the pandemic, companies faced challenged in reduced or eliminated physical contacts. Nevertheless, the element of trust needed to be maximized.

Communication Channels

The pandemic period presented an opportunity for businesses to improve and consolidate existing customer relationships. Informing employees of revised processes like changes to working hours or close personal attention regarding health information are relationship-enhancing moves that demonstrate their value outside of the employment setting. An important impact on valuing employees is enhancing their commitment to customer relationship management (CRM) capabilities. One-to-one interaction in the virtual environment will have positive effects on both small and large businesses.

It is a smart move to increase and digitalize channels that provide customer interactions. All necessary channels should be used, including websites and social media or global platforms like Amazon and Alibaba. First, company websites should be designed to ensure customer confidence. According to Kim, Ferrin, and Rao (2008), users' trust in a website depends on its information quality, the company's reputation, privacy tendencies, and security.

Research on trust places value on data sharing. It is more challenging to establish trust online (Zimmer et al., 2010). For instance, people do not share personal information via websites, even if it offers them an advantage. The design and branding of a website increase customer trust (Chang, Hsu, Chen, & Kuo, 2017; Fimberg & Sousa, 2020). According to Delone and Mclean (2003), a website's quality can be viewed in the following dimensions: (1) system quality; (2) information quality; and (3) service quality. System quality consists of the general performance evaluation of the website. Information quality refers to the information produced by the site and the site's speed. Service quality is made up of customer perceptions about the service they receive from the site. Security certificates and branding by third parties also increase trust and user experience (UX). Broadcasting a chatbox or WhatsApp customer interaction option opens more channels and has positive results. Quick responses to customer requests also increase the site's preference rating. These factors impact users' intentions to interact with a website.

Another communication/service strategy is to offer recommender engine services to customers within the scope of personalized marketing. This benefits companies with an extensive scale of customer data because it increases sales (Beheraa et al., 2020).

Distribution Network

A study during the COVID-19 period revealed that satisfaction is the most critical variable affecting the use of food delivery applications (FDA). Other essential determinants include the suitability of technology, trust, performance expectation, and social impact (Zhao & Bacao, 2020). Particularly during the pandemic crisis, companies focused on convenience. In product-based sectors, digitizing distribution and delivery services provide a competitive advantage for both small and large businesses. For instance, contracted online sales sites have established their distribution structures by employing third parties (small markets, barbers, etc.). On the other hand, logistics/distribution companies started contactless delivery, adding door-to-door service and security code options. Drone deliveries are expected to increase in the future.

Customer Contact Points and Payment Systems

A crucial stage in the customer experience involves the interaction of customers, products, and services. This stage should consider new trends regarding virtual strategies. Improvements should be performed with an innovative perspective, as described in the business model or product/service improvement. An example of this stage is the city scooter sharing program. Scooter sharing, or vehicle-sharing systems that create value for customers, is increasingly popular. Users of this innovative business model use the Internet to locate and pick up the vehicle (scooter) within specific cities. The user then leaves the vehicle in a location of their choice. Payment occurs via credit card for the time and distance used. The second example of this stage involves the Burberry brand's in-store experience. Burberry began using radio waves to show adaptations of fashion products in its stores. In other words, customers could select and watch a product video on a giant screen in the store. In collaboration with Google, Burberry has created a project on lip recognition. Thus, when customers kiss the smartphone screen, they send a Burberry kiss to the person they desire (Gellweiler & Krishnamurthi, 2020).

AI and data analysis can improve in-store experiences. These technologies can analyze customers' movements to enhance the shopping experience (for example, distribute information or create question and answer kiosks in the store). Future technologies to enhance customers' experiences include gamification and sound. Gamification includes in-store technological games with rewards to attract younger shoppers. Sound technologies will analyze customers' moods via voice tones. These technologies can develop algorithms to suggest products to the customer (Globaltechmagazine, 2020).

Revolut, one of the world's largest innovative fintech banks, offered superior services to its customers during the pandemic process by foregoing charges on money transfers and/or account operations. The company's customers were given virtual credit cards to make contactless transactions and ATM withdrawals through an application developed by Apple. Revolut developed social responsibility projects, infrastructure for campaigns to aid healthcare personnel struggling with COVID-19. It presented the opportunity to switch to crypto money to support customers who lost income and offered interest advantages. It also partnered and supported local companies (Gouveia, Perun, & Daradkeh, 2020). The EasyPay brand, on the other hand, offered a service for small firms to receive orders by phone and online, as well as inform payment to support local trade (Gouveia, Perun, & Daradkeh, 2020).

It would be a rational strategy for all companies to cooperate with low-cost fintech organizations. In doing so, companies can facilitate and digitize customer transactions during a crisis like the pandemic.

Post-Sales Stage

Today's marketing approaches aim at long-term, mutually beneficial relationships between companies and customers. Therefore, strategies should protect interaction in the post-sales period. First, companies must maintain regular contact with clients. During a crisis period, it is necessary to utilize all channels to share reassuring communication campaigns, including health and information bulletins. Personalized communication is beneficial to both the company and client via digital platforms as discussed throughout this study.

FUTURE RESEARCH DIRECTIONS

A digital world experiences rapid change. The pandemic process impacted research and global trends. Additional topics for studying virtual strategies and consumer behaviors include:

1. Changes in consumer preferences based on regional and product categories
2. New business models and products/services emerging from the pandemic process
3. Changes in customer satisfaction and loyalty during the pandemic process
4. Effects of website security certificates on trust and user experience
5. Impacts of accelerating information exchanges with customers
6. Effects of VR products and service promotions on customer preferences

CONCLUSION

Clearly, the pandemic has changed the world and affected consumers' preferences. Thus the occurring changes aren't surprising and seem to fit in with the theories of consumer behavior. The consumers who have come face to face with the risk of death or losing their health and gained the consciousness of this have acted according to the fear of death or the survival instinct. These behaviors are completely based on instincts. The increase in the consumption of food, hygiene, and healthy nutrition materials, making more research before the shopping analytically can be explained like this. Similarly, the interesting fact that there is no decrease in luxury goods may be a result of people wanting to connect to life. Consumer spending, which fell sharply in the first month of the pandemic, recovered rapidly. In the early periods of the pandemic, behavioral changes related to consumers' safety and survival instincts emerged. So it can be claimed that the trust factor in people has become even more important during the pandemic. Another proof can be presented for this claim and it is that Expenditures were directed toward packaged food, healthy life, and cleaning products. Shopping methods were digitalized to be contactless. It can be argued that many processes are now more functional and economical. So the main point to get from this section is the necessity of the trust factor to have discoursed more. Firms have to take this necessity seriously. Hence, some of the strategies that improve the trust factor from the detailed suggestions above are the following:

On the other hand, the pandemic has not created a new trend. Instead, it has accelerated an existing digitalization trend and offered an opportunity for businesses to transition to new models for products and services. Crises also involve chance. Some companies, especially smaller businesses, found opportunities to enhance competition and customers. For this reason, it is crucial to find and implement digital/virtual strategies to improve customer experiences:

1. To get customer information through digital tools, to observe them with digital tools, getting their data and interpreting them, using technologies
2. Providing employees with an opportunity to work remotely and participate in professional and personal development offerings
3. Digitalize products and services to promote functionality, usefulness, health, and affordability. For instance, using Industry 4.0 technologies in production, enriching the interaction with the customers through AR and VR, making digital innovations in distribution and payment channels that offer fast and contactless service assurance
4. Digitalize distribution networks and payment systems
5. Digitalize customer experiences through virtual tools in the product and service phase
6. Develop digital interactions to monitor customers and build trust
7. Developing interactions that will improve the trust by observing the customers, making web sites and social media tools informative and trustworthy
8. Taking action regarding E-WOM that will encourage the customers

The second important point the writer has made considering the change in consumer behavior in this section is that it is necessary to focus on products and services that will connect them to life while they are staying at home or by themselves, as an alternative to socialization, and increase their joy of life. As it is mentioned in the suggestions sections, the change in luxury goods' use (like the transition from luxury car to spa), doing at-home activities or exercising shows that humans are in a tendency to improve their life quality as well as their trust and feel more. In that case, managers must develop strategies that will satisfy consumers' demands, develop products and services that will increase the joy of life, or turn product/service use into a positive life experience. This situation also strongly corresponds to modern marketing understanding (customer experience/personalization) and strategies. These strategies which will be more significant especially if done through personalized analysis using customer data or big data will help the customer connect with the firm.

As it is stated in this section, the pandemic has not created a new trend in the world. Rather, it has accelerated the digitalization trend and also given the opportunity of transitioning to newer business models which have been backdated for many products/services and business models. The fact that every crisis bears an opportunity within and some firms have come out of previous crises even greater hold opportunities, especially for smaller firms. As long as they can grasp the change in the world, more precisely competition, and customers. That's why it is extremely important to find and apply digital/virtual strategies towards customers fast and to the point. It is more probable for firms that gain the trust of their customers on the digital media by applying the suggestions given above, present products/

services or experiences that will give reliance, make them feel good, and connect to life to survive the pandemic stronger.

In summary, the pandemic will kill companies and strengthen survivors. Digitalization, which supports equal opportunities in competition, has accelerated with the pandemic. A promising future awaits those brands that adapt to the changes and connect with customers in a virtual, competitive field.

REFERENCES

Accenture. (2020, November 23). *The Big Value Shift*. https://www.accenture.com/sk-en/insights/strategy/big-value-shift

Adams, F. G. (1964). Consumer Attitudes, Buying Plans, and Purchases of Durable Goods: A Principal Components, Time Series Approach. *The Review of Economics and Statistics*, *46*(4), 347–355. doi:10.2307/1924042

Agur, I., Peria, S. M., & Rochon, C. (2020, July 1). *Digital Financial Services and the Pandemic: Opportunities and Risks for Emerging and Developing Economies. IMF COVID-19 Special Series*. https://www.imf.org/en/Search#q=agur%20peria&sort=relevancy

Ajzen, I. (1991). The theory of planned behavior. *Organizational Behavior and Human Decision Processes*, *50*(2), 179–211. doi:10.1016/0749-5978(91)90020-T

Beheraa, R. K., Gunasekaran, A., & Guptac, S. (2020). Personalized digital marketing recommender engine. *Journal of Retailing and Consumer Services*, *53*, 101799. Advance online publication. doi:10.1016/j.jretconser.2019.03.026

Belch, G. (1975) Belief system and differential role of the self-concept. *Advertising and Consumer Research,* (5), 320-325. http://acrwebsite.org/volumes/9443/volumes/v05/NA-05

Campbell, D., & Frei, F. (2010). Cost structure, customer profitability, and retention implications of self-service distribution channels: Evidence from customer behavior in an online banking channel. *Management Science*, *56*(1), 4–24. doi:10.1287/mnsc.1090.1066

Chang, K.-C., Hsu, C.-L., Chen, M.-C., & Kuo, N.-T. (2017). How a branded website creates customer purchase intentions. *Total Quality Management & Business Excellence*, *30*(3-4), 422–446. doi:10.1080/14783363.2017.1308819

Conway, J. (2020, September 10). *Impact of the coronavirus pandemic on the global FMCG market - Statistics & Facts*. https://www.statista.com/topics/6248/covid-19-impact-on-the-fmcg-market-worldwide/

Cox, N., Ganong, P., Noel, P., Vavra, J., Wong, A., Farrell, D., & Greig, F. (2020). *Initial Impacts of the Pandemic on Consumer Behavior: Evidence from Linked Income, Spending, and Savings Data*. University of Chicago, Becker Friedman Institute for Economics Working Paper No. 2020-82. doi:10.2139srn.3633008

Czarniewski, S. (2014). Changes in consumer behavior in the market and the value of companies. *European Journal of Research and Reflection in Management Sciences*, *2*(2), 61–68.

DeLone, W., & McLean, E. (2003). The model of information systems success: A ten-year update. *Journal of Management Information Systems, 19*(4), 9–30. doi:10.1080/07421222.2003.11045748

Erdoğan, U. (2008). *Tüketici davranış modellerinin tüketici pazarları için tasarlanan ürünlere etkisi* [Master's Thesis, Marmara University]. Marmara University Thesis Collection. https://katalog.marmara.edu.tr/eyayin/tez/T0061510.pdf

Fernazdez-Rovira, C., Valdés, J. A., Molleví, G., & Nicolas-Sans, R. (2021). The digital transformation of business. Towards the datafication of the relationship with customers. *Technological Forecasting and Social Change, 162*(20339), 120339. Advance online publication. doi:10.1016/j.techfore.2020.120339

Fimberg, K., & Sousa, S. (2020). The Impact of Website Design on Users' Trust Perceptions. In Advances in Creativity, Innovation, Entrepreneurship and Communication of Design. AHFE 2020. Advances in Intelligent Systems and Computing. doi:10.1007/978-3-030-51626-0_34

Gathergood, J., & Guttman-Kenney, B. (2020, October 17). *The English Patient: Evaluating Local Lockdowns Using Real-Time COVID-19 & Consumption Data.* https://arxiv.org/abs/2010.04129

Gellweiler, C., & Krishnamurthi, L. (2020). Editorial: How Digital Innovators Achieve Customer Value. *Journal of Theoretical and Applied Electronic Commerce Research, 15*(1), 0. Advance online publication. doi:10.4067/S0718-18762020000100101

Globaltechmagazine. (2020). *Geleceğin en önemli 5 perakende teknolojisi neler olacak.* https://www.globaltechmagazine.com/2020/10/30/gelecegin-en-onemli-5-perakende-teknolojisi-neler-olacak/

Gouveia, L. B., Perun, M., & Daradkeh, Y. I. (2020). Dijital Transformation And Customer Services: The Banking Revolution. *International Journal of Open Information Technologies, 8*(7), 124–128.

Gursoy, D., Ouyang, Z., Nunkoo, R., & Wei, W. (2019). Residents' impact perceptions of and attitudes towards tourism development: A meta-analysis. *Journal of Hospitality Marketing & Management, 28*(3), 306–333. doi:10.1080/19368623.2018.1516589

Hashem, T. (2020). Examining the Influence of COVID 19 Pandemic in Changing Customers' Orientation towards E-Shopping. *Modern Applied Science, 14*(5), 59–76. doi:10.5539/mas.v14n8p59

Hernaez, F. (2020, October 15). *World Luxury Tracking: Between new constraints & new expectations.* https://www.ipsos.com/en/world-luxury-tracking-2020

Ikeda, K., & Marshall, A. (2019). Strategies for competing in markets enabled by digital platforms. *Strategy and Leadership, 47*(1), 30–36. doi:10.1108/SL-10-2018-0097

Ipsos. (2020, March). *Koronavirüs, Hane İçi Hızlı Tüketim Ürünleri Harcamalarına Nasıl Etki Ediyor?* https://www.ipsos.com/tr-tr/koronavirus-hane-ici-hizli-tuketim-urunleri-harcamalarina-nasil-etki-ediyor

Isaeva, N., Gruenewald, K., & Saunders, M. (2020). Trust theory and customer services research: Theoretical review and synthesis. *Service Industries Journal, 1*(33), 1031–1063. doi:10.1080/02642069.2020.1779225

Islamoglu, A. H., & Altunışık, R. (2010). *Tüketici Davranışları.* Beta Basım.

Jacobides, M. G., & Reeves, M. (2020, October 1). Adapt Your Business to the New Reality. *Harvard Business Review Turkey*, *10*, 78–85.

Kim, D. J., Ferrin, D. L., & Rao, H. R. (2008). A Trust-Based Consumer Decision-Making Model in Electronic Commerce: The Role of Trust, Perceived Risk, and Their Antecedents. *Decision Support Systems*, *44*(2), 544–564. doi:10.1016/j.dss.2007.07.001

Kim, M. J., Lee, C.-K., & Jung, T. (2020). Exploring Consumer Behavior in Virtual Reality Tourism Using an Extended Stimulus-Organism-Response Model. *Journal of Travel Research*, *59*(1), 69–89. doi:10.1177/0047287518818915

Kimberly, A. (2020, December 27). *Consumer Spending Statistics and Current Trends*. https://www.thebalance.com/consumer-spending-trends-and-current-statistics-3305916?utm_source=emailshare&utm_medium=social&utm_campaign=shareurlbuttons

Kotler, P. (1965). Behavioral Models for Analyzing Buyers. *Journal of Marketing*, *29*(4), 37–45. doi:10.1177/002224296502900408

Lantos, G. P. (2015). *Consumer behavior in action: Real-life applications for marketing managers*. Routledge. doi:10.4324/9781315705439

Liguori, E. W., & Pittz, T. G. (2020). Strategies for small business: Surviving and thriving in the era of COVID-19. *Journal of the International Council for Small Business.*, *1*(2), 106–110. doi:10.1080/26437015.2020.1779538

Lin, A. J., Li, E. Y., & Lee, S. Y. (2018). Dysfunctional customer behavior in cross-border e-commerce: A justice-affect-behavior model. *Journal of Electronic Commerce Research*, *19*(1), 36–54.

Lock, S. (2020a, October 20). Forecasted change in revenue from the travel and tourism industry due to the coronavirus (COVID-19) pandemic worldwide from 2019 to 2020. *Global change in travel and tourism revenue due to COVID-19 2019-2020*. https://www.statista.com/forecasts/1103426/covid-19-revenue-travel-tourism-industry-forecast

Lock, S. (2020b, November 30). *Year-over-year daily change in seated restaurant diners due to the coronavirus (COVID-19) pandemic worldwide from February 24 to November 28, 2020*. Daily year-on-year impact of COVID-19 on global restaurant dining Feb-Nov 2020. https://www.statista.com/statistics/1103928/coronavirus-restaurant-visitation-impact/

McCracken, G. (1988). *Culture and consumption: New approaches to the symbolic character of consumer goods and activities*. Indiana University Press.

McKinsey. (2020, October 26). Consumer sentiment and behavior continue to reflect the uncertainty of the COVID-19 crisis. *McKinsey & Company COVID-19 Consumer Pulse surveys, conducted globally September 18-30, 2020*. https://www.mckinsey.com/business-functions/marketing-and-sales/our-insights/a-global-view-of-how-consumer-behavior-is-changing-amid-covid-19

Mukherjee, S. (2020, October 26). *Adapting to pandemic-driven consumer behaviour changes*. https://www.researchworld.com/adapting-to-pandemic-driven-consumer-behaviour-changes/

Odabaşı, Y., & Barış, G. (2002). *Tüketici Davranışı*. MediaCat Akademi.

Olson, J. M., & Zanna, M. P. (1993). Attitudes and attitude change. *Annual Review of Psychology*, *28*(3), 117–154. doi:10.1146/annurev.ps.44.020193.001001

Peppers, D., & Rogers, M. (2004). *Managing Customer Experience and Relationships: A Strategic Framework*. John Wiley & Sons.

Turan, A. H. (2011). Determinations Of Customers Internet Shopping Behavior: Empricial Test With The Theory of Planned Behavior (TPB). *Doğuş Üniversitesi Dergisi, 12*(1), 128-143. http://journal.dogus.edu.tr/index.php/duj/article/view/12

TutD. (2020, July 26). FinTech and the COVID-19 Pandemic: Evidence from Electronic. doi:10.2139srn.3660987

Voinea, L., & Filip, A. (2011). Analyzing the main changes in new consumer buying behavior during economic crisis. *International Journal of Economic Practices and Theories*, *1*(1), 14–19.

Wang, H. (2015). Analysis on the Changes in Consumer Behavior and Marketing Countermeasure. In *SHS Web of Conferences* (*Vol. 17*). EDP Sciences. 10.1051hsconf/20151701007

Wang, S., Ngamsiriudom, W., & Hsieh, C. H. (2015). Trust disposition, trust antecedents, trust, and behavioral intention. *Service Industries Journal*, *35*(10), 555–572. doi:10.1080/02642069.2015.1047827

William Wilkie. (1986). *Consumer Behavior*. John Wiley and Sons.

Zhao, Y., & Bacao, F. (2020). What factors determining customer continuingly using food delivery apps during 2019 novel coronavirus pandemic period? *International Journal of Hospitality Management*, *91*, 102683. doi:10.1016/j.ijhm.2020.102683 PMID:32929294

Zhu, G., & Gao, X. (2019). The digital sales transformation featured by precise retail marketing strategy. *Expert Journal of Marketing*, *7*(1), 72–76.

Zimmer, J. C., Arsal, R. A., Al-Marzouqc, M., & Varun, G. (2010). Investigating online information disclosure: Effects of information relevance, trust and risk. *Information & Management*, *47*(2), 115–123. doi:10.1016/j.im.2009.12.003

KEY TERMS AND DEFINITIONS

Augmented Reality (AR): Enrichment of real-life assets via computers.

Consumer Behavior: Decisions and activities by a person or group to meet their needs.

Consumer Preferences: Choices by consumers regarding their consumption of products and/or services.

Digitalization: Transferring information to digital media.

Internet of Things (IoT): Physical assets communicating with each other and big systems in a digital environment.

User Experience: Experiences of an online user with a service provider.

Virtual Reality (VR): Projecting images via digital tools.

Virtual Strategy: Path followed by a company in a virtual environment to achieve organizational goals.

Chapter 12
Sensationalism vs. Information During COVID-19 in Ecuador:
A Framing Theory-Based View

Rebeca Sánchez-Figuera
Universidad Técnica de Manabí, Ecuador

Fernando Casado Gutiérrez
Universidad Técnica de Manabí, Ecuador

Arturo Luque González
https://orcid.org/0000-0002-7447-7560
Universidad Tecnica de Manabí, Ecuador & Universidad del Rosario, Colombia

Jorge García-Guerrero
https://orcid.org/0000-0002-6524-8168
Universidad de Córdoba, Ecuador

ABSTRACT

The different frames used in the COVID-19 coverage in Ecuador by the national and international press were analyzed through their Twitter accounts. This allowed the examination of which aspects of the pandemic were given greater prominence by each newspaper. The study was based on five generic frames, between 17 March and 16 April 2020. The exploration of these frames was carried out by means of an intersubjective content analysis, using four previously trained encoders. The dominant frames for COVID-19 in Ecuador varied according to the media group studied. 1) The concept of heterogeneity was confirmed within framing theory, according to which a single reality, understood as a textual and visual construct, is addressed in multiple ways by the selection of certain aspects that are given greater emphasis or priority; 2) international newspapers and, to a lesser extent, the national press showed their propensity to "internalize" the dynamic of sensationalism; and 3) there are discrepancies in the interests of the readerships with respect to the dominant frames in the media.

DOI: 10.4018/978-1-7998-7164-4.ch012

INTRODUCTION

On 29 February, 2020, the first case of COVID-19, also referred to as coronavirus, was confirmed in Ecuador. The disease spread rapidly throughout the country's 24 provinces, initially leading to significant levels of infection in Guayas, Pichincha, Manabí, Los Ríos and Azuay (El Universo, 2020a). A day after the World Health Organization (WHO) declared the outbreak a pandemic on March 12, 2020, Ecuador announced a national health emergency in order to implement greater prevention and containment measures and avoid mass infection (El Comercio, 2020a). On March 16, the state of emergency decree was signed into law, coming into force the following day to provide for measures such as a curfew, the involvement of police and the armed forces in the implementation of containment, the total suspension of all non-essential face-to-face work, the banning of domestic flights and interprovincial coach and rail transport, as well as the closure of public services in general (Secom, 2020).

The measures were not sufficient to stop the spread of the virus and, as of April 23, 2020, 11,183 cases of infection and 560 deaths were officially reported (El Universo, 2020b), while the total excess deaths—almost certainly attributable to the epidemic—were 15 times higher according to an analysis of data from the official death records by The New York Times (2020), released the same day. Guayaquil, Ecuador's main port and the second most populous city, was the hardest hit, accounting for 68.4% of cases as of April 20 (Millán, 2020). Acosta (2020, p.1) provided a dramatic description of the outbreak in the city, "hundreds of families devastated by the death of a family member, corpses everywhere, including abandoned corpses, hundreds of infected health workers, and thousands of people who are torn between starving to death as they seek daily sustenance on the streets or dying of coronavirus". The scale of the emergency in Guayaquil was such that it became a focus of attention in the media, leading to the need to discuss their key role in this first pandemic of the 21st century (Dircom, 2020).

The objective of this research was to carry out a comparative analysis of the news coverage of the COVID-19 outbreak in Ecuador, in both national and international newspapers, through its framing on the social network, Twitter. To achieve this, approximate answers were sought to the following questions: Which are the predominant news frames of the pandemic in Ecuador? What are the similarities and differences between the news frames of the national and international press? What news events does each respond to? To achieve this, a content analysis was carried out using the keywords "coronavirus", "COVID", "Ecuador", as used in Twitter posts published by the following Ecuadorian newspapers: El Universo, El Comercio, Expreso, La Hora; and the international newspapers, El Espectador (Colombia), El Tiempo (Colombia) El Clarín (Argentina), La Nación (Argentina), El Mundo (Spain) and El País (Spain). The significance of this study arises from its innovative comparative analysis of journalistic publications about COVID-19 in Ecuador, being one of the countries most affected by the pandemic in Latin America. It also contributes to the lines of research into the pandemic in the field of journalism 3.0, thereby enriching knowledge within the social sciences in a context of significant production of literature in the applied sciences.

Framing as a Limitless, Multidirectional Element

Framing theory has evolved considerably and become widely used since its origin in the 1970s, yet the term lacks a unanimous conceptualization (Weaver, 2007; Tuchman, 1978). There is also a lack of agreement on its precise definition and delimitations, with various contradictory positions having emerged (Cacciatore, Scheufele, & Iyengar, 2015; McCombs, 2006).

The processes of framing connect politicians and other opinion leaders to the public, mainly through the media. This is a most effective relationship although issues can be observed and interpreted in different ways, multiplying and complicating their application and effective scope. Hence the need to structure information by creating a bridge to comprehension, principally through a frame that lends meaning and holds the interest (Valkenburg, Semetko & De Vreese, 1999). Therefore, reality as perceived through the news, understood to be a textual and visual construct, necessarily admits different interpretations by each individual. Additionally, a news story is influenced by the surrounding circumstances of the process of its construction, including clear design parameters, production techniques, context, flexibility, necessities and requirements.

Frames, according to Reese (2001, p.11), allow us "*to structure with meaning the social world*" In fact, framing theory introduces the component of meaning to the facts themselves, as well as other associated interaction processes (De Vreese, 2005). The concept of heterogeneity also appears to be a strength in the face of multifactorial dilemmas (Reese; 2007; D'Angelo, 2002). In other words, a selection is made of certain aspects of a reality—even one that is fabricated— that are given greater emphasis or priority, including parameters such as value judgments, importance, solutions or simply the behavior to be applied through different techniques (Entman, 1993). This then transcends from the prime cause (physical or logical) that produces the news event to the audience, who must then decode it through endogenous processes of interpretation and understanding. All this is conditioned by the opinions held by the public, which may be poorly informed or absent altogether (Chong & Druckman, 2007; Zaller 1992; Converse 1964). Here, news as a construct delimits reality, acting as an osmotic membrane between perception itself and one part of reality. Consequently, in Hirschman's view, "*Vacillation, indifference, or weakly held opinions have long met with utmost contempt, while approval and admiration have been bestowed on firmness, fullness, and articulation of opinion*" (1989, p.76).

Twitter: Tool or Dystopia?

Twitter, as a dissemination tool, is a means of communication of somewhat unconventional attributes (Zhao et al., 2011). It defines itself as a microblogging service through message dissemination allowing open and free access. Twitter collects information on all activity in its network in order to offer additional services of publicity and impact to add to the 280 characters allowed in each message (prior to 2017, this was a 140 maximum). The potentially high impact is one of its greatest strengths as Twitter boasts a monthly average of 330 million active users (Clement, 2019). It operates on the basis of the followers of an account registered through the @ sign followed by the username (e.g. @bbcnews) and other features, such as trending topics (those attracting the greatest activity of the day), retweets (news stories that have been published in another account and are then shared), and hashtags (words or phrases that are prefixed by the # symbol), which create a trend around a slogan (e.g., #MakeAmericaGreatAgain). Twitter establishes an asymmetric process of interaction in which different interests converge to form a thematic agenda through different frames (Sicilia, Díaz & Langa, 2013), the impact of which is becoming increasingly evident (Murthy, 2018). The main objective is to create an impact on the public (Boulianne, 2009; Kenski & Stroud, 2006) through continuous messages and responses (Lovejoy, Waters, & Saxton, 2012; Small, 2011). As a result, it is a worthy object of study as a mechanism that introduces synergies, political debate and non-regulated elements (Hamdy & Gomaa, 2012). Indeed, information and the opinion of people from outside the media can be incorporated to provide vital elements of news that are an alternative to that of traditional journalism. Government news releases or stories cast by the establishment media, which are defined by their adherence to the traditional processes of communication, can all be called into question.

Framing Theory as Currently Applied to Twitter

Recent studies focusing on framing theory demonstrate the dynamism and vigor that its conceptual precepts continue to manifest (Luque et al., 2020). Proof of this are the nearly 17 thousand citations that Entman's classic (1993) "Framing: Toward clarification of a fractured paradigm", has accrued, according to the statistics of Microsoft Academic (as of June 2020). Contemporary research around framing and its application to Twitter has numerous proponents, underlining the importance of this theoretical field. First, these cover a wide diversity of topics, ranging from the newsworthiness of genetically modified mosquitoes (Wang & Guo, 2018) to users of train travel (Nisar & Prabhakar, 2018). Through framing theory applied to Twitter, the divergent narratives of social networks and the media have been documented. Controversial characters such as Edward Snowden are depicted as media heroes and media traitors (Qin, 2015); in the murder of journalist Jamal Khashoggi, influencers on Twitter were instrumental in creating narrative frames for or against Saudi Arabia's regional agenda (Abrahams & Leber, 2020).

Conflict, as expressed in general terms, is another common topic of interest for framing-related research. Consequently, warfare is a theme in which framing theory has flourished. Following Entman's claim that governments construct frames for the media through which to present their policies to the public in a positive light (1993), Manor and Crilley (2018) conducted an analysis of the war in Gaza in 2014 as framed through the Twitter account of Israel's foreign minister. Elsewhere, frames have been used in the analysis of the Taliban's resurgence in Afghanistan and their strategies, via Twitter, for the recruitment of adherents in central and south Asia, as well as to reach receptive audiences in the West (Drissel, 2015).

The fascination of war notwithstanding, the favored theme of communication research into framing has consistently been elections. It would be an impossible and endless task to cover all of the studies in this field; however, there are several outstanding recent papers that are essential references for the present study. In the context of electoral campaigns, Walter and Ophir (2019) reproduced the competitive frames of the topics and strategy used by Cappella and Jamieson (1997) to examine the Twitter communication of the top twelve candidates in the U.S. Republican Party primaries of 2016. Vlatkovic (2018) conducted a study through framing theory of the new communication paradigm on Twitter imposed by Donald Trump during the last U.S. presidential election. Other studies into electoral analysis focus on visual framing, taking as a reference the images published on Twitter and used to influence the perception of the audience in Spain's 2015 municipal elections (Quevedo, Portalés & Salomé, 2016). Beyond the Western electoral context are studies of framing and the personalization of politics through the use of Twitter in the 2014 Indian elections that helped bring relative outsider Narendra Modi to power (Bajaj, 2017). Current framing theory has already begun to produce various studies applied to the context of COVID-19. Lin and Le Pham (2020) assessed how The New York Times established the following frames on its pandemic coverage: "the novel coronavirus is a deadly Chinese coronavirus" and "the Chinese government is to blame for the spread of COVID-19." Other research has applied the use of framing and Twitter to the analysis of the different frames used in the context of the pandemic crisis in the Canadian media (Poirier et al., 2020). The effects of the COVID-19 pandemic and the frames through which it has been presented to the public is the focal point of this present study.

The Use of Generic Frames in Communication Research

Various methodological tools have been developed to study the use of framing to determine the most emphasized aspects of a topic that are used to influence the recipient of a message. Two epistemological approaches can be distinguished within media framing research (De Vreese, 2005; De Vreese, Peter & Semetko, 2001) "*a generic approach to frames and an issue-specific approach*" (Idoyaga et al., 2012, p.33). Generic frames cut across different themes, so that they may be applied to the analysis of various facts, contexts and spaces. In contrast, specific frames refer to particular facts, with categories of analysis confined to a certain topic. The pioneers of the line of research into generic frames (Semetko & Valkenburg, 2000; Valkenburg, Semetko & De Vreese, 1999) identify five main frames: conflict, consequences, human interest, morality and attribution of responsibility. These are to be further defined in the next section, according to the objectives of the research.

However, many authors have chosen to build custom frames adapted to their object of study following analysis of a sample on Twitter. This is the case of Supovitz and Reinkordt (2017), who analyzed the use of this social network by opponents of certain education policies, which generated various frames used to communicate their values to the public. Another recent approach is that developed by Johnson, Lee and Goldwasser (2017) for the classification of political discourse on Twitter, which combines linguistic characteristics and ideological indicators in order to refine the application of frames to this social network.

Digital platforms and the transnational flow of information affect our understanding of framing as a tool for the analysis of political conflicts. As this flow grows, media systems are increasingly affected and network environments and the emerging logic of digital platforms become more complex (Knüpfer & Entman, 2018). As a consequence, certain analyses seek to address how terrorism is framed on Twitter in this complex network usage of ever-increasing volumes of information, users and interactions (Kwon, Chadha, & Pellizzaro, 2017).

METHODOLOGY

The study of tweets linked to COVID-19 in Ecuador was carried out through an analysis of deductive exploratory content, within the ambit of framing theory, to verify the existence of previously defined generic frames in the two media groups that make up the sample. The study period ran from March 17, 2020, when the state of emergency decree came into force, until April 16, a month later. Ecuador suggests itself as a relevant case study due to the wide dissemination, on Twitter, of images of corpses piling up in public spaces as a result of the collapse of the health system, a situation that had a great impact on society. The crisis was described by the digital newspaper El Periódico in the following terms:

"What is happening in the country's public health system? They don't come to collect the dead from people's houses, they leave them on the sidewalks, they collapse in front of hospitals, no one wants to pick them up," decried the mayor of Guayaquil, Cynthia Viteri. The stories are indeed shocking. Families have to live with coffins in their midst, waiting for them to be removed, or gather round the deceased, barely shrouded in a blanket, counting down the hours until someone comes to take the body from the floor. (2020)

These stark images that went viral on social media, and the public debate provoked by them, lend a specific identity to the Ecuadorian experience of the pandemic that makes it stand out from others, even more so when framed in the regional context of the collapse of the health system and the inability of the authorities to deal with the crisis.

To meet the objective of analyzing news coverage of COVID-19 in national and international newspapers in Ecuador, the social network, Twitter, was selected. This was due to its widespread use as a tool for the dissemination of news, as established by Kwak et al. in their article "What is Twitter, a Social Network or a News Media?" in which they point out that the majority of trending topics (over 85%) "are headline news or persistent news in nature" (2010).

Characterization of the Sample

The sample is drawn from two groups of newspapers—national and international—with established reputations or wide circulations: El Universo (Ecuador), El Comercio (Ecuador), Expreso (Ecuador), La Hora (Ecuador), El Espectador (Colombia), El Tiempo (Colombia) El Clarín (Argentina), La Nación (Argentina), El Mundo (Spain) and El País (Spain). These are described below.

El Universo, based in Guayaquil, is considered the leading newspaper in Ecuador. In 2007, it was consolidated as the media conglomerate with the second highest turnover in the country, after the Isaiah group, and currently has 2.1 million followers on Twitter. El Comercio is the leading newspaper in the city of Quito and has the second largest circulation in Ecuador. At the time of research, it had 1.7 million followers on Twitter. Expreso, founded in 1973 in Guayaquil, currently has 754.3 thousand followers on Twitter. La Hora uniquely has a national edition and ten regional editions, with a presence in almost the whole country. Currently it has 564.9 thousand followers on Twitter (Casado & Sánchez, 2017).

El Tiempo is the most widely disseminated newspaper in Colombia and is also in the top five publications in Latin America by circulation. It currently has 7 million followers on Twitter. El Espectador, Colombia's oldest newspaper, traditionally is the second most widely read national paper, after El Tiempo; it currently has 5.2 million followers on Twitter. El Clarín, which enjoys the largest circulation in Argentina, is second only to Spain's El País as the most widely read Spanish language daily newspaper. It has 3.1 million followers on Twitter. La Nación, Argentina's oldest newspaper, ranks second to El Clarín in the country and has 3.4 million followers on Twitter. El País, the foremost Spanish newspaper in terms of readership is also one of the most influential in the Americas, a region to which it devotes a significant part of its coverage; it has 7.6 million followers on Twitter. Finally, El Mundo, in second place in terms of circulation in Spain, claims to be "*the world leader in electronic information, on the Internet, in Spanish*" ranking 12th of the most visited websites in Spain, ahead of its main competitor, El País; it has 3.7 million followers on twitter (Casado, 2015, p.27).

Units of Analysis

In the selection and extraction of the relevant tweets for this study, the MAXQDA program, version 2020, was used in order to collect units of analysis with novel, condensed or specific meanings, that is, shortcut words (Charmaz, 2006). To this end, from the sample of international media, a selection was made of those that referred to Ecuador (Guayaquil, Quito, Ecuador), amassing a total of 168 units of analysis; at the same time, from the national media sample, the selection focused on those that referred to the "coronavirus" or "COVID" in "Ecuador", for a total of 2515 units of analysis.

The 168 tweets analyzed from international media came from the following sources: 54 in El Clarín, 41 in El Espectador, 22 in El País, 22 in El Tiempo, 21 in La Nación and 8 in El Mundo, while the 2515 tweets in the national media correspond to 999 in El Universo, 721 in El Comercio, 515 in La Hora and 280 in Expreso.

Frame Building in the Context of COVID-19

The exploration of the frames was made by content analysis (Benoit, 2013; Nuendorf & Kumar, 2015), a technique that delves into the structure of the tweets and detects the adscription of the units of analysis within each general frame "*in a systematic, objective, replicable, valid way*" (Ruiz, 1996, p.193). To this end, an empirical methodology is established of an intersubjective nature (Alvarez Ossa, 2016), in which four encoders interact in the characterization of the sample units. To establish the reliability of the study, the encoders went through a process of practical training, based on a 20-item guide, which had previously been used in a pilot experiment that allowed the necessary adjustments to be made to the items.

In order to establish the frames, the aspects of the event that is the focus of the news story have the greatest influence, and answers must be provided to questions such as "who did what?" and "for what purpose?" (Ardevol-Abreu, 2015). Therefore, when operating the frames, they must be adapted to the reality of COVID-19 in Ecuador, following the approach of Gamson and Modigliani (1989). In order to identify the similarities and/or differences in the development of news coverage of the pandemic in Ecuador by national and international newspapers on Twitter, generic frames on the scale proposed by Semetko and Valkenburg (2000) were used: conflict, consequences, human interest, morality and responsibility (De Vreese, Peter & Semetko, 2001). These are detailed below.

The frame of conflict refers to disputes or antagonisms between individuals, groups and institutions as a strategy to capture as wide an audience as possible. Examples of this frame in the newspaper La Hora include: "The mayor of #Guayaquil, @CynthiaViteri6, accuses the Government of #Ecuador of having left them 'alone' to face the health emergency and is calling for international aid to combat the pandemic" (Twitter, 2020a); and in El País: "The text that Podemos uses to call for an investigation into a 'criminal organization' of fake news cites two cases in which images of coffins and corpses are falsely attributed to Spain, which were actually taken in Italy and Ecuador" (Twitter, 2020).

The frame of consequences includes texts expressing the social and economic consequences of the coronavirus on individuals, groups, institutions or countries (Neuman et al., 1992). An example of social consequences in El Universo is, "#Ecuador ranks second in number of deaths due to #coronavirusCOVID19 in Latin America" (Twitter, 2020a); and an example of economic consequences in La Hora states, "#Ecuador will face the worst economic crisis in its history" (Twitter, 2020b).

The frame of human interest takes into consideration those publications that focus on the theme of coronavirus from the human or emotional angle, showing specific cases of people or groups involved. Generally speaking, human narratives are aimed at provoking sensations, emotions or impressions, and may be regarded as techniques of sensationalism. An example in the newspaper El Universo is, #Coronavirus in #Ecuador: "We wrapped the bodies of my sister and her husband in plastic and waited 4 days for them to be taken away" (Twitter, 2020b); and in La Nación, "Coronavirus in Ecuador: they had a dead man in the car and tried to pass him off as asleep" (Twitter, 2020).

The morality frame includes publications framed in religious debates or social or moral prescriptions (García-Romero et. al., 2018, Luque 2018). An example in La Hora is, "People of #SantoDomingo trusted to faith to overcome the #coronavirus pandemic" (Twitter, 2020c); and in El Comercio, "#QuédateEn-

Casa [#StayAtHome] and follow these rules to correctly comply with the #cuarentena [#quarantine] for the coronavirus. Overcoming the #covid19 emergency is everyone's responsibility" (Twitter, 2020).

The responsibility frame concerns all tweets that attribute responsibility for problems or solutions arising from coronavirus to the government and other state institutions, or to certain individuals (such as the President of the Republic, Vice President and others), or groups (the public, doctors, scientists), whether in a positive or negative light. An example in El Espectador is, "Otto Sonnenholzner, the unexpected leader of the coronavirus crisis in Ecuador" (Twitter, 2020); or in La Hora, "The public appears unaware of social distancing in the Wholesale Market" (Twitter, 2020d).

The proposed items allowed measurement of the presence/absence of news frames in the texts on COVID-19 in Ecuador. By means of a binary numbering system, where "yes" equals 1 and "no" is 0 for each set item, the dominant frame was established in each analyzed text (the frame that received the greatest number of affirmative responses). The items are derivations of the generic categories of Semetko and Valkenburg (2000), as described above.

RESULTS AND DISCUSSION

Frame Reliability

To evaluate the reliability of the intersubjective coding process of frames, the nominal analysis procedure put forward by Holsti (1969) was employed, using the following formula:

Reliability = 2M x N1+N2

Where M represents the number of coding decisions on which two encoders agree, while N1 and N2 express the total coding decisions of Analyst 1 and Analyst 2 respectively.

Once the result was obtained, a subsample of 15% was taken. Of the 2515 tweets related to COVID-19 in Ecuador, a subsample of 377 tweets was randomly selected, of which the first encoder and second encoder matched 358 reviews, resulting in an agreement of 0.938 (i.e. 93.8%). Taking into account that the minimum level of agreement that must be reached to attest to the reliability of the frames is 0.8 (80%) (Igartua, 2006), the high degree of reliability of the categorization process was established.

The Frames of COVID-19 in Ecuador

The publications on Twitter were all consulted between March 17 and April 16, 2020, in the relevant newspapers, from which those stories with the keywords "coronavirus", "COVID", "Ecuador" were extracted. According to the results, the dominant frames on coronavirus or COVID-19 in Ecuador were different depending on the group of media studied, with a greater presence of the consequences frame in the national press, unlike the international press where the human interest frame was most apparent.

Table 1. Frames

Generic frames	Results: positive answers (1) or negative answers (0)
Conflict Frame	
The news refers to discrepancies between individuals, groups and institutions	
The news suggests a reproach to an individual, group or institutions	
The story alludes to two or more parts of the problem or topic	
The story is construed by alluding to the victors and the vanquished	
Consequences Frame	
The news contains data on infections and deaths	
The text alludes to the effects of coronavirus on health and education systems, food, employment, public services, leisure and entertainment, including sport	
The news mentions present, past or future economic losses or gains	
The story refers to various events that are a direct or indirect consequence of the coronavirus.	
Human Interest Frame	
The news shows a specific case of the topic or problem	
The text reports on the impact of coronavirus on certain individuals or groups of people	
The story delves into the emotions or private lives of the actors or protagonists	
The news suggests the media's interest in creating sensations, emotions or impressions through the stories told	
Morality Frame	
The news contains an ethical or moral message	
The text refers to morality, God, or to other religious principles	
The news includes specific requirements that suggest how action should be taken in the context of coronavirus	
The news refers to the axiological values of justice	
Responsibility Frame	
The text, directly or indirectly, indicates an individual's responsibility for the issue of coronavirus	
The responsibility attributed is positive or negative	
The news suggests solutions to the coronavirus problem	
The news suggests that the problem requires urgent action	
Source: compiled by the author based on García-Romero et al., (2018)	

In the national press, the consequences frame dominated by 62%, which corresponds to a social context of a strong news demand for the effects of the pandemic on the internal reality of the country, especially information linked to the numbers of infections and deaths. At the same time, this sits within a regional environment in which newspapers strive to maintain legitimacy in the face of the "infodemic" and so-called "fake news" phenomena. This is highlighted in the recent study, "From viral to tribal", according to which "the press today reasserts its authority as a reliable platform for information and opinion," after a period of crisis arising from the difficulties in moving from its traditional business model to the digital (Vega, 2020). The struggle to consolidate themselves as reliable sources for their, mainly national, readerships compounds the concern of the Ecuadorian media for news that is contextualized and stays close to official versions.

Figure 1. Frequency of generic frames in national media
Source: own elaboration

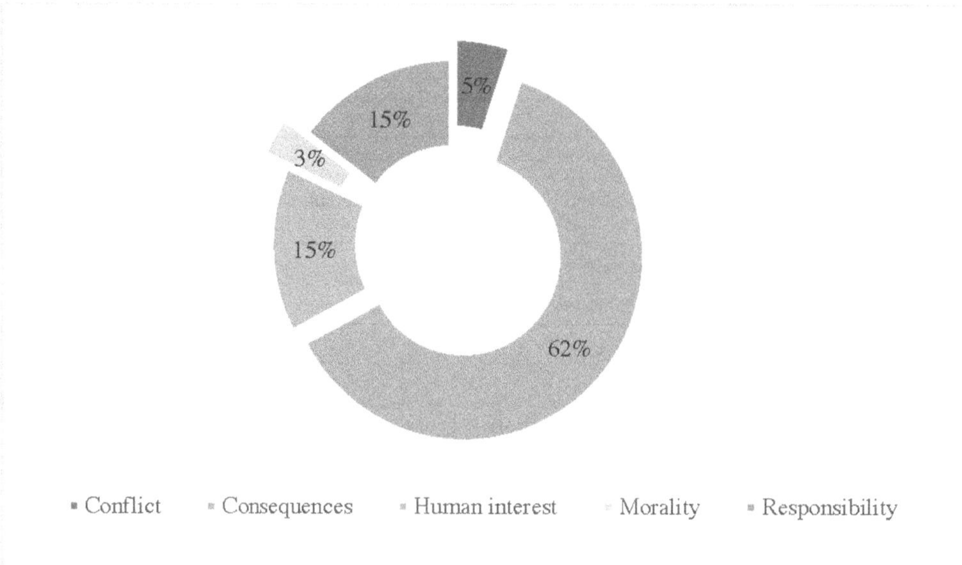

Figure 2. Frequency of generic frames in international media
Source: own elaboration

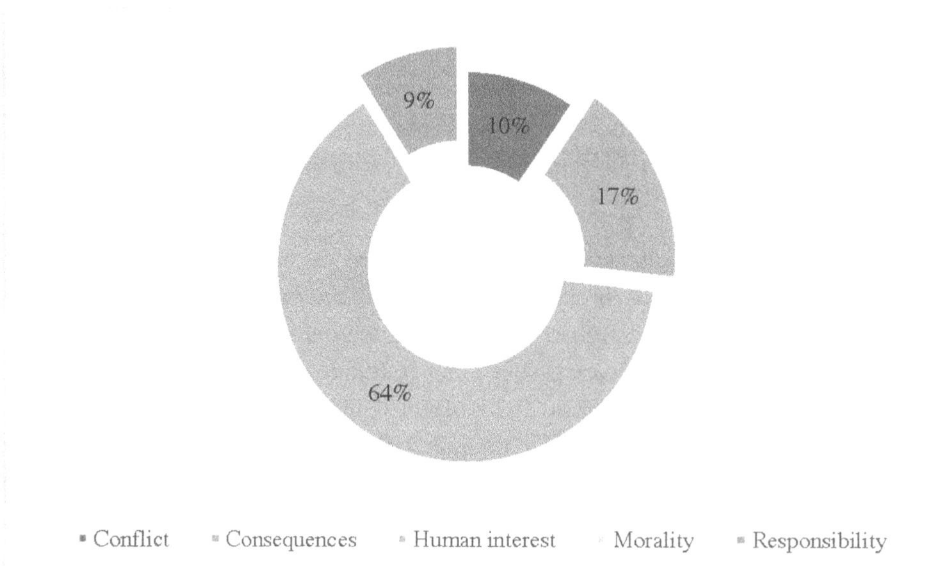

In the international press, the human interest frame dominated by 64%, which may be interpreted as part of the commercial strategy of that media group to attract greater audiences through a sense of the morbidly spectacular at the expense of the contextualization of news about the situation of COVID-19 in Ecuador (Bennett, Swenson & Wilkinson, 1992). This media group chose largely to report on the mass deaths, in many cases accompanied by gratuitous details, as well as focus on the feelings and emotions of the people affected.

According to these findings, as differentiated by national newspapers, El Universo and La Hora contributed most to the framing of consequences, unlike El Comercio and Expreso, which, while favoring this same frame, structured a greater number of their publications through the frames of responsibility and human interest. El Comercio took the greatest interest in the actions of prevention and containment by state agencies, mainly by the executive branch. However, together with Expreso, a significant percentage of news coverage addressed the human interest angle, which suggests a deliberate intention of creating sensations, emotions or impressions through the stories told. Both newspapers are part of the so-called "serious press" in Ecuador, yet, on several occasions, they have shown flexibility in promoting public opinion on the situation of COVID-19 in Ecuador in the search for angles that are more entertaining and commercially appealing. This can also be seen, although to a lesser extent, in the cases of La Hora and El Universo. This situation calls into question the classic duality of the serious press versus tabloid reporting; as Redondo-García (2012, p.237) explains, "*the traditional division between informative journalism and sensationalist journalism has been rethought by various researchers who understand that this stark separation does not hold water, given the process of thematic and formal contamination that the media experience, without exceptions*".

Figure 3. Generic frames on Coronavirus in Ecuador, in percentages, by national newspaper
Source: own elaboration

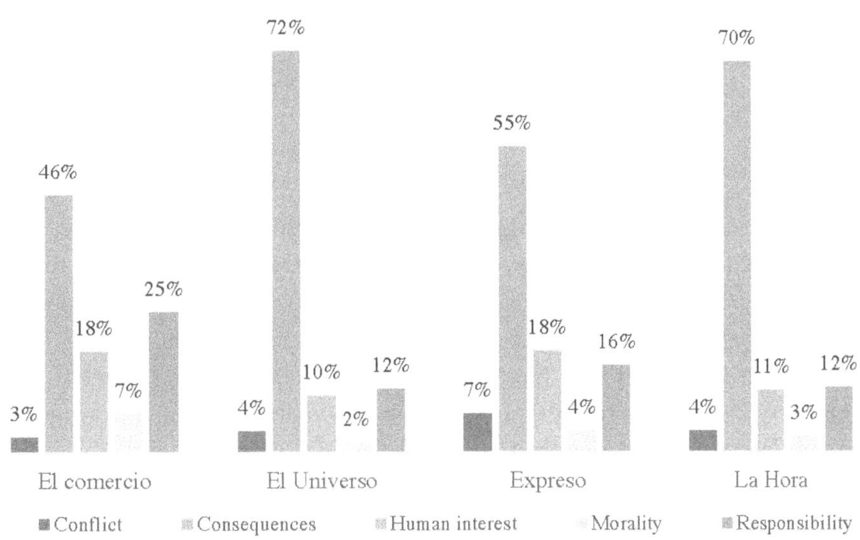

Within the group of international newspapers, El Mundo y La Nación recorded the highest percentage of news interpreted through the human interest frame, unlike El País, the "least tainted" in its morbid attraction to catastrophic aspects; nevertheless, half of its news focused on the spectacular and the banal in its reporting of facts about the coronavirus in Ecuador (Aksoy & Robins, 2002). Generally speaking, this group of newspapers blurred the traditionally clear boundary that separates rigorous and reliable journalism from sensational journalism, through reporting in which the scrutiny and entertainment of the tabloid format was more in evidence. In terms of content, the publications in this frame related to dramatic and shocking stories of infection and death, mainly in the city of Guayaquil, with a liberal accompaniment of controversial photographs and videos of corpses abandoned in public spaces, piled up in morgues and hospitals, or cremated by relatives. There were also reports from citizens affected by the collapse of the health system and a lack of government response.

Figure 4. Generic frames of the coronavirus in Ecuador by international newspaper, in percentages
Source: own elaboration

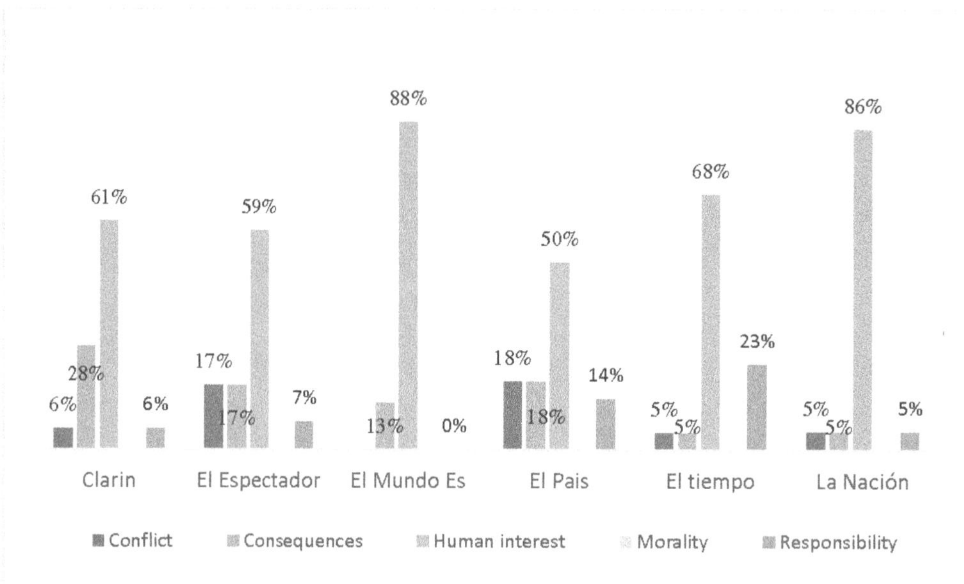

The results in Figure 5 show that, although in the national press there is a greater dissemination of retweets and favorites belonging to the consequences frame, there are times when this tendency does not apply. On March 28, the human interest frame peaked significantly, coinciding with the going viral of the harshest images that documented the inability of the Ecuadorian authorities to deal with the dead left on the streets. In fact, audiences gave much more attention to sensational images and stories than to information about COVID-19 in the frame of consequences, which most Ecuadorian newspapers focused on. This has its parallel in the sensationalization of politics (Bouza, 2007).

Figure 5. Retweets and favorites per day by frame in national newspapers
Source: own elaboration

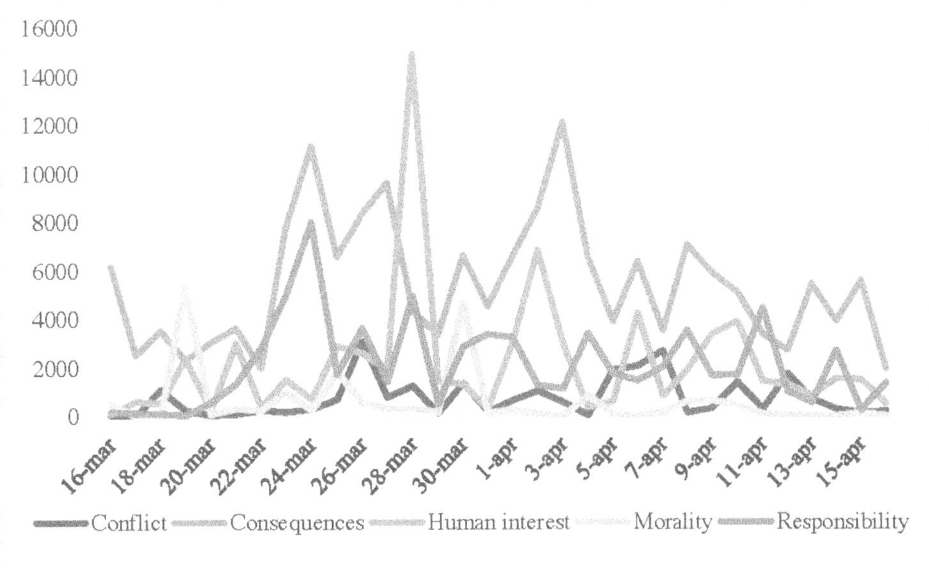

Figure 6. Retweets and favorites by frame per day in national newspapers
Source: own elaboration

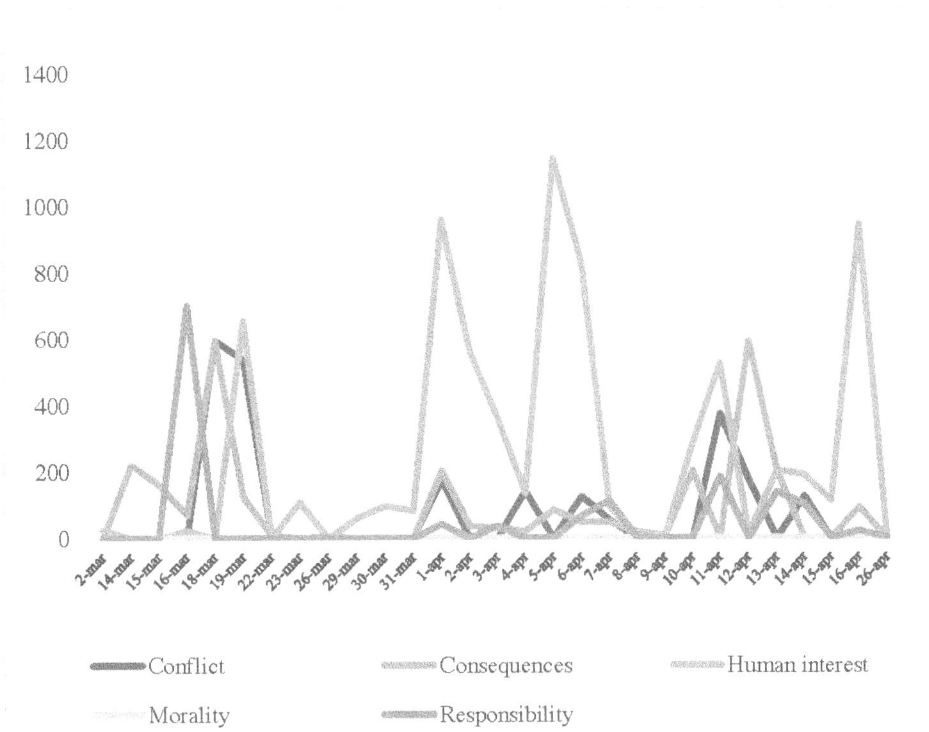

Figure 6, in reference to retweets and international media favorites, shows that these coincide with the frame of human interest. As in the international newspapers, there are spikes on the days when newspapers posted a large number of tweets to coincide with the times when the authorities were overwhelmed by the number of coronavirus deaths and their apparent lack of response had a greater international impact. The peak of tweets in the responsibility frame, posted on March 16, coincided with the blockade of Guayaquil Airport by municipal vehicles ordered by the mayor, Cynthia Viteri.

CONCLUSION

The application of the generic frames of Semetko and Valkenburg (2000) to the news coverage of COVID-19 in Ecuador confirms their usefulness in comparative works on frame-building on Twitter, regardless of the time or place to which they are applied. By using generic framing that is well established in the literature on political communication, the conclusions of this study are well placed to contribute to the generalizations that are needed to strengthen the theoretical-methodological corpus of framing.

The comparative analysis highlighted the difference between the national and international media in their treatment of the COVID-19 outbreak in Ecuador, as well as the importance of dramatic stories in those frames. Twitter users showed great interest in sensational publications, at times far-removed from the the most prevalent frames in the news.

In the national press, the frame of consequences predominates in a social context of strong news demand brought about by the effects of the pandemic on the internal situation of the country, especially information linked to the numbers of infections and deaths. The approach of national media is further influenced by their rivalry and struggle to consolidate their credibility in the face of the "infodemic" and fake news phenomena. Meanwhile, the international press, distanced both geographically and socially from this reality, focused its news through the frame of human interest, responding to a commercial strategy to capture larger audiences by way of the morbid and the spectacular. At the same time, the contextualization of the news stories surrounding COVID-19 in Ecuador was rejected. This media group largely reported from the perspective of the feelings and emotions of those affected, often with gratuitous details.

With their origin in the same reality of the coronavirus in Ecuador, two news constructs emerge in the national and international press. This confirms the concept of heterogeneity in framing theory, according to which, a single reality, understood as a textual and visual construct, is addressed in multiple ways through the selection of certain aspects to which greater emphasis or priority are given. In this way, the media has an impact on the interpretation of the coronavirus pandemic in Ecuador by its audience and, at the same time, journalism is conditioned by the opinions of the same readership. The differentiated construction of dominant frames in the national and international press was mediated by factors such as the context (social, cultural, political, media type, geographical) in which such frames were created, the journalistic needs of each media group, its value judgments, as well as the requirements of its audiences, editorial teams, and other aspects.

The international newspapers have confirmed the tendency of the so-called "serious press" to "internalize" sensationalist techniques in the pursuit of wider readerships and greater profit. Although to a much lesser extent, the national media has also resorted to the use of these techniques when offered inputs (the dramatic, the unusual and the controversial) by which to create attractive news products. Furthermore, in both groups of media, these are frequently adorned with accessory details that exploit the attraction that people feel toward death and related aspects, even if this leads to the newspapers' mimicking the style of the tabloid and degrading themselves as representatives of quality news reporting, with few exceptions. Such findings show the loss of validity of the classic division between informative journalism and tabloid journalism.

Dissonance between the news frame and the interests of national media audiences in the face of extraordinary events—such as that represented by the viral images of corpses in public spaces—was also identified in the Guayaquil outbreak crisis. This indicates the interest of the audience in sensational images of this type rather than those of a more sober informative character. The sensationalization of politics is evident as audiences readily consume and disseminate those stories colored by the morbid and the spectacular. The impact itself becomes the story rather than the news event. This audience behavior can easily be measured by newspapers using tools such as Twitter and they, in turn, publish sensationalist pieces with greater frequency in the clear knowledge that these are in great demand and, therefore, bring greater economic returns. This objective is pursued to the detriment of journalistic quality and, consequently, the weakening of one of the pillars of every democracy.

REFERENCES

Abrahams, A., & Leber, A. (2020). Framing a murder: Twitter influencers and the Jamal Khashoggi incident. *Mediterranean Politics*, 1-13. doi:10.1080/13629395.2019.1697089

Acosta, A. (2020). El coronavirus en los tiempos del Ecuador [The coronavirus in Ecuador's times]. *Fundación Carolina*. Retrieved from https://www.fundacioncarolina.es/wp-content/uploads/2020/04/AC-23.-2020.pdf

Aksoy, A., & Robins, K. (2002). *Banal transnationalism: The difference that television makes.* University of Oxford. Transnational Communities Programme. Retrieved from http://www.transcomm.ox.ac.uk/working%20papers/WPTC-02-08%20Robins.pdf

Álvarez-Ossa, M. (2016). La subjetividad e intersubjetividad: un camino en la comprensión de lo cultural [Subjectivity and intersubjectivity: a path to understand culture]. *Revista Linhas. Florianópolis, 17*(34), 323-336. https://dx.doi.org/ doi:10.5965/1984723817342016323

Ardévol-Abreu, A. (2015). Framing o teoría del encuadre en comunicación. Orígenes, desarrollo y panorama actual en España [Framing theory in communication research. Origins, development and current situation in Spain]. *Revista Latina de Comunicación Social, 70*, 423–430. doi:10.4185/RLCS-2015-1053

Aruguete, N., & Koziner, N. S. (2014). La cobertura mediática del "7D" en la prensa argentina. Aplicación de encuadres noticiosos genéricos a los principales diarios nacionales [The media coverage of "7d" in the argentine press. application of generic news frames to major national newspapers]. *Anuario Electrónico de Estudios en Comunicación Social. Disertaciones, 7*(1), 129–165.

Bajaj, S. G. (2017). The Use of Twitter during the 2014 Indian General Elections. Framing, Agenda-Setting, and the Personalization of Politics. *Asian Survey, 57*(2), 249-270. Retrieved from https://bit.ly/34HoeYW

Bennett, E. M., Swenson, J. D., & Wilkinson, J. S. (1992). Is the Medium the Message? An Experimental Test With Morbid News. *The Journalism Quarterly, 69*(4), 921–928. doi:10.1177/107769909206900411

Bennett, W. L. (2016). *News: The politics of illusion*. University of Chicago Press.

Benoit, W. (2013). Content Analysis in Political Communication. In E. P. Bucy & L. Holbert (Eds.), *Sourcebook for Political Communication Research Methods, Measures, and Analytical Techniques* (pp. 268–279). Routledge.

Berná-Sicilia, C., Pérez-Díaz, P. L., & Arroyas-Langa, E. (2013). La construcción del relato sobre la "Ley Wert": un análisis de los encuadres interpretativos del debate en Twitter [The "Wert Law" narrative construction: an analysis of the interpretive frames of the debate on Twitter]. In *Redes sociales y lo 2.0 y 3.0*. Visión Libros.

Boulianne, S. (2009). Does internet use affect engagement? A meta-analysis of research. *Political Communication*, *26*(2), 193–211. https://dx.doi.org/10.1080/

Bouza, F. (2007). La telenovelización de la política (del nacionalcatolicismo al mirón comunitario). In J. Almaraz & J. Carabaña (Eds.), *Lo que hacen los sociólogos, libro-homenaje a Carlos Moya* [Policy's telenovelization (from national-Catholicism to community voyeur)] (pp. 363–373). Centro de Investigaciones Sociológicas.

Cacciatore, M., Scheufele, D., & Iyengar, S. (2015). The End of Framing as we Know it … and the Future of Media Effects. *Mass Communication & Society*, *19*(1), 7–23. doi:10.1080/15205436.2015.1068811/

Cañás, M. (2020). *La evidencia en tiempos de coronavirus (COVID-19)* [Evidence in times of coronavirus (COVID-19)]. Retrieved from http://evidencia.org.ar/index.php/Evidencia/article/view/4285/1851

Cappella, J. N., Joseph, N., Jamieson, K. H., & Hall, K. (1997). *Spiral of cynicism: The press and the public good*. Oxford University Press on Demand.

Casado-Gutiérrez, F. (2015). *Antiperiodistas. Confesiones de las agresiones mediáticas contra Venezuela* [Anti-journalists. Confessions of the media attacks against Venezuela]. Akal.

Casado-Gutiérrez, F., & Sánchez-Figuera, R. (2017). *La comunicación en tiempos de la Revolución Ciudadana: hablan los periodistas* [Communication in times of the Citizen Revolution: journalists talk]. Ciespal.

Charmaz, K. (2006). *Constructing grounded theory: A practical guide through qualitative analysis*. Sage.

Chew, C., & Eysenbach, G. (2010). Pandemics in the age of Twitter: Content analysis of Tweets during the 2009 H1N1 outbreak. *PLoS One*, *5*(11). Advance online publication. doi:10.1371/journal.pone.0014118

Chong, D., & Druckman, J. N. (2007). Framing theory. *Annual Review of Political Science*, *10*, 103–126. doi:10.1146/annurev.polisci.10.072805.103054

Clement, J. (2019). *Twitter: number of monthly active users 2010-2019*. Statista. Retrieved from https://www.statista.com/statistics/282087/number-of-monthly-active-twitter-users/#statisticContainer

Converse, P. E. (1964). The nature of belief sys-tems in mass publics. In D. E. Apter (Ed.), *Ideology and Dis-content* (pp. 206–261). Free.

D'Angelo, P. (2002). News framing as a multiparadigmatic research program: A response to Entman. *Journal of Communication*, *52*, 870–888. doi:10.1111/j.1460-2466.2002.tb02578.x

De Vreese, C.H. (2005). News framing: Theory and typology. *Information Design Journal & Document Design, 13*(1), 51-62.

De Vreese, C. H., Peter, J., & Semetko, H. A. (2001). Framing politics at the launch of the euro: A crossnational comparative study of frames in the news. *Political Communication, 18*, 107–122. doi:10.1080/105846001750322934

Delgado-López, E., & Martín-Martín, A. (2020). *La viralidad de la ciencia defectuosa: el contagioso impacto mediático de un preprint en bioRxiv sobre el coronavirus y sus efectos en la comunicación científica* [The virality of flawed science: the contagious media impact of a coronavirus-related preprint on bioRxiv and its effects on scientific communication]. doi:10.13140/RG.2.2.12666.44485

Dircom. (2020, April 21). El papel de los medios de comunicación ante la pandemia del COVID-19 [Media role during the COVID-19 pandemic]. *Asociación de Directivos de Comunicación.* Retrieved from http://www.dircom.org/actualidad-dircom/item/10381-el-papel-de-los-medios-de-comunicacion-ante-la-pandemia-del-covid-19

. doi:

Drissel, D. (2015). Reframing the Taliban insurgency in Afghanistan: new communication and mobilization strategies for the Twitter generation. *Behavioral Sciences of Terrorism and Political Aggression,* 97-128. https://doi.org/ doi:10.1080/19434472.2014.986496

El Comercio. (2020a, March 12). *Presidente declara emergencia sanitaria en el Ecuador por el coronavirus covid-19* [President declares a health emergency in Ecuador due to the covid-19 coronavirus]. Retrieved from El Comercio: https://www.elcomercio.com/video/ecuador-medidas-emergencia-coronavirus-covid.html

El Comercio [@elcomerciocom]. (2020, March 23). *Home* [Twitter page]. Twitter. Retrieved from https://t.co/RmwgTPYxlR

El Espectador [@elespectador]. (2020, April 6). *Home* [Twitter page]. Twitter. Retrieved from https://t.co/2M7njbCqrM

El País [@el_pais]. (2020, April 2). *Home* [Twitter page]. Twitter. Retrieved from https://t.co/SLfMLlxTzt

El Periódico. (2020, April 2). *Muertos en las calles: la imagen que resume la crisis del coronavirus en Ecuador* [Death on the streets: the image that sums up the coronavirus crisis in Ecuador]. Retrieved from El Periódico: https://www.elperiodico.com/es/internacional/20200402/muertos-en-las-calles-la-imagen-que-resume-la-crisis-sanitaria-en-ecuador-7914370

El Universo. (2020a, April 11). *En 5 provincias del Ecuador el coronavirus se expande de forma comunitaria* [In 5 provinces of Ecuador the coronavirus spreads at community level]. Retrieved from El Universo: https://www.eluniverso.com/noticias/2020/04/12/nota/7811271/5-provincias-coronavirus-se-expande-forma-comunitaria

El Universo. (2020b, April 23). *Casos de coronavirus en Ecuador, 23 de abril 11h00: 22 160 contagiados, 560 fallecidos* [Cases of coronavirus in Ecuador, April 23th 11h00: 22,160 infected, 560 deaths]. Retrieved from El Universo: https://www.eluniverso.com/noticias/2020/04/23/nota/7821111/casos-coronavirus-ecuador-23-abril-11h00-10-contagiados-5

El Universo [@eluniversocom]. (2020a, March 31). *Home* [Twitter page]. Twitter. Retrieved from https://t.co/FI6zHPVbqd

El Universo [@eluniversocom]. (2020b, April 6). *Home* [Twitter page]. Twitter. Retrieved from https://t.co/fJzLwvWM0e

Entman, R. (1993). Framing: Toward clarification of a fractured paradigm. *Journal of Communication, 43*, 51–58.

Entman, R. (2004). *Proyection of Power. Framing News, public opinión and U.S. Foreign Policy*. University of Chicago Press.

Franzosi, R., Doyle, S., McClelland, L.E., Rankin, C.P., & Vicari, S. (2013). Quantitative narrative analysis software options compared: PC-ACE and CAQDAS (ATLAS. ti, MAXqda, and NVivo). *Quality & Quantity: International Journal of Methodology, 47*(6), 3219-3247. doi:10.100711135-012-9714-3

García-Romero, E., Ruiz-San Román, J. A., & Serrano-Oceja, J. F. (2018). *Google es noticia. Transformación de los marcos informativos sobre Google en la prensa española. Google is in the news. Transformation of the news frames about Google in the Spanish press.* Academic Microsoft. Retrieved from https://academic.microsoft.com/paper/2810706329/related

Giménez, J. (2020). *Coronavirus y desinformación: la otra pandemia.* Retrieved from http://sedici.unlp.edu.ar/bitstream/handle/10915/94170/Documento_completo.pdf?sequence=1&isAllowed=y

Grabe, M. E., Zhou, S., & Barnett, B. (2001). Explicating sensationalism in television news: Content and the bells and whistles of form. *Journal of Broadcasting & Electronic Media, 45*(4), 635–655. doi:10.120715506878jobem4504_6

Hamdy, N., & Gomaa, E. H. (2012). Framing the Egyptian uprising in Arabic language newspapers and social media. *Journal of Communication, 62*(2), 195–211. doi:10.1111/j.1460-2466.2012.01637.x

Hirschman, A. O. (1989). Having opinions—One ofthe elements of well-being. *The American Economic Review, 79*(2), 75–79. doi:10.2307/1827734

Holsti, O. R. (1969). *Content analysis for the social sciences and humanities.* AddisonWesley.

Idoyaga, N., Valencia, J. F., Gil-de Montes, L., & Ortiz, G. (2012). Efectos del Framing y representaciones sociales de epidemias sanitarias: El Caso de la Gripe A. *Escritos de Psicologia, 5*(3), 31–42. doi:10.5231/psy.writ.2012.0211

Igartua, J. (2006). *Métodos cuantitativos de investigación en comunicación* [Quantitative research methods in Communication]. Editorial Bosch S.A.

Jarren, O. (2008). Media democracy. *The international encyclopedia of communication.* Retrieved from https://onlinelibrary.wiley.com/doi/abs/10.1002/9781405186407.wbiecm024

Johnson, K., Lee, I.-T., & Goldwasser, D. (2017). Ideological Phrase Indicators for Classification of Political Discourse Framing on Twitter. *Second Workshop on Natural Language Processing and Computational Social Science*, 90-99. doi: 10.18653 / v1 / W17-2913

Kenski, K., & Stroud, N. J. (2006). Connections between Internet use and political efficacy, knowledge, and participation. *Journal of Broadcasting & Electronic Media*, *50*(2), 173–192. doi:10.120715506878jobem5002_1

Knüpfer, C., & Entman, R. (2018). Framing conflicts in digital and transnational media environments. *Media, War & Conflict*, 476–488. doi:10.1177/1750635218796381

Kuckartz, U. (2010). *Realizing mixed-methods approaches with MAXQDA*. Philipps-Universität.

Kwak, H., Lee, C., Park, H., & Moon, S. (2010). What is Twitter, a social network or a news media? *Proceedings of the 19th International Conference on World Wide Web - WWW '10*. doi:10.1145/1772690.1772751

Kwon, H., Chadha, M., & Pellizzaro, K. (2017). Proximity and Terrorism News in Social Media: A Construal-Level Theoretical Approach to Networked Framing of Terrorism in Twitter. *Mass Communication & Society*, *26*, 1–26. doi:10.1080/15205436.2017.1369545

La Hora [@lahoraecuador]. (2020a, April 10). *Home* [Twitter page]. Twitter. Retrieved from https://t.co/xOiDhd5l5w

La Hora [@lahoraecuador]. (2020b, April 14). *Home* [Twitter page]. Twitter. Retrieved from https://t.co/e2eAsSdIO0

La Hora [@lahoraecuador]. (2020c, April 5). *Home* [Twitter page]. Twitter. Retrieved from https://bit.ly/3erTxZX

La Hora [@lahoraecuador]. (2020d, April 27). *Home* [Twitter page]. Twitter. Retrieved from https://t.co/2EIbfH4yoi

La Nación [@LANACION]. 2020, April 15). *Home* [Twitter page]. Twitter. Retrieved from https://t.co/ndkDfqPwBq

Lin, S., & Le Pham, H. (2020). *Who's Playing the Blame Game? – An Analysis of Media Framing of China and COVID-19 in The New York Times*. Heidelberg Center for American Studies. Retrieved from https://hcagrads.hypotheses.org/2966

Lovejoy, K., Waters, R., & Saxton, G. (2012). Engaging stakeholders through Twitter: How nonprofit organizations are getting more out of 140 characters or less. *Public Relations Review*, *38*(2), 313–318. doi:10.1016/j.pubrev.2012.01.005

Luque, A. (2018). Corruption in the transnational textile industry: An exception or the rule? *Empresa y humanismo, 21*(2), 123-184.

Luque, A., Maniglio, F., Casado, F., & García-Guerrero, J. (2020). Transmedia Context and Twitter as Conditioning the Ecuadorian Government's Action. The Case of the "Guayaquil Emergency" during the COVID-19 Pandemic. *Trípodos*, *2*(47), 47–68.

Manor, I., & Crilley, R. (2018). Visually framing the Gaza War of 2014: The Israel Ministry of Foreign Affairs on Twitter. *Media, War & Conflict*, *11*(4), 369–391. doi:10.1177/1750635218780564

Martín-Barato, A., López-Doblas, M., Luque-Martín, N., & March-Cerdá, J. C. (2020). *Fake news y bulos contra la seguridad y la salud durante la crisis del coronavirus* [Fake news and hoaxes against safety and health during the coronavirus crisis]. Escuela Andaluza de Salud Pública. Retrieved from https://bit.ly/2YNgUHf

McCambridge, J., Hawkins, B., & Holden, C. (2014). Vested interests in addiction research and policy. The challenge corporate lobbying poses to reducing society's alcohol problems: Insights from UK evidence on minimum unit pricing. *Addiction (Abingdon, England)*, *109*(2), 199–205. doi:10.1111/add.12380

McCombs, M. (2006). *Estableciendo la agenda. El impacto de los medios en la opinión pública y en el conocimiento* [Setting the agenda. The impact of the mass media on public opinion and knowledge]. Paidós.

McCombs, M. (2018). *Setting the agenda: Mass media and public opinion*. Maxwell McComs.

Michalski, R. S. (1983). A Theory and Methodology of Inductive Learning. In R. S. Michalski, J. G. Carbonell, & T. M. Mitchell (Eds.), *Machine Learning. Symbolic Computation*. Springer., doi:10.1007/978-3-662-12405-5_

Microsoft Academic. (2020). *Unleash the Power of Semantic Search*. Retrieved from Microsoft Academic: https://bit.ly/2YOnm0H

Millán, A. (2020, April 2). *Coronavirus: ¿por qué Ecuador tiene el mayor número de contagios y muertos per cápita de covid-19 en Sudamérica?* [Coronavirus: why does Ecuador have the highest covid-19 rate of infections and deaths *per capita* in South America]. https://www.bbc.com/mundo/noticias-america-latina-52036460

Murthy, D. (2018). *Twitter*. Polity Press.

Neuendorf, K. A., & Kumar, A. (2016). Content Analysis. In G. Mazzoleni (Ed.), *The International Encyclopedia of Politi-cal Communication*. doi:10.1002/9781118541555.wbiepc065

Neuman, W. R., Just, M. R., & Crigler, A. N. (1992). *Common knowledge*. University of Chicago Press.

Nisar, T., & Prabhakar, G. (2018). Trains and Twitter: Firm generated content, consumer relationship management and message framing. *Transportation Research Part A, Policy and Practice*, *113*, 318–334. doi:10.1016/j.tra.2018.04.026

Poirier, W., Ouellet, C., Rancourt, M.-A., Justine, B., & Dufresne, Y. (2020). (Un)Covering the CO-VID-19 Pandemic: Framing Analysis of the Crisis in Canada. *Canadian Journal of Political Science*, 1–7. Retrieved from https://doi.org/ doi:10.1017/S0008423920000372

Qin, J. (2015). Hero on Twitter, Traitor onNews: How Social Media and Legacy News Frame Snowden. *The International Journal of Press/Politics*, *20*(2), 166–184. doi:10.1177/1940161214566709

Quevedo, R., Portalés, M., & Salomé, B. (2016). The image use on Twitter during the 2015 municipal election campaign in Spain. *Revista Latina de Comunicación Social*, *71*, 85–107.

Redondo-García, M. (2012, October 18). El sensacionalismo y su penetración en la prensa española de calidad. El "caso McCann" en El País, El Mundo y ABC [The Penetration of Sensationalism in the Quality Spanish Press. McCann Case in Newspapers El País, El Mundoand ABC]. *Estudios sobre el Mensaje Periodístico, 19*(1). Advance online publication. doi:10.5209/rev_ESMP.2013.v19.n1.42519

Reese, S. (2007). The framing project: A bridging model for media research revisited. *Journal of Communication, 57*, 148–154. doi:10.1111/j.1460-2466.2006.00334.x

Reese, S. D. (2001). A bridging model for media research. In S. Reese, O. Gandy Jr, & A. Grant (Eds.), *Framing public life: perspectives on media and our understanding of the social world* (Vol. N). Lawrence Erlbaum.

Ruiz, J. (1996). *Metodología en la investigación cualitativa* [Methodology in qualitative research]. Universidad de Deusto.

Sarabia, S. (2020). La salud mental en los tiempos del coronavirus [Mental health in the time of coronavirus]. *Neuropsiquia, 83*(1), 3–4. doi:10.20453/rnp.v83i1.3680

Secom. (2020). El presidente Lenín Moreno decreta Estado de Excepción para evitar la propagación del COVID-19 [President Lenín Moreno decrees the state of emergency to prevent the spread of COVID-19]. *Secretaría Nacional de Comunicación de la Presidencia de Ecuador*. Retrieved from https://www.comunicacion.gob.ec/el-presidente-lenin-moreno-decreta-estado-de-excepcion-para-evitar-la-propagacion-del-covid-19/

Semetko, H., & Valkenburg, P. (2000). Framing European Politics: A Content Analysis of Press and Television News. *Journal of Communication, 50*, 93–109. doi:10.1111/j.1460-2466.2000.tb02843.x

Shelby, T. (2014). Racism, moralism, and social criticism 1. *Du Bois Review, 11*(1), 57–74. doi:10.1017/S1742058X14000010

Sicilia, C. B., Díaz, P. L. P., & Langa, E. A. (2013). La construcción del relato sobre la 'ley wert': un análisis de los encuadres interpretativos del debate en Twitter [The "Wert Law" narrative construction: an analysis of the interpretive frames of the debate on Twitter]. In *Redes sociales y lo 2.0 y 3.0*. Retrieved from https://bit.ly/2EPAE5W

Supovitz, J., & Reinkordt, E. (2017). Keep your eye on the metaphor: The framing of the Common Core on Twitter. *Education Policy Analysis Archives, 25*(30), 1–29. doi:10.14507/epaa.25.2285

The New York Times. (2020, April 23). El número de muertos en Ecuador durante el brote está entre los peores del mundo [The death toll in Ecuador during the outbreak is among the worst in the world]. *The New York Times*. Retrieved from https://www.nytimes.com/es/2020/04/23/espanol/america-latina/virus-ecuador-muertes.html

Tuchman, G. (1978). *Making news*. Free Press.

Valkenburg, P. M., Semetko, H. A., & De Vreese, C. H. (1999). The effects of news frames on readers' thoughts and recall. *Communication Research, 26*(5), 550–569. doi:10.1177/009365099026005002

Van Gorp, B. (2007). The constructionist approach to framing: Bringing culture back. *Journal of Communication, 57*, 60–78. doi:10.1111/j.0021-9916.2007.00329.x

Vega, F. (2020, March 24). Los medios tradicionales recuperan poder y credibilidad con la pandemia provocada por el Coronavirus [Traditional media regain power and credibility due to the Coronavirus pandemic]. *Comscore Social para América Latina*. Retrieved from https://www.comscore.com/lat/Prensa-y-Eventos/Blog/Los-medios-tradicionales-recuperan-poder-y-credibilidad-con-la-pandemia-provocada-por-el-Coronavirus

Venegas, R. (2006). La similitud léxico-semántica en artículos de investigación científica en español: Una aproximación desde el Análisis Semántico Latente [The Lexical-Semantic Similarity in Scientific Research Articles in Spanish: An Approach from Latent Semantic Analysis]. *Revista Signos*, *39*(60), 75–106. doi:10.4067/S0718-09342006000100004

Vlatković, S. (2018). New Communication Forms and Political Framing: Twitter in Donald Trump's Presidential Campaign. *AM Journal*, *16*, 123-134. Retrieved from http://dx.doi.org/10.25038 /am.v0i16.25

Walter, D., & Ophir, Y. (2019). The Elephant and the Bird: Republican Candidates' Use of Strategy. *Journal of Communication*, *13*, 23. Retrieved from https://www.ijoc.org/index.php/ijoc/article/view/11808

Wang, W., & Guo, L. (2018). Framing genetically modified mosquitoes in the online news and Twitter: Intermedia frame setting in the issue-attention cycle. *Public Understanding of Science (Bristol, England)*, *27*(8), 937–951. doi:10.1177/0963662518799564

Weaver, D. H. (2007). Toughts on agenda-setting, framing and priming. *Journal of Communication*, *57*, 142–147. doi:10.1111/j.1460-2466.2006.00333.x

Weller, K., Bruns, A., Burgess, J., Mahrt, M., & Puschmann, C. (2014). Twitter and society. *QUT ePRINTS*, 89. Retrieved from https://bit.ly/3b8o3qC

Wimmer, R. D., & Dominick, J. R. (1996). *La investigación científica de los medios de comunicación. Una introducción a sus métodos* [Mass Media Scientific investigation. An introduction to its methods]. Bosch Casa Editorial S.A.

Wu, S. M., Hofman, J. A., Mason, W., & Watts, J. D. (2011). Who Says What to Whom on Twitter. *International World Wide Web Conference Committee*, 705-714. Retrieved from https://bit.ly/2EP9EDA

Zaller, J. (1992). *The Nature and Origins of Mass Opinion*. Cambridge Univ. Pres.

Zhao, W. X., Jiang, J., Weng, J., He, J., Lim, E. P., Yan, H., & Li, X. (2011). Comparing Twitter and Traditional Media Using Topic Models. In Advances in Information Retrieval. ECIR 2011. Lecture Notes in Computer Science (vol. 6611). Springer. https://doi.org/ doi:10.1007/978-3-642-20161-5_34

Chapter 13
International Trade in the Context of the COVID-19 Pandemic

Giga Abuseridze
Riga Stradins University, Latvia

ABSTRACT

This chapter overviews the relationship between international trade and the WTO law, international trade strategy, as well as labour standards, human rights, and the public health in the context of the COVID-19 pandemic crisis. It is stated that the most effective way to overcome the crisis is timely and effective information-sharing since informed community can make better decisions on trade issues. The urgency of effective measures and implementation of new WTO regulations are believed to be vital for providing fair trade in the present circumstances. The right trade policies would not only revive the trade and recover the time lost to the crisis but would also shift toward a more sustainable and inclusive future. The author claims that, in view of the pandemic, the efforts of policymakers and business leaders to find ways to achieve trade balance should imply greater coherency between trade, labour standards, public health, and human rights objectives.

INTRODUCTION

Throughout the eighteenth and nineteenth centuries and into the twentieth, many countries limited the competitiveness of foreign goods in order to foster native industries by using the tariff. A tariff is a tax on imported goods that raises their price, thus making similar domestically produced goods more economically attractive. Tariffs were a significant source of income for many governments before they had revenue from income and sales taxes. However, the need for reduced tariffs was advocated by many countries, beginning in the nineteenth and throughout the twentieth centuries. Many countries opened up their national markets to foreign goods by reducing tariffs in return for similar liberalisation by others, because "the key to sustaining increased free trade is to maintain balanced benefits in this process, a concept called *reciprocity* - each government gives similar levels of concessions in order to balance

DOI: 10.4018/978-1-7998-7164-4.ch013

the benefits from the agreements made" (Buterbaugh & Fulton, 2007). The increase of international free trade has been encouraged principally with the goal of solidifying peace and distributing economic development across "national boundaries by means of multinational negotiations and agreements", in short, "it deals with attempts to liberalize markets" in the world.

However, the current COVID-19 pandemic and challenges have called international trade and related relationships, inclusive the tariffs, human rights, public health and different spheres of trade, into question. Against this background, there is a clear need to keep trade flowing, firstly, to ensure the supply of essential products and secondly, to send a signal of confidence for the global economy. Trade is essential to save both lives and livelihoods. In parallel with the adoption of relevant changes, democratic processes as well as the existence and exercise of fundamental civil liberties and political rights should be maintained to generate the social conditions most conducive to economic development (Abuseridze, 2020).

INTERNATIONAL RULES FOR INTERNATIONAL TRADE

Globalization and international trade need to be properly managed if they are to be of benefit to all humankind. Former GATT and WTO director-general, Peter Sutherland, wrote in 1997: 'The greatest challenge facing the world is the need to create an international system that not only maximizes global growth but also achieves a greater measure of equity, a system that both integrates emerging powers and assists currently marginalized countries in their efforts to participate in worldwide economic expansion. The most important means available to secure peace and prosperity into the futures is to develop effective multilateral approaches and institutions' (Sutherland, 1997). One of the most effective means of addressing this crisis is through timely, accurate information as the informed public is better positioned to make sound decisions including on questions related to trade.

But what exactly is the role of legal rules and, in particular, international legal rules in international trade? How do international trade rules allow countries realize the gains of international trade? Of course, under normal conditions, there are basically four related reasons why there is a need for international trade rules. First, countries must be restrained from adopting trade-restrictive measures both in their own interest and in that of the world economy. International trade rules restrain countries from taking trade-restrictive measures. National policy-makers may come under considerable pressure from influential interest groups to adopt trade-restrictive measures in order to protect domestic industries from import competition. Such measures may benefit the specific, short-term interests of the groups advocating them but they very seldom benefit the general economic interest of the country adopting them. 'Governments know very well, that by tying their hands to the mast, reciprocal international pre-commitments help them to resist the siren-like temptations from rent-seeking, interest groups at home' (Sutherland, 1997). Countries also realise that, if they take trade-restrictive measures, other countries will do so too. This may lead to an escalation of trade-restrictive measures, a disastrous move for international trade and for global economic welfare. International trade rules help to avoid such escalation. Second and closely related reason why international trade rules are necessary is the need of traders and investors for a degree of security and predictability. International trade rules offer a degree of security and predictability. Traders and investors operating, or intending to operate in a country that is bound by such legal rules will be able to predict better how that country will act in the future on matters affecting their operations in that country. A third reason why international trade rules are necessary is that national governments alone simply cannot cope with the challenges presented by globalization. International trade rules serve to ensure that countries only maintain national regulatory measures that are necessary for the protection of the above key societal values (Jackson, 1998). Furthermore international trade rules may introduce a degree of harmonization of domestic regulatory measures and thus ensure an effective, international protection of these societal values. As fourth and final reason why international trade rules are necessary is the need to achieve a greater measure of equity in international economic relations. Without international trade rules, binding and enforceable on the rich as well as the poor, and rules recognizing the special needs of developing countries, many of these countries would not be able to integrate fully in the world trading system and derive an equitable share of the gains of international trade. However, for international trade legal rules to play these multiple roles, such rules have, of course, to be observed. It is clear that international trade rules are not always adhered to. All countries and their people benefit from the existence of rules on international trade making the trading environment more predictable and stable. However, provided the rules take into account their specific interest and needs, developing countries, with generally limited economic, political and military power, should benefit even more from the existence of rules on international trade.

If we look at all this from a pandemic perspective, in many areas of trade, WTO members are required to establish or maintain one or more "Enquiry Points" to answer reasonable enquiries of governments, traders and other interested parties and provide relevant documents and information. In emergency situations, such as the COVID-19 pandemic, access to information on product requirements and certification procedures can be crucial, as it can minimize or avoid delays or rejections at customs points. According to WTO, the trade impact of the crisis has differed dramatically across regions, with relatively modest declines in trade volumes in Asia and stronger contractions in Europe and North America. While the WTO trade forecast only covers merchandise trade, the increasingly important services sector has also been hit hard by COVID-19. WTO estimates suggest that the volume of this trade fell around 27% during the pandemic, with travel and transport-related sectors, which are important sources of exports for low-income countries, hit hardest (WTO, 2020).

For international trade legal rules to play these multiple roles, such rules have, of course, to be observed. It is clear that international trade rules are not always adhered to. All countries and their people benefit from the existence of rules on international trade making the trading environment more predictable and stable. However, provided the rules take into account their specific interest and needs, developing countries, with generally limited economic, political and military power, should benefit even more from the existence of rules on international trade. The weaker countries are likely to suffer most where the law of the jungle reigns. They are more likely to thrive in a rules-based, rather than a power-based, international trading system.

International trade law consists of, on the one hand, numerous bilateral or regional trade agreements and, on the other hand, of multilateral trade agreements. Examples of bilateral and regional trade agreements are manifold. COVID-19 has spawned new trade restrictions and threatens to widen old trade divisions.

BASIC RULES AND PRINCIPLES OF WTO LAW

The law of the WTO is complex and specialized. It deals with a broad spectrum of issues, ranging from tariffs, import quotas and customs formalities to intellectual property rights, food safety regulations and national security measures. However, six groups can be distinguished:

1. The principle of non-discrimination;
2. The rules on market access, including rules on transparency;
3. The rules on unfair trade;
4. The rules on conflicts between trade liberalizations and other societal values and interests;
5. The rules in special and differential treatment for developing countries; and
6. A number of key institutional and procedural rules relating to decision-making and dispute settlement (Bossche, 2005).

These basic rules and principles of WTO law make up what is commonly referred to as the multilateral trading system. According to these rules, the complex approaches/measures of the organization during the pandemic are important. It should be noted that, the WTO's latest Trade Monitoring Report on G20 trade measures shows a slowdown in the number and coverage of trade-restrictive and trade-facilitating measures on goods implemented by G20 countries between mid-May and mid-October 2020, primarily as a result of the sharp decline in overall global trade since the COVID-19 outbreak. The report also documents numerous trade-facilitating and support measures introduced by G20 economies in response to the economic downturn in order to prepare the ground for a strong economic recovery (WTO, 2020).

Forty one new COVID-19 trade and trade-related measures were recorded for G20 economies between May and October 2020. Some 34% of the measures were extensions of existing measures originally implemented in the early stages of the pandemic. Most of these measures were adopted on a temporary basis. Of the measures implemented during the review period (For example, duties on raw hide and skins, and exoneration for SMEs), (44%) were of a trade facilitating nature (according to preliminary estimates by the WTO Secretariat, the trade coverage of the COVID-19 trade facilitating measures implemented during the review period amounted to USD 129.6 billion (including exports and based on annual 2019 trade figures). And twenty-three measures (56%) could be considered trade restrictive. Export bans continue to account for more than 90% of all restrictive measures recorded (WTO, 2020).

The reduction or elimination of import tariffs and import taxes make up one-third of trade facilitating measures taken during the review period. Certain G2O economies reduced their tariffs on a variety of goods such as PPE, sanitizers, disinfectants, medical equipment and medicine/drugs. In many cases, tariff reductions were also accompanied by exemptions from VAT and other taxes. Regarding exports, the termination of export bans (for example, hydroxychloroquine, ventilators, PPE/masks, hand sanitizers, and certain food products) make up one-third of trade facilitating measures, followed by the elimination of export duties (11%) (For example, duties on raw hide and skins, and exoneration for SMEs).

On the other hand, G20 economies had also been repealing facilitating measures which had been implemented. For instance, around 21% of COVID-19 specific facilitating measures have been terminated (According to preliminary estimates by the WTO Secretariat, the trade coverage amounted to USD 37.2 billion (including exports and based on annual 2019 trade figures), (WTO, 2020).

As of mid-October 2020, 68 COVID-19 measures affecting trade in services were compiled for G20 economies with most of them being trade-facilitating in nature (Measures have been compiled for Australia, Brazil, Canada, China, the European Union, France, Germany, India, Indonesia, Italy, Japan, the Republic of Korea, Mexico, the Kingdom of Saudi Arabia, South Africa, Turkey, the United Kingdom, and the United States).

By mid-October 2020, some 255 formal notifications and communications on COVID-19

trade-related measures had been received by the Secretariat from WTO Members and Observers, including from G20 economies. Some WTO Members notified multiple times under the same subject area. Notifications focused largely on SPS, TBT and QRs. About two-thirds of the overall notifications were related to SPS and TBT measures, such as trade in PPE, food, live animals and medical equipment. Many of these measures aimed at streamlining certification procedures, and moving towards more electronic/digital procedures, including electronic certification, to facilitate access to PPE and other medical equipment necessary to combat the pandemic, and to food. Some also focused on COVID-19 risks from international trade in live animals. In the case of the QR notifications, members notified prohibitions and restrictions on the export of PPE, sanitizers and disinfectants, and pharmaceuticals were recorded. Some Members also restricted the export of foodstuffs and notified them to the Committee on Agriculture. Around half of the export restrictive measures were notified as temporary.

The measures taken are vital and highlight the effective work of the organization, which should ensure trade stability, simplicity neutrality and economic stability in parallel with the pandemic. According to the author, special priority is given to timely measures and the creation of the necessary legal framework both for managing a pandemic and in case of force majeure.

INTERNATIONAL TRADE STRATEGY

Free Trade among nations is largely seen as the key to economic growth, peace and better standards of living, leading to a happier state of human existence at a global level (Krugman, 1979). The General Agreement on Tariffs and Trade (GATT) was formed in 1947 with a treaty signed by 23 countries, and signed into international law on January 1, 1948. The world witnessed in the 1930s and 1940s, enshrined the philosophy of free trade using the principles of non-discriminations (also known as Most Favoured Nation Obligation) and the elimination of quantitative restrictions. This Philosophy of free trade continues to this day in the form of GATT 1994 (Annex 1 A to the World Trade Organization Agreement). The Philosophy of free Trade, however, has not gone unchallenged. Over time, the world has become more aware of the global effects of environmental degradation and the exploitation of the economically disadvantaged and the young by commercial enterprises. Social and ethical issues in the context of trade have taken on new meaning and non-governmental organization (WTO) and the philosophy of free trade as enshrined in GATT 1994, so much so that there is widespread agreement that trade needs to acquire a human face (Carr, 2010).

Since the formation of the World Trade Organization, international trade has been subject to WTO regulations based on a simple, stable and liberal regulatory framework. Today all members of the WTO must adhere to certain principles as they make trade policy. They must automatically extend the best trade conditions granted to one member to every other nation that belongs to the WTO. They must treat products of foreign firms in the same way they do products of local firms. Policymakers cannot discriminate between imported products originating in different countries and domestically produced goods. If member states do not adhere to the rules, they may find their trade policies subject to trade disputes at the WTO. Likewise, countries have considerable flexibility under WTO rules to protect human rights at home or abroad.

The author claims that the current legal framework of the WTO is based on mandatory changes, improvements and adaptations against the background of globalization and COVID-19. It makes trade relations more flexible, reduces trade tensions, thus proving its clear advantage over GATT legislation. According to the author, the WTO plays an important role for the intergovernmental community, given its substantial jurisdiction and the existence of an effective mechanism for multilateral international agreements concluded within its framework. Its importance in modern international relations is especially evident in view of the list of areas covered by this organization, including intellectual property, protection of human rights, labor rights, environmental protection, technical barriers to trade and other important aspects. One of the reasons for the success of the WTO, in author's opinion is the effective implementation mechanism of international agreements between the member states, the unimpeded functioning of which has been guaranteed by the Dispute Settlement Mechanism established at Uruguay Round. Its effectiveness is confirmed by interstate disputes in the WTO, the sentences of which are always distinguished by an effective enforcement mechanism. An exception is the recent escalation of trade tensions between the United States and China, of which the author is critical. However, according to the author, the WTO maintains a balance of power since small member states can express their views on the development of world trade, using all the mechanisms to protect their interests. These facts allow us to conclude that the organization greatly contributes to the interpretation and development of international law.

It can be assumed that the universal jurisprudence of the WTO trade regime provides for the process of trade liberalization, which makes trade policy more flexible and effective. WTO successfully replaced GATT and eliminated the vicious sides of jurisprudence. However, despite the effectiveness of the WTO and its universal legislation, the pandemic has endangered its normal functioning.

However, what should be the trading strategy in the COV-19 pandemic? Given the current difficult situation the pandemic and the ensuing structural changes can only add to the feeling that WTO rules have been conceived in a context that differs substantially from the one we are living in, increasing the risk of a loss of legitimacy. The rules-based trading system is threatened with irrelevance, and the inability of the WTO to play an active role in coordinating responses since the outbreak of the crisis does not help to assuage these concerns. Preserving coordination and stability in international trade relationships is thus more essential now than ever and should be the priority of any European trade policy response. It is, however, utterly challenging, both because of the frailty of the existing multilateral trading system and because of the necessity to make trade a lever, not an obstacle, to legitimise public objectives such as health, security and sustainable development. A rigid application of existing rules is unlikely to work, given their eroded legitimacy and the ñaws already apparent in their enforcement. A multilateral agreement to reform the WTO would be the best solution that would allow for an updating of the rules, organising of mutually proðtable grand bargains and coordinating of responses to global challenges. Unfortunately, it is clearly out of reach in the near future. A more pragmatic approach is needed, building upon political understandings and piecemeal reform, combining all available levels of political dialogue - at the WTO but also in the G20 and other international forums - so as to retain the trading system's consistency, but also to allow it more ñexibility (Jean, 2020).

It is important for member countries to set priorities that will ensure trade recovery and income growth. Respond Recover and Grow should be the priority in the short-term perspective. It is vital to take the following actions:

1. Identify the trade impact of COVID-19 on its key export sectors;
2. Trade restrictions need to be reinstated in accordance with security measures, taking into account digital delivery technologies;
3. Develop anti-crisis roadmaps to improve transport and logistics capabilities and manage risk;
4. High-level negotiations aimed at strengthening the existing strategy and striving for a sustainable, stable future.

These measures will be preventive in nature to address future challenges and overcome the current crisis.

LABOUR STANDARDS, HUMAN RIGHTS AND PUBLIC HEALTH IN THE WTO

Human rights and trade rules, including WTO rules, are based on the same values: individual freedom and responsibility, non-discrimination, rule of law, food security and welfare through peaceful cooperation among individuals. Policymakers gradually developed new rules to achieve both trade and human rights objectives. For example, in the early nineteenth century, England signed treaties with the U.S., Portugal, Denmark, and Sweden to ban trade in slaves. In the late nineteenth century, the US, England, Australia and Canada banned trade in goods made by conflict labor. These efforts stimulated international cooperation. In 1919, the signatories of the Treaty of Versailles created the International Labor Organization (ILO); its members agreed that state failure to protect labor rights could distort trade and undermine labor rights in other countries (Percy & Bidwell, 1939).

The trade labor linkage has a long history (Charnovitz, 1987). It has become one of the most contentious contemporary issues in trade and labour policy circles and debates (Langille,1997). The idea of using international labour standards to protect workers from economic exploitation was first promoted by individual social reformers in Europe in the first half of the nineteenth century during the early stages of the industrial revolution. The work of these reformers was later taken over by various non-governmental organizations. Calls for international labour legislation increased dramatically during the second half of the nineteenth century and found expression in various international organizations that were formed (often international associations of trade unions).

The unprecedented global crisis has brought the human rights issue into question; the risks and dangers that the virus has created in our daily life have been identified.

The global public health crisis, accompanied by economic and social crises, will have a lasting impact on both the global economy, people and societies. Hence, along with trade stability and economic survival, it is important to take care of human rights both during and after a crisis.

The author claims that the protection of life, health, social and economic rights should be a fundamental principle for the countries. All members of the WTO should adhere to certain principles as they make trade policy. They must automatically extend the best trade conditions granted to every other nation that belongs to the WTO. Policymakers cannot discriminate between products originating in different countries nor between imported or domestically produced goods. If member states don't adhere to the rules, they may find their trade policies subject to trade disputes at the WTO. The author thinks, within these structures, countries have considerable flexibility under WTO rules to protect human rights at home or abroad. Member states can use trade waivers and exception to promote human rights abroad or at home. They occasionally bring up human rights during accessions and trade policy review. Furthermore, human rights concerns have seeped in into WTO and GATT negotiations, although many WTO members still see human rights concerns as "non-trade" issues. Author recommends as follow:

1. Make a policy determination that trade and human rights should be coordinated (Respond to public concerns, make strategies to address globalization more coherent);
2. Reform national trade policymaking process (for example: develop a channel for human rights concerns to enter the policymaking process. Set up an advisory system);

3. Task advisors to weigh human rights concerns (ask the rights questions when making public policy decision);
4. Create coalition of the willing at the WTO (member states should jointly request the WTO to study the relationship between WTO rules and human rights rules);
5. Clarify relationship (member states should request that WTO staff examine how social labelling and procurement policies can be designed so they do not distort trade);
6. Explore human rights impact assessments (governments and foundations should fund research and testing of human rights assessments);

The author believes that trade and human rights should be coordinated and countries should exercise considerable flexibility under the WTO rules to protect human rights at home or abroad. All these issues are related to how states tried decades long to allocate jurisdiction between legislative and judicial functions within each state, among states themselves, among state and international organizations and between international organizations.

WTO member states must fulfil their human rights and WTO obligations in good faith, so as to exclude conflict between these two sets of legislation. The author believes that the WTO's flexible legislation can allow it. Accordingly, in light of the inherent flexibility of many of the WTO obligations, including Articles XX and XXI of GATT, WTO Members can simultaneously respect both their human rights and their WTO rights and obligations.

The author claims, that since the WTO adjudicating bodies do not determine whether human rights have been violated or respected, the states should act consistently with international law.

CORE LABOUR STANDARDS (CLS) AS HUMAN RIGHTS

Various CLS have been characterized as human rights the UN Universal Declaration of Human Rights, the subsequent international Covenant on Civil and Political Rights, and International Covenant on Economics, social and Cultural rights. The ILO's 1998 Declaration of Fundamental Principles and Rights at Work enumerates a short list of core international labour standards that are defined more fully in eight background Covenants incorporated by reference, namely, freedom of association and collective bargaining, the elimination of forced labour, the elimination of child labour, and the elimination of discrimination in employment, which is also consistent with the characterization of certain core labour standards or rights as human rights, especially that guarantee basic freedom of choice in employment relations (Trebilcock, Howse, 2005). Labour standards have been used in the Generalized System of Preferences a preferential system to provide duty free access to exports of developing countries by (most notably) the European Union and the United States of America. Currently, there is a revision of the EU's GSP scheme, the potential implications of which may be considerable given that the new GSP plus scheme appears to target not only ratification of the fundamental Conventions, but also application of Conventions in line with comments from the ILO supervisory bodies. This has the potential to be very problematic for employers.

Anartya Sen argues in his book "Development as Freedom" that basic goals of development can be conceived of in universalistic terms where individual well-being can plausibly be viewed as entailing certain basic freedoms irrespective of cultural context:

1. Freedom to engage in political criticism and association;
2. Freedom to engage in market transactions;
3. Freedom from the ravages of preventable or curable disease;
4. Freedom from the disabling effects of illiteracy and lack of basic education;
5. Freedom from extreme material privation (Sen, 1999).

According to Sen, these freedoms have both intrinsic and instrumental value. Importantly, in contrast to the unfair competition and race to the bottom rationales for linking international trade policy and international labour standards, the human rights perspective focuses primarily on the welfare of citizens in exporting, not importing countries. The assumption underlying this concern for basic or universal human rights is that failure to respect them in any country is either a reflection of the decision of unrepresentative or repressive governments rather than the will of the citizens or a sign of the majoritarian oppression of minorities, for example, children, women or racial religious minorities; alternatively, there may be paternalistic concerns that citizens in other countries have made uninformed or ill-advised choices to forgo these basic rights.

In my view, the linkage of international trade policy, including trade or other economic sanctions, with CLS that reflect basic or universal human rights is a cogent one. When citizens in some countries observe gross or systematic abuses of human rights in other countries, the possible range of reactions open to them include diplomatic protests, withdrawal of ambassadors, cancellation of air landing rights, trade sanctions or more comprehensive economic boycotts, or at the limit, military intervention.

Arguing that doing nothing is always or often the most appropriate response is inconsistent with the very notion of universal human rights. In extreme cases, such as war crimes, apartheid, the threat of chemical warfare in the case of Iraq, genocide in the case of Serbia, or the Holocaust in the case of Nazi Germany, excluding a priori economic sanctions form the menu of possible options seems indefensible. Whether it is the most appropriate option may, of course, be context specific and depend both on the seriousness of the abuses and on the likely efficacy of the response choice of instrument. But it is sufficient for present purposes to restate the point that to the extent that CLS are appropriately characterized as basic or universal human rights, a linkage between trade policy and such labour standards is not only defensible but arguably imperative, in contrast to the other two rationales for such a linkage which, despite their much longer historical lineage, are largely spurious and inconsistent with the central predicates of a liberal trading system. However, CLS viewed as basic or universal human rights, by promoting human freedom of choice, are entirely consistent with a liberal trading regime that seeks to ensure other human freedoms, in particular the right of individuals to engage in market transactions with other individuals without discrimination on the basis of country of location (Cleveland, 2002). Having said this scope and definition of the class human rights viewed as sufficiently universal as to warrant potentially the imposition of trade sanctions for their violation is problematic in various respects. Even CLS are not susceptible to uncontentious understandings of their scope. The scope of many economic, social and cultural rights is controversial (Ignatieff, 2001). These controversies do not obviate the normative force of the rights themselves, but do have implications for the choice of instrument and choice of institutional arrangement for addressing the trade policy-labour standards linkage, to which we now turn. As regards developing country: From a developing country perspective, the conventional wisdom is that unlike the case with developed countries, increased integration with the world economy will be beneficial to less skilled workers. But this does not seem to be supported by the available empirical evidence, which suggests that many developing countries experienced rising wage inequality after opening to international trade. It appears possible that there is a pervasive skill bias in globalization. It is also uncertain what prospects international trade offers in creating jobs in developing countries, particularly those located in Africa and Latin America.

With regard to the role of labor standards in a pandemic, international labour standards are a useful decent work compass in the context of the crisis response to the COVID-19 outbreak. Firstly, respecting key provisions of ILS relating to occupational safety and health, working arrangements, protection of specific categories of workers, nondiscrimination, social security or employment protection ensures that workers, employers and government can maintain decent work while adjusting to the socio-economic consequences of the COVID-19 pandemic. Secondly, a wide range of ILO labour standards on employment, social protection, wage protection, SMEs promotion or workplace cooperation contain specific guidance on policy measures that would encourage a human-centred approach to the crisis and to its recovery. Their guidance extends to the specific situation of certain categories of workers, such as nursing personnel, domestic workers, migrant workers, seafarers or fishers, who are very vulnerable in the current context. Respect for these standards further contributes to a culture of social dialogue and workplace cooperation that is key to building the recovery and preventing a downward spiral in employment and labour conditions during and after the crisis. ILS establish a fair and equitable framework and embody resilience in front of concrete situations in the world of work and are fundamental to any long-lasting and sustainable response to pandemics, including COVID-19 (ILO, 2020).

FOOD SAFETY AND HEALTH POLICY PERSPECTIVE

International trade can also hurt the right to health directly or indirectly (Palkova & Abuseridze, 2020). In this case it should be mentioned that the Regional Committee for the Eastern Mediterranean of WHO discussed in its Forty-fifth Session the impact of the GATT Agreements on health and passed a resolution urging Member States to: A. Ensure that ministries of health are represented on national committees entrusted with the task of studying the negative impact of World Trade Organization agreements on the health sector; B. Conduct studies to coordinate response to the World Trade Organization health-related agreements in cooperation with the Regional Office. WHO expressed its concerns in a statement at the Third WTO Ministerial Conference as follows - trade and public health should not be discussed in isolation from each other. Decisions made outside the health sector have tremendous influence on health outcomes, especially in poor societies. WHO supports the main purpose of promoting trade, that is, to improve living conditions and to raise real income. It strongly reaffirms that health is central to this development goal. The benefits to be derived from expanding trade should further the goal of improving the health of the population, especially that of poor or marginalized groups who may find themselves excluded from the process of economic growth (WTO, 1999).

Just as international trade is an essential element of national food security policy, it is also an essential requirement of a properly functioning and sustainable global food trade system that could enable the achievement of food security for all. To pick a topical example, recognizing the value of collective food security policies will be vital in ensuring the successful completion of the Doha Development Agenda (DDA). From a global security perspective therefore the slow progress on the agricultural proposals in the DDA is particularly worrying, as the current system discourages production diversification both in terms of products and geography. Indeed, many international food security initiatives are now focused on the need for accurate information. The Agricultural Market Information System (AMIS) uses a

G20 initiative which acknowledges that there is a need to enhance global food security by encouraging information sharing, improving data reliability and increasing transparency, and introducing a global early warning system. Currently such initiatives are principally inter-State. Effective participation by the private sector would require such initiatives be increasingly focused towards providing useful input for agricultural producers themselves (Ewing-Chow & Slade, 2016). Currently, it is the import-depended countries and most vulnerable sectors of society that suffer most from our global failure to achieve collective food security. The challenges and uncertainties presented by COVID-19 make this about more than just fairness towards countries facing food security challenges: it is about our collective global survival.

The issue of food safety is also important that gives rise to keen debate. The author claims that the pandemic has had a considerable impact on food security, especially in developing countries. How can this problem be solved in view of the complete dependence of developing countries on the imported food so that the crisis caused by the pandemic does not affect food security?

There are many ways to minimize the impact of the external shock caused by the pandemic on food safety. However, the author sees the most justified solution of the problem in expanding local production, especially in those countries where food production is feasible. On average, African countries spend over 70 billion USA dollars on food imports, while most of the continent's arable land (approximately 446 million hectares) is unused. Therefore, the developing countries on this continent have good potential and an appropriate institutional framework to produce more food. The exploitation of this potential would enable the countries of the African continent to reduce large food imports and ensure food security at the regional level.

In addition to minimizing local food safety risks, it is also an excellent opportunity for all sectors of the population to have adequate access to food, which also addresses hunger.

Particular importance is attached to the use of financial institutions and the EU investment assistance platform. The industrious application of these opportunities would allow developed countries to expand production locally, address hunger and create new jobs. Ultimately, this will create food autonomy for states and reduce dependence on food imports.

Proceeding from the above mentioned the author claims, that in view of the risks to health equity and access, empirical studies on the impact of reducing trade barriers on health equity, efficiency, access, or quality are vitally important. Studies should be carried out under the auspices of the WTO or by order of the organization. Particular attention should be paid to the well-coordinated work of trade experts and medical professionals to minimise the risks to health equity from liberalisation of services trade, and ensure that any resulting economic gains in health-related service sectors generate tangible public health benefits. The author argues that such a strategy that prioritizes human development and public health goals would enable to achieve a more suitable trade balance.

CONCLUSION

It is important that all actors, especially governments ensure effective information-sharing since informed community can make better decisions, which also has a preventive character. Particular importance is attached to issues of human rights, ensuring labor standards and regulations of WTO. The author believes that along with the efforts of countries, the high public responsibility of citizens is also important. Pandemic and the shock caused by it is revealing weaknesses in the way services are delivered and inequalities that impede access to them. Effective solutions and timely public information help us to respond to the immediate priorities and develop prevention strategies for the future, including developing countries in which respond, recover and grow should be priority in the short-term perspective.

In addition, research into the impact of the pandemic on areas such as human rights, social and political life, trade, economics, etc. should be continued so that the countries manage to emerge from the crisis with minimal losses, on the one hand and be prepared for better protection of human rights in possible future crises, strengthening of socio-economic systems and effective crisis management, on the other.

The author claims that access to information on pandemics should be mandatory for all WTO member states, which implies the right of every person to freely receive and disseminate information in accordance with Article 19 of the UN Universal Declaration of Human Rights.

It is important to monitor WTO member states, which on the one hand would speed up the import of products, ensure the prevention of bureaucracy at border checkpoints and simplify customs procedures, especially for the goods of public health network and foodstuffs.

Simplified and expedited procedures should be established for the import of pharmaceutical products and special medical equipment. Appropriate measures should also be taken in relation to developing countries to ensure the timely supply of food and basic items.

Finally, the unprecedented shock caused by the pandemic and the ensued global public health crisis, accompanied by economic and social crises, will have a lasting impact on world economies as well as on individuals and societies. Therefore, in addition to saving the economy, it is important to take care of human rights. Every step taken by governments to fight the virus should entail primarily the protection of such essential rights as the right to life and the right to health, in accordance with the Universal Declaration of Human Rights, the World Health Organization and the World Trade Organization. All these perspectives are similarly common and vitally important for all the WTO members, especially for developing countries, which aspire to join this organization, and especially amidst the pandemics.

REFERENCES

Abuseridze, G. (2020). Political Stability and Trade Agreements. *Bulletin of the Georgian Natioanl Academy of Science*.

Bidwell, P. (1939). *The Invisible Tariff: A Study of the Control of Imports into the Inited States*. New York: Council on Foreign Relations.

Bossche, P. (2005). *The Law and Policy of the World Trade Organization*. Cambridge University Press. doi:10.1017/CBO9781139165143

Butrrbaugh, K., & Fulton, R. (2007). *The WTO Primer: Tracing Trade's Visible Hand through Case Studies*. Palgrave Macmillan. doi:10.1057/9780230610309

Carr, I. (2010). *International Trade Law*. Routledge.

Charnovitz, S. (1987). The Influence of International Labor Standards on the World Trading System: An Historical Overview. *International Labor Review, 126*(5).

Cleveland, S. (2002). Human Rights and International Trade: a Theory of Compatibility. *Journal of International Economic Law, 5*(1).

Ewing-Chow, M., & Slade, M. (2016). *International Trade and Food Security*. Edvard Edgar Publishing. doi:10.4337/9781785361890

Ignatieff, M. (2001). *Human Rights as Politics and Idolatry*. Princeton University Press. doi:10.1515/9781400842841

International Labor Organisation. (2020). *ILO Standards and COVID-19*. Retrieved from Interantional Labour Organisation: https://socialprotection.org/discover/publications/ilo-standards-and0covid-19-coronavirus-key-provisions-international-labor

Jackson, J. (1998). Global Economic and International Economic Law. *Journal of International Economic Law*.

Jean, S. (2020). How the COVID-19 Pandemic is Reshaping the Trade Landscape and What to do about it. *Journal of Intereconomics*.

Krygman, P. (1979). Increasing Returns, Monopolistic Competition and International Trade. *Journal of International Economics*, *9*(4), 469–479. doi:10.1016/0022-1996(79)90017-5

Langille. (1997). Eight Ways to Think about International Labor Standards. *Journal of World Trade*.

Palkova, K. Abuseridze, G. (2020). Human Rights and Labor Standards from the Public Health Perspectives in the World Trade Organization: Challenges and Possible Solutions. *Journal of Economics Studies and Research*.

Sen, A. (1999). *Development as Freedom*. Oxford University Press.

Sutherland, P. (1997). Beyond the Market, a Different Kind of Equity. *International Herald Tribune*.

Trebilcock, M., & Howse, R. (2005). *The Regulation of International Trade*. Routledge. doi:10.4324/9780203978566

World Trade Organization. (1999). *The Third World Trade Organisation's Ministerial Conference*. Retrieved from The WTO Ministerial Conference Website: https://www.wto.org/english/thewto_e/minist_e/min99_e/english/about_e/presspack_english.pdf

World Trade Organization. (2020). *Trade set to plunge as COVID-19 pandemic upends global economy*. Retrieved from https://www.wto.org/english/news_e/pres20_e/pr855_e.htm

World Trade Organization. (2020). *WTO report shows slowdown in G20 trade restrictions as COVID-19 impacts world economy*. Retrieved from https://www.wto.org/english/news_e/news20_e/trdev_18nov20_e.htm

KEY TERMS AND DEFINITIONS

Core Labour Standards: Framework of internationally agreed conventions which determine minimum expectations of rights at work. Although core labour standards represent fundamental human rights they are not applied in many circumstances and for many reasons. Successful implementation of core labour standards can directly contribute to poverty elimination.

Doha Development Agenda: Multilateral trade negotiations round among the WTO members. Its aim was to achieve major reform of the international trading system through the introduction of lower trade barriers and revised trade rules.

European Union: An international organization comprising 27 European countries and governing common economic, social, and security policies. Originally confined to western Europe, the EU undertook a robust expansion into central and eastern Europe in the early 21st century.

G20: An international forum, made up of 19 countries and the European Union, representing the world's major developed economies. Together, the G20 members represent 85% of global GDP, 75% of international trade and two-thirds of the world's population.

General Agreement on Tariffs and Trade: The first multilateral free trade agreement that first took effect in 1948 as an agreement between 23 countries, and it remained in effect until 1995. It was replaced by the World Trade Organization.

International Labor Organization: The U.N. agency that brings together governments, employers and workers of 187 member States to set labour standards, develop policies and devise programmes promoting decent work for all women and men.

United Nations: An international organization founded in 1945 after the Second World War by 51 countries committed to maintaining international peace and security, developing friendly relations among nations and promoting social progress, better living standards and human rights.

World Health Organization: The directing and coordinating authority for health within the United Nations system, responsible for providing leadership on global health matters.

World Trade Organization: The only global international organization dealing with the rules of trade between nations. At its heart are the WTO agreements, negotiated and signed by the bulk of the world's trading nations and ratified in their parliaments. The goal is to help producers of goods and services, exporters, and importers conduct their business.

Chapter 14
Gulf Business Environment for the Arabic Family Firms:
Evidence From Oman During the COVID-19 Pandemic

Irfan Saleem
https://orcid.org/0000-0002-1564-6053
Sohar University, Oman

Tahir Masood Qureshi
https://orcid.org/0000-0002-1749-2297
American University in the Emirates, UAE

Muntazir Hussain
Sohar University, Oman

Amitabh Verma
Sohar University, Oman

ABSTRACT

The purpose of this chapter is to understand the business environment for the family businesses in the Gulf Cooperation Council (GCC) based on the theoretical foundation of organisational ecology and open system perspective during the COVID-19 pandemic. More specifically, the reader can understand the business environment of the family firms and how firms can recover from the pandemic by fighting against the infodemic in the GCC region. The authors have used a survey to collect data online from the family firms from Oman during the first and second waves of COVID-19 (i.e., Feb.-Dec. 2020). The results of the study demonstrate that business infodemic negatively moderates the linkage between the business environment-innovation performance nexus and positively moderates between the business environment-commerce association. This research implies the scanning of the Gulf business environment and continuous innovation by family-owned enterprises is vital to avoid a U-shaped recovery in the Arab economies.

DOI: 10.4018/978-1-7998-7164-4.ch014

INTRODUCTION

Seven pandemics have been recorded in the last 130 years of human's history, including COVID-19. Nevertheless, the recently COVID-19 epidemic has not only the worsen the world's economies but also the business environment in the Gulf region, including top-performing economies of the Gulf Cooperation Council (GCC). When family businesses face the dual challenge of survival and growth in a turbulent gulf business environment, then the family firm's survival becomes difficult without scanning for the business environment of oil-dependent GCC economies like Oman, Saudi Arabia, Qatar, Kuwait and UAE. For instance, family firms may avoid investing in innovate business plans due to potential social, technological, political and economic factors.

Family firms in the emerging market are unique and somewhat different from the western family-owned enterprises (Saleem et al., 2019). The research on Arabian family firms is also scarce when we talk about the business environment in specific (Mariotti et al., 2020). For instance, a recent study reveals that the families mainly control the corporations in the GCC. However, ownership concentration in the family firms of the GCC does not influence the family firm's performance (Matinez-Garcia et al. 2020). Similarly, a recently published statistical report about 692 listed firms in the GCC by Family business in the Arab World confirms that mostly the families own the company in the GCC region. Thus family firms in the GCC are suffering from the recent pandemic and need to understand the post-pandemic business environment for survival. For instance, the report reveals that financial firms in Kuwait, Oman and Qatar have a higher degree of ownership concentration than those in the UAE Saudi Arabia, and Bahrain (Basco et al., 2020).

Furthermore, a shareholder is found to be positively related to a firm's size in the GCC and the families as the largest shareholder across the GCC countries, with Qatar having the lowest proportion the UAE having the highest (Basco et al., 2020; Matinez-Garcia et al. 2020). The key shareholders of the GCC business, the ownership concentration, the ownership identity and control mechanisms of the family firms are presented in Appendix 2, which demonstrate the significance of studying the family firms in the GCC. Thus further investigation is required, how the family firms can further expand the business by scanning the business environment of the GCC.

The COVID-19 has also caused wide spread of both inaccurate and accurate information about the business environment. The business infodemic is the type of disinformation, which is circulated during the period of economic distress and a health crisis like COVID -19 to gain a short term profit and to kill the competition (Okan et al., 2020). Such disinformation is usually based on rumours in the market, deception of the underestimated business environment, and gossipy (See, e.g. Bunker, 2020). The business infodemic is generally spread by social media such as WhatsApp, YouTube and Facebook have confused not only the business leaders of multinationals firms operating in the GCC but also the family firms. Because such disinformation not only impacts negatively on the performance of the family businesses in general but has consequences for employees in the form of job loss, psychological and physical health, poor performance for the expatriate - workforce working (Mariotti et al., 2020) in the GCC region since last many decades. Sooner or later, the COVID-19 maybe finished; nevertheless, the role of infodemic may continue on the Gulf's businesses for several more years to come, and economic recovery could be in many shapes.

The objectives of this chapter include followings:

- To familiarise readers with the GCC business environment.

- To describe the business environment in terms of social, technological, political, environmental and legal factors in the GCC and its impact during COVID-19.
- To explain the moderating role of the business infodemic during a recent health crisis.
- To forecast how the family firms can recover from crisis and fight against the business infodemic in the GCC region.

This chapter has introduced the business environment of the GCC and family firms in the GCC. In the subsequent sections, we have developed the proposed conceptual model to link business environment and family firms' outcomes, related methodology, research findings and implications for critical stakeholders operating family businesses in the GCC region in the post-pandemic business environment.

LITERATURE REVIEW

A business that is run and owned by a single family since the last few generations can be termed a family firm (Gómez-Mejía et al., 2007; Mariotti et al., 2020). Theoretically speaking no organisation can survive without a conducive business environment; Infodemic - a hybrid of incorrect and correct information during COVID-19 has made this environment more challenging for a family firm (Bunker, 2020). However, according to ecology theory of the firm, the firms usually fight for the survival and growth like any creature (Hannan & Freeman, 1977) and family firm are one of the oldest forms of the business (Zellweger et al., 2012). In this regard, we can assume that the family firm has to interact with the business environment and this interaction based on the theoretical assumptions of an open system perspective within which a firm usually operates (Scott, & Davis, 2015). For example, classical grocery stores owned by the Arab family in the GCC are trying to use mobile applications to deal with this pandemic by scanning for a technical environment. Another theory which support interaction of the firm is with the business environment is resource dependence theory (Pfeffer & Salancik, 2003). For instance, the Bank of Muscat is dependent on human capital from its external environment, and the Central Bank of Oman provide the governing rules to the Bank of Muscat. Lastly, we should understand the stakeholder theory perspective of the organisational (Freeman, 1999) before scanning the business environment of the Persian Gulf. The firm interacts and deals with its critical stakeholders for survival and growth; which include employees, suppliers and society at large. For instance, an oil-producing plant in the Gulf region usually employs the plant managers and labour from Asian countries. At the same time, they have to be socially responsible by taking care of employee during the pandemic by providing them sanitisers and not destroying waste in the sea in an unethical way. So, based on Organisational Ecology, Stakeholder Theory, Open System Perspective, and Resource Dependence perspectives; the purpose of this chapter is to understand the post-pandemic business environment for the Family Businesses (Mariotti et al., 2020).

GULF BUSINESS ENVIRONMENT

The six GCC nations have transformed their infrastructure from deserts to Skyscrapers based on their aims (Ramady, 2012). For instance: UAE wanted to become the world's new tourist and cultural attraction; Qatar aimed at building the foundations for a knowledge economy and hopes to be an international destination for world events and conferences; Bahrain worked very hard trying to establish a reputation as a global financial centre; Saudi Arabia attempted to become the region's industrial and economic powerhouse. Otherwise, Kuwait would still be a small fishing and smuggling location; Saudi Arabia would be mostly dependent on annual Hajj (pilgrimage) for its foreign exchange. Bahrain, along with Qatar and Abu Dhabi, would be dependent on pearling trade (Mishrif, 2018). But the GCC countries are and can attract large foreign investments, and are getting ready to change their local laws to encourage investments.

A collection of external factors which affect the firm's performance and usually are uncontrollable comprise of the business environment (Palmer & Hartley, 2013). The example for such factors includes customer's needs, product's supply and demand in the market, suppliers, ownership structure in the family firm (Mariotti et al., 2020), legislation by government, evolution in technology, social demography, product life cycle and economic changes.

Economic Environment is one of the critical factors that may also affect any family business operating in the gulf region: These factors such include interest rates, inflation, exchange rates, recession due to COVID-19 pandemic and value-added tax usually affect family business performance. The economies of the GCC countries are oil-dependent and are observing the shocks due to recent pandemic. The economic indicators are sound and stable for the last many years. For instance, GCC economies have reduced inflation by controlling the money supply and financing budget deficits by issuing bonds, rather than printing money. So, there is a 0.8 per cent increase in the prices of consumer goods and services in the GCC over the last 12 months to April 2020[1]. Similarly, In 2020 the exchange rate Vs US$ are stable since many previous years, i.e. 0.38 (Bahraini Dinar), 0.31 (Kuwaiti Dinar), 0.38 (OMR), 3.64 (Qatari Rial), 3.75 (Saudi Riyal) and 3.67 (United Arab Emirates Dirham). That is why we have not included the economic factor as a key independent variable.

Political environment may be regarded as the activity concerned with determining the rules under which we live in a society like Oman. The political environment refers to the actions of a government that impact business operations—for instance, kingdom, monarch, Majles Al-Umma and democracy. Although there is no political instability in the GCC countries, nevertheless, due to the recent demise of Omani[2] and Kuwaiti[3] rules, we have added this variable.

Technological environment of the GCC refers to the state of technological developments such as the rate of technological advancement - for instance, 5G- Mobile Technology – a fifth-generation standard for a broadband cellular network like Omantel in Oman. Technical introduction and adoption of the GCC are also changing form grocery stores to high tech oil and gas industry. So explaining the impact, of tech-factors can also help us to understand the GCC economic environment in the post-pandemic era. Although other factors related to pollution are equally crucial environmental factor are not part of our scope due to unavailability of primary data form our target population.

Hypothesis Development

Generally speaking, the scanning of environmental factors that may impact the business outcomes include economic, political, legal, social, ecological and technological factors (Elearn, 2018). However, during this pandemic, the businesses have faced the issue of infodemic. The term *business infodemic* is the news that is may or may not be accurate and usually harm the performance of the company (Brown2019). The Competitors and business opportunists spread such rumours inform of disinformation. Technically speaking, jointly, "information" and "epidemic" is usually referred to as infodemic and coined in 2003 and frequently being related to the pandemic of this century, i.e. COVID-19 (Okan et al., 2020). Due to the business infodemic, the established relationship between the business environment factors and business performance indicators can be weakened or strengthen (See Bunker, 2020). For example, let's talk about the technological factor impacting business performance (Hu et al., 1999). If a company - like a grocery store - during the pandemic - is opting for a mobile app then as compare to competitors the company may outperform and the disinformation in the market about facemasks during the first week may give them higher sales volume. Accordingly to scholars, the environment factors economic, political, legal, social, ecological and technological can play a positive role for vigilant businesses (Elearn, 2018; Hannan, & Freeman, 1977; Pfeffer& Salancik 2003). In contrast, the business environment related external factors may also harm all forms of businesses and may result in the closure of the family business during the pandemic (Elearn, 2018; Zellweger et al., 2012). Similarly, we can take the example of social and cultural factors that may have a positive effect in the case of family firms as they know society very well. Generally speaking, an individual's social environment usually include surroundings influenced by physical structures, family relationships, institutions and local culture. However, the social climate of the family business may consist of the customs, values, and beliefs of any society, like Oman, in which the family business operates. So social factor may affect the firm's innovation performance and commerce at the same time. We should understand that in most of the Gulf countries, the gross national income is either coming from oil or the trade and commerce across the Gulf and high-tech economies.

Gulf Business Environment and Firm's Outcomes

Scanning the business environment in the Gulf region is the key to ensure the family firm's performance (Matinez-Garcia et al., 2020; Saleem et al., 2019) because most of the family firms are collaborating with multinational firms. For example, if we talk about the political environment of the region is relatively stable for the GCC region, which includes stable economies like Oman, Saudi Arabia, UAE, Bahrain and Qatar. Social environment - in terms of social values and culture - of the Persian Gulf is identical, and most of the people move across the region free of visa for the business and employment purposes, and networking is equally essential (Al-Abdallah, Khair, & Elmarakby, 2021). This free movement and synchronised social values across the Arabs can ensure the harmonious social-environment for the Arab family business growth across the Gulf counties and help them to diversify the business. In the recent pandemic the technological environment remained turbulent (Bunker, 2020), and technology acceptance is the key for survival and growth for the family firms irrespective of size and type of the family business (Hu et al., 1999; Zhu et al., 2004). This technological adoption is also changing the legal environment of the region. The gulf counties have started legislating to deal with potential e-Business related issues to protest the consumer rights. So, based on the discussion above, we may hypothesise the following:

Hypothesis One: Business Environment has a positive impact on the firm's level outcomes in Arab Family Firms.

Business Infodemic as a Moderator

Infodemic is the disinformation spread during the recent pandemic, and most of the opportunists have taken advantage during the current health and financial crisis. For instance, the business of facemasks and vaccine. According to literature, "information" and "epidemic" is usually referred to as infodemic (Okan et al., 2020). Technically speaking, this term is a hybrid of incorrect and correct information, coined in

2003 and frequently being related to the COVID 19 – pandemic. The infodemic can play a crucial role during the crisis in this social-media age. Identification of accurate information has become a challenge for the customers without proper research about the product being offered by family firms. For instance, Let's assume that the stable political and economic environment of Oman, can help to innovate and increase commerce and trade across the region for a family firm. Nevertheless, during this pandemic, the disinformation about the economic figure and death of his majesty Qaboos bin Said (Jan 10, 2020) can demotivate the family firms and thus nexus between the business Business Environment factors, and the innovation performance of the family firm in Oman could be negatively moderated due to the infodemic (Bunker, 2020; Okan et al., 2020). Similarly, recent technology acceptance during pandemic most of the firms have to trust the mobile applications to reach the customer (e.g. FoodPanda and Talabat) and these mobile applications are collecting a lot of data about customers and firms and playing a classical role of the middleman. So, these tech-firms can become a source of infodemic for the relatively smaller family-firms in the GCC. So, based on the discussion above, we may hypothesise the following:

Hypothesis Two: Business Infodemic negatively moderates the relationship between Business Environment factors and the innovation performance of the Arab family firm.

In continuation of the discussion in the proceeding section of hypothesis regarding the negative role of the infodemic between business environment – innovation, we can further assume that this business infodemic can play a role to disrupt the trade and commerce across the gulf counties during the pandemic and most of the food and travelling related family businesses may close due to missing resilience at individual and organisational levels (Prayag et al., 2019). For example, we may assume that the Arab family firm has a proper understanding of social and political environment but at the same time business affiliation with the top preformatting business group usually plays a vital role in the middle east (Gedefaw Birhanu, & Wezel, 2020). So, just observing the Gulf's political stability in terms of same rulers in most of the Gulf is not enough. The powerful groups and family businesses have their say and network. This robust network linked internally with government and externally across the GCC may impact the commerce across the GCC, and at the same time, infodemic can play a role to weaken the linkage between the business environment indicators and the commerce of the family firm (Al-Abdallah, Khair, & Elmarakby, 2021; Basco et al., 2020). So we assume the following:

Hypothesis Three: Business Infodemic negatively moderates the relationship between Business Environment and the commerce of the Arab family firm.

In the above section, we have hypothesised the role of the impact of the business environment on the firm's level outcomes and the moderating role of the infodemic by connecting the context of Arab family firms (See Figure 1). The next sections are dedicated to present the methodology, measure of concepts, data analysis and discussion.

METHODOLOGY AND MEASURE

The data was collected from the various family businesses operating in Sohar city of Oman using an online survey. Descriptive characteristics of the sample are present in Table 1. Most of the respondent of

Arab family firms were having about 50 employees. The Age of the family firms was mostly 5-10 years. The majority of the Arabs are the CEOs of the family firms, and the firms are top management involve people from the first and second generation, and they are part of the corporate boards. Similarly, family firm management usually trusts the older employees in Oman and usually keep consulting the senior employees by allowing him as affiliate director for the family-owned enterprise. We can see the gender diversity is low; however, there is the diversified workforce in term of expatriates (40%). Nevertheless, a family firm likes to hire the employee if s/he is in the blood relation with the top-management.

Measurement of the Concepts

According to the literature cited in the preceding section, the business environment usually consists of four factors that may impact the business, i.e. political, economic, social and technological factors. We have tried to proxy key indicators like political, social and technical using Likert scale and primary data response of the family business employees and manager. However, we are not using the qualitative technique to measure economic factors; instead, we have relied on presenting economic variables like inflation, Riyal- US dollar ratio and other indicators as part of our descriptive analysis.

The six items scale was adapted from the study of Hu et al. (1999) based on the technology acceptance model to proxy for the '*Technological Environment*'. However, we have used the theme of '*Intention to us'*. We used four items scale to measure, *'Political and Legal Environment'*, which is adapted from the research study of Zhu et al. (2004). Eight items were adapted from Singelis et al. (1995) was used to proxy the '*Social and Cultural Environment'* factors.

Latel, Okan et al. (2020) have generated two items scale to measure our moderating variable, i.e. *business infodemic*, we have adopted the same for our study. *Impact on commerce' scale* was measured using a four items scale and this scale is also adapted from the study of Zhu et al. (2004). The two items scale for 'Analysis of the *Business Environment'* and four items scale for '*Innovation Performance* were adopted from the study of Maydeu-Olivares and Lado (2003).

Refer to Table 2. this study a series of confirmatory factor analyses helped to archive a better model with the TLI (Tucker–Lewis Index) above 0.90 and RMSEA (Root-Mean Square Error of Approximation) score was below 0.05 (X^2 = 1364.20; p £ .001; CMIN/df = 1.58; RMSEA = .05; CFI .92 TLI = .92, according to Byrne (2013).). All the indicators had significant factor loadings on relevant constructs with average loading from 0.86 to 0.93.

RESULTS AND DISCUSSION

The study found exciting relationships between business environment factors and dependent and control variables. Roughly all the environmental factors found statistically significant. For example, we found negative associations between Business Infodemic, Social environment, Analysis of the Business Environment, information performance and commerce (See Table 3). So our results are partially consistent with previous studies (see Elearn, 2018; Palmer & Hartley, 2013)

Multiple regression analysis was run to test the impact of Business Infodemic, Technological Environment, Political and Legal Environment, Social and Cultural Environment on Innovation performance and Commerce for the Arab Family firms. Following table present the impact of business environment factors and Business Infodemic on dependent variables Innovation performance and commerce. The model explained 19 per cent variation. We also found that *Technological Environment* was positively impacting the innovation-related performance (β=-0.16;p<0.5) of the family firms while *Business Infodemics* was negatively impacting and the performance of the family firms (β=--0.27;p<0.001). these findings are matching with the previous studies (Hu et al, 1999; Zhu, Kraemer, & Dedrick, 2004). However, those Arab family firms who performed the *analysis of the business environment* were having a good effect on regional commerce within the Gulf States (β=-0.54;p<0.001) but no impact was found on the innovation performance of the family firms (See Table 4). So, this result regarding innovation is alarming and inconsistent with previous studies (Zhu, Kraemer, & Dedrick, 2004). Unless the family firms operating in the GCC, do not go for radical innovation in various sector, these companies may lose the pace of regional economic growth, which is already low as the world is shifting from Oil to sustainable and renewable energy sources.

In Table 5, we can observe that environmental factors explain 12 per cent variation of innovation performance among family business operating in Oman. The findings are somewhat steady with older research (see e.g. Elearn, 2018) and confirm the ecological perspective of firms (Hannan & Freeman, 1977)

We can also watch that business infodemic is negatively moderating between for the technological environment – innovation performance (β=-0.47;p<0.01) and the Social and Cultural Environment – innovation performance (β=-0.08;p<0.01). These results unique findings and the contribution of our research (Brown, 2019; Mariotti, Marzano, & Piscitello, 2020).

In Table 5, we can observe that environmental factors explain 41 per cent variation of innovation performance among family business operating in Oman. However, against our hypothesised model, we can also lookout that business infodemic is positively moderating between for the Political and Legal Environment – Commerce (β=0.27;p<0.01). So, the regional political situation is stable at the macro level, but the power of business groups in the GCC is playing a key role nevertheless (Al-Abdallah, Khair & Elmarakby, 2021). Moreover, the Social and Cultural Environment – Commerce (β=-0.08;p<0.01) nexus has a negative but statically significant relationship. One key reason could be that due to disinformation some family firms may be having more sales for a shorter period. We collected data during the lockdown of COVID-19 during two waves, which is why we think that facemasks and related medical products were costly during this period; opportunists would have made money due to disinformation in the market. Thus, the relationship between business environment factors - commerce is positively moderated by business infodemic. These findings are somewhat steady with recent research (see e.g. Gedefaw Birhanu, & Wezel, 2020; Okan et al, 2020), who thinks that business groups play a key role to generate demand of some products with business infodemic. These findings are partially inconsistent with older studies due to reasons discussed (Basco et al, 2020; Mishrif, 2018; Ramady, 2012; Saleem, Lamarque, & Hasan, 2020).

SOLUTIONS AND RECOMMENDATIONS

Lately, one of a critical issue during the recent pandemic was a broad spread of disinformation in the industry, which is why the responsibility of the top management team of family firms is to properly scan the Gulf business environment before thinking for the growth or to start of a new family business's subsidiary. The Arab family firms need to be vigilant about business infodemic by competitors and international counterparts in the GCC by adopting for the latest technologies. For instance, being aware of the political network and power of the business group can help to neutralise the role of infodemic

(Al-Abdallah, Khair & Elmarakby, 2021; Gómez-Mejía et al., 2007). Nevertheless, smaller family firms are at risk of exposing to informatics at the same time (Bunker, 2020). Similarly, the role of rescanning the technological environment is critical, and the middleman role of tech-firms like FoodPanda needs to be legislated if resulting in loss of the customer base for the Arab family firms in the Gulf region.

According to recent research by Harvard business school[4], understanding the economic shock is vital, and this pandemic has a diverse effect on oil-driven economies. The oil consumption is at a record low, and the economies are shifting for green and environment-friendly solutions. The economic recoveries will have various shock shapes, i.e. V- Shape, L-Shape and U-shape. The supply side of the economy in the Gulf region has mostly disrupted due to low oil demand. As harder, the supply side in the GCC region has been hit during COVID 19 pandemic, so less money is being injected in the businesses of the gulf region in terms of credit and loans. So it may take more time to recover the economic productivity for the family firms. The ideal recovery was V – Shape recovery, where economic growth dipped in the GCC countries and should have been recovered by the first quarter of the year 2021. The subsequent costly recovery is U – Shaped where the Gulf region's actual growth may not reach to the pre-crisis economic growth trend due to a slower growth rate as compared to the year 2020. The L-Shaped recovery –meagre foreign direct investment- could be the worst scenario for the GCC economies, including Omani family firms. So a dual-edged sword of the COVID 19 pandemic, i.e. financial system shock and epic frees of the real economy needs a unique policy in the Gulf region. The Gulf economies do not have any existing playbook to deal with this double edge sword. A million-dollar question is How to avoid L- Shape recovery for the family firms operating in the Gulf region? Based on our analysis about the impact of environmental factors, we can only trust on innovation and critical business environment factors promoting innovation performance of the Arabic family firms, including Oman. For instance, on the medical side, the vaccine and capacity building in the health sector needs investment from family firms and larger business groups in the GCC. On the economic policy side, the Governers of the GCC region need policy innovation. For example, in Oman[5], the Central bank Oman, inject additional liquidity of about OMR 8 billion in the first quarter of the year 2020. Nevertheless, the innovate is required in the distribution of this amount. One way out could be interest-free loans to adjust mortgage rents and payment of salary for employees. These potential solutions could make a real difference in post-pandemic Arab economies.

FUTURE RESEARCH DIRECTIONS

Based on this research study, we can recommend that scholars not only needs to study the external factor in terms of the business environment for the family firms but focusing on the internal factors employees commitments, and individual level needs to be explored using lense of the socio-emotional perspective of the family firms in the Arab region (Berrone, Cruz, & Gomez-Mejia, 2012;). One of the critical research areas that need to be examined during the pandemic is organisational resilience, psychological resilience and planned resistance for the life satisfaction of the employees (see, e.g. Prayag et al., 2019). Another area of business research is to find the role alliance in Arab family firms across countries (Al-Abdallah, Khair& Elmarakby, 2021). Moreover, regarding the business environment, scholars can study the role of economic factors using secondary data, improvement in the world's environment during lockdown and analysis of business laws devised during the pandemic (see, e.g. Mariotti et al. 2020; Saleem et al., 2020) but the study of social and political factors at firms' level using data from expatriates can be a unique cutting edge research for the family firms operating in the Arab world (Basco et al., 2020;

Gedefaw Birhanu & Wezel, 2020). Future research can also be conducted to further understanding of the paradigms related to evolution and failure of the family firms in the GCC using the theoretical lenses of organisational ecology and open system perspective (Hannan & Freeman, 1977; Pfeffer & Salancik, 2003). One unique study can be conducted to test the impact of family ownership (Matinez-Garcia, et al., 2020) socio-emotional wealth and moderating role concerning business environment factors and firm's level outcomes for larger family-based business groups (Basco et al, 2020; Saleem et al., 2019). Lastly, the future study can compare the financial crisis of 2007 with the recent economic crunch on Arab family firms due to pandemic by collecting panel data across the Gulf countries including Bahrain, Kuwait, UAE, Saudia Arabia and Qatar.

CONCLUSION

In the chapter, we have talked about the business environment of the GCC in general by testing our conceptual model. We tested the moderating role of the business infodemic to address the recent call for further research during the economic crunch. We can conclude that during the pandemic the business infodemic has played a positive role by improving the commence of the short term business opportunities. However, business infodemic has negatively impacted the relationship between the business environment and innovation performance of the family firms in the Gulf region. Overall we found that the technological environment has positively impacted the organisational outcomes, and business infodemic has negatively affected the performance of the family firms in the GCC. So the Arab family firms need to avoid the business infodemic by competitors and multinational importers by properly scanning for the business technological social and political environment in the GCC region by adopting for the latest technologies, focusing on innovation and taking unique policy measure to avoid U-Shaped recovery in the GCC region.

REFERENCES

Al-Abdallah, G., Khair, N., & Elmarakby, R. (2021). The Impact of Social Networking Sites on Luxury Vehicles Purchase Decision Process in Gulf Cooperation Council Countries. *Journal of International Consumer Marketing*, 1–19. doi:10.1080/08961530.2020.1867023

Basco, R., & Ghaleb, F. (2020). *Ownership Concentration in the Listed Firms in the Gulf Corporation Council: implications for corporate governance, Statistical Report.* Family Business in the Arab World (FBAW). Accessed from https://familyfirmblog.files.wordpress.com/2020/09/ownership-concentration-report.pdf

Berrone, P., Cruz, C., & Gomez-Mejia, L. R. (2012). Socioemotional wealth in family firms: Theoretical dimensions, assessment approaches, and agenda for future research. *Family Business Review*, *25*(3), 258–279. doi:10.1177/0894486511435355

Brown, K. (2019). How Your Company's Culture Can Adapt to an Ever-Changing World. *Harvard Business Review.* https://hbr.org/sponsored/2019/10/how-your-companys-culture-can-adapt-to-an-ever-changing-world

Bunker, D. (2020). Who do you trust? The digital destruction of shared situational awareness and the COVID-19 infodemic. *International Journal of Information Management, 55*, 102201. doi:10.1016/j.ijinfomgt.2020.102201 PMID:32836649

Byrne, B. M. (2013). *Structural equation modelling with AMOS: Basic concepts, applications, and programming*. Routledge.

Elearn. (2018). *Business Environment: Management Extra*. Elsevier.

Freeman, R. E. (1999). Divergent stakeholder theory. *Academy of Management Review*, *24*(2), 233–236.

Gedefaw Birhanu, A., & Wezel, F. C. (2020). The competitive advantage of affiliation with business groups in the political environment: Evidence from the Arab Spring. *Strategic Organization*. Advance online publication. doi:10.1177/1476127020952174

Gómez-Mejía, L. R., Haynes, K. T., Núñez-Nickel, M., Jacobson, K. J., & Moyano-Fuentes, J. (2007). Socioemotional wealth and business risks in family-controlled firms: Evidence from Spanish olive oil mills. *Administrative Science Quarterly*, *52*(1), 106–137. doi:10.2189/asqu.52.1.106

Hannan, M. T., & Freeman, J. (1977). The population ecology of organisations. *American Journal of Sociology*, *82*(5), 929–964. doi:10.1086/226424

Hu, P. J., Chau, P. Y., Sheng, O. R. L., & Tam, K. Y. (1999). Examining the technology acceptance model using physician acceptance of telemedicine technology. *Journal of Management Information Systems*, *16*(2), 91–112. doi:10.1080/07421222.1999.11518247

Mariotti, S., Marzano, R., & Piscitello, L. (2020). The role of family firms' generational heterogeneity in the entry mode choice in foreign markets. *Journal of Business Research*. Advance online publication. doi:10.1016/j.jbusres.2020.10.064

Matinez-Garcia, I., Basco, R., Gomez-Anson, S., & Boubakri, N. (2020). Ownership concentration in the Gulf Cooperation Council. *International Journal of Emerging Markets*. doi:10.1108/IJOEM-03-2020-0290

Maydeu-Olivares, A., & Lado, N. (2003). Market orientation and business economic performance. *International Journal of Service Industry Management*, *14*(3), 284-309.

Mishrif, A. (2018). *Economic Diversification in the Gulf Region* (Vol. 1). Palgrave Macmillan.

Okan, O., Bollweg, T. M., Berens, E. M., Hurrelmann, K., Bauer, U., & Schaeffer, D. (2020). Coronavirus-related health literacy: A cross-sectional study in adults during the COVID-19 infodemic in Germany. *International Journal of Environmental Research and Public Health*, *17*(15), 5503. doi:10.3390/ijerph17155503 PMID:32751484

Palmer & Hartley. (2013). *The Business Environment*. McGraw-Hill Edication.

Pfeffer, J., & Salancik, G. R. (2003). *The external control of organisations: A resource dependence perspective*. Stanford University Press.

Prayag, G., Spector, S., Orchiston, C., & Chowdhury, M. (2019). Psychological resilience, organisational resilience and life satisfaction in tourism firms: Insights from the Canterbury earthquakes. *Current Issues in Tourism*, *23*(10), 1216–1233. doi:10.1080/13683500.2019.1607832

Ramady, M. A. (Ed.). (2012). *The GCC economies: Stepping up to future challenges*. Springer Science & Business Media. doi:10.1007/978-1-4614-1611-1

Saleem, I., Lamarque, E., & Hasan, R. (2020). State and self-regulation for better governance: An Implication of Collibration. *International Journal of Law and Management*. doi:10.1108/IJLMA-05-2020-0128

Saleem, I., Siddique, I., & Ahmed, A. (2019). An extension of the Socioemotional wealth: Insights from an Asian sample. *Journal of Family Business Management*, *10*(4), 293–312. doi:10.1108/JFBM-04-2019-0022

Scott, W. R., & Davis, G. F. (2015). *Organisations and organising: Rational, natural and open systems perspectives*. Routledge. doi:10.4324/9781315663371

Singelis, T. M., Triandis, H. C., Bhawuk, D. P., & Gelfand, M. J. (1995). Horizontal and vertical dimensions of individualism and collectivism: A theoretical and measurement refinement. *Cross-Cultural Research*, *29*(3), 240–275. doi:10.1177/106939719502900302

Zellweger, T. M., Kellermanns, F. W., Chrisman, J. J., & Chua, J. H. (2012). Family control and family firm valuation by family CEOs: The importance of intentions for transgenerational control. *Organization Science*, *23*(3), 851–868. doi:10.1287/orsc.1110.0665

Zhu, K., Kraemer, K. L., & Dedrick, J. (2004). Information technology payoff in e-business environments: An international perspective on value creation of e-business in the financial services industry. *Journal of Management Information Systems*, *21*(1), 17–54. doi:10.1080/07421222.2004.11045797

KEY TERMS AND DEFINITIONS

COVID 19: 'CO' stands for the corona, 'VI' for the virus, 'D' for the disease and 19 refer to the year 2019.

Ecological Environment: The environmental aspects include climate, and climate changes like global working affecting industries such as tourism, agriculture and farming.

Economic Environment: The economic factors such as interest rates, inflation, exchange rates, recession due COVID 19 and value-added tax usually affect family business performance and are generally uncontrollable.

External Business Environment: A collection of external and internal and factors which affect the firm's performance and usually are uncontrollable. The example for such factors includes customer's needs, product's supply and demand in the market, suppliers, ownership structure in the family firm, legislation by government, evolution in technology, social demography, product life cycle and economic changes.

Family Firm: A business that is run and owned by a single family since the last few generations.

GCC: The Gulf Cooperation Council (GCC) is a regional union of Persian-Gulf region with common economic and political interests. The GCC was created on May 25, 1981, and six Arabian states are included, i.e. United Arab Emirates, Oman, Bahrain, Qatar, Saudi Arabia and Kuwait.

Infodemic: Jointly, "information" and "epidemic" is usually referred to as infodemic. Technically speaking, this term is a hybrid of incorrect and correct information, coined in 2003 and frequently being related to the pandemic of this century, i.e., COVID-19.

Legal Environment: Understanding of legal environment clarifies the family firm to know what is legal and what is illegal to trade ethically and successfully in a particular economic region like GCC such as employee's health and safety laws and consumer protection laws.

Open System Perspective: The perspective argues that a family firm cannot survive or operate in isolation. In that view, a family firm is affected and controlled from external factors such as the political, economic, technological and social environment.

Political Environment: Politics may be regarded as the activity concerned with determining the rules under which we live in a society like Oman. The political environment refers to the actions of a government that impact business operations—for instance, kingdom, monarch, Majles Al-Umma and democracy.

Resource Dependence Theory: This theory assumes that an organisation, including family business, engages in business transactions with stakeholders (e.g. suppliers) and institutes in its business environment to acquire useful resources. So resource acquisition impacts organisational behaviour.

Social Environment: Generally speaking, an individual's social environment usually include surroundings influenced by physical structures, family relationships, institutions and local culture. However, the social climate of the family business may consist of the customs, values, and beliefs of any society, like Oman, in which the family business operates.

Stakeholder Theory: A stakeholder is any individual or an organisation who is directly or indirectly affects a family business. The stakeholders are usually impacted or impacted by the outcomes of the firms, for instance, the government, Omani society, expatriate workforce and ecology in general. For this chapter, we are more interested in the external stakeholder of the family business firm; thus, we may not be discussing employees, organisational culture and other stakeholders contributing for the internal business environment of the firm.

Technological Environment: This factor environment for business refers to the state of technological developments such as the rate of technological advancement - for instance, 5G- Mobile Technology – a fifth-generation standard for a broadband cellular network like Omantel in Oman.

ENDNOTES

1 Statistics https://www.gccstat.org/ lasted accessed on November 11, 2020.

2 Omani Leader https://www.theguardian.com/world/2020/jan/11/sultan-of-oman-dies-state-media-announces lasted accessed on November 11, 2020.

3 Gulf economy and Kuwait https://www.economist.com/middle-east-and-africa/2020/09/30/the-death-of-kuwaits-emir-robs-the-gulf-of-a-real-diplomat lasted accessed on November 11, 2020.

4 Understanding the Economic Shock https://www.youtube.com/watch?v=RK2IfGPSqO0&t=33s&ab_channel=HarvardBusinessReview

5 Oman Government measures to address COVID-19 https://home.kpmg/om/en/home/insights/2020/04/Oman%20Government%20measures%20to%20address%20COVID-19.html

APPENDIX 1

Figure 1. Conceptual Model

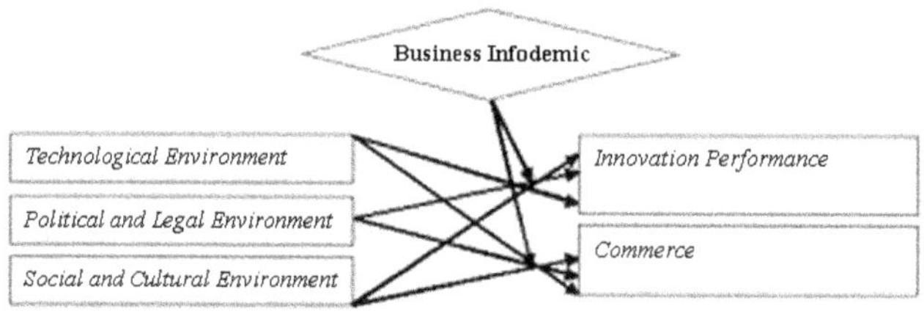

Table 1. Descriptive characteristics of the sample

Variable		Percentage %
Size of the Family firm (Number of Employees)	1-50 51-100 101-150 151-200 >200	59.0 19.2 05.1 01.3 15.4
Family Firm's Age	>40 31-40 21-30 11-20 5-10 < 5	07.7 10.3 12.8 12.8 25.6 30.8
Independent CEO	Family Related CEO Non- Family CEO	96.2 03.8
Generations involved in the same family business	1 2 3	46.1 43.6 10.3
Family members ratio in corporate board	Below 25% 26-50% 51-75% 76-100%	09.0 09.0 20.5 61.5
An old employee as a board Member	Yes No	41.0 59.0
Gender	Female Male	07.70 92.3
Diversity at Family Firms	Arabs Expats Relation to Family Other	17.7 42.3 20.5 19.5

Table 2. Validity of instruments

Variable	CR	AVE	MSV	ASV
1. Technological Environment	0.91	0.56	0.18	0.10
2. Political and Legal Environment	0.91	0.69	0.28	0.06
3. Business Infodemic	0.86	0.56	0.537	0.17
4. Social and Cultural Environment	0.86	0.61	0.289	0.14
5. Innovation Performance	0.93	0.70	0.287	0.09
6. Commerce	0.93	0.68	0.283	0.14
7. Analysis of the Business Environment	0.899	0.642	0.537	0.145
Note: Threshold of Convergent validity: AVE > .50; Discriminant validity: AVE > MSV; Convergent Reliability ≥ .70; CR = Composite Reliability. AVE = Average Variance Extracted. MSV = Maximum Shared Variance. ASV = Average Squared Shared Variance				

Table 3. Correlations and Descriptive

Variable	M	SD	1	2	3	4	5	6	7
1. Technological Environment	3.18	0.66	1						
2. Political and Legal Environment	2.70	0.97	0.16*	1					
3. Business Infodemic	2.08	0.76	-0.31**	.51**	1				
4. Social Environment	3.66	0.74	0.39**	.07	-.17**	1			
5. Innovation Performance	3.93	0.55	0.35**	.08	-.11+	.49**	1		
6. Commerce	3.94	0.54	0.22**	.10	-.13*	.44**	.46**	1	
7. ABE (Control)	3.83	0.61	0.10	.08	-.09	.40**	.43**	.65**	1
Note: Analysis of the Business Environment (ABE); n=128**p < 0.01; *p < 0.05.,+ p < 0.10									

Table 4. Direct Impact of Environmental Factors

Variable Name	Model 1	Model 2
1. Technological Environment	0.16*	0.01
2. Business Infodemic	-0.27***	0.01
3. Political and Legal Environment	0.07	0.11+
4. Social and Cultural Environment	0.10	0.10+
Controls		
1. Industry (Oil and Gas / Tourism)	-0.03	-0.10
2. Firm Size	0.07	0.04
3. Generation	-0.01	0.00
4. Family CEO	0.01	.11
5. ABE	-.069	0.54***
Model Specification		
R^2	0.19	0.46
Adjusted R^2	0.16	0.44
F-test	5.88***	21.13***
Note: +p <.10 ; *p<.05; **p<.01; ***p<.001. Model 1: Innovation Performance (dependent variable); Model 2: Commerce (dependent variable). N =128.		

Table 5. Business Infodemic as Moderator

Variable Name	Model 1A	Model 1B
1. BI X Technological Environment	-.47**	-.48**
3. BI X Political and Legal Environment	.17	0.16
3. BI X Social and Cultural Environment	-.09*	-.08**
Controls		
1. Industry (Oil and Gas / Tourism)	-0.07	-
2. Firm Size	0.11	-
3. Generation	0.01	-
4. Family CEO	0.01	-
Model Specification		
R^2	0.15	0.13
Adjusted R^2	0.12	0.12
F-Test	4.99***	8.99**
Note: +p <.10; *p<.05; **p<.01; ***p<.001. Innovation Performance (dependent variable); N =128. Business Infodemic (BI)		

Table 6. Business Infodemic as Moderator

Variable Name	Model 2A	Model 2B
1. BI X Technological Environment	.08	.08
3. BI X Political and Legal Environment	.27**	.24**
3. BI X Social and Cultural Environment	.34***	.37***
Controls		
1. Industry (Oil and Gas / Tourism)	.047	-
2. Firm Size	.030	-
3. Generation	.087+	-
4. Family CEO	-.061	-
Model Specification		
R^2	.43	.42
Adjusted R^2	.41	.414
F-Test	21.13***	41.05***
Note: +p <.10; *p<.05; **p<.01; ***p<.001. Commerce (dependent variable). N =128.		

APPENDIX 2

Figure 2.

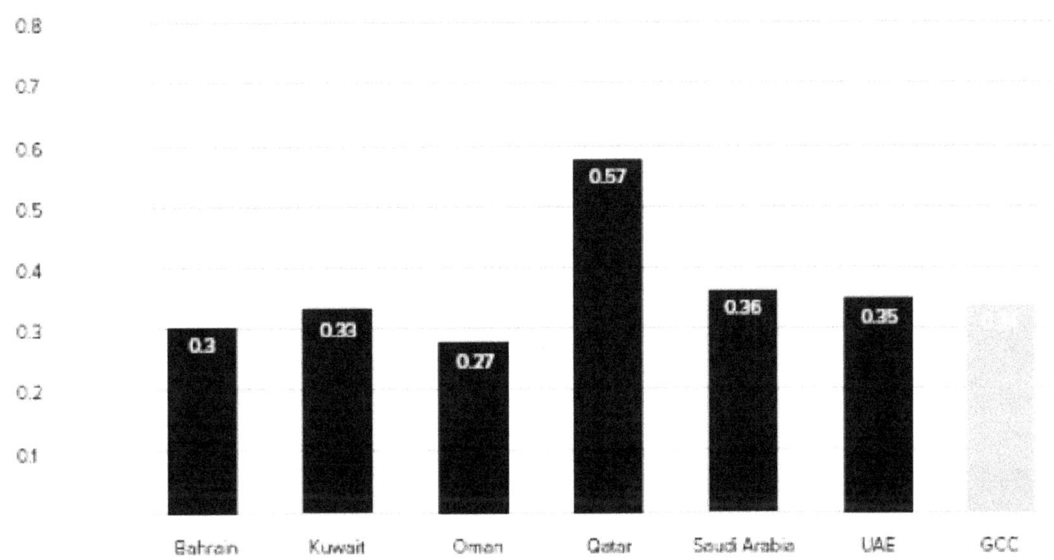

Figure 3.

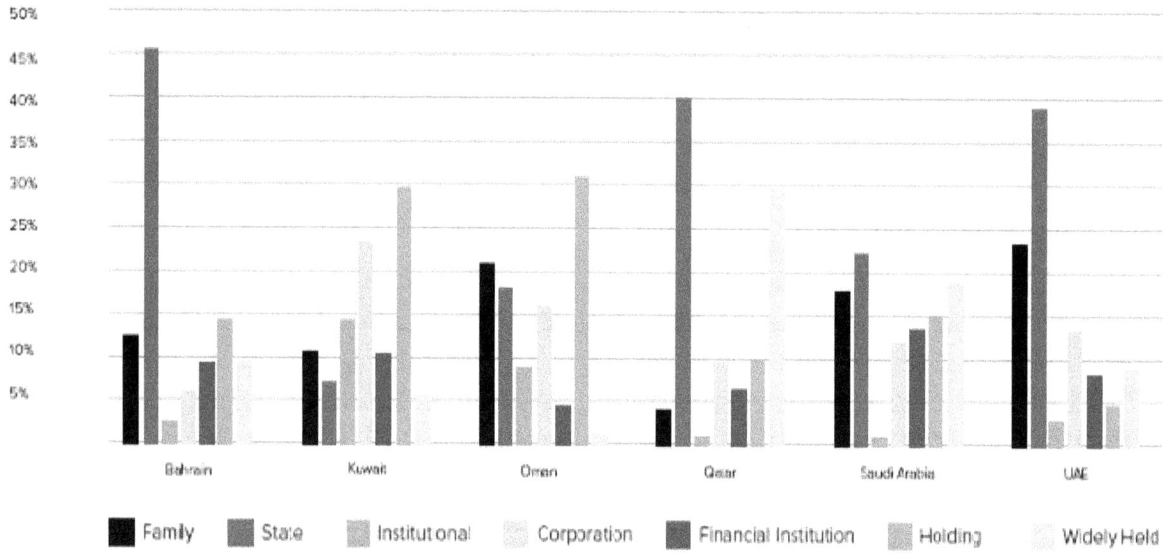
50%
45%
40%
35%
30%
25%
20%
15%
10%
5%
Bahrain
Kuwait
Oman
Qatar
Saudi Arabia
UAE
Family
State
Institutional
Corporation
Financial Institution
Holding
Widely Held

Figure 4.
Source: Basco et al. (2020: pages 16, 36 and 55)

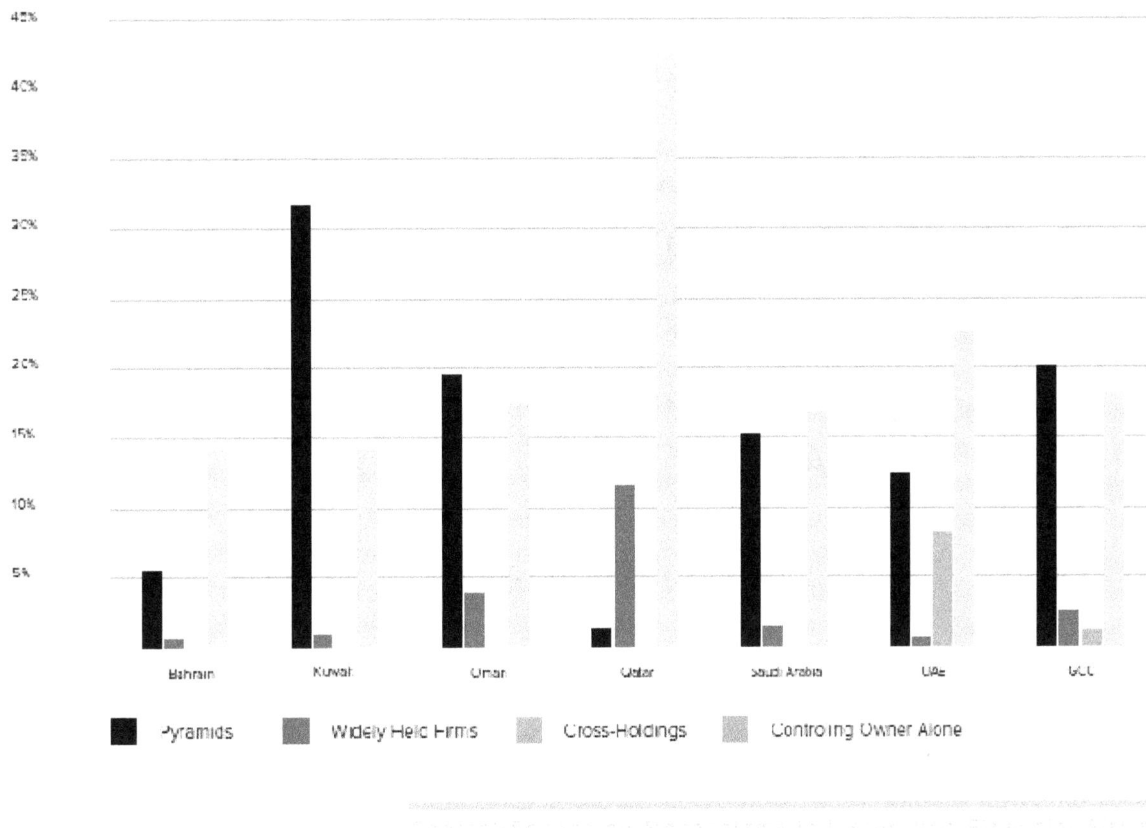

Chapter 15
Social Media Literacy and COVID-19 Awareness for Faculty Resilience in a Moderated Mechanism:
An Empirical Study

Fatema Johara
Bangladesh Army International University of Science and Technology, Bangladesh

Md. Abu Taher
University of Chittagong, Bangladesh & University Grants Commission, Bangladesh

Md. Aftab Uddin
https://orcid.org/0000-0002-9101-7451
University of Chittagong, Bangladesh

ABSTRACT

The educational institutions face tremendous challenges due to the sudden transition from traditional brick and mortar to online or distance learning in this neo-normal pandemic situation. Meanwhile, the present study examines the influence of faculties' social media literacy and knowledge and awareness of COVID-19 on their resilience via persuasion and coping behavior. Following the essence of the deductive reasoning approach in a positivism paradigm, the study used the partial least square-based structural equation modeling (PLS-SEM) technique to analyze the data. The study collected data using a random sampling method, and results revealed that social media literacy and knowledge and awareness of COVID-19 positively influenced persuasion. Engaging persuasion also positively predicts faculties' resilience. Surprisingly, the study found no significant moderating influence coping behavior. The findings of this study imply beneficial insights for policymakers and educators for ensuring an educational environment. Limitations and directions for future research are also described.

DOI: 10.4018/978-1-7998-7164-4.ch015

INTRODUCTION

The outbreak of coronavirus disease (COVID-19) shattered the world and attempted to transition to a society described as neo-normal life (Dwivedi et al., 2020). Besides, WHO (World Health Organization) is trying to slump the accelerating spread of COVID-19. Amidst the crisis, the global epidemic of misinformation—spreading rapidly through social media platforms and other outlets—poses a severe problem for public health (El Rayess et., 2018; Flostrand, Pitt, & Kietzmann, 2019; Laato et al., 2020). The advent of this historic pandemic was so sudden and abrupt that it did not provide enough time to prepare for such a situation (Dawson & Golijani-Moghaddam, 2020; Garfin, 2020; Shechter et al., 2020).

This COVID-19 pandemic also enforced all forms of class paradigm to shift on-default to the online mode of classes (Quezada, Talbot, & Quezada-Parker, 2020). The world is witnessing a unique kind of situation where education for all study levels is being imparted through online classes using the Internet (Bao, 2020; Ferdig et al, 2020). Avoiding close contact, such as social distancing, leads to nearly total closure of schools, shops, malls, festivals, rituals, colleges, universities, etc. (Das et al., 2021; Khan et al., 2021). This outbreak gives rise to a sudden increase in a variety of educational technologies, such as YouTube, Learning Management Systems, Digital Databases, Internet Streaming Or Broadcasting, repositories such as the Open Educational Tools (RET), etc. that provide online classes as the only alternative to traditional ways of teaching (Alea et al., 2020). In a similar vein, educational institutions of Bangladesh, willingly or unwillingly, also have started teaching online (Hasan & Bao, 2020).

Immediate and widespread sharing of misleading information outside of expert circles before it has been thoroughly vetted (e.g., preprints) can be dangerous, especially in a pandemic (El Rayess et al., 2018; Flostrand et al., 2019). A pandemic is a rapidly evolving setting in which researchers and academics are always learning and contributing to government policy dynamic adjustments. Compounding this information vortex is that governments rarely make policy decisions solely based on empirical evidence where the political interest is vital, and the two are frequently at the crossroads. Even information given out by government agencies across the world has turned out to be inaccurate at times, leading to more confusion (Newton, 2020).

Faculty resilience has become more vibrant than ever since the inception of COVID-19 (Garfin, 2020; Zia, 2020). Like other businesses and industries, education and learning are also affected by the infodemics, and trying to find ways to mitigate the probable risks (Ferdig et al., 2020; Izumi et al., 2020). While universities are the key players in the education sector, few research studies are focused on addressing these challenges to faculty members' resilience (Alea et al., 2020; Hasan & Bao, 2020). Consequently, the increased use of computers and smartphones is responsible for the rapid dissemination of information through the internet and social media, but such data lacks sufficient quality guarantees (Xu et al., 2020). This situation is extremely concerning because it undermines the trust in educational institutions and their program.

This study intends to offer a collective insight into many of the key issues and underlying complexities affecting the faculty members' resilience in higher educational institutions arising from COVID-19 through social media literacy, knowledge and awareness of COVID, coping behavior, and engaging persuasion. Indeed, faculty members are also not immune to infodemics, and they, too, have been bombarded with information about COVID-19 from all sorts of official and unofficial sources. Notably, there is still little awareness in higher educational institutions about the influence of infodemic on faculty members' engaging persuasion and resilience. Nevertheless, numerous questions remain untouched in connection with what is happening, predominantly those related to practice and why. Therefore, more research is needed to identify the mechanisms by which infodemic affects the faculty members' engaging persuasion and resilience.

Surprisingly, there are no data in the South Asian context, especially in Bangladesh, where local factors might influence information-seeking behavior and the channeling of misinformation. It becomes more challenging to grasp the concern's vital information when facts, rumors, and concerns mingle and spread. This chapter's potential contribution is to unearth the associations among social media literacy, knowledge and awareness, coping behavior, and engaging persuasion on faculty members' resilience affected by the COVID-19 pandemic. With more support and funding, Bangladesh can adapt to the challenge and become even stronger than before.

BACKGROUND

Social Media Literacy

Social media is an eminent resource for social networking where users can extend their offline-online relationships or create new social ties (Schreurs & Vandenbosch, 2020). Livingstone (2014) defined social media literacy as the ability to decode, evaluate, and communicate text, image, device, etc., with any social interaction platform maintaining anonymity, privacy, and confidentiality. Furthermore, Schreurs and Vandenbosch (2020) recognized it as using social media in meaningful and efficient ways by users of technological and cognitive competencies for social networking and online communication. Finally, media literacy is specifically designed to offer participants the required critical discretion to connect with the media in a secure and timely manner (Schreurs & Vandenbosch, 2020).

Knowledge and Awareness

Perceived awareness can be characterized as a person's ability to directly observe, perceive, recognize or be conscious of events or activities in their immediate environment (Rahman & Sathi, 2020; Roy et al., 2020). When people understand the harmful effects of COVID-19 on themselves and others, they are more likely to feel the responsibilities entrusted to them. In medical science research, it was found that the health professionals were better conscious regarding the disease, and they had positive attitudes (Mishra et al., 2016). Xu et al. (2020) assessed the knowledge, awareness, and actions of COVID-19 among various Central Chinese population groups to provide useful findings to support other COVID-19 countries and regions. Furthermore, higher education advisors are positively inspired to inform university students about special needs, such as hearing and vision impairment, because of the hazards and difficulties of learning materials, pedagogy, supervision, implementation and psychology (Alea et al., 2020).

Persuasion

The origins of persuasion can be identified from ancient Greek and Roman theorists to modern-day thinkers and investigators (Feezel, 2018). Traditionally, persuasion referred to the human communication intended to influence others' unbiased behavior and choices (Fullana et al., 2020; Oinas-Kukkonen & Harjumaa, 2009; Shechter et al., 2020). According to Persichetti (2020), persuasion, as Wittgenstein put it in On Certainty (1969) (OC), seems like an interpretation of something behind our eyes, and we never thought of it the same way. Similarly, social influence characteristics within a persuasive context include social learning, social contrast, behavioral influence of social development and implementation, cooperation, competition and appreciation (Tikka & Oinas-Kukkonen, 2017). With reduced motivation and capacity to interpret messages, peripheral information such as the availability of an online privacy statement becomes an essential factor for persuasion (Beldad, de Jong, & Steehouder, 2010). Moreover, the profound impact of digital and social media on persuasive communication should also be carefully observed by educators (Feezel, 2018).

Coping Behavior

Traditionally, coping is characterized as cognitive and behavioral needs to master, react, or mitigate direct and indirect expectations and inconsistencies between them (Folkman & Lazarus, 1980). In psychology research, coping means a change in the intentional effort to deal with relational or emotional problems and an endeavor to minimize or overcome stress (Wang et al., 2016). Furthermore, coping behavior is also used to describe why and how people can live and deal with stress without experiencing severe psychologically adverse effects (Horvath & Massey, 2018). The study by Zheng, Luo, and Ritchie (2021) supports the current protective model based on the research on the coping and resilience of people shows that 'travel fear' can lead to different coping policies that increase the psychological strength of people and use of careful behavior, minimize 'travel fear' and encourage world travel after COVID-19. Thus, coping is a way to respond to a stressor using one or more accessible techniques and approaches (Dawson & Golijani-Moghaddam, 2020; MacIntyre, Gregersen, & Mercer, 2020; Ye et al., 2020). Coping behavior among faculties during COVID-19 refers to their preparation to cope up with changing requirements of offering teaching, academic, and administrative supports to their universities and students in this neo-normal life (Sobaih, Hasanein, & Abu Elnasr, 2020).Furthermore, McQuillan et al. (2020) found that the workshops deliberately integrate resilient realistic coping mechanisms and careful leaders in graduates' transition.

Faculty Resilience

Resilience is the capacity to recover from trouble and cope with long-term negative interactions (Horvath & Massey, 2018). A wide range of studies has considered it as a means of alleviating or eliminating stress or ensuring that regular compassion fatigue does not result in severe psychological implications (Lee et al., 2019; O'Dowd et al., 2018). According to a recent work conducted by Fergusson et al. (2020), it is an individual's psychological trait that represents the mechanism to adjust during stress or trauma and to promote the ability of the individual to adapt and recover his/her environment in the face of adversity. Studies have shown that individuals with high tolerance are more able to respond to their workplace and have the resilience to adjust to obstacles, stress, conflicts, or disagreements (Gupta & Sharma, 2018; Saad & Elshaer, 2020; Ye et al., 2020). From the ideation of Mosheva et al. (2020), the present study defines resilience as faculties' capacity to cope, adapt, and thrive with the negativities and consequences of the COVID-19 pandemic.

LITERATURE REVIEW

Social Media Literacy for Engaging Persuasion

In this regard, Festl (2020) highlighted that media literacy is increasingly seen as the gateway to human growth, living standards, and wellbeing. Besides, engagement in the media literacy program was significantly linked with information-seeking behaviors, media comprehension, and news-analysis expertise (Martens & Hobbs, 2015). Ikhalia et al. (2019) presented observations as to why online social networks contribute to user behavior changes on a magnitude. Netizens may be engaged in social activities on the online platform in a variety of contexts. Unlike other industries, persuasive educators should also begin to recognize the massive adoption of digital media on persuasion (Feezel, 2018). Studies of Youn and Shin (2020) and Chen and Cheng (2019) showed that the heightened literacy on social media increased an individual's engaged persuasion. Faculties' adequate social media literacy can effectively help them craft the right decision during COVID-19 (Garfin, 2020; Zia, 2020). The following hypothesis is developed:

H1. Social media literacy influences faculties' persuasion.

Knowledge and Awareness for Engaging Persuasion

People would be worried about the possible implications if they knew the negative consequences of failing to perform specific tasks. The COVID-19 not only causes humanitarian crises across the globe but also affects all aspects of life, as well as the teaching profession where academics have used digital sites to reach and communicate out to students, webinars have become substitute classes, parents have been called to track at home, and students have been dispossessed of social contact between peers (Sobaih et al., 2020). The outbreak eventually motivates scholars and academics to plan distant learning programs and switch from traditional teaching to online teaching that demands planned transition (Phan & Dang, 2017). Faculties prevented from fake and uncensored information on COVID, are highly likely to engage in heightening persuasion. Immensely, accurate news and information on COVID will enhance faculties' understanding of the means and modes in engaging academic pursuits. Thus, it can be hypothesized as follows:

H2. Knowledge and awareness of COVID influence faculties' persuasion.

Engaging Persuasion for Faculties' Resilience

Well-designed persuasion among faculties shapes them, envisioning the steps to be taken during any crisis. The study of Alea et al. (2020) evidenced that faculties in the Philippines ensured their transition from face-to-face to online and distance learning to deliver their lessons. For ensuring social distancing, educators crafted need-based training and workshops for everyone to keep pace with distant learning (Alea et al., 2020; Darling-Hammond et al., 2020). Tikka and Oinas-Kukkonen (2017) stressed that collaboration must exist between persuasion to resilience to take effective compliance action through charitable appeals where participants have taken similar action to achieve a common purpose. Austin and Gregory (2020) identified valuable insights into the work environment to make a meaningful contribution towards individual resilience via shared accountability between staff and management during the period of pandemics and disasters. Institutional, administrative and faculty resilience depends on a supportive atmosphere in such a way that individuals collaborate to carry out both institutional activities and to empower each other to achieve career aspirations and potential outcomes (Bickel, 2009). In a way, the study hypothesizes as follows:

H3. Faculties' persuasion influences their resilience during COVID-19.

Moderating Influence of Coping Behavior

When people fall prey to stressful situations, coping mechanisms can be used to resolve outcomes or experiences (Zheng et al., 2021). Compared to other careers, teaching is often referred to as one of the most demanding and stressful occupations. The extent of teaching stress has increased with the emergence of COVID-19, where a phase of transition has compounded workloads to a digital platform because many academics have not yet been equipped. Still, the implications seem to be severely demanded (MacIntyre et al., 2020). Faculties' advance response strategies or avoiding coping mechanisms strengthen or weaken the influence of social media literacy and knowledge and awareness of COVID19 on persuasion. When faculties have an adequate understanding of coping techniques during this pandemic, their social media literacy consequences on persuasion rise and vice-versa. Thus, the following hypotheses are developed:

H4. The influence of social media literacy on persuasion increases when coping behavior rises and vice versa.
H5. Knowledge and awareness improve persuasion when coping behavior is high and vice versa.

Figure 1 demonstrates the research model highlighting the influences of social media literacy and knowledge and awareness of COVID-19 on faculties' persuasion. It also shows the influence of persuasion on faculties' resilience. Additionally, the research model also exhibits the moderating effect of coping behavior on the impacts of social media literacy and knowledge and awareness of COVID-19 on faculties' persuasion.

RESEARCH METHODS

Research Settings

The present chapter used a deducting reasoning approach to conduct the research, and a quantitative research technique was adopted to execute the research design. Multi-item scales were collected from prior studies, and the self-administered questionnaire survey was administered to collect the required data. The study used cross-sectional data by maintaining social distancing through cross-sectional data due to the emergence of COVID-19. The poll survey is designed using Google-doc form. The questionnaire was rolled out using social media, such as LinkedIn, Twitter, Facebook, and Email services, because the COVID-19 issue highly recommends the snowball technique (Das et al., 2021).

Figure 1.

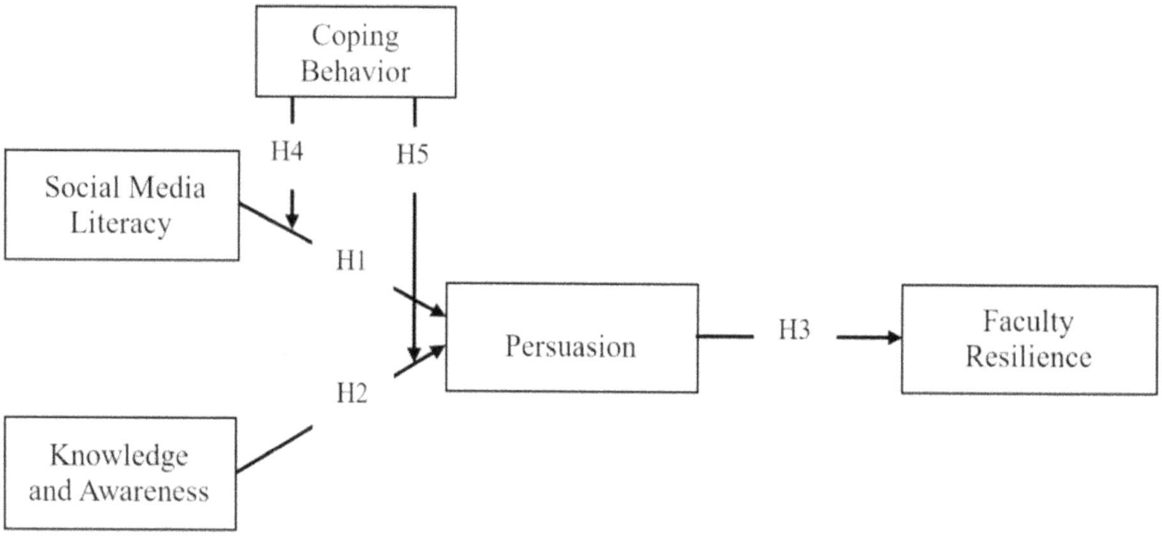

Data Collection Procedure

The current research collected responses from faculties who have been serving as teachers at universities in Bangladesh. Amidst this crisis, teachers are also the victims of the novel coronavirus due to educational institutes' closure since March 2020. It got worse when Bangladesh's government urged all educational institutes to reopen their virtual classrooms using the Zoom, Facebook, and Google meeting networks. The infrastructural supports available to academic institutions, and the technical know-how of teachers were not adequate. We collected data from faculties in this changing neo-normal time. Accordingly, we requested university teachers to respond the survey through social media who have access to the internet connection with English proficiency. The response was voluntary, and the respondents had the option to withdraw themselves at any time during the data collection process. To ensure the accuracy and prompt response, we assured privacy, anonymity, and confidentiality of their data.

Participants' Information

The university profession represents diverse characteristics among participants. The present study received 165 responses from teachers who serve in different universities in Bangladesh. Considering the respondents' homogeneity, i.e., university teachers in Bangladesh, and the analytic software used in this study, i.e., SmartPLS-based structural equation modeling (SPLS-SEM), the number of respondents are deemed acceptable (Fan, Mahmood, & Uddin, 2019). Moreover, there is no prescriptive rule of thumb on the unanimous sample size. Yet, Hair Jr. et al.(2017) and Hair Jr et al. (2014) endorsed the use of 120 to 150 samples for applying when the data normality can be ensured inhomogeneous cases with no missing data (Fan et al., 2019). Thus, our 165 responses are within the threshold limit.

The majority of the respondents were lecturers (42 percent), followed by associate professors (38 percent), professors (13 percent), and others (7 percent). University teaching profession is still male-dominated with 72 percent male teachers and 28 percent female teachers. Teachers with Master Degrees

(83 percent) outnumbered others with Ph.D. and post-Doctorate (17 percent). A large segment among the respondents completed their Master Degrees. The respondents' age ranges from 23 to 50 years, with a mean age of 32.97 years. The respondents used social media for 2.69 hours on an average each day.

Method Bias

Previous studies reported an enormous possibility of method bias when the response of items representing numerous scales is collected from the same source (Podsakoff, MacKenzie, Lee, & Podsakoff, 2003; Podsakoff, MacKenzie, & Podsakoff, 2012). Thus, we took several precautions to limit response bias. First, we asked the respondents to respond to our survey voluntarily and assured their anonymity and privacy of the supplied data that guaranteed the accuracy of their responses. Second, cross-sectional data increases the chance of a growing correlation among the responses; thus, we checked the collinearity issue by investigating the variance inflation factor. The study has no problem with the former because the variance inflation factor is less than 5-10 (Field, 2018, p. 534) that prevents the bias and contamination from normality (Kim, 2019; Mahmood, Uddin, & Luo, 2019). Additionally, we conducted Harman's one-factor test that asserts that not a single factor explains more than 50 percent of the overall predictability (Fuller et al., 2016).

Measurement Tools

The present chapter adopted survey measures from prior studies (**Appendix 1**). Social media literacy, coping behavior, persuasion, and faculty resilience are measured by Ak (2020), Carver, Scheier, and Weintraub (1989), and Azevedo and Shane (2019), respectively. Due to the scale's unavailability, we developed a scale following the method reported in Eom, Han, and Song (2020) and Hasan and Bao (2020). We adopted the mixed method-quantitative approach by conducting the pilot study and –qualitative method through an online focus group study among potential respondents comprising teachers with diverse backgrounds in terms of gender, religion, institution, geographical location, etc. The scale representing knowledge and awareness on COVID is based on the conceptualization of previous studies of Shi et al. (2020) and, Sajed and Amgain (2020). Moreover, we structured the scale that accommodated multiple perspectives from both deductive and inductive reasoning based on the strength of the mixed research method (Das et al., 2021; Hasan & Bao, 2020). We made few modifications to the items for contextualizing those items for increasing their readability and understandability (Mahmood et al., 2019; Uddin et al., 2020; Uddin, Mahmood, & Fan, 2019; Uddin, Priyankara, & Mahmood, 2020).

Analytical Technique

The study used structural equation modeling (SEM) over other regression techniques. SEM's supremacy over other regression analytics lies in its robustness and exhaustiveness as it simultaneously analyzes both measurement model and structural model holistically (Hair Jr. et al., 2017). Additionally, MacKinnon et al. (2002) asserted that SEM suits better when the study aims to investigate a mediated mechanism. We used partial least square-based structural equation modeling (PLS-SEM) to analyze and report the results. Thus, SmartPLS 3.7 package is used to analyze the results because this tool is flexible and adequate to analyze the result even if the sample size is minimal (such as 100 observation) (Azim et al., 2019; Fan et al., 2019). The PLS-SEM using SmartPLS is a powerful and flexible multivariate analytical tool that assists in exploring underlying constructs and their relationships (Hair et al., 2017; Hair Jr. et al., 2017). Additionally, it uses bootstrapping of 5000 cases to estimate p-values and t-statistics.

FINDINGS

Assessment of Measurement Model

The assessment of the measurement model, in **Table 1,** includes convergent validity and discriminant validity. We estimated Cronbach's Alpha (CA), composite reliability (CR), and average variance extracted (AVE). Both CA and CR above 0.70 are considered the cut-off value, and the AVE score above 0.50 is the minimum threshold limit (Fornell & Larcker, 1981; Hair Jr. et al., 2017). **Table 1** showed that the minimum cut-off points of CA ($Persuasion_{CA}$=0.825), CR ($Persuasion_{CR}$=0.825), and AVE (Knowledge and $awareness_{AVE}$ =0.606) are maintained (Fornell & Larcker, 1981; Hair Jr. et al., 2017). Thus, convergent validity is ensured. We also observed the square root of all latent variables' AVEs, whether it exceeds its correlation with other variables. Table 1 also revealed that any scale's AVE's square root is higher than its correlation with other variables. Hence, discriminant validity is also confirmed.

Hypothesis Testing using the Structural Model

The structural model examines beta-coefficient (β), significance level, and R^2. Whereas β refers to the strength of the relationship, R^2 reflects the overall predictability of the model. Regarding the overall predictability of R^2, Cohen (1977) attested that R^2 values over 0.00, 0.13, and 0.26 are considered non-significant, tangent, and significant, respectively. **Figure 2** demonstrates that the minimum R^2_{FR} in this model is 0.278, which is substantial.

Table 2 highlighted the summary of the results. In hypothesis 1, we hypothesized that social media literacy influences persuasion. Estimates in Table 2 showed that the influence is significant (β=0.486, p=0.000). Thus, H1 is supported. In hypothesis 2, it is predicted that knowledge and awareness affect persuasion, and estimates showed a positive and significant influence (β=0.417, p=0.000). Hence, H2 is also supported. Finally, we proposed in hypothesis 3 that persuasion significantly explains faculties' resilience. Table 2 revealed that influence is also significant and positive (β=0.527, p=0.000). Therefore, H3 is also supported.

The study also crafted the moderating effects of coping behavior on observed associations with persuasion. In H4, previous literature suggested a moderating influence of coping behavior on the association between social media literacy and persuasion. **Table 2** demonstrated that the influence is not significant ($\beta_{SML*CB®EP}$=0.024, p=0.799). Hence, coping behavior's moderating influence on the relationship between social media literacy and persuasion is not supported. Finally, hypothesis 5 formulated the moderating effect of coping behavior on the relationship between knowledge and awareness on COVID-19 and persuasion. Surprisingly, this moderating effect is also found insignificant ($\beta_{KA*CB ® EP}$ = 0.041, p=0.650). Therefore, H5 is also not supported.

Figure 2.
CB. *Coping behavior,* **SML.** *Social media literacy,* **KA.** *Knowledge and awareness*

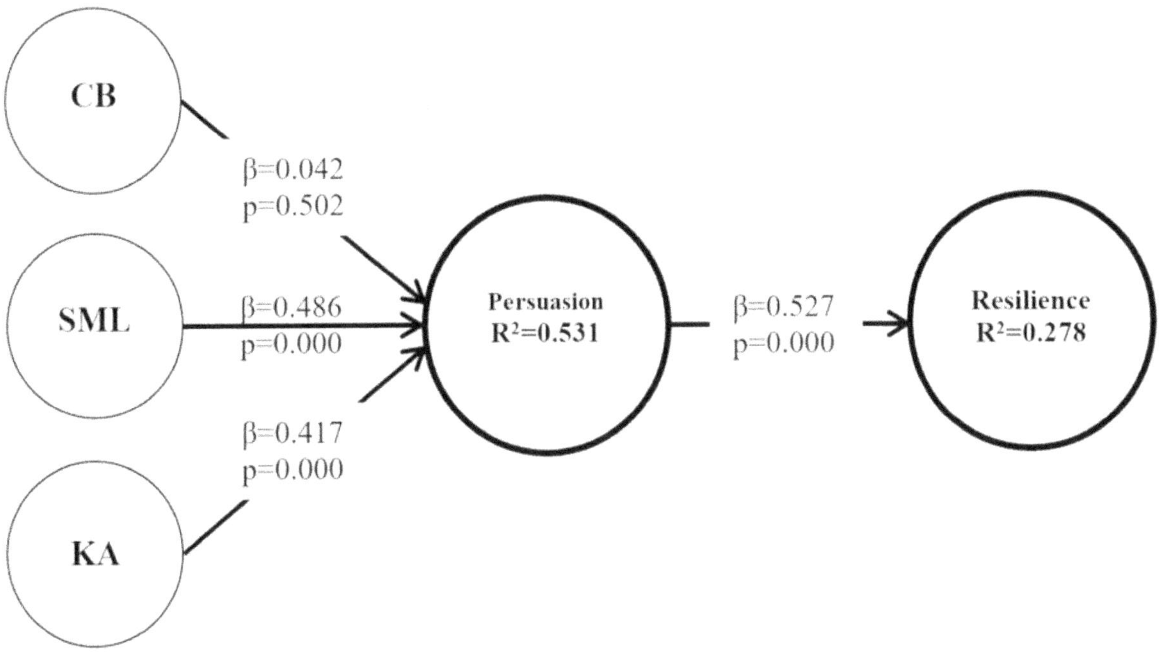

DISCUSSION

To date, little is known about the mechanics of faculty resilience and its predictors in this neo-normal life. Therefore, there is ambiguity in understanding the influence of the infodemic among faculty members (Hasan & Bao, 2020; Sobaih et al., 2020). Because of the technological breakthrough and the sudden upsurge of COVID-19 shifts in student demographics, higher university costs, and rivalry, higher education transforms from traditional teaching to online learning (Tesar, 2020). This study demonstrates how neo-normal life shaped higher educational institutions and faculties' resilience employing moderated and mediated mechanism.

This chapter's specific aim was to provide a coherent understanding of many of the significant concerns and fundamental complications affecting the resilience of the faculty members due to the outbreak of COVID-19 through social media literacy, knowledge and awareness of COVID, and coping with misleading and engaging behavioral information about COVID. The present study used a deducting justification approach to study and collected responses from faculties teaching at universities in Bangladesh and found that social media literacy and knowledge and awareness affect persuasion. Estimates have had a positive and significant effect.

Moreover, persuasion substantially explains the resilience of faculties and shows that influence is significant. The result stated that when faculty members choose their rational behavior, such as adopting the right technologies to conduct online mode, their resilience in a demanding situation improves (Austin & Gregory, 2020). Being a faculty member is challenging during this pandemic; knowing how to deal with stress is an invaluable skill that is developed through training programs on the job and off the job.

Table 1. Estimates on convergent and discriminant validities

Variables	1	2	3	4	5	6	7	8	9	10	11	12
1. Age	1											
2. Gender	-.247**	1										
3. Education	.501**	-.201*	1									
4. Position	.677**	-.260**	.599**	1								
5. TS	-.186*	.123	-.195*	-.168*	1							
6. CB	-.174*	.067	-.073	-.083	.165*	0.812						
7. Persuasion	-.065	-.191*	-.056	.011	-.028	0.250**	0.810					
8. FS	-.039	-.117	-.053	.022	.048	0.262**	0.527**	0.844				
9. IG	.128	-.239**	.145	.178*	-.118	0.185*	0.533**	0.272**	0.906			
10. KA	.028	-.069	.026	.101	-.001	0.233**	0.549**	0.188*	0.293**	0.779		
11. TS	.000	-.206**	-.014	.075	.019	0.250**	0.472**	0.234**	0.432**	0.149*	0.843	
12. TE	.041	-.353**	.088	.083	.062	0.075*	0.361**	0.235**	0.303**	0.121*	0.489**	0.894
Mean	32.969	-	-	-	2.686	3.923	4.034	4.031	4.125	4.115	3.948	3.013
SD	5.338	-	-	-	2.223	0.559	0.496	0.527	0.697	0.479	0.572	0.933
CA	-	-	-	-	-	0.829	0.825	0.867	0.891	0.838	0.865	0.958
CR	-	-	-	-	-	0.886	0.884	0.908	0.932	0.885	0.908	0.965
AVE	-	-	-	-	-	0.660	0.656	0.713	0.821	0.606	0.711	0.800

. Correlation is significant at the 0.01 level (2-tailed), *. Correlation is significant at the 0.05 level (2-tailed), **TS. Time spent, **CB.** Coping behavior, **FR.** Faculty resilience, **IG.** Information gathering, **KA.** Knowledge and awareness of COVID-19, **TS.** Trustworthiness, **TE.** Technical expertise, **SD.** Standard deviation, **CA.** Cronbach's Alpha, **CR.** Composite reliability, **AVE.** Average variance extracted.

The findings of the influence of social media literacy and knowledge and awareness to engage persuasion asserted that improving the faculties' literacy on using social media and understanding the credential of fake and accurate news explain their persuasion, such as eliciting the right choice in a vulnerable situation. The result approves that the exhaustive understanding of social medias' pros and cons can lead them to make wise decisions by drawing a clear divide between right and wrong use of it.

Table 2. Estimates on hypotheses testing

Hypothesis	Path relations	β	STERR	t-value	p-value	Decision
H1	SML → PS	0.486	0.086	5.661	0.000	Supported
H2	KA → PS	0.417	0.080	5.237	0.000	Supported
H3	PS → FR	0.527	0.057	9.331	0.000	Supported
H4	SML*CB → PS	0.024	0.095	0.255	0.799	Not supported
H5	KA*CB → PS	0.041	0.090	0.455	0.650	Not supported

SML. Social media literacy, **PS.** Persuasion, **KA.** Knowledge and awareness of COVID-19, **FR.** Faculty resilience, **CB.** Coping behavior

Furthermore, in the wake of apparent ambiguity with no proven vaccine, a piece of accurate knowledge and awareness to contain the spread of the outbreak by accurately understanding the difference between misinformation and prudent facts can strengthen the persuasion further. Additionally, the study expects the faculties to pay attention to accurate news or information credentials for making a rational decision even in a critical situation by having accurate information from social media information overloads.

Also, we endeavored to examine the moderating effects of coping behavior on the association between social media literacy and persuasion and the relationship between knowledge and awareness of COVID-19 and persuasion. Surprisingly, the study showed insignificant moderating effects of coping behavior on both connections. Results on moderating effects postulate that the relative importance of those antecedents described above are bearing so profound effects on persuasion that coping behavior matters little to them. It asserts that social media literacy and knowledge and awareness matter a lot to teachers in their persuasion during the pandemic.

RECOMMENDATIONS

The present study increasingly requires appropriate knowledge and awareness across a broad spectrum of variations and individualized experience to the conventional comprehensive framework of persuasion and faculty resilience. Until higher educational institutions identify new mechanisms, there will be a lack of availability of a considerable amount of knowledge and awareness programs. If it happens otherwise, neither higher education institutions nor society will be able to withstand the catastrophic consequences. Thus, concerned authorities, higher education authorities, university grants commission, and the ministry of education must pay attention to formulate essential policy interventions of censoring information and knowledge regarding the pandemic. It is also customary that higher educational institutions will initiate sufficient programs to build the productive belief of technology knowledge, mainly social media usage, by providing numerous programs to catch up with the neo-normal life.

FUTURE RESEARCH DIRECTIONS

The present study demonstrates significant contributions to advance knowledge and literature in higher educational institutions in a neo-normal-COVID-19 context. Nonetheless, this research is not defect-free. First, the sample size is relatively small, considering the size of faculties in Bangladeshi universities. Thus, more samples are attested to examine the estimates if it results in the same. The sample size might prevent the generalizability of the findings. The present study used cross-sectional data, which is one of the significant limitations of the result because it collected data from the same sources over the observed variables. To limit the limitations, future researchers might go for the time-lagged survey or multi-wave survey to ensure the findings' robustness and generalizability. Finally, the present study is quantitative that fails to gauge the inference. Thus, including qualitative thorough interviews or case studies and quantitative methods might prevent the causality issue.

CONCLUSION

This study examines teachers' resilience due to the emergence of social media literacy and awareness of COVID-19 amidst pandemic through the influence of engaging persuasion in a moderated mechanism with coping behavior. Consequently, the study considered Bangladeshi university teachers, considering the severity of the higher education scenario after the outbreak that demands the tech-enabled pedagogy's sophistication. In a similar vein, the result concludes that a significant proportion of faculty members can engage in persuasion and resilience. We recommend faculty members to be resilient to the degree that they exhibit implicit resilience and predictive response to rampant changes. The contingency planning for a range of possible uncertainties and willingness to build strategies might significantly promote hypothesized associations. Such interactions apply to the current state and approve these invaluable insights to help better faculty members find themselves in atmospheric pressure and related challenges. Moreover, the policy-makers relating to higher education need massive resource commitment to stimulate energies (i.e., coping, engaging persuasion, and awareness) and teachers' capabilities (i.e., social media literacy) to be a good fit with the changing skill-sets in this pandemic situation.

ACKNOWLEDGMENT

The present study acknowledges the constructive comments of reviewers, associate editor and editor-in-chief that really worked to develop the current study at this stage. Authors are also thanking respondents who gave their responses in this study. Finally, the assistance of Ahmed Ishmum Uddin (graduate student of the Department of Human Resource Management, University of Chittagong, Bangladesh) was crucially helpful for the present research.

REFERENCES

Ak, N. Y. (2020). Development of Internet literacy self-efficacy scale for pre-service teachers. *Turkish Journal of Education*, *9*(2), 179–204.

Alea, L. A., Fabrea, M. F., Roldan, R. D. A., & Farooqi, A. Z. (2020). Teachers' Covid-19 awareness, distance learning education experiences and perceptions towards institutional readiness and challenges. *International Journal of Learning, Teaching and Educational Research*, *19*(6), 127–144.

Austin, Z., & Gregory, P. (2020). Resilience in the time of pandemic: The experience of community pharmacists during COVID-19. *Research in Social & Administrative Pharmacy*. Advance online publication. doi:10.1016/j.sapharm.2020.05.027 PMID:32499160

Azevedo, A., & Shane, M. J. (2019). A new training program in developing cultural intelligence can also improve innovative work behavior and resilience: A longitudinal pilot study of graduate students and professional employees. *International Journal of Management Education*, *17*(3), 100303. doi:10.1016/j.ijme.2019.05.004

Azim, M. T., Fan, L., Uddin, M. A., Jilani, M. M. A. K., & Begum, S. (2019). Linking transformational leadership with employees' engagement in the creative process. *Management Research Review*, *42*(7), 837–858. doi:10.1108/MRR-08-2018-0286

Bao, W. (2020). COVID-19 and online teaching in higher education: A case study of Peking University. *Human Behavior and Emerging Technologies*, *2*(2), 113–115. doi:10.1002/hbe2.191 PMID:32510042

Beldad, A., de Jong, M., & Steehouder, M. (2010). How shall I trust the faceless and the intangible? A literature review on the antecedents of online trust. *Computers in Human Behavior*, *26*(5), 857–869. doi:10.1016/j.chb.2010.03.013

Bickel, J. (2009). Faculty resilience and career development: Strategies for strengthening academic medicine. In T. R. Cole, T. J. Goodrich, & E. R. Gritz (Eds.), *Faculty Health in Academic Medicine: Physicians, Scientists, and the Pressures of Success* (pp. 83–92). Humana Press. doi:10.1007/978-1-60327-451-7_7

Carver, C. S., Scheier, M. F., & Weintraub, J. K. (1989). Assessing coping strategies: A theoretically based approach. *Journal of Personality and Social Psychology*, *56*(2), 267–283. doi:10.1037/0022-3514.56.2.267 PMID:2926629

Chen, Z. F., & Cheng, Y. (2019). Consumer response to fake news about brands on social media: The effects of self-efficacy, media trust, and persuasion knowledge on brand trust. *Journal of Product and Brand Management*, *29*(2), 188–198. doi:10.1108/JPBM-12-2018-2145

Cohen, J. (1977). *Statistical Power Analysis for the Behavioral Sciences*. Academic Press.

Darling-Hammond, L., Flook, L., Cook-Harvey, C., Barron, B., & Osher, D. (2020). Implications for educational practice of the science of learning and development. *Applied Developmental Science*, *24*(2), 97–140. doi:10.1080/10888691.2018.1537791

Das, A. K., Jilani, M. M. A. K., Uddin, M. S., Uddin, M. A., & Ghosh, A. K. (2021). Fighting ahead: Adoption of social distancing in COVID-19 outbreak through the lens of theory of planned behavior. *Journal of Human Behavior in the Social Environment*, 1–21. Advance online publication. doi:10.1080/10911359.2020.1833804

Dawson, D. L., & Golijani-Moghaddam, N. (2020). COVID-19: Psychological flexibility, coping, mental health, and wellbeing in the UK during the pandemic. *Journal of Contextual Behavioral Science*, *17*, 126–134. doi:10.1016/j.jcbs.2020.07.010 PMID:32834970

Dwivedi, Y. K., Hughes, D. L., Coombs, C., Constantiou, I., Duan, Y., Edwards, J. S., Gupta, B., Lal, B., Misra, S., Prashant, P., Raman, R., Rana, N. P., Sharma, S. K., & Upadhyay, N. (2020). Impact of COVID-19 pandemic on information management research and practice: Transforming education, work and life. *International Journal of Information Management*, *102211*, 102211. Advance online publication. doi:10.1016/j.ijinfomgt.2020.102211

El Rayess, M., Chebl, C., Mhanna, J., & Hage, R.-M. (2018). Fake news judgement: The case of undergraduate students at Notre Dame University-Louaize, Lebanon. *RSR. Reference Services Review*, *46*(1), 146–149. doi:10.1108/RSR-07-2017-0027

Eom, T., Han, H., & Song, H. (2020). Discovering the perceived attributes of CBT destination travelers in South Korea: A mixed method approach. *Tourism Management*, *77*, 104013. doi:10.1016/j.tourman.2019.104013

Fan, L., Mahmood, M., & Uddin, M. A. (2019). Supportive Chinese supervisor, innovative international students: A social exchange theory perspective. *Asia Pacific Education Review*, *20*(1), 101–115. doi:10.100712564-018-9572-3

Feezel, J. D. (2018). The evolution of communication pedagogy. *Journal of Communication Pedagogy, 1*(1), 3–8. doi:10.31446/JCP.2018.02

Ferdig, R. E., Baumgartner, E., Hartshorne, R., Kaplan-Rakowski, R., & Mouza, C. (2020). Teaching, technology, and teacher education during the covid-19 pandemic: Stories from the field. Waynesville, NC: Association for the Advancement of Computing in Education (AACE).

Fergusson, L., van der Laan, L., Shallies, B., & Baird, M. (2020). Work, resilience and sustainable futures: The approach of work-based research to problems and their solutions. *Journal of Work-Applied Management, 12*(1), 22–41. doi:10.1108/JWAM-11-2019-0036

Festl, R. (2020). Social media literacy & adolescent social online behavior in Germany. *Journal of Children and Media*, 1–23. doi:10.1080/17482798.2020.1770110

Field, A. (2018). *Discovering Statistics Using IBM SPSS Statistics* (5th ed.). Sage Publications Inc.

Flostrand, A., Pitt, L., & Kietzmann, J. (2019). Fake news and brand management: A Delphi study of impact, vulnerability and mitigation. *Journal of Product and Brand Management, 29*(2), 246–254. doi:10.1108/JPBM-12-2018-2156

Folkman, S., & Lazarus, R. S. (1980). An analysis of coping in a middle-aged community sample. *Journal of Health and Social Behavior, 21*(3), 219–239. doi:10.2307/2136617 PMID:7410799

Fornell, C., & Larcker, D. F. (1981). Evaluating structural equation models with unobservable variables and measurement error. *JMR, Journal of Marketing Research, 18*(1), 39–50. doi:10.1177/002224378101800104

Fullana, M. A., Hidalgo-Mazzei, D., Vieta, E., & Radua, J. (2020). Coping behaviors associated with decreased anxiety and depressive symptoms during the COVID-19 pandemic and lockdown. *Journal of Affective Disorders, 275*, 80–81. doi:10.1016/j.jad.2020.06.027 PMID:32658829

Fuller, C. M., Simmering, M. J., Atinc, G., Atinc, Y., & Babin, B. J. (2016). Common methods variance detection in business research. *Journal of Business Research, 69*(8), 3192–3198. doi:10.1016/j.jbusres.2015.12.008

Garfin, D. R. (2020). Technology as a coping tool during the COVID-19 pandemic: Implications and recommendations. *Stress and Health, 34*(4), 555–559. doi:10.1002mi.2975 PMID:32762116

Gupta, N., & Sharma, V. (2018). Relationship between leader member exchange (LMX), high-involvement HRP and employee resilience on extra-role performance: Mediating role of employee engagement. *Journal of Indian Business Research, 10*(2), 126–150. doi:10.1108/JIBR-09-2017-0147

Hair, J. F. Jr, Hult, G. T., Ringle, C. M., & Sarstedt, M. (2014). *A primer on partial least squares structural equation modeling (PLS-SEM)*. SAGE Publications, Inc.

Hair, J. F. Jr, Hult, G. T. M., Ringle, C. M., & Sarstedt, M. (2017). *A Primer on Partial Least Squares Structural Equation Modeling (PLS-SEM)*. Sage Publication.

Hair, J. F., Hult, G. T. M., Ringle, C. M., Sarstedt, M., & Thiele, K. O. (2017). Mirror, mirror on the wall: A comparative evaluation of composite-based structural equation modeling methods. *Journal of the Academy of Marketing Science, 45*(5), 616–632. doi:10.100711747-017-0517-x

Hasan, N., & Bao, Y. (2020). Impact of "e-Learning crack-up" perception on psychological distress among college students during COVID-19 pandemic: A mediating role of "fear of academic year loss". *Children and Youth Services Review*, *118*, 105355. doi:10.1016/j.childyouth.2020.105355 PMID:32834276

Horvath, M. A. H., & Massey, K. (2018). The impact of witnessing other people's trauma: The resilience and coping strategies of members of the Faculty of Forensic and Legal Medicine. *Journal of Forensic and Legal Medicine*, *55*, 99–104. doi:10.1016/j.jflm.2018.02.012 PMID:29486433

Ikhalia, E., Serrano, A., Bell, D., & Louvieris, P. (2019). Online social network security awareness: Mass interpersonal persuasion using a Facebook app. *Information Technology & People*, *32*(5), 1276–1300. doi:10.1108/ITP-06-2018-0278

Izumi, T., Sukhwani, V., Surjan, A., & Shaw, R. (2020). Managing and responding to pandemics in higher educational institutions: initial learning from COVID-19. *International Journal of Disaster Resilience in the Built Environment*. doi:10.1108/IJDRBE-06-2020-0054

Khan, A. G., Kamruzzaman, M., Rahman, M. N., Mahmood, M., & Uddin, M. A. (2021). Quality of life in the COVID-19 outbreak: Influence of psychological distress, government strategies, social distancing, and emotional recovery. *Heliyon*, *7*(3), e06407. Advance online publication. doi:10.1016/j.heliyon.2021.e06407 PMID:33688587

Kim, J. H. (2019). Multicollinearity and misleading statistical results. *Korean Journal of Anesthesiology*, *72*(6), 558–569. doi:10.4097/kja.19087 PMID:31304696

Laato, S., Islam, A. K. M. N., Islam, M. N., & Whelan, E. (2020). What drives unverified information sharing and cyberchondria during the COVID-19 pandemic? *European Journal of Information Systems*, *29*(3), 288–305. doi:10.1080/0960085X.2020.1770632

Lee, Y.-R., Lee, J.-Y., Kim, J.-M., Shin, I.-S., Yoon, J.-S., & Kim, S.-W. (2019). A comparative study of burnout, stress, and resilience among emotional workers. *Psychiatry Investigation*, *16*(9), 686–694. doi:10.30773/pi.2019.07.10 PMID:31455062

Livingstone, S. (2014). Developing social media literacy: How children learn to interpret risky opportunities on social network sites. *Communications*, *39*(3), 283–303. doi:10.1515/commun-2014-0113

MacIntyre, P. D., Gregersen, T., & Mercer, S. (2020). Language teachers' coping strategies during the Covid-19 conversion to online teaching: Correlations with stress, wellbeing and negative emotions. *System*, *94*, 102352. doi:10.1016/j.system.2020.102352

MacKinnon, D. P., Lockwood, C. M., Hoffman, J. M., West, S. G., & Sheets, V. (2002). A comparison of methods to test mediation and other intervening variable effects. *Psychological Methods*, *7*(1), 83–104. doi:10.1037/1082-989X.7.1.83 PMID:11928892

Mahmood, M., Uddin, M. A., & Luo, F. (2019). Influence of transformational leadership on employees' creative process engagement: A multi-level analysis. *Management Decision*, *57*(3), 741–764. doi:10.1108/MD-07-2017-0707

Martens, H., & Hobbs, R. (2015). How media literacy supports civic engagement in a digital age. *Atlantic Journal of Communication*, *23*(2), 120–137. doi:10.1080/15456870.2014.961636

McQuillan, N., Wightman, C., Moore, C., McMahon-Beattie, U., & Farley, H. (2020). Developing resilient graduates to be future workplace leaders. *Higher Education, Skills and Work-Based Learning*. doi:10.1108/HESWBL-11-2019-0162

Mishra, P., Bhadauria, U. S., Dasar, P. L., Kumar, S., Lalani, A., Sarkar, P., ... Vyas, S. (2016). Knowledge, attitude and anxiety towards pandemic flu a potential bio weapon among health professionals in Indore City. *Przegląd Epidemiologiczny*, *70*(1), 41–45, 125–127. PMID:27344473

Mosheva, M., Hertz-Palmor, N., Dorman Ilan, S., Matalon, N., Pessach, I. M., Afek, A., Ziv, A., Kreiss, Y., Gross, R., & Gothelf, D. (2020). Anxiety, pandemic-related stress and resilience among physicians during the COVID-19 pandemic. *Depression and Anxiety*, *37*(10), 965–971. doi:10.1002/da.23085 PMID:32789945

Newton, K. (2020). Government Communications, Political Trust and Compliant Social Behaviour: The Politics of Covid-19 in Britain. *The Political Quarterly*, *91*(3), 502–513. doi:10.1111/1467-923X.12901 PMID:32904826

O'Dowd, E., O'Connor, P., Lydon, S., Mongan, O., Connolly, F., Diskin, C., McLoughlin, A., Rabbitt, L., McVicker, L., Reid-McDermott, B., & Byrne, D. (2018). Stress, coping, and psychological resilience among physicians. *BMC Health Services Research*, *18*(1), 730. doi:10.118612913-018-3541-8 PMID:30241524

Oinas-Kukkonen, H., & Harjumaa, M. (2009). Persuasive systems design: Key issues, process model, and system features. *Communications of the Association for Information Systems*, *24*(1), 485–500. doi:10.17705/1CAIS.02428

Phan, T. T. N., & Dang, L. T. T. (2017). Teacher readiness for online teaching: A critical review. *International Journal of Open Distance E-Learning*, *3*(1), 1–16.

Podsakoff, P. M., MacKenzie, S. B., Lee, J.-Y., & Podsakoff, N. P. (2003). Common method biases in behavioral research: A critical review of the literature and recommended remedies. *The Journal of Applied Psychology*, *88*(5), 879–903. doi:10.1037/0021-9010.88.5.879 PMID:14516251

Podsakoff, P. M., MacKenzie, S. B., & Podsakoff, N. P. (2012). Sources of method bias in social science research and recommendations on how to control it. *Annual Review of Psychology*, *63*(1), 539–569. doi:10.1146/annurev-psych-120710-100452 PMID:21838546

Quezada, R. L., Talbot, C., & Quezada-Parker, K. B. (2020). From bricks and mortar to remote teaching: A teacher education programme's response to COVID-19. *Journal of Education for Teaching*, *46*(4), 1–12. doi:10.1080/02607476.2020.1801330

Rahman, A., & Sathi, N. J. (2020). Knowledge, attitude, and preventive practices toward COVID-19 among bangladeshi internet users. *Electronic Journal of General Medicine, 17*(5).

Roy, D., Tripathy, S., Kar, S. K., Sharma, N., Verma, S. K., & Kaushal, V. (2020). Study of knowledge, attitude, anxiety & perceived mental healthcare need in Indian population during COVID-19 pandemic. *Asian Journal of Psychiatry*, *51*, 102083. doi:10.1016/j.ajp.2020.102083 PMID:32283510

Saad, S. K., & Elshaer, I. A. (2020). Justice and trust's role in employees' resilience and business' continuity: Evidence from Egypt. *Tourism Management Perspectives*, *35*, 100712. doi:10.1016/j.tmp.2020.100712

Sajed, A. N., & Amgain, K. (2020). Corona virus disease (COVID-19) outbreak and the strategy for prevention. *Europasian Journal of Medical Sciences*, *2*(1), 1–4. doi:10.46405/ejms.v2i1.38

Schreurs, L., & Vandenbosch, L. (2020). Introducing the social media literacy (SMILE) model with the case of the positivity bias on social media. *Journal of Children and Media*, •••, 1–18. doi:10.1080/17482798.2020.1809481

Shechter, A., Diaz, F., Moise, N., Anstey, D. E., Ye, S., Agarwal, S., Birk, J. L., Brodie, D., Cannone, D. E., Chang, B., Claassen, J., Cornelius, T., Derby, L., Dong, M., Givens, R. C., Hochman, B., Homma, S., Kronish, I. M., Lee, S. A. J., ... Abdalla, M. (2020). Psychological distress, coping behaviors, and preferences for support among New York healthcare workers during the COVID-19 pandemic. *General Hospital Psychiatry*, *66*, 1–8. doi:10.1016/j.genhosppsych.2020.06.007 PMID:32590254

Shi, Y., Wang, J., Yang, Y., Wang, Z., Wang, G., Hashimoto, K., . . . Liu, H. (2020). Knowledge and attitudes of medical staff in Chinese psychiatric hospitals regarding COVID-19. *Brain, Behavior, & Immunity - Health, 4*. doi:10.1016/j.bbih.2020.100064

Sobaih, A. E. E., Hasanein, A. M., & Abu Elnasr, A. E. (2020). Responses to COVID-19 in higher education: Social media usage for sustaining formal academic communication in developing countries. *Sustainability*, *12*(16), 6520. doi:10.3390u12166520

Tesar, M. (2020). Towards a post-COVID-19 'new normality?' physical and social distancing, the move to online and higher education. *Policy Futures in Education*, *18*(5), 556–559. doi:10.1177/1478210320935671

Tikka, P., & Oinas-Kukkonen, H. (2017). Contributing or receiving-the role of social interaction styles in persuasion over a social networking platform. *Personal and Ubiquitous Computing*, *21*(4), 705–721. doi:10.100700779-017-1027-z

Uddin, M. A., Alam, M. S., Mamun, A. A., Khan, T.-U.-Z., & Akter, A. (2020). A study of the adoption and implementation of enterprise resource planning (erp): Identification of moderators and mediator. *Journal of Open Innovation*, *6*(1), 2–19. doi:10.3390/joitmc6010002

Uddin, M. A., Mahmood, M., & Fan, L. (2019). Why individual employee engagement matters for team performance? Mediating effects of employee commitment and organizational citizenship behaviour. *Team Performance Management*, *25*(1/2), 47–68. doi:10.1108/TPM-12-2017-0078

Uddin, M. A., Priyankara, H. P. R., & Mahmood, M. (2020). Does a creative identity encourage innovative behaviour? Evidence from knowledge-intensive IT service firms. *European Journal of Innovation Management*, *23*(5), 877–894. doi:10.1108/EJIM-06-2019-0168

Wang, Y., Keller, J. C., Huang, C., & Fanjoy, R. O. (2016). An exploratory study: Correlations between occupational stressors, coping mechanisms, and job performance among Chinese aviation maintenance technicians. *Journal of Aviation Technology and Engineering*, *5*(2), 69–80. doi:10.7771/2159-6670.1129

Xu, H., Gonzalez Mendez, M. J., Guo, L., Chen, Q., Zheng, L., Chen, P., Cao, X., Liu, S., Sun, X., Zhang, S., & Qiao, Y. (2020). Knowledge, awareness, and attitudes relating to the COVID-19 pandemic among different populations in central china: Cross-sectional survey. *Journal of Medical Internet Research, 22*(10), e22628. doi:10.2196/22628 PMID:32886623

Ye, Z., Yang, X., Zeng, C., Wang, Y., Shen, Z., Li, X., & Lin, D. (2020). Resilience, social support, and coping as mediators between COVID-19-related stressful experiences and acute stress disorder among college students in China. *Applied Psychology: Health and Well-Being*. doi:10.1111/aphw.12211

Youn, S., & Shin, W. (2020). Adolescents' responses to social media newsfeed advertising: The interplay of persuasion knowledge, benefit-risk assessment, and ad scepticism in explaining information disclosure. *International Journal of Advertising, 39*(2), 213–231. doi:10.1080/02650487.2019.1585650

Zheng, D., Luo, Q., & Ritchie, B. W. (2021). Afraid to travel after COVID-19? Self-protection, coping and resilience against pandemic 'travel fear'. *Tourism Management, 83*, 104261. doi:10.1016/j.tourman.2020.104261

Zia, A. (2020). Exploring factors influencing online classes due to social distancing in COVID-19 pandemic: a business students perspective. *The International Journal of Information and Learning Technology*. doi:10.1108/IJILT-05-2020-0089

KEY TERMS AND DEFINITIONS

Coping Behavior: Coping behavior is the cognitive and behavioral response of an individual that helps ensure balance in expectations and inconsistencies.

Faculty Resilience: Faculty resilience is the capability of faculty to recover themselves from any adversity and revive them to fit in any unforeseen psychological issues.

Knowledge and Awareness: Knowledge and awareness of COVID-19 refer to observation, collection, synthesis, understanding, and conscious evaluation of the events in the immediate environment.

Persuasion: Persuasion is a rational choice that directs toward accepting new events or behavior in a particular situation through changing attitude.

Social Media Literacy: Social media literacy refers to the acquaintance, adoption, and productive use of social media technology in any given setting.

Table 3. Survey measures

Social media literacy	
SML1	I can distinguish whether information on the web is subjective or scientific.
SML2	I can create videos on the web (e.g. GoAnimate, Powtoon, etc.).
SML3	I can distinguish whether information on the web is trustworthy.
SML4	I can solve software-related Internet access problems
SML5	I can create podcasts.
SML6	I can solve other Internet access problems
SML7	I can use Google search techniques.
SML8	I can use online library databases.
SML9	I can create blogs.
SML10	I can distinguish trustworthy web sites.
SML11	I can create posters or concept maps (e.g. Bubbl.us, Easel.ly, etc.).
SML12	I can distinguish whether the source of information on the web is scientific or not.
SML13	I can solve hardware-related Internet access problems.
SML14	I can use academic reference programs (e.g. Mendeley, Evernote, etc.).
Engaging persuasion	
EP1	Apply the knowledge
EP2	Curiosity developed
EP3	Intention to reuse
EP4	Extra cautious
Coping behavior	
CB1	When I have a question about the situation, I search for information
CB2	I turn to work or other substitute activities to take my mind off things
CB3	I use alcohol or drugs to make myself feel better
CB4	I enjoy the jokes about the situation
Faculty resilience	
FR1	I can adapt when changes occur.
FR2	I can deal with whatever comes my way.
FR3	I tend to bounce back after illness, injury or hardships.
FR4	Having to cope with stress can make me stronger
Knowledge and awareness of COVID-19	
KA1	I have proper knowledge of the COVID-19 epidemic provided by the World Health Organization (WHO).
KA2	I am aware of the risks for people and me due to COVID-19.
KA3	I am conscious of how to protect others and myself in the COVID-19 epidemic.
KA4	I believe that frequent hand washing, maintain proper sneezing, and coughing etiquette will reduce infection from COVID-19.
KA5	I consider staying home is crucial to maintain social distance in the COVID-19 epidemic.

Chapter 16
Stock Market Price and Company Performance Between Two Major Downturns:
The Financial Crisis and the COVID-19 Pandemic

Larissa Batrancea
Babes-Bolyai University, Cluj-Napoca, Romania

ABSTRACT

The chapter investigates the degree to which stock market prices were influenced by company financial performance during the period March 2007–September 2020, which included both the beginning of the global financial crisis and the ongoing COVID-19 pandemic crisis. Using quarterly financial data retrieved from the first 34 companies listed on the New York Stock Exchange according to their transaction volumes, empirical results show that, in the period between the two crises, stock market metrics including price to earnings, price to sales, price to book value, and price to free cash flow were shaped by financial performance indicators such as gross margin ratio, operating margin ratio, earnings before interest, taxes, depreciation and amortization margin, pretax margin, and net profit margin.

INTRODUCTION

A stock market is a dynamic environment in which share prices are influenced by a variety of factors from macroeconomic, financial and political to psychological, cultural or even natural ones (Basher, Haug & Sadorsky, 2012; Batrancea & Nichita, 2015; Batrancea, Nichita & Batrancea, 2012; Batrancea, Batrancea & Moscviciov, 2009a, 2009b; Batrancea et al., 2018; Benlagha, 2020; Garcia-Vega, Zeng & Keane, 2020; Graham, 2003; Hirsch & Kass, 2012; Hirshleifer, Hsu & Li, 2020; Hong & Li, 2020; Hsing, 2011; Lin, 2012; Malkiel, 2007; Rudzkis & Valkavičienė, 2014; Ornelas & de Carvalho, 2020;

DOI: 10.4018/978-1-7998-7164-4.ch016

Padungsaksawasdi, Treepongkaruna & Brooks, 2019; Patra & Poshakwale, 2007; Siddiqui, Mahmood & Margaritis, 2020; Shiller, 2003; Shleifer, 2000; Villanueva & Feinstein, 2020; Wen et al., 2019).

Despite the multitude of factors, both seasoned investors and aspiring newbies decide to join this market aiming to maximize their investments – ideally on the bull market – either on the short run or on the long run. Like any other dynamic ground, the stock market has its own written and unwritten rules. In this regard, investment gurus such as Warren Buffet (chairman and the largest shareholder of the American company Berkshire Hathaway) famously stated that the first rule of investing was "Never lose money", while the second rule was "Never forget rule no.1". According to Warren Buffet, any purchasing decision on the stock market should be preceded by a thorough analysis of the company financial statements and reports in order to understand the business behind the stock. Only after investors grasp the characteristics of the business and its perspective of growth should they buy any shares.

Crunching numbers within financial statements and not letting oneself be influenced by skyrocketing prices, rumors (Kiymaz, 2001; Rose, 1951) or word-of-mouth communication (Argan, Sevil & Yalama, 2014) would be a rational strategy that could prevent investors from falling into the so-called "winner's curse" (i.e., buying an overpriced share). To a certain degree, the well-known principle of "thinking before you speak" could be translated as "analyzing before you buy" for savvy players in the stock market world. In this regard, Warren Buffet wittingly concludes that it is "far better to buy a wonderful company at a fair price than a fair company at a wonderful price".

In this day and age, people interested in investing on the stock market are certainly not running short of advice coming from wealthy professionals, scholars and even Nobel Prize winners. For instance, Lynch (2000: 12) explains his investment strategy in simple words: "I own stocks where results depend on ancient fundamentals: a successful company enters new markets, its earnings rise, and the share price follows along".

By means of various interviews with "super-traders" such as Paul Tudor Jones, Anthony Saliba or Mark Weinstein, Schwager (2012) gives account of how these executives have become legendary in this ever-changing environment. In his follow-up book, Schwager (2020: 323–324) notes that "there is no single formula for succeeding in the markets. [...] Trading success is not about finding the right approach but instead finding the right approach for you".

Richard Thaler, the 2017 Nobel Prize in Economics winner and co-founder of the successful Fuller & Thaler Asset Management hedge fund, believes that the best investment strategy comprises three key elements:

1. owning a diversified portfolio, which should include mostly shares;
2. examining the portfolio once a year;
3. ignoring daily news.

Thaler's rationale is sensible and straightforward. Investing in multiple companies at the same time can protect investors from losing everything if one business in their portfolio undergoes financial difficulties or goes bankrupt. Yearly examination of portfolios develops a long-term thinking and trains investors to put financial stability and steady returns ahead of one-time gains. Last but not least, eliminating noise generated by everyday news can prevent investors from selling otherwise profitable stocks under momentary impulses triggered by rumors, herding behavior (Bikhchandani & Sharma, 2000; Christie & Huang, 1995; Demirer, Kutan & Chen, 2010; Lin, Tsai & Lung, 2013; Munkh-Ulzii et al., 2018) or temporary difficulties of a company. As the same Buffet explains, the stock market can be seen as "a device for transferring money from the impatient to the patient".

Nevertheless, even if investors may act cautiously and calculate every step, there are certain periods of economic downturn that cannot be prevented in due time and may have overall severe consequences. It is the case of the 2007–2008 global financial crisis (Batrancea, Batrancea & Moscviciov, 2009c, 2009d; Batrancea et al., 2013) and the ongoing COVID-19 pandemic crisis (Ashraf, 2020; Lyócsa et al., 2020), during which economic activities around the globe have experienced recurring lockdown measures in the attempt to curb the virus spread.

The book chapter brings forward a causality analysis between company financial performance (measured through different financial indicators) and stock market prices amid these two major crises by using data retrieved from the financials of the first 34 companies listed on the New York Stock Exchange (NYSE). The choice of NYSE was motivated by the importance of this stock market for investors and traders around the world. Empirical data will, therefore, elicit the evolution of stock metrics for these major NYSE players during the period March 2007 – September 2020.

The chapter is organized as follows. Section two includes the literature review and explores relevant studies on distinct categories of factors driving stock market metrics. Section three describes the research method, formulates hypotheses and discusses empirical results. The last section presents concluding remarks, discusses study limitations and pictures future research directions.

LITERATURE REVIEW

The following paragraphs will briefly present some of the most important variables reported in the literature that are said to influence stock market metrics. As previously mentioned, variables are included into categories such as macroeconomic, financial, political, psychological, cultural and natural.

Macroeconomic and Financial Determinants of Stock Market Metrics

Before any major crash similar to the 1929 Great Depression was even conceived to be happening again, Chen, Roll and Ross (1986) showed that variables such as the spread between long and short interest rates, industrial production, spread between high-grade and low-grade bonds, as well as expected and unexpected inflation significantly influenced market prices.

Using data from the Karachi Stock Exchange for the period 1998–2009, Khan and Zaman (2012) investigated the effect of various macroeconomic factors (i.e., consumer price index; exchange rate; exports; foreign direct investments; gross domestic product; money supply M2; oil prices) on stock prices. Empirical results estimated via multiple regressions with fixed effects reported that stock prices were positively influenced by GDP and exchange rate, while consumer price index mitigated the outcome variable. Chang et al. (2019) focused on the same stock market for the time frame September 1997 – June 2018 and concluded that the exchange rate, interest rate and trade balance had a negative influence on stock prices, whereas consumer price index and industrial production augmented stock prices.

Based on monthly data from the US and Canada, Bhuiyan and Chowdhury (2020) studied the degree to which money supply and interest rate impacted the composite and sectoral stock indices. Empirical results corresponding to the period 2008–2018 reported that stock prices were positively influenced by money supply and negatively influenced by interest rate on the US market. Canadian stock prices showed no significant influence of these predictors. Interestingly enough, the levels of money supply and interest rate within the US did play an important role on Canadian stock prices but not the other way around.

Besides macroeconomic factors, stock market metrics are also influenced by *financial variables* such as bank diversification, company performance, liquidity, solvency, dividend policy, various expenditure categories etc. (e.g., Anwaar, 2016; Foye, 2013; Kim, Kwon & Oh, 2016; Rahaman & Chowdhury, 2017).

In this regard, Brammer, Brooks and Pavelin (2006) analyzed the relationship between company social performance (captured via social activity outlays) and stock market returns for UK companies. Authors concluded that higher levels of social performance triggered lower stock returns levels.

Alexakis, Patra and Poshakwale (2010) focused on the Athens Stock Exchange for the period 1993–2006 in order to examine stock predictability based on accounting information. Empirical results reported that stocks selected based on certain financial indicators yielded higher returns than stock selected via other criteria.

Nassirzadeh, Salehi and Sarvghadi (2015) investigated the impact of various financial predictors (e.g., profitability, liquidity, solvency) on the trading volume of 67 companies listed on the Tehran Stock Exchange during the period March 21, 2010 – March 20, 2014[1] and concluded that only liquidity indicators had a significant influence.

Edirisuriya, Gunasekarage and Dempsey (2015) analyzed the impact of bank diversification on stock returns in Bangladesh, India, Pakistan and Sri Lanka for the period 1999–2012. Empirical results showed that market-to-book values reached higher levels when the commercial banks in South Asian countries diversified their portfolios and generated income from non-interest activities.

Grieco (2017) proposed a new empirical model showing that the degree of company innovativeness (measured via the expenditures for research and development) significantly influenced stock market performance for ambiguity-averse investors.

Political Determinants of Stock Market Metrics

Market prices react in general not only to economic and financial factors, but also to political changes within countries (Riley & Luksetich, 1980; Schneider & Tröger, 2006).

For instance, Füss and Behtel (2007) focused on the partisan politics theory and their empirical results supported the theoretical assumptions: returns registered by small companies increased with the probability of having a right-wing coalition ruling the federal government. Using data from 37 countries for the period 1985–2004, Mosley and Singer (2008) found that political factors such as capital-account openness and shareholder protections played a significant role in market valuations.

Furió and Pardo (2014) tested the partisan theory on returns yielded by the Spanish stock market and found evidence that the political orientation of the government triggered different returns throughout an entire mandate. Lehkonen and Heimonen (2015) conducted a panel investigation on data from 49 emerging markets during the time span 2000–2012 and reported that democracy and political risk shaped market returns. Moreover, higher returns were yielded by lower political risks, as expected.

Psychological Determinants of Stock Market Metrics

Despite the fact that classical economic theory depicts investors as rational calculators and profit maximizers, they often make investment decisions based on perceptions, beliefs, sentiments, biases, third-party influence, all of which defocus rational judgment and computations (Dhaoui, 2015; Thaler, 2015; Thaler & Sunstein, 2009).

Chang (2020) analyzed the relationship between herding behavior and stock returns from the renewable energy and fossil fuel energy sectors using daily data from Europe, the US and Asia. Authors chose the period March 24, 2000 – May 29, 2020 in order to capture three major crises (i.e., global financial crisis, SARS epidemic, COVID-19 pandemic) and concluded that investors were more prone towards herding behavior after the crises because of asset loss aversion.

According to Huang et al. (2014), there seemed to be a significant relationship between investor sentiment and stock returns across different industries. That is, an optimist sentiment among investors was positively linked to stock returns, while pessimistic sentiments had no effects in any industry. In the same vein, Griffith, Najand and Shen (2020) analyzed the effect of emotions on stock returns and reported that stress and fear strongly influenced market returns. Using 22,504 social media posts shared by microbloggers, Sun et al. (2020) showed that social interaction moderated the relationship between investor sentiment and stock returns.

Mbanga, Darrat and Park (2019) tackled the same topic while using aggregate stock market data. Authors concluded that the effect of investor sentiment on stock returns was mediated by investor attention, but to various degrees, depending on the stock size. Namely, in the case of large and medium stocks, the effect lasted only a short period. In the case of small stocks, the effect lasted longer.

Cultural and Natural Determinants of Stock Market Metrics

Lastly, although one may believe that such factors could hardly have an impact on stock prices, the literature counts cultural and natural phenomena as drivers of significant changes on stock markets (Hirshleifer & Shumway, 2003; Pizzutilo & Roncone, 2017; Saunders, 1993; Singh, Li & Roca, 2017).

Brown, Chua and Mitchell (2002) conducted an engaging and compelling analysis on the Shanghai and Shenzhen stock markets for the period 1994–2002 in order to study the impact of culture on price clustering (i.e., price propensity to include certain numbers instead of others). Authors concluded that the prices of shares owned by Chinese companies or Chinese individual taxpayers were more likely to have number *eight* as their last digit rather than number *four*[2]. Hence, Chinese culture was regarded as a significant determinant since the pattern was not identified for shares owned by foreign companies or foreign individual taxpayers. Starting from the cultural dimensions introduced by Geert Hofstede, Zhou et al. (2019) reported that countries with small cultural distance registered similar volatility levels on their national stock markets.

From the category of natural phenomena, Cagle (1996) focused on the study of how the dangerous category 4 Hurricane Hugo influenced insurer stock prices. Empirical results showed that insurers highly exposed to damage claims registered mitigating prices after the hurricane, while less exposed insurance companies went unaffected. Jiang et al. (2019) analyzed how extreme weather conditions (captured by temperature, humidity, sunshine duration) influenced returns on the Hong Kong and Shenzhen stock exchange markets. According to results, only Shenzhen returns were significantly impacted by the weather.

METHOD AND RESULTS

In order to capture the evolution of the stock market metrics between the two major crises, the present chapter uses quarterly data from the first 34 companies listed on the New York Stock Exchange, ranked according to their transaction volumes (for the complete list, see the Appendix).

Companies included in the sample carry out various economic activities, such as: athletic footwear, apparel, equipment and accessories manufacturing; automotive manufacturing; consumer goods; e-commerce; entertainment; financial services; graphics design for gaming market; healthcare; insurance and reinsurance; internet services; investment services; media; medical devices and healthcare; movie production; pharmaceuticals; retail; semiconductor manufacturing; soft drinks manufacturing; software; telecommunications.

The time frame chosen for analyses was March 2007 (quarter 1) – September 2020 (quarter 3). For the purpose of computing various indicators, financial data were taken from company financial statements.

The following indicators were selected to represent stock market metrics, since they convey important information about the company's attractiveness in the eyes of investors with regards to earnings, revenues, net value and cash flow. In other words, analyzing the evolution of these indicators should constitute a top priority for any investor willing to expand stock portfolio.

- *Price to earnings* ratio (*PE*), which indicates the ratio of the price per share to its earnings per share. A high value of the indicator could show that either company shares are overvalued or investors expect high growth rates;
- *Price to sales* ratio (*PES*), which is computed by dividing the share price by sales per share;
- *Price to book value* ratio (*PBV*), which is determined to compare the market price with the company book value;
- *Price to free cash flow* ratio (*PFCF*), which is used to compare the market price of a company share to the amount of operating cash flow (FCF) associated with one share.

With respect to the company financial performance, the following indicators were considered relevant since they capture all types of performance from gross profit to net profit. Investors are interested in such indicators because, at the end of the day, they purchase stocks expecting that the company's capacity of generating profit increases and exceeds their initial investments. Hence, econometric models will use these predictors:

- *Gross margin* ratio (*GM*), calculated as a ratio of gross margin (determined as the difference between revenue and cost of goods sold) to revenue. The indicator captures the profit level generated by a company after deducting its cost of goods sold (i.e., COGS);
- *Operating margin* ratio (*OPM*), determined as a ratio of operating income (or profit) to net sales;
- *Earnings before interest, taxes, depreciation and amortization margin* (*EBITDAM*), which is computed by dividing EBITDA and revenue. EBITDA is determined by adding net income, interest, taxes, depreciation and amortization;
- *Pretax margin* ratio (*PRTXM*), which is determined as a ratio of earnings before tax to total sales;
- *Net profit margin* ratio (*NPM*), which captures the company net profit generated by one unit of revenue gained. The indicator is computed by dividing net income to total revenue.

Descriptive Statistics

The following paragraphs give account on the measures of central tendency and variation regarding the nine variables of interest.

Table 1. Descriptive statistics

Indicators	PE	PES	PBV	PFCF	GM	OPM	EBITDAM	NPM	PRETXPM
Mean	40.7021	23.4489	29.4954	933.4971	0.5601	0.1989	0.2724	0.1540	0.2100
Median	16.4700	2.4050	3.0900	15.7200	0.5598	0.1911	0.2597	0.1374	0.1902
Maximum	10234.00	36434.00	1187.670	74454.14	1.0000	0.7860	0.9329	0.7360	0.8321
Minimum	0.0000	0.0162	–686.3600	0.0000	0.0663	–0.4036	–0.3655	–0.2997	–0.3864
Std. Dev.	263.4175	851.6142	154.4165	5465.075	0.2167	0.1303	0.1733	0.1116	0.1499
Skewness	33.2627	42.7423	5.9574	6.6398	0.2143	0.8248	0.7436	0.7542	1.0815
Kurtosis	1246.705	1827.937	39.0581	52.8329	2.3893	5.0449	3.8029	4.3704	4.9796
Jarque-Bera test	1.18***	2.54***	110084.2***	202688.6***	42.5532***	526.3298***	213.5067***	317.5728***	657.3265***
Observations	1829	1830	1832	1829	1835	1830	1794	1835	1835

Source: Author's computations.
Note: *** indicates significance at the 1% level.

Table 1 displays the mean, median and standard deviation values for all the variables of interest. Regarding the standard deviation, data showed that *PFCF* and *PES* had registered the largest volatility, while *NPM* had registered the lowest volatility. Skewness values showed that all variables were right-skewed. According to the kurtosis values, eight variables had leptokurtic distributions and one variable had a platykurtic distribution.

Moreover, by conducting the Jarque-Bera test (which investigates whether data are normally distributed), it became evident that data were non-normally distributed at the 1% level.

Correlation Analysis

Correlation analysis was used as a second set of investigations in order to control for possible multicollinearity problems that could bias empirical estimates. Tables 2 presents the pairwise Pearson correlation coefficients between all variables chosen.

Table 2. Correlation coefficients for the nine variables of interest

Indicators	PE	PES	PBV	PFCF	GM	OPM	EBITDAM	NPM	PRETXPM
PE	1								
PES	–0.0020	1							
PBV	–0.0002	–0.0034	1						
PFCF	–0.0057	–0.0024	0.9052	1					
GM	–0.0024	0.0146	–0.0678	–0.0723	1				
OPM	–0.0942	0.0147	0.0560	0.0471	0.5623	1			
EBITDAM	–0.0312	0.0033	–0.0001	–0.0068	0.3773	0.7279	1		
NPM	–0.0925	0.0818	0.0535	0.0474	0.5073	0.8074	0.6422	1	
PRETXPM	–0.0859	0.0689	0.0413	0.0309	0.5694	0.8060	0.71681	0.8095	1

Source: Author's computations.

As can be seen from Table 2, no multicollinearity problems were identified with respect to the variables of interest since they are not highly correlated.

Econometric Models

Four multiple linear regressions models were estimated via panel data analysis by means of the EViews version 9.0 statistical software. Four research hypotheses were formulated in this regard:

- *H1: There is a linear dependence between performance ratios (GM, OPM, EBITDAM, NPM, PRETXPM) and PE.*
- *H2: There is a linear dependence between performance ratios (GM, OPM, EBITDAM, NPM, PRETXPM) and PES.*
- *H3: There is a linear dependence between performance ratios (GM, OPM, EBITDAM, NPM, PRETXPM) and PBV.*
- *H4: There is a linear dependence between performance ratios (GM, OPM, EBITDAM, NPM, PRETXPM) and PFCF.*

Econometric models had the following general format:

$$Z_{it} = a_0 + a_1 V_{1it} + a_2 V_{2it} + a_3 V_{3it} + a_4 V_{4it} + a_5 V_{5it} + {}'_i + {},_t + \mu_{it}$$

in which,

- a_0 denotes the intercept;
- a_i denotes the coefficient of the predictors, taking values from 1 to 5;
- *V* denotes the predictors;
- *i* denotes the company's activity;
- *t* denotes the selected time frame (q1–2007; q3–2020);
- δi denotes the fixed effects, which take into account time-invariant company-specific factors;

- θi denotes the fixed effects, which take into account common shocks (in this case, the world financial crisis and the COVID-19 crisis);
- εi_t denotes the error term.

Empirical analyses also considered company-specific unobserved effects (δi_j in order to compensate for the omission of other factors influencing stock market metrics. Moreover, since common shocks have an impact on outcome variables, econometric models were estimated with and without cross-section fixed effects (see Table 3).

Table 3. Econometric models estimating the outcome variables price to earnings ratio (PE), price to sales ratio (PES), price to book value ratio (PBV) and price to free cash flow ratio (PFCF)

	Model 1 $PE = a_0 + a_1 GM + a_2 OPM + a_3 EBITDAM + a_4 NPM + a_3 PRETXPM + \delta + \theta + \varepsilon$		Model 2 $PES = a_0 + a_1 GM + a_2 OPM + a_3 EBITDAM + a_4 NPM + a_3 PRETXPM + \delta + \theta + \varepsilon$		Model 3 $PBV = a_0 + a_1 GM + a_2 OPM + a_3 EBITDAM + a_4 NPM + a_3 PRETXPM + \delta + \theta + \varepsilon$		Model 4 $PFCF = a_0 + a_1 GM + a_2 OPM + a_3 EBITDAM + a_4 NPM + a_3 PRETXPM + \delta + \theta + \varepsilon$	
Constant	31.1226* (1.6852)	109.2915* (1.6101)	50.2785 (0.8452)	–457.5114** (–2.0715)	36.2240*** (5.1065)	12.06940* (2.205018)	835.1456*** (4.6933)	106.4536 (0.4506)
GM	110.3897*** (3.0886)	–186.2427 (–1.3628)	–97.8854 (–0.8506)	724.4531* (1.6345)	–64.9582*** (–4.7825)	3.2682 (0.3076)	–1660.584*** (–4.8242)	–57.8325 (–0.1220)
OPM	–321.0495** (–2.4832)	–46.8849 (–0.2859)	–2069.826*** (–4.9647)	–1831.712*** (–3.4337)	117.3047*** (2.3586)	14.4922 (1.0978)	3139.374*** (2.5175)	–438.0380 (–0.7676)
EBITDAM	150.5878*** (2.7672)	242.2632* (1.7149)	–286.0898* (–1.6312)	–131.3935 (–0.2861)	–53.9013*** (–2.5734)	–4.9608 (–0.4476)	–1362.247*** (–2.5966)	1278.590** (2.6023)
NPM	–123.5685 (–1.0243)	–85.8663 (–0.5521)	1466.174*** (3.7690)	1228.328*** (2.4274)	5.7837 (0.1244)	12.7204 (1.0134)	203.6477 (0.1750)	186.1155 (0.3438)
PRETXPM	–49.7426 (–0.4447)	–32.9957 (–0.1851)	1396.282*** (3.8718)	1357.635*** (2.3435)	22.8217 (0.5297)	–17.2095 (–1.2040)	295.7116 (0.2741)	–576.4644 (–0.9302)
Cross-section effects	No	Yes	No	Yes	No	Yes	No	Yes
Time fixed effects	Yes	Yes	Yes	Yes	Yes	Yes	Yes	Yes
Prob.>*F*	0.0000	0.0000	0.0005	0.0000	0.0103	0.0000	0.1036	0.0000
R^2	0.0509	0.0997	0.0559	0.0882	0.0407	0.9601	0.0396	0.8814
Adjusted R-squared	0.0185	0.0509	0.0237	0.0388	0.0080	0.9579	0.0068	0.8749
***F*-statistic**	1.5699	2.0413	1.7362	1.7835	1.2440	444.2576	1.2085	136.9581
Observations	1788	1788	1789	1789	1792	1794	1789	1789

Source: Author's computations.

Note: Robust *t*-statistics are indicated in parentheses; *, **, *** show statistical significance at the 10%, 5% and 1% levels. Prob.>*F* denotes the probability of not considering fixed effects. Multicollinearity was tested with variance inflation and no problems were identified. Homoskedasticity was investigated with the Harvey and Breusch-Pagan-Godfrey tests and both statistics rejected the null hypothesis.

DISCUSSIONS ON EMPIRICAL RESULTS

The **first model (M1)** without cross-section effects revealed that 5.09% of the changes in price to earnings ratio was due to the predictors gross margin, operating margin and earnings before interest, taxes, depreciation and amortization margin ($F = 1.57$, $p < 0.001$). Namely, when GM increased by one unit, PE would follow the same trend with 110.39 units. Should OPM grow by one unit, PE would decrease by 321.05 units. By the same token, an increase in EBITDAM would generate an increase of 150.59 units in PE. When cross-section effects were taken into consideration, the variance explained by the predictors reached 9.97% ($F = 2.04$, $p < 0.001$). EBITDAM was the predictor whose influence remained significant: when it increased by one unit, PE would augment by 242.26 units.

According to the **second model** (**M2**) with no cross-section effects, empirical results showed that the price to sales ratio was impacted by the chosen independent variables, which explained 5.59% of its variance ($F = 1.74$, $p < 0.001$). That is, when OPM and EBITDAM increased by one unit, price to sales mitigated by 2069.83 and 286.09 units, respectively. Moreover, a one-unit change in NPM and PRETXPM would trigger an increase of 1466.17 and 1396.28 units in price to sales. After cross-section effects were added to the model, the percentage of explained variance reached 8.82% ($F = 1.78$, $p < 0.001$). In this case, only the influence of EBITDAM did not reach significance. In other words, when GM increased by one unit, PS rose by 724.45 units, while if OPM followed the same trend, PS would decrease by 1831.71 units. Both NPM and PRETXPM yielded positive results on PS: should these variables increase by one unit, PS would augment by 1228.33 units and 1357.64 units, respectively.

The **third model** (**M3**) lacking cross-section effects indicated that 4.07% of the variance in price to book value ratio was determined by the chosen predictors ($F = 1.24$, $p < 0.001$). For this model, the influence of GM, OPM and EBITDAM proved to be significant. Namely, when GM rose by one unit, PBV ratio decreased by 64.96 units. Should OPM increase by one unit, PBV ratio would follow a similar trend with 117.30 units. Last but not least, when EBITDAM increased by one unit, PVB ratio would mitigate by 53.90 units. When the empirical model included cross-section effects, none of the independent variables reached significance.

Based on the **fourth model** (**M4**) with no cross-section effects, 3.96% of the variance in price to free cash flow ratio was generated by the chosen predictors ($F = 1.21$, $p < 0.001$). Namely, when gross margin rose by one unit, price to free cash ratio would decrease by 1660.58 units. Along the same lines, a matching increase in OPM would be followed by a 3139.37 rise in PFCF ratio. Moreover, should EBITDAM increase by one unit, the outcome variable would mitigate by 1362.25 units. In the presence of cross-section effects, 88.14% of the variance in the PFCF ratio was explained by EBITDAM ($F = 136.96$, $p < 0.001$). That is, when this particular predictor increased by one unit, the dependent variable PFCF would augment by 1278.59 units.

CONCLUSIONS

This book chapter investigated the degree to which financial performance influenced stock market prices of the first 34 large companies listed on the New York Stock Exchange. The period of analysis ranged from the first quarter of 2007 until the third quarter of 2020, selected so as to capture both the global financial crisis and the COVID-19 pandemic crisis. The indicators chosen to measure stock market prices were price to earnings ratio, price to sales ratio, price to book value ratio and price to free cash flow ratio. Company performance was captured by means of indicators such as gross margin ratio, operating margin ratio, earnings before interest, taxes, depreciation and amortization margin, pretax margin ratio and net profit margin ratio.

The financial indicators that exerted the most consistent influence on stock returns for models with and without cross-section effects were operating margin ratio and earnings before interest, taxes, depreciation and amortization margin. The least consistent were the pretax margin ratio and the net profit margin ratio.

Figure 1. The evolution of price to earnings ratio (PE) for the company sample

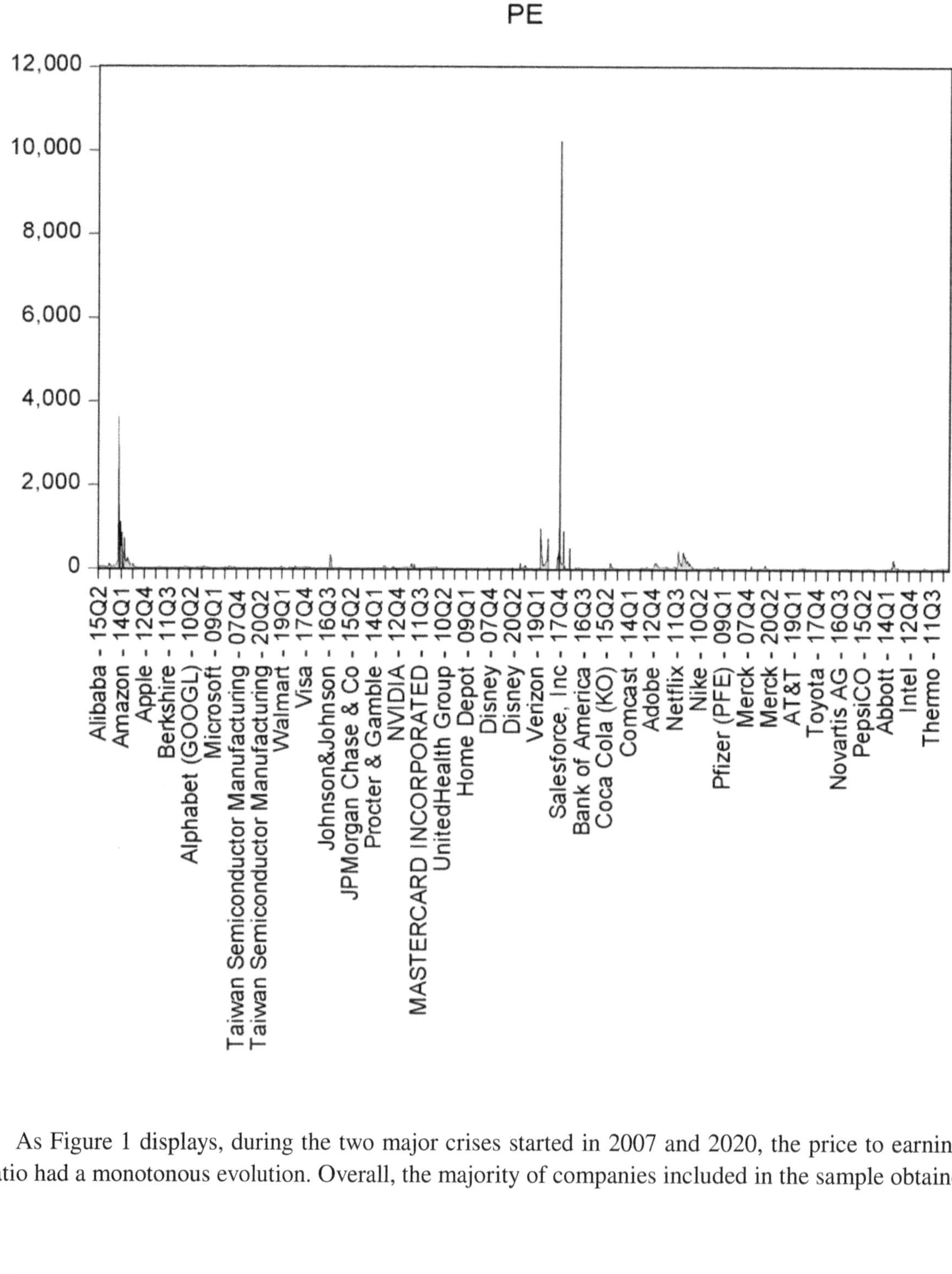

As Figure 1 displays, during the two major crises started in 2007 and 2020, the price to earnings ratio had a monotonous evolution. Overall, the majority of companies included in the sample obtained similar metrics, with few exceptions. Among the companies that registered the biggest market price fluctuations, one could mention Adobe, Alibaba, Amazon, Apple, Verizon, Salesforce, Netflix and Nike.

Figure 2. The evolution of price to book value ratio (PBV) for the company sample

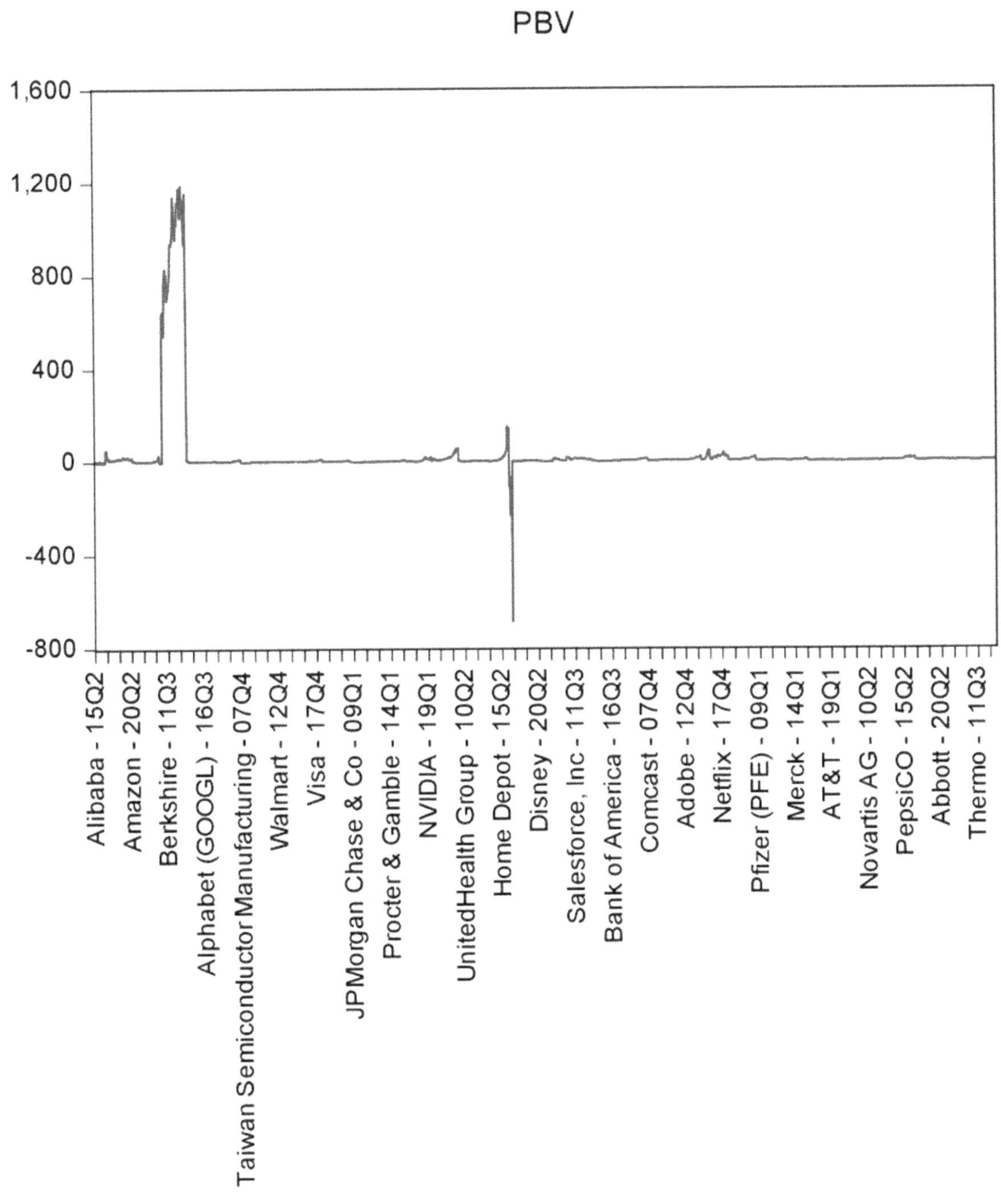

Figure 3. The evolution of price to free cash flow ratio (PFCF) for the company sample

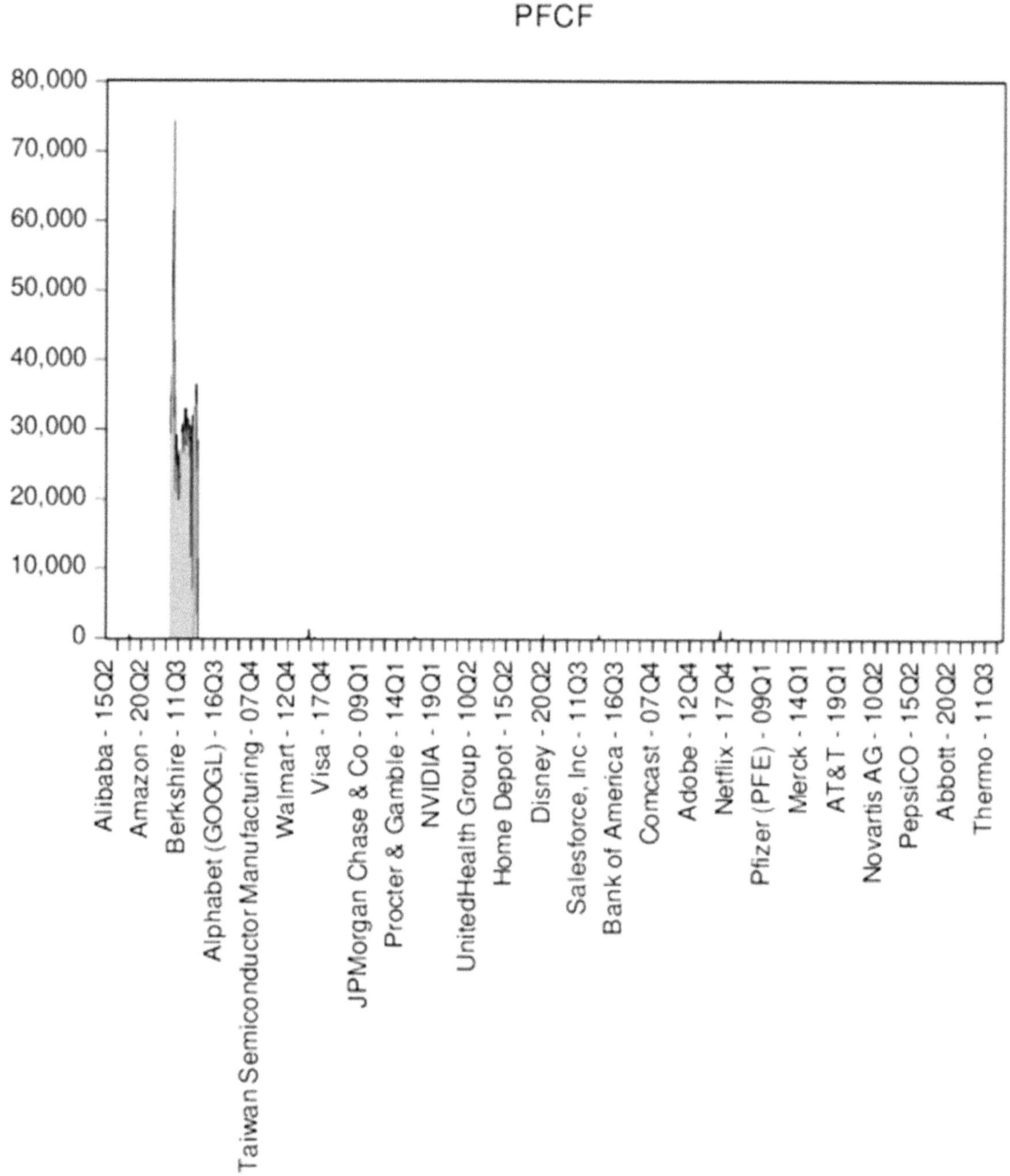

Once again, the majority of companies reported a positive price to book value ratio, which could mean that financial downturns were overcome through increasing investments. In this regard, the highest stock market metric was reported by the company Berkshire Hathaway (run during the last 50 years by Warren Buffet). The lowest price to book value ratio was registered by Home Depot, the largest and well-known home improvement retailer in USA.

As shown by Figure 3, the majority of companies registered a constant price to free cash flow ratio during March 2007 – September 2020. Again, Berkshire Hathaway stood out by reporting the highest stock market metric.

In terms of study limitations, future research endeavors could focus on a bigger number of companies with a wider range of economic activities and listed on different stock markets around the world. This could also facilitate the running of comparisons between different stock markets and their metrics. Future studies could also extend the time frame across several decades in order to capture other financial downturns such as the 1997 Asian financial crisis or the dotcom bubble.

The chapter also provided important insights regarding the evolution of stock returns and emphasized the top companies that managed to generate steady financial returns amid turbulent times.

Overall, stock markets are as complex as the players who interact within these environments: sometimes monotonous and predictable, other times capricious and unpredictable; sometimes calculated and rational, other times biased and erratic. At the end of the day, market prices are "a kind of public opinion" (Rose, 1951: 461), filtering a myriad of information and keeping only the ones that favor a particular purpose.

REFERENCES

Alexakis, C., Patra, T., & Poshakwale, S. (2010). Predictability of stock returns using financial statement information: Evidence on semi-strong efficiency of emerging Greek stock market. *Applied Financial Economics*, *20*(16), 1321–1326. doi:10.1080/09603107.2010.482517

Anwaar, M. (2016). Impact of firms' performance on stock returns (evidence from listed companies on FTSE-100 Index London, UK). *Global Journal of Management and Business Research: D Accounting and Auditing*, *16*(1), 1–9.

Argan, M., Sevil, G., & Yalama, A. (2014). The effect of the word-of-mouth communication on stock holdings and trades: Empirical evidence from an emerging market. *Journal of Behavioral Finance*, *15*(2), 89–98. doi:10.1080/15427560.2014.914029

Ashraf, B. N. (2020). Stock markets' reaction to COVID-19: Cases or fatalities? *Research in International Business and Finance*, *54*, 101249. doi:10.1016/j.ribaf.2020.101249

Basher, S. A., Haug, A. A., & Sadorsky, P. (2012). Oil prices, exchange rates and emerging stock markets. *Energy Economics*, *34*(1), 227–240. doi:10.1016/j.eneco.2011.10.005

Batrancea, I., Moscviciov, A., Sabau, C., & Batrancea, L. M. (2013). Banking crisis: Causes, characteristics and solutions. *Proceedings of the DIEM*, *2013*, 16–29.

Batrancea, L., Batrancea, I., & Moscviciov, A. (2009a). The analysis of the entity's liquidity-A means of evaluating cash flow. *Journal of International Finance and Economics*, *9*(1), 92–98.

Batrancea, L., Batrancea, I., & Moscviciov, A. (2009b). Treasury flow analysis in Romanian companies. *International Journal of Business Research*, *9*(1), 57–62.

Batrancea, L., & Nichita, A. (2015). Which is the best government? Colligating tax compliance and citizens' insights regarding authorities' actions. *Transylvanian Review of Administrative Sciences*, *11*(44), 5–22.

Batrancea, L., Nichita, A., Batrancea, I., & Gaban, L. (2018). The strength of the relationship between shadow economy and corruption: Evidence from a worldwide country-sample. *Social Indicators Research, 138*(3), 1119–1143. doi:10.100711205-017-1696-z

Batrancea, L., Nichita, R. A., & Batrancea, I. (2012). Tax non-compliance behavior in the light of tax law complexity and the relationship between authorities and taxpayers. *Scientific Annals of the "Alexandru Ioan Cuza". University of Iasi Economic Sciences, 59*(1), 97–106.

Batrancea, L. M., Batrancea, I., & Moscviciov, A. (2009c). *Evolution of global financial crisis.* Industrial Revolutions, from the Globalization and Post-globalization Perspective, Vol. IV: Banking, Accounting and Financial Systems from the 21t Century Perspective. *Lucian Blaga University of Sibiu, 16th International Conference – IECS 2009*, 36–41.

Batrancea, L. M., Batrancea, I., & Moscviciov, A. (2009d). The roots of the world financial crisis. *Annals of the Faculty of Economics, 3*(1), 57–62.

Benlagha, N. (2020). Stock market dependence in crisis periods: Evidence from oil price shocks and the Qatar blockade. *Research in International Business and Finance, 54*, 101285. Advance online publication. doi:10.1016/j.ribaf.2020.101285

Bhuiyan, E. M., & Chowdhury, M. (2020). Macroeconomic variables and stock market indices: Asymmetric dynamics in the US and Canada. *The Quarterly Review of Economics and Finance, 77*, 62–74. doi:10.1016/j.qref.2019.10.005

Bikhchandani, S., & Sharma, S. (2000). *Herd behavior in financial markets: A review.* IMF Working Paper WP/00/48.

Brammer, S., Brooks, C., & Pavelin, S. (2006). Corporate social performance and stock returns: UK evidence from disaggregate measures. *Financial Management, 35*(3), 97–116. doi:10.1111/j.1755-053X.2006.tb00149.x

Brown, P., Chua, A., & Mitchell, A. (2002). The influence of cultural factors on price clustering: Evidence from Asia-Pacific stock markets. *Pacific-Basin Finance Journal, 10*(3), 307–332. doi:10.1016/S0927-538X(02)00049-5

Cagle, J. A. B. (1996). Natural disasters, insurer stock prices, and market discrimination: The case of Hurricane Hugo. *Journal of Insurance Issues, 19*(1), 53–68.

Chang, B. H., Meo, M. S., Syed, Q. R., & Abro, Z. (2019). Dynamic analysis of the relationship between stock prices and macroeconomic variables: An empirical study of Pakistan stock exchange. *South Asian Journal of Business Studies, 8*(3), 229–245. doi:10.1108/SAJBS-06-2018-0062

Chang, C. L., McAleer, M., & Wang, Y. A. (2020). Herding behavior in energy stock markets during the global financial crisis, SARS and ongoing COVID-19. *Renewable & Sustainable Energy Reviews, 134*, 110349. Advance online publication. doi:10.1016/j.rser.2020.110349

Chen, N.-F., Roll, R., & Ross, S. A. (1986). Economic forces and the stock market. *The Journal of Business, 59*(3), 383–403. doi:10.1086/296344

Christie, W. G., & Huang, R. D. (1995). Following the pied piper: Do individual returns herd around the market? *Financial Analysts Journal, 51*(4), 31–37. doi:10.2469/faj.v51.n4.1918

Demirer, R., Kutan, A. M., & Chen, C.-D. (2010). Do investors herd in emerging stock markets?: Evidence from the Taiwanese market. *Journal of Economic Behavior & Organization, 76*(2), 283–295. doi:10.1016/j.jebo.2010.06.013

Dhaoui, A. (2015). What does matter in economy today: When human psychology drives financial markets. *The Arab Economics and Business Journal, 10*(1), 39–47. doi:10.1016/j.aebj.2014.12.002

Edirisuriya, P., Gunasekarage, A., & Dempsey, M. (2015). Bank diversification, performance and stock market response: Evidence from listed public banks in South Asian countries. *Journal of Asian Economics, 41*, 69–85. doi:10.1016/j.asieco.2015.09.003

Foye, J. (2013). *The relationship between financial ratios and stock market returns in the East European members of the EU* (Doctoral dissertation). University of Ljubljana, Faculty of Economics.

Furió, D., & Pardo, Á. (2014). Partisan politics theory and stock market performance: Evidence from Spain. *Revista Española de Financiación y Contabilidad, 41*(155), 371–392. doi:10.1080/02102412.2012.10779729

Füss, R., & Bechtel, M. M. (2008). Partisan politics and stock market performance: The effect of expected government partisanship on stock returns in the 2002 German federal election. *Public Choice, 135*(3-4), 131–150. doi:10.100711127-007-9250-1

Garcia-Vega, S., Zeng, X. J., & Keane, J. (2020). Stock returns prediction using kernel adaptive filtering within a stock market interdependence approach. *Expert Systems with Applications, 160*, 113668. Advance online publication. doi:10.1016/j.eswa.2020.113668

Graham, B. (2003). *Intelligent investor: The definitive book of value investing*. HarperCollins Publishers.

Grieco, D. (2017). Innovation and stock market performance: A model with ambiguity-averse agents. *Journal of Evolutionary Economics, 28*(2), 287–303. doi:10.100700191-017-0537-1

Griffith, J., Najand, M., & Shen, J. (2020). Emotions in the stock market. *Journal of Behavioral Finance, 21*(1), 42–56. Advance online publication. doi:10.1080/15427560.2019.1588275

Hirsch, J. A., & Kass, D. A. (2012). *The little book of stock market cycles*. John Wiley & Sons.

Hirshleifer, D., Hsu, P.-H., & Li, D. M. (2020). Innovative originality, profitability, and stock returns. *Review of Financial Studies, 31*(7), 2553–2605. doi:10.1093/rfs/hhx101

Hirshleifer, D., & Shumway, T. (2003). Good day sunshine: Stock returns and the weather. *The Journal of Finance, 58*(3), 1009–1032. doi:10.1111/1540-6261.00556

Hondroyiannis, G., & Papapetrou, E. (2001). Macroeconomic influences on the stock market. *Journal of Economics and Finance, 25*(1), 33–49. doi:10.1007/BF02759685

Hong, Y., & Li, Y. (2020). House price and the stock market prices dynamics: Evidence from China using a wavelet approach. *Applied Economics Letters, 27*(12), 971–976. doi:10.1080/13504851.2019.1649359

Hsing, Y. (2011). Impacts of macroeconomic variables on the stock market in Bulgaria and policy implications. *East-West Journal of Economics and Business*, *16*(2), 41–53.

Huang, C., Yang, X., Yang, X. G., & Sheng, H. (2014). An empirical study of the effect of investor sentiment on returns of different industries. *Mathematical Problems in Engineering*, *545723*, 1–11. Advance online publication. doi:10.1155/2014/545723

Jiang, Z., Kang, S. H., Cheong, C., & Yoon, S.-M. (2019). The effects of extreme weather conditions on Hong Kong and Shenzhen Stock Market Returns. *International Journal of Financial Studies*, *7*(4), 70. doi:10.3390/ijfs7040070

Khan, M. N., & Zaman, S. (2012). Impact of macroeconomic variables on stock prices: Empirical evidence from Karachi Stock Exchange, Pakistan. In M. Zhu (Ed.), Business, economics, financial sciences, and management. Advances in intelligent and soft computing (pp. 227–233). Berlin: Springer. doi:10.1007/978-3-642-27966-9_32

Kim, H.-Y., Kwon, O., & Oh, G. (2016). A causality between fund performance and stock market. *Physica A*, *443*, 439–450. doi:10.1016/j.physa.2015.08.041

Kyimaz, H. (2001). The effects of stock market rumors on stock prices: Evidence from an emerging market. *Journal of Multinational Financial Management*, *11*(1), 105–115. doi:10.1016/S1042-444X(00)00045-1

Lehkonen, H., & Heimonen, K. (2015). Democracy, political risks and stock market performance. *Journal of International Money and Finance*, *59*, 77–99. doi:10.1016/j.jimonfin.2015.06.002

Lin, C.-H. (2012). The comovement between exchange rates and stock prices in the Asian emerging markets. *International Review of Economics & Finance*, *22*(1), 161–172. doi:10.1016/j.iref.2011.09.006

Lin, W. T., Tsai, S.-C., & Lung, P.-Y. (2013). Investors' herd behavior: Rational or irrational? *Asia-Pacific Journal of Financial Studies*, *42*(5), 755–776. doi:10.1111/ajfs.12030

Lynch, P. (2000). *One up on Wall Street: How to use what you already know to make money in the market*. Simon & Schuster.

Lyócsa, Š., Baumöhl, E., Výrost, T., & Molnár, P. (2020). Fear of the coronavirus and the stock markets. *Finance Research Letters*, *36*, 101735. doi:10.1016/j.frl.2020.101735 PMID:32868975

Malkiel, B. G. (2007). *A random walk down Wall Street: The time-tested strategy for successful investing* (9th ed.). W.W. Norton & Company.

Mbanga, C., Darrat, A. F., & Park, J. C. (2019). Investor sentiment and aggregate stock returns: The role of investor attention. *Review of Quantitative Finance and Accounting*, *53*(2), 397–428. doi:10.100711156-018-0753-2

Mosley, L., & Singer, D. A. (2008). Taking stock seriously: Equity-market performance, government policy, and financial globalization. *International Studies Quarterly*, *52*(2), 405–425. doi:10.1111/j.1468-2478.2008.00507.x

Munkh-Ulzii, B. J., McAleer, M., Moslehpour, M., & Wong, W.-K. (2018). Confucius and herding behavior in the stock markets in China and Taiwan. *Sustainability*, *10*(12), 4413. doi:10.3390u10124413

Nassirzadeh, F., Salehi, M., & Sarvhadi, R. (2015). The effect of financial indicators on trading volume of the listed companies on the Tehran Stock Exchange. *International Business Research*, *8*(5), 176–194. doi:10.5539/ibr.v8n5p176

Ornelas, J. R. H., & de Cravalho, P. J. C. (2020). Short-selling costs and asymmetric price response to economic shocks: A transaction cost explanation to price overshooting. *International Journal of Finance & Economics*, ijfe.1876. Advance online publication. doi:10.1002/ijfe.1876

Padungsaksawasdi, C., Treepongkaruna, S., & Brooks, R. (2019). Investor attention and stock market activities: New evidence from panel data. *International Journal of Financial Studies*, *7*(30), 30. Advance online publication. doi:10.3390/ijfs7020030

Patra, T., & Poshakwale, S. (2007). Economic variables and stock market returns: Evidence from Athens stock exchange. *Applied Financial Economics*, *16*(13), 993–1005. doi:10.1080/09603100500426523

Pizzutilo, F., & Roncone, V. (2017). Red sky at night or in the morning, to the equity market neither a delight nor a warning: The weather effect re-examined using intraday stock data. *European Journal of Finance*, *23*(14), 1280–1310. doi:10.1080/1351847X.2016.1151808

Rahaman, M. M., & Chowdhury, M. A. F. (2017). Impact of financial performance on stock price of non-bank financial institutions (NBFI) in Bangladesh: Dynamic Panel Approach. In P. Ordóñez de Pablo (Ed.), *Managerial strategies and solutions for business success in Asia* (pp. 199–211). IGI Global. doi:10.4018/978-1-5225-1886-0.ch011

Riley, W. B., & Luksetich, W. A. (1980). The market prefers republicans; Myth or reality. *Journal of Financial and Quantitative Analysis*, *15*(3), 541–560. doi:10.2307/2330399

Rose, A. M. (1951). Rumor in the stock market. *Public Opinion Quarterly*, *15*(3), 461–486. doi:10.1086/266330

Rudzkis, R., & Valkavičienė, R. (2014). Econometric models of the impact of macroeconomic processes on the stock market in the Baltic countries. *Technological and Economic Development of Economy*, *29*(4), 783–800. doi:10.3846/20294913.2014.949901

Saunders, E. M. (1993). Stock prices and Wall Street weather. *The American Economic Review*, *83*(5), 1337–1345.

Schneider, G., & Tröger, V. E. (2006). War and the world economy: Stock market reactions to international conflicts. *The Journal of Conflict Resolution*, *50*(5), 623–645. doi:10.1177/0022002706290430

Schwager, J. D. (2012). *Market wizards: Interviews with top traders*. John Wiley & Sons. doi:10.1002/9781119203469

Schwager, J.D. (2020). *Unknown market wizards: The best traders you've never heard of.* Petersfield: Harriman House.

Shiller, R. J. (2003). From efficient markets theory to behavioral finance. *The Journal of Economic Perspectives*, *17*(1), 83–104. doi:10.1257/089533003321164967

Shleifer, A. (2000). *Inefficient markets: An introduction to behavioral finance*. Oxford University Press. doi:10.1093/0198292279.001.0001

Siddiqui, A., Mahmood, H., & Margaritis, D. (2020). Oil prices and stock markets during the 2014–16 oil price jump: Asymmetries and speed of adjustment in GCC and oil-importing countries. *Emerging Markets Finance & Trade*, *56*(15), 3678–3708. doi:10.1080/1540496X.2019.1570497

Singh, V., Li, B., & Roca, E. (2017). How pervasive is the effect of culture on stock market linkages? Evidence across regions and economic cycles. *Applied Economics*, *49*(42), 4209–4230. doi:10.1080/00036846.2017.1279268

Sun, Y., Liu, X., Chen, G., Hao, Y., & Zhang, Z. (2020). How mood affects the stock market: Empirical evidence from microblogs. *Information & Management*, *57*(5), 103181. doi:10.1016/j.im.2019.103181

Thaler, R. H. (2015). *Misbehaving: The making of behavioral economics*. W.W. Norton & Company.

Thaler, R. H., & Sunstein, C. R. (2009). *Nudge: Improving decisions about health, wealth, and happiness*. Penguin Books.

Villanueva, O. M., & Feinstein, S. (2020). Stock price reactivity to earnings announcements: The role of the Cammer/Krogman factors. *Review of Quantitative Finance and Accounting*. Advance online publication. doi:10.100711156-020-00943-4

Wen, F., Xiao, J., Xia, X., Chen, B., Xiao, Z., & Li, J. (2019). Oil prices and Chinese stock market: Nonlinear causality and volatility persistence. *Emerging Markets Finance & Trade*, *55*(6), 1247–1263. doi:10.1080/1540496X.2018.1496078

Zhou, X., Cui, Y., Wu, S., & Wang, W. (2019). The influence of cultural distance on the volatility of the international stock market. *Economic Modelling*, *77*, 289–300. doi:10.1016/j.econmod.2018.10.005

KEY TERMS AND DEFINITIONS

Book Value: Net worth as reported in company financial statements.

Cash Flow: Difference between cash inflows and cash outflows registered by a company during a fiscal year, from operating, investing and financing activities. It is reported in the company financial statement bearing the same name.

Earnings: Company income, before or after tax payments.

Financial Performance: The capacity of a company to generate profit and wealth by using its resources.

Investment: Allocation of money for purchasing an asset, which aims to generate income or profit.

Prices: Values of goods and services, set during economic transactions.

Sales: Revenue generated by a company from selling goods and/or services.

Stock Market: Regulated marketplace, where company shares can be bought and sold by individuals and firms.

ENDNOTES

1 In 2010, March 21 was the first day of Iranian New Year (also called "Nowruz"), which coincided with the first day of the fiscal year.

2 In Chinese culture, number 8 and other numbers ending with the digit 8 are considered extremely lucky because the pronunciation of eight ("bā", in Mandarin Chinese) is similar with "making a fortune". Number 4 and other numbers ending in four are generally associated with bad luck because its pronunciation (i.e., "sì") is similar to the word "death". No wonder that most of time those last digits within prices migrated away from number 4.

APPENDIX

The 34 companies listed on the New York Stock Exchange, which were included in the sample, were the following (in alphabetical order):

- Abbott;
- Adobe;
- Alibaba;
- Alphabet;
- Amazon;
- Apple;
- AT&T;
- Bank of America;
- Berkshire Hathaway;
- Coca Cola;
- Comcast;
- Disney;
- Home Depot;
- Intel;
- Johnson & Johnson;
- JP Morgan Chase;
- Mastercard;
- Merck;
- Microsoft;
- Netflix;
- Nike;
- Novartis;
- NVIDIA;
- PepsiCo;
- Pfizer;
- Procter & Gamble;
- Salesforce;
- Taiwan Semiconductor Manufacturing;
- Thermo Fisher Scientific;
- Toyota;
- United Health Group;
- Verizon;
- Visa;
- Walmart.

Chapter 17
The Impact of Misinformation and Preferences of News Sources on Institutional Trust Perception in the COVID-19 Process

Selman Selim Akyüz
Selcuk University, Turkey

ABSTRACT

During the COVID-19 pandemic, the flow of misinformation that appeared in the mass media and especially on social media and was defined as "Infodemic" by the World Health Organization (WHO). In this study, the relationship between the level at which 1.319 social media users in Turkey have been exposed to misinformation during the COVID-19 process, and their views on which sources spread suspicious and misinformation the most and the level of trust in institutions during the pandemic process were investigated. Participants followed developments in the pandemic on social media; 61% were exposed to false information about COVID-19 every day, and most encountered suspicious information on Facebook and Twitter. Social media users who participated in the study found that the institutions they least trusted were the World Health Organization (WHO), pharmaceutical companies, political opposition of Turkey, and traditional media.

INTRODUCTION

Trust is one of the most important determinants in the Healthy Execution and reproduction of both interpersonal and social relations. Problems can arise in terms of cohabitation and public order when people do not trust each other, different social groups and institutions. From a sociological point of view a high level of trust increases the trend of interpersonal and public order cooperation. Trust reproduces

DOI: 10.4018/978-1-7998-7164-4.ch017

cooperation and cooperation reproduces trust. Low-trust societies seem to be quite poor in terms of social capital (Sargut, 2003).

Pandemics arise as periods when social trust is irreparably weakened in the long term. This effect in Spanish flu (Akbaş, 2020), has led to increased social uncertainty and insecurity throughout the world in the Covid-19 process (Siders & Ward, 2020). People have problems trusting individuals and societies due to the lack of knowledge about who and how to transmit the disease to them as well as institutions for reasons such as the fear, level of danger and treatment caused by the disease.

During the first 6 months of the outbreak there are studies that show that people's trust in institutions has increased (Bunker, 2020) but after the outbreak has completed one year, in this sense, the number of studies that reveal the picture in Turkey is limited.

The World Health Organization has defined "Infodemic" and has taken important decisions to combat it. This "false information outbreak" (Akyüz, 2020) has led to the spread of misinformation about measures and treatment an another threat that endangers human health. Deaths have been caused by underestimating the disease by believing false information or by improper prevention and treatment practices (Spring, 2020b).

In the literature section of the study, information and researches on trust and intitutional trust, social media, misinformation and the Covid-19 process were discussed. In the second part, field research from quantitative research methods was applied and a survey was conducted with 1.319 people reached via the internet. During the Covid-19 process, participants tried to determine their views on news consumption habits, misinformation and perception of trust.

INSTUTIONAL TRUST PERCEPTION AND PANDEMIC PROCESS

Looking at the definitions made about the concept of trust, it seems that some of the definitions focus on expectation on the other side and some on the desire to remain vulnerable to the other side (Kalemci Tüzün, 2007) It is defined as confidence, sense of involvement, and trust without fear and doubt (Aslan, 2016).

Institutional trust is defined as the trust that individuals have in political, social and economic institutions and the system. Preliminary determinants of trust are expressed as knowledge and institution-based trust, account, cognitive and personality-based trust. Knowledge-based trust is built on the predictability of the other: *"Knowing the other adequately and being able to predict their behavior". In this context, the knowledge-based trust relationship is not about threat or fear, but about the relationship based on the knowledge that the sides have about each other* (Kalemci Tüzün, 2007).

Lack of knowledge about people, institutions and events makes it difficult to recognize and makes it difficult to create a sense of trust. The Covid-19 pandemic originated in obscurity. The world was forced to meet this major outbreak, which occurred almost a hundred years after the Spanish flu, but problems in the production and access of scientific knowledge to humans have made it difficult to know the virus and its effects.

Individuals' sense of confidence that their lives are under their control has been undermined and the environment of uncertainty has increased threat perception and anxiety (Doğan & Düzel, 2020). In this context, the pandemic exists as a major crisis that shakes the social and economic order as well as the sense of trust in institutions, causing uncertainty, fear, anxiety (Bozkurt, Zeybek, & Aşkın, 2020). Uncertainty about disease and virus also reduces confidence in science (Kreps & Kriner, 2020).

Trust in government institutions is a distinct indicator of social trust. However, mostly cross-sectional analyses provide limited causal evidence regarding the relationship between institutional trust and social trust. In contrast to the cultural approach, which claims that social trust is a deep foundation, some studies reveal the possibility of social trust changing. Time and experiences that shape trust in government institutions play an important role in this change. It is inevitable that problems in the management of institutions will undermine not only those who govern, but also trust in institutions (Sønderskov & Dinesen, 2016).

During the Covid-19 pandemic, studies were conducted to measure social confidence. The Study in the UK reveals data comparing the periods, January 2020-May 2020 (Bunker, 2020). Among the government and its subsidiaries, non-governmental organizations (NGO), business and media, the government was ranked as the most trusted institution in May while it ranked third in January. A study conducted in Italy shows that trust in institutions has increased significantly (75%) compared to before the outbreak (Falcone, et al., 2020)

In Europe, Bargain and Aminjonov (2020) found that in areas with a level of trust in national policymakers, there was less behavior of following restrictions and social distance recommendations and less calls for people with low political confidence to stay at home.

A study conducted in Azerbaijan also showed that confidence in public institutions and the government increased during the pandemic period (Selamzade, Korkmazer, Bostan, & Yusifbeyli, 2020) Both studies show that trust in media is low compared to official sources of information, and trust in social media has fairly low level of trust compared to traditional media.

Research conducted in Turkey also shows that confidence in the government and its affiliates was high during the first period of the outbreak (Dönmez & Gürbüz, 2020). A study in April 2020 found that 75 per cent of respondents relied on information from the minister of health, doctors and goverment statements about the virus. It was determined that television news was more trusted as a source of information than social media news (Universal McCann, 2020).

There is an inverse correlation between trust level and usage of news source. People use social media more often but have less confidence. This frequency of use can lead to misinformation and decreased trust in institutions. According to Peter Dahlgren (2018),, the transition from the enterprise-professional model to the network-based algorithmic model, that is, to new media, has led to an erosion of trust that has visibly affected everyone.

Van Dijk and Alinead (2020) note that social media platforms can undermine public confidence in institutions and expert knowledge, while also being used by authorities to reach a wide audience to maintain trust. After Dutch Prime Minister Rutte's announcement, citing scientific evidence of the government's initial practices, a study found that public confidence in the government increased from 45 percent to 73 percent.

It has been found that Fahrettin Koca, the Minister of Health in Turkey, has created trust after effective information on Twitter during the pandemic and the number of followers has increased 12 times, reaching one of both users in the country (Bilgiç & Akyüz, 2020).

Research by the Reuters Institute of Journalism (2020) at the University of Oxford shows that confidence in media and news is generally declining in the world. Media researches (Cömlekçi & Başol, 2019; Güz & Yanık, 2020; Balcı & Bekiroğlu, 2014), if the level is low confidence in mass media then social media, which is defined as the main current in comparison with traditional media due to their corporate structures reveals that trust is higher. Periods of increased confidence in the mainstream media are generally noted as periods of crisis. A similar increase in interest and confidence is observed during the pandemic period.

THE PROBLEM OF MISINFORMATION IN THE COVID-19 PROCESS

"ISIS gathered followers from the internet". "Teens who want to look like their faces on Instagram filters get plastic surgery". "Internet lynch mob kills dozens in India over fake news". These sentences are from a production called Social Dilemma (Orlowski, 2020) which has caused controversy in both ordinary viewers and academic circles. The film's intro concludes with two striking sentences: *"We have moved from the age of information to the age of misinformation"*.

The internet has opened the door to the information age, but the user in the center of new media, social media platforms in the Arab Spring, social movements such as Occupy Wall Street show revealed the problems disinformation and fake news. A transition from the information age to the "Misinformation Age" has begun.

The term "Post Truth" (Keyes, 2019), used to describe the period when communication has changed significantly. This term has become an important definition for this new period in which truth is judged by evidence, not knowledge, but perception, point of view, the relationship between benefit and harm. In his book of the same name as the definition, Keyes notes that "truth has been replaced by believability" in today's world, while focusing on the causes of lies and deception throughout human history. New media with its structure that makes it easier to lie and spread, has become an "ethics-free zone" where fraud is met with incentives, not sanctions.

At the base of the emergence of social media as a problematic place in terms of trust is the fact that it is an uncontrolled space and a medium suitable for the dissemination of misinformation, as it provides ordinary users with the opportunity to produce content.

The user-centered structure of social media has increased the diversity of resources and content, and content has started to spread faster and easier through interaction. Digital-born news distributors have shown that news in the media does not have to be produced only by professionals, causing users to prefer new media tools than traditional media (Vosoughi, Roy, & Aral, 2018).

Confidence in the continuity of the role of sociality and communication is crucial but face to face communication in virtual space where attributed to safely apply practices in daily life or in institutions maintaining contact to establish a relationship can lead to problems. On social media, users can use a computer software, comments on products are manipulative, news can only be what a filter bubble offers you. Unconditional trust causes misinformation to spread further and cause harm (Silverman, 2020).

The concept of misinformation came to the agenda of the academy after the definition of "fake news" began to be discussed in the information ecosystem. Although in some definitions, the concept of misinformation, which includes fake news, has also been used, but the main characteristics agreed in the definition of fake news are that it is intentionally produced and intended to cause harm, as well as similar characteristics to real news (Gelfert, 2018).

Deliberately produced fake news is defined as disinformation and is produced for the purpose of reputation or physical damage, material expectation, political interest. In mesenformation, there is a situation where users who share misinformation do not realize that the content is false/fake. Wardle (2020) says it was an example of misenformation that social media users shared unconfirmed information or erroneously associated images/videos without realising they were not involved in the incident.

In the production of misinformation to the lack of malicious intent or in bad faith (cognitive biases, simple errors, such as entertainment), it may be possible to classify by looking on the internet. But features are always laid out with great precision to produce a fake content, they cannot be carried by actors or asymmetric emitting propaganda in the examples, as different political actors have the opportunity to wear masks in disguise and therefore may increase the risk of error in determining the types of fake news (Foça, 2019).

Looking at the forms of production of fake/false news, names have also been made for different types. Wardle and Derakhshan (2017) states that there are 7 types of intentional (disinformation) and unintentional (misenformation) false news:

- Satire and parody
- Misleading content
- Imposter content
- Fabricated content
- False connection
- False context
- Manipulated content

Figure 1. Types of mis- and disinformation

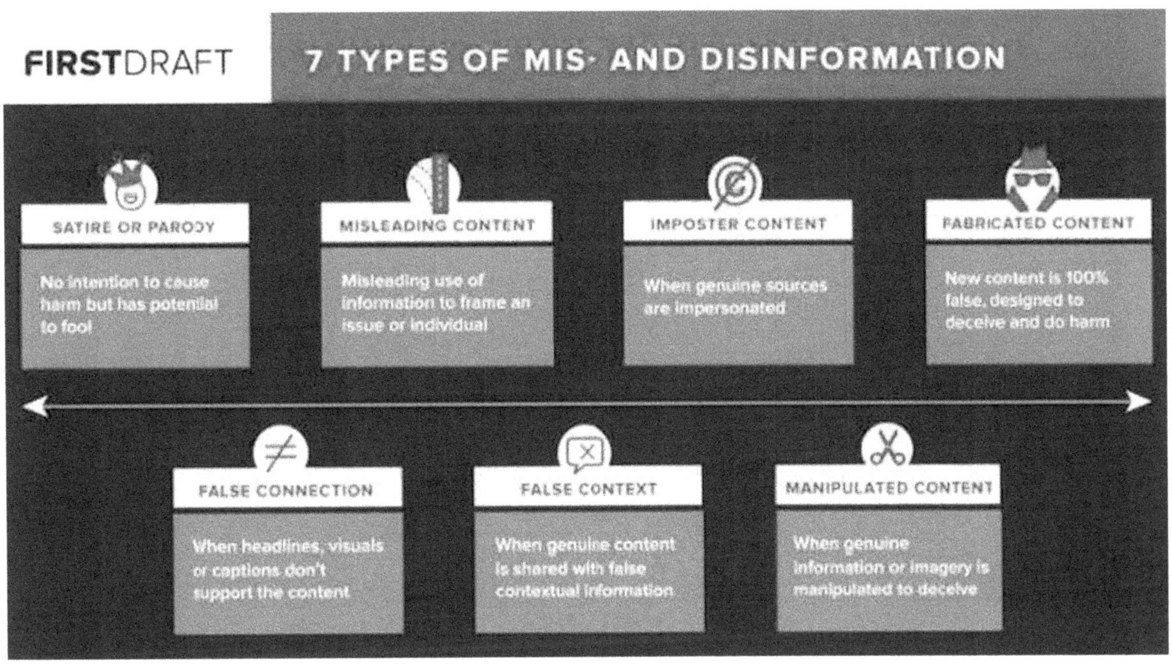

Misinformation and disinformation is not only produced by ordinary social media users, professional or voluntary troll associations, political, ideological and terrorist groups, firms can insert false information and fake news into the information ecosystem for the purpose of causing harm (Unal & Taylan, 2017). The COVID-19 (Coronavirus Disease 2019) virus has emerged as an important crisis period, the most suitable environments for the spread of fake news. During times of crisis, the increase in disinformation and misinformation on social media has also threatened human health (Yerlikaya, 2020).

"Believable lies" can go beyond the credibility of news and manipulation of opinions in new media and reach the dimensions that threaten the safety and health of people. The falsehood of the word "no one dies from a lie", which is used in Turkish, is often confirmed in the period.

Examples of disinformation include deceptive advertising (in business and politics), government propaganda, manipulated photos, fake documents, fake maps, internet fraud, fake websites, and manipulated Wikipedia entries (Fallis, 2015).

Fallis (2015) states that disinformation can generally be considered a subgenre of false information used for misinformation, and emphasizes the existence of a clear purpose of deception, as in black propaganda. The terminology related to Propaganda and disinformation is based on two periods of experience (Romerstein, 2009): World Wars and the Cold War. While propaganda is perceived as a more neutral term, such as spreading an opinion, Romerstein (2009) notes that the propaganda administrations of Germany and the Soviet Union have turned counter-propaganda activities into disinformation by imposing heavy negatives on the grip.

It is now possible to spread tags, fake images, links using millions of bot accounts, as well as trolls managed by real users, send unsolicited emails, spam and make it easy to discredit a person online or pretend that they are being strongly criticized (Wild & Godart, 2020). Moreover, with the development of technology on this issue, the capabilities of bots that imitiate human behavior have increased and a period has begun in which people will have long conversations with software without realizing that it is a bot.

Figure 2. Fake image claiming alcohol kills coronavirus (Özdemir, 2020)

During the Covid-19 pandemic, approximately 800 people who drank fake alcohol to protect themselves from the disease died in Iran due to fake news reports (Güler, 2020). The American priest who caught the virus and died because of conspiracy theories or beliefs by underestimating the disease and failing to comply with the precautions was also reflected in the news as an important example during this period (Boorstein, 2020)

After spreading claims and conspracy theories such as "The coronavirus has defeated alcohol", "the pandemic is a planned experiment", "planned to reduce the population" or conversely "virus is not different from the flu" The World Health Organization has described this information as "Infodemic" which spreads faster than the virus and has announced action plans.

The term of infodemic is explained as "the vast accumulation of knowledge that occurs during an pandemic, some of which are true and some of which are false, spread as quickly as the virus, and complicate the health organization (WHO, 2020).

During the Covid-19 pandemic, thousands of fake news and false information about the characteristics of the virus, transmission, effects of the disease, methods of prevention and treatment, practices of competent institutions and governments were produced and millions of people were negatively affected by this information. 75 platforms from more than 70 countries of 188 platforms that are members of the International Fact Checking Network (IFCN) and with non-members, were forced to combat the pandemic of false information in the first period of the pandemic (Büyükafşar, 2019).

January-August 2020 period, 8.688 suspicious information circulating in 40 languages around the world was found to be false (Poynter, 2020). Spreading in the traditional and social media, 315 claims on Covid-19 were examined by fact checking platforms and 94 percent of this information was found to be false in January-June 2020 period in Turkey (Akyüz, 2020).

Unidentified audio recordings, especially from WhatsApp, have caused panic about the disease. Facebook, Twitter, Youtube and Google have made important decisions to combat misinformation. Whatsapp announced a 70 percent reduction in the spread of unidentified messages after deciding to reduce the limit forwarded messages (Bilge, 2020). Facebook has given the IFCN a million dollars in support to continue fact checking fake news during the epidemic (Hutchinson, 2020).

Brennen and colleagues (2020) found in the false information report on COVID-19 that 37% of the misinformation spread during the pandemic was newly fabricated, 3% was parody, and 59% was a reformed version of previous false claims. Daniel Funke (2020), author of the fact checking platform Politifact, has prepared an analysis of conspiracy theories that have been shared 18 thousand times on Facebook and consist of 2 thousand words. Funke has been said the most commonly used words were *"Dr. Fauci, Bill Gates, hydrosichloroquine, vaccines, dollars and Chinese laboratories"*. These words also point to misinformation about treatment and the prevalence of conspiracy theories.

A BBC investigation revealed 7 actors who spread false and fake information about Coronavirus as pranksters, fraudsters, politicians, conspiracy theorists, insiders (those who provide information from within authorized agencies), relatives and famous people (Spring, 2020a). A joint study by 5 European fact checking platforms also found that the most common issues of coronavirus misinformation are the claim that the virus is human production, incorrect treatment and vaccine information, masks and protective equipment, claims about 5G, avoidance of infection, Bill Gates and seasonal flu comparisons with coronavirus (AFP, Correctiv, Pagella, Maldita and Full Fact, 2020).

In another study, the structure of false content was examined. In the Covid-19 process, reconstructed content was saw higher interaction than fabricated content, according to social media data collected. Three different subspecies of misinformation have been identified that reconstruct existing information. The most common type of misinformation, "misleading content" (29 percent), contained some accurate information, but the details made them false or misleading. This information had been reconstructed, selected and changed in context. Wardle (2020) has given notable examples:

One much-shared post was medical advice that combined both true and false information about how to treat and prevent the virus, and was offered as if it were from someone's uncle. While some recommendations, such as washing hands, match medical opinions, other recommendations do not. For example, one claims: "This new virus is not heat-resistant and only dies at 26/27 degrees. He hates the sun". But that's not true. Because although the heat kills the virus, 27 degrees Celsius is not high enough to do so.

While some of suspicious/false contents is deliberately misinformation presented by ordinary people or health professionals who are not experts in infectious diseases, many disinformation material and conspiracy theory affecting billions of people have also been heavily circulated in both traditional and new media.

There are studies that show that people deliberately follow and spread these theories because they believe, while those who are unintentionally exposed to conspiracy theories also tend to believe (Douglas & Sutton, 2008). Conspiracy theories have been active on social media. The structure of new media and the increased time spent online while under lockdown has enabled these theorists, who challenge evidence-based views, to explore new strategies. So misinformation has reached people with increasing intensity (Morrish, 2020).

January-June 2020 period, Akyuz's research in Turkey (Akyüz, 2020) revealed internet sites and social media accounts of fact checking platforms in the number of visitors and interactions a 400 percent increase. People who are more likely to be exposed to misinformation also have an increased need for true information.

Although the growth of the problem of mis/disinformation has a high impact on the structure of new media that causes it to be circulated and spread, the fact that users are ready to believe such information also increases the effectiveness of fake news.

Factors in the spread misinformation and fake news can be listed as follows.

- Declining of trust in traditional media
- Sharpening the political bias of media organizations
- Increasing polarization in societies
- The problem of media literacy
- Inadequate precautions of social media platforms
- Algorithms
- Locking users in echo chambers by following users close to their own views only

METHODOLOGY

In this section, there are topics related to news sources of social media users during Covid-19 period, applying of misinformation and trust perception research to institutions and selection of participants, measuring intruments, data collection and statistical analysis used.

Table 1. Reliability values of the questionnaire

Cronbach Alpha	Number of Items
0,814	10

Applying of Research and Sampling

The research universe consists of internet and social media users in Turkey. The survey was conducted using a form prepared over the internet, the layer and quota were determined and users of different demographics were reached. For this reason, the simple random sampling technique was only not used. The research has a parametric design. In addition to receiving support from accounts with a large number of followers on Facebook and Twitter, users living in different cities have also been reached privately. Necessary explanations were made during the publication and sharing of the questionnaire. 1. 319 users participated in the survey held in December 2020.

Measuring Instruments and Questions of Research

In the question form, answers to the following questions were sought to measure participants ' preferences for news sources, exposure to misinformation and the level of trust in institutions during the Covid-19 process.

1. From which sources have internet and social media users followed the developments related to Covid-19?
2. To what extent and in what mass media have users encountered misinformation?
3. At what level do users trust decision-making institutions and the media in the pandemic process?
4. Do news sources preferences have an impact on the level of trust?

Consistent results between the behavior of following social media platforms and the platform and actors in which misinformation is shared suggest that the study has structural validity.

Statistical Analyses

Data from the survey participants was entered through a program called SPSS 17.0 and appropriate statistical analyses were applied to achieve the results. Since the study had a descriptive research pattern, multiple frequency analysis and central tendency statistics were applied. The reliability level of the scale has been determined to be high.

FINDINGS

In this part of the study, findings from field research conducted with 1.319 users are included. Descriptive statistics, regression analysis, correlation analysis and one-way analysis of variance were used to obtain descriptive and relational findings.

Demographic Characteristics of Participants

Table 2. Gender, age and education

	Group	Frequency	Percentage
Age	15-24	359	27.3
	25-34	412	31.2
	35-44	383	29.0
	45 +	165	12.5
Educational Status	Primary and Middle School	39	3.0
	High School	285	21.5
	Bachelor's Degree	812	61.6
	Post-graduate	183	13.9
Gender	Female	922	69.9
	Male	397	30.1

69.9 percent of the survey participants were male and 30.1 percent were female.

The highest number of users participated in the 25-34 age range (31.2%). The 15-24 age group is 27.3 percent, the 35-44 age group is 29.0 percent, and the over 45 age group is 12.5 percent. Participation in the survey is observed from all age groups.

At the distribution related to the level of education, it was determined that 61.6 percent of the participants with the most university graduates, 3 percent of primary graduates, 21.6 percent of high school, and 13.9 percent of post-graduates participated in the research.

Table 3. Cities where participants live

City	Percentage
1.İstanbul	27.0
2. Konya	16.0
3. Ankara	9.9
4. Bursa	5.2
5. Antalya	3.4
6. İzmir	3.4

Table 4. Frequency of participants using social media platforms

Social media platform	Mean
1.Whatsapp	4,15
2. Youtube	3,42
3. Twitter	3,19
4. Instagram	3,10
5. Facebook	2,23
6. Tiktok	1,18

Table 5. Mass media following developments related to Covid-19

Mass media	Mean
1.Social media	3,86
2.News websites	3,22
3.Television	2,79
4. Newspaper	1,46

Users of 74 cities in Turkey participated in the study. The highest turnout is from Istanbul with 27.2 percent. The other highest turnout is from Ankara, Konya, Izmir, Bursa, Antalya, Kocaeli and Elazig.

Using of News Sources, Encounter With Misinformation and General Levels of Trust

Participants in the study noted that the social media platform they use most is WhatsApp. Youtube and Twitter use is still high and the least used platforms are Tiktok and Facebook.

Social media is noted as the most followed mass media with developments related to Covid-19. Television, one of the traditional media tools, is preferred in the third place as a news source after internet websites.

Table 6. Frequency of exposure to suspicious/misleading information regarding Covid-19

Frequency	Percentage
1.Every day	58,8
2.Once a week	24,0
3.A few times a week	7,1
4.Rarely	8,3
5.I have never exposed to	1,8

Table 7. Frequency of suspicious/misleading information about Covid-19 on social media platforms

Social media platform	Mean
1. Twitter	3,32
2. Facebook	3,30
3.İnstagram	2,98
4. Youtube	2,73
5. Whatsapp	2,72
6.Tiktok	2,41

Table 8. Frequency of sharing suspicious/misleading information in sources

Social media platform	Mean
1.Ordinary social media users	3,47
2.Anonymous accounts with high followings	3,29
3.Politicians	3,25
4.Accounts/pages of television channel and newspapers	3,12
5.News websites	3,10
6.Journalists, reporters and columnists	3,07

Asked how often they were exposed to suspicious/misleading information on Covid-19 on the internet and social media, 58.8 percent of respondents said they encountered it every day and 24 percent several times a week. The proportion of users who say they have never met is 1.8 per cent.

Participants stated that they encountered the most suspicious/misleading information about Covid-19 on Twitter and Facebook, while the platforms encountered with the least misinformation were Tiktok and Whatsapp.

Table 9. Level of trust in institutions and decision makers

	Mean
1.Doctors/Scientists	3,47
2.Minister of Health Fahrettin Koca	3,19
3.Minister of health	3,09
4.Covid-19 Science Board	2,97
5.Goverment	2,89
6.Social media	2,45
7.World Health Organization (WHO)	2,33
8.Tratidional media (TV, newspaper…)	2,24
9.Pharmaceutical companies	1,97
10.Political opposition	1,95

In the survey, participants were asked which actors shared more suspicious/misleading information on the internet and social media and it was determined that ordinary social media users were in the first place. It seems that the other two sources that share misleading information at a high rate are anonymous accounts/phenomena with high followers and politicians.

As part of the research, participants were asked about their trust in institutions, decision makers and the media, taking into account the Covid-19 process, participants expressed the highest level of trust in doctors/scientists, Minister of health Fahrettin Koca and Ministry of Health. The least trusted institutions are the political opposition in Turkey, pharmaceutical companies, the traditional media and the World Health Organization.

Correlation Between Information Sources, Trust Level and Vaccine Attitude

Table 10. Correlation between the level of trust in the WHO and vaccine attitude

WHO	Are you going to get a Covid-19 vaccine?		
	Yes	No	I'm ambivalent
Definitely I don't trust	24,8	48,1	27,1
I don't trust	36,8	28,7	34,6
Middling	41,4	16,9	41,7
I trust	41,7	12,3	46,1
Definitely I trust	42,6	23,0	34,4
		Percentage	

The correlation between the findings of the study has also been tested. It has been observed that there is a significant relationship between trust in institutions and attitude to vaccination. Users with low levels of trust in institutions have been found to have negative attitudes about vaccination. 48.1 percent of respondents who said they had absolutely no confidence in the World Health Organization said they would not get vaccinated.

Table 11. Correlation between trust level of Covid-19 Science Board and vaccine attitude

Covid-19 Science Board	Are you going to get a Covid-19 vaccine?		
	Yes	No	I'm ambivalent
Definitely I don't trust	16,3	59,7	24,0
I don't trust	24,8	34,1	41,1
Middling	34,5	24,7	40,7
I trust	44,8	18,8	36,4
Definitely I trust	54,4	16,3	29,4
		Percentage	

Table 12. Correlation between the level of trust in doctors/scientists and vaccine attitude

Doctors/scientists	Are you going to get a Covid-19 vaccine?		
	Yes	No	I'm ambivalent
Definitely I don't trust	20	66,4	13,6
I don't trust	30,1	39.0	30.9
Middling	23,1	37.0	39.8
I trust	40,1	18,6	41,2
Definitely I trust	49,4	19,8	30,8
		Percentage	

Table 13: Correlation between trust level of government and vaccine attitude

Goverment	Are you going to get a Covid-19 vaccine?		
	Yes	No	I'm ambivalent
Definitely I don't trust	32,7	34,0	33,3
I don't trust	33,5	31,3	35,2
Middling	29,3	28,3	42,4
I trust	34,7	27,3	38,0
Definitely I trust	44,3	28,0	27,6
		Percentage	

Between the level of trust in pharmaceutical companies, the ministry of health and the Minister of Health Fahrettin Koca with the attitude of the vaccine has been found a close relationship. In this section, the highest level of correlation has been found among users who did not trust the Covid-19 Science Board and doctors/scientists. It has been found that 59.7 percent of respondents who said they absolutely did not trust the Covid-19 board (table 8) and 66.4 percent of those who said they did not trust doctors and scientists said they would not get vaccinated (table 9).

Table 14: Correlation between trust and level of information acquisition from social media

Frequency of information acquisition about Covid-19 on social media	Level of trust in Health Minister Fahrettin Koca				
	Definitely I don't trust	I don't trust	Middling	I trust	Definitely I trust
Very few	17,3	6,2	24,7	30,9	21,0
Sometimes	16,4	10,0	29,1	22,7	21,8
Middle	13,7	17,2	23,8	20,7	24,7
Often	15,4	21,8	18,7	24,9	19,2
Too often	18,8	13,7	21,7	20,0	25,8
			Percentage		

Table 15: Correlation between trust and level of information acquisition from television

Frequency of information acquisition about Covid-19 on television	Level of trust in Health Minister Fahrettin Koca				
	Definitely I don't trust	I don't trust	Middling	I trust	Definitely I trust
Very few	28,4	18,8	19,7	16,2	16,8
Sometimes	18,5	19,5	23,9	22,4	15,6
Middle	10,0	13,6	27,2	25,7	23,6
Often	10,5	17,0	19,8	25,5	27,1
Too often	12,6	9,4	17,8	24,1	36,1
			Percentage		

A low significance correlation was found between the level of trust in the government and the attitude of vaccination. The "yes" and "no" answers of respondents who don't trust the government has been determined in close proportions. Participants who said "I absolutely trust" had a high rate of responding positively to the vaccine question (44.3%).

It has been determined that the level of trust of users who followed coronavirus information on social media and those who followed it on television was different. The level of trust in institutions other than the World Health Organization and pharmaceutical companies was found to be lower in social media users. The level of trust in the ministry of health, Coronavirus Science Board, Health Minister Fahrettin Koca and the government has been found to be higher in users who followed the information of Covid-19 from television.

Participants who stated that they followed the developments on Covid-19 "frequently" and "very often" from social media had a confidence level of 22.8 percent, while participants who used television frequently had an average confidence level of 31.6 percent.

CONCLUSION

The increased use of digital tools has led to a radical shift in people's sources of information. From the monopolistic and controlled structure of traditional media, new media has been moved to contribute to the diversity of resources and freedom of expression. But in this transition, problems of misinformation and disinformation have also emerged, which negatively affect the relations of democracy and trust.

During the Covid-19 process, people followed developments and information about the pandemic mainly from social media and were exposed to an outbreak of misinformation as well as an pandemic caused by the virus. This process has reduced people's distance and confidence in each other due to virus as well as affected their trust in institutions.

In this study, a survey was conducted for 1.319 internet and social media users. During the Covid-19 process, participants mainly used social media and internet news sites as news sources and preferred Whatsapp, Twitter and YouTube in social media tools.

It has been determined that those who use New Media tools encounter suspicious/misleading information about Covid-19 very often (almost every day) and most often on Facebook and Twitter. It is noteworthy that the level of encounter with false information on WhatsApp, which is one of the main means of spreading misinformation during the pandemic, is low. Users express the spread of misinformation on social media rather than traditional media, noting that misinformation is most commonly spread by ordinary social media users, anonymous accounts with high followers and politicians.

This conclusion coincides with researches that shows that real users rather than bots spread false information and fake news on social media araştırmalarla (Vosoughi, Roy, & Aral, 2018). One notable result of the study is that users point out that more politicians than news organizations share misinformation. This finding can also be considered as suspicious or misleading information intended to be used as a tool of political discourse.

The study's findings on trust also reveal significant results. It was determined that the average level of trust of participants, institutions and persons was low in general terms. The only category indicated by high confidence has been doctors/scientists. It is important to have high confidence in experts and scientists in the pandemic that has emerged with its unknowns. In terms of trust in institutions and decision makers, higher trust in the ministry of health and Minister of Health Fahrettin Koca is stated. 67.5 per cent of respondents indicated a medium to high level of confidence in the minister.

A high level of trust in scientists is found, while a low level of trust in the Covid-19 Science Board of the Ministry of Health is noted.

Among the options offered to participants, the lowest level of trust has been stated in the political opposition in Turkey. The pharmaceutical companies, traditional media and the World Health Organization was the other institutions with the lowest level of trust. It is believed that the high expectations for the management of the pandemic and the raising of some claims and criticisms (Yücel, 2020) about it may have an effect on the low level of trust in WHO. Research conducted around the world and in Turkey shows that interest and trust in television increased during the pandemic (Reuters Institute, 2020), (Universal McCann, 2020), while social media is more preferred as a source of news and is more trusted than traditional media. It is believed that between the first period of the pandemic and the period in which the study was conducted, people's attitudes about trust may have changed, and that the survey was conducted with internet and social media users may have an impact on this result.

Based on the data, the correlation between information sources and trust level has been also examined and it was determined that users who followed the information related to Covid-19 on social media had a lower level of trust in institutions than users who followed them on television. It can be estimated that the level of trust is low because social media is the main area of disinformation of misinformation, and discussions about the government and related organizations withholding information are mainly conducted on social media.

A significant correlation has been found between the level of trust in institutions and the attitude of the vaccine, especially participants with a low level of trust in the World Health Organization, doctors/scientists and the Covid-19 Science Board had a negative attitude to the vaccine.

FUTURE RESEARCH DIRECTIONS

During the pandemic period, many areas of study emerged in terms of mass communication and new media. Research that will reveal the levels of trust in scientific knowledge, treatment and preventive measures, as well as the reasons for people being affected by media messages will contribute to the field.

In this period, there is anxiety in people especially about vaccination and restriction measures. Detailed analysis of mis- and disinformation will allow us to understand the relationship between people's belief levels of conspiracy theories and in false information and their attitudes to restraint and vaccination.

ACKNOWLEDGMENT

This study has been presented orally at UYSAD International Management and Social Sciences Conference on 15-16 January 2021.

REFERENCES

Akbaş, E. (2020). Covid-19'un Toplumsal Etkileri, Kovid-19 ve Sonrası: Disiplinlerarası Bir Yaklaşım. *ULİSA*, *12*(3), 5–9.

Akyüz, S. S. (2020). Yanlış Bilgi Salgını: COVID-19 Salgını Döneminde Türkiye'de Dolaşıma Giren Sahte Haberler. *Akdeniz Üniversitesi İletişim Fakültesi Dergisi*, (34), 422–444.

Aslan, S. (2016). Türkiye'de sosyal sermaye bileşenlerinden güven hakkında bir değerlendirme. *C.Ü. İktisadi ve İdari Bilimler Dergisi, 17*(2), 181-204.

Balcı, Ş., & Bekiroğlu, O. (2014). Medyanın kritik ve süreğen dönemeci: Üniversite öğrencilerinin gözünden medya haberlerinin güvenilirliği. *Selçuk İletişim*, *8*(2), 192–217.

Bargain, O., & Ulugbek, A. (2020). Trust and Compliance to Public Health Policies in Times of COVID-19. *IZA Discussion Papers*, *192*(13205), 1–21. doi:10.1016/j.jpubeco.2020.104316 PMID:33162621

Bilge, N. (2020). *Whatsapp'ta yönlendirilen mesajlar yüzde 70 azaldı*. Digital Report. Retrieved November 2020, from, https://digitalreport.com.tr/whatsappta-yonlendirilen-mesajlar-yuzde-70-azaldi-teknoloji-13594/

Bilgiç, A., & Akyüz, S. S. (2020). Türkiye'de Covid-19 Pandemisi Döneminde Sağlık Bakanı Fahrettin Koca'nın Sosyal Medya Kullanımı: Twitter Paylaşımları İçerik Analizi. *Gaziantep University Journal of Social Sciences, 19*,231-243.

Boorstein, M. (2020). *Prominent Virginia pastor who said 'God is larger than this dreaded virus' dies of covid-19*. Retrieved July 17, 2020, from Washington Post: https://www.washingtonpost.com/religion/2020/04/13/virginia-pastor-church-dies-coronavirus/

Bozkurt, Y., Zeybek, Z., & Aşkın, R. (2020). Covid-19 Pandemisi: Psikolojik etkileri ve terapötik müdahaleler. İstanbul Ticaret Üniversitesi Sosyal Bilimler Dergisi, Bahar,304-318.

Brennen, J. S., Simon, F., Howard, P. N., & Nielsen, R. N. (2020). *Types, Sources, and Claims of COVID-19 Misinformation*. Reuters Institute Report, Factsheet, April 2020.

Bunker, D. (2020). Who do you trust? The digital destruction of shared situational awareness and the COVID-19 infodemic. *International Journal of Information Management*, *55*, 1–6. doi:10.1016/j.ijinfomgt.2020.102201 PMID:32836649

Büyükafşar, M. (2019). *Haber ve doğruluk ilişkisi: "Yalan haber" ve haber doğrulama pratikleri. Yayınlanmamış doktora tezi*. Marmara Üniversitesi Sosyal Bilimler Enstitüsü.

Cömlekçi, M., & Başol, O. (2019). Sosyal medya haberlerine güven ve kullanıcı teyit alışkanlıkları üzerine bir inceleme. *Galatasaray İletişim Dergisi*, (30), 55–77.

Dahlgren, P. (2018). Media, knowledge and trust: The deepening epistemic crisis of democracy. *Javnost: The Public*, *25*(1-2), 20–27. doi:10.1080/13183222.2018.1418819

Dijk, J. V., & Alinead, D. (2020). Social Media and Trust in Scientific Expertise: Debating the Covid-19 Pandemic in The Netherlands. *Social Media + Society*, *6*(4), 1–11.

Doğan, M., & Düzel, M. (2020). Covid-19 özelinde korku-kaygı düzeyleri. *Turkish Studies*, *15*(4), 739–752.

Dönmez, İ., & Gürbüz, S. (2020). Üniversite Öğrencilerinin Covid-19 Virüsü Hakkında Bilişsel Yapılarının Belirlenmesi. *MANAS Sosyal Araştırmalar Dergisi*, *9*(4), 2159–2172. doi:10.33206/mjss.763029

Falcone, R., Coli, E., Felletti, S., Sapienza, A., Castelfranchi, C., & Paglieri, F. (2020). All We Need Is Trust: How the COVID-19 Outbreak Reconfigured Trust in Italian Public Institutions. *Frontiers in Psychology*, *11*(11), 1–17. doi:10.3389/fpsyg.2020.561747 PMID:33132966

Foça, M. A. (2019). *Sözlük: Yanlış bilginin en yaygın yedi türü*. Retrieved May 2020, from https://teyit.org/sozluk-yanlis-bilginin-en-yaygin-7-turu

Funke, D. (2020). *Fact-checking a Facebook conspiracy about Bill Gates, Dr. Fauci and COVID-19*. Politifact. Retrieved April 2020, from https://www.politifact.com/article/2020/apr/14/fact-checking-facebook-conspiracy-about-bill-gates/

Gelfert, A. (2018). Fake News: A Definition. *Informal Logic*, *38*(1), 84–117. doi:10.22329/il.v38i1.5068

Güler, B. (2020). *İran'da sahte içkiden ölenlerin sayısı 800'e yaklaştı*. Retrieved June 22, 2020 from Anadolu Ajansı: https://www.aa.com.tr/tr/dunya/iranda-sahte-ickiden-olenlerin-sayisi-800e-yaklasti/1822904

Güz, N., & Yanık, H. (2020). Toplumsal sorumluluk yaklaşımı ve güven bağlamında medya ve kamuoyu araştırmaları arasındaki ilişki. *Gümüşhane Üniversitesi İletişim Fakültesi Dergisi*, *8*(1), 298–336.

Hutchinson, A. (2020). Facebook Launches New, Million-Dollar Grant Programs to Support Fact-Checkers and Local Newsrooms. *SocialMediaToday*. Retrieved April 2020, from https://www.socialmediatoday.com/news/facebook-launches-new-million-dollar-grant-programs-to-support-fact-checke/574325/

Kalemci Tüzün, İ. (2007). Güven, Örgütsel Güven ve Örgütsel Güven Modelleri. *Karamanoğlu Mehmetbey Üniversitesi Sosyal ve Ekonomik Araştırmalar Dergisi*, (2), 93–118.

Keyes, R. (2019). *Hakikat Ötesi Çağ: Günümüz dünyasında yalancılık ve aldatma*. Deli Dolu.

Kreps, S., & Kriner, D. (2020). Model uncertainty, political contestation, and public trust in science: Evidence from the COVID-19 pandemic. *Science Advances*, *6*(43), 1–12. doi:10.1126ciadv.abd4563 PMID:32978142

Morrish, L. (2020). *The 2020 rabbit hole: Why conspiracy theories draw people in*. Ocak 2021 tarihinde First Draft: https://firstdraftnews.org/latest/rabbit-hole/adresindenalındı

Orlowski, J. (Director). (2020). *Social Dilemma* [TV Movie]. ABD.

Özdemir, S. (2020). *Alkolün Koronavirüs'ü Öldürdüğü İddiası*. Dogrulugu Ne? Retrieved January 9, 2021, from https://dogrulugune.org/alkolun-koronavirusu-oldurdugu-iddiasi/

Poynter. (2020). *The CoronaVirusFacts/DatosCoronaVirus Alliance Database*. Poynter. Retrieved August 2020, from https://www.poynter.org/ifcn-covid-19-misinformation/

Reuters Institute. (2020). *Reuters Digital News Report 2020*. Oxford University. Retrieved May 2020, from reutersinstitute.politics.ox.ac.uk: https://reutersinstitute.politics.ox.ac.uk/sites/default/files/2020-06/DNR_2020_FINAL.pdf

Sargut, A. (2003). *Kurumsal alanlardaki örgüt yapılarının oluşmasında ve ekonomik işlemlerin yürütülmesinde güvenin rolü. In Sosyal Bilimlerde Güven*. Vadi.

Selamzade, F., Korkmazer, F., Bostan, S., & Yusifbeyli, G. (2020). COVID-19 Pandemisinin Toplum Üzerine Etkisi: Azerbaycan Örneği. *Turkiye Klinikleri Journal of Health Sciences*, *5*(2), 278–287. doi:10.5336/healthsci.2020-75559

Siders, D., & Ward, M. (2020). A fight over data infiltrates Trumpworld's response to coronavirus. *Science Advances*, *6*(43), 1–12.

Silverman, C. (2020). *Dezenformasyon ve medya manipülasyonunu araştırmak. In Dezenformasyon ve medya manipülasyonu üzerine doğrulama el kitabı*. European Journalism Center-Teyit.

Spring, M. (2020a). *Coronavirus: The seven types of people who start and spread viral misinformation*. BBC. Retrieved January 2020 from, https://www.bbc.com/news/blogs-trending-52474347

Spring, M. (2020b). *ABD'de Koronavirüsün sahte olduğunu düşünen rahip, Covid-19'dan öldü*. Retrieved December 2020, from BBC Türkçe: https://www.kisa.link/OjNq

Ünal, R., & Taylan, A. (2017). Sağlık iletişiminde yalan haber-yanlış enformasyon sorunu ve doğrulama platformları. *Atatürk İletişim Dergisi*, (14), 81–100.

Universal McCann. (2020). *Universal McCann'den Türkiye'nin Korona Günleri araştırması*. Retrieved December 2020, from MediaCat: https://mediacat.com/universal-mccannden-turkiyenin-korona-gunleri-arastirmasi/

Vosoughi, S., Roy, D., & Aral, S. (2018). The spread of true and false news online. *Science*, *357*(6380), 1146–1151. doi:10.1126cience.aap9559 PMID:29590045

Wardle, C. & Derakhshan, H. (2017). *Information Disorder: Toward an interdisciplinary framework for research and policy making*. Council of Europe report DGI (2017) 09.

Wardle, C. (2020). *Bilgi düzensizliği çağı. In Dezenformasyon ve Medya Manipülasyonu Üzerine Doğrulama El Kitabı*. European Journalism Center-Teyit.

WHO. (2020). *1st WHO Infodemiology Conference*. Retrieved October 2020, from World Health Organization: https://www.who.int/news-room/events/detail/2020/06/30/default-calendar/1st-who-infodemiology-conference

Wild, J., & Godart, C. (2020). *Bot, cyborg ve yapay hareketliliği saptamak. C. Silverman içinde, Dezenformasyon ve Medya Manipülasyonu üzerine Doğrulama El Kitabı*. European Journalism Center-Teyit.

Yerlikaya, T. (2020). Koronavirüs ile Mücadelede Yeni Risk Alanı: İnfodemi. *SETA Perspektif*, (269), 1–4.

Yücel, H. (2020). Dünya Sağlık Örgütü'nün Koronavirüs Yönetimi. *SETA Analiz*, (324), 7–17.

KEY TERMS AND DEFINITIONS

COVID-19: COVID-19 is the disease caused by a new coronavirus called SARS-CoV-2. WHO first learned of this new virus on 31 December 2019, following a report of a cluster of cases of 'viral pneumonia' in Wuhan, People's Republic of China.

Disinformation: Disinformation is false or misleading information that is spread deliberately to deceive. Disinformation in new media include deceptive advertising, propaganda, fake news, fake websites/accounts imitating one person or news organization.

Fake News: Fake news is false or misleading content that is similar in structure to news and is usually prepared to deceive people on internet and social media.

Infodemic: The term of infodemic is explained as the vast accumulation of knowledge that occurs during a pandemic, some of which are true and some of which are false, spread as quickly as the virus, and complicate the health organization.

Misinformation: False information that is spread, regardless of whether there is intent to mislead.

Pandemic: It is a term used for epidemics that spread in more than one country or continent around the world and affect a very wide area.

Social Media: Social media are interactive digitally mediated technologies that facilitate the creation or sharing of information ve ideas of expression via and networks.

Trust: It is defined as confidence, sense of involvement and trust without fear and doubt.

Chapter 18
The Impacts of the COVID-19 Outbreak on the Education Sector:
Evidence From Pakistan

Syed Arslan Haider
Sunway University, Malaysia

Azeem Gul
National University of Modern Languages, Pakistan

Bilal Anwar
University of Sahiwal, Pakistan

Shehnaz Tehseen
https://orcid.org/0000-0002-4039-0256
Sunway University, Malaysia

Shahid Iqbal
Bahria University, Pakistan

ABSTRACT

The COVID-19 outbreak has prevented students from contributing towards the economic growth of Pakistan. It first disrupted the education system in China and later entered Pakistan to close all levels of educational institutions/sectors since the middle of March 2020. This study aims to highlight the COVID-19 outbreak's effects on educational sector in Pakistan. Pakistan's overall public sector expenditure as a percentage of GDP before the pandemic was already low as compared to regional level, but due to the pandemic, it has dropped down significantly. This study seeks to answer two important questions: (1) What are the impacts of COVID-19 outbreak on Pakistan? (2) Will the closure of educational institutions impact the economic growth of Pakistan? According to empirical and theoretical findings, the results show that the lack of school education for a long period of time will contribute towards unskilled human capital. The COVID-19 outbreak has impacted student learning activities, which may increase the drop-out rates, loss of mental health, and consequently, may impact the economic growth of Pakistan later.

DOI: 10.4018/978-1-7998-7164-4.ch018

INTRODUCTION

The outbreak of Covid-19 in 2019 after the 1918 influenza pandemic has been recorded as the worst pandemic of the contemporary era. Surging in China and infecting every country has deeply impacted socioeconomic indicators worldwide. In one hand, the shock of the pandemic has seriously disrupted most advanced economies of the world such as the United States, China, India, Japan, and beyond and on the other hand, developing nations such as Pakistan especially has experienced this shock at the socioeconomic domain when it hit Karachi city an economic hub of the nation. The pandemic swept across the nation in few weeks where its effects were observed in the form of nationwide socioeconomic lockdown (Williams, 2021). This study is aimed at highlighting the effects of the pandemic in the form of Covid-19 on education and the economic growth of Pakistan. This is study is unique as this approach provides a theoretical understanding of the pandemic effects on the nation. Also, the study has used various independent variables to highlight its impacts on the education and economic growth of Pakistan.

The study is divided into many sections. First, previous pandemics and the current Covid-19 have been highlighted. Second, the study has utilized different economics and social theories which is useful by providing an explanatory power to the current study. Third, a brief overview has shown the current education system in Pakistan as compared to the regional and international educational system of other countries. Fourth, the study has highlighted the impacts of education in Pakistan and the relationship of education with other indicators. The study has also examined the relationship of education with the economy as a major indicator. The concluding part of the study has examined the pandemic's causal relationship with the socioeconomic system of Pakistan. The current study is useful in many aspects by inviting further debates on the topic which would be useful for the policy formulation aiming at addressing issues related to social and economic indicators in regards to education.

AN OVERVIEW OF PANDEMICS

Human history has recorded numerous epidemics including smallpox, cholera, dengue, acquired immune deficiency syndrome (AIDS), influenza, respiratory infections severe acute respiratory syndrome (SARS), West Nile disease, and tuberculosis. The flu pandemic is an unpredictable but repetitive event that can have serious consequences for communities around the world. The flu epidemic has hit nearly three times every century since the 1500s, or almost every 10-50 years. In the 20th century, there were three pandemics called the "Spanish flu" in 1918-1919, the "Asian flu" in 1957-1958, and the "Hong Kong flu" in 1968-1969. (Covid-19 and Children, 2020). Each pandemic affected human life and economic development. Recently, the origin of this catastrophic Covid-19 outbreak (Cov-19OB) first froze social mobility in Wuhan city in Hubei Province of China and the rest of the world. In December 2019, patients were reported with clinical features resembling viral pneumonia (Huang et al., 2020). Chinese researchers named initially as nCoV, but the International Committee on Taxonomy of Virus called it as Severe Acute Respiratory Syndrome Coronavirus-2 (SARS-CoV-2). World Health Organization (WHO) on the same day named pneumonia as Covid-19. Later, WHO declared Covid-19 as the Sixth Public Health of Emergency Service (SPHEC) on January 30, 2020. China's bordering countries such as Pakistan with the first infected case was detected on February 26, 2020, in the city of Karachi, Sindh Province. The estimated population of Karachi is 204.65 million. The virus easily swept across the country and has currently become an epidemic (Abid, 2020). The total number of confirmed cases indicates in Figures 1 and 2 which shows that the virus multiplied more from April 2020 to July 2, 2020 (ZME Science, 2020).

Figure 1. Total confirmed cases

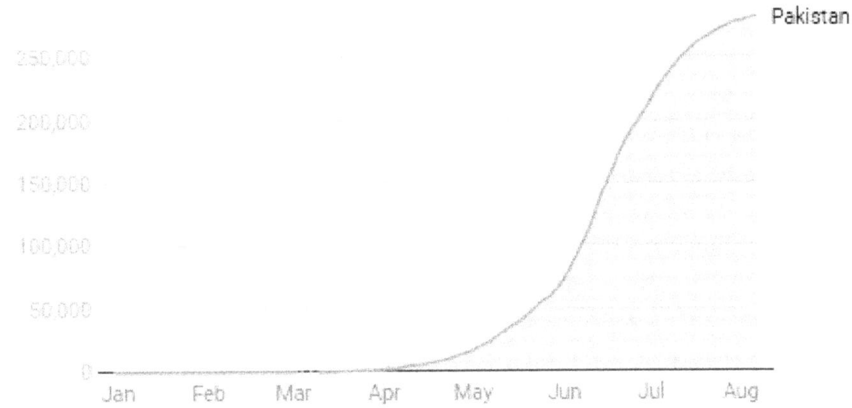

Figure 2. Total fatalities reported per day

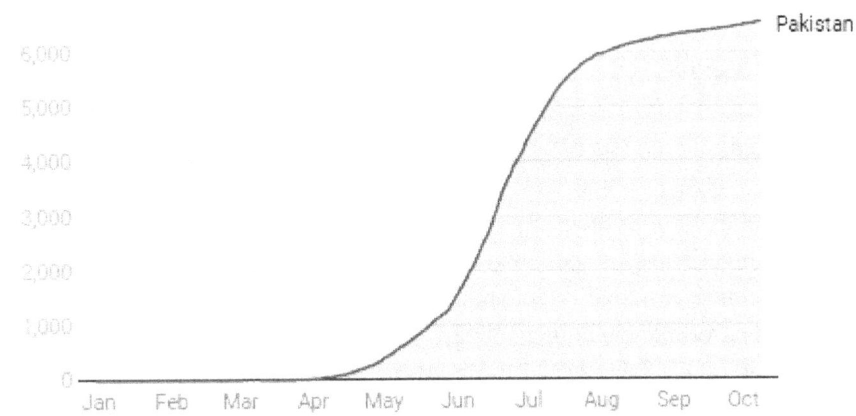

Later, Covid-19 spread via traveling to other cities, and the same day another case was confirmed in Islamabad (Waris et al., 2020). According to fresh data, the total number of infected cases has crossed over 6,153, and 287, 300 are the confirmed cases in August 2020 in Pakistan. With this, Pakistan was on the cusp of Cov-19OB in March 2020. This pushed the country to ban international flights in March 2020. This action made the Pakistani people not travel for unnecessary things. It was followed by a lockdown of all socio-economic activities in the country. The Prime Minister of Pakistan officially announced a lockdown of the country on March 22, 2020 (Srivastava et al., 2020). Lockdown has also closed all educational institutions worldwide including Pakistan. Cov-19OB has affected almost 46,803,407 enrolled students in Pakistan. Sector-wise enrollments comprise: pre-primary level 8,636,383, secondary level 13,357618, and tertiary level 1,878,101 are out of their schools, colleges, and universities (Saeed, 2020).

Education is the foundation of international progress; that is why its sustainability is so important to the growth and development of all nations. Education over the past several centuries had faced many challenges ranging from changes in the school curriculum to the closure of educational institutions due to student or staff protests, outbreaks, and/or instability in national administration where the Pakistani education system does not prefer. Pakistan's education system has been plagued by challenges such as curriculum changes that lead to educational challenges, student violence, and possible outbreaks of diseases that may / may not lead to school closures.

The Coronavirus epidemic has affected education systems around the world, leading to the widespread closure of schools in the affected countries. As of March 28, 2020, more than 1.7 billion students have been illiterate due to non-formal schools due to the epidemic. In addition, school closures due to COVID-19 highlighted various social and economic problems, including student debt (Mamun & Ullah, 2020), digital learning, food insecurity and homelessness, and access to child care, health care, and housing (Mustafa, 2020). The recent outbreak of infectious diseases has led to widespread school closures worldwide with varying degrees of activity. This study aims to explore the Covid-19 outbreak's impacts on education in Pakistan. First, the paper has highlighted education as the basic human capital mobilizer conceptually to understand its role towards economic growth (EG) of Pakistan. Second, the study has briefly explored the previous history of education. Finally, the current paper shows the Covid-19 outbreak's impacts on learners' physical and mental developments such as dropouts' issues, mental development such as mental stress, and other related issues.

ANALYTICAL FRAMEWORK

Many theoretic and economic models have examined the impacts of education on the EG of a country. Developing countries such as Pakistan and others are spending on education to accelerate economic growth. Investment in education in the early childhood of the nation advances problem-solving skills, learning skills, communication skills, personal skills for self-management, and social skills (Patrinos, 2016). Previous studies have revealed the correlation between educational expenditure and economic growth. The high rate of enrollment in higher education leads towards the higher EG rate of a country. The investment in human capital has been tested in Pakistan, the United States (US), and other countries to determine the impact of education on economic growth. It has been revealed that it has a positive impact on the Gross Domestic Product (GDP) of a country. The countries with high enrollment in schools grow faster in terms of per capita income leading to more productivity in a country (Eric & Ludger, 2007). Bils & Klenow (2000) have worked to show the causality of educational spending and GDP. They have used the Granger causality model which has revealed positive impacts on the economy of a country to accelerate EG (Reza and Valeecha, 2012).

Prior models such as the neoclassical models have examined the contribution of education towards economic growth. In the 1960s, the empirical studies of Shultz and Denison revealed that the Western economies flourished with the increasing enrollment in schools, colleges, and universities. Other studies were conducted regarding the impacts of education on the national growth of a country such as period Gary Becker, Jacob Mincer (1955—75) have found that it increases earnings or estimated rate of returns (Teixeira, 2014). A survey was conducted to determine the impact of education on the EG of Ghana and Mexico in 1984. The results showed that a 1% increase was detected in Mexican national economic growth and 23% of Ghana (Ozturk, 2001).

According to neoclassical growth theories, there are three mechanisms of education to impact EG. First, it develops and increases human capital inherent in the labor force which in turn enhances productivity. This leads to a high level of equilibrium of output. Second, according to endogenous growth theories, it creates innovative capability of the economy which leads to greater knowledge regarding technologies and products which promotes growth. Third, education helps to diffuse and transmit knowledge about new technologies produced in the developed world for the developing countries. Along with these theories, empirical studies have found that the indicator of education has affected the EG (Hanushek & Wobamann, 2010).

Education in Pakistan

In developing countries like Pakistan, the education sector is an international outlier in terms of gender gaps. According to the United Nations Education, Scientific, and Cultural Organization (UNESCO), the current situation has forced 190 countries to close their educational institutions including Pakistan and other countries across the world. The pandemic has impacted around 1.6 billion students that is a 91% student population worldwide. In order to keep the students safe, Pakistan has closed down all educational institutions since mid-March 2020 and implemented a social distancing policy to prevent the spread of the virus (Hazirullah, 2020). Before the outbreak of Covid-19, Pakistan has been reported by United Nations International Children's Emergency Fund (UNICEF) showing the major challenge of the world's second-highest number of out-of-school children where 22.8 million children aged 15-16 out of school which are comprising of 44 percent of the population in this age of group. This condition becomes more severe when children with age of 5-9 not attending schools. The record has shown that 5 million children comprising in this age of group. This situation doubles with age of 11.4 million adolescent between the age of 10-14 indicating that they are not receiving formal education. The severity of challenges for education sector in Pakistan exacerbated by many factors where among such factors are: gender, poor socio-economic condition and the geographic indicators (UNICEF, 2020). Pakistan as the record has shown facing extreme challenge to the education sector, however, with arrival of novel Coronavirus as an independent variable has pushed the country into another challenge.

The closure of educational institutions associated with the slash to growth of Pakistani economy. According to Moody's projection Mogaji (2020), about overall EG of Pakistan, the growth rate of Pakistan was reduced by 2.9% in the mid of March 2020 and by the end of March 2020, the growth rate was further reduced to 2% from the 2.9%. The real GDP loss is now 3% in the mid of June 2020. The projection of both Moody's and Asian Development Bank (ADB) are in line with the growth estimation of Pakistan. The Pakistani authorities have projected loss to GDP by PKR 2.5 trillion due to many factors such as supply shocks, disruption foreign trade, and suspension of operations of service and manufacture industries in the third week of March 2020. The Planning Commission of Pakistan has declared that the Covid-10 infection would lead to a 0.8-1.3% loss in the GDP. This situation would bring the EG to fall from 3.3% to 2.5% (Sareen, 2020). In the education sector, Pakistan is spending less as compared to other countries as a percent of GDP. For example, out of 80 countries, the government spending on education is less as compared to 4.21% of other countries. In case of Pakistan the public expenditure on education was recorded 2.9% in the FY 2017.The detail of public spending on education percentage of GDP from 1971 to 2015 is shown in the Figure 3 (Pakistan: Education spending, percent of GDP, 2020).

Figure 3. Pakistan-education spending, percent of GDP

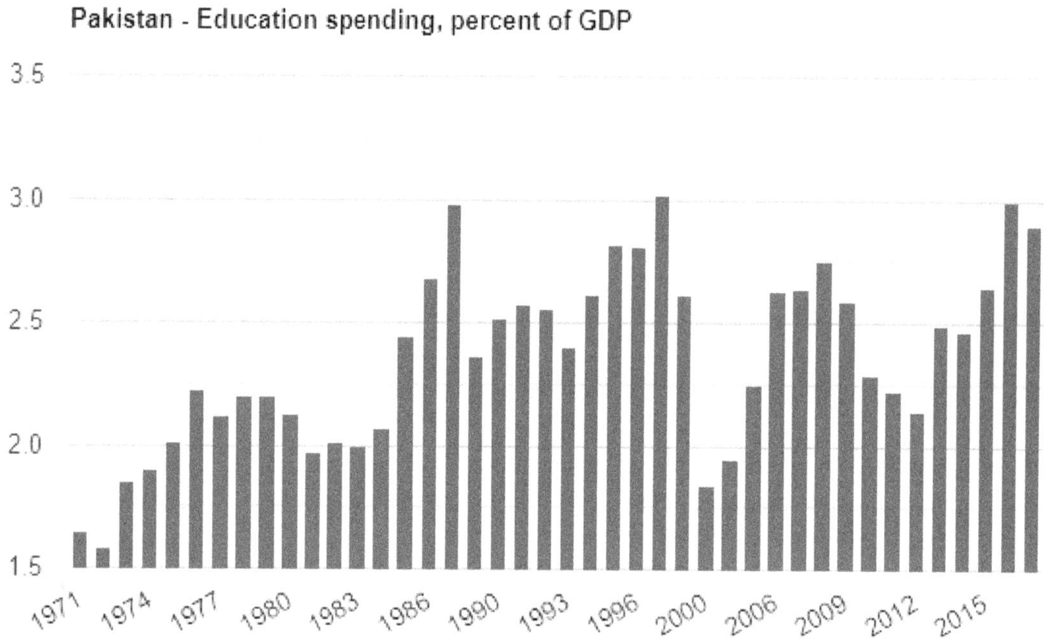

The public expenditure on education as a percentage to GDP has declined continually in the region in the FY 2018 of Pakistan. According to economic survey of Pakistan for FY 2018-19, public expenditure on education was estimated 2.4% which was lowest in the region. The United Nations Development Program (UNDP) has reported that Pakistan has ranked 150th out of 189 countries with Human Development Indicator (HDI) value of 0.562. The educational indictors have shown that only Afghanistan lies behind in the region in this context. Other countries improved HDI as compared to Pakistan. The data provided by FY 2018-19 has shown an increase in expenditure on education since 2013-14. Although spending on education sector in Pakistan has increased since 2013-14, it is still the least in global context. In 2018-19, Pakistan spent only 2.4% in this sector which ranks it 150 out of 189. Moreover, Pakistan is at second last within the south Asian region which has spent on education sector (Amin, 2019).

However, the public expenditure on education to GDP has decreased in the current economic survey of Pakistan. Overall GDP growth of the country has estimated contracted by 0.38% against the revised projected target of 2.4% in the FY 2020. The loss to the GDP growth has come from many sectors performing negatively such as industry recorded -2.64%, service sector recorded -3.4%, transport and communication recorded -7.1% and manufacturing contracted by 22.9%for April-June 2020 (Editorial, 2020). The contraction to the GDP growth has significantly affected the budget for public spending on education in FY 2019-20. This loss to the GDP by over PKR 3 trillion has claimed by Advisor to the Prime Minster on Finance and Revenue Dr. Abdul Hafeez Shiekh due to the Covid-19 pandemic (Amin, 2019).

The reduction in the public expenditure for Education Affairs and Services in the federal budget has come down from PKR 97.155 billion to 77.362 billion in the 2019-20 revised allocation. The current has decreased by 20.5%. The current reduction has affected the higher education that is lowest percentage in the region. The budget for Higher Education Commission (HEC) under the Public Sector Development Program (PSDP) has declined from PKR 35.830 billion to PKR 28.64 billion in 2020. This was later revised downward to PKR 30.961 billion for 2019-20. However, HEC has demanded PKR 55 billion under the PSDP for 2019-20. The government allocation for Education Affairs and Service has declined from PKR 2.831 billion to PKR 77.262 for Pre-primary and Primary Education Affairs for 2019-20. The amount allocated in the 2018-19 budgets was PKR 10.120 billion. This amount was further distributed in total PKR 6.718 billion for Secondary Education Affairs and Services, the budget for Tertiary Education Affairs and Services has declined from71.824 billion to PKR 65.233 billion in the 2019-20 (Amin, 2019).

METHODOLOGY

This research led to a systematic review of the literature, which discussed in more detail the subject of research in the field. The advantage of systematic literature reviews is that it allows researchers to report on the most relevant subjects and to apply critical evaluations of these sources. As Dochy (2006) argues, the procedure aims to reduce bias and increase the strength of the study. This study focuses on education sector by looking at the general views submitted by previous researchers, with the aim of proposing an appropriate theoretical framework. This means that this systematic review of literature should have focused on topics most closely related to the field. For this we studied the available books, journal articles, newspaper articles and news channels which enlightened me about many aspects of the Covid-19 pandemic. The present study is based on observation. Additionally, secondary sources were utilized to analyze and interpret to know what other researchers have examined.

Impacts of Covid-19 Outbreak

Apart from reduction of public expenditure on education that is caused by shrinking of EG, the closure of educational institute due to current Covid-19 pandemic has adverse impacts on social and economic costs particularly for the most vulnerable and marginalized girls and boys of the community in Pakistan. This leads to exacerbate the existing disparities in the education system and other aspects of their lives. According to UNESCO, the learning is interrupted which affects children and youth. They are deprived to grow and develop. Under privileged students are facing disproportionate disadvantages and have fewer opportunities beyond their schools. The longer school closure caused other adverse impacts such as dropout rates, increased exposure to violence and exploitation, social isolation, decreasing human mental development, high economic costs for the parents and other adverse impacts (UNESCO, 2020).

Student Dropout Rate in Pakistan

Student dropout rate is an adverse effect of many factors but the most important one in Pakistan is due to poverty. Low socioeconomic status leads to poverty. It has a large, pervasive, and persistent influence on an education of children in a family. Although other factors such as culture also contribute to dropout rate from schools, colleges and universities in Pakistan, however, the most striking is the cause of poverty before the pandemic and the current situation will trigger to the worst situation. Pakistan is the second highest in the world after Nigeria with 5.5 million children out of schools and with more illiterate adults after India and China (UNESCO, 2020). Moreover, Pakistan is among 21 countries with learning crisis due to number of indices such as enrollment, dropout rates, performance, and literacy (Ahmed et al, 2014). Poverty has triggered both the national level financing education and as well as the international level to ensure more enrollment and less dropout rate from the school in Pakistan. According to UNESCO, one out of four children will not be completing primary school by 2030 (Ahmed, 2019). Poverty has hit hard girl education in Pakistan amid the pandemic.

Impact on Girl Education

Findings have shown that women literacy rate contributes towards economic growth and economic development of a country. In this regard, an efficient educational system affects advancement of a society positively when everyone has equal access to education in that country (Parveen, 2008). Despite revelation of these findings in some countries like Pakistan human capital is not supported by economic development and economic growth. History has shown that Pakistan has recorded adequate GDP growth rate, however, the indices such as human development has been a neglected indicator (Husain, Qasim, & Sheikh, 2003). Women comprising half of population in Pakistan; however, experts have found that it has faced major discrimination in the form of women empowerment through education (Hasani, 2013). By empowering women in the form of education it would not only reduce educational discrimination but also would lead to more economic growth of Pakistan.

Girl education is an independent variable positively affecting poverty in a nation which leads to poverty reduction. Examples include in the African and Middle Eastern countries. In these countries socioeconomic positions have become more stable of women and other affects have observed in the form of reduction in the fertility rate (Dauda, 2012). In the case of Pakistan, studies conducted have revealed so far that there is a long U-shaped relationship female labor force and economic development. The outcome of this relationship has caused more female labor force participation in the market and more economic development (Mujahid & Zafar, 2012). The Table 1 below provides the detail of correlation of female education (Hassan, & Rafaz, 2017).

Table 1. Correlation of education

	Female Education	Labor Force	GDP	Education Expenditure
Female Education	**1.000**			
Labor Force	0.398	**1.000**		
GDP	0.454	0.962	**1.000**	
Education Expenditure	-0.06	0.198	0.373	**1.000**

These variables in the table such as female education female, labor force, GDP and educational expenditure have correlation. Regarding female education has affected their participation the market place positively in the form of providing labor force and overall economic growth in the country. In one hand, the above data has revealed that the more a female labor force participation in the market the more it has affected economic growth positively, however, the data has revealed it has negative impacts on the economic growth as regards to less expenditure on their education in any country. The correlation of female education has negatively affected besides negligible allocation of fund to women education in Pakistan the other independent variable has also negatively affected by the outbreak of Covid-19 girls' education in Pakistan. Additional detail of gender inequalities is highlighted below as Figure 4 (UN Women Pakistan, 2020).

Figure 4. Gender inequalities

Poverty and Gender Gap

Previous empirical and theoretical studies have revealed that low socioeconomic condition disrupts education in all countries including Pakistan. Economic crisis that is emerging out of Covid-19 pandemic in Pakistan may result in increased poverty (Shah et al, 2019). Gender gap has been associated with the problems of sustainable development of Pakistan. Women play pivotal role in the development of economy. However, the current situation has not only triggered the global gender discrimination but also in Pakistan, according to UNESCO, the school closure will hit hard girls and will lead to dropout rate particularly adolescent girls disproportionally to entrench the gender gap further (UNESCO, 2020). According to UNDP, gender gap has widened during the outbreak of previous attack of infectious diseases such as Ebola in Sierra Leonne (UNESCO, 2020). Many studies indicate adverse effects of COVID-19 on low-income countries including Pakistan (UNESCO, 2020).

Impact on Democracy

The adverse effects of declining economic growth of Pakistan due to Covid-19 may generate and exacerbate issues associated with democracy, terrorism, economic growth, leadership, conflicts. Education is a soul of democracy. Democracy is crucial for Pakistan for its economic development which will impact the education sector. As Franklin Roosevelt has said in a message for American Education week on September 27, 1938, "Democracy cannot succeed unless those who express their choice are prepared to choose wisely" (Davis, 2021). The guardian of democracy is education. In this sense, education prepares citizens to choose wisely and freely (Kominiak, 2019). Lack of education in Pakistan has created terrorists' groups in Pakistan which has jeopardized the national and international security of people. The lack of access to education to every child in Pakistan has not promoted the economic growth. The existing studies have identified that education is a key to economic development (Quddus, 2018).

Impacts on Children's Parents

The pandemic has also negatively affected the physical and mental health of Pakistanis. Many of the labour migrants from the Middle East have returned to Pakistan amid the Pandemic. There are reports that many migrants from the UAE have come to Pakistan without pay (Turak, 2020). The UNDP has warned that socioeconomic impacts are far more than a health crisis. Socioeconomic impacts will increase poverty and inequalities in the most affected countries. This will escalate and jeopardize lives and livelihoods in years to come (UNDP, 2020). People believe that lower SE ranking in the society impacts family relationships. What if Covid-19 exacerbates and lowers the economic ranking of Pakistani families? Mental stress and turbulent family relationship are the natural outcomes of joblessness. Lower socioeconomic prevents you in pro-social behaviors to work voluntarily and help others and thus build lack of moral development.

According to UNICEF, an estimated 22.8 million Pakistani kids between 6-16 years of age are out of schools in Pakistan. This has ranked Pakistan as the world's second largest number of out-Of-School Children (OOSC). The OOSC makes 44% of total population of Pakistan. Children of age 5-9 comprising 5 million are not enrolled in school and it becomes double after primary school age. This makes 11.4 million adolescents between the age 10-14 not receiving formal educations in Pakistan (UNICEF, 2020). The dropout rate is based on many factors but the most seminal is the economic ranking of a family which determines school enrollment of their children. The arrival of novel Corona virus has severed this situation because many daily wages worker, private jobs keepers are out from their work places that would make the parents unable to impart the right of education to their children. In this context by highlighting another independent variable where its study needs here would help us is income loss due to pandemic which has caused income inequalities particularly the most marginalized.

Income Loss due to Covid-19

It has been estimated that 930,000 children drop-out rate expected both at the primary and secondary educational level. The previous discussion has shown that about 22 million children are not attending schools in Pakistan and this would be representing an increase by 4.2 percent. A record where various barriers have already affected children in Pakistan out of schools, but the current pandemic affecting a family income level may exacerbate the drop-out rate alarmingly. The estimated drop-out rate is based on income elasticity of education for multifarious socioeconomic quintiles. This situation is based on Pakistan's growth estimates in June 2020 which were estimated to be -4.4 percent (World Bank Predicts Sharpest Decline of Remittances in Recent History, 2020). It is argued that income is only one aspect impacting education (Field, 2010). In case of Pakistan the Covid-19 pandemic have affected its national economic growth so far estimated by various sources. The report released by UK-based Economic Intelligence Unit (EIU) has highlighted the impacts of pandemic on the GDP of Pakistan to contract by 1.6% in the fiscal year 2020-21 and will grow in the next fiscal year 2020-21 by 2.9%. The negative impacts of pandemic on the balance of payments will be supplemented with the help of International Monetary Fund (IMF), multilateral and bilateral donors. With this, the currency of the country will be depreciated against the US dollar by 17.7 from an annual average of RS160.8: US$1 in 2020 to RS1768.5:US$1 in 2024. As the current pandemic has global ramification this will slow down the overseas worker's remittance with a sharp decline. The employment will further plummet to 11.8% in 2020-21 and thus will be continued to go further down to 9.4% in 2021-22. The increase in unemployment will stay the same in the 2021-23. However, there will be decrease in the unemployment up to 8.4% during 2023-24. (Mustafa, 2020). To reduce the adverse economic impacts of Covid-19 on the economy and other social adverse effects the government has approached towards IMF along with other donors for financial support in the middle of 2020.

Table 2. Major economic indicators

Economic Indicators	IMF	IMF	IMF	World	Bank	ADB	ADB
	FY20(Pre Covid-1)	FY20 (Post-Covdi-19)	FY21	FY (Post-Covid-19)	FY21	FY(Pre-Covid-19	FY21(Post-Covid-19)
Real GDP Growth Rate (%)	2.4	-1.5	2.0	-1.3	0.9	2.6	3.2
Inflation (%)	11.8	11.3	8.0	11.8	9.5	11.5	8.3
Fiscal Deficit (% of GDP)	-7.2	-9.2	-6.5	-9.5	-8.7	-8.0	-
Export Growth(%)	5.6	-2.1	-4.7	-19.7	-5.3	-	-
Imports Growth (%)	-8.8	-16.0	3.0	-26.3	-7.7	-	-
Remittance Growth (%)	3.4	-4.8	-1.5	-6.5	-6.0	-	-
Current Account Deficit (%) of GDP	-2.2	-1.7	-2.4	-1.9	-2.0	-2.8	-2.4
Debt (%) of GDP	84.6	89.8	87.8	90.6	91.8	-	-

Pakistan had already been struggling to make the current account and fiscal deficit stable, but the pandemic has exacerbated the vulnerabilities to its economy. IMF while observing the impacts on the economy has suggested to Pakistan to continue fiscal consolidation. The country has already high and unsustainable debt to hit 90% of the total value of national economy. Due to the increasing of burden of public health crisis Pakistan's took decision to seek debt relief from the G20 countries for the stability of fiscal and current account deficit. On the other side, IMF has asked to freeze salaries of government employees. The ministry of finance of the country has considered to abolish 67,000 vacant posts every one year due the current pandemic. Moreover, to squeeze current expenditure a ban on purchase of vehicles had also been under discussion (Rana, 2020). International donors such as IMF has conditioned its financial support for Pakistan in some areas in order to keep the economy of Pakistan on track.

Since the government decision to apply lock down in the country, the GDP has shown downward trend. For example, the stock market's benchmark KSE-100 Index plunged down by over 25% in March 2020. The forex reserves of the country slumped 12% from $12.8 billion to $11.2 billion in March and it has further decreased by USD72.90 million in August 2020. Major reason behind the slump is the panic selling of debt and equities. According the State Bank of Pakistan (SBP), the policy rate has decreased by 2% which has led to a total of about $1.5 billing leaving Pakistani Market Treasury Bills (MTBs) and Pakistani Investment Bonds (PIBs) (World Bank, 2020). According to the World Bank data the remittance has also declined from 23% to $17 billion in 2020 with a total of $22.5 billion in 2019 (World Bank, 2020). Lockdown of Pakistan has its own adverse impacts on the economic growth of Pakistan. The weak economy has no capacity to absorb the shock of the anemic.

According to UN Conference on Trade and Development (UNCTAD) estimates Pakistan is placed among hard-hit countries by the global pandemic of Corona virus, causing $2-3 trillion financing deficit in 170 developing countries (Salik, 2020). The Covid-19 has caused to shrink the faltering economy of Pakistan leading to contract the GDP finally. It has far-reaching ramification for other social indicators such as education and health. Bothe education and health are a form of human capital. Without advancing human capital a country will remain less developed (Lonska &Mietule, 2015). Developing country such as Pakistan fall below many countries in South Asia in the education sector the current pandemic has further worsen the situation. It is predicted on the bases of previous research that Pakistan will face barrage of social implication due to its economic fall in the short and long-run if not managed through timely rigorous states polices, the social consequences will be thorny for the people of Pakistan. Table 2 below shows the estimations of leading world financial organization of the Covid-19 impacts on the economy of Pakistan (News Desk, 2020).

CONCLUSION AND RECOMMENDATIONS

The researchers, policy makers and practitioners are of opinion that an active role of government is indispensable in balancing between the conflicting objectives of saving lives and saving economy. For this purpose, the government needs to enforce smart lock down and allocate more resources to provide better medical facilities to the masses. Furthermore, the responsibility lies with the government to assure the continuous supply of essential services, provision of financial aid to those who lost their jobs, prevent the disruption of economy. The developing countries like Pakistan are prone to demand and supply shocks and these shocks have exerted adverse impact on the development process of the economy. Covid-19 outbreak has impacted learning system of Pakistan at all level with additional social and economic consequences. Empirical and theoretical studies have identified that education is a human development indicator that has contributed towards accelerating economic growth of Pakistan. In the midst of the epidemic where students do not go to school, most learning centers turn to e-learning which includes regular communication with teachers in the classroom to the visual classroom using the internet and technology such as phones, computers and tablets. The study revealed that most families in Pakistan do not have access to the internet, which has led to the suspension of the Ministry of Education in Pakistan because most students do not have internet access. Those who have access to the Internet also complain about the high cost of data access to full access to this service and improve their home reading. Some respondents argued that the online learning presented by the Department and other schools is very effective but accessibility has been a problem because you will need technological devices such as smart phones or computers and the internet to be able to access them. This made studying at home during the epidemic a challenge for them.

It is also said that learning is best achieved by using the right teaching materials with the right intention during the process. There is no doubt that it is true that many families in Pakistan do not have the resources to help their children learn and even if they are available, it is not enough to include education. This has made learning some concepts, especially those that are not considered very difficult for students in this time of school closure and closure. However, students' dropout and enrollments rate are policy issues since Pakistan's independence. The major cause behind fewer enrollments and more dropout rate is poverty at the state and the family level. This has not created skilled people and hence the economic growth rate have downward trajectory. Additional social consequences of disruption in education among learners in Pakistan may create interrupted learning, poor nutrition, stress on teachers, parents are not prepared for distance learning, challenges of distance learning, health related issue among students, high economic costs, increased dropout rates, increased exposure to violence and exploitation, social isolation and it may have students' assessment issues. Pakistan was already among the poorest countries at regional and global level to impart standard education. The future export strategies should protect the interest of exporters through a sufficient stimulus package. The formulation and implementation of bold, consistent and proper government policies is the key to take Pakistan economy away from the future losses of Covid-19 pandemic. The proper utilization of existing resources may assist the revival of educations sector of the country.

Table 3. Sources of data

Publishers	Links
Google Scholar	https://scholar.google.com/
SAGE	https://journals.sagepub.com/
American Economic Association	https://www.aeaweb.org/
Elsevier	https://www.elsevier.com/
Taylor and Francis	https://www.tandfonline.com/

Table 4. List of abbreviations

Cov-19OB	Covid-19 Outbreak
EG	Economic Growth
AIDS	Acquired immunodeficiency syndrome
SARS	severe acute respiratory syndrome
WHO	World Health Organization
SPHEC	sixth public health of emergency service
GDP	Gross Domestic Product
UNESCO	United Nations Education, Scientific and Cultural Organization
ADB	Asian Development Bank
UNDP	United Nations Development Program
HDI	Human Development Indicator
HEC	Higher Education Commission
PSDP	Public Sector Development Program
UNICEF	United Nations International Children's Emergency Fund
OOSC	out-Of-School Children
EIU	Economic Intelligence Unit
IMF	International Monetary Fund
MTBs	Market Treasury Bills
PIBs	Pakistani Investment Bonds
UNCTAD	Conference on Trade and Development

REFERENCES

Abid, K., Bari, Y. A., Younas, M., Tahir Javaid, S., & Imran, A. (2020). <covid19> Progress of COVID-19 Epidemic in Pakistan. *Asia-Pacific Journal of Public Health, 32*(4), 154–156. doi:10.1177/1010539520927259 PMID:32429679

Adverse Consequences of School Closure. (n.d.). *UNESCO*. Retrieved from: https://en.unesco.org/covid19/educationresponse/consequences

Ahmed, A. (2019, July 10). One in Four Pakistani won't Complete Primary Education by 2030: UNESCO. *Dawn*. Retrieved from: https://www.dawn.com/news/1493212

Ahmed, I. (2014). Critical Analysis of the Problems of Education in Pakistan: Possible Solutions. *International Journal of Evaluation and Research in Education, 3*(2). Advance online publication. doi:10.11591/ijere.v3i2.1805

Ahmed, J. (2020, March 23). Pakistan's First Corona Virus Death Exposes Nations' Vulnerability. *Reuter*. Retrieved from: https://www.reuters.com/article/us-health-coronavirus-pakistan-insight/pakistans-first-coronavirus-death-exposes-nations-vulnerability-idUSKBN21A0X1

Ahsan, A. (2020, May 6). The Covid-19 Emergency and Prioritizing Public Health in Pakistan. *Dawn*. Retrieved from: https://www.dawn.com/news/1545501

Bils, M., & Klenow, P. J. (2000). Does schooling cause growth? *The American Economic Review, 90*(5), 1160–1183. doi:10.1257/aer.90.5.1160

Bucci & Alberto. (2019). *Human Capital and Economic Growth: The Impact of health, Education and Demographic Change*. Palgrave Macmillan. Retrieved from: https://www.amazon.com/Human-Capital-Economic-Growth Demographic/dp/3030215989

Chakraborty, I., & Maity, P. (2020). Covid-19 Outbreak: Migration, effects on Society, Global Environment and Prevention. *The Science of Total Environment*. totenv.2020138882 doi:10.1016/J.Sci

Cohen, D., & Alleyne, G. A. O. (2002). *Economic Growth and Poverty Reduction*. World Health Organization. Retrieved from https://apps.who.int/iris/bitstream/handle/10665/42492/9241590092.pdf;jsessionid=0C522FB211DB2AB686E2CE5FEF9F9CE5?sequence=1

Covid-19 and Children. (2020). *UNICEF*. Retrieved from: https://data.unicef.org/topic/covid-19-and-children/

Covid-19 School Closure Around the World will hit Girls Hardest. (2020). *UNESCO*. Retrieved from: https://enunescoorh/news/covid-school-closure-around-world-hit-gilrs–hardest

Dauda, R. O. S. (2013). Does female education promote economic performance? Evidence from Nigeria. *International Journal of Economics and Finance, 5*(1), 201–209.

Davis, M. (2021). 3 Franklin Roosevelt and the Challenges of the Democratic Majority. In *Politics as Usual* (pp. 37-49). Cornell University Press. doi:10.1515/9781501757419-005

Dochy, F. (2006). A guide for writing scholarly articles or reviews for the Educational Research Review. *Educational Research Review*, *4*(1-2), 1–21.

Education: Giving Every Child the Right to Education. (n.d.). *UNICEF*. Retrieved from: https://www.unice.org/pakistan/education

Field, F. (2010). *The Foundation Years: preventing poor children becoming poor adults*. The report of the Independent Review on Poverty and Life Chances.

Fligauf, E., & Ayres, A. (2020). Coronavirus in South Asia, March 24, 2020: Outbreak in Pakistan and India on Lock Down. *Council on Foreign Relations*. Retrieved from: https://www.cfr.org/blog/coronavirus-south-asia-march-24-2020-outbreak-pakistan-and-india-lockdown

Hanusheck, E. A., & Wobmann, L. (2010). Education and economic growth. *International Encyclopedia of Education, 2*. doi:10.2139srn.960379

Hasani, Z. (2013). Factors affecting the level of female employment in Iran. *Technical Journal of Engineering and Applied Sciences*, *3*(14), 1424–1431.

Hassan, S. A., & Rafaz, N. (2017). The role of female education in economic growth of Pakistan: A time series analysis from 1990-2016. *International Journal of Innovation and Economic Development, 3*(5), 83-93.

Hazirullah. (2020, May 1). Covid-19 and Education: Unequal learning loss. *The Nation*. Retrieved from: http//nation.com.pk/01-May-2020/Covid-19-and-education-unequal-learning-loss

Huang, C., Wang, Y., Li, X., Ren, L., Zhao, J., & Hu, Y. (2020). Clinical features of patients infected with 2019 novel coronavirus in Wuhan, China. *Lancet*, *395*, 497–506.

Husain, F., Qasim, M. A., & Sheikh, K. H. (2003). An analysis of public expenditure on education in Pakistan. *Pakistan Development Review*, *42*(4), 771–780.

Kominiak, T. (2019). *On Veterans Day: Understanding the Vital Role of Education in our Democracy*. Retrieved from: k12insight.com/trusted/veterans-day-scholls/

Lonska, J., & Mietule, I. (2015). The Impact of Human Capital Development on the Economic and Social Development of a Country: Empirical Study. *Environmental Technology*. Retrieved from: doi:10.17770/etr2015vol2.268

Lonska, J., & Mietule, I. (2015). The Impact of Human Capital Development on the Economic and Social Development of a Country: Empirical Study. *Environmental Technology*. Retrieved from: doi:10.17770/etr2015vol2.268

Mamun, M. A., & Ullah, I. (2020). COVID-19 suicides in Pakistan, dying off not COVID-19 fear but poverty? –The forthcoming economic challenges for a developing country. *Brain, Behavior, and Immunity*. doi:10.1016/j.bbi.2020.05.028

Mattson, D. (2017). Different Indicators of Socioeconomic Status and their Relative Importance as Determinants of Health in Old Age. *International Journal for Equity in Health*. doi:10.118612939-017-0670-3

Mogaji, E. (2020). Financial vulnerability during a pandemic: Insights for coronavirus disease (COVID-19). *Mogaji. E (Norwalk, Conn.)*, 57–63.

Mujahid, N., & uz Zafar, N. (2012). Economic growth-female labour force participation nexus: An empirical evidence for Pakistan. *Pakistan Development Review*, 565–585.

Mustafa, K. (2020, May 9). Impact of Covid-19 Pandemic: Pak GDP to contract by 1.6pc in Current Fiscal, Says economic Intelligence Unit. *The News*. Retrieved from: https://www.thenews.com.pk/print/656244-impact-of-covid-19-pandemic-pak-gdp-to-contract-by-1-6pc-in-current-fiscal-economist-intelligence-unit

Mustafa, N. (2020). Impact of the 2019–20 coronavirus pandemic on education. *International Journal of Health Preferences Research*, 1-12.

News Desk. (2020). *Unemployment in Pakistan to rise in FY21 even after combating COVID-19 successfully*. Retrieved from: https://mettisglobal.news/unemployment-in-pakistan-to-rise-in-fy21-even-after-combating-covid-19-successfully

Ozturk, I. (2001). *The Role of education in Economic Development: A Theoretical Perspective*. Retrieved from: https://mpra.ub.uni-muenchen.de/9023/

Pakistan: Covid-19 2020 Dashboard. (2020). Retrieved from: https://pakwired.com/the-pakistan-coronavirus-disease-tracker/

Pakistan: Education spending, percent of GDP. (2020). *Pakistan: Public spending on education, percent of GDP, 1971 – 2017*. Retrieved from: https://www.theglobaleconomy.com/Pakistan/Education_spending/

Parveen, S. (2008). Female education and national development: As viewed by women activists and advocates. *Bulletin of Education & Research*, *30*(1), 33–41.

Patrinos, A. H. (2016). *Why Education matters for Economic Development*. World Bank.

Quddus. (2018). Role of Education in Democracy. *Daily Times*. Retrieved from: https://dailytimes.com.pk/233967/role-of-education-in-democracy/

Rana, S. (2020, June5). IMF Urges Pakistan to Freeze Government Salaries. *The Express Tribune*. Retrieved from: https://tribune.com.pk/story/2235689/2-imf-urges-pakistan-freeze-govt-salaries

Razum, O., & Amzat, J. A. (2014). *Functionalist Perspective on Health*. Retrieved from: https://www.researchgate.net/publication/300827734_Functionalist_Perspective_on_Health

Reza, A., & Valeecha, S. (2012). Impact of Education on economic growth-Economic Analysis. *Journal of Business and Management*, *5*(4).

Saeed, A. (2020, May 9). The impact of Covid-19 0n education in Pakistan. *Centre for Research and Security Studies*. Retrieved from: http//crssblog.com/the-impact-of-Covid-19-on-education-in-Pakistan/

Salik, N. (2020). Impact of Covid-19 on Economy of Pakistan. *Institute of Strategic Studies*. Retrieved from: http://issi.org.pk/issue-brief-on-impact-of-covid-19-on-economy-of-pakistan/

Shah, D., Haider, G., & Taj, T. (2019). Causes of Dropout Rate at Primary Level in Pakistan. *International Journal of Curriculum and Instruction*, *11*(2), 38–74.

Srivastava, S., Kumar, A., Bauddh, K., Gautam, A. S., & Kumar, S. (2020). 21-Day lockdown in India dramatically reduced air pollution indices in Lucknow and New Delhi, India. *Bulletin of Environmental Contamination and Toxicology*, *105*, 9–17.

Suman & Asgher. (2012). Ashgar Reza and Suman Valeecha, "Impact of Education on Economic Growth of Pakistan-Econometric Analysis. *Journal of Business and Management*, *5*(4). http://www.iosrjournals.org/iosr-jbm/papers/Vol5-issue4/D0542027.pdf?id=5376

Teixeira, P. N. (2014). Gary Becker's early work on human capital–collaborations and distinctiveness. *IZA Journal of Labor Economics*, *3*(1), 1–20.

Turak, N. (2020, July 10). Pakistan Expects UAE Remittance to be Slashed as Pandemic Hits Migrant Workers. *CNBC News*. Retrieved from: https://www.cnbc.com/2020/07/10/pakistan-sees-remittances-hit-as-pandemic-hits-migrant-workers.html

UN Women Pakistan. (2020). *Gendered Impact and Implications of COVID-19 in Pakistan*. Retrieved from: https://asiapacific.unwomen.org/en/digital-library/publications/2020/04/gendered-impact-and-implications-of-covid-19-in-pakistan#view

UNICEF. (2020). *Education: Giving Every Child the Right to Education*. Retrieved from: https://www.unicef.org/pakistan/education

Waris, A., Khan, A. U., Ali, M., Ali, A., & Baset, A. (2020). COVID-19 outbreak: current scenario of Pakistan. *New Microbes and New Infections*, 100681. Retrieved from doi:10.1016/j.nmni.2020.100681

Williams, G. A. (2021). Understanding the Preferences for Online Learning: Online MBAs in Malaysia. In Advancing Innovation and Sustainable Outcomes in International Graduate Education (pp. 194-208). IGI Global.

Wobamann, L., & Hanushek, E. A. (2010). Education and Economic Growth. *International Encyclopedia of Education, 2*. Retrieved from: http://hanushek.stanford.edu/publications/education-and-economic-growth

World Bank Predicts Sharpest Decline of Remittances in Recent History. (2020). *World Bank*. Retrieved from: https://www.worldbank.org/en/news/press-release/2020/04/22/world-bank-predicts-sharpest-decline-of-remittances-in-recent-history

ZME Science. (2020). *Coronavirus in Pakistan — live updates, cases, and news*. Retrieved from: https://www.zmescience.com/medicine/coronavirus-updates-news-pakistan/

KEY TERMS AND DEFINITIONS

COVID-19 Outbreak (Cov-19OB): It is also known as the coronavirus pandemic, is an ongoing pandemic of coronavirus disease 2019 (COVID-19) caused by (SARS-CoV-2).

Economic Growth (EG): Economic growth is the increase in the production of economic goods and services, compared to one period to another. It can be measured by design or actual terms (set of monetary values).

Gross Domestic Product (GDP): It is the total value or market value of all completed goods and services produced within national borders over a period of time. As a comprehensive measure of a complete domestic product, it serves as a complete credit card for the economic life of a particular country.

Higher Education Commission (HEC): A legal entity established by the government of Pakistan. Its main functions are funding, administration, control, and accreditation of higher education institutions in the country. The commission is responsible for developing higher education policy and quality assurance to meet international standards and to provide accredited educational qualifications, development of new institutions and promotion of existing institutions in Pakistan.

Human Development Indicator (HDI): It is integrated indicator of lifetime statistics, education (literacy rate, total enrollment at various levels and attendance), and individual indicators, which are used to rank countries into four categories of people.

International Monetary Fund (IMF): The international financial institution, based in Washington, DC, with 190 countries working to promote global financial cohesion, safeguard financial stability, facilitate international trade, promote high employment and sustainable economic growth, and reduce global poverty while from time to time depending on the World Bank for its resources.

United Nations Education, Scientific, and Cultural Organization (UNESCO): It was born on 16 November 1945. UNESCO has 195 members and 8 Joint Members and is governed by the General Conference and the Executive Board. The Secretariat, headed by the Director-General, implements the decisions of the two organizations. The organization has more than 50 offices worldwide and is headquartered in Paris.

United Nations International Children's Emergency Fund (UNICEF): Promotes the rights and well-being of all children. In partnership with its partners, it is working in 190 countries and territories to translate this commitment into action, with a special focus on reaching the most vulnerable and marginalized children, to the benefit of all children, everywhere.

World Health Organization (WHO): The United Nations special public body dedicated to public health worldwide.

Compilation of References

Abid, K., Bari, Y. A., Younas, M., Tahir Javaid, S., & Imran, A. (2020). <covid19> Progress of COVID-19 Epidemic in Pakistan. *Asia-Pacific Journal of Public Health*, *32*(4), 154–156. doi:10.1177/1010539520927259 PMID:32429679

Abrahams, A., & Leber, A. (2020). Framing a murder: Twitter influencers and the Jamal Khashoggi incident. *Mediterranean Politics*, 1-13. doi:10.1080/13629395.2019.1697089

Abuseridze, G. (2020). Political Stability and Trade Agreements. *Bulletin of the Georgian Natioanl Academy of Science.*

Accenture. (2020, November 23). *The Big Value Shift*. https://www.accenture.com/sk-en/insights/strategy/big-value-shift

Account Chamber of Russian Federation. (2020). *Social Impact of the COVID-19 Pandemic and Inclusiveness*. Government of Russian Federation.

Acosta, A. (2020). El coronavirus en los tiempos del Ecuador [The coronavirus in Ecuador's times]. *Fundación Carolina*. Retrieved from https://www.fundacioncarolina.es/wp-content/uploads/2020/04/AC-23.-2020.pdf

Adams, F. G. (1964). Consumer Attitudes, Buying Plans, and Purchases of Durable Goods: A Principal Components, Time Series Approach. *The Review of Economics and Statistics*, *46*(4), 347–355. doi:10.2307/1924042

Adner, R. (2002). When are technologies disruptive? A demand-based view of the emergence of competition. *Strategic Management Journal*, *23*(8), 667–688. doi:10.1002mj.246

Adverse Consequences of School Closure. (n.d.). *UNESCO*. Retrieved from: https://en.unesco.org/covid19/education-response/consequences

Agarwal, K., Fortune, L., Heintzman, J. C., & Kelly, L. L. (2020). Spiritual experiences of long-term meditation practitioners diagnosed with breast cancer: An interpretative phenomenological analysis pilot study. *Journal of Religion and Health*, *59*(5), 1–17. doi:10.100710943-020-00995-9 PMID:32062734

Aguinis, H., & Bakker, R. M. (2020). Time is of the essence: Improving the conceptualization and measurement of time. *Human Resource Management Review*, *100763*(March), •••. doi:10.1016/j.hrmr.2020.100763

Agung, I. M. (2020). *Memahami Pandemi Covid-19 Dalam Perspektif Psikologi Sosial.* Psikobuletin: Buletin Ilmiah Psikologi.

Agur, I., Peria, S. M., & Rochon, C. (2020, July 1). *Digital Financial Services and the Pandemic: Opportunities and Risks for Emerging and Developing Economies. IMF COVID-19 Special Series*. https://www.imf.org/en/Search#q=agur%20peria&sort=relevancy

Ahmadov, G., & Veziroglu, V. (2003). *Sumgayit and the People in Sumgayit.*

Ahmed, A. (2019, July 10). One in Four Pakistani won't Complete Primary Education by 2030: UNESCO. *Dawn*. Retrieved from: https://www.dawn.com/news/1493212

Ahmed, J. (2020, March 23). Pakistan's First Corona Virus Death Exposes Nations' Vulnerability. *Reuter.* Retrieved from: https://www.reuters.com/article/us-health-coronavirus-pakistan-insight/pakistans-first-coronavirus-death-exposes-nations-vulnerability-idUSKBN21A0X1

Ahmed, I. (2014). Critical Analysis of the Problems of Education in Pakistan: Possible Solutions. *International Journal of Evaluation and Research in Education*, *3*(2). Advance online publication. doi:10.11591/ijere.v3i2.1805

Ahsan, A. (2020, May 6). The Covid-19 Emergency and Prioritizing Public Health in Pakistan. *Dawn*. Retrieved from: https://www.dawn.com/news/1545501

Ajzen, I. (1991). The theory of planned behavior. *Organizational Behavior and Human Decision Processes*, *50*(2), 179–211. doi:10.1016/0749-5978(91)90020-T

Akbaş, E. (2020). Covid-19'un Toplumsal Etkileri, Kovid-19 ve Sonrası: Disiplinlerarası Bir Yaklaşım. *ULİSA*, *12*(3), 5–9.

Ak, N. Y. (2020). Development of Internet literacy self-efficacy scale for pre-service teachers. *Turkish Journal of Education*, *9*(2), 179–204.

Aksoy, A., & Robins, K. (2002). *Banal transnationalism: The difference that television makes*. University of Oxford. Transnational Communities Programme. Retrieved from http://www.transcomm.ox.ac.uk/working%20papers/WPTC-02-08%20Robins.pdf

Akyüz, S. S. (2020). Yanlış Bilgi Salgını: COVID-19 Salgını Döneminde Türkiye'de Dolaşıma Giren Sahte Haberler. *Akdeniz Üniversitesi İletişim Fakültesi Dergisi*, (34), 422–444.

Al-Abdallah, G., Khair, N., & Elmarakby, R. (2021). The Impact of Social Networking Sites on Luxury Vehicles Purchase Decision Process in Gulf Cooperation Council Countries. *Journal of International Consumer Marketing*, 1–19. doi:10.1080/08961530.2020.1867023

Alase, A. (2017). The interpretative phenomenological analysis (IPA): A guide to a good qualitative research approach. *International Journal of Education and Literacy Studies*, *5*(2), 9–19. doi:10.7575/aiac.ijels.v.5n.2p.9

Alea, L. A., Fabrea, M. F., Roldan, R. D. A., & Farooqi, A. Z. (2020). Teachers' Covid-19 awareness, distance learning education experiences and perceptions towards institutional readiness and challenges. *International Journal of Learning, Teaching and Educational Research*, *19*(6), 127–144.

Alexakis, C., Patra, T., & Poshakwale, S. (2010). Predictability of stock returns using financial statement information: Evidence on semi-strong efficiency of emerging Greek stock market. *Applied Financial Economics*, *20*(16), 1321–1326. doi:10.1080/09603107.2010.482517

Ali, W. (2020). Online and remote learning in higher education institutes: A necessity in light of COVID-19 pandemic. *Higher Education*, *10*(3), 16–25.

Allakhverdieva, L., & Gabzalilova, V. (2007). Migration and Labor Market. In Z. M. Zayonchkovskaya (Ed.), *Methodology and Study Methods Migration Processes* (pp. 294–315). Center for Migration Studies.

Alliance for Patriont of Georgia. (2020). *Our Program*. Retrieved November 11, 2020, from http://patriots.ge/ka/program

Alperovich, V. (2002). *Social Gerontology*. Rostov State University Journal.

Al-Senaidi, S., Lin, L., & Poirot, J. (2009). Barriers to adopting technology for teaching and learning in Oman. *Computers & Education*, *53*(3), 575–590. doi:10.1016/j.compedu.2009.03.015

Al-tawfiq, J. A., Zumla, A., & Memish, Z. A. (2014). ScienceDirect Travel implications of emerging coronaviruses : SARS and MERS-CoV. *Travel Medicine and Infectious Disease*, *12*(5), 422–428. doi:10.1016/j.tmaid.2014.06.007 PMID:25047726

Altbach, P., & de Wit, H. (2020, April 4). Post pandemic outlook for HE is bleakest for the poorest. *University World News*. Retrieved from https://www.universityworldnews.com/post.php?story=20200402152914362

Álvarez-Ossa, M. (2016). La subjetividad e intersubjetividad: un camino en la comprensión de lo cultural [Subjectivity and intersubjectivity: a path to understand culture]. *Revista Linhas. Florianópolis, 17*(34), 323-336. https://dx.doi.org/doi:10.5965/1984723817342016323

Amankwah-amoah, J. (2020). Note : Mayday, Mayday, Mayday! Responding to environmental shocks : Insights on global airlines' responses to COVID-19. *Transportation Research Part E, Logistics and Transportation Review*, *143*(September), 1–9. doi:10.1016/j.tre.2020.102098 PMID:33013185

Ammar, A., Trabelsi, K., Brach, M., Chtourou, H., Boukhris, O., Masmoudi, L., ... Ahmed, M. (2020). Effects of home confinement on mental health and lifestyle behaviours during the COVID-19 outbreak: Insight from the" ECLB-COVID19" multi countries survey. *Biology of Sport*, *38*(1), 9–21. doi:10.5114/biolsport.2020.96857 PMID:33795912

Anischenko, L. (2020). Vivchennya okremikh aspects in the injection of EPIDEMIS COVID-19 on the psychosomatic manifestation of the inhabitants of the pivnich regions of Ukraine. *Preview of the covid-19 pandemic: distant psychological awareness*.

Anisimov, V. (2003). *Molecular and Physiological Mechanisms of Aging*. Journal Nauka.

Anthony Fauci's security is stepped up as doctor and face of U.S. coronavirus response receives threats. (2020). *The Washington Post*. Retrieved from https://www.washingtonpost.com/politics/anthony-faucis-security-is-stepped-up-as-doctor-and-face-of-us-coronavirus-response-receives-threats/2020/04/01/ff861a16-744d-11ea-85cb-8670579b863d_story.html

Anthony Fauci's security is stepped up as doctor and face of U.S. coronavirus response receives threats. (2020, April 2). *The Washington Post*. Retrieved from https://www.washingtonpost.com/politics/anthony-faucis-security-is-stepped-up-as-doctor-and-face-of-us-coronavirus-response-receives-threats/2020/04/01/ff861a16-744d-11ea-85cb-8670579b863d_story.html

Anwaar, M. (2016). Impact of firms' performance on stock returns (evidence from listed companies on FTSE-100 Index London, UK). *Global Journal of Management and Business Research: D Accounting and Auditing*, *16*(1), 1–9.

Ardévol-Abreu, A. (2015). Framing o teoría del encuadre en comunicación. Orígenes, desarrollo y panorama actual en España [Framing theory in communication research. Origins, development and current situation in Spain]. *Revista Latina de Comunicación Social*, *70*, 423–430. doi:10.4185/RLCS-2015-1053

Argan, M., Sevil, G., & Yalama, A. (2014). The effect of the word-of-mouth communication on stock holdings and trades: Empirical evidence from an emerging market. *Journal of Behavioral Finance*, *15*(2), 89–98. doi:10.1080/15427560.2014.914029

Arora, A. K., & Srinivasan, R. (2020). Impact of pandemic COVID-19 on the teaching-learning process: A study of higher education teachers. *Prabandhan: Indian Journal of Management*, *13*(4), 43–56. doi:10.17010/pijom/2020/v13i4/151825

Aruguete, N., & Koziner, N. S. (2014). La cobertura mediática del "7D" en la prensa argentina. Aplicación de encuadres noticiosos genéricos a los principales diarios nacionales [The media coverage of "7d" in the argentine press. application of generic news frames to major national newspapers]. *Anuario Electrónico de Estudios en Comunicación Social. Disertaciones*, *7*(1), 129–165.

Ashraf, B. N. (2020). Stock markets' reaction to COVID-19: Cases or fatalities? *Research in International Business and Finance*, *54*, 101249. doi:10.1016/j.ribaf.2020.101249

Asimov, I. (1971). *Isaac Asimov's Treasury of Humor*. Houghton Mifflin Company.

Aslan, S. (2016). Türkiye'de sosyal sermaye bileşenlerinden güven hakkında bir değerlendirme. *C.Ü. İktisadi ve İdari Bilimler Dergisi, 17*(2), 181-204.

Assunção Flores, M., & Gago, M. (2020). Teacher education in times of COVID-19 pandemic in Portugal: National, institutional, and pedagogical responses. *Journal of Education for Teaching*, *46*(4), 1–10. doi:10.1080/02607476.2020.1799709

Austin, Z., & Gregory, P. (2020). Resilience in the time of pandemic: The experience of community pharmacists during COVID-19. *Research in Social & Administrative Pharmacy*. Advance online publication. doi:10.1016/j.sapharm.2020.05.027 PMID:32499160

Azevedo, J.P., Hasan, A., Goldemberg, D., Iqbal, S.A., & Geven, K. (2020). *Simulating the potential impacts of covid-19 school closures on schooling and learning outcomes: a set of global estimates*. Academic Press.

Azevedo, A., & Shane, M. J. (2019). A new training program in developing cultural intelligence can also improve innovative work behavior and resilience: A longitudinal pilot study of graduate students and professional employees. *International Journal of Management Education*, *17*(3), 100303. doi:10.1016/j.ijme.2019.05.004

Azim, M. T., Fan, L., Uddin, M. A., Jilani, M. M. A. K., & Begum, S. (2019). Linking transformational leadership with employees' engagement in the creative process. *Management Research Review*, *42*(7), 837–858. doi:10.1108/MRR-08-2018-0286

Bajaj, S. G. (2017). The Use of Twitter during the 2014 Indian General Elections. Framing, Agenda-Setting, and the Personalization of Politics. *Asian Survey, 57*(2), 249-270. Retrieved from https://bit.ly/34HoeYW

Balcı, Ş., & Bekiroğlu, O. (2014). Medyanın kritik ve süreğen dönemeci: Üniversite öğrencilerinin gözünden medya haberlerinin güvenilirliği. *Selçuk İletişim*, *8*(2), 192–217.

Bao, W. (2020). COVID-19 and online teaching in higher education: A case study of Peking University. *Human Behavior and Emerging Technologies*, *2*(2), 113–115. doi:10.1002/hbe2.191 PMID:32510042

Bargain, O., & Ulugbek, A. (2020). Trust and Compliance to Public Health Policies in Times of COVID-19. *IZA Discussion Papers*, *192*(13205), 1–21. doi:10.1016/j.jpubeco.2020.104316 PMID:33162621

Bartik, A. W., Bertrand, M., Cullen, Z., Glaeser, E. L., Luca, M., & Stanton, C. (2020). The impact of COVID-19 on small business outcomes and expectations. *Proceedings of the National Academy of Sciences of the United States of America*, *117*(30), 17656–17666. doi:10.1073/pnas.2006991117 PMID:32651281

Basco, R., & Ghaleb, F. (2020). *Ownership Concentration in the Listed Firms in the Gulf Corporation Council: implications for corporate governance, Statistical Report.* Family Business in the Arab World (FBAW). Accessed from https://familyfirmblog.files.wordpress.com/2020/09/ownership-concentration-report.pdf

Basher, S. A., Haug, A. A., & Sadorsky, P. (2012). Oil prices, exchange rates and emerging stock markets. *Energy Economics*, *34*(1), 227–240. doi:10.1016/j.eneco.2011.10.005

Bashir, S. (2020, September 12). The Impact Of Covid-19: How Pakistani Workers Are Living With The New Reality. *Dawn News*. Retrieved from https://www.dawn.com/news/1560876

Batrancea, L. M., Batrancea, I., & Moscviciov, A. (2009c). *Evolution of global financial crisis*. Industrial Revolutions, from the Globalization and Post-globalization Perspective, Vol. IV: Banking, Accounting and Financial Systems from the 21t Century Perspective. *Lucian Blaga University of Sibiu, 16th International Conference – IECS 2009*, 36–41.

Batrancea, I., Moscviciov, A., Sabau, C., & Batrancea, L. M. (2013). Banking crisis: Causes, characteristics and solutions. *Proceedings of the DIEM, 2013*, 16–29.

Batrancea, L. M., Batrancea, I., & Moscviciov, A. (2009d). The roots of the world financial crisis. *Annals of the Faculty of Economics*, *3*(1), 57–62.

Batrancea, L., Batrancea, I., & Moscviciov, A. (2009a). The analysis of the entity's liquidity-A means of evaluating cash flow. *Journal of International Finance and Economics*, *9*(1), 92–98.

Batrancea, L., Batrancea, I., & Moscviciov, A. (2009b). Treasury flow analysis in Romanian companies. *International Journal of Business Research*, *9*(1), 57–62.

Batrancea, L., & Nichita, A. (2015). Which is the best government? Colligating tax compliance and citizens' insights regarding authorities' actions. *Transylvanian Review of Administrative Sciences*, *11*(44), 5–22.

Batrancea, L., Nichita, A., Batrancea, I., & Gaban, L. (2018). The strength of the relationship between shadow economy and corruption: Evidence from a worldwide country-sample. *Social Indicators Research*, *138*(3), 1119–1143. doi:10.100711205-017-1696-z

Batrancea, L., Nichita, R. A., & Batrancea, I. (2012). Tax non-compliance behavior in the light of tax law complexity and the relationship between authorities and taxpayers. *Scientific Annals of the "Alexandru Ioan Cuza". University of Iasi Economic Sciences*, *59*(1), 97–106.

Bauer, L. B., Bloch, D., & Merkert, R. (2020). Ultra Long-Haul: An emerging business model accelerated by COVID-19. *Journal of Air Transport Management*, *89*(August), 101901. doi:10.1016/j.jairtraman.2020.101901 PMID:32839647

Bayramova, Y., & Gasimov, Ch. (2012). Features of bioelectrical activity of brain in long-lived in Astana district. Azerbaijan Academy of Ascience, Collection of Scientific Papers of Institute of Physiology named after Garayev, A. and Society of Physiologists.

Beheraa, R. K., Gunasekaran, A., & Guptac, S. (2020). Personalized digital marketing recommender engine. *Journal of Retailing and Consumer Services*, *53*, 101799. Advance online publication. doi:10.1016/j.jretconser.2019.03.026

Belch, G. (1975) Belief system and differential role of the self-concept. *Advertising and Consumer Research,* (5), 320-325. http://acrwebsite.org/volumes/9443/volumes/v05/NA-05

Beldad, A., de Jong, M., & Steehouder, M. (2010). How shall I trust the faceless and the intangible? A literature review on the antecedents of online trust. *Computers in Human Behavior*, *26*(5), 857–869. doi:10.1016/j.chb.2010.03.013

Belhadi, A., Kamble, S., Jabbour, C. J. C., Gunasekaran, A., Ndubisi, N. O., & Venkatesh, M. (2020). Manufacturing and service supply chain resilience to the COVID-19 outbreak: Lessons learned from the automobile and airline industries. *Technological Forecasting and Social Change*, *120447*(November). doi:10.1016/j.techfore.2020.120447 PMID:33518818

Benlagha, N. (2020). Stock market dependence in crisis periods: Evidence from oil price shocks and the Qatar blockade. *Research in International Business and Finance*, *54*, 101285. Advance online publication. doi:10.1016/j.ribaf.2020.101285

Bennett, E. M., Swenson, J. D., & Wilkinson, J. S. (1992). Is the Medium the Message? An Experimental Test With Morbid News. *The Journalism Quarterly*, *69*(4), 921–928. doi:10.1177/107769909206900411

Bennett, W. L. (2016). *News: The politics of illusion*. University of Chicago Prcss.

Benoit, W. (2013). Content Analysis in Political Communication. In E. P. Bucy & L. Holbert (Eds.), *Sourcebook for Political Communication Research Methods, Measures, and Analytical Techniques* (pp. 268–279). Routledge.

Berdyashev, G. (2003). *Ecological and Genetic Factors of Aging and Longevity*. Journal Nauka.

Berge, Z. L., & Mrozowski, S. E. (1999). *Barriers to Online Teaching in Elementary, Secondary, and Teacher Education*. UMBC Faculty Collection. doi:10.21432/T2P59B

Berná-Sicilia, C., Pérez-Díaz, P. L., & Arroyas-Langa, E. (2013). La construcción del relato sobre la "Ley Wert": un análisis de los encuadres interpretativos del debate en Twitter [The "Wert Law" narrative construction: an analysis of the interpretive frames of the debate on Twitter]. In *Redes sociales y lo 2.0 y 3.0*. Visión Libros.

Berrone, P., Cruz, C., & Gomez-Mejia, L. R. (2012). Socioemotional wealth in family firms: Theoretical dimensions, assessment approaches, and agenda for future research. *Family Business Review*, *25*(3), 258–279. doi:10.1177/0894486511435355

Berthoud, R., & Blekesaune, M. (2007). *Persistent Employment Disadvantage*. The University of Essex.

Bhuiyan, E. M., & Chowdhury, M. (2020). Macroeconomic variables and stock market indices: Asymmetric dynamics in the US and Canada. *The Quarterly Review of Economics and Finance*, *77*, 62–74. doi:10.1016/j.qref.2019.10.005

Bickel, J. (2009). Faculty resilience and career development: Strategies for strengthening academic medicine. In T. R. Cole, T. J. Goodrich, & E. R. Gritz (Eds.), *Faculty Health in Academic Medicine: Physicians, Scientists, and the Pressures of Success* (pp. 83–92). Humana Press. doi:10.1007/978-1-60327-451-7_7

Bidwell, P. (1939). *The Invisible Tariff: A Study of the Control of Imports into the Inited States*. New York: Council on Foreign Relations.

Bikhchandani, S., & Sharma, S. (2000). *Herd behavior in financial markets: A review*. IMF Working Paper WP/00/48.

Bilge, N. (2020). *Whatsapp'ta yönlendirilen mesajlar yüzde 70 azaldı*. Digital Report. Retrieved November 2020, from, https://digitalreport.com.tr/whatsappta-yonlendirilen-mesajlar-yuzde-70-azaldi-teknoloji-13594/

Bilgiç, A., & Akyüz, S. S. (2020). Türkiye'de Covid-19 Pandemisi Döneminde Sağlık Bakanı Fahrettin Koca'nın Sosyal Medya Kullanımı: Twitter Paylaşımları İçerik Analizi. *Gaziantep University Journal of Social Sciences, 19*,231-243.

Bils, M., & Klenow, P. J. (2000). Does schooling cause growth? *The American Economic Review*, *90*(5), 1160–1183. doi:10.1257/aer.90.5.1160

Biron, M., De Cieri, H., Fulmer, I., & Lin, C. H. (2019, May). (Veronica), Mayrhofer, W., Nyfoudi, M., … Sun, J. M. (James). (2020). Structuring for innovative responses to human resource challenges: A skunk works approach. *Human Resource Management Review*, *100768*. Advance online publication. doi:10.1016/j.hrmr.2020.100768

Biryukov, I. (2019). Sports spirituality as a subject of theological and philosophical consideration. *Servis+, 4*. Retrieved from: https://cyberleninka.ru/article/n/sportivnaya-duhovnost-kak-predmet-teologo-filosofskogo-rassmotreniya

Biryukov, I. (2020). *Spirituality. Tradition. Education. Sacred meanings of bodily practices*. EPD AGPU.

Biryukov, I. (2020). *Sports spirituality concept*. EPD ASPU.

Boorstein, M. (2020). *Prominent Virginia pastor who said 'God is larger than this dreaded virus' dies of covid-19*. Retrieved July 17, 2020, from Washington Post: https://www.washingtonpost.com/religion/2020/04/13/virginia-pastor-church-dies-coronavirus/

Bossche, P. (2005). *The Law and Policy of the World Trade Organization*. Cambridge University Press. doi:10.1017/CBO9781139165143

Boulianne, S. (2009). Does internet use affect engagement? A meta-analysis of research. *Political Communication*, *26*(2), 193–211. https://dx.doi.org/10.1080/

Bouza, F. (2007). La telenovelización de la política (del nacionalcatolicismo al mirón comunitario). In J. Almaraz & J. Carabaña (Eds.), *Lo que hacen los sociólogos, libro-homenaje a Carlos Moya* [Policy's telenovelization (from national-Catholicism to community voyeur)] (pp. 363–373). Centro de Investigaciones Sociológicas.

Bozkurt, Y., Zeybek, Z., & Aşkın, R. (2020). Covid-19 Pandemisi: Psikolojik etkileri ve terapötik müdahalcler. İstanbul Ticaret Üniversitesi Sosyal Bilimler Dergisi, Bahar,304-318.

Bozkurt, A., & Sharma, R. C. (2020). Emergency remote teaching in a time of global crisis due to CoronaVirus pandemic. *Asian Journal of Distance Education*, *15*(1), i–vi.

Brammer, S., Brooks, C., & Pavelin, S. (2006). Corporate social performance and stock returns: UK evidence from disaggregate measures. *Financial Management*, *35*(3), 97–116. doi:10.1111/j.1755-053X.2006.tb00149.x

Brennen, J. S., Simon, F., Howard, P. N., & Nielsen, R. N. (2020). *Types, Sources, and Claims of COVID-19 Misinformation*. Reuters Institute Report, Factsheet, April 2020.

Brizek, M. G., Frash, R. E., McLeod, B. M., & Patience, M. O. (2020). Independent restaurant operator perspectives in the wake of the COVID-19 pandemic. *International Journal of Hospitality Management*, *93*, 102766. doi:10.1016/j.ijhm.2020.102766 PMID:33230361

Brom, C., Lukavský, J., Greger, D., Hannemann, T., Straková, J., & Švaříček, R. (2020, July). Mandatory home education during the covid-19 lockdown in the czech republic: A rapid survey of 1st-9th graders' parents. *Frontiers in Education*, *5*, 103. doi:10.3389/feduc.2020.00103

Brown, K. (2019). How Your Company's Culture Can Adapt to an Ever-Changing World. *Harvard Business Review*. https://hbr.org/sponsored/2019/10/how-your-companys-culture-can-adapt-to-an-ever-changing-world

Brown, P., Chua, A., & Mitchell, A. (2002). The influence of cultural factors on price clustering: Evidence from Asia-Pacific stock markets. *Pacific-Basin Finance Journal*, *10*(3), 307–332. doi:10.1016/S0927-538X(02)00049-5

Buabeng-Andoh, C. (2012). Factors influencing teachers adoption and integration of information and communication technology into teaching: a review of the literature. *International Journal of Education and Development Using ICT*, *8*(1).

Bucci & Alberto. (2019). *Human Capital and Economic Growth: The Impact of health, Education and Demographic Change*. Palgrave Macmillan. Retrieved from: https://www.amazon.com/Human-Capital-Economic-Growth Demographic/dp/3030215989

Bunker, D. (2020). Who do you trust? The digital destruction of shared situational awareness and the COVID-19 infodemic. *International Journal of Information Management*, *55*, 102201. doi:10.1016/j.ijinfomgt.2020.102201 PMID:32836649

Butrrbaugh, K., & Fulton, R. (2007). *The WTO Primer: Tracing Trade's Visible Hand through Case Studies*. Palgrave Macmillan. doi:10.1057/9780230610309

Butz, D., & Slautina, I. (2020). Formation of a student's personality during a pandemic. Pedagogical sciences: Questions of theory and practice, 170-172.

Büyükafşar, M. (2019). *Haber ve doğruluk ilişkisi: "Yalan haber" ve haber doğrulama pratikleri. Yayınlanmamış doktora tezi*. Marmara Üniversitesi Sosyal Bilimler Enstitüsü.

Bykhovets, K., Kogan-Lerner, L. (2020). The COVID-19 pandemic as a multifactorial traumatic situation. *Social and Economic Psychology*, *2*(18), 291-308.

Byrne, B. M. (2013). *Structural equation modelling with AMOS: Basic concepts, applications, and programming*. Routledge.

Cacciatore, M., Scheufele, D., & Iyengar, S. (2015). The End of Framing as we Know it … and the Future of Media Effects. *Mass Communication & Society*, *19*(1), 7–23. doi:10.1080/15205436.2015.1068811/

Cagle, J. A. B. (1996). Natural disasters, insurer stock prices, and market discrimination: The case of Hurricane Hugo. *Journal of Insurance Issues*, *19*(1), 53–68.

Campbell, D., & Frei, F. (2010). Cost structure, customer profitability, and retention implications of self-service distribution channels: Evidence from customer behavior in an online banking channel. *Management Science*, *56*(1), 4–24. doi:10.1287/mnsc.1090.1066

Cañás, M. (2020). *La evidencia en tiempos de coronavirus (COVID-19)* [Evidence in times of coronavirus (COVID-19)]. Retrieved from http://evidencia.org.ar/index.php/Evidencia/article/view/4285/1851

Cappella, J. N., Joseph, N., Jamieson, K. H., & Hall, K. (1997). *Spiral of cynicism: The press and the public good.* Oxford University Press on Demand.

Carr, I. (2010). *International Trade Law.* Routledge.

Carver, C. S., Scheier, M. F., & Weintraub, J. K. (1989). Assessing coping strategies: A theoretically based approach. *Journal of Personality and Social Psychology*, *56*(2), 267–283. doi:10.1037/0022-3514.56.2.267 PMID:2926629

Casado-Gutiérrez, F. (2015). *Antiperiodistas. Confesiones de las agresiones mediáticas contra Venezuela* [Anti-journalists. Confessions of the media attacks against Venezuela]. Akal.

Casado-Gutiérrez, F., & Sánchez-Figuera, R. (2017). *La comunicación en tiempos de la Revolución Ciudadana: hablan los periodistas* [Communication in times of the Citizen Revolution: journalists talk]. Ciespal.

Cassidy, E., Reynolds, F., Naylor, S., & De Souza, L. (2011). Using interpretative phenomenological analysis to inform physiotherapy practice: An introduction with reference to the lived experience of cerebellar ataxia. *Physiotherapy Theory and Practice*, *27*(4), 263–277. doi:10.3109/09593985.2010.488278 PMID:20795878

Cepoi, C. O. (2020). Asymmetric dependence between stock market returns and news during COVID19 financial turmoil. *Finance Research Letters*, *36*, 101658. doi:10.1016/j.frl.2020.101658 PMID:32837370

Chakraborty, I., & Maity, P. (2020). Covid-19 Outbreak: Migration, effects on Society, Global Environment and Prevention. *The Science of Total Environment*. totenv.2020138882 doi:10.1016/J.Sci

Chang, B. H., Meo, M. S., Syed, Q. R., & Abro, Z. (2019). Dynamic analysis of the relationship between stock prices and macroeconomic variables: An empirical study of Pakistan stock exchange. *South Asian Journal of Business Studies*, *8*(3), 229–245. doi:10.1108/SAJBS-06-2018-0062

Chang, C. L., McAleer, M., & Wang, Y. A. (2020). Herding behavior in energy stock markets during the global financial crisis, SARS and ongoing COVID-19. *Renewable & Sustainable Energy Reviews*, *134*, 110349. Advance online publication. doi:10.1016/j.rser.2020.110349

Chang, K.-C., Hsu, C.-L., Chen, M.-C., & Kuo, N.-T. (2017). How a branded website creates customer purchase intentions. *Total Quality Management & Business Excellence*, *30*(3-4), 422–446. doi:10.1080/14783363.2017.1308819

Charmaz, K. (2006). *Constructing grounded theory: A practical guide through qualitative analysis*. Sage.

Charnovitz, S. (1987). The Influence of International Labor Standards on the World Trading System: An Historical Overview. *International Labor Review, 126*(5).

Chaudhary, N. S., Phoolka, S., Sengar, R., & Pande, S. (2019). Whistleblowing in Indian higher education sector: A qualitative study. *International Journal of Learning and Change*, *11*(2), 145–168. doi:10.1504/IJLC.2019.101662

Cheng, D. (2013). The development of the service industry in the modern economy: Mechanisms and implications for China. *China Finance and Economic Review*, *1*(1), 3. doi:10.1186/2196-5633-1-3

Chen, N.-F., Roll, R., & Ross, S. A. (1986). Economic forces and the stock market. *The Journal of Business*, *59*(3), 383–403. doi:10.1086/296344

Chen, R. J. (2010). Investigating models for preservice teachers' use of technology to support student-centered learning. *Computers & Education*, *55*(1), 32–42. doi:10.1016/j.compedu.2009.11.015

Chen, Z. F., & Cheng, Y. (2019). Consumer response to fake news about brands on social media: The effects of self-efficacy, media trust, and persuasion knowledge on brand trust. *Journal of Product and Brand Management*, *29*(2), 188–198. doi:10.1108/JPBM-12-2018-2145

Chew, C., & Eysenbach, G. (2010). Pandemics in the age of Twitter: Content analysis of Tweets during the 2009 H1N1 outbreak. *PLoS One*, *5*(11). Advance online publication. doi:10.1371/journal.pone.0014118

Chkhenkeli, M. (2020). *We Overcome Challenges.* Retrieved November, 05, 2020, from http://mes.gov.ge/content.php?lang=geo&id=10320

Choi, T. M. (2020). Innovative "Bring-Service-Near-Your-Home" operations under Corona-Virus (COVID-19/SARS-CoV-2) outbreak: Can logistics become the Messiah? *Transportation Research Part E, Logistics and Transportation Review*, *140*(March), 101961. doi:10.1016/j.tre.2020.101961 PMID:32346356

Chong, D., & Druckman, J.N. (2007). Framing theory. *Annual Review of Political Science, 10*, 103-126. . doi:10.1146/annurev.polisci.10.072805.103054

Christie, W. G., & Huang, R. D. (1995). Following the pied piper: Do individual returns herd around the market? *Financial Analysts Journal*, *51*(4), 31–37. doi:10.2469/faj.v51.n4.1918

Christopher, M. (2000). The agile supply chain: Competing in volatile markets. *Industrial Marketing Management*, *29*(1), 37–44. doi:10.1016/S0019-8501(99)00110-8

Chung, E., Subramaniam, G., & Dass, L. C. (2020). Online learning readiness among university students in Malaysia amidst COVID-19. *Asian Journal of University Education*, *16*(2), 46–58. doi:10.24191/ajue.v16i2.10294

Cifuentes-Faura, J. (2020). Infodemics during COVID-19: Resources and recommendations to combat it. *Online Information Review*. Advance online publication. doi:10.1108/OIR-08-2020-0352

Clement, J. (2019). *Twitter: number of monthly active users 2010-2019.* Statista. Retrieved from https://www.statista.com/statistics/282087/number-of-monthly-active-twitter-users/#statisticContainer

Cleveland, S. (2002). Human Rights and International Trade: a Theory of Compatibility. *Journal of International Economic Law, 5*(1).

Cohen, D., & Alleyne, G. A. O. (2002). *Economic Growth and Poverty Reduction.* World Health Organization. Retrieved from https://apps.who.int/iris/bitstream/handle/10665/42492/9241590092.pdf;jsessionid=0C522FB211DB2AB686E2CE5FEF9F9CE5?sequence=1

Cohen, J. (1977). *Statistical Power Analysis for the Behavioral Sciences.* Academic Press.

Cömlekçi, M., & Başol, O. (2019). Sosyal medya haberlerine güven ve kullanıcı teyit alışkanlıkları üzerine bir inceleme. *Galatasaray İletişim Dergisi*, (30), 55–77.

Converse, P. E. (1964). The nature of belief sys-tems in mass publics. In D. E. Apter (Ed.), *Ideology and Dis-content* (pp. 206–261). Free.

Conway, J. (2020, September 10). *Impact of the coronavirus pandemic on the global FMCG market - Statistics & Facts.* https://www.statista.com/topics/6248/covid-19-impact-on-the-fmcg-market-worldwide/

Covid-19 and Children. (2020). *UNICEF.* Retrieved from: https://data.unicef.org/topic/covid-19-and-children/

COVID-19 Coronavirus Pandemic. (2020).https://www.worldometers.info/coronavirus/?

COVID-19 Dashboard by the Center for Systems Science and Engineering. (2020). https://coronavirus.jhu.edu/map.html

Covid-19 School Closure Around the World will hit Girls Hardest. (2020). *UNESCO.* Retrieved from: https://enunescoorh/news/covid-school-closure-around-world-hit-gilrs–hardest

Cox, N., Ganong, P., Noel, P., Vavra, J., Wong, A., Farrell, D., & Greig, F. (2020). *Initial Impacts of the Pandemic on Consumer Behavior: Evidence from Linked Income, Spending, and Savings Data.* University of Chicago, Becker Friedman Institute for Economics Working Paper No. 2020-82. doi:10.2139srn.3633008

Cultural-historical activity psychology in extreme situation: the pandemic challenge. (2020). *Chelovek, 4,* 7-40.

Curley, A., Dichter, A., Krishnan, V., Riedel, R., & Saxon, S. (2020). *Coronavirus: Airlines brace for severe turbulence.* McKinsey. Retrieved from https://www.mckinsey.com/industries/travel-logistics-and-transport-infrastructure/our-insights/coronavirus-airlines-brace-for-severe-turbulence

Czarniewski, S. (2014). Changes in consumer behavior in the market and the value of companies. *European Journal of Research and Reflection in Management Sciences, 2*(2), 61–68.

D'Angelo, P. (2002). News framing as a multiparadigmatic research program: A response to Entman. *Journal of Communication, 52,* 870–888. doi:10.1111/j.1460-2466.2002.tb02578.x

Dahlgren, P. (2018). Media, knowledge and trust: The deepening epistemic crisis of democracy. *Javnost: The Public, 25*(1-2), 20–27. doi:10.1080/13183222.2018.1418819

Dain, K., & Pappadopulos, E. (2020). *Opinion: Depression, anxiety, insomnia — health workers, and the side effects of COVID-19.* Retrieved September 22, 2020, from https://www.devex.com/news/opinion-depression-anxiety-insomnia-health-workers-and-the-side-effects-of-covid-19-97607

Darling-Hammond, L., Flook, L., Cook-Harvey, C., Barron, B., & Osher, D. (2020). Implications for educational practice of the science of learning and development. *Applied Developmental Science, 24*(2), 97–140. doi:10.1080/10888691.2018.1537791

Das, A. K., Jilani, M. M. A. K., Uddin, M. S., Uddin, M. A., & Ghosh, A. K. (2021). Fighting ahead: Adoption of social distancing in COVID-19 outbreak through the lens of theory of planned behavior. *Journal of Human Behavior in the Social Environment,* 1–21. Advance online publication. doi:10.1080/10911359.2020.1833804

Das, L., & Raut, R. (2014). Impact of changes in Service Sector in India in shaping the future of Business & Society. *Procedia Economics and Finance, 11,* 795–803. doi:10.1016/S2212-5671(14)00243-3

Dauda, R. O. S. (2013). Does female education promote economic performance? Evidence from Nigeria. *International Journal of Economics and Finance, 5*(1), 201–209.

Davis, M. (2021). 3 Franklin Roosevelt and the Challenges of the Democratic Majority. In *Politics as Usual* (pp. 37-49). Cornell University Press. doi:10.1515/9781501757419-005

Davitashvili, L., & Tandiashvili, N. (2018). *Action Program. Third National Environmental Action Program of Georgia 2017-2021*. United Nations Development Program.

Dawson, D. L., & Golijani-Moghaddam, N. (2020). COVID-19: Psychological flexibility, coping, mental health, and wellbeing in the UK during the pandemic. *Journal of Contextual Behavioral Science*, *17*, 126–134. doi:10.1016/j.jcbs.2020.07.010 PMID:32834970

De Vreese, C. (2005). News framing: Theory and typology. *News Framing: Theory and Typology*, 13(1), 51-62.

De Vreese, C.H. (2005). News framing: Theory and typology. *Information Design Journal & Document Design, 13*(1), 51-62.

De Vreese, C. H., Peter, J., & Semetko, H. A. (2001). Framing politics at the launch of the euro: A crossnational comparative study of frames in the news. *Political Communication*, *18*, 107–122. doi:10.1080/105846001750322934

Delgado-López, E., & Martín-Martín, A. (2020). *La viralidad de la ciencia defectuosa: el contagioso impacto mediático de un preprint en bioRxiv sobre el coronavirus y sus efectos en la comunicación científica* [The virality of flawed science: the contagious media impact of a coronavirus-related preprint on bioRxiv and its effects on scientific communication]. doi:10.13140/RG.2.2.12666.44485

DeLone, W., & McLean, E. (2003). The model of information systems success: A ten-year update. *Journal of Management Information Systems*, *19*(4), 9–30. doi:10.1080/07421222.2003.11045748

Demirer, R., Kutan, A. M., & Chen, C.-D. (2010). Do investors herd in emerging stock markets?: Evidence from the Taiwanese market. *Journal of Economic Behavior & Organization*, *76*(2), 283–295. doi:10.1016/j.jebo.2010.06.013

Dewi, W. A. F. (2020). Dampak Covid-19 terhadap implementasi pembelajaran daring di Sekolah Dasar. *Edukatif: Jurnal Ilmu Pendidikan*, *2*(1), 55–61. doi:10.31004/edukatif.v2i1.89

Dhaoui, A. (2015). What does matter in economy today: When human psychology drives financial markets. *The Arab Economics and Business Journal*, *10*(1), 39–47. doi:10.1016/j.aebj.2014.12.002

Dijk, J. V., & Alinead, D. (2020). Social Media and Trust in Scientific Expertise: Debating the Covid-19 Pandemic in The Netherlands. *Social Media + Society*, *6*(4), 1–11.

Dipboye, R. L., & Foster, J. B. (2002). Multi-level theorizing about perceptions of organizational politics. *Research in Multi-Level Issues*, *1*(1), 255–270. doi:10.1016/S1475-9144(02)01035-4

Dircom. (2020, April 21). El papel de los medios de comunicación ante la pandemia del COVID-19 [Media role during the COVID-19 pandemic]. *Asociación de Directivos de Comunicación*. Retrieved from http://www.dircom.org/actualidad-dircom/item/10381-el-papel-de-los-medios-de-comunicacion-ante-la-pandemia-del-covid-19

Dochy, F. (2006). A guide for writing scholarly articles or reviews for the Educational Research Review. *Educational Research Review*, *4*(1-2), 1–21.

Doğan, M., & Düzel, M. (2020). Covid-19 özelinde korku-kaygı düzeyleri. *Turkish Studies*, *15*(4), 739–752.

Dönmez, İ., & Gürbüz, S. (2020). Üniversite Öğrencilerinin Covid-19 Virüsü Hakkında Bilişsel Yapılarının Belirlenmesi. *MANAS Sosyal Araştırmalar Dergisi*, *9*(4), 2159–2172. doi:10.33206/mjss.763029

Doremalen, V. (2020). Aerosol and Surface Atability of SARS-CoV-2 as Compared with SARS-CoV-1. *English Journal of Medicine*.

Drissel, D. (2015). Reframing the Taliban insurgency in Afghanistan: new communication and mobilization strategies for the Twitter generation. *Behavioral Sciences of Terrorism and Political Aggression*, 97-128. https://doi.org/ doi:10.1080/19434472.2014.986496

Durodiй, B. (2020). *Handling Uncertainty and Ambiguity in the COVID-19 Pandemic*. https://psycnet.apa.org/fulltext/2020-37336-001.html

Dwivedi, Y. K., Hughes, D. L., Coombs, C., Constantiou, I., Duan, Y., Edwards, J. S., Gupta, B., Lal, B., Misra, S., Prashant, P., Raman, R., Rana, N. P., Sharma, S. K., & Upadhyay, N. (2020). Impact of COVID-19 pandemic on information management research and practice: Transforming education, work and life. *International Journal of Information Management*, *102211*, 102211. Advance online publication. doi:10.1016/j.ijinfomgt.2020.102211

Edirisuriya, P., Gunasekarage, A., & Dempsey, M. (2015). Bank diversification, performance and stock market response: Evidence from listed public banks in South Asian countries. *Journal of Asian Economics*, *41*, 69–85. doi:10.1016/j.asieco.2015.09.003

Education: Giving Every Child the Right to Education. (n.d.). *UNICEF*. Retrieved from: https://www.unice.org/pakistan/education

Edwards, A. (Ed.). (2012). *New Technology and Education*. Continuum Publishing Corporation.

El Comercio [@elcomerciocom]. (2020, March 23). *Home* [Twitter page]. Twitter. Retrieved from https://t.co/RmwgTPYxlR

El Comercio. (2020a, March 12). *Presidente declara emergencia sanitaria en el Ecuador por el coronavirus covid-19* [President declares a health emergency in Ecuador due to the covid-19 coronavirus]. Retrieved from El Comercio: https://www.elcomercio.com/video/ecuador-medidas-emergencia-coronavirus-covid.html

El Espectador [@elespectador]. (2020, April 6). *Home* [Twitter page]. Twitter. Retrieved from https://t.co/2M7njbCqrM

El País [@el_pais]. (2020, April 2). *Home* [Twitter page]. Twitter. Retrieved from https://t.co/SLfMLlxTzt

El Periódico. (2020, April 2). *Muertos en las calles: la imagen que resume la crisis del coronavirus en Ecuador* [Death on the streets: the image that sums up the coronavirus crisis in Ecuador]. Retrieved from El Periódico: https://www.elperiodico.com/es/internacional/20200402/muertos-en-las-calles-la-imagen-que-resume-la-crisis-sanitaria-en-ecuador-7914370

El Rayess, M., Chebl, C., Mhanna, J., & Hage, R.-M. (2018). Fake news judgement: The case of undergraduate students at Notre Dame University-Louaize, Lebanon. *RSR. Reference Services Review*, *46*(1), 146–149. doi:10.1108/RSR-07-2017-0027

El Universo [@eluniversocom]. (2020a, March 31). *Home* [Twitter page]. Twitter. Retrieved from https://t.co/FI6zHPVbqd

El Universo [@eluniversocom]. (2020b, April 6). *Home* [Twitter page]. Twitter. Retrieved from https://t.co/fJzLwvWM0e

El Universo. (2020a, April 11). *En 5 provincias del Ecuador el coronavirus se expande de forma comunitaria* [In 5 provinces of Ecuador the coronavirus spreads at community level]. Retrieved from El Universo: https://www.eluniverso.com/noticias/2020/04/12/nota/7811271/5-provincias-coronavirus-se-expande-forma-comunitaria

El Universo. (2020b, April 23). *Casos de coronavirus en Ecuador, 23 de abril 11h00: 22 160 contagiados, 560 fallecidos* [Cases of coronavirus in Ecuador, April 23th 11h00: 22,160 infected, 560 deaths]. Retrieved from El Universo: https://www.eluniverso.com/noticias/2020/04/23/nota/7821111/casos-coronavirus-ecuador-23-abril-11h00-10-contagiados-5

Elearn. (2018). *Business Environment: Management Extra*. Elsevier.

Ellepola, A., & Rajapakse, R. P. (2020). *Foreseeable psychological impact of COVID 19 in Sri Lanka*. https://www.researchgate.net/publication/340522703

Emmungil, L., & Akleylek, S. (2008). Technical requirements for online education support. *Proceedings of 8th International Educational Technology Conference*, 607-609.

Entman, R. (1993). Framing: Toward clarification of a fractured paradigm. *Journal of Communication, 43*, 51–58.

Entman, R. (2004). *Proyection of Power. Framing News, public opinión and U.S. Foreign Policy*. University of Chicago Press.

Eom, T., Han, H., & Song, H. (2020). Discovering the perceived attributes of CBT destination travelers in South Korea: A mixed method approach. *Tourism Management, 77*, 104013. doi:10.1016/j.tourman.2019.104013

Erdoğan, U. (2008). *Tüketici davranış modellerinin tüketici pazarları için tasarlanan ürünlere etkisi* [Master's Thesis, Marmara University]. Marmara University Thesis Collection. https://katalog.marmara.edu.tr/eyayin/tez/T0061510.pdf

Etzkowitz, H., & Leydesdorff, L. (2000). The dynamics of innovation: From National Systems and "Mode 2" to a Triple Helix of university–industry–government relations. *Research Policy, 29*(2), 109–123. doi:10.1016/S0048-7333(99)00055-4

European Union Agency for Fundamental Rights. (2020). *Fundamental Rights Report*. Luxemburg: Office of European Union.

Ewing-Chow, M., & Slade, M. (2016). *International Trade and Food Security*. Edvard Edgar Publishing. doi:10.4337/9781785361890

Falcone, R., Coli, E., Felletti, S., Sapienza, A., Castelfranchi, C., & Paglieri, F. (2020). All We Need Is Trust: How the COVID-19 Outbreak Reconfigured Trust in Italian Public Institutions. *Frontiers in Psychology, 11*(11), 1–17. doi:10.3389/fpsyg.2020.561747 PMID:33132966

Fan, L., Mahmood, M., & Uddin, M. A. (2019). Supportive Chinese supervisor, innovative international students: A social exchange theory perspective. *Asia Pacific Education Review, 20*(1), 101–115. doi:10.100712564-018-9572-3

Farmer, L. B., & Byrd, R. (2015). Genderism in the LGBTQQIA community: An interpretative phenomenological analysis. *Journal of LGBT Issues in Counseling, 9*(4), 288–310. doi:10.1080/15538605.2015.1103679

Feezel, J. D. (2018). The evolution of communication pedagogy. *Journal of Communication Pedagogy, 1*(1), 3–8. doi:10.31446/JCP.2018.02

Fehr, A., & Perlman, S. (2015). Coronaviruses: An Overview of their Replication and Pathogenesis. *Methods in Molecular Biology (Clifton, N.J.), 1282*, 1–23. doi:10.1007/978-1-4939-2438-7_1 PMID:25720466

Ferdig, R. E., Baumgartner, E., Hartshorne, R., Kaplan-Rakowski, R., & Mouza, C. (2020). Teaching, technology, and teacher education during the covid-19 pandemic: Stories from the field. Waynesville, NC: Association for the Advancement of Computing in Education (AACE).

Fergusson, L., van der Laan, L., Shallies, B., & Baird, M. (2020). Work, resilience and sustainable futures: The approach of work-based research to problems and their solutions. *Journal of Work-Applied Management, 12*(1), 22–41. doi:10.1108/JWAM-11-2019-0036

Fernazdez-Rovira, C., Valdés, J. A., Molleví, G., & Nicolas-Sans, R. (2021). The digital transformation of business. Towards the datafication of the relationship with customers. *Technological Forecasting and Social Change, 162*(20339), 120339. Advance online publication. doi:10.1016/j.techfore.2020.120339

Festl, R. (2020). Social media literacy & adolescent social online behavior in Germany. *Journal of Children and Media*, 1–23. doi:10.1080/17482798.2020.1770110

Field, F. (2010). *The Foundation Years: preventing poor children becoming poor adults*. The report of the Independent Review on Poverty and Life Chances.

Field, A. (2018). *Discovering Statistics Using IBM SPSS Statistics* (5th ed.). Sage Publications Inc.

Fimberg, K., & Sousa, S. (2020). The Impact of Website Design on Users' Trust Perceptions. In Advances in Creativity, Innovation, Entrepreneurship and Communication of Design. AHFE 2020. Advances in Intelligent Systems and Computing. doi:10.1007/978-3-030-51626-0_34

Fligauf, E., & Ayres, A. (2020). Coronavirus in South Asia, March 24, 2020: Outbreak in Pakistan and India on Lock Down. *Council on Foreign Relations.* Retrieved from: https://www.cfr.org/blog/coronavirus-south-asia-march-24-2020-outbreak-pakistan-and-india-lockdown

Flostrand, A., Pitt, L., & Kietzmann, J. (2019). Fake news and brand management: A Delphi study of impact, vulnerability and mitigation. *Journal of Product and Brand Management, 29*(2), 246–254. doi:10.1108/JPBM-12-2018-2156

Foça, M. A. (2019). *Sözlük: Yanlış bilginin en yaygın yedi türü.* Retrieved May 2020, from https://teyit.org/sozluk-yanlis-bilginin-en-yaygin-7-turu

Folkman, S., & Lazarus, R. S. (1980). An analysis of coping in a middle-aged community sample. *Journal of Health and Social Behavior, 21*(3), 219–239. doi:10.2307/2136617 PMID:7410799

Fornell, C., & Larcker, D. F. (1981). Evaluating structural equation models with unobservable variables and measurement error. *JMR, Journal of Marketing Research, 18*(1), 39–50. doi:10.1177/002224378101800104

Foye, J. (2013). *The relationship between financial ratios and stock market returns in the East European members of the EU* (Doctoral dissertation). University of Ljubljana, Faculty of Economics.

Franzosi, R., Doyle, S., McClelland, L.E., Rankin, C.P., & Vicari, S. (2013). Quantitative narrative analysis software options compared: PC-ACE and CAQDAS (ATLAS. ti, MAXqda, and NVivo). *Quality & Quantity: International Journal of Methodology, 47*(6), 3219-3247. doi:10.100711135-012-9714-3

Freeman, R. E. (1999). Divergent stakeholder theory. *Academy of Management Review, 24*(2), 233–236.

Fullana, M. A., Hidalgo-Mazzei, D., Vieta, E., & Radua, J. (2020). Coping behaviors associated with decreased anxiety and depressive symptoms during the COVID-19 pandemic and lockdown. *Journal of Affective Disorders, 275*, 80–81. doi:10.1016/j.jad.2020.06.027 PMID:32658829

Fuller, C. M., Simmering, M. J., Atinc, G., Atinc, Y., & Babin, B. J. (2016). Common methods variance detection in business research. *Journal of Business Research, 69*(8), 3192–3198. doi:10.1016/j.jbusres.2015.12.008

Funke, D. (2020). *Fact-checking a Facebook conspiracy about Bill Gates, Dr. Fauci and COVID-19.* Politifact. Retrieved April 2020, from https://www.politifact.com/article/2020/apr/14/fact-checking-facebook-conspiracy-about-bill-gates/

Furió, D., & Pardo, Á. (2014). Partisan politics theory and stock market performance: Evidence from Spain. *Revista Española de Financiación y Contabilidad, 41*(155), 371–392. doi:10.1080/02102412.2012.10779729

Füss, R., & Bechtel, M. M. (2008). Partisan politics and stock market performance: The effect of expected government partisanship on stock returns in the 2002 German federal election. *Public Choice, 135*(3-4), 131–150. doi:10.100711127-007-9250-1

Gafurov, I., Ibragimov, G., Kalimullin, A. & Alishev, T. (2020). Transforming Higher Education During a Pandemic: Pain Points. *Higher Education in Russia, 10,* 101-112.

García-Romero, E., Ruiz-San Román, J. A., & Serrano-Oceja, J. F. (2018). *Google es noticia. Transformación de los marcos informativos sobre Google en la prensa española. Google is in the news. Transformation of the news frames about Google in the Spanish press.* Academic Microsoft. Retrieved from https://academic.microsoft.com/paper/2810706329/related

Garcia-Vega, S., Zeng, X. J., & Keane, J. (2020). Stock returns prediction using kernel adaptive filtering within a stock market interdependence approach. *Expert Systems with Applications*, *160*, 113668. Advance online publication. doi:10.1016/j.eswa.2020.113668

Garfin, D. R. (2020). Technology as a coping tool during the COVID-19 pandemic: Implications and recommendations. *Stress and Health*, *34*(4), 555–559. doi:10.1002mi.2975 PMID:32762116

Gathergood, J., & Guttman-Kenney, B. (2020, October 17). *The English Patient: Evaluating Local Lockdowns Using Real-Time COVID-19 & Consumption Data.* https://arxiv.org/abs/2010.04129

Gavidia, M. (2020). *How Has COVID-19 Affected Mental Health, Severity of Stress Among Employees?* Retrieved December 11, 2020, from https://www.ajmc.com/view/how-has-covid19-affected-mental-health-severity-of-stress-among-employees

Gedefaw Birhanu, A., & Wezel, F. C. (2020). The competitive advantage of affiliation with business groups in the political environment: Evidence from the Arab Spring. *Strategic Organization*. Advance online publication. doi:10.1177/1476127020952174

Gelfert, A. (2018). Fake News: A Definition. *Informal Logic*, *38*(1), 84–117. doi:10.22329/il.v38i1.5068

Gellweiler, C., & Krishnamurthi, L. (2020). Editorial: How Digital Innovators Achieve Customer Value. *Journal of Theoretical and Applied Electronic Commerce Research*, *15*(1), 0. Advance online publication. doi:10.4067/S0718-18762020000100101

Geo News. (2020). *Pakistan's exports increase by 7.2% amid the COVID-19 pandemic*. Retrieved December 5, 2020, from https://www.geo.tv/latest/321785-pakistans-exports-increase-by-72-amid-covid-19-pandemic

Georgian Labor Party. (2020). *Election Program.* Retrieved November 18, 2020, from Labour. ge: http://www.labor.ge/ka/chvens-shesakheb/programa

Gill, M. J. (2015). A phenomenology of feeling: Examining the experience of emotion in organizations. *New Ways of Studying Emotions in Organizations*, *11*, 29–50. doi:10.1108/S1746-979120150000011003

Giménez, J. (2020). *Coronavirus y desinformación: la otra pandemia.* Retrieved from http://sedici.unlp.edu.ar/bitstream/handle/10915/94170/Documento_completo.pdf?sequence=1&isAllowed=y

Giovannella, C., Passarelli, M., & Persico, D. (2020). Measuring the effect of the Covid-19 pandemic on the Italian learning Ecosystems at the steady-state: A school teachers' perspective. *Interaction Design and Architecture (s) Journal (IxD&A)*, (45).

Global Compact for Migration. (2018). *Global Compact for Safe, Orderly, and Regular Migration.* Global Compact for Migration.

Globaltechmagazine. (2020). *Geleceğin en önemli 5 perakende teknolojisi neler olacak*. https://www.globaltechmagazine.com/2020/10/30/gelecegin-en-onemli-5-perakende-teknolojisi-neler-olacak/

Goddard, J., & Vallance, P. (2012). The civic university and the leadership of place. B A. O. In R. Capello (Ed.), *Universities, Cities and Regions: Loci for Knowledge and Innovation Creation (cmp* (pp. 43–63). Routledge.

Gómez-Mejía, L. R., Haynes, K. T., Núñez-Nickel, M., Jacobson, K. J., & Moyano-Fuentes, J. (2007). Socioemotional wealth and business risks in family-controlled firms: Evidence from Spanish olive oil mills. *Administrative Science Quarterly*, *52*(1), 106–137. doi:10.2189/asqu.52.1.106

Goodell, J. W. (2020). COVID-19 and finance: Agendas for future research. *Finance Research Letters*, *101512*. Advance online publication. doi:10.1016/j.frl.2020.101512 PMID:32562472

Gouveia, L. B., Perun, M., & Daradkeh, Y. I. (2020). Dijital Transformation And Customer Services: The Banking Revolution. *International Journal of Open Information Technologies*, *8*(7), 124–128.

Government of Georgia. (2020). *Decision About the Mandatory Quaranteen.* Retrieved November, 11, 2020, from http://gov.ge/indexphp?lang_id=GEO&sec_id=541&info_id=78080

Government of Georgia. (2020). *Georgia-COVID-19 Rapid Response Project. Natural and Social Impact Management Framework.* Retrieved November, 11, 2020, from https://www/moh.gov.ge/uploads/files/2021/06.01.21.pdf

Government of Georgia. (2020). *Prevention of Coronavirus Spread in Georgia.* Retrieved November, 15, 2020, from https://stopcov.ge

Grabe, M. E., Zhou, S., & Barnett, B. (2001). Explicating sensationalism in television news: Content and the bells and whistles of form. *Journal of Broadcasting & Electronic Media*, *45*(4), 635–655. doi:10.120715506878jobem4504_6

Graham, B. (2003). *Intelligent investor: The definitive book of value investing*. HarperCollins Publishers.

Gratz, E., & Looney, L. (2020). Faculty resistance to change: an examination of motivators and barriers to teaching online in higher education. *International Journal of Online Pedagogy and Course Design, 10*(1), 1-14.

Greenberg, N., Docherty, M., Gnanapragasam, S., & Wessely, S. (2020). Managing mental health challenges faced by healthcare workers during a covid-19 pandemic. *BMJ (Clinical Research Ed.)*, 368. doi:10.1136/bmj.m1211 PMID:32217624

Grieco, D. (2017). Innovation and stock market performance: A model with ambiguity-averse agents. *Journal of Evolutionary Economics*, *28*(2), 287–303. doi:10.100700191-017-0537-1

Griffith, J., Najand, M., & Shen, J. (2020). Emotions in the stock market. *Journal of Behavioral Finance*, *21*(1), 42–56. Advance online publication. doi:10.1080/15427560.2019.1588275

Grzymala-Busse, A. (2011). Time will tell? temporality and the analysis of causal mechanisms and processes. *Comparative Political Studies*, *44*(9), 1267–1297. doi:10.1177/0010414010390653

Guadagno, L. (2020). *Migrants and the COVID-19 Pandemic: An Initial Analysis*. International Oganization for Migration.

Güler, B. (2020). *İran'da sahte içkiden ölenlerin sayısı 800'e yaklaştı.* Retrieved June 22, 2020 from Anadolu Ajansı: https://www.aa.com.tr/tr/dunya/iranda-sahte-ickiden-olenlerin-sayisi-800e-yaklasti/1822904

Gunay, S., & Kurtulmuş, B. E. (2020). Covid-19 Social Distancing and the Us Service Sector: What Do We Learn? *Research in International Business and Finance*, *101361*. Advance online publication. doi:10.1016/j.ribaf.2020.101361

Gupta, K. P., & Chaudhary, N. S. (2017). Prioritizing the factors influencing whistle blowing intentions of teachers in higher education institutes in India. *Procedia Computer Science*, *122*, 25–32. doi:10.1016/j.procs.2017.11.337

Gupta, N., & Sharma, V. (2018). Relationship between leader member exchange (LMX), high-involvement HRP and employee resilience on extra-role performance: Mediating role of employee engagement. *Journal of Indian Business Research*, *10*(2), 126–150. doi:10.1108/JIBR-09-2017-0147

Gursoy, D., Ouyang, Z., Nunkoo, R., & Wei, W. (2019). Residents' impact perceptions of and attitudes towards tourism development: A meta-analysis. *Journal of Hospitality Marketing & Management, 28*(3), 306–333. doi:10.1080/19368623.2018.1516589

Güz, N., & Yanık, H. (2020). Toplumsal sorumluluk yaklaşımı ve güven bağlamında medya ve kamuoyu araştırmaları arasındaki ilişki. *Gümüşhane Üniversitesi İletişim Fakültesi Dergisi, 8*(1), 298–336.

Haber, J., & Mills, M. (2008). Perceptions of barriers concerning effective online teaching and policies: Florida community college faculty. *Community College Journal of Research and Practice, 32*(4-6), 266–283. doi:10.1080/10668920701884505

Hair, J. F., Hult, G. T. M., Ringle, C. M., Sarstedt, M., & Thiele, K. O. (2017). Mirror, mirror on the wall: A comparative evaluation of composite-based structural equation modeling methods. *Journal of the Academy of Marketing Science, 45*(5), 616–632. doi:10.100711747-017-0517-x

Hair, J. F. Jr, Hult, G. T. M., Ringle, C. M., & Sarstedt, M. (2017). *A Primer on Partial Least Squares Structural Equation Modeling (PLS-SEM)*. Sage Publication.

Hair, J. F. Jr, Hult, G. T., Ringle, C. M., & Sarstedt, M. (2014). *A primer on partial least squares structural equation modeling (PLS-SEM)*. SAGE Publications, Inc.

Hamdy, N., & Gomaa, E. H. (2012). Framing the Egyptian uprising in Arabic language newspapers and social media. *Journal of Communication, 62*(2), 195–211. doi:10.1111/j.1460-2466.2012.01637.x

Hannan, M. T., & Freeman, J. (1977). The population ecology of organisations. *American Journal of Sociology, 82*(5), 929–964. doi:10.1086/226424

Hanusheck, E. A., & Wobmann, L. (2010). Education and economic growth. *International Encyclopedia of Education, 2*. doi:10.2139srn.960379

Hasani, Z. (2013). Factors affecting the level of female employment in Iran. *Technical Journal of Engineering and Applied Sciences, 3*(14), 1424–1431.

Hasan, N., & Bao, Y. (2020). Impact of "e-Learning crack-up" perception on psychological distress among college students during COVID-19 pandemic: A mediating role of "fear of academic year loss". *Children and Youth Services Review, 118*, 105355. doi:10.1016/j.childyouth.2020.105355 PMID:32834276

Hashem, T. (2020). Examining the Influence of COVID 19 Pandemic in Changing Customers' Orientation towards E-Shopping. *Modern Applied Science, 14*(5), 59–76. doi:10.5539/mas.v14n8p59

Hassan, S. A., & Rafaz, N. (2017). The role of female education in economic growth of Pakistan: A time series analysis from 1990-2016. *International Journal of Innovation and Economic Development, 3*(5), 83-93.

Hazirullah. (2020, May 1). Covid-19 and Education: Unequal learning loss. *The Nation*. Retrieved from: http//nation.com.pk/01-May-2020/Covid-19-and-education-unequal-learning-loss

Hernaez, F. (2020, October 15). *World Luxury Tracking: Between new constraints & new expectations*. https://www.ipsos.com/en/world-luxury-tracking-2020

Higher Education in the World. Towards a Socially Responsible University: Balancing the Global with the Local. (2017). https://unesdoc.unesco.org/ark:/48223/pf0000248150

Hirsch, J. A., & Kass, D. A. (2012). *The little book of stock market cycles*. John Wiley & Sons.

Hirschman, A. O. (1989). Having opinions—One ofthe elements of well-being. *The American Economic Review, 79*(2), 75–79. doi:10.2307/1827734

Hirshleifer, D., Hsu, P.-H., & Li, D. M. (2020). Innovative originality, profitability, and stock returns. *Review of Financial Studies*, *31*(7), 2553–2605. doi:10.1093/rfs/hhx101

Hirshleifer, D., & Shumway, T. (2003). Good day sunshine: Stock returns and the weather. *The Journal of Finance*, *58*(3), 1009–1032. doi:10.1111/1540-6261.00556

Holsti, O. R. (1969). *Content analysis for the social sciences and humanities*. AddisonWesley.

Hondroyiannis, G., & Papapetrou, E. (2001). Macroeconomic influences on the stock market. *Journal of Economics and Finance*, *25*(1), 33–49. doi:10.1007/BF02759685

Hong, Y., & Li, Y. (2020). House price and the stock market prices dynamics: Evidence from China using a wavelet approach. *Applied Economics Letters*, *27*(12), 971–976. doi:10.1080/13504851.2019.1649359

Horvath, M. A. H., & Massey, K. (2018). The impact of witnessing other people's trauma: The resilience and coping strategies of members of the Faculty of Forensic and Legal Medicine. *Journal of Forensic and Legal Medicine*, *55*, 99–104. doi:10.1016/j.jflm.2018.02.012 PMID:29486433

How physical activity improves mood and health. (2020). *Armavirskij sobesednik*.

Hsing, Y. (2011). Impacts of macroeconomic variables on the stock market in Bulgaria and policy implications. *East-West Journal of Economics and Business*, *16*(2), 41–53.

Hua, Z., Yangb, Z., & Lib, Q. (2020). *Infodemiological study on COVID-19 epidemic and COVID-19 infodemic*. doi:10.20944/preprints202002.0380.v3

Huang, C., Wang, Y., Li, X., Ren, L., Zhao, J., & Hu, Y. (2020). Clinical features of patients infected with 2019 novel coronavirus in Wuhan, China. *Lancet*, *395*, 497–506.

Huang, C., Yang, X., Yang, X. G., & Sheng, H. (2014). An empirical study of the effect of investor sentiment on returns of different industries. *Mathematical Problems in Engineering*, *545723*, 1–11. Advance online publication. doi:10.1155/2014/545723

Huang, R. H., Liu, D. J., Tlili, A., Yang, J. F., & Wang, H. H. (2020). *Handbook on facilitating flexible learning during educational disruption: The Chinese experience in maintaining undisrupted learning in COVID-19 outbreak*. Smart Learning Institute of Beijing Normal University.

Huang, R. H., Liu, D. J., Tlili, A., Yang, J. F., & Wang, H. H. (2020). *Handbook on Facilitating Flexible Learning during Educational Disruption: The Chinese Experience in Maintaining Undisrupted Learning in COVID-19 Outbreak*. Smart Learning Institute of Beijing Normal University.

Huber, B. (2016). The Role of Universities in Society. B C. Y. In N. C. Liu (Ed.), *Matching Visibility and Performance. Global Perspectives on Higher Education* (pp. 92–138). Sense Publishers. doi:10.1007/978-94-6300-773-3_5

Hu, P. J., Chau, P. Y., Sheng, O. R. L., & Tam, K. Y. (1999). Examining the technology acceptance model using physician acceptance of telemedicine technology. *Journal of Management Information Systems*, *16*(2), 91–112. doi:10.1080/07421222.1999.11518247

Husain, F., Qasim, M. A., & Sheikh, K. H. (2003). An analysis of public expenditure on education in Pakistan. *Pakistan Development Review*, *42*(4), 771–780.

Hutchinson, A. (2020). Facebook Launches New, Million-Dollar Grant Programs to Support Fact-Checkers and Local Newsrooms. *SocialMediaToday*. Retrieved April 2020, from https://www.socialmediatoday.com/news/facebook-launches-new-million-dollar-grant-programs-to-support-fact-checke/574325/

Hu, Z., Yang, Z., & Li, Q. (2020). *Infodemiological study on COVID-19 epidemic and COVID-19 infodemic*. Research Square.

Idoyaga, N., Valencia, J. F., Gil-de Montes, L., & Ortiz, G. (2012). Efectos del Framing y representaciones sociales de epidemias sanitarias: El Caso de la Gripe A. *Escritos de Psicologia, 5*(3), 31–42. doi:10.5231/psy.writ.2012.0211

Igartua, J. (2006). *Métodos cuantitativos de investigación en comunicación* [Quantitative research methods in Communication]. Editorial Bosch S.A.

Ignatieff, M. (2001). *Human Rights as Politics and Idolatry*. Princeton University Press. doi:10.1515/9781400842841

Ignatovich, O. (2020). Psychological prophylaxis of panika and zasobi podolannya. In V. Ribalka (Ed.), *Psychological Prevention and Hygiene in the Anti-COVID-19 Pandemic*. Institute of Pedagogical Education and Education for Young People Ivan Zyazyun of the National Academy of Sciences of Ukraine.

Iivari, N., Sharma, S., & Ventä-Olkkonen, L. (2020). Digital transformation of everyday life–How COVID-19 pandemic transformed the basic education of the young generation and why information management research should care? *International Journal of Information Management, 55*, 102–183. doi:10.1016/j.ijinfomgt.2020.102183 PMID:32836640

Ikeda, K., & Marshall, A. (2019). Strategies for competing in markets enabled by digital platforms. *Strategy and Leadership, 47*(1), 30–36. doi:10.1108/SL-10-2018-0097

Ikhalia, E., Serrano, A., Bell, D., & Louvieris, P. (2019). Online social network security awareness: Mass interpersonal persuasion using a Facebook app. *Information Technology & People, 32*(5), 1276–1300. doi:10.1108/ITP-06-2018-0278

IMF. (2020) https://www.imf.org/en/Publications/WEO/Issues/2020/04/14/weo-april-2020

Impact of COVID-19 on people's livelihoods, their health and our food systems. (2020.). Joint statement by ILO, FAO, IFAD, and WHO.

Infodemic. (2019). In *Meriam Webster dictionary*. Academic Press.

Information and analytical report on the results of the survey on the state of use of distance learning technologies in higher education institutions of Ukraine. (2020). State Service for the Quality of Education of Ukraine.

International Air Transport Association. (2020). *Airport Development Reference Manual*. Retrieved from https://www.iata.org/en/publications/store/airport-development-reference-manual/

International Labor Organisation. (2020). *ILO Standards and COVID-19*. Retrieved from Interantional Labour Organisation: https://socialprotection.org/discover/publications/ilo-standards-and0covid-19-coronavirus-key-provisions-international-labor

International Labor Organization. (2020). *How to Protect Workers Migrants in Conditions Pandemic COVID-19*. International Labor Organization.

Iontsev, V. (1999). *International Migration for Population: Theory and History of Studying*. Dialogue.

Ipsos. (2020, March). *Koronavirüs, Hane İçi Hızlı Tüketim Ürünleri Harcamalarına Nasıl Etki Ediyor?* https://www.ipsos.com/tr-tr/koronavirus-hane-ici-hizli-tuketim-urunleri-harcamalarina-nasil-etki-ediyor

Isaeva, N., Gruenewald, K., & Saunders, M. (2020). Trust theory and customer services research: Theoretical review and synthesis. *Service Industries Journal, 1*(33), 1031–1063. doi:10.1080/02642069.2020.1779225

Islamoglu, A. H., & Altunışık, R. (2010). *Tüketici Davranışları*. Beta Basım.

ISO 26000:2010 social responsibility. (2010). https://www.iso.org/standard/42546.html

Izumi, T., Sukhwani, V., Surjan, A., & Shaw, R. (2020). Managing and responding to pandemics in higher educational institutions: initial learning from COVID-19. *International Journal of Disaster Resilience in the Built Environment*. doi:10.1108/IJDRBE-06-2020-0054

Jackson, J. (1998). Global Economic and International Economic Law. *Journal of International Economic Law*.

Jacobides, M. G., & Reeves, M. (2020, October 1). Adapt Your Business to the New Reality. *Harvard Business Review Turkey*, *10*, 78–85.

Jarren, O. (2008). Media democracy. *The international encyclopedia of communication*. Retrieved from https://onlinelibrary.wiley.com/doi/abs/10.1002/9781405186407.wbiecm024

Jarus, O. (2020). *20 of the worst epidemics and pandemics in history*. Retrieved December 26, 2020, from https://www.livescience.com/worst-epidemics-and-pandemics-in-history.html

Jean, S. (2020). How the COVID-19 Pandemic is Reshaping the Trade Landscape and What to do about it. *Journal of Intereconomics*.

Jiang, Z., Kang, S. H., Cheong, C., & Yoon, S.-M. (2019). The effects of extreme weather conditions on Hong Kong and Shenzhen Stock Market Returns. *International Journal of Financial Studies*, *7*(4), 70. doi:10.3390/ijfs7040070

Jiménez-Pavón, D., Carbonell-Baeza, A., & Lavie, C. J. (2020). Physical exercise as a therapy to fight against the mental and physical consequences of COVID-19 quarantine: Special focus in older people. *Progress in Cardiovascular Diseases*, *63*(3), 386–388. doi:10.1016/j.pcad.2020.03.009 PMID:32220590

Jirásek, I. (2018). Religion and Spirituality in Sport. In *Oxford Research Encyclopedia of Psychology*. Retrieved from https://oxfordre.com/psychology/view/10.1093/acrefore/9780190236557.001.0001/acrefore-9780190236557-e-149

Johnson, K., Lee, I.-T., & Goldwasser, D. (2017). Ideological Phrase Indicators for Classification of Political Discourse Framing on Twitter. *Second Workshop on Natural Language Processing and Computational Social Science*, 90-99. doi: 10.18653 / v1 / W17-2913

Kalemci Tüzün, İ. (2007). Güven, Örgütsel Güven ve Örgütsel Güven Modelleri. *Karamanoğlu Mehmetbey Üniversitesi Sosyal ve Ekonomik Araştırmalar Dergisi*, (2), 93–118.

Karamova, N., Gasimov, Ch., Teymurova, N. (2018). Features of memory and excitement process in long-living persons. *European Journal of Technical and Natural Sciences*.

Karpinskaya, E. (2020). COVID-19: Effects for Higher Education. *Russian International Affairs Council: analytics and commentary*. Retrieved from https://russiancouncil.ru/analytics-and-comments/analytics/covid-19-effekty-dlya-vysshego-obrazovaniya/#short

Kaup, S., Jain, R., Shivalli, S., Pandey, S., & Kaup, S. (2020). Sustaining academics during COVID-19 pandemic: The role of remote teaching-learning. *Indian Journal of Ophthalmology*, *68*(6), 1220. doi:10.4103/ijo.IJO_1241_20 PMID:32461490

Keelery, S. (2020). *India – estimated economic impact of COVID-19 by sector 2020*. Statista. Available at: www.statista.com/statistics/1107798/india-estimated-economic-impact-of-coronavirus-by-sector/

Keengwe, J., Onchwari, G., & Wachira, P. (2008). The use of computer tools to support meaningful learning. *AACE Journal*, *16*(1), 77–92.

Kenny, R. (2020). *How Can We Combat Post-Lockdown Anxiety?* Retrieved September 12, 2020, from https://www.thehrdirector.com/business-news/employee-engagement/one-simple-tip-from-mental-health-experts-to-boost-staff-wellbeing-and-combat-post-lockdown-workplace-anxiety/

Kenski, K., & Stroud, N. J. (2006). Connections between Internet use and political efficacy, knowledge, and participation. *Journal of Broadcasting & Electronic Media*, *50*(2), 173–192. doi:10.120715506878jobem5002_1

Keyes, R. (2019). *Hakikat Ötesi Çağ: Günümüz dünyasında yalancılık ve aldatma*. Deli Dolu.

Khan, M. N., & Zaman, S. (2012). Impact of macroeconomic variables on stock prices: Empirical evidence from Karachi Stock Exchange, Pakistan. In M. Zhu (Ed.), Business, economics, financial sciences, and management. Advances in intelligent and soft computing (pp. 227–233). Berlin: Springer. doi:10.1007/978-3-642-27966-9_32

Khan, A. G., Kamruzzaman, M., Rahman, M. N., Mahmood, M., & Uddin, M. A. (2021). Quality of life in the COVID-19 outbreak: Influence of psychological distress, government strategies, social distancing, and emotional recovery. *Heliyon*, *7*(3), e06407. Advance online publication. doi:10.1016/j.heliyon.2021.e06407 PMID:33688587

Kimberly, A. (2020, December 27). *Consumer Spending Statistics and Current Trends*. https://www.thebalance.com/consumer-spending-trends-and-current-statistics-3305916?utm_source=emailshare&utm_medium=social&utm_campaign=shareurlbuttons

Kim, D. J., Ferrin, D. L., & Rao, H. R. (2008). A Trust-Based Consumer Decision-Making Model in Electronic Commerce: The Role of Trust, Perceived Risk, and Their Antecedents. *Decision Support Systems*, *44*(2), 544–564. doi:10.1016/j.dss.2007.07.001

Kim, H.-Y., Kwon, O., & Oh, G. (2016). A causality between fund performance and stock market. *Physica A*, *443*, 439–450. doi:10.1016/j.physa.2015.08.041

Kim, J. H. (2019). Multicollinearity and misleading statistical results. *Korean Journal of Anesthesiology*, *72*(6), 558–569. doi:10.4097/kja.19087 PMID:31304696

Kim, M. J., Lee, C.-K., & Jung, T. (2020). Exploring Consumer Behavior in Virtual Reality Tourism Using an Extended Stimulus-Organism-Response Model. *Journal of Travel Research*, *59*(1), 69–89. doi:10.1177/0047287518818915

Kindström, D., Kowalkowski, C., & Sandberg, E. (2013). Enabling service innovation: A dynamic capabilities approach. *Journal of Business Research*, *66*(8), 1063–1073. doi:10.1016/j.jbusres.2012.03.003

King, A. A., & Baatartogtokh, B. (2015). How useful is the theory of disruptive innovation? *MIT Sloan Management Review*, *57*(1), 77.

Knüpfer, C., & Entman, R. (2018). Framing conflicts in digital and transnational media environments. *Media, War & Conflict*, 476–488. doi:10.1177/1750635218796381

Kominiak, T. (2019). *On Veterans Day: Understanding the Vital Role of Education in our Democracy*. Retrieved from: k12insight.com/trusted/veterans-day-scholls/

König, J., Jäger-Biela, D. J., & Glutsch, N. (2020). Adapting to online teaching during COVID-19 school closure: Teacher education and teacher competence effects among early career teachers in Germany. *European Journal of Teacher Education*, 1–15.

Kotler, P. (1965). Behavioral Models for Analyzing Buyers. *Journal of Marketing*, *29*(4), 37–45. doi:10.1177/002224296502900408

Kowalkowski, C., Gebauer, H., Kamp, B., & Parry, G. (2017). Servitization and deservitization: Overview, concepts, and definitions. *Industrial Marketing Management*, *60*, 4–10. doi:10.1016/j.indmarman.2016.12.007

Krainov, V., Maslenkova, E., & Chelidze, N. (2007). Impact of Migration on the Economy. In Z. M. Zayonchkovskaya (Ed.), *Methodology and Study Methods Migration Processes* (pp. 294–315). Center for Migration Studies.

Kreps, S., & Kriner, D. (2020). Model uncertainty, political contestation, and public trust in science: Evidence from the COVID-19 pandemic. *Science Advances*, *6*(43), 1–12. doi:10.1126ciadv.abd4563 PMID:32978142

Krueger, D., Uhlig, H., & Xie, T. (2020). *Macroeconomic dynamics and reallocation in an epidemic* (No. w27047). National Bureau of Economic Research. https://www.nber.org/papers/w27047.pdf

Krygman, P. (1979). Increasing Returns, Monopolistic Competition and International Trade. *Journal of International Economics*, *9*(4), 469–479. doi:10.1016/0022-1996(79)90017-5

Kuckartz, U. (2010). *Realizing mixed-methods approaches with MAXQDA*. Philipps-Universität.

Kumar, D. (2010). *Pros and cons of online education*. North Carolina State University.

Kumar, S., & Managi, S. (2020). Does Stringency of Lockdown Affect Air Quality? Evidence from Indian Cities. *Economics of Disasters and Climate Change*, *4*(3), 481–502. doi:10.100741885-020-00072-1 PMID:32838121

Kutter, J., Sporonken, P., Fraaij, R., Founchier, A., & Herfst, S. (2018). Transmission Route of Respiratory Visruses Among Humans. *Current Opinion in Virology*, *28*, 142–151. doi:10.1016/j.coviro.2018.01.001 PMID:29452994

Kwak, H., Lee, C., Park, H., & Moon, S. (2010). What is Twitter, a social network or a news media? *Proceedings of the 19th International Conference on World Wide Web - WWW '10*. doi:10.1145/1772690.1772751

Kwiek, M. (2003). The Social functions of the university in the context of the changing State. *Market Relations*, 2-31.

Kwon, H., Chadha, M., & Pellizzaro, K. (2017). Proximity and Terrorism News in Social Media: A Construal-Level Theoretical Approach to Networked Framing of Terrorism in Twitter. *Mass Communication & Society*, *26*, 1–26. doi:10.1080/15205436.2017.1369545

Kyimaz, H. (2001). The effects of stock market rumors on stock prices: Evidence from an emerging market. *Journal of Multinational Financial Management*, *11*(1), 105–115. doi:10.1016/S1042-444X(00)00045-1

La Hora [@lahoraecuador]. (2020a, April 10). *Home* [Twitter page]. Twitter. Retrieved from https://t.co/xOiDhd5l5w

La Hora [@lahoraecuador]. (2020b, April 14). *Home* [Twitter page]. Twitter. Retrieved from https://t.co/e2eAsSdIO0

La Hora [@lahoraecuador]. (2020c, April 5). *Home* [Twitter page]. Twitter. Retrieved from https://bit.ly/3erTxZX

La Hora [@lahoraecuador]. (2020d, April 27). *Home* [Twitter page]. Twitter. Retrieved from https://t.co/2EIbfH4yoi

La Nación [@LANACION]. 2020, April 15). *Home* [Twitter page]. Twitter. Retrieved from https://t.co/ndkDfqPwBq

Laato, S., Islam, A. K. M. N., Islam, M. N., & Whelan, E. (2020). What drives unverified information sharing and cyberchondria during the COVID-19 pandemic? *European Journal of Information Systems*, *29*(3), 288–305. doi:10.1080/0960085X.2020.1770632

Lai, C. C., Shih, T. P., Ko, W. C., Tang, H. J., & Hsueh, P. R. (2020). Severe acute respiratory syndrome coronavirus 2 (SARS-CoV-2) and coronavirus disease-2019 (COVID-19): The epidemic and the challenges. *International Journal of Antimicrobial Agents*, *55*(3), 105924. doi:10.1016/j.ijantimicag.2020.105924 PMID:32081636

Lai, J., Ma, S., Wang, Y., Cai, Z., Hu, J., Wei, N., Wu, J., Du, H., Chen, T., Li, R., Tan, H., Kang, L., Yao, L., Huang, M., Wang, H., Wang, G., Liu, Z., & Hu, S. (2020). Factors Associated With Mental Health Outcomes Among Health Care Workers Exposed to Coronavirus Disease 2019. *JAMA Network Open*, *3*(3), e203976. doi:10.1001/jamanetworkopen.2020.3976 PMID:32202646

Langille. (1997). Eight Ways to Think about International Labor Standards. *Journal of World Trade*.

Lantos, G. P. (2015). *Consumer behavior in action: Real-life applications for marketing managers*. Routledge. doi:10.4324/9781315705439

Lathifah, Z. K., Helmanto, F., & Maryani, N. (2020). The practice of effective classroom management in COVID-19 time. *International Journal of Advanced Science and Technology*, *29*(7), 3263–3271.

Lee, D., & Profeli, E. (2015). Youths' socialization to work and school within the family. *International Journal for Educational and Vocational Guidance*, *15*(2), 145–162. doi:10.100710775-015-9302-x PMID:26101556

Lee, Y.-R., Lee, J.-Y., Kim, J.-M., Shin, I.-S., Yoon, J.-S., & Kim, S.-W. (2019). A comparative study of burnout, stress, and resilience among emotional workers. *Psychiatry Investigation*, *16*(9), 686–694. doi:10.30773/pi.2019.07.10 PMID:31455062

Lehkonen, H., & Heimonen, K. (2015). Democracy, political risks and stock market performance. *Journal of International Money and Finance*, *59*, 77–99. doi:10.1016/j.jimonfin.2015.06.002

Letter of the Ministry of Education and Science /1/9-154 . (2020).

Leung, N., Chu, D. K. W., Shiu, E. Y. C., Chan, K.-H., McDevitt, J. J., Hau, B. J. P., Yen, H.-L., Li, Y., Ip, D. K. M., Peiris, J. S. M., Seto, W.-H., Leung, G. M., Milton, D. K., & Cowling, B. J. (2020). Respiratory Virus Shedding in Exhaled Breath and Efficacy of Face Masks. *Nature Medicine*, *26*(5), 676–680. doi:10.103841591-020-0843-2 PMID:32371934

Levy, G. (2007). The relationship of Parkinson disease with aging *(pp. 12-42)*. *Archives of Neurology*, *64*(9). doi:10.1001/archneur.64.9.1242 PMID:17846263

Liguori, E. W., & Pittz, T. G. (2020). Strategies for small business: Surviving and thriving in the era of COVID-19. *Journal of the International Council for Small Business.*, *1*(2), 106–110. doi:10.1080/26437015.2020.1779538

Limb, M. (2016). The world will lack 18 million health workers by 2030 without adequate investment, warns UN. *BMJ (Clinical Research Ed.)*, *1*, 1. https://www.who.int/hrh/com-heeg/bmj.i5169.full.pdf. doi:10.1136/bmj.i5169 PMID:27660102

Lin, S., & Le Pham, H. (2020). *Who's Playing the Blame Game? – An Analysis of Media Framing of China and COVID-19 in The New York Times*. Heidelberg Center for American Studies. Retrieved from https://hcagrads.hypotheses.org/2966

Lin, A. J., Li, E. Y., & Lee, S. Y. (2018). Dysfunctional customer behavior in cross-border e-commerce: A justice-affect-behavior model. *Journal of Electronic Commerce Research*, *19*(1), 36–54.

Lin, C.-H. (2012). The comovement between exchange rates and stock prices in the Asian emerging markets. *International Review of Economics & Finance*, *22*(1), 161–172. doi:10.1016/j.iref.2011.09.006

Lin, W. T., Tsai, S.-C., & Lung, P.-Y. (2013). Investors' herd behavior: Rational or irrational? *Asia-Pacific Journal of Financial Studies*, *42*(5), 755–776. doi:10.1111/ajfs.12030

Lipsitch, M., Phil, D., Swerdlow, D. L., & Finelli, L. (2020). Defining the Epidemiology of Covid-19— Studies Needed. *The New England Journal of Medicine*, *382*(13), 1194–1196. doi:10.1056/NEJMp2002125 PMID:32074416

Litvinova, S. (2011). *Age-related changes in the parameters of saccadic eye movements in healty condition and in Parkinson's disease*. Human Physiology.

Livingstone, S. (2014). Developing social media literacy: How children learn to interpret risky opportunities on social network sites. *Communications*, *39*(3), 283–303. doi:10.1515/commun-2014-0113

Lloyd, S. A., Byrne, M. M., & McCoy, T. S. (2012). Faculty-perceived barriers of online education. *Journal of Online Learning and Teaching*, *8*(1).

Lock, S. (2020a, October 20). Forecasted change in revenue from the travel and tourism industry due to the coronavirus (COVID-19) pandemic worldwide from 2019 to 2020. *Global change in travel and tourism revenue due to COVID-19 2019-2020*. https://www.statista.com/forecasts/1103426/covid-19-revenue-travel-tourism-industry-forecast

Lock, S. (2020b, November 30). *Year-over-year daily change in seated restaurant diners due to the coronavirus (COVID-19) pandemic worldwide from February 24 to November 28, 2020*. Daily year-on-year impact of COVID-19 on global restaurant dining Feb-Nov 2020. https://www.statista.com/statistics/1103928/coronavirus-restaurant-visitation-impact/

Lonska, J., & Mietule, I. (2015). The Impact of Human Capital Development on the Economic and Social Development of a Country: Empirical Study. *Environmental Technology*. Retrieved from: doi:10.17770/etr2015vol2.268

Lovejoy, K., Waters, R., & Saxton, G. (2012). Engaging stakeholders through Twitter: How nonprofit organizations are getting more out of 140 characters or less. *Public Relations Review*, *38*(2), 313–318. doi:10.1016/j.pubrev.2012.01.005

Luque, A. (2018). Corruption in the transnational textile industry: An exception or the rule? *Empresa y humanismo, 21*(2), 123-184.

Luque, A., Maniglio, F., Casado, F., & García-Guerrero, J. (2020). Transmedia Context and Twitter as Conditioning the Ecuadorian Government's Action. The Case of the "Guayaquil Emergency" during the COVID-19 Pandemic. *Trípodos*, *2*(47), 47–68.

Lynch, P. (2000). *One up on Wall Street: How to use what you already know to make money in the market*. Simon & Schuster.

Lyócsa, Š., Baumöhl, E., Výrost, T., & Molnár, P. (2020). Fear of the coronavirus and the stock markets. *Finance Research Letters*, *36*, 101735. doi:10.1016/j.frl.2020.101735 PMID:32868975

MacIntyre, P. D., Gregersen, T., & Mercer, S. (2020). Language teachers' coping strategies during the Covid-19 conversion to online teaching: Correlations with stress, wellbeing and negative emotions. *System*, *94*, 102352. doi:10.1016/j.system.2020.102352

Mackey, T. K., & Liang, B. A. (2012). Lessons from SARS and H1N1/A: Employing a WHO-WTO forum to promote optimal economic-public health pandemic response. *Journal of Public Health Policy*, *33*(1), 119–130. doi:10.1057/jphp.2011.51 PMID:22048060

MacKinnon, D. P., Lockwood, C. M., Hoffman, J. M., West, S. G., & Sheets, V. (2002). A comparison of methods to test mediation and other intervening variable effects. *Psychological Methods*, *7*(1), 83–104. doi:10.1037/1082-989X.7.1.83 PMID:11928892

Mahajan, S. (2020). *Technological, social, pedagogical issues must be resolved for online teaching* [Web log post]. Available at: https://indianexpress.com/article/opinion/columns/india-coronavirus-lockdown-online-education-learning-6383692/

Mahesh, S. (2020). *A need now but no replacement: teachers share concerns about online classes during COVID-19* [Web log post]. Available at: www.newindianexpress.com/education/2020/may/06/a-need-now-but-no-replacement-teachers-share-concerns-about-online-classes-during-covid-19-2139605.html

Mahmood, M., Uddin, M. A., & Luo, F. (2019). Influence of transformational leadership on employees' creative process engagement: A multi-level analysis. *Management Decision*, *57*(3), 741–764. doi:10.1108/MD-07-2017-0707

Malkiel, B. G. (2007). *A random walk down Wall Street: The time-tested strategy for successful investing* (9th ed.). W.W. Norton & Company.

Mamun, M. A., & Ullah, I. (2020). COVID-19 suicides in Pakistan, dying off not COVID-19 fear but poverty? –The forthcoming economic challenges for a developing country. *Brain, Behavior, and Immunity*. doi:10.1016/j.bbi.2020.05.028

Mandel, A., & Veetil, V. P. (2020). The economic cost of covid lockdowns: An out-of-equilibrium analysis. *Economics of Disasters and Climate Change*, *4*(3), 431–451. Advance online publication. doi:10.100741885-020-00066-z PMID:32838118

Manor, I., & Crilley, R. (2018). Visually framing the Gaza War of 2014: The Israel Ministry of Foreign Affairs on Twitter. *Media, War & Conflict*, *11*(4), 369–391. doi:10.1177/1750635218780564

Mariotti, S., Marzano, R., & Piscitello, L. (2020). The role of family firms' generational heterogeneity in the entry mode choice in foreign markets. *Journal of Business Research*. Advance online publication. doi:10.1016/j.jbusres.2020.10.064

Mariupol State University. (2019). http://en.mdu.in.ua/

Marshall, D. (2020). *Taking Care of your Mental Health in the Face of Uncertainty*. American Foundation of Suicide Prevention. Retrieved from https://www.easton.wednet.edu/docs/3-18-20-MentalHealthSupport.pdf

Martens, H., & Hobbs, R. (2015). How media literacy supports civic engagement in a digital age. *Atlantic Journal of Communication*, *23*(2), 120–137. doi:10.1080/15456870.2014.961636

Martín-Barato, A., López-Doblas, M., Luque-Martín, N., & March-Cerdá, J. C. (2020). *Fake news y bulos contra la seguridad y la salud durante la crisis del coronavirus* [Fake news and hoaxes against safety and health during the coronavirus crisis]. Escuela Andaluza de Salud Pública. Retrieved from https://bit.ly/2YNgUHf

Matinez-Garcia, I., Basco, R., Gomez-Anson, S., & Boubakri, N. (2020). Ownership concentration in the Gulf Cooperation Council. *International Journal of Emerging Markets*. doi:10.1108/IJOEM-03-2020-0290

Mattson, D. (2017). Different Indicators of Socioeconomic Status and their Relative Importance as Determinants of Health in Old Age. *International Journal for Equity in Health*. doi:10.118612939-017-0670-3

Maydeu-Olivares, A., & Lado, N. (2003). Market orientation and business economic performance. *International Journal of Service Industry Management*, *14*(3), 284-309.

Mbanga, C., Darrat, A. F., & Park, J. C. (2019). Investor sentiment and aggregate stock returns: The role of investor attention. *Review of Quantitative Finance and Accounting*, *53*(2), 397–428. doi:10.100711156-018-0753-2

McCambridge, J., Hawkins, B., & Holden, C. (2014). Vested interests in addiction research and policy. The challenge corporate lobbying poses to reducing society's alcohol problems: Insights from UK evidence on minimum unit pricing. *Addiction (Abingdon, England)*, *109*(2), 199–205. doi:10.1111/add.12380

McCombs, M. (2006). *Estableciendo la agenda. El impacto de los medios en la opinión pública y en el conocimiento* [Setting the agenda. The impact of the mass media on public opinion and knowledge]. Paidós.

McCombs, M. (2018). *Setting the agenda: Mass media and public opinion*. Maxwell McComs.

McCracken, G. (1988). *Culture and consumption: New approaches to the symbolic character of consumer goods and activities*. Indiana University Press.

McKinsey. (2020, October 26). Consumer sentiment and behavior continue to reflect the uncertainty of the COVID-19 crisis. *McKinsey & Company COVID-19 Consumer Pulse surveys, conducted globally September 18-30, 2020*. https://www.mckinsey.com/business-functions/marketing-and-sales/our-insights/a-global-view-of-how-consumer-behavior-is-changing-amid-covid-19

McQuillan, N., Wightman, C., Moore, C., McMahon-Beattie, U., & Farley, H. (2020). Developing resilient graduates to be future workplace leaders. *Higher Education, Skills and Work-Based Learning*. doi:10.1108/HESWBL-11-2019-0162

MHRD. (2020a). *Students to continue their learning by making full use of the available digital e-Learning platforms – Shri Ramesh Pokhriyal 'Nishank'*. Available at: https://pib.gov.in/PressReleasePage.aspx?PRID=1607521

MHRD. (2020b). *UGC guidelines on examinations and academic calendar for the universities in view of COVID-19 and subsequent lockdown.* **Error! Hyperlink reference not valid.**Available at: https://pib.gov.in/PressReleasePage.aspx?PRID=1619368

MHRD. (2020c). *National education policy 2020.* Available at: https://static.pib.gov.in/WriteReadData/userfiles/NEP_Final_English_0.pdf

Michalski, R. S. (1983). A Theory and Methodology of Inductive Learning. In R. S. Michalski, J. G. Carbonell, & T. M. Mitchell (Eds.), *Machine Learning. Symbolic Computation.* Springer., doi:10.1007/978-3-662-12405-5_

Microsoft Academic. (2020). *Unleash the Power of Semantic Search.* Retrieved from Microsoft Academic: https://bit.ly/2YOnm0H

Millán, A. (2020, April 2). *Coronavirus: ¿por qué Ecuador tiene el mayor número de contagios y muertos per cápita de covid-19 en Sudamérica?* [Coronavirus: why does Ecuador have the highest covid-19 rate of infections and deaths *per capita* in South America]. https://www.bbc.com/mundo/noticias-america-latina-52036460

Ministry of Environment and Natural Resources of Georgia. (2020). Third International Enviromental Action Program of Georgia (2017-2012). Tbilisi: Author.

Mishra, S. V. (2020). *COVID-19, online teaching, and deepening digital divide in India.* SocArXiv.

Mishra, P., Bhadauria, U. S., Dasar, P. L., Kumar, S., Lalani, A., Sarkar, P., ... Vyas, S. (2016). Knowledge, attitude and anxiety towards pandemic flu a potential bio weapon among health professionals in Indore City. *Przegląd Epidemiologiczny, 70*(1), 41–45, 125–127. PMID:27344473

Mishrif, A. (2018). *Economic Diversification in the Gulf Region* (Vol. 1). Palgrave Macmillan.

Mogaji, E. (2020). Financial vulnerability during a pandemic: Insights for coronavirus disease (COVID-19). *Mogaji. E (Norwalk, Conn.)*, 57–63.

Morrish, L. (2020). *The 2020 rabbit hole: Why conspiracy theories draw people in.* Ocak 2021 tarihinde First Draft: https://firstdraftnews.org/latest/rabbit-hole/adresindenalındı

Mosheva, M., Hertz-Palmor, N., Dorman Ilan, S., Matalon, N., Pessach, I. M., Afek, A., Ziv, A., Kreiss, Y., Gross, R., & Gothelf, D. (2020). Anxiety, pandemic-related stress and resilience among physicians during the COVID-19 pandemic. *Depression and Anxiety, 37*(10), 965–971. doi:10.1002/da.23085 PMID:32789945

Mosley, L., & Singer, D. A. (2008). Taking stock seriously: Equity-market performance, government policy, and financial globalization. *International Studies Quarterly, 52*(2), 405–425. doi:10.1111/j.1468-2478.2008.00507.x

Moustakas, C. (1994). *Phenomenological Research Methods.* Sage Publications. doi:10.4135/9781412995658

Mujahid, N., & uz Zafar, N. (2012). Economic growth-female labour force participation nexus: An empirical evidence for Pakistan. *Pakistan Development Review*, 565–585.

Mukherjee, S. (2020, October 26). *Adapting to pandemic-driven consumer behaviour changes.* https://www.research-world.com/adapting-to-pandemic-driven-consumer-behaviour-changes/

Munkh-Ulzii, B. J., McAleer, M., Moslehpour, M., & Wong, W.-K. (2018). Confucius and herding behavior in the stock markets in China and Taiwan. *Sustainability, 10*(12), 4413. doi:10.3390u10124413

Murgatroyd, S. (2020). COVID-19 and online learning: A SWOT analysis of users' perspectives on learning management system of University of Education, Winneba, Ghana. *International Journal of Learning. Teaching and Educational Research, 19*(9), 382–401.

Murthy, D. (2018). *Twitter*. Polity Press.

Mustafa, K. (2020, May 9). Impact of Covid-19 Pandemic: Pak GDP to contract by 1.6pc in Current Fiscal, Says economic Intelligence Unit. *The News*. Retrieved from: https://www.thenews.com.pk/print/656244-impact-of-covid-19-pandemic-pak-gdp-to-contract-by-1-6pc-in-current-fiscal-economist-intelligence-unit

Mustafa, N. (2020). Impact of the 2019–20 coronavirus pandemic on education. *International Journal of Health Preferences Research*, 1-12.

Nassirzadeh, F., Salehi, M., & Sarvhadi, R. (2015). The effect of financial indicators on trading volume of the listed companies on the Tehran Stock Exchange. *International Business Research, 8*(5), 176–194. doi:10.5539/ibr.v8n5p176

National Statistics of Georgia. (2020). *Population and Demography*. Retrieved November, 05, 2020, from https://www.geostat.ge/ka/modules/categories/316/mosakhleoba-da-demografia

NCOC. (2020). *SOPs*. Retrieved October 13, 2020, from https://ncoc.gov.pk/sop.php

Nemov, R. (2001). Psychology. Book 3. Moscow: Academic Press.

Neuendorf, K. A., & Kumar, A. (2016). Content Analysis. In G. Mazzoleni (Ed.), *The International Encyclopedia of Politi-cal Communication*. doi:10.1002/9781118541555.wbiepc065

Neuman, W. R., Just, M. R., & Crigler, A. N. (1992). *Common knowledge*. University of Chicago Press.

News Desk. (2020). *Unemployment in Pakistan to rise in FY21 even after combating COVID-19 successfully*. Retrieved from: https://mettisglobal.news/unemployment-in-pakistan-to-rise-in-fy21-even-after-combating-covid-19-successfully

Newton, K. (2020). Government Communications, Political Trust and Compliant Social Behaviour: The Politics of Covid-19 in Britain. *The Political Quarterly, 91*(3), 502–513. doi:10.1111/1467-923X.12901 PMID:32904826

Nguyen, H., Nguyen, M., Do, B., Tran, C., Nguyen, T., Pham, K., Pham, L., Tran, K., Duong, T., Tran, T., Duong, T., Nguyen, T., Nguyen, Q., Hoang, T., Nguyen, K., Pham, T., Yang, S.-H., Chao, J., & Duong, T. (2020). *People with Suspected COVID-19 Symptoms Were More Likely Depressed and Had Lower Health-Related Quality of Life: The Potential Benefit of Health Literacy*. https://pubmed.ncbi.nlm.nih.gov/32244415/

Nisar, T., & Prabhakar, G. (2018). Trains and Twitter: Firm generated content, consumer relationship management and message framing. *Transportation Research Part A, Policy and Practice, 113*, 318–334. doi:10.1016/j.tra.2018.04.026

Nisha Chanana, S. (2020). Employee engagement practices during COVID-19 lockdown. *Journal of Public Affairs, 2*. https://www.ncbi.nlm.nih.gov/pmc/articles/PMC7536939/

O'Dowd, E., O'Connor, P., Lydon, S., Mongan, O., Connolly, F., Diskin, C., McLoughlin, A., Rabbitt, L., McVicker, L., Reid-McDermott, B., & Byrne, D. (2018). Stress, coping, and psychological resilience among physicians. *BMC Health Services Research, 18*(1), 730. doi:10.118612913-018-3541-8 PMID:30241524

Obergriesser, S., & Stoeger, H. (2020). Students' emotions of enjoyment and boredom and their use of cognitive learning strategies–How do they affect one another? *Learning and Instruction, 66*, 101285. doi:10.1016/j.learninstruc.2019.101285

Odabaşı, Y., & Barış, G. (2002). *Tüketici Davranışı*. MediaCat Akademi.

Oinas-Kukkonen, H., & Harjumaa, M. (2009). Persuasive systems design: Key issues, process model, and system features. *Communications of the Association for Information Systems, 24*(1), 485–500. doi:10.17705/1CAIS.02428

Okan, O., Bollweg, T. M., Berens, E. M., Hurrelmann, K., Bauer, U., & Schaeffer, D. (2020). Coronavirus-related health literacy: A cross-sectional study in adults during the COVID-19 infodemic in Germany. *International Journal of Environmental Research and Public Health, 17*(15), 5503. doi:10.3390/ijerph17155503 PMID:32751484

Okoro, J., Ekeroku, A., Nweze, B., Odionye, T., Nkire, J., Onuoha, M., Ezeonwuka, C., & Owoh, J. (2020). *Attitude and preventive practices towards COVID-19 disease and the impact of awareness training on knowledge of the disease among correctional officers.* https://emeraldopenresearch.com/articles/2-51/v1

Olenich, T., Terarakelyants, V., Shestopalova, O., & Biryukov, I. (2020). Sport spirituality as an educational innovation (evidenced-based study). *E3S Web Conference: Innovative Technologies in Science and Education.*

Olson, J. M., & Zanna, M. P. (1993). Attitudes and attitude change. *Annual Review of Psychology, 28*(3), 117–154. doi:10.1146/annurev.ps.44.020193.001001

Onder, G., Rezza, G., & Brusaferro, S. (2020). Case-fatality rate and characteristics of patients dying in relation to COVID-19 in Italy. *Journal of the American Medical Association, 323*(18), 1775–1776. doi:10.1001/jama.2020.4683 PMID:32203977

Organization of Security and Cooperation in Europe and Association for the Prevention of Torture. (2020). *Guidance Monitoring Places of Detention through the COVID-19 Pandemic*. Office for Democratic Institutions and Human Rights.

Orlowski, J. (Director). (2020). *Social Dilemma* [TV Movie]. ABD.

Ornelas, J. R. H., & de Cravalho, P. J. C. (2020). Short-selling costs and asymmetric price response to economic shocks: A transaction cost explanation to price overshooting. *International Journal of Finance & Economics*, ijfe.1876. Advance online publication. doi:10.1002/ijfe.1876

Orzhel, O. (2017). Social responsibility of universities as a factor in shaping the culture of quality of higher education. In Worldview priorities of humanization of higher education: monograph (pp. 140-155). Kyiv: Institute of higher education.

Ostopolets, I., Kurilchenko, I., & Ulyanova, T. (2020). Psychic deprivation in the minds of quarantine and self-isolation in connection with COVID-19. Contemporary Issues of Digital Economy and Society. Wyższa Szkoła Techniczna w Katowicach.

Özdemir, S. (2020). *Alkolün Koronavirüs'ü Öldürdüğü İddiası*. Dogrulugu Ne? Retrieved January 9, 2021, from https://dogrulugune.org/alkolun-koronavirusu-oldurdugu-iddiasi/

Ozturk, I. (2001). *The Role of education in Economic Development: A Theoretical Perspective.* Retrieved from: https://mpra.ub.uni-muenchen.de/9023/

Padungsaksawasdi, C., Treepongkaruna, S., & Brooks, R. (2019). Investor attention and stock market activities: New evidence from panel data. *International Journal of Financial Studies, 7*(30), 30. Advance online publication. doi:10.3390/ijfs7020030

Paiola, M., & Gebauer, H. (2020). Internet of things technologies, digital servitization and business model innovation in BtoB manufacturing firms. *Industrial Marketing Management, 89*(March), 245–264. doi:10.1016/j.indmarman.2020.03.009

Pakistan: Covid-19 2020 Dashboard. (2020). Retrieved from: https://pakwired.com/the-pakistan-coronavirus-disease-tracker/

Pakistan: Education spending, percent of GDP. (2020). *Pakistan: Public spending on education, percent of GDP, 1971 – 2017*. Retrieved from: https://www.theglobaleconomy.com/Pakistan/Education_spending/

Palkova, K. Abuseridze, G. (2020). Human Rights and Labor Standards from the Public Health Perspectives in the World Trade Organization: Challenges and Possible Solutions. *Journal of Economics Studies and Research*.

Palmer & Hartley. (2013). *The Business Environment*. McGraw-Hill Edication.

Park, D., & Shin, K. (2012). *The service sector in Asia: is it an engine of growth?* Asian Development Bank Economics Working Paper Series, 322.

Partiebi. ge. (2020). *Compare the Results- Environment Protection*. Retrieved December, 11, 2020, from https://partiebi.ge/2020/geocompeare?party1=10&party2=9&party3=&theme=83

Partiebi.ge. (2020). *Compare the Results - Healthcare*. Retrieved December, 11, 2020, from pttps://partiebi.ge/2020/geo/compeare?party1=10&party2=9&party3=&theme=76.

Parveen, S. (2008). Female education and national development: As viewed by women activists and advocates. *Bulletin of Education & Research*, *30*(1), 33–41.

Pathak, N. V. (2020). Experiencing Online Education. *Purakala*, *31*(40), 211–215.

Patra, T., & Poshakwale, S. (2007). Economic variables and stock market returns: Evidence from Athens stock exchange. *Applied Financial Economics*, *16*(13), 993–1005. doi:10.1080/09603100500426523

Patrinos, A. H. (2016). *Why Education matters for Economic Development*. World Bank.

Peart, A., Lewis, V., Barton, C., & Russell, G. (2020). Healthcare professionals providing care coordination to people living with multimorbidity: An interpretative phenomenological analysis. *Journal of Clinical Nursing*, *29*(13/14). PMID:32221995

Peppers, D., & Rogers, M. (2004). *Managing Customer Experience and Relationships: A Strategic Framework*. John Wiley & Sons.

Peralta, H., & Costata, F. A. (2007). *Teachers's competence and confidence regarding the use of ICT*. Sísifo-Educational Sciences Journal.

Pfeffer, J., & Salancik, G. R. (2003). *The external control of organisations: A resource dependence perspective*. Stanford University Press.

Phan, T. T. N., & Dang, L. T. T. (2017). Teacher readiness for online teaching: A critical review. *International Journal of Open Distance E-Learning*, *3*(1), 1–16.

Phutela, N., & Dwivedi, S. (2020). A qualitative study of students' perspective on e-learning adoption in India. *Journal of Applied Research in Higher Education*, *12*(4), 545–559. doi:10.1108/JARHE-02-2019-0041

Pizzutilo, F., & Roncone, V. (2017). Red sky at night or in the morning, to the equity market neither a delight nor a warning: The weather effect re-examined using intraday stock data. *European Journal of Finance*, *23*(14), 1280–1310. doi:10.1080/1351847X.2016.1151808

Plotnikova, Y. (2011). *Human longevity as a socio-demographic phenomenon*. Dissertation for the degree of Candidate of Social Sciences.

Podsakoff, P. M., MacKenzie, S. B., Lee, J.-Y., & Podsakoff, N. P. (2003). Common method biases in behavioral research: A critical review of the literature and recommended remedies. *The Journal of Applied Psychology, 88*(5), 879–903. doi:10.1037/0021-9010.88.5.879 PMID:14516251

Podsakoff, P. M., MacKenzie, S. B., & Podsakoff, N. P. (2012). Sources of method bias in social science research and recommendations on how to control it. *Annual Review of Psychology, 63*(1), 539–569. doi:10.1146/annurev-psych-120710-100452 PMID:21838546

Poirier, W., Ouellet, C., Rancourt, M.-A., Justine, B., & Dufresne, Y. (2020). (Un)Covering the COVID-19 Pandemic: Framing Analysis of the Crisis in Canada. *Canadian Journal of Political Science*, 1–7. Retrieved from https://doi.org/ doi:10.1017/S0008423920000372

Poynter. (2020). *The CoronaVirusFacts/DatosCoronaVirus Alliance Database*. Poynter. Retrieved August 2020, from https://www.poynter.org/ifcn-covid-19-misinformation/

Prayag, G., Spector, S., Orchiston, C., & Chowdhury, M. (2019). Psychological resilience, organisational resilience and life satisfaction in tourism firms: Insights from the Canterbury earthquakes. *Current Issues in Tourism, 23*(10), 1216–1233. doi:10.1080/13683500.2019.1607832

Press Trust of India. (2020). *From technological queries to distress calls, teachers struggle with challenges posed by lockdown*. Available at: www.ndtv.com/education/from-technological-queries-to-distress-calls-teachers-struggle-with-challenges-posed-by-lockdown-2208957

Pringle, J., Drummond, J., McLafferty, E., & Hendry, C. (2011). Interpretative phenomenological analysis: A discussion and critique. *Nurse Researcher, 18*(3), 20–24. doi:10.7748/nr2011.04.18.3.20.c8459 PMID:21560922

Prottas, D. J., Cleaver, C. M., & Cooperstein, D. (2016). Assessing faculty attitudes towards online instruction: A motivational approach. *Online Journal of Distance Learning Administration, 19*(4).

Punit, I.S. (2020). *For many of India's teachers, online classes amid lockdown have been an awful experience*. Available at: https://scroll.in/article/961738/for-many-of-indias-teachers-online-classes-amid-lockdown-have-been-an-awful-experience

Qin, J. (2015). Hero on Twitter, Traitor onNews: How Social Media and Legacy News Frame Snowden. *The International Journal of Press/Politics, 20*(2), 166–184. doi:10.1177/1940161214566709

QS-ERA. (2020). *COVID-19: a wake-up call for Indian internet service providers*. Available at: www.igauge.in/news/2020/4/covid-19-a-wake-up-call-for-indian-internet-service-providers

Quddus. (2018). Role of Education in Democracy. *Daily Times*. Retrieved from: https://dailytimes.com.pk/233967/role-of-education-in-democracy/

Quevedo, R., Portalés, M., & Salomé, B. (2016). The image use on Twitter during the 2015 municipal election campaign in Spain. *Revista Latina de Comunicación Social, 71*, 85–107.

Quezada, R. L., Talbot, C., & Quezada-Parker, K. B. (2020). From bricks and mortar to remote teaching: A teacher education programme's response to COVID-19. *Journal of Education for Teaching, 46*(4), 1–12. doi:10.1080/02607476.2020.1801330

Radha, R., Mahalakshmi, K., Kumar, V. S., & Saravanakumar, A. R. (2020). E-Learning during a lockdown of a covid-19 pandemic: a global perspective. *International Journal of Control and Automation, 13*(4), 1088-1099.

Rahaman, M. M., & Chowdhury, M. A. F. (2017). Impact of financial performance on stock price of non-bank financial institutions (NBFI) in Bangladesh: Dynamic Panel Approach. In P. Ordóñez de Pablo (Ed.), *Managerial strategies and solutions for business success in Asia* (pp. 199–211). IGI Global. doi:10.4018/978-1-5225-1886-0.ch011

Rahman, A., & Sathi, N. J. (2020). Knowledge, attitude, and preventive practices toward COVID-19 among bangladeshi internet users. *Electronic Journal of General Medicine, 17*(5).

Ramaci, T., Barattucci, M., Ledda, C., & Rapisarda, V. (2020). Social Stigma during COVID-19 and its impact on HCWs outcomes. *Sustainability*, *12*(9), 3834. doi:10.3390u12093834

Ramady, M. A. (Ed.). (2012). *The GCC economies: Stepping up to future challenges.* Springer Science & Business Media. doi:10.1007/978-1-4614-1611-1

RamijM.SultanaA. (2020). Preparedness of Online Classes in Developing Countries amid COVID-19 Outbreak: A Perspective from Bangladesh. doi:10.2139srn.3638718

Rana, S. (2020, June5). IMF Urges Pakistan to Freeze Government Salaries. *The Express Tribune.* Retrieved from: https://tribune.com.pk/story/2235689/2-imf-urges-pakistan-freeze-govt-salaries

Rapaccini, M., Saccani, N., Kowalkowski, C., Paiola, M., & Adrodegari, F. (2020). Navigating disruptive crises through service-led growth: The impact of COVID-19 on Italian manufacturing firms. *Industrial Marketing Management*, *88*(May), 225–237. doi:10.1016/j.indmarman.2020.05.017

Razum, O., & Amzat, J. A. (2014). *Functionalist Perspective on Health.* Retrieved from: https://www.researchgate.net/publication/300827734_Functionalist_Perspective_on_Health

Redondo-García, M. (2012, October 18). El sensacionalismo y su penetración en la prensa española de calidad. El "caso McCann" en El País, El Mundo y ABC [The Penetration of Sensationalism in the Quality Spanish Press. McCann Case in Newspapers El País, El Mundoand ABC]. *Estudios sobre el Mensaje Periodístico*, *19*(1). Advance online publication. doi:10.5209/rev_ESMP.2013.v19.n1.42519

Reese, S. (2007). The framing project: A bridging model for media research revisited. *Journal of Communication*, *57*, 148–154. doi:10.1111/j.1460-2466.2006.00334.x

Reese, S. D. (2001). A bridging model for media research. In S. Reese, O. Gandy Jr, & A. Grant (Eds.), *Framing public life: perspectives on media and our understanding of the social world* (Vol. N). Lawrence Erlbaum.

Reuters Institute. (2020). *Reuters Digital News Report 2020.* Oxford University. Retrieved May 2020, from reutersinstitute.politics.ox.ac.uk: https://reutersinstitute.politics.ox.ac.uk/sites/default/files/2020-06/DNR_2020_FINAL.pdf

Reza, A., & Valeecha, S. (2012). Impact of Education on economic growth-Economic Analysis. *Journal of Business and Management*, *5*(4).

Ribalka, V. (Ed.). (2020). *Psychological prophylaxis and hygiene of specialties in the anti-pandemic COVID-19.* Institute of Pedagogical Education and Education for Young People Ivan Zyazyun of the National Academy of Sciences of Ukraine.

Richard, M. (2016). Influenza "A" Virus via Respiratoty aeroslos or Droplets as it Relates to Pnademic Potential. *FEMS Microbiology Reviews*, *40*, 68–85. doi:10.1093/femsre/fuv039 PMID:26385895

Riley, P. (2011). Attachment theory and the teacher-student relationship: A practical guide for teachers, teacher educators and school leaders. New York: Routledge.

Riley, W. B., & Luksetich, W. A. (1980). The market prefers republicans; Myth or reality. *Journal of Financial and Quantitative Analysis*, *15*(3), 541–560. doi:10.2307/2330399

Rose, A. M. (1951). Rumor in the stock market. *Public Opinion Quarterly, 15*(3), 461–486. doi:10.1086/266330

Rothkopf, D. (2003). Article. *The Washington Post.*

Rouadi, N. E., & Anouti, M. F. (2020). The online learning experiment in the intermediate and secondary schools in Lebanon during the coronavirus (COVID-19) crisis. *Online Learning, 7*(7), 14466-14485.

Roy, D., Tripathy, S., Kar, S. K., Sharma, N., Verma, S. K., & Kaushal, V. (2020). Study of knowledge, attitude, anxiety & perceived mental healthcare need in Indian population during COVID-19 pandemic. *Asian Journal of Psychiatry, 51*, 102083. doi:10.1016/j.ajp.2020.102083 PMID:32283510

Rudzkis, R., & Valkavičienė, R. (2014). Econometric models of the impact of macroeconomic processes on the stock market in the Baltic countries. *Technological and Economic Development of Economy, 29*(4), 783–800. doi:10.3846/20294913.2014.949901

Ruiz, J. (1996). *Metodología en la investigación cualitativa* [Methodology in qualitative research]. Universidad de Deusto.

Ryan, G.W., & Bernard, H.R. (2000). *Data management and analysis methods.* Academic Press.

Saad, S. K., & Elshaer, I. A. (2020). Justice and trust's role in employees' resilience and business' continuity: Evidence from Egypt. *Tourism Management Perspectives, 35*, 100712. doi:10.1016/j.tmp.2020.100712

Saeed, A. (2020, May 9). The impact of Covid-19 0n education in Pakistan. *Centre for Research and Security Studies.* Retrieved from: http//crssblog.com/the-impact-of-Covid-19-on-education-in-Pakistan/

Saini, D., & Chaudhary, N. S. (2019). What drives research in higher education? An Indian context. *Journal of Applied Research in Higher Education.*

Sajed, A. N., & Amgain, K. (2020). Corona virus disease (COVID-19) outbreak and the strategy for prevention. *Europasian Journal of Medical Sciences, 2*(1), 1–4. doi:10.46405/ejms.v2i1.38

Salat, D. (2001). Selective presentation and degeneration within the prefrontal cortex in aging and Alzheimer disease. *Archives of Neurology, 658*(1). PMID:11559311

Saleem, I., Lamarque, E., & Hasan, R. (2020). State and self-regulation for better governance: An Implication of Collibration. *International Journal of Law and Management.* doi:10.1108/IJLMA-05-2020-0128

Saleem, I., Siddique, I., & Ahmed, A. (2019). An extension of the Socioemotional wealth: Insights from an Asian sample. *Journal of Family Business Management, 10*(4), 293–312. doi:10.1108/JFBM-04-2019-0022

Salik, N. (2020). Impact of Covid-19 on Economy of Pakistan. *Institute of Strategic Studies.* Retrieved from: http://issi.org.pk/issue-brief-on-impact-of-covid-19-on-economy-of-pakistan/

Samra, C. (1986). *Aspects of internalization.* International Universities Press.

Sandesh, R., Shahid, W., Dev, K., Mandhan, N., Shankar, P., Shaikh, A., & Rizwan, A. (2020). Impact of COVID-19 on the mental health of healthcare professionals in Pakistan. *Cureus, 12*(7), 1–5. doi:10.7759/cureus.8974 PMID:32775056

Sarabia, S. (2020). La salud mental en los tiempos del coronavirus [Mental health in the time of coronavirus]. *Neuropsiquia, 83*(1), 3–4. doi:10.20453/rnp.v83i1.3680

Sargut, A. (2003). *Kurumsal alanlardaki örgüt yapılarının oluşmasında ve ekonomik işlemlerin yürütülmesinde güvenin rolü. In Sosyal Bilimlerde Güven.* Vadi.

Sauer, L. (2020). *What Is Coronavirus?* Retrieved from Hopkins Medicine: https://www.hopkinsmedicine.org/health/conditions-anddiseases/coronavirus

Saunders, E. M. (1993). Stock prices and Wall Street weather. *The American Economic Review*, *83*(5), 1337–1345.

Schneider, G., & Tröger, V. E. (2006). War and the world economy: Stock market reactions to international conflicts. *The Journal of Conflict Resolution*, *50*(5), 623–645. doi:10.1177/0022002706290430

Schreurs, L., & Vandenbosch, L. (2020). Introducing the social media literacy (SMILE) model with the case of the positivity bias on social media. *Journal of Children and Media*, ●●●, 1–18. doi:10.1080/17482798.2020.1809481

Schwager, J.D. (2020). *Unknown market wizards: The best traders you've never heard of.* Petersfield: Harriman House.

Schwager, J. D. (2012). *Market wizards: Interviews with top traders*. John Wiley & Sons. doi:10.1002/9781119203469

Scott, W. R., & Davis, G. F. (2015). *Organisations and organising: Rational, natural and open systems perspectives*. Routledge. doi:10.4324/9781315663371

Secom. (2020). El presidente Lenín Moreno decreta Estado de Excepción para evitar la propagación del COVID-19 [President Lenín Moreno decrees the state of emergency to prevent the spread of COVID-19]. *Secretaría Nacional de Comunicación de la Presidencia de Ecuador*. Retrieved from https://www.comunicacion.gob.ec/el-presidente-lenin-moreno-decreta-estado-de-excepcion-para-evitar-la-propagacion-del-covid-19/

Selamzade, F., Korkmazer, F., Bostan, S., & Yusifbeyli, G. (2020). COVID-19 Pandemisinin Toplum Üzerine Etkisi: Azerbaycan Örneği. *Turkiye Klinikleri Journal of Health Sciences*, *5*(2), 278–287. doi:10.5336/healthsci.2020-75559

Semetko, H., & Valkenburg, P. (2000). Framing European Politics: A Content Analysis of Press and Television News. *Journal of Communication*, *50*, 93–109.

Sen, A. (1999). *Development as Freedom*. Oxford University Press.

Senaklen, P., & Arifen, I. (2014). *International Politics, Modern Theories, and Tasks*. Ilia State University.

Serrano, F., & Kazda, A. (2020). The future of airport post COVID-19. *Journal of Air Transport Management*, *89*(May), 101900. doi:10.1016/j.jairtraman.2020.101900 PMID:32834696

Shah, D., Haider, G., & Taj, T. (2019). Causes of Dropout Rate at Primary Level in Pakistan. *International Journal of Curriculum and Instruction*, *11*(2), 38–74.

Sharma, A. K. (2020). COVID-19: creating a paradigm shift in India's education system. *Economic Times Blog*. Available at: https://economictimes.indiatimes.com/blogs/et-commentary/covid-19-creating-a-paradigm-shift-in-indias-education-system/

Shea, P. (2007). Bridges and barriers to teaching online college courses: A study of experienced online faculty in thirty six colleges. *Journal of Asynchronous Learning Networks*, *11*(2), 73–128.

Shechter, A., Diaz, F., Moise, N., Anstey, D. E., Ye, S., Agarwal, S., Birk, J. L., Brodie, D., Cannone, D. E., Chang, B., Claassen, J., Cornelius, T., Derby, L., Dong, M., Givens, R. C., Hochman, B., Homma, S., Kronish, I. M., Lee, S. A. J., ... Abdalla, M. (2020). Psychological distress, coping behaviors, and preferences for support among New York healthcare workers during the COVID-19 pandemic. *General Hospital Psychiatry*, *66*, 1–8. doi:10.1016/j.genhosppsych.2020.06.007 PMID:32590254

Shelby, T. (2014). Racism, moralism, and social criticism 1. *Du Bois Review*, *11*(1), 57–74. doi:10.1017/S1742058X14000010

Shenoy, V., Mahendra, S., & Vijay, N. (2020). COVID 19 lockdown technology adaption, teaching, learning, students engagement and faculty experience. *Mukt Shabd Journal*, *9*(4), 698–702.

Shi, Y., Wang, J., Yang, Y., Wang, Z., Wang, G., Hashimoto, K., . . . Liu, H. (2020). Knowledge and attitudes of medical staff in Chinese psychiatric hospitals regarding COVID-19. *Brain, Behavior, & Immunity - Health, 4*. doi:10.1016/j.bbih.2020.100064

Shiller, R. J. (2003). From efficient markets theory to behavioral finance. *The Journal of Economic Perspectives, 17*(1), 83–104. doi:10.1257/089533003321164967

Shleifer, A. (2000). *Inefficient markets: An introduction to behavioral finance*. Oxford University Press. doi:10.1093/0198292279.001.0001

Sicilia, C. B., Díaz, P. L. P., & Langa, E. A. (2013). La construcción del relato sobre la 'ley wert': un análisis de los encuadres interpretativos del debate en Twitter [The "Wert Law" narrative construction: an analysis of the interpretive frames of the debate on Twitter]. In *Redes sociales y lo 2.0 y 3.0*. Retrieved from https://bit.ly/2EPAE5W

Siddiqui, A., Mahmood, H., & Margaritis, D. (2020). Oil prices and stock markets during the 2014–16 oil price jump: Asymmetries and speed of adjustment in GCC and oil-importing countries. *Emerging Markets Finance & Trade, 56*(15), 3678–3708. doi:10.1080/1540496X.2019.1570497

Siders, D., & Ward, M. (2020). A fight over data infiltrates Trumpworld's response to coronavirus. *Science Advances, 6*(43), 1–12.

Sikharulidze, A., Abulashvili, G., & Kunchulia, I. (2020). *Georgia's 2030 Climate Change Strategy and 2021-2023 Action Plan*. Ministry of Environmental Protection and Agriculture of Georgia.

Silverman, C. (2020). *Dezenformasyon ve medya manipülasyonunu araştırmak. In Dezenformasyon ve medya manipülasyonu üzerine doğrulama el kitabı*. European Journalism Center-Teyit.

Singelis, T. M., Triandis, H. C., Bhawuk, D. P., & Gelfand, M. J. (1995). Horizontal and vertical dimensions of individualism and collectivism: A theoretical and measurement refinement. *Cross-Cultural Research, 29*(3), 240–275. doi:10.1177/106939719502900302

Singh, V., Li, B., & Roca, E. (2017). How pervasive is the effect of culture on stock market linkages? Evidence across regions and economic cycles. *Applied Economics, 49*(42), 4209–4230. doi:10.1080/00036846.2017.1279268

Škare, M., Soriano, D. R., & Porada-Rochoń, M. (2020). Impact of COVID-19 on the travel and tourism industry. *Technological Forecasting and Social Change*, (November). Advance online publication. doi:10.1016/j.techfore.2020.120469

Slyusarevsky, M., Nayd'onovoi, L., & Voznesenskoy, O. (Eds.). (2020). Materials of the online seminars "Awareness of quarantine: distance psychological assistance and education". Academic Press.

Smith, J. A., & Osborn, M. (2003). Interpretative phenomenological analysis. Qualitative Psychology: A Practical Guide to Research Methods, 53-80.

Smith, J. A. (1996). Beyond the divide between cognition and discourse: Using interpretative phenomenological analysis in health psychology. *Psychology & Health, 11*(2), 261–271. doi:10.1080/08870449608400256

Smith, J. A. (2011). Evaluating the contribution of interpretative phenomenological analysis. *Health Psychology Review, 5*(1), 9–27. doi:10.1080/17437199.2010.510659

Smith, J. A., & Eatough, V. (2007). *Interpretative phenomenological analysis. Analysing Qualitative Data in Psychology*.

Smith, P. K., Smith, C., Osborn, R., & Samara, M. (2008). A content analysis of school anti-bullying policies: Progress and limitations. *Educational Psychology in Practice, 24*(1), 1–12. doi:10.1080/02667360701661165

Sobaih, A. E. E., Hasanein, A. M., & Abu Elnasr, A. E. (2020). Responses to COVID-19 in higher education: Social media usage for sustaining formal academic communication in developing countries. *Sustainability, 12*(16), 6520. doi:10.3390u12166520

Society and Pandemic: Experience and Lessons from COVID-19 Fighting in Russia. (2020). IPK Pareto-Print LLC.

Son, C., Hegde, S., Smith, A., Wang, X., & Sasangohar, F. (2020). Effects of COVID-19 on college students' mental health in the United States: An interview survey study. *Journal of Medical Internet Research, 22*(9), 1–36. doi:10.2196/21279 PMID:32805704

Spring, M. (2020a). *Coronavirus: The seven types of people who start and spread viral misinformation.* BBC. Retrieved January 2020 from, https://www.bbc.com/news/blogs-trending-52474347

Spring, M. (2020b). *ABD'de Koronavirüsün sahte olduğunu düşünen rahip, Covid-19'dan öldü.* Retrieved December 2020, from BBC Türkçe: https://www.kisa.link/OjNq

Srivastava, S., Kumar, A., Bauddh, K., Gautam, A. S., & Kumar, S. (2020). 21-Day lockdown in India dramatically reduced air pollution indices in Lucknow and New Delhi, India. *Bulletin of Environmental Contamination and Toxicology, 105*, 9–17.

Stadnytskyi, V., Bax, E., Bax, A., & Anfinrud, P. (2020). The Airborne Lifetime of Small Speech Droplets and Their Potential Importance in SARS-CoV-2 Transmission. Proceedings of National Academy of Science of the United States of America, 117.

Stoffregen, J. D., Pawlowski, J. M., Ras, E., Tobias, E., Šćepanović, S., Fitzpatrick, D., Mehigan, T., Steffens, P., Przygoda, C., Schilling, P., Friedrich, H., & Moebs, S. (2016). Barriers to open e-learning in public administrations: A comparative case study of the European countries Luxembourg, Germany, Montenegro. *Technological Forecasting and Social Change, 111*, 198–208. doi:10.1016/j.techfore.2016.06.030

Strong, A., & Welburn, J. W. (2020). *An Estimation of the Economic Costs of Social-Distancing Policies.* RAND Corporation.

Suman & Asgher. (2012). Ashgar Reza and Suman Valeecha, "Impact of Education on Economic Growth of Pakistan-Econometric Analysis. *Journal of Business and Management, 5*(4). http://www.iosrjournals.org/iosr-jbm/papers/Vol5-issue4/D0542027.pdf?id=5376

Sun, Y., Liu, X., Chen, G., Hao, Y., & Zhang, Z. (2020). How mood affects the stock market: Empirical evidence from microblogs. *Information & Management, 57*(5), 103181. doi:10.1016/j.im.2019.103181

Supena, A., Umboh, D., Tarusu, D. T., & Kalengkongan, J. (2020, August). Learning Strategies in Elementary Schools During COVID-19 Pandemic in North Sulawesi. In *Proceeding of International Conference on Teaching and Science Education* (Vol. 1, No. 1, pp. 12-19). 10.31098/ictase.v1i1.14

Supovitz, J., & Reinkordt, E. (2017). Keep your eye on the metaphor: The framing of the Common Core on Twitter. *Education Policy Analysis Archives, 25*(30), 1–29. doi:10.14507/epaa.25.2285

Sutherland, P. (1997). Beyond the Market, a Different Kind of Equity. *International Herald Tribune.*

Sutherland, S. (2014). Team teaching: Four barriers to native English speaking assistant teachers' ability to model native English in Japanese classrooms. *Asian EFL Journal: Quarterly Journal, 16*(2), 156–180.

Swafford, P. M., Ghosh, S., & Murthy, N. (2006). The antecedents of supply chain agility of a firm: Scale development and model testing. *Journal of Operations Management, 24*(2), 170–188. doi:10.1016/j.jom.2005.05.002

Talwar, R. (2020). *Help Navigating Covid-19 Impacts on Your Business*. Available at: https://troymedia.com/business/help-navigating-covid-19-impacts-on-yourbusiness/

Tamm, S., Fakhri, S., Martisiute, L., & Lee, M. (2019). *Disadvantages of E-Learning*. Retrieved from e-student.org: https://estudent.org/disadvantages-of-e-learning/

Taylor, C. R. (2002). E-learning: The second wave. *T and D*, *56*(10), 24–31.

Teixeira, P. N. (2014). Gary Becker's early work on human capital–collaborations and distinctiveness. *IZA Journal of Labor Economics*, *3*(1), 1–20.

Tellier, R. (2009). Aerosol Transmission of Influenza "A" Virus: A Review of New Studies. *Journal of Social Interface.*, *6*(suppl_6), 783–790. doi:10.1098/rsif.2009.0302.focus PMID:19773292

Tesar, M. (2020). Towards a post-COVID-19 'new normality?' physical and social distancing, the move to online and higher education. *Policy Futures in Education*, *18*(5), 556–559. doi:10.1177/1478210320935671

Thaler, R. H. (2015). *Misbehaving: The making of behavioral economics*. W.W. Norton & Company.

Thaler, R. H., & Sunstein, C. R. (2009). *Nudge: Improving decisions about health, wealth, and happiness*. Penguin Books.

The National University of Life and Environmental Sciences of Ukraine. (2020). https://nubip.edu.ua/en

The New York Times. (2020, April 23). El número de muertos en Ecuador durante el brote está entre los peores del mundo [The death toll in Ecuador during the outbreak is among the worst in the world]. *The New York Times*. Retrieved from https://www.nytimes.com/es/2020/04/23/espanol/america-latina/virus-ecuador-muertes.html

The Parliament of Georgia. (1995). *The Constitution of Georgia*. Author.

The priest of the Holy Trinity Cathedral created a health group in Armavir. (2020). *Armavirskij sobesednik*.

The Resolution of the Cabinet of Ministers of Ukraine Nº 211 "On prevention of the spread of the coronavirus COVID-19 on the territory of Ukraine ". (2020).

The storm of the first weeks: how higher education stepped into the reality of a pandemic. (2020). National Research University Higher School of Economics.

Tikka, P., & Oinas-Kukkonen, H. (2017). Contributing or receiving-the role of social interaction styles in persuasion over a social networking platform. *Personal and Ubiquitous Computing*, *21*(4), 705–721. doi:10.100700779-017-1027-z

Titov, A. (2020). Distance learning in self-isolation. *Actual Scientific Research in the Modern World, 5*(61),128-130.

Trebilcock, M., & Howse, R. (2005). *The Regulation of International Trade*. Routledge. doi:10.4324/9780203978566

Tronvoll, B., Sklyar, A., Sörhammar, D., & Kowalkowski, C. (2020). Transformational shifts through digital servitization. *Industrial Marketing Management*, *89*(February), 293–305. doi:10.1016/j.indmarman.2020.02.005

Trothen, T. (2019). Sport, Spirituality, and Religion: New Intersections and Global Challenges. *Religions*, *10*, 1–8.

Tryma, K. (2019). Cooperation between Higher Education Institutions and Non-governmental Organizations in Higher Education: International Discourse. *International Scientific Journal of Universities and Leadership*, *2*(8), 102–107. doi:10.31874/2520-6702-2019-8-2-102-107

Tse, A. C. B., & Leo Sin, S. S. (2006). Crisis management and recovery: How restaurants in Hong Kong responded to SARS. *International Journal of Hospitality Management*, *25*(1), 3–11. doi:10.1016/j.ijhm.2004.12.001 PMID:32287848

Tuchen, S., Arora, M., & Blessing, L. (2020). Airport user experience unpacked: Conceptualizing its potential in the face of COVID-19. *Journal of Air Transport Management, 89*(June), 101919. doi:10.1016/j.jairtraman.2020.101919 PMID:32874022

Tuchman, G. (1978). *Making news*. Free Press.

Turak, N. (2020, July 10). Pakistan Expects UAE Remittance to be Slashed as Pandemic Hits Migrant Workers. *CNBC News*. Retrieved from: https://www.cnbc.com/2020/07/10/pakistan-sees-remittances-hit-as-pandemic-hits-migrant-workers.html

Turan, A. H. (2011). Determinations Of Customers Internet Shopping Behavior: Empricial Test With The Theory of Planned Behavior (TPB). *Doğuş Üniversitesi Dergisi, 12*(1), 128-143. http://journal.dogus.edu.tr/index.php/duj/article/view/12

TutD. (2020, July 26). FinTech and the COVID-19 Pandemic: Evidence from Electronic. doi:10.2139srn.3660987

Uddin, M. A., Alam, M. S., Mamun, A. A., Khan, T.-U.-Z., & Akter, A. (2020). A study of the adoption and implementation of enterprise resource planning (erp): Identification of moderators and mediator. *Journal of Open Innovation, 6*(1), 2–19. doi:10.3390/joitmc6010002

Uddin, M. A., Mahmood, M., & Fan, L. (2019). Why individual employee engagement matters for team performance? Mediating effects of employee commitment and organizational citizenship behaviour. *Team Performance Management, 25*(1/2), 47–68. doi:10.1108/TPM-12-2017-0078

Uddin, M. A., Priyankara, H. P. R., & Mahmood, M. (2020). Does a creative identity encourage innovative behaviour? Evidence from knowledge-intensive IT service firms. *European Journal of Innovation Management, 23*(5), 877–894. doi:10.1108/EJIM-06-2019-0168

Uğur, N. G., & Akbıyık, A. (2020). Impacts of COVID-19 on global tourism industry: A cross-regional comparison. *Tourism Management Perspectives, 36*(September), 100744. doi:10.1016/j.tmp.2020.100744 PMID:32923356

UN Women Pakistan. (2020). *Gendered Impact and Implications of COVID-19 in Pakistan*. Retrieved from: https://asiapacific.unwomen.org/en/digital-library/publications/2020/04/gendered-impact-and-implications-of-covid-19-in-pakistan#view

Ünal, R., & Taylan, A. (2017). Sağlık iletişiminde yalan haber-yanlış enformasyon sorunu ve doğrulama platformları. *Atatürk İletişim Dergisi*, (14), 81–100.

UNESCO. (2020). *COVID-19 Educational Disruption and Response*. UNESCO. Available at: https://en.unesco.org/covid19/educationresponse

UNICEF. (2020). *Education: Giving Every Child the Right to Education*. Retrieved from: https://www.unicef.org/pakistan/education

United Nations Assembly. (2019). *Global Compact for Safe, Orderly and Regular Migration*. Report A/RES/73/195. Author.

United Nations International Cildren's Emergency Fund. (2020). *UN agencies welcome the first relocation of unaccompanied children from Greece*. Retrieved October 18, 2020, from www.unicef.org: www.unicef.org/eca/press-releases/un-first-relocation-greece

United Nations. (1951). *Convention Relating to the Status of Refugees*. United Nations Office.

United Nations. (1979). *Handbook on Procedures and Criteria for Determining Refugee Status under the 1951 Convention and the 1067 Protocol relating to the Status of Refugees*. United Nations for Human Rights.

United Nations. (2007). *Practical Strategies to Promote Social Integration*. United Nations Office.

United Nations. (2019). *Population Division International Migration 2019. ReportSTESA/SER.A/438.* Department of Economic and Social Affairs.

United Nations. (2019). *Population Division International Migration. ST/ESA/SER.A/438.* Department of Economic and Social Affairs.

United Nations. (2019). *Report ST/ESA/SER.A/438. Global Compact for Safe, Orderly, and Regular Migration 2019.* United Nations General Assembly.

United Nations. (2020). *Joint United Nations Program on HIV/AIDS. Human Rights in COVID-19. Lessons from the HIV Epidemic: an Effective Community Response.* United Nations Office for Human Rights.

United Nations. (2020). *United Nations Development Program. Comprehensive Analysis of Human Rights and COVID-19. Rapid Self-Assessment of Business Areas.* United Nations Office for Human Rights.

United States Environmental Protection Agency. (1969). *Summary of the National Enviromental Policy Act.* Retrieved November 17, 2020 from https://www.epa.gov/law-regulations/summary-national-enviromental-policy-act

Universal McCann. (2020). *Universal McCann'den Türkiye'nin Korona Günleri araştırması.* Retrieved December 2020, from MediaCat: https://mediacat.com/universal-mccannden-turkiyenin-korona-gunleri-arastirmasi/

Uotila, J. (2018). Punctuated equilibrium or ambidexterity: Dynamics of incremental and radical organizational change over time. *Industrial and Corporate Change, 27*(1), 131–148. doi:10.1093/icc/dtx018

Valkenburg, P. M., Semetko, H. A., & De Vreese, C. H. (1999). The effects of news frames on readers' thoughts and recall. *Communication Research, 26*(5), 550–569. doi:10.1177/009365099026005002

Van Gorp, B. (2007). The constructionist approach to framing: Bringing culture back. *Journal of Communication, 57,* 60–78. doi:10.1111/j.0021-9916.2007.00329.x

Vega, F. (2020, March 24). Los medios tradicionales recuperan poder y credibilidad con la pandemia provocada por el Coronavirus [Traditional media regain power and credibility due to the Coronavirus pandemic]. *Comscore Social para América Latina.* Retrieved from https://www.comscore.com/lat/Prensa-y-Eventos/Blog/Los-medios-tradicionales-recuperan-poder-y-credibilidad-con-la-pandemia-provocada-por-el-Coronavirus

Venegas, R. (2006). La similitud léxico-semántica en artículos de investigación científica en español: Una aproximación desde el Análisis Semántico Latente [The Lexical-Semantic Similarity in Scientific Research Articles in Spanish: An Approach from Latent Semantic Analysis]. *Revista Signos, 39*(60), 75–106. doi:10.4067/S0718-09342006000100004

Verma, G., Campbell, T., Melville, W., & Park, B.Y. (2020). *Science teacher education in the times of the COVID-19 pandemic.* Academic Press.

Villanueva, O. M., & Feinstein, S. (2020). Stock price reactivity to earnings announcements: The role of the Cammer/Krogman factors. *Review of Quantitative Finance and Accounting.* Advance online publication. doi:10.100711156-020-00943-4

Visnjic, I. K., & Van Looy, B. (2013). Servitization: Disentangling the impact of service business model innovation on manufacturing firm performance. *Journal of Operations Management, 31*(4), 169–180. doi:10.1016/j.jom.2013.02.001

Vlatković, S. (2018). New Communication Forms and Political Framing: Twitter in Donald Trump's Presidential Campaign. *AM Journal, 16,* 123-134. Retrieved from http://dx.doi.org/10.25038 /am.v0i16.25

Voinea, L., & Filip, A. (2011). Analyzing the main changes in new consumer buying behavior during economic crisis. *International Journal of Economic Practices and Theories, 1*(1), 14–19.

Volonsenkova, E., Kabachenko, P., & Tarasova, E. (2007). Migration Policy. Migration Management Processes. In Z. M. Zayonchkovskaya (Ed.), *Methodology and Study Methods Migration Processes* (pp. 9–13). Center for Migration Studies.

Vosoughi, S., Roy, D., & Aral, S. (2018). The spread of true and false news online. *Science, 357*(6380), 1146–1151. doi:10.1126cience.aap9559 PMID:29590045

Walter, D., & Ophir, Y. (2019). The Elephant and the Bird: Republican Candidates' Use of Strategy. *Journal of Communication, 13*, 23. Retrieved from https://www.ijoc.org/index.php/ijoc/article/view/11808

Wang, H. (2015). Analysis on the Changes in Consumer Behavior and Marketing Countermeasure. In *SHS Web of Conferences* (*Vol. 17*). EDP Sciences. 10.1051hsconf/20151701007

Wang, S., Ngamsiriudom, W., & Hsieh, C. H. (2015). Trust disposition, trust antecedents, trust, and behavioral intention. *Service Industries Journal, 35*(10), 555–572. doi:10.1080/02642069.2015.1047827

Wang, W., & Guo, L. (2018). Framing genetically modified mosquitoes in the online news and Twitter: Intermedia frame setting in the issue-attention cycle. *Public Understanding of Science (Bristol, England), 27*(8), 937–951. doi:10.1177/0963662518799564

Wang, Y., Keller, J. C., Huang, C., & Fanjoy, R. O. (2016). An exploratory study: Correlations between occupational stressors, coping mechanisms, and job performance among Chinese aviation maintenance technicians. *Journal of Aviation Technology and Engineering, 5*(2), 69–80. doi:10.7771/2159-6670.1129

Wardle, C. & Derakhshan, H. (2017). *Information Disorder: Toward an interdisciplinary framework for research and policy making*. Council of Europe report DGI (2017) 09.

Wardle, C. (2020). *Bilgi düzensizliği çağı. In Dezenformasyon ve Medya Manipülasyonu Üzerine Doğrulama El Kitabı*. European Journalism Center-Teyit.

Waris, A., Khan, A. U., Ali, M., Ali, A., & Baset, A. (2020). COVID-19 outbreak: current scenario of Pakistan. *New Microbes and New Infections*, 100681. Retrieved from doi:10.1016/j.nmni.2020.100681

Watson, J., & Gemin, B. (2008). *Socialization in online programs. Promising practices in online learning*. North American council for online learning. (ERIC Document Reproduction Service ED509631)

Weaver, D. H. (2007). Toughts on agenda-setting, framing and priming. *Journal of Communication, 57*, 142–147. doi:10.1111/j.1460-2466.2006.00333.x

Weekly epidemiological update. (n.d.). Retrieved December 6, 2020, from https://www.who.int/publications/m/item/weekly-epidemiological-update---1-december-2020

Weller, K., Bruns, A., Burgess, J., Mahrt, M., & Puschmann, C. (2014). Twitter and society. *QUT ePRINTS*, 89. Retrieved from https://bit.ly/3b8o3qC

Wen, F., Xiao, J., Xia, X., Chen, B., Xiao, Z., & Li, J. (2019). Oil prices and Chinese stock market: Nonlinear causality and volatility persistence. *Emerging Markets Finance & Trade, 55*(6), 1247–1263. doi:10.1080/1540496X.2018.1496078

Wenzel, M. (2020). Strategic responses to crisis. *Strategic Management Journal, 42*(March), 7–18. doi:10.1002mj.3161

WHO. (2020). *1st WHO Infodemiology Conference*. Retrieved October 2020, from World Health Organization: https://www.who.int/news-room/events/detail/2020/06/30/default-calendar/1st-who-infodemiology-conference

Wild, J., & Godart, C. (2020). *Bot, cyborg ve yapay hareketliliği saptamak. C. Silverman içinde, Dezenformasyon ve Medya Manipülasyonu üzerine Doğrulama El Kitabı*. European Journalism Center-Teyit.

William Wilkie. (1986). *Consumer Behavior*. John Wiley and Sons.

Williams, G. A. (2021). Understanding the Preferences for Online Learning: Online MBAs in Malaysia. In Advancing Innovation and Sustainable Outcomes in International Graduate Education (pp. 194-208). IGI Global.

Wimmer, R. D., & Dominick, J. R. (1996). *La investigación científica de los medios de comunicación. Una introducción a sus métodos* [Mass Media Scientific investigation. An introduction to its methods]. Bosch Casa Editorial S.A.

Wobamann, L., & Hanushek, E. A. (2010). Education and Economic Growth. *International Encyclopedia of Education, 2*. Retrieved from: http://hanushek.stanford.edu/publications/education-and-economic-growth

World Bank Predicts Sharpest Decline of Remittances in Recent History. (2020). *World Bank*. Retrieved from: https://www.worldbank.org/en/news/press-release/2020/04/22/world-bank-predicts-sharpest-decline-of-remittances-in-recent-history

World Health Organization. (2020). *Coronavirus Disease (COVID-2019) situation reports*. Retrieved from https://www.who.int/emergencies/diseases/novel-coronavirus-2019/situation-reports/

World Health Organization. (2020). *Population-based age-stratified seroepidemiological investigation protocol for coronavirus 2019 (COVID-19) infection, 26 May 2020*. World Health Organization.

World Trade Organization. (1999). *The Third World Trade Organisation's Ministerial Conference*. Retrieved from The WTO Ministerial Conference Website: https://www.wto.org/english/thewto_e/minist_e/min99_e/english/about_e/presspack_english.pdf

World Trade Organization. (2020). *Trade set to plunge as COVID-19 pandemic upends global economy*. Retrieved from https://www.wto.org/english/news_e/pres20_e/pr855_e.htm

World Trade Organization. (2020). *WTO report shows slowdown in G20 trade restrictions as COVID-19 impacts world economy*. Retrieved from https://www.wto.org/english/news_e/news20_e/trdev_18nov20_e.htm

Wu, S. M., Hofman, J. A., Mason, W., & Watts, J. D. (2011). Who Says What to Whom on Twitter. *International World Wide Web Conference Committee*, 705-714. Retrieved from https://bit.ly/2EP9EDA

Xu, D., & Jaggars, S. S. (2013). Adaptability to online learning: Differences across types of students and academic subject areas. *The Journal of Higher Education*, *85*(5). Advance online publication. doi:10.1353/jhe.2014.0028

Xu, H., Gonzalez Mendez, M. J., Guo, L., Chen, Q., Zheng, L., Chen, P., Cao, X., Liu, S., Sun, X., Zhang, S., & Qiao, Y. (2020). Knowledge, awareness, and attitudes relating to the COVID-19 pandemic among different populations in central china: Cross-sectional survey. *Journal of Medical Internet Research*, *22*(10), e22628. doi:10.2196/22628 PMID:32886623

Ye, Z., Yang, X., Zeng, C., Wang, Y., Shen, Z., Li, X., & Lin, D. (2020). Resilience, social support, and coping as mediators between COVID-19-related stressful experiences and acute stress disorder among college students in China. *Applied Psychology: Health and Well-Being*. doi:10.1111/aphw.12211

Yerlikaya, T. (2020). Koronavirüs ile Mücadelede Yeni Risk Alanı: İnfodemi. *SETA Perspektif*, (269), 1–4.

Youn, S., & Shin, W. (2020). Adolescents' responses to social media newsfeed advertising: The interplay of persuasion knowledge, benefit-risk assessment, and ad scepticism in explaining information disclosure. *International Journal of Advertising*, *39*(2), 213–231. doi:10.1080/02650487.2019.1585650

Yücel, H. (2020). Dünya Sağlık Örgütü'nün Koronavirüs Yönetimi. *SETA Analiz*, (324), 7–17.

Yuen, A. H., & Ma, W. W. (2008). Exploring teacher acceptance of e-learning technology. *Asia-Pacific Journal of Teacher Education*, *36*(3), 229–243. doi:10.1080/13598660802232779

Zalewska, J. (2019). Practice Theory Revisited: How Flexible Meta-habit Complements Habitus. *Polish Sociological Review*, *205*, 65–84.

Zaller, J. (1992). *The Nature and Origins of Mass Opinion*. Cambridge Univ. Pres.

Zarocostas, J. (2020). How to fight an infodemic. *Lancet*, *395*(10225), 676. doi:10.1016/S0140-6736(20)30461-X PMID:32113495

Zellweger, T. M., Kellermanns, F. W., Chrisman, J. J., & Chua, J. H. (2012). Family control and family firm valuation by family CEOs: The importance of intentions for transgenerational control. *Organization Science*, *23*(3), 851–868. doi:10.1287/orsc.1110.0665

Zhang, R., Zhang, A., Wung, Y., & Molina, M. (2020). Conference on Social Science. In *Identifying airborne transmission as the DOminant route for the spread of COVID-19*. National Academy of Science of the United States of America.

Zhang, W., Wang, Y., Yang, L., & Wang, C. (2020). Suspending classes without stopping learning: China"s education emergency management policy in the Covid-19 outbreak. *Journal of Risk and Financial Management*, *13*(55), 1–6. doi:10.3390/jrfm13030055

Zhao, W. X., Jiang, J., Weng, J., He, J., Lim, E. P., Yan, H., & Li, X. (2011). Comparing Twitter and Traditional Media Using Topic Models. In Advances in Information Retrieval. ECIR 2011. Lecture Notes in Computer Science (vol. 6611). Springer. https://doi.org/ doi:10.1007/978-3-642-20161-5_34

Zhao, Y., & Bacao, F. (2020). What factors determining customer continuingly using food delivery apps during 2019 novel coronavirus pandemic period? *International Journal of Hospitality Management*, *91*, 102683. doi:10.1016/j.ijhm.2020.102683 PMID:32929294

Zheng, D., Luo, Q., & Ritchie, B. W. (2021). Afraid to travel after COVID-19? Self-protection, coping and resilience against pandemic 'travel fear'. *Tourism Management*, *83*, 104261. doi:10.1016/j.tourman.2020.104261

Zhou, X., Cui, Y., Wu, S., & Wang, W. (2019). The influence of cultural distance on the volatility of the international stock market. *Economic Modelling*, *77*, 289–300. doi:10.1016/j.econmod.2018.10.005

Zhu, G., & Gao, X. (2019). The digital sales transformation featured by precise retail marketing strategy. *Expert Journal of Marketing*, *7*(1), 72–76.

Zhu, K., Kraemer, K. L., & Dedrick, J. (2004). Information technology payoff in e-business environments: An international perspective on value creation of e-business in the financial services industry. *Journal of Management Information Systems*, *21*(1), 17–54. doi:10.1080/07421222.2004.11045797

Zia, A. (2020). Exploring factors influencing online classes due to social distancing in COVID-19 pandemic: a business students perspective. *The International Journal of Information and Learning Technology*. doi:10.1108/IJILT-05-2020-0089

Zimmer, J. C., Arsal, R. A., Al-Marzouqc, M., & Varun, G. (2010). Investigating online information disclosure: Effects of information relevance, trust and risk. *Information & Management*, *47*(2), 115–123. doi:10.1016/j.im.2009.12.003

Ziv, A. (1984). *Personality and Sense of Humor*. Springer.

ZME Science. (2020). *Coronavirus in Pakistan — live updates, cases, and news*. Retrieved from: https://www.zmescience.com/medicine/coronavirus-updates-news-pakistan/

Zvolensky, M. J., Garey, L., Rogers, A. H., Schmidt, N. B., Vujanovic, A. A., Storch, E. A., Buckner, J. D., Paulus, D. J., Alfano, C., Smits, J. A. J., & O'Cleirigh, C. (2020). Psychological, addictive, and health behavior implications of the COVID-19 pandemic. *Behaviour Research and Therapy*, *134*(May), 103715. doi:10.1016/j.brat.2020.103715 PMID:32891956

About the Contributors

Emilia Alaverdov, Ph.D. in Political Science, associate professor, Faculty of Law and International Relations since 2011. She received her bachelor's degree in Languages and Literature, has been awarded a qualification of Philologist of English Language and Literature and Spanish Language and Literature, Ilia Chavchavadze State University, Tbilisi, Georgia. Has a master's degree in International Relations and Politics from the Diplomatic Academy of Georgia. She defended her doctoral thesis, "Islamic Factor in the History and Modern Russia" at Georgian Technical University and was awarded a Ph.D. degree in Political Science in 2013. Her research interests include religion, migration, and European and Russian studies. She is an editor of 2 books, has participated in 48 international scientific conferences (among them majority abroad) and published more than 15 articles, and 3 book chapters.

Muhammad Waseem Bari is an assistant professor at Lyallpur Business School, Government College University Faisalabad, Pakistan. Dr. Waseem earned his Ph.D. degree from the Beijing Institute of Technology, China. He has broad insight into the topics of organizational sciences and has published several papers in high-quality impact factor journals. Dr. Waseem is also an editor of three books on tourism and Knowledge Management, article editor, and reviewer of several impact factor journals. He has vast experience in banking and the FMCG industries. His research areas are knowledge management, psychological contract, innovation, organizational changes, and tourism.

* * *

Muhammad Abrar is an associate professor of Business Administration and currently, he is serving as director Lyallpur business school at Government College University, Faisalabad, Pakistan. He is a well-known scholar in his research areas (Product Innovation, TQM, Digital Marketing, etc.). Many high impact factor articles are to his credit.

Giga Abuseridze, Ph.D candidate of Legal Science, researcher and lecturer at Riga Staradins University since 2015. He received his bachelor's degree in law, Tbilisi State Universit, Tbilisi, Georgia. He has a master's degree in Law from the University of Latvia, Riga, Latvia. His research profile is focused on international trade issues, transformation of trade system, WTO, DCFTA etc. One of his main areas of interest is also Law and Diplomacy. He is the author 16 scientific papers (also published in Scopus and WoS), several policy papers and international research projects. He has participated in 20 international scientific conferences. He is fluent in the following languages: Georgian, English, Russian and Latvian.

Natalia Afanasieva, Doctor Psychological Sciences, Associate Professor, Department of Psychology of Activities in Special Conditions, National University of Civil Defense of Ukraine, Kharkiv, Ukraine. ORCID: https://orcid.org/0000-0003-3341-1845.

Selman Akyüz has a bachelor's degree in public relations. His master's degree in local television journalism. He completed his doctoral studies with the thesis "Neutrality perception of mass media users in Turkey within the framework of hostile media effect". He is an assistant professor in the department of radio, television and cinema at the Faculty of communication of Selcuk University. His fields of study are relationship of media and politics, politic cinema, disinformation, fake news, and television news.

Larissa Batrancea is Associate Professor at Babes-Bolyai University Cluj-Napoca, Romania. She received her PhD in economics from Babes-Bolyai University and completed a postdoctoral program at the Romanian Academy in Bucharest, ranking first among 134 fellows. She holds a BA and an MA in economics, a BSc and an MSc in mathematics, all awarded by Babes-Bolyai University. She was visiting professor, invited researcher and completed training programs at universities from Austria, Brazil, Denmark, Germany, Italy, the Netherlands, Russia, Spain, Sweden, USA. Her publications comprise 30 books and book chapters as editor, author, translator (Routledge, Springer, Elsevier, IGI Global) and numerous articles in outlets such as Journal of Economic Psychology, Social Indicators Research, Economic Research-Ekonomska Istraživanja, Eastern European Economics. She conducts research on tax behavior, financial analysis, behavioral public finance, experimental economics, neuroeconomics, cognitive neuroscience. She activated as PI and member in 16 grants and received 13 prizes in research and teaching.

Fernando Casado Gutierrez is an international analyst born in Córdoba, Spain. Graduated in Law and PhD in Social Communication, he is a tenured professor at the Institute of High National Studies of Ecuador and a teacher in the Master of Public International Law at the Bolivarian University of Venezuela. He has written the books Introduction to Human Rights from a Bolivarian and Revolutionary perspective and in 2015 with the Akal publishing house another book entitled Anti-journalists: confessions of media attacks against Venezuela.

Manana Darchashvili, doctor of history, professor of Georgian Technical University; researcher at Research Institute for Political Studies. She graduated from the Tbilisi State University, Faculty of History in 1985. Then she received her second higher education in Legal Studies at Tbilisi Business and Marketing Institute in 1999. Later she pursued her advanced study course at Tbilisi State University and became a Doctor of History in 2005. Research Interest: Elections and Political Parties, International Relations, Religious Factor in International Relations, Cultural Politics, Political Parties, International Organizations. She participated in 48 international conferences, is the author of - 39 scientific articles and 2 study courses, editor of 4 monographs, supervisor of 3 Ph.D. theses.

Vikas Garg, PhD, is the Director Executive Programs Management Domain at Amity University Uttar Pradesh, Greater Noida Campus, India. He is UGC NET qualified with 15 years of academic experience. His areas of specialization are accounting and finance, and his major interests are in financial markets, financial reporting, and analysis. He is a lifetime member of the Indian Commerce Association, Indian Accounting Association, and Indian Management Association. He is certified in Customer

Relationship Management from the Indian Institute of Management Bangalore, India. He has published numerous research papers in various Scopus- and ABDC-indexed international and national journals. He holds many copyrights and patents and has organized many national and international conferences. He is associated with several universities as an external guide for research scholars and has conducted many workshops at institutions.

Syed Arslan Haider is a PhD scholar in the Department of Management at Sunway University Business School, Malaysia. He received his BS in Computer Science and Master in Project Management from the Capital University of Science and Technology, Pakistan. He is active in research in the areas of Knowledge management, Innovation, Leadership, Organizational Culture and Project Complexity. His research appeared in good journals such as Journal of Knowledge Management, Abasyn Journal of Social Sciences and many others Scopus indexed journals. He is a Project Manager of Soulmate Construction Company in Pakistan.

Iqbal Hussain is PhD Scholar at Government College University, Faisalabad and specialize in the field of marketing. He earned his MSBA from NUML, Pakistan.

Muntazir Hussain has developed an acute interest for research and discovering new things in association with academia and research. He has a keen interest to contribute to both theoretical and practical research in the field of finance.

Shahid Iqbal has received his PhD from University of Engineering and Technology, Taxila Pakistan. He is currently working as an Assistant professor at Bahria University, Islamabad, Pakistan. His area of interest includes Engineering Management, Project Management and Technology Management.

Fatema Johara received her Ph.D. in Accountability & Performance Measurement from the Universiti Sains Malaysia, Penang, Malaysia in 2020. She did her Master of Philosophy in Management and M.B.A in Accounting Information Systems. In 2007 she was hired as a lecturer of Accounting by the Faculty of Business Administration at the University of Science & Technology Chittagong and is currently the Associate Professor and Head, Department of Business Administration of Bangladesh Army International University of Science & Technology. She is a regular reviewer of the Journal of Research in Marketing and Entrepreneurship. She has also worked as co-editor for the proceedings of the International Conference on Business, Sustainability, and Innovation (ICBSI), 2018. Moreover, currently, she is the editorial member for BAIUST Academic Journal. She is the best paper award recipient of the ICBSI, 2018. She writes and presents widely on issues of talent management practices, faculty engagement, Islamic work ethics, faculty resilience, entrepreneurship, and faculty performance.

Natavan Karamova, Doctor of Philosophy in Biology, associate professor, Institute of Physiology named after academician Abdulla Garayev under the Azerbaijan National Academy of Sciences and Western Caspian University. She is the author of 32 scientific articles, 1 book, and 4 study courses, and a participant of 51 international conferences. Natavan Karamova is a member of the editorial boards of several scientific journals. Her research interest is Philosophy, psychology, biology, and public awareness. She is fluent in the following languages: Azerbaijani, Russian and English.

Lubna Akhlaq Khan is currently working as Assistant professor of English under the Higher Education Department, Punjab. She is a PhD scholar in Linguistics at the National University of Modern Languages, Islamabad. Her articles have been published in various HEC recognized national and international journals. She has also presented her papers in different national and international conferences including Language, Gender and Hate Speech orgaized by Ca Foscari, University of Venice, Venice, Italy. Furthermore, she is an HEC scholar for indigenous PhD scholarship. Her research interests include: Gender and Language, Humor studies, Anthropological linguistics, Paremiology and folklore.

Qurrahtulain Khan is an assistant professor. Currently, she is working as a faculty member in the Department of Public Administration, University of Kotli, Kotli, Azad Jammu and Kashmir. Her research interests are leadership behaviors, knowledge management, and organizational changes.

Arturo Luque is full professor at the Technical University of Manabí, Ecuador, and member of Euro-Mediterranean Observatory on Public Policies and Democratic Quality at the University King Juan Carlos (Spain). He holds a Ph.D. in Social Sciences and Law and a Master of two years about Labor Relations. He supervises several doctoral theses (Ph.D.) in Córdoba (Spain) and in the Basque Country (GEZKI Institute) like a director and co-director. It has 54 indexed articles and his latest publications includes topics about corporate social (Ir)responsibility (How corporate social (ir)responsibility in the textile sector is defined, and its impact on ethical sustainability: An analysis of 133 concepts), transnational companies (The transnational textile companies relationship with environment: a Delphi analysis approach) and their relations with ethics (Corruption in the transnational textile industry: an exception or the rule?), social economy and cooperative system like economic alternative (Socially responsible public management: case spinning development in Ecuador), media analysis and social conflicts (Analysis of the indigenous uprising of Ecuador, 2019).

Tahir Masood is a research-oriented academic professional and his interest in finding practical solutions for the industry make him a regular consultant and trainer for the corporate world. Dr Masood has 36 research contributions in journals of repute, in addition to two books and 15 international conference presentations. Being a member of world high ranked societies like Academy of Management and Society of Human Resource Management, he is actively functioning different roles as a reviewer, session chair and doctoral examiner. In an entrepreneurial capacity, he organizes numerous conferences, symposiums and training for academia and industry. He has a PhD in Human Resource Management, along with World Bank/IFCToT and ToMT Certifications.

Iryna Ostopolets, Candidate of Pedagogical Sciences, Associate Professor of the Department of General Psychology, Donbass State Pedagogical University, Slovyansk, Ukraine. ORCID: https://orcid.org/0000-0001-7315-2062.

Neha Puri, PhD, is Assistant Professor in Amity College of Commerce & Finance, Amity University Uttar Pradesh, India. She has written study material books for Pan African students. Besides this, numerous research papers, chapters, book reviews are on her credit. Her publications have appeared in Inderscience, Springer, Thomas Reuters, and so on. Her expert area is Financial Reporting, Accounting Fundamentals, International Financial Reporting Standards and Cost Accounting.

Irfan Saleem obtained his doctorate from Sorbonne Business School France. Currently, he is affiliated with the Sohar University (SU) of Oman. Dr Irfan was affiliated with the University of Central Punjab before joining SU for a decade in the capacity of Director BBA program, Assistant Professor, Principal investigator and conference Secretory of ICIBM 2020. He has an extensive national and international experience of Higher Education Sector. Dr Irfan won the Emerald award Case study competition in 2018. Lately, he is researching about Psychological implications in the time of COVID -19 Pandemic. His research interests include Family Business Governance, Leadership and Entrepreneurship in Emerging Markets. Currently, he is teaching Gulf Business Environment at SU, Oman.

Rebeca Sánchez-Figuera is a professor at the Technical University of Manabí. Sociologist graduated at the Central University of Venezuela in 2004. Master on Research on Latin American Studies & International Relations in the Simon Bolívar University (2014-2016). Member of the Research Team in Critical Studies for Social Justice at the Technical University of Manabí.

Mustafa Şehirli finished his bachelor's degree at Istanbul Technical University Management Engineering Department (1994) and his post-graduate degree at Marmara University Middle East Institution Economy Department, after a long time he completed his doctorate in Maltepe University Management Department. He continues his academic life at The University of Health Sciences (as Ass. Prof.) and studies especially in the field of marketing. He worked as a manager in the VW Group and other companies in Turkey. He also has an International Coaching School Certificate.

Rizwan Shabbir is Assistant Professor in the Lyallpur Business School, Government College University, Faisalabad. He got his PhD of Marketing Management from Huazhong University of Science and Technology, China. He has earned his MS from Lund University, Sweden. His research interests include value-creation, industrial marketing, branding and cross-cultural difference in decision making. He has published in international journals, including Asia Pacific Journal of Marketing and Logistics, Psychology Research and Behavior Management and Frontiers in Psychology.

Nataliia Svitlychna, Candidate of Pedagogical Sciences, Associate Professor of the Department of Psychology of Activities in Special Conditions, Social and Psychological Faculty, National University of Civil Defense of Ukraine, Khark iv, Ukraine. ORCID: https://orcid.org/0000-0001-7891-6295.

Md. Abu Taher, PhD, Department of Management (University of Chittagong, Bangladesh) has been teaching and conducting research in the area of human resource management, ILO, and industrial relations for more than two decades. Dr. Taher served the University of Chittagong as Dean in the Faculty of Business Administration and Chairman of the Department of Management. Besides, he was also Treasurer of Bangladesh Open University and Pro-Vice Chancellor of Southeast University (Private) in Bangladesh. Currently, Dr. Taher has been appointed as the Member of the University Grants Commission of Bangladesh. Additionally, Dr. Taher is also working as Director, Board of Directors, Jibon Bima Corporation, Dhaka. Dr. Md. Abu Taher has published more than 100 research papers in peer reviewed journals and conference proceedings.

Shehnaz Tehseen (PhD in Management) is working as a full-time senior lecturer and Programme Leader of BSc (Honours) in International Business Programme in Department of Management, Sunway University Business School, Sunway University, Malaysia. Her research interests lie in the areas of entrepreneurship, ethnic entrepreneurship, SMEs, cultural orientations, innovation, entrepreneurial competencies, retail sector, human resource management, strategic management, marketing, tourism, and organizational behaviour. She is an active researcher with more than 40 publications. She is also an editorial team member of some international journals including Journal of Management Sciences, Durreesamin Journal, and Journal of Global Business Insights.

Kateryna Tryma is a Senior Researcher of the Unit for cooperation between universities and society Institute of Higher Education, NAESU. Her responsibilities include enhancing the learning environment through instruction, applied research, and service that support the institutional mission. Prior to becoming Senior Researcher, she worked as a Senior Lecturer at Mariupol State University in Mariupol. The researcher gained broad theoretical, practical and teaching experience with specializations in the following areas: global civil society and global democracy, NGOs, e-civil organizations and information security. Kateryna got PhD in Political Sciences in 2011, the theme of thesis: "Globalization as a factor for the transformation of Ukrainian civil society (NGOs analysis)". She is the contributor to more than 30 research theses. She has 2 Masters degrees: Company Economics, Donetsk National University of Economics and Trade named after M. I.Tugan-Baranovsky, Kryvyi Rih and International Relations, Mariupol State University (2005). Scientific interests: NGOs, civil society, the European Union.

Md. Aftab Uddin, PhD, is an Associate Professor in the Department of Human Resource Management, University of Chittagong, Bangladesh 4331. He does research on industrial psychology, cognitive psychology, environmental psychology, and AI in workplace, which were published in Bangladesh, Brazil, Canada, China, India, Iran, Japan, Malaysia, Thailand, Pakistan, Romania, Slovenia, South Korea, Switzerland, United Arab Emirates, United Kingdom, and United States. He published more than 60 research papers with indexations SSCI, SCIE, CPCI, ESCI, ABDC, ABS, Scopus, etc. Beside, he is a regular reviewer of Asia Pacific Education Review, IEEE Access, International Journal of Business Innovation and Research, Journal of Business Research, Journal of Environmental Planning and Management, Management Research Review, Psychology Research and Behavior Management, Sage Open, etc.

Amitabh Verma is working as Assistant Professor, Business Department, Sohar University, Oman. He received his Master of Computer Application in the year 2005, PhD in Management in 2015. He has over 13 years of experience in both teaching and research. His research interest includes DSS, Database Management, Data Mining, MIS, E-Business, AI & Cloud Computing. He has published research papers in international journals and conferences. He is a member of IAENG (International Association of Engineers) and a life member of Indian Society for Technical Education.

Index

A

B

C

D

E

F

G

H

I

J

K

L

M

N

O

P

R

S

T

U

www.ingramcontent.com/pod-product-compliance
Lightning Source LLC
LaVergne TN
LVHW060406300926
849162LV00006B/1359